PLANNING and ORGANIZING for SOCIAL CHANGE

Action Principles From
Social Science Research

Jack Rothman

1974   Columbia University Press
New York and London

Library of Congress Cataloging in Publication Data

Rothman, Jack.
  Planning and organizing for social change.

  Includes bibliographies.
  1. Evaluation research (Social action programs)—
United States.   2. Community development—Research—
United States.   I. Title.
H62.R674   309.2'62   74-4434
ISBN 0-231-03774-0
ISBN 0-231-08335-1 (pbk.)

TO MY FATHER
 JOSEPH ROTHMAN
Who came a long distance to escape oppression
and taught me to care about some important things

Staff For The Project

Principal Investigator

Jack Rothman, Ph.D.

Reviewers and Abstractors

Stephen M. Aigner	Judith P. Gordon	Kathleen T. Okonski
Ronald Beck	Carol L. Hoffer	Linda Ann Paul
Ann Chomet	Carol Jean Jue	Irene A. Reep
Charles Chomet	Marcia Kahn	Karen J. Syed
John L. Erlich	Joseph Katan	Celeste Sturdevant
Susan Erlich	Melvyn R. Lawson	Frances C. Tauritz
David W. Finkbiner	Gretchen A. Lucht	Edgar H. Turkle
Harry Finkelstein	Robert P. McNeal	Gary E. Ulrich
David M. Fram	Lynne C. Morris	Ellen Weiland

Preparation of Original Drafts of Chapters

Practitioner Roles	Jack Rothman
Organizational Behavior	Joseph Katan
Political and Legislative Behavior	David M. Fram and Ronald Beck
Participation	Lynne Morris
Diffusion and Adoption of Innovations	Paul McNeal
Movement and Assimilation of Populations	Harry Finkelstein

This investigation was supported by National Institute of Mental Health Research Grant Number MH 161125

Acknowledgments

THIS BOOK is a production utilizing the efforts and energies of a large supporting cast, as the extensive staff listing in the front matter reveals. Among the latter, I would like especially to thank Joseph Katan and Lynne Morris for their aid in various staff roles. NIMH provided essential financial resources without which the undertaking would not have been possible; Jack Wiener of the Applied Research Branch merits special acknowledgment. Louis Ferman, through the Institute of Labor and Industrial Relations at the University of Michigan, gave initial support in the pilot phase.

John L. Erlich was from the beginning a solid friend and advocate, always available with encouragement, advice, and criticism, as well as valuable editorial assistance.

Thanks are due to my colleagues Edwin J. Thomas for introducing me through his writings to the possibilities of research utilization as a formal technical process, and to Jesse Gordon who, by way of his course on Empirical Bases of Clinical Practice, suggested the idea of applying the process to community change issues. Arthur Dunham and Joyce Kornbluh displayed both kindness and stamina in reading substantial portions of the preliminary draft and making numerous helpful suggestions. Other critical readers, both colleagues and students, included Steven Burghardt, Lou Ferman, Neal Gilbert, Murray Gruber, Jesse Gordon, Roger McNeally, Robert Morris, Meyer Schwartz, Charles Levy, and Milan Dluhy.

I was aided substantially by Belita Cowan, who participated in copyediting the manuscript, and by William Dyer, who prepared the excellent comprehensive index.

Many others, both directly and indirectly, have helped make this compendium a reality.

Foreword

THIS BOOK is a landmark in the history of the relationship between the social sciences and the field of social welfare. That relationship is a long and complicated one, but its overarching characteristic is the failure of scholars on both sides to translate social science findings into fully usable knowledge for practitioners. With the great proliferation of social science theory and research in recent decades, this failure has become more evident, and the field of social welfare has suffered all the more. The time was thus long past due for someone to ask, as Professor Rothman did: "Suppose a very wide range of social-science research studies covering a designated period of time were systematically reviewed, codified, and given an applied formulation; could the resulting product provide tools and strategies for planners and community workers?" He goes on to observe that "It was his assumption that the outcome would be positive and that, indeed, the effort could culminate in a substantial increase in the knowledge base available to those who wish to seriously engage in social change and social adaptation at the community level." Professor Rothman's assumption about his undertaking has, in my judgment, been more than borne out. This book is an outstanding demonstration that social-science findings can be codified and translated in ways which make them of extreme value to social work and human-service practitioners.

The task was, to say the least, a huge one, even though Professor Rothman chose to limit his search of the literature to materials published over six years. Social-science materials are scattered among dozens of journals and periodicals, unpublished reports and manuscripts, and of course books; consequently, reviewing the literature just of the six years is in itself formidable. No fulltime practitioners could conceivably keep abreast of it, even were he or she disposed to try. Moreover, the results of various research projects vary greatly in theoretical sophistication and the soundness of methodology; practitioners should not have to be burdened with the hard task of forming judgments about the adequacy of each article read. Finally, equally sound research often leads to contradictory results, giving rise to the need for cautiously informed interpretations of the possible causes of conflicts, and the directions that further research might take to resolve them. In all of these respects, and many more, the practitioner rightly deserves the aid of scholars in both the human services and the social sciences. And it is precisely that aid which this book provides.

Teachers in every field of practice will find this volume an indispensable sourcebook, and all the more so because of its method of organization. First, the material reviewed is logically grouped, with ready-at-hand bibliographic references, so that student assignments to read and evaluate the material for themselves may be easily made. Second, the derived social-science generalizations are clearly and logically organized, so that critical discussion can be facilitated. Finally, the implications of these generalizations for practice are spelled out in a cogent and relevant way, so that students may both apply and test them in their own field-training experiences. All in all, then, this volume should greatly enrich the student's class and field experience.

It is not, one should quickly add, a book one sits down to read from cover to cover. The work is, for the time period spanned, virtually encyclopedic. Still, it is a pleasure to read. One opens to any section only to be drawn quickly to the fascinating summaries and appraisals of social-science findings, and more especially to the insightful applications to practice afforded by the author. It is a book to return to time and again, until its fullness and richness has been wholly absorbed. To sum up, I consider this book more than a significant intellectual and professional experiment successfully concluded; it is a model for all future efforts of its kind.

RICHARD A. CLOWARD
Professor
Columbia University School of Social Work
July 1974

Contents

PLANNING and ORGANIZING for SOCIAL CHANGE

Introduction

THE PRIMARY purpose of this book is to provide a core of basic social-science research knowledge to social planners and community workers in a variety of human-service fields (such as community mental health, race relations, social work, public health, city planning, community development, public administration, and adult education), for use in guiding their strategies and actions. It is concerned with the systematic application of research findings to practical aspects of community action and planned social change in order to deal with contemporary social problems.

I view this book not as adding one further study to previous examinations that have been made concerning community processes and community problem solving. It is rather one based on an analysis of a pool of close to a thousand research studies and a synthesis of the results of almost five hundred of such empirical investigations. Numerous discussions have taken place in the past concerning whether social-science research has much of a practical nature to offer to community planners and community activists. Opinions have been expressed on both sides of the issue, often in strong and fervent terms. The book speaks to this question by attempting to demonstrate practical use of generalizations from social science to enhance social practice and policy formation.

Suppose a very wide range of social-science research studies covering a designated period of time were systematically reviewed, codified, and given an applied formulation; could the resulting product provide tools and strategies for planners and community workers? It was the assumption of the author that the outcome would be positive and that, indeed, the effort could culminate in a substantial increase in the knowledge base available to those who wish to seriously engage in social change and social adaptation at the community level.[1]

[1] The study, supported by NIMH, which was the basis for this publication had the title, "Toward An Empirical Research Base for Community Organization Practice."

It is not to be assumed that social-science research is the only (or necessarily the most effective) source for informing or improving community intervention. Practical wisdom gleaned from front line experience in directly confronting community issues is a highly significant teacher. Likewise the insights of novelists, poets, and social critics often reflect the earliest or most innovative approaches to perceiving and dealing with social problems. Social-science research reflects only one of a number of ways of gaining a cognitive hold on social reality or for finding points of leverage for manipulating it. It was my intention to give this particular approach a thoroughgoing systematic test, to exploit it vigorously, and to see where it leads. Essentially the endeavor represents my long-standing interests in both social science and social change, and a desire to exercise these intertwined interests in a frame of reference that consolidates both dimensions, to wit, in a demonstration of the concrete contribution of social science for achieving social change objectives.

In language and format this volume is particularly oriented to students training for community work in various professional schools. However the modalities of intervention, or action guidelines, that are given offer strategies and tools for community operatives of many types both in grass-roots social change and in human-service and planning organizations, whether paid or volunteer, professionally trained or not, community specialists or direct service workers. While I ordinarily refer linguistically to the "practitioner," one may also conceive of a generic community-level change agent. That is to say, the action formulations are stated so as to approximate scientific principles available for use by any individual or organization concerned with social change.

In a similar vein, the guidelines are not intended exclusively for professionals from any single discipline or field of practice. My basic discipline is sociology and my primary professional field of experience is social work. The outlook here, however, will be eclectic, so that my occupation will not become also my preoccupation.

I have come to my subject with certain points of view (read biases) that ought perhaps to be made explicit at the outset so that the reader will have a better "feel" for the literary terrain. In the first place, the book is concerned with social goals, with the structuring of new social arrangements and provisions. These are value-laden areas, and they have not been approached from an underlying position of neutrality.

My social perspective involves a commitment to the elimination of social injustices and economic inequities. This implies working toward a social structure where concepts of the common good or of the collective fate of the community are brought into better balance with a professed preoccupation with "individualism." In other words, the public welfare broadly viewed is of higher moment on a scale of human values than is private profit.

My general outlook is that of a nondoctrinaire, humanistic, exploratory social democrat; my basic posture is a personalistic, skeptical leaning to the left. This skepticism precludes an all-embracing acceptance of any one approach as the true and only path to the better community down the road. Too often the visionary zealots of today become the hardened tyrants of tomorrow, and new meritorious social programs are carried forward with stilted, brutalizing rigidity by routine administrative clerks.

In a previous work I suggested that there are a number of different available avenues for social change, including rationalistic social planning, militant social action, and participatory self-help community development. These approaches to a lesser or greater degree are incremental in character, involve differing utilization of conflictual and cooperative tactics, imply varying reliance on technical expertise in planning as contrasted to mobilization of populations and interest groups, have to do with the delivery of specific services and provisions to people who need them in juxtaposition to reconstitution of broader societal structures, and assume a vantage point either as manager or provider within given social institutions or as critic and disrupter outside of them.[2]

Substantively, the content of this book is responsive to these varied, short-run alternative modes of action. In drawing action guidelines I deliberately pursued such wide, multiple applications, on the assumption that both social planning and social action, for example, can be

[2] These modes of action and their practice ramifications are elaborated in Jack Rothman, "Three Models of Community Organization Practice" in *Strategies of Community Organization: A Book of Readings,* Fred Cox et al., eds. (Itasca, Illinois: Peacock Publishers, 1970), pp. 20–36. (Revised edition, 1974).

used to bring about desirable social goals if implemented by an individual dedicated to such purposes. A given finding regarding organizational behavior, for example, will ordinarily be treated in terms of its implications for organizational or institutional maintenance as well as for what it conveys regarding organizational vulnerability. Clearly the same concept can be applied differently for different social units—as in the instance of an antiestablishment organizer using knowledge about organizational maintenance to enhance the stability of a grassroots militant group. (Although objectivity was attempted in terms of the range and character of possible applications, this was naturally subject to influence by the value orientation indicated earlier.)

Another matter of "point of view" ought to be aired initially, one that is more narrowly professional in scope, but that will require more expanded discussion to explicate. The contents of this volume are written to provide knowledge that will enhance the competency of community workers by helping them to become more precise and effective in achieving intended outcomes. It is assumed that professional change agents do indeed seek to produce ends of specific types and that they hold the responsibility and should increasingly acquire the capability to achieve such ends. Such goals are of course mediated through the interplay of various constituencies and interested parties, as for example clients, board members, organizational supervisors, and political elites. Frequently the community practitioner sees his fundamental role as facilitating decision-making capacity on the part of these relevant actors. Nevertheless, as Morris has suggested, "The exercise of professional leadership requires us to select our goals for action. . . . Our concern with helping others to make up their minds does not excuse us from the obligation of making up our own." [3] Schwartz states this notion somewhat differently, pointing out that often the "modest professional" feels constrained to express his views to those with whom he is associated. Still, "If a man has lived with a problem, reflected upon it, studied it, has been trained to deal with the problem, then he is morally committed to expressing an opinion. The professional role is one of bringing to bear expert opinion supported

[3] Robert Morris, "Community Planning for Health—The Social Welfare Experience," in *Public Health Concepts in Social Work Education* (New York: Council on Social Work Education, 1962), pp. 168–69.

by facts and to place his views on display openly in the committee square." [4] Schwartz hypothesizes that the reluctance to "impose" on a group perhaps cloaks a delusion of omnipotence; somehow if the practitioner voices his opinion everyone will automatically fall in line behind him. The complex, politically tinged reality of most contemporary community work leads one to doubt that this could occur with regularity.

As these words were being composed, one of my students wrote in a class paper of the need for practitioners to protect a reasonable degree of independence of thought and freedom of action from the intrusion of both community elites and administrative superordinates on the one hand, and grass-roots clients and pressure groups on the other. She expressed her concern as follows:

> The planner may be in the precarious position of having to weigh professional goals and criteria of good social planning against the interests of his would be "bosses"—existing agencies and supervisors seeking to maintain themselves at all costs; business, civic or political leaders trying to propel their vested interests; citizens groups espousing "participation" while eyeing fuller pocketbooks.

It is likely that social progress will be propelled best through a convergence of formal-technical and informal-lay elements of society—in other words through the blending of "experts" and "people" (or professionals and clients). "Experts" may contribute at least substantive factual information regarding a particular problem or situation, knowledge concerning generally recognized intervention techniques and processes, and a sense of broader social or value considerations pertaining to the situation. "People" may contribute at least a sense of their peculiar desires, aspirations, and special interests related to a given situation, the reality of the situation as perceived experientially by them, and an assessment of what procedures or processes might be uniquely appropriate to deal with it in their special context.

Litwak and Meyer [5] attack this question somewhat differently from

[4] Meyer Schwartz, "Our Voluntary Committee Life," *Journal of Jewish Communal Service,* 32, no. 3 (Spring 1956): 235–42.

[5] Eugene Litwak and Henry J. Meyer, "The School and The Family: Linking Organizations and External Primary Groups," in *The Uses of Sociology* Paul F. Lazarsfeld et al., eds. (New York: Basic Books, 1967), pp. 522–43.

a useful sociological perspective, telling us that most social processes are composed of "uniform" and "nonuniform" aspects—the former recurrent and predictable; the latter idiosyncratic and emergent. In their analysis, bureaucratic structures (composed of experts) are best equipped to deal with uniform matters; primary groups (composed of locally based people) are best able to deal with nonuniform matters. Since most social situations, state Litwak and Meyer, encompass both, the ability to perform uniform as well as nonuniform tasks is called for:

> We argue that most areas of social endeavor must take account of both uniform and nonuniform tasks and therefore will be most effectively carried on when both bureaucratic and primary-group organizational forms are involved. This is not to say that at any time the balance between uniform and nonuniform aspects of a given social task may not change. It is only to say that in principle both aspects will be involved and both must, in the achievement of most social objectives, be considered. (p. 532)

The relative weighting of inputs into this amalgam, then, may vary from situation to situation. But if the expert is to put his concepts into effect he must be prepared to see that his contribution, even if by vigorous assertion, becomes part of the domain of discourse and action. Underplaying one's role in this connection may be as detrimental as overexerting it, if a meaningful balance is to be achieved.

Also inhibiting to effectiveness is the practitioner who intuitively acts on the imperative of making a professional impact, but who feels this may be undemocratic or improper. He consequently confounds the situation by blurring the character of his role performance in his own eyes as well as in the eyes of others. How much more "manipulating" is this advocate of self-determination who deludes himself or misleads, confuses, or deceives his clients into thinking that he is making a lesser professional impact on the situation than he really is? One may want for good reasons to maintain low public awareness of the extent of one's influence or effect, but this is different from not recognizing it—or denying it.

Many practitioners in the human-service fields cripple their effectiveness through a muddy engagement with terms such as "self-determination," "participatory democracy," and "manipulation." This is not to say that such concepts are unimportant or meaningless, but their application is highly complex, and not particularly aided by philosophical sloganeering. In making a study of the self-determination notion, one observer points out a number of contingencies that shape its applicability: clients may be ambivalent or contradictory concerning their true desires; reality constraints such as legal restrictions, conditions of health, or financial insufficiencies may limit certain wishes; one man's desires may impinge on the prerogatives of others, to the point sometimes of destroying those who are closest to him or oppressing those at a further distance. Human worth, the author concludes, is of greater utility as a concept in giving value direction to professional behavior. "If what the client wants will result in the exploitation of others or the degradation of himself, the worker should try to help him change his desires." [6]

Research studies of community processes which are reported in this book have found that broad public participation may have deleterious effects on such social goals as desegregation of school systems, fluoridation of drinking water, and the passage of mileage proposals to improve public education. A change agent seeking to promote such goals would do well to ponder relative values and alternative social benefits attached to various courses of action. The well known political tactic of keeping the situation cool while getting your own supporters out is one not to be dismissed lightly.

Contrary to much rhetorical expression, "enabling," or "participation," is not the method of choice in all situations. If a community change agent is to be only a docile, automatic expediter of whatever decisions are made by others, then human-service professional schools are greatly overtraining their students. If the practitioner does not stand ready to thwart the wishes of those around him that promote racism, hatred, or exploitation, his function is tarnished.

This is not to say that a practitioner needs always to be assertive and directive in his activities; although at times he may choose to be, and occasionally he must be. Surely, while oriented toward particular social objectives, the practitioner needs to be guided also by the outlook and wishes of others, to be highly sensitive about when to hold back

[6] Saul Bernstein, "Self-Determination: King or Citizen in the Realm of Values?" *Social Work* 5, no. 1 (January 1960): 7–8.

or to defer to other affected, informed, or interested publics. Opportunity for citizen choice is an objective that should be optimized whenever feasible; and if the practitioner's reasoned intention is to increase participation, research-based strategies to support that aim will be found in this volume.

It might make life easier if there were a single, invariant prescribed role: to dominate all decisions or, contrariwise, to be accommodatingly facilitative. Actually the practitioner may be at either of these extremes from time to time. However most of the time he is somewhere in the middle. Simple, unidimensional formulas are comforting, but they reflect neither what occurs in the real world of action or the imperatives necessary for making an impact on a complicated human fabric of interacting individuals and social structures.

Important as they are, value questions such as these are not given prominence in this volume; [7] the function of the book is to make change agents more knowledgeable from a "scientific" standpoint. This should enable them to better manipulate their relevant world. That evocative term is deliberately used because, frowned upon as it is, "manipulation" is the business of the professional—acting on or changing the social or physical environment in some valued direction (architects aim to create more beautiful or functional buildings, doctors better health, teachers more informed or creative citizens). Being calculating in goal-oriented activity needs to be sorted out from engaging in dishonest, illegal, arrogant, or despotic behavior.

In some of the human-service fields, in particular social work, value considerations have disproportionately dominated discourse. This work aims to counterbalance such valid concern by shifting attention to such equally critical matters as competence, incisiveness, and predictability in performance. Allowing that change agents and those they work with have goals, we shall focus on what social-science research literature has to say about potentially efficacious means for reaching them.

In assessing the current state of knowledge in social planning for human services a student of the subject was lead to declare:

[7] These matters are discussed at greater length by the author in "An Analysis of Roles and Goals in Community Organization Practice" in *Readings in Community Organization Practice* Ralph M. Kramer and Harry Specht, eds. (Englewood Cliffs: Prentice Hall, Inc., 1969), pp. 260–68.

At the present time, much of the knowledge base of social planning is a haphazard collection of practical principles and sundry truisms such as "Planning begins with dissatisfaction," "Participation of all important interests is necessary," "Involve the power structure," and "Obstacles to planning must be identified and overcome." Some attempts have been made to develop a theoretical base, and some principles are supported by empirical data gathered for the purpose, but in most cases this data is not substantial. Planners have hardly begun the long-term effort that will be required to identify the variables that influence planning, to specify the types of relationships existing among these variables, and to create useful concepts that summarize and organize the variables and their relationships.[8]

It is to that overriding long-term objective that this particular scholarly undertaking is resolutely directed. It will endeavor to contribute one incremental step to the developmental chain of effort involved in the process of acquiring scientific knowledge.

This book was written out of respect and affection for knowledge, a passion for social justice, and an urge to construct theories and techniques that might improve the human condition. It springs from diverse influences and has various shadings of purpose. Its author is a man-in-the-middle: call him an applied scientist, or a scientific practitioner; the better choice is uncertain. The tension between the interlocked motivations and purposes may have brought about occasional unevenness or ambiguity in this exposition. Are the writer's real roots in the academic world or the world of action and service? Perhaps the tension cannot be resolved, and indeed it may serve as a catalyst for newer, more creative formulations: not theory *or* practice, but theory *about* practice. Lewin said there is nothing as practical as a good theory. Let us see.

JACK ROTHMAN
Ann Arbor, Michigan

[8] James J. Callahan, Jr., "Obstacles and Social Planning," *Social Work* 18, no. 6 (Winter 1973): 70–79.

Part One
Overview

Chapter One
Purpose and Process

THIS BOOK is responsive to the reverberations of what we have come to know as the "knowledge explosion." In particular it aims to present to those engaged in social planning, community work, and social action what the outpouring of recent social-science research has to say concerning intervention strategies and programs.

It is evident that writings on purposive community change are highly scattered through a wide spectrum of journals from many fields. No single journal exists that concentrates or specializes in this area. It is extremely difficult for busy, deeply involved practitioners and activists to keep up with this burgeoning literature of various disciplines or to obtain a coherent picture of what patterns or tendencies are being shaped by researchers studying dimensions of community processes from different vantage points. Nor indeed, have academicians mastered this problem. That practitioners and academicians tend to have different orientations and to use different languages compounds the problem of utilization of research data by people in the field.

Accordingly, in this project we have broadly surveyed the relevant scientific literature for appropriate materials, specifically those journals which emphasize community variables, research outcomes, and also evidence an applied orientation; the aim was to discover in the literature (and unpublished materials as well) reasonably validated empirical referents to guide community practice and to synthesize this material in one publication. Throughout the study criteria related to *systematic and controlled investigation* of phenomena were employed in order to select only studies of appropriate "hardness" for the data pool.

The point here is not that there is an absence of pertinent literature. Many works touching on various aspects of community structure or planned community change are currently available, but largely in disarray as far as the practitioner is concerned. Most of these writings have one or more deficiencies: an inadequate base of empirical research, faulty conceptualization, a level of theoretical abstraction that does not sufficiently address application, or an emphasis on one or another limited band of the range of forms of community action. The difficulties in obtaining a stronger conceptual base for community practice were articulated by a group of application-minded social scientists: "In some cases we were unable to locate change agents who could deal abstractly with their diagnostic techniques and their principles and methods of inducing change. This split between those who act and those who conceptualize was particularly and rather painfully conspicuous among change agents working at the level of community systems." [1]

Several researchers have made note of the sparse acquaintanceship that community practitioners have with available social-science knowledge. Roland Warren, for example, maintains that sociology can make an important contribution to community organization by providing background about the social context (particularly the community setting) in which practice takes place as well as about the process of social change. Nevertheless, when Warren reviewed several practitioner-oriented journals over a five-year period, he found surprisingly inadequate references to the relevant sociological literature in articles dealing with community matters, and he discovered that research findings in key areas such as voluntary organizations or structural aspects of social problems were "virtually neglected." [2] Significant works by such contributors as Sower, Coleman, and Banfield were entirely or nearly entirely absent. Warren found that his personal bibliography on community contained many more items than the total number of citations found in all the pertinent articles he reviewed in these practitioner journals.

Another study was carried out directly with human-service workers

[1] Ronald Lippitt, Jeanne Watson, Bruce Westley, *The Dynamics of Planned Change* (New York: Harcourt, Brace and Company, 1958), p. 17.

[2] Roland Warren, "Application of Social Science Knowledge to the Community Organization Field," *Journal of Education for Social Work* 3, no. 1 (Spring 1967): 60–72.

practicing in health and welfare areas.[3] Workers filled out questionnaires that tested their familiarity with sociological information pertaining to socially and economically disadvantaged groups. It was found that a stereotyped attitude set rather than factually based knowledge controlled answers. Not only was the general level of knowledge low, but a degree of formal education attained among respondents made no difference concerning the amount of social knowledge manifested in responses to the questionnaires.

By collecting community-level research findings and organizing them into conceptual categories which are of relevance to the practitioner—such as participation, organizational innovation, or the use of intervention roles—this work will aim to acquaint the community change agent with relevant social-science information, providing a broader and better substantiated knowledge base to guide his practice than is currently available.

Existing Models of Research Retrieval Studies

The effort being attempted was given encouragement and was informed by analogous work in several other fields. At the intrapsychic level, Goldstein, Heller, and Sechrest have compiled research findings in psychotherapy to provide guidelines to the clinician on such matters as interpersonal attraction in the therapy relationship, resistance to behavior change, transfer of therapeutic learning, and composition of psychotherapy groups.[4] Collins and Guetzkow have made a similar compilation in the area of decision making in small groups, drawing largely from literature in small-group research.[5] These authors propounded generalizations concerning such issues as direct and indirect sources of power in decision-making groups, obstacles to effective interpersonal relations, participant satisfaction, and leadership traits and

---

[3] Lois Pratt, "Level of Sociological Knowledge among Health and Social Workers," *Journal of Health and Social Behavior* 10, no. 1 (March 1969): 59–65.

[4] Arnold P. Goldstein, Kenneth Heller, and Lee B. Sechrest, *Psychotherapy and the Psychology of Behavior Change* (New York: John Wiley and Sons, 1966).

[5] Barry E. Collins and Harold Guetzkow, *A Social Psychology of Group Process for Decision Making* (New York: John Wiley and Sons, 1964).

roles. While their volume is not specifically designed for practitioners, it does concern itself with the practical aspects of improving decision making in small groups.

An early significant work employing the methodology suggested here is Robin Williams's *The Reduction of Intergroup Tensions*. Williams's project incorporated 101 propositions, including techniques and procedures for improving relations among various racial and ethnic groups. The study collated research on programs conducted by human-relations agencies and suggested programmatic initiatives based on the effects of information and education, of contact and collaboration among contending groups, of legislation and law enforcement, and of different social arrangements among groups. Williams also provided background research information on such matters as origins of hostility, types of conflict, and reactions of minority groups. Examples of propositions by Williams illustrate the orientation toward application incorporated in the book:

> Prejudices are most likely to be changed by the imparting of information about the object of prejudice when learners themselves actively participate in gathering the relevant information.
> Hostility is decreased by any activity which leads members of conflicting groups to identify their own values and life-activities in individuals of the other group. To be most effective this requires devices for inducing personal identification before the introduction of group labels. Dictum: Personalize, Personalize, Personalize.[6]

Some additional related studies in fairly specific subareas include Rogers's, having to do with the diffusion of innovations, and another by Price on organizational management.[7]

More encyclopedic and ambitious is the volume by Berelson and Steiner,[8] which attempts to codify all available social-science knowl-

[6] Robin M. Williams, Jr., *The Reduction of Intergroup Tensions: A Survey of Research on Problems of Ethnic, Racial and Religious Group Relations* (New York: Social Science Research Council, 1947), pp. 65, 66.

[7] Everett Rogers, *The Diffusion of Innovations* (New York: Free Press, 1962); revised edition, with F. F. Shoemaker, *Communication of Innovations,* 1972; James L. Price, *Organization Effectiveness: An Inventory of Research* (Homewood, Ill.: Dorsey Press, 1968).

[8] Bernard Berelson and Gary A. Steiner, *Human Behavior: An Inventory of Scientific Findings* (New York: Harcourt, Brace and World, 1964).

edge concerning "human behavior." This book involves, in large measure, generalizations concerning a great range of individual and social processes, with no particular attention to application principles.

The above are some extant examples of the type of compilation being attempted in this volume. The review should enable the reader to become familiar with the domain of endeavor and to place the current work in a relevant contemporary context.

Overview of Related Community Literature

It might be of value in orienting the reader to the setting of this project to briefly review and characterize the available general literature in the area. Some writings attempt to portray or codify "practice wisdom" accumulated by those familiar with community work, usually in a single professional field such as social work, public health, education, or community development,[9] or with reference to a particular social-

[9] SOCIAL WORK. Arthur Dunham, *Community Welfare Organization: Principles and Practice* (New York: Thomas Y. Crowell, 1958), revised edition, *The New Community Organization,* 1970; Campbell G. Murphy, *Community Organization Principles* (Boston: Houghton Mifflin, 1954); C. King, *Organizing for Community Action* (New York: Harper, 1948); H. D. Green, *Social Work Practice in Community Organization* (New York: Whiteside and Morrow, 1954); A. Hillman, *Community Organization and Planning* (New York: Macmillan, 1950); R. Johns and David F. DeMarche, *Community Organization and Agency Responsibility* (New York: Association Press, 1951); Ernest Harper and Arthur Dunham, *Community Organization in Action: Basic Literature and Critical Comments* (New York: Association Press, 1959). George Brager and Harry Specht, *Community Organizing* (New York: Columbia University Press, 1973); Arnold Gurin and Robert Perlman, *Community Organization and Social Planning* (New York: John Wiley & Sons, 1972).

PUBLIC HEALTH. American Public Health Association, *A Guide to Medical Care Administration* (New York: American Public Health Association, 1965); Munel Bliss Wilbur, *Community Health Services* (Philadelphia: Sanders, 1962); *Area-Wide Planning for Hospitals and Related Health Facilities* (Washington, D.C.: U.S. Government Printing Office, 1961), Public Health Service Publication #855.

EDUCATION. G. McClosky, *Education and Public Understanding* (New York: Harper, 1959): M. R. Sumpting and Y. Engstrom, *School Community Relations: A New Approach* (New York: McGraw-Hill, 1966); National Society for the Study of Education, *Citizen Cooperation for Better Schools,* 53d Yearbook (Chicago: University of Chicago Press, 1954).

COMMUNITY DEVELOPMENT. Richard Franklin, *Patterns of Community Development* (Washington, D.C.: Public Affairs Press, 1966); United Nations, *Social Progress*

problem area such as housing, juvenile delinquency, or the aging.[10] These books often give considerable attention to technique and programmatic consideration devoid of theoretical structure. Other authors attempt to examine case studies and inductively draw implications for action therefrom.[11] Still another approach revolves around a set of

---

through Community Development (New York: United Nations, 1955); Peter DuSavtory, *Community Development in Ghana* (London: Oxford University Press, 1958); T. R. Batten, *Communities and Their Development* (London: Oxford University Press, 1957).

[10] HOUSING. Fern M. Colbern, *The Neighborhood and Urban Renewal* (New York: National Federation of Settlements and Neighborhood Centers, 1963); D. H. Webster, *Urban Planning and Municipal Public Policy* (New York: Harper, 1958); *Working Together for Urban Renewal* (Chicago: Joint Committee on Housing and Welfare of the National Association of Housing and Redevelopment Officials and National Social Welfare Assembly, 1958); "Community Organization in Public Housing and Urban Renewal," in *National Conference on Social Welfare: Community Organization, 1959* (New York: Columbia University Press, 1959).

JUVENILE DELINQUENCY. William E. Ames, et al., *Action Programs for Delinquency Prevention* (Springfield, Illinois: Thomas, 1965); Robert McIver, *The Prevention and Control of Delinquency* (New York: Atherton Press, 1966); *New Approaches to Prevention and Control of Juvenile Delinquency* (Washington, D.C.: Office of Juvenile Delinquency and Youth Development, 1965).

AGING. *Program Planning for Strengthening Services to the Aging through Public Welfare Agencies* (Chicago: American Public Welfare Association, 1965); *Seminar on Community Planning for Older Adults,* Proceedings of a seminar held at Brandeis University, August 27–September 1, 1961 (New York: United Funds and Councils of America, 1962); U.S. President's Council on Aging and Administration on Aging, *A Guide to Community Action* (Washington, D.C.: U.S. Government Printing Office, 1966); Welfare Council of Metropolitan Chicago, *Community Services for Older People: The Chicago Plan* (Chicago: Wilcox and Follett, 1952).

[11] J. Abrahamson, *A Neighborhood Finds Itself* (New York: Harper, 1959); *Adams County Public Assistance Study: A Community Organization Record* (New York: Council on Social Work Education, 1955); S.R. Gordon, *The Reorganization of the Winston County Unemployment Relief Board* (New York: Association Press, 1949); Alexander F. Miller, *Crisis Without Violence* (New York: Anti-Defamation League of B'nai B'rith, 1964); *A Neighborhood Acts to Improve Its Living Conditions* (New York: Council on Social Work Education, 1956); Jean and Jess Ogden, *These Things We Tried* (Charlottesville: University Press of Virginia, 1947); B. D. Paul, *Health, Culture and Community: Case Studies of Public Reactions to Health Programs* (New York: Russell Sage Foundation, 1955); J. T. Reid, *It Happened to Taos* (Albuquerque: University of New Mexico Press, 1947); E. H. Spicer, *Human Problems in Technological Change: A Casebook* (New York: Russell Sage Foundation, 1952); Jack Walker, *Sit-Ins in Atlanta* (New York: McGraw-Hill and Co.); Eagleton Institute, *Case Studies in Practical Politics,* no. 34.

moral principles, which are presumed to guide the practitioner in an
ethical as well as an efficacious manner.[12]

One of the most widely used volumes is Murray Ross's *Community
Organization: Theory and Principles,*[13] which has the defects of
datedness, a bias toward a participatory, highly consensual mode of
action, and use of a circumscribed range of social-science literature
drawn largely from social psychology. Another much-used book is
The Dynamics of Planned Change by Lippitt, Watson, and Westley.[14]
This volume has the virtue of examining common elements of intervention at the individual, group organizational, and community levels;
its concomitant limitation is that it gives proportionately slight emphasis to the community dimension. Also, in juxtaposition to the approach
here, the generalizations are essentially based on a large number of
case studies, rather than on empirical research per se. A volume by
Morris and Binstock[15] focuses on that aspect of community organization which involves the activities by social-planning practitioners,
oriented toward changing the policies of formal organizations. It draws
primarily on literature pertaining to organizational theory and includes
some original comparative community research. Another volume by
Goodenough gives a social anthropology perspective on change efforts
in rural communities in underdeveloped societies.[16] This work is confined theoretically to a self-help, cooperative mode of social change
and has an overriding psychologically oriented stance. Change effort is
viewed from the vantage point of modifying the self-image or personal

[12] William W. and L. J. Biddle, *The Community Development Process* (New York:
Holt, Rinehart and Winston, 1965); Richard W. Poston, *Democracy Is You* (New York:
Harper and Brothers, 1953).

[13] Murray G. Ross, *Community Organization: Theory and Principles* (New York:
Harper and Brothers, 1955). This book was reissued in 1967 with little change. It cannot
be considered updated except for some newer bibliographical references.

[14] Ronald Lippitt, Jeanne Watson, and Bruce Westley, *The Dynamics of Planned
Change: A Comparative Study of Principles and Techniques* (New York: Harcourt, Brace
and Company, 1958).

[15] Robert Morris and Robert H. Binstock, *Feasible Planning for Social Change* (New
York: Columbia University Press, 1966).

[16] Ward Hunt Goodenough, *Cooperation in Change: An Anthropological Approach to
Community Development* (New York: The Russell Sage Foundation, 1963).

sense of identity on the part of individuals and groups in the society.

Writings in the field of urban planning and design likewise either lean toward rather pragmatic atheoretical formulations,[17] or conceptions on a more grandiose theoretical plane,[18] not translated into language or application tools immediately usable to the community planner and activist.

Some existing collections draw applied types of materials from social sciences, but with little or no attempt to synthesize these materials or to inform the community practitioner in a practical way.[19] A more successful work of this genre has been issued by the National Association of Social Workers.[20]

Other social-science volumes deal with theories of community structure and process with little applicability.[21] Besides this there has been a bewildering barrage of strictly social-science writings in areas of special concern to community practice such as power structure, political processes, race relations, social stratification, and the like. As stated earlier, Warren in one of the few systematic studies on the ex-

[17] The Editors of *Fortune, The Exploding Metropolis* (Garden City, New York: Doubleday, 1958): Jane Jacobs, *The Death and Life of Great American Cities* (New York: Random House, 1961).

[18] Harvey S. Perloff (ed.), *Planning and the Urban Community* (Pittsburgh: Carnegie Institute of Technology and the University of Pittsburgh Press, 1961); Paul Goodman and Percival Goodman, *Communitas: Means of Livelihood and Ways of Life* (New York: Vintage, 1960).

[19] Alvin Gouldner and S.M. Miller (eds.), *Applied Sociology: Opportunities and Problems* (New York: The Free Press, 1965); Arthur B. Shostak, *Sociology in Action: Case Studies in Social Problems and Directed Social Change* (Homewood, Illinois: The Dorsey Press, 1966); Warren G. Bennis, Kenneth D. Benne and Robert Chin (eds.) *The Planning of Change: Readings in the Applied Behavioral Sciences* (New York: Holt, Rinehart and Winston, 1961); P.F. Lazerfeld, William H. Sewell, and H.L. Wilensky, *The Uses of Sociology* (New York: Basic Books, 1967).

[20] Henry S. Maas (ed.), *Five Fields of Social Service: Review of Research* (New York: National Association of Social Workers, 1966), revised edition, *Research in The Social Services: A Five Year Review,* 1971.

[21] Nelson Lowry, et al., *Community Structure and Change* (New York: Macmillan Co., 1960); Roland Warren, *The Community in America* (Chicago: Rand McNally, 1963); Irwin Sanders, *The Community,* 2d ed. (New York: Ronald Press, 1966); Paul K. Hatt and A. J. Reiss Jr., *Cities and Society: The Revised Reader in Urban Sociology* (Glencoe, Illinois: The Free Press, 1957).

tent to which this literature has been applied in community organization came to grim and discouraging conclusions.[22]

Hopefully I have made a case for the need for the kind of comprehensive review and codification of research data, with an eye on application, which is the concern of this volume. I shall next amplify the methodology used in this venture.

Methodology of the Study

I have scaled down my description of the methodology to the minimum required for the reader to move expeditiously into the text that follows. In the Appendix is a fuller discussion and analysis of the methodology, including an explication of its limitations, which is necessary in order to assess substantive aspects of the body of this report.

The major retrieval approach entailed a thorough, detailed search of a selected group of thirty journals which had been found to contain, in relatively large proportions, specific kinds of pertinent data. These journals were examined rigorously over a six-year period, 1964–70. Sociological journals received particular emphasis, but journals in the fields of political science, applied anthropology, psychology, social psychology, and in several professional practice fields were also very seriously considered.

The journals selected for study were those which contained proportionately larger numbers of articles with the following characteristics:
   a. empirical research findings
   b. community contexts or community change variables
   c. an applied emphasis offering potential action derivatives—either directly or indirectly.

The general rule was to seek out articles that were fairly close to the "stuff" of community practice or whose findings could be applied fairly readily and obviously to community practice. Preference was given to evaluative studies of, for example, change projects, studies of

[22] Roland Warren, "Application of Social Science Knowledge to the Community Organization Field," *Journal of Social Work Education* (Council on Social Work Education) 3 (Spring 1967): 60–72.

community planning, committee processes, investigations of participation in civic action, and voluntary associations. Broad studies of such subjects as anomie or social stratification were generally excluded. Some degree of flexibility and prudent use of judgment was necessary here in making selections.[23] There were certain advantages and some drawbacks in this procedure. There is value in bringing together research findings that are close to the actual operations of community-organization practice; questions of economy and manageability speak to this approach. However, holding to empirical research findings may yield a loss with regard to "insight" and theory materials. In terms of placing boundaries on the inquiry and giving the research retrieval and utilization approach a full test, this limitation was accepted.

The level of abstraction aimed for was "middle-range" theory or modest empirical generalization. The effort was directed at being able to describe regularities in the way certain change processes occur, or to anticipate to some degree outcomes of some types of interventions aimed at particular goals under given general conditions.

Studies included in this investigation were not scrutinized in terms of the adequacy or sophistication of research design. This would have been an extremely time-consuming procedure, and sufficient information for evaluation of this type was often unavailable. Studies that upon inspection were seen to contain obvious deficiencies in sample adequacy or representativeness, or in logical or statistical treatment, were eliminated. It was assumed that the more defendable generalizations or action principles would emerge from a convergence of the cumulative findings of a sizable number of studies rather than from the conclusions of any single study.

---

[23] Some available writings suggest procedures for the selection and application of social-science knowledge. See, for example, Edwin Thomas, "Selecting Knowledge from Behavioral Science" and "Types of Contributions Social Science Makes to Social Work" in, *Behavioral Science for Social Workers* Edwin J. Thomas, ed. (New York: The Free Press, 1967). See also *Building Social Work Knowledge: Report of a Conference* (New York: National Association of Social Workers, 1964); Ruth Leed and Thomasina Smith (eds.) *Using Social Science Knowledge in Business and Industry: Report of a Seminar* (Homewood, Illinois: Richard D. Irwin Inc., 1963); Rensis Likert and Samuel P. Hays Jr. (eds.), *Some Applications of Behavioral Research* (New York, UNESCO Publications Center, 1957).

The primary strategy in retrieval process was to survey selected journals that contained materials relevant to the project. The use of indices and similar procedures was found to yield a considerable amount of irrelevant or unusable material under any topic used for search purposes, such as community participation or formal organizations. Many of the articles are conjectural or in the realm of "pure" theory which is not easily transformable into action principles.

Through a preliminary review of journals by the investigator as well as a student project on the subject,[24] a somewhat extensive and yet circumscribed listing of relevant journals for this study was composed. These journals are indicated below:

I. *The Disciplines*
   A. *Applied Anthropology*
      American Anthropologist
      Human Organization
   B. *Political Science*
      American Political Science Review
      Journal of Politics
      Midwest Journal of Political Science
   C. *Psychology and Social Psychology*
      American Behavior Scientist
      Applied Behavioral Science
      Human Relations
      Journal of Human Relations
      Journal of Social Issues
      Public Opinion Quarterly
   D. *Sociology*
      Administrative Science Quarterly
      American Journal of Sociology
      American Sociological Review
      Journal of Health and Social Behavior
      Rural Sociology
      Social Forces
      Social Problems
      Trans-Action

[24] Edmond A. Penn, "Where to Find Community Organization Research" (University of Michigan, 1966, Mimeographed).

E. *Others*
Journal of Conflict Resolution
Urban Affairs Quarterly

II. *The Professions*
A. *Adult Education*
Adult Education
Adult Leadership
B. *City Planning*
Journal of the American Institute of Planners
C. *Community Mental Health*
American Journal of Orthopsychiatry
Community Mental Health Journal
D. *Public Administration*
Public Administration Review
E. *Public Health*
American Journal of Public Health
F. *Social Work*
Social Service Review
Social Work

The parameters of the periodical study, then, were these thirty journals and the time dimension 1964–70. Reviewers simply examined a given journal, article by article, over the time frame of the study. They identified all relevant articles according to the specified criteria, prepared a standardized abstract on these, and coded the subject matter into all appropriate categories into which it fit. (A copy of the report form is in Appendix B.)

This core plan was augmented in several ways:

1. Dissertations in social work for the same time period were screened and abstracted.
2. The more informal social-science network was tapped through a systematic review of professional papers delivered at Sociology and Social Work Conferences in 1968 and 1969.
3. More "fugitive" reports and writings were surveyed through use of the *Digest of Urban and Regional Research*.
4. Pertinent books and reports that came to the attention of the project staff were included in the data pool. There was no systematic survey of such materials, but when an especially relevant work intruded itself upon staff consciouness it was not ignored.

The list of journals plus the first three items mentioned above constituted the universe within which a systematic search for appropriate research articles was conducted. In addition, an attempt was made to utilize existing data banks and abstracting services and files. This latter exploration yielded very little of practical utility for the project. In all, 921 research reports were retrieved and processed in the project.

Generalizations and application principles reported here were developed (and constrained) by the universe from which we retrieved our data and the methods used. The procedure has limitations and may appear artificial to some critics. No doubt important studies and writers escaped our net. Still, we hope to have achieved reasonably good coverage of social-science research findings in the recent past.

Research reports were coded in terms of some sixteen "Practice Issue Areas." These were areas considered to be of relevance to community planners and activists. The Issue Areas originally were selected inductively, on the basis of my first-hand familiarity with practitioners and their concerns and modes of action. Following a trial period in using the composed categories to review the literature, two new categories were added which were found to be present in the literature to a substantial degree. These included Diffusion and Adoption of Innovations, and Movement and Assimilation of Populations. These are categories that social scientists addressed more than practitioners, but that had strong practice implications. A listing of the main Issue Areas investigated will be found below, with those to be reported on in this volume marked with an asterisk. It was not possible to complete the analysis and processing of all areas in the time allotted for the project. However, because of overlap among subject areas, material from some uncovered areas was included in covered areas—for example, Political and Legislative process subsuming some aspects of Community Decision making, and Planning Processes.

Communication
Community Decision Making
* Diffusion and Adoption of Innovations
* Legislative Political Governmental Processes
* Movement and Assimilation of Populations
* Organizational Management
* Participation

Planning Processes
Power Structure of the Community
* Practitioner Roles
Resistance to Change
Structure and Delivery of Services
Social Influence
Strategy

The retrieved studies were coded according to these specific categories. Generalizations were composed by working within each category and grouping together studies dealing with the same delimited topical area. From these consensus findings inferred application principles (or action guidelines) were constructed.

The inductive nature of our investigation mitigated against the use of an overarching theoretical framework embracing the entire work. However, the presentation of Issue Areas in the book suggests a logical ordering of concepts. We start with the practitioner–change agent and the various roles he plays in engineering the change process. At the heart of practice lies such an individual, who engages himself analytically in a fluid and complex social situation. This change agent is the ultimate intended user of these materials and fundamentally it is to help enhance his effectiveness that they are written.

Organizational frameworks are crucial in the community intervention process, and we concentrate on these next. Most practitioners are based in agencies or action groups, which provide them with change opportunities and resources while at the same time place constraints on their freedom of action. Such organizations typically provide salary or give basic legitimation. In addition to working through employing agencies or sponsoring organizations, practitioners are recurrently directing their attention to target organizations of various kinds— friendly, hostile or disinterested; resistant or favorable; to gain support or change policies—just to mention a few relevant dimensions.

Organizations are located within a community system of one kind or another. While various subsystems and facets of community might be explored, we have chosen to focus on the political-legislative aspect of community. On the one hand this is viewed as a key subsystem in terms of leverage for community decision making, and on the other it is neglected by some community practitioners, particularly those who are so preoccupied with professionalism that they retreat from the brash and unscrupulous tone that frequently surrounds the political process.

Having surveyed three social aggregate levels—practitioner roles, organizational factors, and political processes—we shall next take up the matter of participation, which emphasizes to a greater degree the client perspective in community practice. Many practitioners see involvement of community participants either as an ethical imperative or as a necessary strategic vehicle for pursuing practice goals. Obtaining an adequate level of client participation often becomes a key practice task.

We shall turn to two change processes in the community: diffusion of innovations, and movement and assimilation of populations. The first is in the "planned change" category. In their programmatic activities, practitioners often seek to promote new ideas, techniques, or service arrangements. The diffusion chapter deals with dissemination of such programs, directed at population groups in the community or at organizational units of various kinds. Movement of populations may be seen as a more "natural" community change process characteristic of the contemporary period. Here the practitioner will typically be more reactive, attempting to control the form or speed of movement in order to minimize dilatory effects of population mobility.

In each of these areas we shall present both generalizations (or consensus findings) descriptive of pertinent social phenomena, and parallel action principles regarding the manipulation of the phenomena in the interests of creating more equitable or humane circumstances.

Description of Presentation Format

The thrust of the study is toward developing generalizations based on consensus findings in the data (several studies in different locales and with different populations arriving at a similar conclusion). These generalizations are built substantially from the original studies and hence by and large make statements about the nature of social phenomena (example: status inconsistency has been found to be associated with a predisposition to participate in social movements). From the generalizations we developed a series of derivations called "action guidelines," which are intended to translate generalizations into their logical applied formulations (example: in seeking participants for social-action programs, the practitioner would be well advised to recruit from among community residents having characteristics of status inconsistency). These action guidelines require the injection of inference, which moves the generalization one step beyond its immediate scientific formulation. We have attempted to keep the leap from findings to their utilization small in order to preserve their original scientific character. The action guidelines may be viewed as emergent hypotheses concerning approaches to intervention, which are in turn an outgrowth of social-science research findings and hence have a firmer, more substantive foundation than is usually characteristic of writings about community organization.

Following the statement of a generalization, the reader will find listed numbers that indicate the studies on which it was based. These numbers refer to the bibliography, which follows that particular practice issue area. In addition there is an assessment of strength of literature support, which the staff attached to that generalization. The range is from one plus (+) or low literature support to four pluses (+ + + +) or high literature support. When there are many studies, of good quality, all confirming a given generalization, a higher rating is indicated. However, when a generalization is based on only one or two studies, or where the studies appear weak, or where there are conflicting findings, a lower rating is given. These literature support ratings should not be viewed as "scientific" or rigorous. They represent the staff's informed judgment based on familiarity with the content and configuration of findings, which is shared with the reader. So long as the judgmental and tentative character of these ratings is acknowledged they may prove helpful to the reader.

It might be added that upon close inspection, most instances of what appeared initially to be conflicts among findings became qualifications or specialized expressions of general statements. Thus, subgeneralizations often emerged from what at first glance appeared to be antithetical in the data. Where inconsistencies remained (an equal number of positive and negative findings, with no clear difference in the quality of the research) no generalization was formulated, although sometimes the factual information indicating the discrepancy was conveyed in the text.

It might serve to clarify the presentation format if one brief example were given in greater detail. The following illustration is taken from the practice issue area on Organizational Behavior and concerns one aspect of agency structural arrangements.

1. GENERALIZATION: Organizations that operate under conditions of high degree of certainty (internally or externally) tend to be characterized by centralization in decision making. Further, this relationship is associated with efficiency of operation. Conversely, where there are relatively high degrees of uncertainty, modes of operation and effectiveness are associated with decentralization in decision making.

2. Listing of Research Studies Compatible with the Proposition

Aiken, M. and J. Hage. "Routine Technology, Social Structure and Organizational Goals." *Administrative Science Quarterly* 14, no. 3 (1969):366–75.

Bar-Yosef, R. and O. S. Schild. "Pressures and Defenses in Bureaucratic Rules." *American Journal of Sociology* 71, no. 6 (1966):665–73.

Klatzky, S. R. "Organizational Size, Complexity and Coordination: Alternative Hypotheses." Paper presented at the American Sociological Association Meeting, San Francisco, 1969.

Lawrence, P. and J. W. Lorsch. "Differentiation and Integration in Complex Organizations." *Administrative Science Quarterly* 12, no. 1 (1967):1–47.

Simpson, R. L. and W. H. Gulley. "Goals, Environmental Pressures and Organizational Characteristics." *American Sociological Review* 27, no. 3 (1962):344–51.

Kaufman, H., *The Forest Ranger* (Baltimore: Johns Hopkins Press, 1960).

Eisenstadt, S. N. and L. Katz. "Some Sociological Observations in the Response of Israeli Organizations to New Immigrants.'' *Administrative Science Quarterly* 5, no. 1 (1960):113–33.

3. Literature Support

Strong (+ + + +). Several good studies in support, no studies in opposition. Also, a well-established base of theory lends credence to the generalization.

4. Action Guidelines: Practitioners in organizations functioning in a context of relatively high degrees of certainty should consider a centralized structure in order to increase efficiency of operation. Practitioners in organizations functioning under relatively high degrees of uncertainty should consider decentralized structural arrangements in order to increase effectiveness.

The basic process employed progresses from research generalizations to derived action statements. In the text itself we provide illustrative examples of studies, definitions of terms, limiting conditions constraining implementation, etc. The abbreviated version reveals the skeletal structure of presentation. A more general, theoretical discussion of the research utilization process that underlies the entire work will be found in the concluding chapter.

On Employing the Utilization Study

Several points of clarification are necessary in order to facilitate the reader's use of this material. The form of the presentation was derived inductively from the pool of studies in given practice issue areas. Chapters were composed from findings in specific issue areas. We discovered that the amount, level, and character of studies in these different issue areas varied considerably. For example, there were a great number of studies in the literature dealing with participation, although participation in its own right does not constitute a highly-developed, comprehensive school of theory or scholarly endeavor. Thus, Part Five possesses a high level of density, resulting from an attempt to consolidate a huge amount of information within a relatively small amount of space with few conventional theoretical categories. Although the presentation is allotted two chapters, a sense of density remains.

Part two has a different character. Practitioner role performance is a fairly amorphous area in which not many studies were found and in which there is an almost total absence of conventional theoretical superstructure. Hence, generalizations were based on fewer instances of common research findings; more opportunity existed to report discursively on the details and methodology of studies. The organizational research area is still different, however, in that there are a moderate number of studies dealing with human-service organizations falling within the framework of a fairly common and established discipline of research and theory. The strategy of presentation overall was to allow the writing to emanate from the particular character or state of research and theory, rather than to fit findings mechanically into a standardized format.

As stated earlier, one study may have various facets or a number of application potentialities, so that it can appear in more than one practice issue area. Thus the reader may find some repetition of studies or even ideas in a number of different chapters. In part this is dictated by the desire to make chapters to the greatest degree possible self-contained, so that one might be able to find the maximum information under a given general subject without having to skim throughout the entire book. While this makes for some degree of duplication, the gain was thought to be greater than the loss.

While the generalizations emerge directly from research findings, action guidelines require a cognitive "leap" from the findings to their application. This leap includes the exercise of inference, conjecture, and imagination. In a sense, it is the most creative component of the study. To the greatest degree possible, the staff "stayed close to the findings" in fashioning application derivations. Wild flights of fancy were resisted and avoided. Nevertheless, the reader should be aware that most of the original studies (designed and conducted from the perspective of social scientists) were of social phenomena, not of mechanisms or processes to deliberately change social phenomena. Hence, action guidelines go one step beyond the primary data in most instances; they constitute *intervention principles* for use by the practitioner, and provide better direction for affecting practice outcomes than most other written materials available. At the same time, they might be viewed alternatively as a series of *emergent intervention hypotheses* for future research, since in their existing formulation they have not directly been tested scientifically. It should also be acknowledged that the action guidelines cannot be applied in a mechanistic, cookbook manner. Many situational (community, organizational, etc.) and personality factors must be weighed in deciding when, if, and how to utilize a guideline. Clearly, social practice requires a skillful blending of art and science. The material presented here aims to contribute to the scientific component of that amalgam.

For each part of this volume (participation, innovation, etc.) there is a separate bibliography listing all authors whose studies provided the data base for constructing generalizations and action guidelines in that part. In addition, there is a general index listing authors of all studies used in the book, as well as key authors footnoted in the text, whose writings provided general background information but who were not part of the data base. A total of 578 separate reports make up the data base. A comprehensive index of subjects is also provided.

Part Two

*The Practitioner-
Change Agent*

Chapter Two

Practitioner Roles: Variables Affecting Role Performance

INTRODUCTION

WHY CONSIDER the subject of practitioner-change agent roles? In a sense practitioner roles, translated as specific behavioral modes of operation on the part of practitioners, are at the heart of what may be termed intervention or change agentry or practice. An individual who uses knowledge, technical skill, and sensitivity in social interaction, with his own person as a major and direct instrument of impact, often plays a crucial part in professions and movements aiming to modify patterns of social arrangements. This implies that he must have a keen understanding of what roles to assume at what times and how to execute these roles to achieve maximum effect.

The professional literature has dwelt on the concept of role to a considerable degree. That much of this discussion has been largely amorphous in character, without hard evidence or conceptual rigor, is not to say that practitioners may not have been dealing intuitively with a significant core ingredient of their work.

Practitioner or change agent roles have typically been discussed in general, unidimensional terms in writings on community organization. One major trend of thought has pertained to the employment of roles directed at "task" vs. "process" goals: the argument often pursued through normative discourse with writers supporting one or another role orientation on the basis of alleged values or traditions of the profession, or some other philosophical assumption. Thus, sometimes a single role set, such as "enabling," has been set forth as the only legitimate position.[1] In recent years a more relativist perspective has

---

[1] Kenneth L. M. Pray, "When Is Community Organization Social Work Practice?" in *Proceedings, National Conference of Social Work,* 1947 (New York, Columbia University Press, 1948).

been offered [2] as well as a broader range of role categories.[3] For example, Grosser has portrayed the enabler, broker, advocate, and activist in neighborhood work; Sanders uses the analyst, planner, organizer, and program administrator in overseas community development; Ross—for all settings—uses the guide, enabler, expert, and social therapist. Most recently, roles in planning for delinquency control were described by Spergel as enabler, advocate, organizer, and developer. There is indeed much overlap as well as imprecise definition among these typologies, and their character is essentially descriptive. That is to say, they denote classes of activity which are presumed to be typical of all practitioners or of practitioners in more discrete settings. We will carry this discussion of roles one step further by attempting to specify conditions under which roles may ideally be employed under different governing circumstances.

VARIABLES BEARING ON ROLE

In this chapter we shall be concerned with one aspect of role—namely, the types of variables that affect the character or style of role performance. We shall state succinctly two overarching generalizations at the outset and elaborate subsequently in the chapter with specific information from an array of different studies. In the next chapter, we shall deal with a wider range of issues pertaining to role performance.

Although there has been much expository writing on roles, there has been a virtual vacuum in research on practitioner roles in the professional literature. Since this has not been a substantive area of inquiry among social scientists, there are a relatively small number of studies to report on in this section and many of these only in a derivative fashion. It is useful, given the state of the empirical situation, to lean

[2] Jack Rothman, "An Analysis of Goals and Roles in Community Organization Practice," *Social Work,* 9, no. 2 (April 1964): 24–31.

[3] Charles Grosser, "Community Development Programs Serving the Urban Poor," *Social Work* 10, no. 3 (July 1965): 15–21; Irwin Sanders, "Professional Roles and Planned Change," in *Centrally Planned Change: Prospects and Concepts* ed. by Robert Morris (New York: National Association of Social Workers, 1969); Murray Ross, *Community Organization: Theory, Principles and Practice* (New York: Harper and Row, 1967); Irving Spergel, *Community Problem Solving: The Delinquency Example* (Chicago: University of Chicago Press, 1969).

somewhat heavily on a fuller description of individual studies in terms of suggestive implications and research directions. Specific action guidelines will be drawn from these individual studies. Because of this limited evidence, literature support for these guidelines should be considered uniformly low.

Diversity of Role Performance

GENERALIZATION 2:1 When viewed collectively, community practitioners engage in diverse roles covering a wide spectrum of activities and emphases. Empirically speaking, it is not accurate to assume that practitioners are employed in a circumscribed role set, role set taken to mean the repertoire of roles typically employed by the practitioner (+ + + +, 3, 21, 31, 50, 57, 59, 75, 76, 78, 84, 93, 94, 98).

A review of relevant literature, reveals a sizable number of variables that help to clarify conditions governing when one specific role rather than another is brought into play. Accordingly:

GENERALIZATION 2:2 Variables that affect role performance may be classified under the following broad categories:

A. Dynamics of the social change process (+ + + +, 23, 31, 59, 69, 76, 83)
B. Community factors (+ + + +, 11, 50, 53, 78, 93)
C. Organizational factors (+ + + +, 4, 9, 19, 21, 32, 57, 94, 98)
D. Personal attributes of the practitioner (+ + + +, 3, 18, 59, 66, 74, 79, 84)

In developing a sociology of community organization practice, Mayer Zald appears to assume this broad role set for community practice. He asserts that "The skill and diagnostic base of community organization practice is an amalgam of many disciplines. Practitioners draw on a range of disciples, from small-group and psychodynamic theory to economics and political science." [4]

[4] Mayer N. Zald, "Sociology and Community Organization Practice," in *Organizing for Community Welfare* Zald, ed. (Chicago: Quadrangle Books, 1967), p. 31.

In the discussion that follows, we shall suggest effects on roles of specific subvariables, illustrating with a typical study or two from which that variable was drawn.

A. *Dynamics of the Social Change Process* (Social Change Objectives, Stages and the Task Environment)

1. Programmatic or Social-Action Objectives

Morris and Randall (83) report on a comparative study of planning for the elderly in seven different communities. Three distinct planning styles were discovered:

THE ENABLER: much effort devoted to establishing and staffing committees.

THE DEMONSTRATOR: emphasis on implementing a single programmatic approach.

STIMULATOR-INNOVATOR: a freewheeling style involving many interorganizational linkages. Emphasis on prodding numerous already-established organizations and programs to do more than they were already doing for the aged.

The enabler style produced few programmatic results. The demonstrator style produced definite short-range successes, but few innovations. The stimulator style generated multiple short-range results, including innovations in a variety of established agencies. Thus, while aggregate diverse roles were in play, viewing practitioners individually more delimited or stylized roles may be discerned (see Generalization 3.1).

Action Guidelines for planning services and programs are obvious. If the practitioner is seeking specific, predetermined programs the demonstrator style would appear to be the method of choice. If the objective is innovation in programs and the stimulation of existing agencies' operations along the lines of a variety of short-term projects, then the stimulator-innovator style would seem to be indicated. Maximizing interorganizational linkage as in this latter style tends to maximize exchange and adoption of innovations.

A study of national planning in a South American nation (31) arrives at a definition of an innovative planning role which is remarkably close to the Morris and Randall formulation.

2. Stages in the Social Change Process

Evidence from several studies leads one to conceive of a multiplicity of roles which may be used selectively by the same or different practitioners at different phases of a change process. This idea is in a study of decision making in a metropolitan area (76). The authors studied 22 metropolitan planning decisions made over a thirty-year period in the Syracuse area.

One conclusion of the work is that planning is "processual" and requires a set of complementary roles—initiators (idea people), influentials (to support a proposal), brokers (who gain support or effect compromises among various formal organizations), and transmitters (government officials and others who make final decisions). This scheme suggests a series of practitioner roles (or roles and resources of others) that a planning organization needs to command in order to be effective.

In nonviolent social action, it is suggested that one of the major difficulties to be dealt with is the mentality of the "native" or oppressed group, which often tends to accept the inherent superiority of the "settler" or dominant party. Based on a study of staff civil rights activity in the South during the summer of 1967—the Michael Schwerner Memorial Fund Project of the Columbia University School of Social Work—three phases of action and practitioner performance were discerned and recommended (59), suggesting action guidelines as follows:

a. Initially, the practitioner serves as an ACTOR-TEACHER, engaging in direct confrontation with the oppressor in the presence of the oppressed.
b. The practitioner functions as a CATALYST-TEAM MEMBER, actively supporting the oppressed as he begins to assume a confronting role himself.

c. Finally, the practitioner recedes to the role of AD-VOCATE-OBSERVER, standing in the background while the oppressed individual or population, having gained a baseline of psychological strength and organizational ability, confronts the oppressor directly and alone.

These roles evolved from a context wherein the practitioners (mainly whites and Northerners) were members of the oppressor class (white) and yet were attempting to aid the organizational efforts of an oppressed racial minority (Southern blacks). *Whether practitioners who were members of the oppressed class would or should assume similar sequenced roles is an open question.* The author of the study does tend to generalize that "clients" who are trained through this process engage in a similar process with other clients.

Stages in role performance may be associated with stages in psychological adjustments or outlooks through which the practitioner passes. This is implied in a study of 1,000 Peace Corps volunteers (23), in which it was found that three main adjustment periods were traversed:

a. *The Crisis of Engagement* in which workers felt hampered by lack of clarity of task definition, including confusion over interpretation on the part of the local client population.
b. *The Crisis of Acceptance* in which tasks and objectives were more clear, but during which most workers experienced a slow, tedious, and substantially unrewarding struggle.
c. *The Crisis of Reentry* in which, before departure, workers experienced a great deal of separation anxiety—they were beginning to see results, but also realized the extent of the required additional effort.

Situational factors here include untrained or recently trained workers who enter a rather amorphous practice context (typical of many community-development and community-organization settings) in which there are cultural differences between the practitioner and the client population. Overseas community development is one such arena, but middle class practitioners who engage with racial and ethnic minorities in slum environments operate under analogous conditions of cultural distance and are faced with similar enormous problems.

From this study, it may be suggested that initial assistance to the worker by supervisors and trainers should focus on helping him with a role definition, emphasizing realistic goals. At a second stage, emphasis would be on establishing feasible boundaries and perspectives regarding the impact of role performance and dealing with frustration, depression, and anger. At the conclusion, practitioners need to be helped to disengage; their contributions and accomplishments should perhaps be pointed out to them, and they should be informed that provisions for continuity in problem-solving have been made.

3. The Task Environment

Different forms of coordination within organizations are required when the context involves nonuniform tasks in a shifting and uncertain task environment (e.g., the volatile plastics industry), as compared with uniform tasks in a stable and fairly predictable task environment (e.g., the long-standing container manufacturing industry). In the uncertain task environment, a greater percentage of staff members are involved in coordination-integration roles, and they participate to a higher degree in interpersonal communication and management. In the better established container industry for example, staff members operated to a greater degree under standardized decision rules and procedures, which were the major means of coordination. Hierarchical relationships were the norm and roles were more tightly prescribed (69).

It follows that an organization involved in a more nonuniform task environment would establish a greater number of coordination-integration roles, and either seek individuals with strong interpersonal skills to fill them or else train or reward staff with respect to application of interpersonal skills. Conversely, an organization involved in a uniform task environment should establish more managerial types of roles and seek individuals who are more rule- and procedure-oriented (and possess bureaucratic skills).

This subject, including definitions, is elaborated in Generalizations 4.1 and 4.2.

B. *Community Factors* (Community Structure, Cultural Norms, Client Needs)

1. Community Structure

Logic would suggest that a great number of community structural variables may affect the range of roles played by practitioners and how they are performed. For example, it is possible to delineate conditions that facilitate the employment of militant social styles of activity. A comparative study of 20 Community Action Agencies conducted at Brandeis University (50) examined the main aspects of organizational operations. It was found that more militant or adversary programs came about in large cities with a large black population, and areas where a citywide action coalition was established by neighborhood CAA associations. The structure of city government (mayor-council vs. council-manager) was associated with type of militancy (internal adversary vs. external adversary).

In additon to predicting circumstances under which militant roles are more likely to be successful, the study suggests that a local organizer who wishes to foster militant social action should allocate a reasonable proportion of time to activities outside the neighborhood aimed at forming or sustaining a citywide coalition of action groups. Said differently, local organizing roles need to be supplemented by citywide coordination and roles to optimize local social action. This is further elaborated in Generalizations 8.15 and 8.37.

2. Cultural Norms in the Community

It borders on the trite to state that community cultural norms may influence the nature of practice. Several volumes, often with an anthropological or community development theme, have emphasized this notion.[5] However, it remains to provide specific guidelines concerning

[5] Benjamin D. Paul, *Health, Culture and Community* (New York: Russell Sage Foundation, 1955); Solon T. Kimball, and Marian Pearsall, *The Talladega Story: A Study in Community Process* (University, Ala.: University of Alabama Press, 1954); Severn T. Bruyn, *Communities in Action: Pattern and Process* (New Haven: College and Universities Press, 1963); Ward Hunt Goodenough, *Cooperation in Change: An Anthropological Approach to Community Development* (New York: Russell Sage Foundation, 1963); Al-

the interdigitation of cultural norms and practice roles under circumscribed conditions, and to codify these to a greater degree than has been the case heretofore. Three studies will be drawn upon to illustrate how this might occur: 1) a study of a cultural subgroup outside of the United States; 2) a study of a cultural subgroup within the United States; 3) a comparative study of U.S. and foreign population groups.

In the first study (93) an attempt was made to assess the attitudes of mental health personnel in a Peruvian mental hospital. The authors tested psychiatric workers by means of the Custodial Mental Illness Scale (CMI), which was developed by Gilbert and Levinson.[6] The researchers concluded that the Peruvian staff members generally scored very high in custodial orientation, "almost fantastically so as compared with North American performance" on these scales. Subprofessionals in particular evidenced little knowledge of the "right" responses in terms of a psychiatric point of view. Still, based on observations of the staff's performance on wards, there was no evidence of a lack of therapeutic atmosphere. One did not find the tone of punitiveness or forceful domination that would probably be associated with this level of CMI scores in a North American institution.

The authors conclude that in a Latin American culture, which has a more pronounced authority structure, the exercise and acceptance of authority can be manifested with a low degree of conflict. Subordinate status roles do not carry with them to a great degree a sense of violation of personal dignity. Moreover, the personalistic flavor of the general culture permits bureaucratic roles to be carried out with warmth of feeling so that clients are viewed as persons rather than as impersonal objects.

Practitioners in social settings in which authority patterns differ from the popularly conceived "American Way" would do well to avoid assuming dire behavioral consequences in

---

bert Mayer, et al., *Pilot Project India* (Berkeley, California: University of California Press, 1958); Richard W. Poston, *Democracy Speaks Many Tongues* (New York: Harper and Brothers, 1962); Marshall B. Clinard, *Slums and Community Development* (New York: The Free Press, 1966).

[6] Doris C. Gilbert and Daniel J. Levinson, "Ideology, Personality and Institutional Policy in the Mental Hospital," *Journal of Abnormal and Social Psychology*, 53 (1956): 263–71.

interpersonal relations. The practitioner can conserve time and energy by utilizing existing social arrangements rather than attempting to change them or by being unduly inhibited or thwarted by them. A more centralized, hierarchical organizational structure in an authoritarian culture is typical and may still permit implementation of human-relations-oriented practice models. When greater warmth in interpersonal relations in the culture is normal and natural, one may not be required to design a facilitating organizational structure to attain this quality of interaction.

Another study (53) arose out of the disproportionate representation of Chicanos (or Mexican-Americans) in mental health clinics in several California communities. The study attempted to compare the perception, response, and definition of a cross section of Americans and Chicanos with regard to mental illness. The interview schedules were administered to a random sample of groups in two communities. There were 200 questions, which elicited responses to vignettes about situations regarding mental illness.

Twice as many Chicanos described the behavior presented as ill, but referred to it as emotional rather than mental illness. Generally they were more optimistic regarding the possibility of cure and the ability of psychiatry to help. The Chicanos tended to have a family physician more often and tended to consult with him more frequently than other nationalities.

The authors concluded that Chicanos are not necessarily more or less mentally ill, but that they differ in their attitude toward mental illness, possibility of cure, and consultation with a physician.

The study suggests that Chicanos, more than some other groups, appear to recognize illness and seek appropriate help. The mental health planner might therefore emphasize making facilities more available to the clients instead of educating them about mental illness. Because of strong emphasis on the role of the family physician, the planner should lean on this existing resource and incorporate the doctor with his program. In general, this study indicates that the practitioner in his emphasis should not attempt to make the community more receptive to service, but rather should make the services more available to the community.

A cross-cultural perspective is offered in a study by Clark (11), which investigates differences in reactions to communications in different cultural contexts. The experiment created ambiguity by conveying discrepant messages (i.e., those in which expectations about a particular communication are not met) to population groups in two countries. For example, Christ is made to appear associated with a message advocating force. Responses were obtained from a group of United States college students and a similar group of Nigerian students. It was found that the Americans consistently reinterpreted incongruent messages whereas the Nigerians refuted them. Also, Nigerians discredited the source and discredited the issue to a greater degree than did Americans. Americans tended to reinterpret through a process of simplifying the message and reacting to it as a reconstituted whole. Nigerians on the other hand paid attention to the details of the message and tended to reject the overall if the parts did not fit.

Based on this study, a practitioner in attempting to reach or influence an American group of students (say, in a public health education program) would be advised to simplify a message to achieve some global impact. In reaching some other cultural groups (such as certain African students) with a similar program, the practitioner would do well to attend carefully to details and to the matter of consistency among the parts of the message.

3. Client Needs and Responses

Assuming that service needs of clients in the community are of primary importance, client reactions to practitioner initiatives should be a major consideration in shaping roles. A study by McBroom (78) in the more clinical area reflects this. She discerned two practitioner role models or styles in providing public-assistance service. These two styles (High P, psychoanalytical orientation; High S, socialization orientation) were appraised in terms of two categories of clients (Type 1, "chronically dependent"; Type II, "downwardly mobile" or "recovering from crisis"). Clients were asked whether or not they had been helped. Contrary to the author's initial hypothesis, both types of families rated High *P* practitioners as more helpful; Type I families expressed this preference more often than did Type II families. However, in terms of specific actions, both family types reported High *S* as the most helpful, timely, and prompt response in crisis or emergency. These had been classified by McBroom as "socializing" acts and included such behaviors as modeling, intervening in the social network, crisis management, frank and fair discussion of complaints, and development of concrete family goals.

The interpretation that may be imposed on these data is that low-income clients respond well to "socializing" roles having to do with environmental management, but prefer these roles to be performed by practitioners who have heightened sensitivity to the dynamics of personality function. This may have implications for community workers engaged in direct organization work with grass-roots clients or in planning services for low-income groups.

C. *Organizational Factors* (Structure, Institutional Traditions, Nature of Organizational Staff Position, Relative Power of Organizations)

1. Change-Organization Structure
It has been theorized elsewhere that goals, structures, and strategies are closely intertwined in community action. Thus, it was suggested, a "simple" structure is best for social action goals and a "federated" structure is for more integrated, "community responsive" goals.[7] A study of a community welfare council (98) elaborates on this. Neighborhood councils (usually local federated structures) by their composition are restrained from utilizing conflict strategies or roles. If engaged in social action, councils are more likely to take defensive postures which neutralize the opposition rather than aggressive initiatives aimed at overcoming or coercing the other side. The practitioner in federated local councils employs social action roles in moderation, emphasizing a series of roles the researcher encompasses under the "exchange con-

[7] Martin Rein and Robert Morris, "Goals, Structures and Strategies for Social Change," *Social Work Practice*, 1962 (New York: Columbia University Press, 1962), pp. 127–45.

cept.'' These exchange roles are necessitated both by the multiple organizational makeup of the federation, and the usual low resource base of neighborhood councils.

Much of the practitioner's effort in local neighborhood Councils is directed at member satisfaction and retention so as to maximize participation (one of the few power resources of the organization). To accomplish this he employs a "rewards" mode of influence. Sources of reward include goal attainment, procedures through which goals are achieved, and structural manipulations such as offering members appointment to offices or participation in informal cliques.

2. Institutional Traditions

Certain fields of practice or types of agencies tend to develop conventional modes of practice which shape the roles of professionals. For example, metropolitan planning agencies (of the city-planning type) were studied by means of a cluster analysis of typical activities (57). Three types of technical emphasis were found: comprehensive land use and transportation planning; capital improvements and community facilities studies and programming, and "newer" variegated studies in social areas such as urban renewal, housing relocation, and economic development. Agencies were classified as giving varying emphasis to one or another of these approaches. In most cases the first type of technical activity predominated and the author states that in general "metropolitan planning agencies follow the same strategy: a heavy emphasis on traditional comprehensive land use planning; a moderate emphasis on programming community facilities; and a small effort scattered over a miscellany of less conventional concerns.''

A practitioner entering such an institutional network might anticipate the types of roles expected of him.

Another study (94) demonstrated the existence of rather definitive institutional styles in organizations concerned with the rehabilitation of juvenile delinquents. *Custodial* institutions were oriented to obedience–conformity while *treatment* institutions were oriented to reedu-

cation-development. Client programs, staff, and executive leadership
roles varied in patterned ways in these different settings.

To illustrate, executives in the treatment institution, in addition to carrying out the managerial-entrepreneurial roles
implicit in custody, had also to assume missionary roles—
pointing out expansive goals, using terms to evoke a sense
of unceasing effort, provoking staff members to share their
idealistic and innovative inclinations.

3. The Nature of the Office or Staff Position

The nature of the office or staff position occupied by a practitioner,
and the extent of his identification with that position, may affect certain aspects of role performance. Ninety-six top-level administrators
and planners in eleven agencies were interviewed at the federal and
local levels in the United States and Canada (32). Inquiries were made
concerning the publics served by the agency and the role of these
publics in influencing the agency. In general, it was found that administrators do not see public or community groups as a source of policy determination; they prefer that this take place through the staff internal boards, and other governmental bodies. Most administrators feel
that they are influenced most by particular interest groups, not by the
general public. Administrators fell into three distinct types, each of
which turned to different publics as a source of influence. The types
and their influence publics were as follows:

POLITICO: an individual whose primary responsibilities are those of
policymaking, defending the agency before the outside world, and
responding to external pressure on the agency. Politicos are responsive to influence from a wide range of sources.

ADMINISTRATOR: an individual whose tasks are those of general
supervision of subunits and execution of agency programs, such as
the deputy department head of a Canadian provincial department.
Such individuals are responsive to influence from intraorganizational sources.

PROFESSIONAL: an individual whose responsibilities involve primarily the use of professional, technical, or scientific skills, such as
the chief executive of a social welfare or highway department planning unit. Professionals are responsive to influence from professional associations.

This suggests not only a number of different role types but also equally important, a series of external intervention strategies for influencing practitioners, especially those attached to governmental agencies. In the first place, broad "general public" approaches are not likely to be effective. Secondly, one should analyze the style of an official and place him in the appropriate category: politico, administrator, professional. Several dicta follow: Attempt to reach the politico through a variety of sources (especially political ones). Attempt to influence the administrator through internal agency sources. Attempt to influence the professional through his professioal association and identities. Ultimate influence, it may be assumed, comes from the source that has direct authority over the official, such as the legislature or policy board.

In a related investigation (21), top officals in the Wisconsin state government were interviewed. Three categories of functionaries were classified: a) executive officials (top elected officers and members of the governor's staff); b) legislative leaders; and c) administrators (executive heads of the twenty most important state agencies). Interviews focused on the ways in which these men related to and used the communications media, particularly the press. It was found that, compared to other methods, administrators are more likely than other officials to make use of press releases. The governor's office uses press conferences, press briefings, and editorial board meetings to a greater extent than other officials, reflecting the ease with which the governor can meet the reporters' definition of news. Executive officials and legislative leaders are more likely than administrators to cultivate reporters and issue information through individual personal contact. In general, it was found that administrators have less flexibility and less opportunity to exploit the press than do elected officials, either because their view of their own newsworthiness leads them not to seek the notice of the press or because they engage in less newsworthy meetings and activities. The researcher states that the office itself has an impact on components of the press-functionary relationship.

There is an implication here that administrators can learn from elected officials how to make more frequent and creative use of the press, perhaps employing press conferences and personal contacts to a greater extent. This is stated with some degree of reservation, however. Perhaps the patterns of press usage reflect ideal or feasible modalities for different types of offices and position. That is to say, an administrator who becomes highly active with the press makes himself more visible, more competitive with elected officials, and more subject to the vagaries of the electoral system; consequently more vulnerable and temporary. Perhaps the optimal approach to the media for the administrator, who typically seeks a long-range sustained tenure, is through a close working relationship with executive officers and their aides, which might provide both access and "cover." The stability or continuity of the professional in office enhances his limited bases of power because he can acquire contacts and information. Thus, this matter of continuity should be viewed functionally, not solely in terms of expediency or careerism.

4. Relative Power and Resources of the Change Agency

The degree of power available to the practitioner, especially through the resources or prestige of his organization, should have a considerable effect on the roles one can and may optimally play. Several studies of practitioners who operate out of low power organizations suggest a number of roles and strategies that may be employed under such circumstances.

Occasionally a small organization attempts to introduce innovations into another organization over which it has limited authority or power. A case study is the program of the Vera Institute of Justice, an organization that attempts to change policies and procedures of the Police Department in New York City. The Vera Institute is a small, autonomous organization with no direct power over the police department, but with a record of success in influencing highly independent and bureaucratized organization. The case study describes efforts to effect bail reform (so that prisoners charged with minor offenses may be released without bail) and police summons practices. The results of these efforts suggest tactics by which one formal organization with limited power can influence a large hierarchical organization that traditionally emphasizes its autonomy (19).

Action principles derived from this study are as follows:

a. The Vera Institute exercised expertise and legitimacy by acquiring a highly qualified technical staff. It emphasized consensus based on expert roles, rather than coercive roles.

b. A long-term continuing relationship was maintained with persons in the target agency. With the lack of coercive power, referent power roles were exercised (trust, friendship).

c. There was considerable flexibility with regard to the type of staff employed for different projects. Diverse backgrounds and role capabilities were sought. In addition, an ample staff was made available by Vera to initiate projects so that new ventures could be undertaken by the police without additionally burdening their own staff.

d. A demonstration project approach put little pressure on the organization to commit itself to new practices on a system-wide basis until they were adequately validated on a small-scale basis.

e. Finally, in an organization with a strong authority system, the change agency found it advantageous to work from the top down, acquiring approval and legitimation at the top of the hierarchy for each venture.

    Negotiating roles by occupants with expertise or social skills were called for. Considerable resources are necessary to carry out an interorganizational influence pattern such as this. A change organization wishing to employ such a strategy would have to limit itself to one or two organizations which are singled out as targets.

As stated earlier, a welfare council's program may be viewed organizationally as a central unit in a federated structure attempting to influence its constituent units, but possessing little by way of formal authority or power to enforce its wishes. Another study (9) treats the question of modes of influence employed by the council to promote usage of the plan by constituent member agencies. The author made an effort to record all known instances in which the council staff deliberately used the formal recommendations of the plan to influence decisions regarding 17 fields of welfare service. Whenever possible, short follow-up interviews were conducted with the person who reported the utilization. Utilizations were analyzed in such terms as frequency and purpose.

It was found that the staff used the priority recommendations most often for emphasizing policy matters rather than for informational purposes. About half the utilizations were made for direct intervention in the decision-making processes of various target agencies. In general, staff used consensus tactics, long-term relationships with agencies, and intervened directly in change activities. Generally, they were participants in decision making as members of boards or study groups in the target agencies.

There are a number of implications in this for organizations that play a coordinating role with target agencies in a federated structure which gives the change-coordinating agency little formal power. Assuming the patterns utilized in the council studied have some functional rationale, workers under such circumstances may find it useful to emphasize consensus tactics, establish long-term continuing relationships with target agencies as a means of maximizing referent power, and obtain common membership in the target agency units (board, staff study group) as a way of directly influencing decision making in that agency.

The operations of an innovative voluntary social agency, interested in establishing new programs in the community, are analyzed in a suggestive article (4). This agency, with a low degree of direct power, had been able to institute a variety of such new programs and have them absorbed by major "threshold" agencies (public-assistance departments, schools, housing projects, etc.).

Several features of the organization were examined in order to account for its relatively high success rate. The following factors seem particularly salient for an organization that wishes to replicate this experience:

A decentralized mode of administration that permits maximum autonomy to be exercised by program staff in carrying out tasks.

Assignment of staff to delimited ad hoc projects so that these can be taken over or disbanded easily. This requires staff members to be able to assume flexible, multiple roles.

Program cosponsorship with the target or threshold agency, including development of the program in the milieu of that agency. Again, the notion of flexibility in roles pertains, as well as the ability of the staff member to sustain conflicting expectations by two sponsoring agencies during the time that the program is being demonstrated.

In addition, the agency found it useful to supplement the regular staff with students and subprofessionals. This amalgam apparently reinforced the emergence of innovative practice roles.

D. *Practitioner's Personal Attributes* (Personality, Perceptions, Values, Homogeneity with Clients, Training)

1. Practitioner's Personality Attributes

While it is true, as some writers claim,[8] that one can differentiate between role and behavior, and that role can be viewed independently of persons or personalities, the elimination of personality as a consideration in role theory is restrictive. Community and organizational constraints and pressures significantly shape roles that practitioners play; it is likely that the personality structure of the practitioner may give emphasis to prescribed roles or, indeed, create new roles within the organization's normative boundaries or even outside them. The question of who assumes roles related to internal organizational

---

[8] Oscar Oeser and Frank Harary, "Role Structures: A Description in Terms of Graph Theory," in *Role Theory: Concepts and Research,* Bruce J. Biddle and Edwin Thomas, eds. (New York: John Wiley and Sons, 1966).

change and innovation was investigated in a study of 289 staff members in five large social welfare agencies (75). It was found that workers with certain personality traits assumed social change roles to a greater degree. Those more disposed to self-actualization, who were less contented, were more demanding and apt to perceive greater ambiguity and conflict in organizational goals. On a more demographic basis, innovative roles were taken more often by men than women and by group workers rather than caseworkers. Amount of education or agency auspice were not found to be relevant variables.

The above suggests personality traits and other personal characteristics to consider in seeking out practitioners who are more likely to take to intraorganizational change roles— either in terms of recruitment into the organization (hiring) or within the organization (activation).

2. Practitioner Perceptions

Practitioner perceptions of clients or of their problem situations may contribute to their role performance as well as to their effectiveness in the situation. Some 600 middle-management executives were involved in a role play simulation of a conflictual work group situation (74). If the individual designated as group leader saw mainly "problem employees" in the standardized scenario, he was less likely to guide the group to an innovative solution than if he saw "idea people." Solutions in groups where the leader sees "idea people" are more often found acceptable by group members. The group leader's attitude toward members, the author concludes, strongly influences the kind of solution reached by a task-oriented group in problem-solving activity.

The implication here, all things being equal, is that a practitioner who wishes to evolve an innovative solution in group problem solving should perform with an outlook that members are "idea people" and try to convey this to them in his manner. Alternatively, if the practitioner is in a position to select or help to select the chairman or discussion leader, he should urge the promotion of someone who views group members as creative "idea people" rather than of a more task- or problem-oriented individual who lacks this point of view.

3. Value Orientation of Practitioners

As discussed more fully in the next chapter, the value structure of professions cannot be assumed to be monolithic. Practitioners lean in one or another direction in terms of their own personal value systems, and this can influence the roles that are taken.

To illustrate, a study of practitioner reaction to pressure by clients (3) found that the type of response or "defense" was correlated with a sources-of-value type of defense. Practitioners who responded uniquely and autonomously were guided predominantly by a "societal" value orientation. The worker drew from generalized norms extraneous to the bureaucratic organization. Workers who adopted "joint defense" (peer group collective responses) or "buffer defense" (organizational mediator responses) were more likely to be guided by a value system derived from the organization or profession.

What is suggested here is that one might be able to direct a worker's attention to one or another source of value input, depending on how one wants him guided. For example, a Welfare Rights group confronting a rather rigid bureaucratic structure might direct the attention of workers to general societal norms of "fairness" and "democracy" as contrasted to formal organizational norms of "orderliness" and "conformity to agency policy." The Welfare Rights group might also use this material as the basis of a diagnostic tool to determine which workers would be more subject to external value influences.

(This approach would naturally need to be orchestrated within a larger action strategy.)

In another study on the relationship between social class and mental illness among children, the authors found that the subjective nature of psychiatric evaluations allows the practitioner's personal values to influence the diagnostic process. It was suggested that those who emphasize "normal" and "abnormal" criteria in appraising behavior unwittingly view the unskilled as having more problems (80).

Protection of the interests of unskilled individuals would call for turning practitioner orientation away from "abnormality" critera.

In addition, Spergel, in *Community Problem Solving, The Delinquency Example,*[9] shows how each worker's role set is affected by his own value-tinged perceptions of the causes of a problem. For example, he points out that a developer sees the problem of delinquency as individual, group-related, and linked to social influences in the local community. In contrast to this, the organizer sees the delinquency problem as symptomatic of basic defects in the whole structure of society and not in the delinquent himself. The advocate may see the delinquency problem as a failure of institutional arrangements in the courts and public housing projects.

4. Practitioner-Client Racial Homogeneity or Heterogeneity

A controversy has ensued recently over whether whites are able to organize blacks and other minorities effectively, although there has been a long-standing discussion in the literature regarding how necessary or desirable it is for the practitioner to be of the same background as his clientele. By and large, practice wisdom has held that workers can operate effectively across ethnic and racial lines, that appropriate personal attitudes and sensitivities are required to accomplish this, and that the early relationship-forming stage of work may be more complicated and extended under such circumstances.[10] The black militant and other movements have disputed this position. Still, little by way of empirical evidence is available to assess the white-nonwhite worker-client question. We previously cited the Kurzman study (59), which implicitly assumed legitimate white roles with blacks in the South and went on to specify stages in carrying out such roles. A more extensive study (66) of white civil rights activity in the South was conducted on a participant observer basis by the psychologist Charles J. Levy. Levy focused on the trust component in this type of organizational activity and concluded that because of the saliency and magnitude of racism in contemporary America, sufficient trust for effective collaborative action is not currently possible. The dynamics and stages of the development of trust are described in considerable elaboration.

[9] Irving A. Spergel, *Community Problem Solving, The Delinquency Example* (Chicago: The University of Chicago Press, 1969).

[10] Alfred Kadushin, "The Racial Factor in The Interview," *Social Work* 17, no. 3 (May 1972): 88–98.

Based on Levy's book, one would discourage whites from assuming organizing roles with blacks, specifically in the South.

Another study (18), by three sociologists, of civil rights participants lends indirect support to Levy. White activists in SCLC projects perceived criteria of success in terms of "process goals"—building a local organization and developing black pride, running a smooth organization with no friction over dishonesty, and having a cohesive project. The researchers note a possible displacement of goals from "outside" achievement to "inside" harmony. Projects rated more highly were those in which more time was devoted to protesting. A strategy with a tone of conflict was seen as more important than the accomplishment of specific tasks. Militancy appeared to be a way for white workers to "prove" their sincerity or "test" themselves under fire. At the same time, volunteers did not indicate a willingness to stay on (7 percent did) or to return. Also, the experience did not appear to basically alter the political attitudes of volunteers. There was no turn to the left politically or an increase in general alienation.

The authors cast white participation in the movement in terms of "romanticism," and tend to shed doubts on the viability of white organizing efforts with blacks.

Further research which examines factors in addition to those such as trust, may lead to other conclusions or to more specialized roles for whites—perhaps in supportive technical functions, such as legal, statistical, or fund-raising assistance.

We have dealt with only the racial dimension of worker-client homogeneity-heterogeneity. Other aspects need also to be considered—social class, ethnicity, religion, sex. From the discussion above, one might offer the tentative hypothesis that when a group is attempting to gain self-sufficiency or when its group characteristics are central to its immediate objectives, worker homogeneity may be important. At other times the understanding of the practitioner and his ability to relate positively to members of the group, regardless of a homogeneity of personal traits with the group, may be a sufficient basis for effective practice.

5. Amount or Type of Training

A recurrent question in professional literature is, What difference does training make? Do those with training perform differently (different functions, different effectiveness) than those without training? A study by Meuller (84) examined practitioners with and without the M.S.W. in community mental health programs in the state of Wisconsin. The researcher sought to clarify the "social work role implicit in the model of community mental health" through an examination of such factors as allocation of time, occupational and physical life space, sanction, and methods. Meuller concluded that there were major differences in all dimensions pertaining to the kind of activities performed and in criteria for success. Interestingly enough, the two groups were quite similar in the most traditional area (casework), less alike in group, and least alike in community work. Because of the study's confinement to one state and one type of service, we cannot justifiably conclude from this study that all trained and untrained practitioners engage in highly different roles.

The study suggests that in some circumstances the level of social work or other professional education may determine the roles that workers may by legitimation, custom, or predeliction play in practice. This has implications for the planning of services and the differential recruitment and use of personnel. A further discussion of professional-paraprofessional relationships and functions is in chapter 5.

PRACTITIONER ROLE EFFECTIVENESS: DIMENSIONS

Parenthetically, there have been few researh efforts directed at predicting and evaluating community practitioner effectiveness based on personal traits. Two studies that attempted such an evaluation of rural community development practitioners in Southeast Asia arrived at different conclusions. Fahn (29), studied AID rural community development advisors in Laos and Vietnam and Lyden (70) studied Peace Corps volunteers in the Philippines. Lyden found that the more successful workers were less aggressive, more introverted, and had less experience. Fahn concluded that successful practitioners are more democratic-minded and impatient with the rate of social change in the United States. While the dimensions studied are not identical, there is some disparity between "less aggressive" and "more impatient," which are both given as attributes of successful practitioners. Did the cultural situations require different practitioner styles, or were the research instruments faulty, or were different practice requirements salient in each location? Again, here is an area calling for further research. Some hint of the complexity involved in making diagnostic assessments to determine practitioner roles in overseas community development may be gleaned from a study of cross-cultural consultation process (87). The following dimensions are suggested as operating. This schema could provide a useful initial framework for further research effort.

A. Basic issues in structuring the immediate consultation relationship
   1. Relationship between consultant and consultee (this deals with matters of personal "styles," roles that both parties assign to the other—i.e., "friend," "junior colleague," etc.)
   2. Relationships with various segments of the population
   3. The use of time
   4. Revising preconceptions of ends and means
B. Disjunctive trends and their handling
   1. Expectations-disappointment
   2. Condescension-resentment
   3. Malcommunication-alienation
C. Different consultation situations
   1. Degree of "technical" content
   2. Goals
      a. Assistance in carrying out operation
      b. Assistance by teaching or training locals to take over such operations
      c. Institution building
   3. Administrative framework within which work is carried out
   4. Cultural content of the consultation
D. Background factors affecting the consultation: Western "expert"   ·
   1. Organizational status of outside expert
   2. Nationality status of outside expert
   3. Preconceived attitudes of outside expert

E. Hosts
   1. General ethos in the country
   2. History of the country with regard to outside intervention
   3. Demographic and subcultural characteristics of the population
   4. Current political situation

One is left with the feeling that we have barely scratched the surface in attempting to sketch the dimensions affecting the practitioner role; at the same time, what we have offered is a start in giving immediate direction and is suggestive of future lines of research inquiry that may fruitfully be followed. This discussion leads us into a consideration of related issues such as limited vs. extensive role sets, role conflict, role consensus, and the impact of different intervention roles, which will be taken up next.

(The general Bibliography on Practitioner Roles will be found at the end of the next chapter.)

Chapter Three

Practitioner Roles:
Some Dynamics
of Role Performance

IN THE PREVIOUS chapter we postulated that when practitioners are examined in aggregate—let us say, if analyzed in system terms—they are found collectively to employ a wide range of roles. Seen individually or in clusters, however, the practitioners' role sets vary in their scope. In this chapter we shall deal with the scope of role set, as well as with the dynamics of role performance. We shall be concerned with role conflict and its resolution. We shall examine matters of assertiveness and autonomy in role execution, we shall review the literature on professional role orientations, and we shall devote special attention to linking and political roles.

Role Set

Scope of Role Set

GENERALIZATION 3.1: Some practitioners utilize a limited role set, others utilize an extended role set encompassing a range of subroles (+ + +, 9, 17, 39, 54, 55, 77, 78, 83, 98).

As indicated earlier, the community organization literature has often projected the concept of a limited role set. For example, "enabling" roles were for a long time widely accepted as the only ethically legitimate mode of practice. Our review of studies, however, suggests variability among practitioners in employment of roles. Narrow role performance was elucidated in several studies cited in the previous chapter. Morris and Randall (83), for example, found four distinct role types employed by different practitioners engaged in planning for the aged. Chetkow (9) and Weissman (98) noted a specific consensus style of role performance for those working in federated council structures. McBroom (78) discerned separate High *P* and High *S* role emphasis among welfare workers. On the other hand, some investigators have found variability and multiplicity of role performance within the functioning of a single practitioner. Demerath (17) noted that practitioners in family-planning programs in India were engaged in manifold role activities within a given position. Among other things, the same practitioner performed different types of roles according to successive stages of the project to which he was assigned. Neighborhood work with street gangs was also found to require multiple role performance (55). In a series of field investigations conducted in connection with the Community Organization Curriculum Development Project sponsored by the Council on Social Work Education (39), it was found that many practitioners engage in dual sets of roles termed ''analytical'' and ''interactional.''

One approach to conceptualizing the issue views practitioners in terms of *direct roles* with clients (aiding them through immediate personal contact) and *indirect roles* (influencing or aiding clients through intermediary agencies and instrumentalities).[1] Direct roles include enabler, motivator, educator, organizer, and socializer; indirect roles include linker, coordinator, consultant, mediator, advocate, and broker. A limited role set involves either direct or indirect roles, while a multiple set entails some mixture of direct and indirect. Taking this perspective, in the Curriculum Development Project a limited role set would involve implementation of only analytical or only interactional roles, while a multiple role set would include components of both.

3.1A: Multiple role performance is associated with a clientele that is distant or distrustful relative to the practitioner's sponsoring organization (+ +, 54, 77).

This subgeneralization is derived from Mayer's observations of a community development program in India (77) and Katz and Eisten-

---

[1] Barbara Carter, ''Community Practitioner Roles: A Second Look,'' Doctoral Seminar Paper, Ann Arbor: University of Michigan, 1970.

stadt's study of Israel's attempts to assimilate new immigrants (54). In reviewing these studies Zald makes the point that multiple roles may be needed when the clientele is distant from or distrustful of the change agency. "To the extent that members of a target group are suspicious of an agency, communication channels will be blocked. In such a situation a 'multi-purpose' worker will be necessary. His main job will be to establish linkages between the organization and the target group. As these linkages are established, it becomes possible to reintroduce specialists, now trading on the multi-purpose workers' relations." [2] The notion is put in a somewhat different way by Litwak.[3] He states that an organization wishing to influence grass-roots neighborhood populations not in accord with the agency's goals will have to employ linking mechanisms that involve a high degree of intensity. This implies the use of role relationships that are "primary group" in nature, and hence that cover many activities and areas of life. A "detached worker" is suggested as the ideal linkage for this purpose.

3.1B: Decentralized organizational structures foster broader role sets than do centralized structures. Practitioners in decentralized structures have more external or community-oriented roles proportional to internal roles (+, 88).

The above is based on a study of workers in three mental hospitals who completed a written questionnaire concerning their role performance. It was found that a decentralized "team" structure encouraged a broader role orientation. Further, there was a slight tendency for staff in such structures to become more involved in community social issues. One might hypothesize that decentralized staffs, brought in to closer contact with community forces, were to a greater degree confronting a nonuniform task environment; hence they were led to employ a greater range of roles in a more flexible way (see chapter 4, under "Organizations and Their Environments.")

[2] Meyer N. Zald, *Organizing for Community Welfare* (Chicago: Quadrangle Books, 1967), p. 52.

[3] Eugene Litwak, "An Approach to Linkage in 'Grass Roots' Community Organization," in *Strategies of Community Organization: A Book of Readings* Fred Cox et al., eds. (Itasca, Illinois: F. E. Peacock Publishers, 1970), pp. 126–38.

Action Guidelines: Practitioners need to assess whether their tasks require employment of limited or multiple role sets. Many community workers are located in situations calling for an extended role set but define themselves in limited role set terms. In some cases, practitioners are unaware that they have defined themselves unidimensionally and consequently perform ineffectively by constricting the boundaries of their potential role repertoire. Sometimes such limitations are cognitive in etiology (being familiar with only certain potential roles); sometimes they are ideological (only certain roles are considered appropriate from a value standpoint). Frequently such ideological prescriptions are not fully thought through and may be dysfunctional in terms of the objectives the practitioner is seeking. The converse of the problem may also be true, that is to say, practitioners may be employing too wide a range of roles in terms of the objectives being addressed.

Diagnosis of one's role set should hypothetically contribute to effectiveness in community practice. Not only might the practitioner be better able to determine the particular roles to employ under given conditions, but this framework might also help him to move from a limited to an extended role set and back again flexibly as circumstances require. As a rule of thumb, a broader role set is suggested when a practitioner is in a decentralized structure or when he is using a high-intensity approach with distrustful groups. Employing this general framework, experienced practitioners can discern many additional criteria for determining the appropriate scope of role set.

Role Conflict

Role Conflict and Solution Strategies

GENERALIZATION 3.2: Whether engaged in limited or extended role sets, many practitioners experience role conflict in the performance of their functions. A variety of solution strategies to resolve role conflict are employed (+ + +, 17, 34, 36, 56).

Various studies (17, 34, 36), some of which will be described more fully later, detail dimensions of role conflict experienced by community practitioners in the field. Gilbert (34), for example, points up the contrasting expectations placed on OEO Community Action Agency staff members by agency executives and neighborhood client groups. Indeed, it is suggested by Krause (56), in a study of rehabilitation counselors, that conflict is structurally built into some professional roles by specific devices such as legal definitions of the position, workloads, production and time pressures, and cultural barriers to successful completion of objectives.

3.2A: Under conditions of role conflict, solution strategies that are typically employed are a) emphasizing only one set of role expectations; b) balancing competing expectations; c) withdrawing from role performance; d) changing the role definition; e) using aggressive and symbolic adjustment patterns (+ +, 34, 56, 71, 72).

We shall discuss this generalization further in terms of the designated solution strategies.

a. *Selecting out one role for emphasis.* In a study of a shelter house for alcoholics (56), it was found that counselors were expected to play disparate roles of manager, companion, and member of the client community (counselors were former alcoholics). The main solution strategy utilized was the selection of one key role to emphasize. Another study (72) dealt with public officials serving as district counselors in Northern Nigeria. The authors hypothesized that those occupying positions would emphasize one role, and that this would be one that officials personally evaluated as being more legitimate or obligatory. The hypothesis was confirmed, but it should be appraised, however, in terms of a setting with a somewhat authoritarian cultural climate.

b. *Meeting or balancing competing expectations.* Neighborhood coordinators in the Pittsburgh antipoverty program were found to encounter competing expectations concerning the primary focus of their role from neighborhood citizens and the top executives of the organization (34). The executives expected coordinators to exhibit broker and expediter roles, assisting welfare agencies to develop services for neighborhood groups. Neighborhood groups, on the other hand, expected the coordinators to work with and through them in advocate and activist roles, formulating demands for services from the agencies. Coordinators generally maintained their delicate position by presenting a different face to these different constituencies, that is, playing incompatible roles but segmenting them in time for different reference groups.

The particular solution in the Gilbert study involves playing competing or incompatible roles, not compromising them. Compromise is another possibility, however, and will be discussed more fully shortly.

c. *Withdrawal from expected role behavior*
d. *Realistic action to change the role definition*
e. *Aggressive and symbolic adjustment patterns*

The three mechanisms cited above were found in the Krause (56) study of rehabilitation counselors. Withdrawal implies noninvolvement—an apathetic, anomic response. Realistic action to change the role definition suggests a mature, problem-solving posture. However, in the Krause study the situation was structured in such a way as to restrict successful employment of the strategy. Aggressive and symbolic behavior represented an acting out of frustration and anxiety in personalistic terms. Such behavior is generally not task productive, but may help maintain emotional stability on the part of workers when confronting an unresolvable practice task.

These empirical findings on actual behavior mesh well with the conceptual categories of role conflict solution hypothesized by Thomas and Feldman.[4] Their scheme, enumerating the range of logical solution strategies to role conflict, is reproduced below with this author's generally analogous concept indicated in brackets.

---

[4] Edwin J. Thomas and Ronald A. Feldman, *Concepts of Role Theory* (Ann Arbor, Mich.: Ann Arbor Publishers, 1964).

a. *Resolution*

Preferential selection of one or other expectation [selecting out one role for emphasis].

Compromise by meeting sets of opposing role expectations [meeting or balancing competing expectations].

Avoidance by performing in a way which is inconsistent with all sets of role expectations [withdrawal].

b. *Elimination*

Achieving consensus of the role expectations [realistic action to change the role definition].

Removing the individual from the position [realistic action . . .]. Eliminating the position [realistic action . . .].

c. *Coping through psychological reactions* [aggressive and symbolic adjustment patterns].

Action Guidelines: The frequency with which role conflict situations are reported in the research literature suggests that agencies and practitioners should make it a point to diagnose work assignments in terms of potential unproductive role disparities. The solution strategy categories found in the literature and conceptualized by Thomas and Feldman provide possible approaches for dealing with such conflicts. At least on the surface, one ideal solution is "realistic action to change the role definition" by achieving role consensus among competing reference groups, by eliminating the position, or by removing the actor from the situation. Meeting competing expectations through the technique of presenting different faces to different reference groups, as in the Gilbert study, would appear to present serious problems. One wonders whether this technique can be sustained over a long period of time in the public context in which community practice takes place. According to Gilbert the practitioner virtually became two persons, one for each of the two types of organizations to which he related. Eventually credibility may become a problem when a member of one group observes the practitioner at work in the terrain of the other group, or when the practitioner is forced to operate with representatives of both groups at the same time. The workability of this solution pattern appears doubtful, but strictly speaking it is an empirical question that can be investigated further. On the other hand, the ethical integrity of this posture is probably more open to immediate criticism.

The strategy of preferential selection seems to have face validity as an economical approach, and appears experientially to be one that is commonly employed. Assuming that this solution modality is occasionally functional, an agency can systematically select out those key roles that it wishes to see emphasized and train practitioners to focus on these (or help practitioners go through the process of selecting out their own key role). In emphasizing a given role, agencies may be able to socialize practitioners to it by explicating its legitimate or obligatory aspects. Aggressive and symbolic adjustment patterns would appear to be the least productive strategy in the long run, but may help practitioners weather unresolvable task situations in the short run.

Through our literature review we can verify that several of the Thomas and Feldman solution strategies are indeed employed by practitioners in real situations. We cannot, however, on the basis of the research that has come to our attention, make firm assertions concerning what types of solution strategies are most efficacious for what types of role conflicts, structural situations, or practitioners. Obviously this is an area where additional investigation is necessary. A few hints along these lines are available from the following studies.

Compromise as an Effective Strategy

GENERALIZATION 3.3: More effective solution strategies for role conflict appear to involve compromising competing expectancies (+ + + 5, 6, 14, 36, 91, 96).

In several instances where role conflict has been studied, the effective solutions appear not to include personalistic reactions on the one hand, or restructuring of the role situation on the other. Rather, a blending or compromising of expectancies within the existing role situation appears to offer greatest potential. Two somewhat different approaches to this will be described.

3.3A: Role clarity and consensus among actors (in particular between the practitioner and his relevant superordinates) facilitates effective role performance (+ + +, 5, 17, 38, 71, 91, 96).

As we have seen, there can be various ways in which practitioners' roles may be defined. Some evidence suggests that clarity and agreement with regard to role definition may have an important bearing on practice outcomes. In an exploration of this issue (5), 30 county extension directors and their 75 county extension agents were interviewed with regard to a number of dimensions of the agents' role, for example, direction and coordination, extension relations, educational leadership, and personnel management. The degree of consensus between directors and agents regarding role expectations was assessed. In addition, state personnel rated the various directors in terms of efficiency in program development and implementation. It was found that county directors who were rated more effective had a higher consensus on mutual role expectations with their county agents than did those rated less effective.

Additional studies lend further support to this position. Demerath (17) found that lack of role consensus between various program levels impeded a birth control program in India. Gross et al. (38) concluded that lack of clarity concerning new roles thwarted the adoption of innovative educational practices among teachers. Rosen (91) determined in a public welfare bureaucracy that caseworkers exhibited high conformity to behavioral expectations specifically when there was a high degree of consensus between supervisors and the practitioner's work groups. The consensus factor was the key variable in the Rosen study, regardless of the type of influence or compliance mechanism used to achieve a designated role performance. Thomas (96) found that role consensus was positively correlated with fairly objective behavioral criteria of work performance. Lyons (71) found that greater role clarity was correlated with lower job tension, lower job turnover and higher job satisfaction.

3.3B: Practitioners who use compromise as a solution to role conflict are generally viewed as more effective by professional associates and supervisors (+ +, 6, 14).

In a study of professional orientations of social workers, Billingsley (6) found that workers with balanced orientations were more effective, according to the criterion of ratings by supervisors. There
are obviously limitations in relying on this standard, but it is
suggestive. A study conducted in a mental hospital (14) attempted
to determine factors associated with resolving conflicts in the direction of either patient satisfaction or organizational-staff requirements. Workers who used compromise solutions were rated by fellow staff members on the wards as most effective. Those exercising
preferential selection in the patient direction received a medium effectiveness rating; preferential selection in the staff direction received a low rating. It is difficult to assess whether the compromise
solution is most effective in some ultimate sense. It appears, however, to be associated with acceptance from and good working relationships with supervisors and peer staff associates, a condition that
potentially could contribute to productivity.

Action Guidelines: In practice terms, an effort should be
made to "spell out" tasks and functions of practitioners
clearly and to foster mutual agreement among all relevant
actors concerning these. In the Bible and McNabb study (5),
it was found that explicit training of practitioners for new
roles had a positive relationship to consensus on role expectations. To increase organizational and practitioner effectiveness, time may indeed be taken out from ongoing operations to clarify roles and tasks, to communicate these, to
provide training regarding roles if necessary, and to establish means by which consensus on role expectations can
be reached through such instrumentalities as orientation
sessions, staff seminars, or sensitivity training groups. Further, practitioners should be given guidance in methods of
balancing or compromising competing sets of role expectations. There is some evidence available that suggests this
contributes to greater effectiveness, or more precisely, to

gaining approval (and hypothetically cooperation) from supervisors and staff associates in the performance of roles.

This is not to hold that role clarity and role consensus are always functional. Role ambiguity and lack of role consensus, even planfully structured, may serve such ends as worker autonomy, worker creativity, the pursuance of multiple-valued objectives or the maintenance of control by upper-level personnel through keeping workers off balance. When other considerations are set aside, and the issue presents itself in terms of an open organization and rationalistic, task-oriented role performance, then the generalization seems most applicable.

Role Assertiveness

Practitioner Impact

GENERALIZATION 3.4: Practitioners have been found to have the capability to strongly influence community programs (+ +, 2, 35, 46, 90, 92, 98).

How significant are change agents who are involved in community intervention? Several studies indicate that their influence can be considerable. Weissman (98) found that practitioners have much sway in federated or welfare council structures through use of "exchange" modes of influence. Gilbert (35) observed that practitioner interventions were decisive in a Community Action Program that had a new and divided policy board. Earlier writings by Banfield (2) and Rossi (92) have documented the impactful role of paid professionals on community issues through their critical location in and capacity to manipulate bureaucratic institutions. This is not to say that practitioners are uniformly successful in exerting influence, as will be shown shortly. Research indicates, however, that the potentiality of impact exists.

4A: Success in community intervention varies directly with the sheer amount of practitioner activity or energy applied to role performance (+ + , 45, 90).

This proposition is borrowed primarily from the Everett Rogers (90) research utilization study of the diffusion of innovations. By analyzing a series of studies in diffusion, Rogers concluded that "the extent of promotional efforts by change agents is directly related to the rate of adoption of an innovation" (pp. 257–58). The relationship between promotional activity and rapid adoption held in such diverse instances as county extension agents motivating farmers to accept new techniques and automotive companies encouraging high schools to institute driver training programs. Rogers cautions the reader to consider the possibility that there is an interaction between the variables—change agents may direct more of their interventional energies toward programs that are more likely to be adopted.

One study in our pool (45) revealed that those families having more contact with extension agents were more likely to adopt the agents' goals of increased social participation.

Action Guidelines: Guidelines from the general proposition are somewhat intangible. There is encouragement for practitioners to "stay with it"—potentialities for success exist if enough energy is allotted, despite the complexity and general resistances one frequently encounters in community work. Budgeting one's time in giving emphasis to various roles is also requisite. That is to say, if outcome is associated with the amount of promotional activity applied to a given role or task, then one's time should be apportioned diagnostically, rather than either indiscriminantly or in balance among various roles. Those roles (and objectives) viewed as most important should receive a greater share of energy output. This standard might include agency goals, need or inequality in the community, and requirements of the change process itself at a given point in time.

Factors Favoring Role Assertiveness

GENERALIZATION 3.5: Practitioners sometimes underestimate the degree of assertiveness in role performance that would be acceptable to important community actors. This may impose limitations on their effectiveness (+ +, 52, 73, 86).

Two types of elites, business leaders and governmental leaders, were interviewed in Atlanta and in Raleigh, North Carolina, with respect to their attitudes toward city planners (52). In general, favorable attitudes were expressed toward planning activities and planning roles. In Atlanta, the opinion that planners should have a greater amount of influence than they do was expressed by 73 percent of the governmental officials and 81 percent of the economic leaders; in Raleigh the percentages for these groups were 51 percent and 63 percent. Governmental leaders were more likely to contact the professional planner than the board chairmen for advice on planning matters; business leaders might not contact either one. In addition, there was evidence that involvement of elites in planning boards and programs tends to enhance their favorable attitude toward planners. Obviously, planners were in a position to assert more leadership than they did. The same tendency of planners in state agencies to define their scope more narrowly than is necessary is reported elsewhere (73).

Additional evidence is available indicating that practitioners occasionally have faulty perceptions of the expectations of other relative actors and accordingly underestimate their mandate and limit the impact of their role performance (86). One study compared the attitudes of the administrative leaders of the Oregon Education Association with the attitudes of the Association's members (and also examined administrators' perceptions of member's attitudes). It was found that administrators had a greater propensity than members to liberalism and activism. However, administrators tended to overestimate the degree of distance between themselves and the membership. That is to say, members were more liberal and action-oriented than administrators realized. "The teachers were more willing to join teachers' unions, political party organizations, or racial organizations (e.g., NAACP) than leaders believe them to be" (pp. 663–64). Sensing a difference in degree of liberal orientation, the administrative practitioners exaggerated it, and became overly cautious in appraising the options open to them.

3.5A. Assertive or Directive Roles are more appropriate for certain situational contexts than for others (+, 83).

There has been considerable discussion in the literature regarding the merits of process (maintenance-oriented) vs. task (goal-oriented) role performance in working with such task-oriented groups as committees and study groups. This subject has been clouded in murky rhetoric, although there is evidence available to aid clarification. In one study, groups of American and Indian students were brought together to discuss aspects of family life (child-rearing practices and the role of grandparents in the family). This issue was selected because it is one in which there are sharp differences of orientation in the two countries. The discussants were told to attempt to reach agreement within a designated time period. The groups were structured experimentally on either a formal or informal basis. In the informal discussion setting, task-oriented leaders were rated as more effective in achieving consensus; in the formal setting socioemotional leaders were so rated. According to this study, when the objective of the practitioner is to achieve consensus or a "meeting of the minds," he should assume a role that counterbalances the atmosphere of the group setting.

3.5B. Assertive or Directive Roles are more appropriate for some objectives than for others (+, 64).

This statement is based on a study of practitioner intervention in a group work context involving a population of welfare clients. Worker-directed vs. group-directed experimental conditions were evaluated in terms of outcomes. Worker-directed groups were more effective in improving marketing and nutritional practices. The two styles were equivalent for improving practices related to use of credit and to physical health and for reducing the clients' sense of powerlessness. Thus, in this situation, the worker-directed approach is more effective on an overall basis, but its advantages are greater for certain objectives than for others.

3.5C. Assertive or Directive Roles are more appropriate for some community participants or client groups than for others (+, 13).

Of relevance here is a study of planning (13) in a semirural county with a board made up of local citizens who were relatively unsophisticated in their knowledge of planning. In this instance there was a rejection of the expert role of the planner and reaffirmation of traditional rural values. The disparity between the technical training and experience of the planner and lack of information on the part of the board members was visible and extreme. This tended to block use of the expert by local people. Planners in settings such as this might minimize social distance between themselves and citizen participants by playing down the practitioner's use of "expert power" in social planning, and employing to a greater extent other bases of power (such as referent or legitimate power). Alternatively, they might devote considerable energy to the training of board members in technical matters, and extending the longevity on the board of those individuals who become better informed.

Action Guidelines: For various reasons, practitioners have sometimes failed to assume appropriate assertive roles in community intervention. Occasionally there is an underestimation of "what the traffic will bear" with respect to reactions of important community actors and groups. Practitioners should be alert to this possibility; perhaps they should develop better tools for determining attitudes and expectations of others and the nature of boundaries thereby imposed on role performance. In assessing the proper extent of directive role performance, practitioners should take into account the situational context, goals being sought, and attitudes of community participants. In small group or committee situations where the objective is consensual problem solving, there is evidence that the worker should take a more directive, task-oriented role when the group atmosphere is informal. One should lean toward more nondirective, socioemotional roles when the group atmosphere is formal. Target groups that are distrustful or that feel a sense of distance or inferiority with respect to the practitioner may react negatively to the exercise of more assertive roles; hence, the practitioner should be cautious in regard to assertiveness with such clients and constituencies until trust is established, or disparity in knowledge or skill is reduced.

Linking Agent Roles

Linking Formal Organizations and Local Populations

GENERALIZATION 3.6: Numerous studies explicate the existence and importance of a linking agent role for community practitioners. This role involves facilitating communication and contact between human-service organizations and local neighborhood populations (+ + + +, 15, 16, 30, 33, 45, 51, 55, 58, 62, 67, 68, 89, 95).

This proposition has been amplified and given sociological underpinnings in several trenchant theoretical statements by Litwak and Meyer.[5] The core idea is captured in the notion of "balance" regarding the relationship of formal organizations to local primary groups in a contemporary urban context. The authors point out that both primary-like groups (families, neighborhood associations, friendship groups) and formal bureaucracies (schools, social agencies, government bureaus) are essential structural forms for social life and development. Primary-like groups meet socioemotional needs and are effective in dealing with a wide range of idiosyncratic, personalistic events. Formal organizations, on the other hand, are task-oriented and have the capability through technology of dealing with (or programming for) more recurring phenomena.

Further, the two types of organizational life have different natural climates—informal, nepotistic, emotional vs. formal, merit ruled, detached. Each type of structure needs and relies on the other to some extent. Primary groups need formal organizations for technical information, professional services, etc. Formal organizations need primary groups to recruit members and clients, diffuse programs and services, raise funds, etc. At the same time, if the two become too close, their climates may become intertwined and contaminated, to the extent that neither can fulfill its function adequately—for example, a family pro-

[5] Eugene Litwak and Henry J. Meyer, "A Balance Theory of Coordination Between Bureaucratic Organizations and Community Primary Groups," *Administrative Science Quarterly* 11, no. 1 (June 1966): 31–58; "The School and the Family: Linking Organizations and External Primary Groups," *The Uses of Sociology* Paul F. Lazersfeld et al., eds. (New York: Basic Books, 1967), pp. 522–43.

viding love or approval to children strictly on the basis of grades received in school, or a school providing rewards on the basis of affection to the exclusion of professional standards and objective criteria of merit. Consequently, a number of "linking mechanisms" are necessary in order to regulate the amount of distance between these basic groups.

Among the "linking mechanisms" enumerated by Litwak and Meyer are the detached expert, the settlement house (or decentralized neighborhood service facility), the opinion leader, the voluntary organization, the common messenger, mass media, formal authority, and delegated function. Certain mechanisms are said to have greater intensity than others, such as the detached expert and the opinion leader, and thus are more effective for working with and changing attitudes of resistant local populations. When populations are sympathetic to organizational goals, mechanisms of low intensity but wide scope—such as the mass media—may be employed.

This brief sketch conveys a few of the salient components of the theory. The interested reader is urged to delve into the subject further in the references cited. The linking agent role which is reflected in the generalization is close in conception to the Litwak-Meyer detached expert mechanism, examples of which are the agricultural extension agent and the detached street club worker. These professionals have the task of reaching out from a formal organization (university, welfare agency, community mental health center) into local communities in order to be in close contact with, provide services to, and influence grass-roots target groups (including farmers, predelinquent youth, troubled families). With this clarifying backdrop, we can consider a number of refinements concerning the employment of this role.

3.6A. Linking agents typically hold values and norms that are in an intermediate position between the units being articulated (+ +, 47, 65).

An empirical test of this assertion was made through a survey of opinions (47) held by different actors concerning the ideal role of the public-health nurse. Within nonmetropolitan counties of Missouri, personal interviews were conducted with all public-health nurses, random samples of the population in four selected counties, and central administrative personnel. It was found that the norms or the public health nurses were intermediate to the positions of those at the central and local levels. The authors suggest that such an intermediate posture is the most comfortable one for incumbents of linking positions; one might hypothesize that this is also likely to be the most functional role for such individuals to assume. In other words, this descriptive statement of the existing arrangement probably reflects what is workable or "should be." This is given mild additional support in the Lawrence and Lorsch (65) findings that interdepartmental mediators or integrators are most effective when they hold an intermediate point of view.

3.6B. Linking agents manifest considerable variability and nonuniformity in the exercise of their functions. This is probably related to the highly emergent, nonuniform character of the task environment in which they typically operate (+ +, 55).

The authors of one study (55) present data on the activities and contacts of ten detached workers assigned by the Los Angeles County Probation Department to the most active gang neighborhoods in the County. Since this is one of the few detailed empirical studies on such workers, we shall review it more fully. The data reported are designed to illuminate two major problems: 1) how uniform the performances of the ten workers are; 2) how consistent the performance of each worker is within his own area of activity. An attempt is made to delineate some of the major factors that may account for the patterns exhibited in the data.

The workers constituted a heterogeneous group. The gang members were either black or Chicano, as were most of the active gangs in the Los Angeles area during the period of the study. The workers completed a series of reports on their activities during one-week periods. The "daily activities form" provided for a complete description of a worker's time allocations each day and the "contact report form" provided for a listing of each person contacted by the worker as part of the program.

Time spent on the job and accounted for on the form was divided into three categories: 1) "contact time" is that spent in the actual company of youths, parents, and various community adults in the furtherance of the program; 2) "organized time" refers to time spent in youth and parent club meetings, planned sports activities, and so forth; 3) "office time" includes supervisory and staff conferences, talking with other workers, clerical and official reporting duties, and time spent filling out the research forms.

Major findings from the data conclude: 1) in general, interworker variability in use of time is quite high; 2) intraworker consistency is not high; 3) these findings hold with respect to allocation of time, to types of activities and of persons, but not to the content of the interventions with these categories of persons.

Agency policy and supervisory practice stressed flexibility in field-work style in accordance with estimates of the varying necessities of each field situation. This agency policy did not generalize to office time, however, since the exigencies of a large bureaucratic structure and the accountability required of a governmental agency necessitate a good deal of paperwork and other routine practices.

Several conclusions the authors reach regarding group work practice seem equally applicable to community-organization interventions. First, it is suggested that the agency must build into its structure and program a system for tolerating variability in worker style. Second, the authors point out that means must be found to increase field supervision—on-the-spot observation, analysis, and modification of field activity—and to reward worker and supervisor alike on the basis of field performance.

3.6C. Linking agents have frequently been found to approach local target populations through grass-roots opinion leaders, employing a "two-step" process of communication. These local opinion leaders play a significant part in facilitating relationships between formal organizations and local population groups (+ + + +, 30, 58, 95).

We have cited here only a few representative studies dealing with this notion. (Other relevant studies can be found in chapter 9.) One study documented the activities of an informal network of indigenous "gatekeepers" who aided the linkage between newly arrived Spanish-surnamed populations to the urban community and formal organizations providing health care, welfare, legal aid, consumer information, etc. (58). The authors made special note of the informal manner in which these gatekeepers functioned, as well as their incomplete knowledge of resources that local constituencies required.

In an examination of an educational family planning program conducted in Turkish villages, it was found that the village population is conservative regarding birth control, that the indigenous political leader typically is more liberal in this connection, and further, that he is more open to outside influences, including mass media (95). Still another example is a case study of an effort by a Point Four officer to introduce public-health concepts (such as fly control) through films into an agrarian Middle East village (30). The officer experienced resistance until he established informal relationships with indigenous leaders. He then showed the film to the leaders and won their acceptance, after which—with the leaders' legitimation— he was able to show the film to the general village population. Whereas the officer had previously found it difficult to make even small headway, he was now able to institute a regularly scheduled public-health film series.

3.6D. Various professional functionaries at the local level who are not involved with human-service or welfare organizations—such as police, physicians, or clergymen—provide ongoing linkage with service organizations. Community practitioners can hypothetically facilitate the carrying out of their linking-agent role by working through other natural professional linkers (+ + +, 16, 33, 62, 67, 68, 95).

Referral of local people to mental-health and social-work agencies is often made through allied professionals such as doctors, clergymen, and police. A general finding is that such referrals are more likely to take place through such allied professionals than through social work or mental-health personnel, and that differences in use of different referral sources are class related.

To illustrate, one study of state mental health hospital patients (68) shows that fifty percent of mentally ill patients and their families utilize the police for community referral. When a study was made of a sample of patients who used the police and those who used the conventional mental-health network it was found that: a) police are called because they are accessible and are more willing to deal with recalcitrant patients; b) low-income people are more likely to use the police; c) police handle the most serious cases; d) there is a strong relationship between the resource consulted first by each case and the resource initiating hospitalization.

3.6E. The effectiveness of linking agents is hindered when the policies and practices of their sponsoring organizations do not permit adequate service to local organizations. Under such circumstances the linker is in a position to observe the dysfunction at close hand. Successful fulfillment of his task requires influencing service organizations to make behavioral change, in addition to the more usual focal task of influencing local target groups to make behavioral change (+ + +, 15, 89).

Two studies in the public-health field will be drawn upon for illustrative purposes. In the first (15), there is an analysis of the role of the social worker in a child health clinic serving a local public-housing development. As distinguished from other functionaries in the clinic, the social worker had the task of outreach with regard to clients, interpreting programs and procedures, and referring clients to various community services. Severe difficulties encountered in connecting clients with services suggest the importance of modifying the delivery pattern and fostering greater coordination among service organizations. This problem was highlighted in a program evaluation of a welfare baby clinic, also serving and located in a neighborhood public-housing project (89). The author concluded that in referrals to agencies there had been poor follow-up in terms of agency response (as well as low client initiative among those referred). In the sample, 14.1 percent had multiple agency contact with "no overall direction"; only 16.3 percent were found to have achieved good agency care, and this in a task area which is fairly concrete and delimited. The authors contended that the location of linking agents in a public-housing project engaged in an outreach program does not insure substantial provision of organized services to local populations.

Action Guidelines: Practitioners should be alert to situations requiring a linking agent role to facilitate the adequate connecting up of service organizations with local population groups. The linking agent ordinarily assumes normative position between that of the service organization and that of local client groups. To foster effectiveness in execution of the role, service organizations need to recognize this dimension of the role, tolerate such "deviant" attitudes in the direction of client groups on the part of linking agents, and even encourage and train agents to adopt such positions.

Since linking agents operate in a highly nonuniform task environment and exhibit much variability in the exercise of their functions, human-service organizations wishing to employ such roles need to develop and accept flexible structures within which linking agents can operate. Such flexibility can pertain either to a limited number of positions or to departments made up of linking positions. Flexibility entails fluid time schedules, open and multiple role definitions, a low level of formalization (meaning few rules), and a minimum of bureaucratic procedures. Supervision might best take place in the field. Hollister (51) concludes on the basis of his study that organizations wishing to encourage linkage need to use procedures that, "a) allow staff discretion, b) diminish social distance, c) allow the mobilization of third parties, d) rely on organizational initiative, and e) are relatively costly" (p. 153).

Linking agents should take advantage of local opinion leaders in conducting their work. Numerous studies indicate that effectiveness of agents can sometimes be enhanced through a "two-step" approach to local populations, that is to say, by working through the medium of opinion leaders. The practitioner should be equipped with the capacity to pinpoint and make contact with local opinion leaders, win their acceptance, obtain their legitimation for programs, and engage opinion leaders in surrogate functions. Other professional and occupational groups in the local community may be utilized in a similar way. Often police, clergymen, and doctors are already heavily involved in providing linkage (making referrals). Their natural, ongoing activities in the community can be enhanced by: a) increasing the number of clients who contact them or; b) providing them with specialized information or training which will permit such natural occupational linkers to carry out these functions with increased proficiency.

Linking agents need skills not only in influencing local

population groups to make use of existing services, but also in modifying policies and practices of service organizations so as to be more in tune with client needs. Linking agents need skills (or training) in fostering innovation and change in complex organizations. Agencies and supervisors need to accept and even encourage this type of reverse feedback if they are serious about discharging their functions properly and optimizing the linkage function. Perhaps this function can be performed with maximum impact by organizing client groups to make their own claims. Linking agents are advised not to take for granted that agencies manifest an enlightened outlook, and should be prepared to tolerate a reasonably high degree of role strain as an ongoing feature of the job, and should possess the stamina to persevere in interpreting to the agency the intrinsic duality embedded in the role.

Sociological Literature on Professional Roles

Major Role Orientations

GENERALIZATION 3.7: Three basic role orientations have been commonly identified as prevalent among professional workers: professional, bureaucratic, and client orientations. Type of role orientation may differentially affect outlook toward practice (+ + +, 6, 24, 25, 26, 27, 28, 42, 43, 44, 99).

In this formulation, *professional orientation* implies a high concern with professional values and standards, a *bureaucratic orientation* refers to a preoccupation with policies and norms of the employing agency, and *client orientation* connotes a primary attention to the needs of those served by the agency. Another way of stating this is in terms of expectancies; focal reference groups conveying expectations regarding the character of job performance may be professional peers, agency superordinates, or client populations.

This threefold breakdown of role orientations provided the basic analytical framework employed by Epstein in a series of studies dealing with social workers and radicalism (24, 25, 26, 27, 28). Wilensky

(99) earlier categorized professionals in a similar way but with a variation in the terminology: professional-discipline, careerist, and client.
Billingsley (6) broadened the scheme to include a fourth role facet—
community. However, this dimension may be incorporated in part
within the client orientation, and Epstein discovered that among his
various categories of professional workers there was little variation in
community commitment, making the category of low utility in his
analysis.

3.7A. Social workers have a high bureaucratic role orientation,
higher than is true for a number of other professions. For social
workers, agency norms typically affect the worker's outlook to a
greater degree than do professional norms (+ + +, 6, 26, 42).

Epstein compared his data on social-worker role orientations with
previous work analyzing lawyers, engineers, and college professors.
To the question "Whose judgment should count most when your
overall professional performance is judged?" 81 percent of the professors as compared to only 17 percent of the social workers chose
professional colleagues or associations. Social workers chose administrative superiors (65 percent), while only 8 percent of each
group of lawyers and professors chose in this manner. According to
Epstein, "among social workers there seems to exist a hierarchy of
normative commitments beginning with agency norms and ending
with professional commitments" (26, p. 74). Billingsley (6) concludes from his data: "Social workers in our sample are relatively
more bureaucratic than professional in their moral evaluative orientations. Both supervisors and caseworkers in both these agencies are
relatively more oriented to carrying out agency policies and procedures than toward carrying out their professional commitments
when these are in conflict. This is in contrast to other studies of
other professions working in formal organizations which show more
orientation to the profession than to the agency" (p. 403).

While agency norms are predominant, studies reach conflicting
conclusions as to whether professional or client orientations are next
in ascendancy, and as to what the relative strength of client orientation is in social work as compared to other professions. Billingsley
(6) in his study found client orientation to be low as compared to

agency and professional commitments. Epstein (25) found client orientation to be rather high, definitely predominating over professional orientation. Hall (42) concluded that social workers along with nurses have high identity with the principle of service to the public as compared with more established professions. Varley (97) discerns patterned *variations* within the profession regarding dedication to service.

3.7B. A sizable proportion of professional workers exhibit mixed rather than single orientations (+ +, 6, 25, 97).

Wilensky (97) concludes from his study that mixed types of orientation are typical. Through Billingsley's procedures (6) some 30 percent of his sample are categorized as holding mixed orientations. Epstein (25) was able to describe consequences of various types of orientation mixture that were revealed in his investigations.

3.7C. Some evidence suggests that mixed rather than single orientations may be conducive to practice effectiveness (+ +, 6, 22, 25, 54, 93).

The question arises as to whether single (pure) or mixed orientations are preferable, and for what purposes. Several strands of evidence from a number of studies lend support to the superiority of the mixed formula. For example, Billingsley (6) discovered that workers with a combined professional-bureaucratic orientation tended to be rated more highly by their supervisors on overall effectiveness. He places this in the context of Merton's finding that neither of the extreme groups, cosmopolitans or locals, was considered as competent or effective as the middle group. Epstein (25) suggests that combining a professional with a client orientation tended to enhance acceptance of nonconventional political strategies. Hall (43) found that a conflict between professional and organizational norms is not inherent, and Engel's work (22) demonstrated that a framework of moderate bureaucracy tended to enhance the professional's sense of autonomy. On this last point, Wilensky implies that "bureaucracy may enfeeble the service ideal more than it threatens autonomy" (p. 137). What this suggests is that different mixtures may promote different outcomes which in themselves can only be appraised in terms of given values or goals. Is professional autonomy or the service ideal a more desirable end state to pursue?

3.7D. The professional training institute may play a significant part in inculcating a given role set configuration (+ +, 6, 8, 48, 99).

Several studies have either directly or indirectly touched on the impact of professional education in socializing students in directions compatible with given professional norms. The strong socializing influences of psychiatric residency are documented by Bucher (8). In this study, a series of "mechanisms of socialization" in graduate training are pinpointed, including modeling, playing the role of the professional, coaching, and conversion experiences relative to the given professional value system. Bucher describes a socialization process that promulgates a single definition of the profession, fosters professional identity, and structures fairly definitive professional roles. From his comparative study of three professions, Wilensky (99) concludes that the source of role orientations appears to be in professional training, not in the organizational location of practice. He found that scores within each of his professional disciplines were similar regardless of place of employment.

Taking a more delimited look at social work education, Billingsley observes that the strong bureaucratic role orientation expressed by his subjects may be attributed to the fact that social-work training emphasizes an agency point of view—indeed an extremely heavy proportion of the skill development takes place in agency settings under the educational supervision of full-time agency employees. Also the preponderance of practice takes place in formal agency contexts. It is suggested by one study (48) that male social-work students experience a greater degree of socialization or change in value orientation in graduate training than do females.

Action Guidelines: Social workers, and perhaps other human-service professionals (especially from less established professions and those who normally are employed in formal organizations), tend to give heavy weight to the employing agency regarding role orientations. This reliance on agency expectancies may encourage conservatism among workers, undermine professional standards and autonomy, and give preference to administrative prerogatives at the comparative expense of client needs or the service ideal. It seems desirable to balance the current emphasis by raising the saliency of professional and client orientations in workers. To do this does not necessarily require the elimination of a bureaucratic orientation: mixed orientations, according to several studies, are both common and functional. A moderate bureaucratic orientation, for example, joined with a professional one, appears to enhance the worker's sense of professional autonomy. (The significance of mixed role orientations for furthering political and activist roles will be discussed shortly.)

The professional training institute seems to be crucial in shaping role orientations in fledgling professionals. It would seem wise for social-work schools to diminish the central place of agency-bureaucratic considerations in the educational program. Some of the current training responsibility can be taken out of the hands of regular agency personnel, and removed from agency sites to school-run laboratories and open community settings. (The reader is referred to the field instruction volume of the Community Organization Curriculum Development Project for an exposition of a new model of field instruction for community organizers, which increases professional and academic influences and decreases agency influences.) [6]

In addition it might be useful to open up increased opportunities for community organization practice outside of formal agency structures—analogous to private practice in casework. This might also tend to diminish the current pervasive influence of agencies. Some possibilities along these lines include more client-run, indigenous planning and action organizations, independent practitioner-run consulting and service organizations, and, as have emerged in some situations, practitioner communes. The latter may be suitable especially for graduating students and early career professionals.

[6] Jack Rothman and Wyatt Jones, *A New Look at Field Instruction: Education for Professional Application in Social Planning and Community Organization* (New York: Association Press, 1971).

In addition, professional associations might seek to reorder the identities and commitments of members. Client groups and community organizations could also play a part by underscoring their claims to the professional's loyalties, crystalizing their expectations, and communicating with professionals directly on these issues. Community practitioners staffing such groups could help give direction and support to such efforts.

Practitioner Role Autonomy

Factors Conducive to Role Autonomy

GENERALIZATION 3.8: Autonomy in role performance can be facilitated through a number of structural and personal variables (+ + +, 6, 40, 46, 61, 86).

An important aspect of practitioner role pertains to the autonomy or independence with which roles are executed. As is documented in Part Three, professionals tend to place an extraordinarily high value on autonomy. Such factors as job satisfaction, innovativeness, and the maintenance of professional standards have been found to be associated with autonomy (82). At the same time, autonomy may not necessarily be correlated with client satisfaction, as client and practitioner definitions of desirable roles may differ (37, 60).

These brief comments hint at the multiple implications and unclarified issues associated with practitioner autonomy. At the same time it is evident that autonomy is a condition that practitioners strive to achieve and without which their personal sense of worth is often injured. Further, for various practice purposes and community goals, a relatively high degree of role autonomy may be extremely helpful.

3.8A. Autonomy is facilitated by a low level of role specificity (+ + +, 46, 86).

Palumbo (86) surveyed a stratified sample of local public-health departments, interviewing administrators, program heads, and operating-level employees. He attempted to relate various measures of organizational structure to aspects of role performance, in particular the amount of autonomy or power that resided in a given role. The investigation supported his hypothesis that the less specific the role norms for any position in an organization, the more power that position will have. Low role specificity in this study was found also to be correlated with high morale, high productivity and innovation, as well as with professionalism. Harvey (46) correlated role specificity with "technical specificity," that is, job performance that is circumscribed, routine, and governed by rules.

3.8B. Autonomy is facilitated through a decentralized structure that encourages participation in decision making (+ +, 40, 46).

This statement is taken from the Hage and Aiken study (40) of 16 social welfare agencies in the Cleveland area. Interviews were conducted with 314 executives and staff members across a wide spectrum of positions and service agencies—rehabilitation, psychiatric, retardation. Many variables were investigated, using a battery of instruments. Hage and Aiken reported that increased participation in decision making was associated with decreased job codification. Less job codification implies more open roles, permitting a greater degree of individual discretion. Harvey's study, previously cited, yields similar conclusions.

3.8C. Autonomy is facilitated by reduced citizen control of organizational decision making (+, 61).

The basis of this assertion is a piece of historical research by Lappin (61) on stages in the development of community-organization practice. The author traces the emergence of the occupational field through three historical periods: "Movement Phase," "Specialization Phase," and "Professionalization Phase." He finds that the prominent place of the layman and community leader in agencies and organizational processes constitutes a barrier to increased role mastery for the community organizer in the last Phase. According to Lappin's analysis, a reduction in layman control, in conjunction with a philosophy of professional legitimacy, would contribute to increased autonomy and role mastery. Here we become embroiled in the issue of appropriate influence for professionals and various organizational and community actors, hinging on value positions.

Setting aside the philosophical merits of the case and speaking behaviorally, we can say that decreased citizen influence is associated with increased practitioner autonomy.

3.8D. Personal autonomy is facilitated by personal rejection of both bureaucratic and professional role orientations (+, 6).

For this statement we return to the Billingsley study (6). Billingsley was able to discern a practitioner type who was expedient and flexible—not tied either to agency or professional role definitions or constraints. Such an independent practitioner, Billingsley found, rejected both bureaucratic and professional roles, and instead operated autonomously, out of his personal internal belief system. Such a worker was described in the study as innovative, and might also be viewed as autonomous. In some ways autonomy and innovativeness may be similar or overlapping. We shall not enter into a discussion of this issue here. A separate substantive treatment of variables related to worker innovativeness will be found in chapter 9.

Action Guidelines: To foster greater worker autonomy in organizational settings: decrease the level of role specificity attached to his tasks; involve him significantly in organizational decision making; reduce the degree of citizen control and influence over organizational decisions and practitioner performance. To maximize personal autonomy, both bureaucratic and professional norms might be deemphasized. If professional autonomy is to be maximized, professional norms might be retained or strengthened while bureaucratic norms are played down. We shall elaborate on this issue in the next section.

Political and Activist Roles

The roles we have discussed thus far have been in somewhat circumscribed practice contexts: by and large the delivery of human services and the running of human-service agencies. We shall now turn our attention to community practice roles that are fundamentally political in character. Promoting community change—including the provision of better services—often requires the manipulation of legislative and governmental processes, as will be shown in chapter 6. Aspects of the participation of community practitioners and other human-service workers in political affairs and radical movements have received only limited examination in the research literature. We shall focus here on those studies which specifically treat practitioner roles in the political process, and leave broader discussion of political and legislative processes for later coverage. The discussion will be informed in large measure by a series of five articles by Epstein (24, 25, 26, 27, 28), which are derived from his penetrating dissertation study in this area. Since we shall be leaning heavily on this work, it would be well initially to describe its methodology succinctly.

The data in the Epstein study were based on a survey of social workers in New York. A preliminary questionnaire was presented to a group of 125 social workers attending Columbia University summer institutes. In December 1966, a revised version of the questionnaire was mailed to a systematic one-third sample (1,574 subjects) of the membership of the New York City Chapter of the National Association of Social Workers. The total yield was 1,020, a completion rate of some 65 percent. Elimination of retired, part-time, and student members reduced the number to 899 usable questionnaires. In a test of representativeness, respondents and nonrespondents were compared along a number of dimensions. Comparable data for nonrespondents were taken from entries in the 1966 *NASW Directory of Professional Social Workers*. This procedure revealed no significant differences with respect to agency position, agency auspices, type of social work program in which employed, and years since completion of professional degree.

The questionnaire contained a battery of instruments upon which the findings were based. These included measures of role orientation, attitudes toward different styles of political participation, attitudes toward professional issues, participation in professional activities, organizational-professional hierarchical rank. General background information on sex, age, and professional specialization, etc., was also gathered.

The presentation that follows derives largely from Epstein, with the inclusion of several additional studies as they pertain.

In his first article, Epstein discusses attitudes of social workers toward activism, exploring responses in two different institutional or social problem areas: public welfare and public housing. Roles were differentiated according to whether they involved the use of consensus or conflict and whether they entailed going through institutionalized (formally organized, publicly sanctioned) or noninstitutionalized channels. This way of viewing such action preferences is depicted in the following conceptual table:

TABLE 3.1: RESPONSES OF SOCIAL WORKERS
TOWARD ACTIVISM

	Institutionalized	*Noninstitutionalized*
Consensus	1. Conduct studies of housing or welfare needs and make recommendations through expert testimony. 2. Bring together interested groups and agencies to discuss the problem and co-ordinate efforts to plan a program based on the agreement of all participants.	3. Communicate with public officials through letters, personal contacts, and so forth. 4. Provide direct services—e.g. counseling, home-maker services—to demonstrate their value in ameliorating the problem.
Conflict	5. Inform low-income tenants or welfare recipients of their rights and encourage them to file complaints through official housing or welfare agencies. 6. Openly campaign for political candidates or work through political parties that favor proposed reforms.	7. Offer support to community action groups that request help in organizing strikes and protest demonstrations at official housing and welfare agencies. 8. Actively organize low-income people to conduct strikes and protest demonstrations at official housing and welfare agencies.

Respondents were asked to indicate their endorsement of employment of these roles by a hypothetical representative group of social workers, using a seven-point scale ranging from "strongly approve" to "strongly disapprove." Without going into details of the analysis, the following two generalizations are derived from the data.

Tendency toward Conventional Political Roles

GENERALIZATION 3.9: Professionals in general tend toward conventional, low-conflict political roles (+ + +, 12, 20, 27, 28, 48, 49, 97).[7]

A number of additional studies supplement the findings of Epstein regarding this general proposition. For example, Heffernan (49) conducted a pilot investigation based on interviews with directors of social-work agencies in Durham, North Carolina, and Lansing, Michigan, and found a clear avoidance of identification with political parties, a reluctance to campaign openly and a highly "professional" stance. Studies of NASW members by Clark (12) in Massachusetts and Downing et al. (20), in Illinois reveal compatible evidence. Studies by Varley (97) and Hayes and Varley (48) on social workers' values also suggest a conservative, nonpolitical outlook. Based on Epstein's and these investigations, it is possible to posit a number of subpropositions as follows:

3.9A. Professionals generally prefer consensus modes of action, both institutionalized and noninstitutionalized. They strongly favor a professional expert role, which involves the giving of testimony at hearings, submitting factual reports, coordination, and communicating with officials. They generally disapprove of conflictual direct action and partisan political involvement (+ + +, 12, 20, 27, 48, 49, 97).

3.9B. Professionals prefer to rely on established *professional channels* for political expression, such as the "professional associations and agency boards," thereby avoiding public political identification. Such roles are viewed as exhibiting proper professional decorum (+ + +, 12, 27, 49).

3.9C. Most professionals disapprove of actively organizing client protest groups; half reject offering of professional support when requested of them by such groups (+ +, 27).

3.9D. While favoring consensus strategies and roles for profes-

---

[7] The data in the following section lean heavily on studies of social workers. "Professionals," when employed in the generalizations has the more precise meaning of "social workers and perhaps other human-service professionals."

sionals generally, institutionalized conflict roles are also accepted, while noninstitutionalized conflict roles are rejected (+ +, 27).

3.9E. The largest proportion of professional social workers (case-workers) tend especially toward conservative roles, while the much smaller segments (community organization and group work) have a greater propensity toward radical roles (see Generalization 3.12A). The aggregate influence, then, is in the direction of conservative roles (+ +, 27).

Action Guidelines: Social workers (and probably other human-service professionals) tend to eschew conflict and partisan politics. A community practitioner cannot expect to achieve much support from professionals for these activities. Participation of professionals in conflict situations is most likely to occur if the conflict is carried out through institutionalized channels. One possible way of involving professionals in political activities is to engage them in roles in which they are comfortable—such as offering expert opinion through testifying in public hearings or consulting in private conferences. Professionals may also be stimulated to act politically through agency boards and professional associations. The community practitioner should be alert to circumstances in which the mobilization of boards and associations could be politically useful and should know how to drum up such support. It might also be noted that agency boards and professional associations may be instrumentalities through which to escalate political involvement by professionals. These entities may serve in part as political reference groups through which to modify political role expectations.

Perceived Efficacy of Political Roles

GENERALIZATION 3.10: Professionals evaluate the efficacy of radical-conservative role performance differentially according to: a) proximity to the institutional domain of action; b) social class status of the political actors (+ +, 27).

In the Epstein study one institutional area of action, public welfare, was close to the social work profession's central area of interest, while the other, public housing, represented a more peripheral concern. Respondents answered in significantly different ways with regard to role performance in these two areas. Likewise, when respondents were asked to assess the use of different political styles by lower- and middle-class actors, their pattern of response reflected clear differences of outlook regarding appropriate political behavior for these two class groupings. These differences in outlook may be summarized as follows:

3.10A. In institutional areas closer to the central professional domain of social work (such as public welfare), social workers view more conservative roles as more effective for themselves and others. In institutional areas more distant from their central professional domain (such as public housing), social workers are more willing to accept radical roles for themselves and others (+ +, 27).

3.10B. Conventional political roles are viewed as most effective for middle-class actors; radical roles involving protest and conflict are viewed as more effective for lower-class actors (+ +, 27).

3.10C. In areas closer to their central professional domain, social workers project a greater differentiation of roles between themselves and middle-class lay groups. In this context, social workers tend to view themselves as assuming greater leadership roles (+ +, 27).

Action Guidelines: Professionals are more likely to be mobilized for activist roles in areas more removed from their central domain.

The tendency to regard relatively conservative strategies as most effective for low-income people in areas in which professionals are institutionally involved may be translated into actions that reduce the militancy of politically active low-income groups. This suggests that the community practitioner committed to principles of self-help will have to work hard to keep from playing the very roles that may make it impossible to achieve his goals in working with low-income people.

Epstein also looked at whether the worker's basic role conception affected his attitude toward political style. Tendencies toward each of the three basic role orientations discussed in Generalization 3.7 (professional, bureaucratic and client) were determined for the respondents through a modification of Billingsley's role-orientation index. This procedure revealed the following:

Role Orientation and Political Orientation

GENERALIZATION 3.11: Type of practice role orientation (professional, client, bureaucratic) assumed by professionals is associated with acceptance of a radical role perspective (+ +, 25).

Having stated the issue in its most general form, we can make more refined assertions as follows:

3.11A. The greater the client role orientation, the greater the approval of radical roles (+ +, 25).

This is compatible with speculations made by Billingsley and Wilensky in the context of their studies, to the effect that professionals with strong client role orientations may be more willing to violate agency norms that contravene client interests, and are more likely to conceive of their profession in social movement-social change terms.

3.11B. The greater the agency role orientation, the lower the approval of radical roles (+ +, 25).

3.11C. There is no direct relationship between a professional role orientation and either approval or disapproval of radical roles (+ +, 25).

3.11D. Professional role orientation appears to intensify the effects of the other two role orientations; it magnifies the radical tendency of a client orientation and the conservative tendency of a bureaucratic orientation (+ +, 25).

3.11E. In order of ascendency of role orientation, social workers tend to rank bureaucratic roles highest, followed by either client or professional roles. Accordingly, they exhibit a strong orientation to the employing agency, and a weaker orientation to the profession and client groups. This may be assumed to foster a conservative political role orientation in the profession (+ + +, 16, 25, 42).

Billingsley and Hall also found bureaucratic orientation high; differences were found among investigators in relative position of client and professional orientations.

Action Guidelines: Community practitioners wishing to encourage more active or radical political participation by professionals should stress a client role orientation coupled with a professional orientation. A professional outlook should be projected in terms of commitment to and advocacy of the interests of client and community, rather than in terms of agency requirements or narrow conceptions of professionalism.

The "process model" of professions makes the assumption that occupational groups do not exist as a unified entity, but rather as discrete segments of a profession with different interests and different views on a variety of issues.[8] Another question examined was whether different specializations within social work favor different political styles, especially treatment-oriented casework on the one hand and more system- and change-oriented community organization and group work on the other. Does hierarchical rank make a difference regarding preferred political-action methods? When Epstein's data were analyzed in terms of these issues, his study yielded the following conclusion with its relevant refinements:

Structural Variables and Radical Role Support

GENERALIZATION 3.12: Support for radical roles varies according to: a) specialization within the profession; b) hierarchical rank in employing organizations (+ +, 24).

3.12A. Workers with more individual- and treatment-oriented specializations (casework) tend to be less supportive of radical roles. Workers with more system- and change-oriented specializations

[8] Rue Bucher and Anselm Strauss, *Professions in Process, American Journal of Sociology* 66 (January 1961): 325–34.

(community organization and group work) tend to be more supportive of radical roles (+ +, 24).

3.12B. These differences according to specialization are greatest at the line worker level and are reduced at the executive level, where community organizers and group workers move toward the conservative casework posture (+ +, 24).

3.12C. Pressures against radical role orientations are more intense at the upper organizational levels. These conservatizing forces have a greater effect on community organization and group work specialists than on caseworkers, since the potential for radical action is greater among the former (+ +, 24).

3.12D. In institutional areas close to the central professional domain (public welfare), all organizational ranks tend to be uniformly conservative, thereby eliminating differential support for radical roles according to rank (+ +, 24).

3.12E. In institutional areas more distant from the central professional domain (such as public housing), differentials are found to operate (+ +, 24).

3.12F. A professional role orientation by a worker tends to reduce the conservatizing effect of higher rank, that is to say, executives with a high professional orientation are able to retain their earlier radical inclination even while rising in the ranks. (+ +, 24).

3.12G. The tendency for professional orientation to neutralize the conservatizing effect of higher rank is more pronounced for community organization and group work specialists. Casework specialists, who are more conservative initially, move up the ranks with little change in orientation, regardless of the degree of professional identification (+ +, 24).

Action Guidelines: Among social work professionals, community organizers and group workers are more likely to support activist political strategies than their colleagues in casework. There may be similar differentiation in other human-service fields, with greater change-orientation and activism to be found among segments concerned with macrosystems (e.g., community and adult education personnel in the field of education or community psychologists in the field of psychology). Since these are relatively small, marginal segments of the profession, care must be taken to prevent their mobilization for action from having the effect of simply splitting off and isolating a core politically oriented group.

Rank-and-file members offer more potential for recruitment into activist roles in institutional or problem areas relatively distant from the profession's central domain. Community-organization executives are more susceptible to being redirected toward activist roles through increasing the saliency of their professional reference group identity. These executives undergo considerable role conflict and require professional identification as a check on the conservatizing effects of their position, including those of board members and community elites with whom such professionals may come into close and frequent contact.

In what way does professional ideology operate in connection with political roles? One hears much talk of "the value system of the profession" or of "professional norms." Do the human service professions have such a crystalized or integrated value system that guides role behavior in general, or political role performance in particular? Epstein examined this matter with respect to social work and found little support for the notion of a structurally integrated professional community. A wide range of professional measures were brought to bear, including:

ORGANIZATIONAL PROFESSIONALIZATION: Percentage of agency employees with the masters' degree;

PARTICIPATION IN THE PROFESSIONAL COMMUNITY: Involvement in local and national professional association activity, numbers of papers presented to professional groups, published papers, conferences attended, and amount of reading of professional journals;

IDEOLOGY OF PROFESSIONALISM: Attitudinal commitment to political neutrality, professional decorum, affective neutrality, and superiority of the professional's to the client's definition of the latter's needs;

PROFESSIONAL ROLE ORIENTATION: Indices of role orientation of professionals developed by Billingsley, Scott, and Wilensky.

Analysis of these measures leads to a number of conclusions along the following lines:

Professional Value Consensus

GENERALIZATION 3.13: Human-service professions do not appear to be highly integrated with regard to the existence of a delimited uniformly accepted value system (+ + +, 26, also 10, 41, 47, 63, 81, 85, 97).

> 3.13A. Social work is not a structurally integrated professional community. That is to say, there is little correlation among various indices of professionalization within the occupational community, such as extent of organizational professionalization, participation in professional associations, and among various measures of professional role orientation (+ +, 26).
>
> 3.13B. Social workers do not uniformly accept a neutralist professional ideology in role performance (political neutrality, professional decorum, affective neutrality, superiority of professional over client definitions of service). Commitment to this ideology varies among members of the profession (+ +, 26).
>
> 3.13C. Commitment to a neutralist professional ideology is unrelated to other indices of professionalization (organizational professionalization, participation in professional associations, and various measures of professional role orientation) (+ +, 26).

Several studies amplify on value differences within the profession. For example, Varley (97) shows that males and females hold different value positions, Hall (41) finds that geographical and regional differences account for many liberal-conservative value differences, and Lauffer (63) indicates that newer people to the field tend to be less conservative than those already practicing and that divisions occur along lines of specialization. Northwood (85) describes value conflicts among professionals regarding the use of so-called "benign" quotas, and links value positions to personality variables.

The question of a crystallized or uniform value system is a complex one. While the data play down value uniformity, other data suggest *tendencies* in a common value direction. For example,

Meyer, Litwak, and Warren (81) found an overall difference in values between teachers and social workers when tested with the Meyer-McLeod Values Scale. Meyer and McLeod point out one ambiguity when they state that "fully trained social workers, though distinguishable from less trained social workers (as well as school teachers) vary considerably among themselves in their social values" (p. 414).

Chetkow (9) notes some interesting distinctions between the values held by community organization practitioners in coordinating bodies such as welfare councils and those held by social workers in affiliated direct-service agencies. The two different value sets are displayed in Table 3.2, together with yet a third set of values held by lay board members.

TABLE 3.2: COMPARISON OF VALUE SETS

Planning (Council)	Direct-Service (Agency)	Allocative-Fund (Layman)
Desire to document unmet needs, create balance of services	Desire to expand operations to meet specialized needs of more clients	Desire to preserve the status quo, not raise campaign goals each year
Use of all available financial resources	Use of all available financial resources	Ambivalence about growing role of government; preference for voluntarism
Prevention of dependency	Belief in need for therapy for dependent persons	Punitive view of dependency
Belief that services may be ineffective	Belief that agency services are inadequate	Belief that current services are adequate
Hope for negotiated consent, representativeness, cooperation, and coordination	Commitment to practitioner's art, self-maintenance, preservation of organizational autonomy	Desire for efficient administration, cost-per-unit analysis

Action Guidelines: Since there is no unified or crystallized value system to which all professionals subscribe, it is possible for community organization practitioners to select out and give emphasis to those components of the professional norms which support a more activist orientation. This may be one strategy for enhancing political activism. Refinement of such a strategy are suggested in the next generalization.

Professionalization and Political Role Orientation

GENERALIZATION 3.14: Political orientation is affected differentially by different components of professionalization (+ +, 26, 28).

> 3.14A. Greater professional density in an organization (larger proportion of M.S.W.'s) is associated with greater acceptance of radical roles among all workers regardless or specialization, with the influence stronger in group work and community-oriented organizations (+ + , 26).
> 3.14B. A commitment to a neutralist professional ideology is associated with low acceptance of radical roles among all workers, regardless of specialization (+ +, 26).
> 3.14C. A professional role orientation is associated with approval of radical roles among community organizers and group workers, but not among caseworkers (+ +, 28).
> 3.14D. Participation in the professional association has a definite negative influence on approval of radical roles among community organizers and group workers. Among caseworkers, the influence of the association in this regard is weak, although again negative (+ +, 28).

Action Guidelines: Some important strategic directions are suggested. For example, the community practitioner desiring to promote activist tendencies should attempt to undercut the neutralist professional orientation among all professionals. Arguments against retention of this orientation include the fact that it is not uniformly held in the profession and hence is not the only legitimate position to assume to achieve status or recognition. Secondly, the conservatizing and potentially anticlient ramifications of the position could be articulated. Practitioners could work to increase professional density in agencies as a way of fostering an organizational climate conducive to greater activism. More radical professionals (community organizers and group workers) should be encouraged to keep professional peer group identification high, but to keep actual participation in professional-association activities moderate. Such direct involvement with a range of more conservative professionals appears to be associated with a decline in activism among the most radical segments. This observation does not hold to the same degree for caseworker activists.

A final generalization concerns the degree to which there is accurate perception among professionals concerning preferred political roles. The general statement on this may be expressed as follows:

GENERALIZATION 3.15: Human-service professionals tend to underestimate the extent to which approval of radical roles exists in the profession (+ +, 7, 27).

There are two aspects of this statement: 1) peer perception per se; 2) perception of differentials between professionals and board members.

3.15A. There is more support for conflictual modes of social action among rank-and-file social workers than they themselves perceive to be the case (+ +, 27).

From analysis of his data, Epstein found that workers underestimated the extent to which their colleagues were willing to support radical roles—that is, more workers actually indicated such support than respondents thought would do so.

3.15B. Social workers believe that political role preferences of colleagues and board members are congruent; professionals are not perceived as more radical than board members. Some evidence leads to the inferential proposition that social workers do not recognize the extent to which their position is divergent in the radical direction from the position of board members (+, 7, 27).

In a study by Brager of Mobilization for Youth (7), commitment to the radical values of the organization was found to be clearly lower on the part of board members than among executives, supervisors, and practitioners. Some caution needs to be exercised, however, in that another study (1) showed that while community mental health specialists and consultants scored higher on the community Mental Health Ideology Scale than did concerned nonprofessional citizens and board members, citizens scored higher than psychiatrists and psychologists.

Action Guidelines: The main practice principle here is to document and publicize the extent of activist support that exists among professionals. The sense of peer support and group legitimation that would result from such revelation may have the effect of allowing expression of activist tendencies on the part of those who hold these but feel isolated or deviant in their beliefs. An analogous study discovered that in a class of school children, favorable and cooperative attitudes toward the teacher were more widely held than the children believed to be true. When this information was shared, the group climate shifted in a positive direction in terms of relationships with the teacher.[9] A similar phenomenon occurred when the extent of antidiscriminatory attitudes held by members was fed back to members of a fraternity house having racially discriminatory policies.[10]

To close out our discussion of political activist roles, we shall offer one additional statement, which serves as a summary of points made in a number of generalizations throughout this section. We shall use the opportunity to indicate those variables which have the effect of en-

[9] Richard Schmuck, Mark Chestler, and Ronald Lippitt, *Problem-Solving to Improve Classroom Learning* (Chicago: Science Research Associates, 1966).

[10] James B. Lau, "Attitude Change as Related to Change in Perception of the Group Norm" (Doctoral dissertation, University of Michigan, Department of Psychology, 1954.); Andrew Kapos, "Some Individual-Group Determinants of Fraternity Attitudes Toward the Admission of Members of Certain Minority Groups" (Doctoral dissertation, University of Michigan, Department of Social Psychology, 1953).

couraging political and radical role orientations, on the assumption that these roles are underdeveloped and underplayed in the profession, and that the circumstances in the contemporary social situation require additional commitments along these lines by professionals and citizens alike. Accordingly:

Variables Conducive to Activist Roles
(A Recapitulation)

GENERALIZATION 3.16: Factors associated with a more radical role orientation on the part of practitioner include:
   Involvement in more distant institutional areas
   A client orientation
   A professional orientation conjointly with a client orientation
   A professional orientation for community organizers and group workers
   Community organization or group work specialization
   Lower rank in the organizational hierarchy
   High professional density in an organization
   Low commitment to a norm of professional neutrality
   Low participation in professional associations
   A low bureaucratic orientation

CONCLUSION

Discussion of community practitioner roles in the professional literature has generally taken a pragmatic, atheoretical form of discourse. Descriptive writings and even study reports usually have dealt with isolated situations or problems, offering little by way of comparative analysis across discrete contexts. In this chapter we have made an attempt to impose a comparative perspective by synthesizing, in several categories, heterogeneous research touching on the general subject. Three theoretical-conceptual perspectives in particular have been drawn upon to inform this effort—one from role theory, another from linkage theory, and a third from the sociology of the professions.

Only a limited start has been made in this direction; perhaps merely enough to constitute a trial of the utility of further work along these lines. The formulation of more basic theoretical foundations for dealing with practitioner roles is desperately needed to enhance the understanding of this crucial element of intervention for social change.

BIBLIOGRAPHY FOR PART TWO

1. Baker, Frank and Herbert C. Schulberg. "Community Mental Health Ideology, Dogmatism and Political-Economic Conservatism." *Community Mental Health* 5, no. 6 (December 1969): 433–36.

2. Banfield, Edward C. *Political Influence*. New York: Free Press, 1961.

3. Bar Yosef, R. and E. O. Schild. "Pressures and Defenses in Bureaucratic Roles." *American Journal of Sociology* 71, no. 6 (May 1966): 665–73.

4. Bernard, Sydney, Emeric Kurtagh, and Harold Johnson. "The Neighborhood Service Organization: Specialist in Social Welfare Innovation." *Social Work* 13, no. 1 (January 1968): 76–84.

5. Bible, Bond L. and Coy G. McNabb. "Role Consensus and Administrative Effectiveness." *Rural Sociology* 31, no. 1 (March 1966): 5–14.

6. Billingsley, Andrew. "Bureaucratic and Professional Orientation Patterns in Social Casework." *Social Service Review* 38, no. 4 (December 1964): 400–407.

7. Brager, George. "Commitment and Conflict in a Normative Organization." *American Sociological Review* 34, no. 4 (August 1969): 482–91.

8. Bucher, Rue. "The Psychiatric Residency and Professional Socialization." *Health and Social Behavior* 6, no. 4 (Winter 1965): 197–206.

9. Chetkow, B. Harold. "The Planning of Social Service Changes." *Public Administration Review* 27, no. 3 (May–June 1968): 256–83.

10. Chetkow, B. Harold. "Some Factors Influencing the Utilization and Impact of Priority Recommendations in Community Planning." *Social Service Review* 41, no. 3 (September 1967): 271–82.

11. Clark, Cedric C. "Cultural Differences in Reactions to Discrepant Communication." *Human Organization* 27, no. 2 (Summer 1968): 125–31.

12. Clark, Kate M. "Social Workers and Social Action: A Study of Attitudes and Actions." Master's thesis, Smith College, School of Social Work, 1964.

13. Clavel, Pierre. "Planners and Citizen Boards: Some Applications of Social Theory to the Problem of Plan Implementation." *Journal of the American Institute of Planners* 34, no. 3 (May 1968): 130–39.

14. Cotes, Judith. "Conflict Resolution in the Mental Hospital." *Journal of Health and Social Behavior* 7, no. 2 (Summer 1966): 138–42.

15. Cowin, Ruth P., Elizabeth P. Rice, and William M. Schmidt. "Social Work in a Child Health Clinic: A Report of a Demonstration." *American Journal of Public Health* 55, no. 6 (June 1965): 821–31.

16. Cumming, Elaine and Ian and Laura Edele. "Policeman as Philosopher, Guide and Friend, *Social Problems* 12, no. 13 (Winter 1965): 276–86.

17. Demerath, Nicholas J. "Can India Reduce Its Birth Rate? A Question of Moderniza-

tion and Governmental Capacity,'' *Journal of Social Issues* 23, no. 4 (October 1961): 179–95.

18. Demerath, Nicholas J., Gerald Marwell, and Michael T. Aiken. ''Tactics and Tensions in a Summer of Yesteryear: Results of a Panel Analysis of 1965 Southern Civil Rights Workers,'' Paper before American Sociological Association Annual Conference, San Francisco, 1969.

19. Doig, Jameson W. ''Police Problems, Proposals, and Strategies for Change,'' *Public Administration Review* 28, no. 5 (September–October 1968): 393–406.

20. Downing, Ruppert A., Laura N. Izenson, and Ann Montz. ''The Current Role of Social Action in the Social Work Profession.'' Master's thesis, Jane Addams Graduate School of Social Work, University of Illinois, 1966.

21. Dunn, Delmer, ''Transmitting Information to the Press: Differences among Officials.'' *Public Administration Review* 28, no. 5 (September–October 1968): 445–52.

22. Engel, Gloria V. ''The Effect of Bureaucracy on the Professional Autonomy of the Physician.'' *Journal of Health and Social Behavior* 10, no. 1 (March 1969): 30–41.

23. English, Joseph T. and G. Colmen. ''Psychological Adjustment Patterns of Peace Corps Volunteers.'' *Psychiatric Opinion* 3, no. 6 (December 1966): 29–35.

24. Epstein, Irwin. ''Organizational Careers, Professionalization and Social-Worker Radicalism.'' *The Social Service Review* 44, no. 2 (June 1970): 123–31.

25. Epstein, Irwin. ''Professional Role Orientation and Conflict Strategies.'' *Social Work* 15, no. 4 (October 1970): 87–92.

26. Epstein, Irwin. ''Professionalization, Professionalism and Social-Worker Radicalism.'' *Journal of Health and Social Behavior* 11, no. 1 (March 1970): 67–77.

27. Epstein, Irwin. ''Social Workers and Social Action: Attitudes toward Social Action Strategies.'' *Social Work* 13, no. 2 (April 1968): 101–8.

28. Epstein, Irwin. ''Specialization, Professionalization and Social-Worker Radicalism: A Test of the 'Process' Model of the Profession.'' *Applied Social Studies* 2 (1970): 155–63.

29. Fahn, Jane C., ''Some Characteristics of Successful and Less Successful Overseas Community Development Advisors.'' *Adult Education* no. 1 (Fall 1967): 15–23.

30. Fathi, Asghar. ''Leadership and Resistance to Change: A Case From an Underdeveloped Area.'' *Rural Sociology* 30, no. 2 (June 1965): 204–12.

31. Friedman, John. ''Planning or Innovation: The Chile Case.'' *Journal of the American Institute of Planners* 32, no. 4 (July 1966): 194–204.

32. Friedman, Robert, Bernard W. Klein, and John H. Romani. ''Administrative Agencies and the Publics They Serve.'' *Public Administration Review* 26, no. 3 (September 1966): 192–204.

33. Furman, Sylvan, Lili G. Sweat, and Guido M. Crocetti. ''Social Class Factors in the Flow of Children to Outpatient Psychiatric Facilities.'' *American Journal of Public Health* 55 (March 1965): 385–92.

34. Gilbert, Neil. ''Clients or Constituents? A Case Study of Pittsburgh's War on Poverty.'' Dissertation, University of Pittsburgh Graduate School of Social Work, 1968.

35. Gilbert, Neil. "Maximum Feasible Participation? A Pittsburgh Encounter." *Social Work* 14, no. 3 (November 1969): 84–92.

36. Gilbert, Neil. "Neighborhood Coordinator: Advocate or Middleman." *Social Service Review* 43, no. 2 (June 1969): 136–44.

37. Gottesfeld, Harry. "Professionals and Delinquents Evaluate Professional Methods with Delinquents." *Social Problems* 13, no. 1 (Summer 1965): 45–59.

38. Gross, Neal, Joseph B. Giacquinta, and Marilyn Bernstein. "Complex Organizations: The Implementation of Major Organization Innovation." Paper presented at the meeting of the American Sociological Association, Boston, August 1968, pp. 1–27.

39. Gurin, Arnold and Robert Perlman. *Social Planning and Community Organization.* New York: John Wiley, in cooperation with the Council on Social Work Education, 1972.

40. Hage, Jerald and Michael Aiken. "Relationship of Centralization to Other Structural Properties." *Administrative Science Quarterly* 12, no. 1 (June 1967): 74–92.

41. Hall, Julian Craven. "The Conflict between Income Guarantee Proposals and the Value of work." Dissertation, Washington University School of Social Work, 1968.

42. Hall, Richard H. "Professionalization and Bureaucratization." *American Sociological Review* 33, no. 1 (February 1968): 92–104.

43. Hall, Richard H. "Some Organizational Considerations in the Professional-Organizational Relationship." *Administrative Science Quarterly* 12, no. 3 (December 1967): 461–78.

44. Hanlan, Archie. "Organizational Influences on Public Assistance Staff: A Comparative Analysis of Staff Orientations in Three County Welfare Departments. Doctoral Dissertation, University of California, Berkeley, 1967.

45. Hardee, Gilbert J. "Planned Changes and Systematic Linkage in a Five-Year Extension Program with Part-Time Farm Families." *Rural Sociology* 30, no. 1 (March 1965): 23–32.

46. Harvey, Edward. "Technology and the Structure of Organization." *American Sociological Review* 33, no. 2 (1968): 247–59.

47. Hassinger, Edward W. and Charles E. Grubb. "The Linking Role of the Local Public Health Nurse in Missouri." *Rural Sociology* 30, no. 3 (September 1965): 299–310.

48. Hayes, Dorothy D. and Barbara K. Varley. "Impact of Social Work Education on Students' Values." *Social Work* 10, no. 3 (July 1965): 40–46.

49. Heffernan, W. Joseph, Jr. "Political Activity and Social Work Executives." *Social Work* 9, no. 2 (April 1964): 18–23.

50. Florence Heller School for Advanced Studies in Social Welfare. "Community Representation in Community Action Programs." March 1969.

51. Hollister, Clifton David. "Bureaucratic Structure and School-Parent Communication in Eighteen Detroit Elementary Schools." Dissertation, University of Michigan School of Social Work, 1966.

52. Jennings, M. Kent. "Planning and Community Elites in Two Cities." *Journal of the American Institute of Planners* 31, no. 1 (February 1965): 62–68.

53. Karna, Marvin and Robert B. Edgerton. "Perception of Mental Illness in the Mexican American Community." *Archives of General Psychiatry* 20, no. 2 (February 1969): 233–38.

54. Katz, Elihu and S. N. Eistenstadt. "Some Sociological Observations on the Response of Israeli Organizations to New Immigrants." *Administrative Science Quarterly* 5, no. 1 (June 1960): 113–33.

55. Klein, Malcom W. and Neal Snyder. "The Detached Worker: Uniformities and Variances in Work Style." *Social Work* 10, no. 4 (October 1965): 60–68.

56. Krause, Elliott A. "Structured Strain in a Marginal Profession—Rehabilitation Counseling." *Health and Social Behavior* 6, no. 1 (Spring 1965): 55–62.

57. Krueckelberg, Donald A. "A Multivariate Analysis of Metropolitan Planning." *Journal of the American Institute of Planners* 35, no. 5 (September 1969): 319–25.

58. Kurtz, Norman R. "Gatekeepers—Agents in Acculturation." *Rural Sociology* 33, no. 1 (March 1968): 64–70.

59. Kurzman, Paul A. "The Native-Settler Concept: Implications for Community Organization." *Social Work* 14, no. 3 (November 1969): 58–64.

60. Lansing, John B. and Robert W. Murans. "Evaluation of Neighborhood Quality." *Journal of the American Institute of Planners* 35, no. 3 (May 1969): 195–99.

61. Lappin, B. W. "Stages in the Development of Community Organization Work as a Method in Social Work Practice." Dissertation, University of Toronto School of Social Work, 1965.

62. Larson, Richard F. "Clerical and Psychiatric Conceptions of the Clergyman's Role in the Therapeutic Setting." *Social Problems* 11, no. 4 (Spring 1964): 419–28.

63. Lauffer, Armand. "Social Activists Come to Social Work: A Comparison of Community Organization Students with their Peers in Casework." Dissertation, Brandeis University, Florence Heller School, 1968.

64. Lawrence, Harry. "The Effectiveness of Group-Directed vs. Worker-Directed Style of Leadership for Group Work." Dissertation, University of California at Berkeley, 1967.

65. Lawrence, P. R. and J. W. Lorsch. *Organization and Environment: Managing Differentiation and Integration*. Boston: Harvard Business School, 1967.

66. Levy, Charles J. *Voluntary Servitude: Whites in the Negro Movement*. New York: Appleton-Century-Crofts, 1968.

67. Liberman, Robert. "The Part Played by Physicians in the Patient's Path to the Mental Hospital." *Community Mental Health Journal* 3, no. 4 (1967): 325–34.

68. Liberman, Robert. "Police as a Community Mental Health Resource." *Community Mental Health Journal* 5, no. 2 (April 1969): 11–20.

69. Lorsch, Jay W. and Paul R. Lawrence. "Environmental Factors and Organizational Integration." Paper presented for the American Sociological Association, Boston, Massachusetts, 1968.

70. Lyden, Fremont. "Success in the Peace Corps." *Public Administration Review* 26, no. 4 (December 1966): 354.

71. Lyons, Thomas F. "Role Clarity, Need for Clarity, Satisfaction, and Withdrawal." *Organizational Behavior and Human Performance* 6 (January 1971): 99–110.

72. Magid, Alvin. "Dimensions of Administrative Role and Conflict Resolution among Local Officials in Northern Nigeria." *Administrative Science Quarterly* 12, no. 2: 321–38.

73. Maher, Philip, Richard Rubino, and Sureva Seligson. "Status, Effectiveness and Acceptance of Planning and Advanced Programming in State Government." *Digest of Urban and Regional Research* 15, no. 1 (Fall 1968): 125.

74. Maier, Norman R. G. "Acceptance and Quality of Solutions as Related to Leaders' Attitudes toward Disagreement in Group Problem Solving." *Applied Behavioral Science* 1, no. 4 (October–December 1965): 373–86.

75. Markus, Nathan. "Staff Participation in Organizational Change: A Study of the Participation of Staff Members of Social Service Organizations in Activities Aimed at Influencing Changes in the Services and Functions of the Employing Agencies." Dissertation, University of Toronto School of Social Work, 1969.

76. Martin, Roscoe C., et al. *Decisions in Syracuse*. Bloomington, Indiana: University of Indiana Press, 1961.

77. Mayer, Albert, et al. *Pilot Project India*. Berkeley: University of California Press, 1958.

78. McBroom, Elizabeth. "A Comparative Analysis of Social Work Interventions in Two Types of AFDC Families." Dissertation, University of California at Berkeley, 1965.

79. McBroom, Elizabeth. "Helping AFDC Families—A Comparative Study." *Social Service Review* 39, no. 4 (December 1965): 390–98.

80. McDermott, John, Saul Harrison, Jules Schrager, and Paul Wilson. "Social Class and Mental Illness in Children: Observation of Blue Collar Families." *American Journal of Orthopsychiatry* 35, no. 3 (April 1965): 500–505.

81. Meyer, Henry J., Eugene Litwak, and Donald Warren. "Occupational and Class Differences in Social Values: A Comparison of Teachers and Social Workers." *Sociology of Education* 41, no. 3 (Summer 1968): 263–81.

82. Miller, George A. "Professionals in Bureaucracy—Alienation among Industrial Scientists and Engineers." *American Sociological Review* 32, no. 5 (October 1967): 755–68.

83. Morris, Robert and Ollie A. Randall. "Planning and Organization of Community Services for the Elderly." *Social Work* 1, no. 10 (January 1965): 96–103.

84. Mueller, Jeanne. "Social Work Practice and Community Mental Health." Paper, University of Wisconsin School of Social Work, 1968.

85. Northwood, L. K. and Louise Klein. "The Benign Quota, An Unresolved Issue: Attitudes of Agency Personnel." *Phylon* 28, no. 2 (Summer 1965): 109–22.

86. Palumbo, Dennis J. "Power and Role Specificity in Organizational Theory." *Public Administration Review* 29, no. 3 (May–June 1969): 237–48.

87. Rapaport, Robert N. "Some Notes on Para-Technical Factors in Cross-Cultural Consultation." *Human Organization* 23, no. 1 (Spring 1964): 5–10.

88. Riley, John M. "A Comparative Study of Social Worker's Role Orientation in State Mental Hospitals with Differing Organizational Structures." Dissertation, Brandeis University, Florence Heller School, 1967.

89. Robinson, Derek. "Effectiveness of Medical and Social Supervision in a Multiproblem Population." *American Journal of Public Health* 58, no. 2 (February 1968): 10.

90. Rogers, Everett M. *Diffusion of Innovations.* New York: The Free Press, 1962.

91. Rosen, Aaron. "The Influence of Perceived Interpersonal Power and Consensus of Expectations on Conformity of Performance of Public Assistance Workers." Dissertation, University of Michigan School of Social Work, 1963.

92. Rossi, Peter. "Theory, Research and Practice in Community Organization." In *Social Science and Community Action* by Charles P. Adrian et al. East Lansing: Michigan State University Press, 1960.

93. Stein, William W. and E. R. Oetting. "Humanism and Custodialism in a Peruvian Mental Hospital." *Human Organization* 23, no. 4 (Winter 1964): 278–82.

94. Street, David, Robert D. Vinter, and Charles Perrow. *Organization for Treatment.* New York: The Free Press, 1966.

95. Stycos, J. Mayone. "The Potential Role of Turkish Village Opinion Leaders in a Program of Family Planning." *Public Opinion Quarterly* 29, no. 1. (Spring 1965): 120–30.

96. Thomas, Edwin J. "Role Conceptions and Organizational Size." *American Sociological Review* 20, no. 1 (1959): 30–37.

97. Varley, Barbara. "Are Social Workers Dedicated to Service?" *Social Work* 11, no. 2 (April 1966): 84–91.

98. Weissman, Harold H. "An Explanatory Study of a Neighborhood Council." Dissertation, Columbia University School of Social Work, 1966.

99. Wilensky, Harold L. "The Professionalization of Everyone?" *American Journal of Sociology* 70, no. 2 (September 1964): 137–58.

Part Three

The Organizational Framework of Social Change

Chapter Four

Organizational Behavior: Contextual Factors

INTRODUCTION AND OVERVIEW

THE CONCEPT of organization is found at the center of community organization practice. Like the human-service fields in general, community organization is an organizational profession. The overwhelming number of practitioners spend their entire professional careers working in one or another organization, sometimes on behalf of still other organizations. The service outcomes or collective fates of clients and constituents of various types are profoundly affected by organizational structures, climates, and policies.

Zald has stated the issue graphically:

> It is impossible to consider the community organization practitioner without considering the agency context in which he is employed. Indeed, compared to many professions, a much greater part of the variety of practices is determined by the organizational context for the profession. . . . "needs" and "problems" . . . are defined and shaped by the employing agency. The techniques selected to deal with them also depend upon requirements of the organization. Whether the practitioner facilitates, fund raises, or foments, whether he plans, serves as a resource expert, counsels, or agitates is determined by the structure, aims, and operating procedures of the organization that pays the bill. Any useful theory of community organization practice must include concepts and propositions about how community organization agencies shape policies.[1]

In addition to being constrained or influenced by a sponsoring agency, the practitioner's goal is often the modification of policies or practices of some external target organization or institution in the com-

[1] Meyer N. Zald, "Sociology and Community Organization Practice," in *Organizing for Community Welfare*, Zald, ed. (Chicago: Quadrangle, 1967) pp. 33, 35.

munity. Usually, organizations view intervention overtures directed at them less than enthusiastically. Morris and Binstock have discussed this issue in the following way:

> For a number of reasons, organizations are predisposed to resist changes embodied in social planning goals. . . . The propensity of organizations to resist . . . poses important practical questions for the planner. Is it possible to predict or anticipate which target agencies are especially likely to resist? How extensively?
>
> No classification has yet been developed which provides systematic guidance for predictions as to which organization, under what circumstances, will resist certain types of planning goals. . . . For the present, social planners must rely upon a sensitive reading of each new situation against an extensive backdrop of relatively intimate knowledge of the pertinent organizations.[2]

In this chapter, we shall attempt to move the practitioner beyond intuitive, ad hoc engagement with organizations by constructing a limited number of generalizations about organizational behavior. Hopefully, these can provide basic guidance for organizational intervention across particular settings and contexts.

We shall present research findings here which were gleaned from "organizational theory" literature. A very high proportion of the studies are from such journals as *The Administrative Science Quarterly* and the *American Sociological Review*. Many of the studies pertain to business, industrial, and military spheres. Hence, we have exercised judgment in choosing those which were applicable to the human-services field, and (among the various issues that could have been discussed) those which seemed most important or interesting. The subject of innovations in organizations will be treated separately in chapter 9.

Unlike other practice issue areas, organizational research has a definite tradition of theory and research development representing a coherent school of scholarly endeavor. There are more concrete and rigorous theoretical boundaries within which to place studies we reviewed than is true in other sections of this volume. We shall present the reader with some of the general theoretical issues in the field of orga-

[2] Robert Morris and Robert H. Binstock, *Feasible Planning for Social Change,* (New York: Columbia University Press, 1966) pp. 94, 102.

nizational research as a way of introducing the research tradition, and providing a basis for interpreting and evaluating studies. Because of the cognitive and philosophical orientation of the researchers, most of the studies lend themselves to application in terms of administrative and planning issues, rather than social action.

The presentation of research in this chapter moves from broader, contextual aspects of organization behavior to more internal, technical ones. Thus, we shall start with such surrounding factors as organization environment, goals and size (Chapter 4), and work inward to technology and staff (especially professional) considerations within the organization (Chapter 5). General and theoretical discussion pertaining to each area will be distributed within each section rather than being presented together at the outset. The nature of the substantive content lends itself to this interspersed mode of presentation.

ORGANIZATIONS AND THEIR ENVIRONMENTS

The relationship between an organization and its environment has received increasing attention from social scientists. The tendency to concentrate on intraorganizational phenomena is being supplemented of late by an effort to relate organizations to their environments and to view internal characteristics and processes as a product of interaction with external systems. The environment of each organization contains numerous interacting variables such as the value system of the general society; policies and activities of other formal organizations; influences of primary groups and voluntary associations; and resources markets (such as manpower, money, knowledge). Hence, organizations function within a dynamic environment that includes social units and forces of relevance. Evan has conceptualized aspects of this environment as an "organizational set."

A review of the literature reveals that there are two main types of studies: those dealing with the interaction between an organization and a single environmental component, and those dealing with an organization's interaction with a comprehensive environmental system.[3] Sev-

[3] For attempts to construct conceptual frameworks regarding the relationships between organizations and their environments, see F. E. Emery, and E. Trist, "The Causal Texture of Organizational Environments," *Human Relations,* 18, no. 1 (February 1965):

eral studies in the former tradition, for example, discuss the issue of relations among formal organizations; others examine the impact of external values on organizations. The second group of studies combines those components into a unified framework and attempts to offer a typology of whole environments. The Emery and Trist article on "The Causal Texture of Organizational Environments," and the Eisenstadt study of bureaucracy, overbureaucratization, and debureaucratization are conspicuous among these studies. Unfortunately, most of the writings in this area are theoretical, and only a few are based on empirical data derived from field investigation.

We shall attempt here to construct generalizations derived from studies in our retrieval pool that deal directly with the environmental concept. The discussion to follow will lean heavily on the significant Lawrence and Lorsch Study of six firms operating in different industrial environments.

Environmental Certainty and Bureaucratic Structure

GENERALIZATION 4.1: Organizations that operate in a task environment of high certainty and regularity tend to have more pronounced bureaucratic features. Further, this relationship is associated with efficiency of operation. Conversely, when the task environment is uncertain and unpredictable, less pronounced bureaucratic features are typical and desirable (+ + + +, 1, 2, 4, 15, 23, 49).

The term "certainty" describes situations in which events are fairly uniform and recurrent. Operating conditions under such circumstances are fairly stable and predictable. Accordingly, tasks in the organization

---

21–32; M. William Evan, "The Organization Set: Toward a Theory of Interorganizational Relationships," in *Approaches to Organizational Design*, J. D. Thompson, ed. (Pittsburgh: University of Pittsburgh Press, 1966) pp. 173–91; S. N. Eisenstadt, "Bureaucracy, Bureaucratization and Debureaucratization," *Administrative Science Quarterly,* 4 (1959) 302–320; E. Litwak, with J. Rothman, "Toward the Theory and Practice of Coordination between Formal Organizations," in *Organizations and Clients: Essays in the Sociology of Service* by William R. Rosen and Mark Lefton, (Columbus, Ohio: Merrill, 1970) pp. 137–86; E. Litwak and H. J. Meyer, "A Balance Theory of Coordination between Bureaucratic Organizations and Community Primary Groups," American Sociological Review 2, no. 1, pp. 31–58.

can be "programmed," routinized, and often carried out by personnel with minimal training. The complexity of uniform, routine events is less than that associated with nonuniform events. Because of the potential regularity of operations, more formal structured and technical organizational attributes can be brought into play.[4]

4.1A. Organizations that operate under conditions of high certainty tend to be characterized by centralization in decision making (+ , 23, 49).

"Centralization" refers to the concentration of decision making in the upper levels of an organization, with little participation of lower-level members. The term "decentralization" refers to a diffused decision-making structure wherein lower-level members participate, often in conjunction with upper-level members.

Research evidence from a variety of organizational settings suggests that where there is a relatively high degree of certainty concerning environmental factors, decision making is most effective when concentrated at the upper levels of management. This seems valid, since at this level of the organization knowledge of broad areas of organization functioning can be pooled, codified, and then coupled with technical requirements of the total process needed for production of outcomes.

Research findings also suggest that where there is a relatively high degree of uncertainty, decision making that is decentralized or shared among different levels in the organization is conducive to effectiveness. In this situation, knowledge is not easily concentrated at higher levels of the organization, since environmental factors are in flux. Thus, units of the organization directly in touch and dealing with the changing conditions are best equipped to react quickly and make, or share in the making of, decisions.

---

[4] For a useful discussion on uniform—nonuniform organizational environments and impact on organizational variables, see Eugene Litwak, "Models of Bureaucracy Which Permit Conflict" *American Journal of Sociology,* 57, no. 2 (Sept. 1961): 177–84. A more recent discussion is in Eugene Litwak and Jack Rothman, "Impact of Factors of Organizational Climate and Structure on Social Welfare and Rehabilitation Workers and Work Performance," *Working Paper No. 1: National Study of Social Welfare and Rehabilitation Workers, Work and Work Centers* (Washington, D.C.: Department of Health, Education and Welfare, Social and Rehabilitation Service, 1971).

Lawrence and Lorsch's study of organizations in three types of environments offers direct evidence of the relationships among degree of certainty, structure of decision making, and effectiveness. They found that effective organizations in the plastic industry—an industry characterized as new, emergent, and rapidly changing (high degrees of uncertainty)—generally had decentralized decision making. Effective organization in the box manufacturing industry, however, a long-established, stable, and routinized field (high degrees of certainty), had highly centralized decision making. There was an intermediate level of centralization-decentralization in an industrial organization having a moderate degree of environmental certainty.

4.1B. The greater the degree of certainty of an organization's relevant environment, the greater will be the degree of formalization (use of written rules) within the organization (+ + , 4, 15, 31, 32).

As implied above, the main environmental factor having an impact on the organization, according to Lawrence and Lorsch (32), is degree of certainty. They found that an organization's research activities are organized in a separate subsystem, in part because of the high degree of uncertainty that uniquely characterizes the research subenvironment, and the inability of administrators to impose rules on research operations. Why does uncertainty lead to a lower degree of organizational formalization? As in the case of centralization–decentralization, a situation of uncertainty typically cannot be dealt with by strict rules. It demands greater flexibility and autonomy for personnel who are on the front lines, in direct, on-the-spot contact with a fluid task situation. Such decentralized staff members are able to have intimate knowledge of emergent situations and, in order to use this knowledge well, cannot have their hands tied by restricting regulations.

Kaufman's study (31) of the National Forest Service revealed that formalization promoted effectiveness in terms of high quality in the National Forest Program. The upper-level organizational decision makers established goals and developed a codified manual of what Kaufman calls "procedural devices for performing decisions" concerning daily operations for the Forest Ranger. This manual specified the nature of certain tasks and when they were to be performed. In terms of our generalization, the organization was operating under conditions of certainty and the formalized structure was consistent with effective goal achievement.

The impact of an unsure environment consisting of heterogeneous and new clientele on welfare organizations is indicated in the Eisenstadt and Katz (15) and Bar-Yosef and Shild (4) studies of the response of Israeli bureaucratic service organizations to new immigrants. Those studies indicate that the appearance of new heterogeneous clientele created a change in organizational structure resulting in a modification of role prescriptions at the lower levels.

Among other hypothesized structural variables associated with environmental certainty are personal-impersonal relations, merit, and delimitation of rights and duties.

Action Guidelines: Practitioners in organizations functioning in a context of relatively high degrees of certainty should consider a centralized, formalized structure in order to promote effectiveness. Practitioners in organizations functioning under relatively high degrees of uncertainty should consider decentralized, low formalization structural arrangements in order to promote effectiveness.

A practitioner who wishes to reduce an organization's degree of centralization and formalization, viewing this as leverage for more flexibility and openness to change, might attempt to increase the degree of uncertainty in the environment in which the organization operates. One way to increase uncertainty in human-service agency environments is by activating clients and evoking diverse demands among various constituencies.

Judgment must be exercised concerning degree of centralization and formalization. It is not suggested here that an extreme level of centralization is associated with effectiveness. Most social-welfare agencies probably operate optimally under a degree of centralization in the middle range, but may move toward one or another end of this range in order to increase effectiveness. Income maintenance agencies probably can tolerate a greater degree of centralization and reliance on rules than can settlement houses, community mental health centers, or grass-roots social action organizations. Extremes of centralization may lead to moral questions of "dictatorship," operational questions of rigidity, and human questions of personal relationships and identity. One may have to soften task considerations associated with "efficiency" in order to accommodate considerations of organization survival associated with the maintenance features of the system. Most studies indicate that a balance of task and socioemotional factors must be maintained for optimal effectiveness.

In a situation of high centralization, technically oriented leadership is required. Increasing centralization may require technical equipment, forms, routines, etc., that take a good deal of planning and administrative knowhow. Attention must be paid to the latest and most effective equipment, and successful forms and procedures used elsewhere. Monitoring and feedback procedures may be important. A decentralized structure may require a different executive leadership—individuals more attuned to human relations, more willing to share decision making, and capable of providing charismatic as opposed to purely formal leadership (or headship). In the decentralized operation, special mechanisms of coordination may be required in order to maintain coherence in the organization (See Generalization 4.2).

Parallel Environment-Structural Arrangements

GENERALIZATION 4.2: An organization's performance is dependent on its ability to maintain a degree of differentiation between its subsystems as required by subenvironments, but at the same time insure a degree of integration among them consistent with requirements of the total environment (+ , 32).

4.2A. When the environment requires both a high degree of subsystem differentiation and a high degree of integration, integrative devices will tend to emerge (+ , 32).

This generalization also is an outgrowth of the Lawrence and Lorsch studies of organizational behavior (32). The authors based their measure of organizational performance on effectiveness criteria related to profits and growth. Differentiation among units was assessed in terms of such factors as different orientations among members located in various subunits with respect to interpersonal, time, and goal perceptions. Integration among units related to the utilization of integration devices, as for example a coordinator assigned to the role of linking different departments.

The data suggest that organizational subsystems relate to distinct subenvironments. The authors conclude that effective organizations structure themselves on the basis of differentiation and integration. Separate substructures are needed to deal with unique subenvironments. At the same time integration is required among these substructures in order to give the organizations the capability of dealing with an overall environmental complex. According to this study, integrative devices tend to emerge when too much emphasis on differentiation hinders the organization's capacity to confront its total environment. This investigation is one of the first attempts to research very broad aspects of organization-environment interaction. As such, it offers some immediate operational hints to practitioners and also serves as a baseline study for further research on the subject.

Action Guidelines: In designing the structure of an organization, the internal departments might be planned according to the structure of the environment. Organizational tasks involving confrontation with different subenvironments should be concentrated in separate units. Integration devices should be used in order to maintain an appropriate degree of coordination among the different units.

Time Orientation and Environmental Feedback

GENERALIZATION 4.3: The time orientations of organization members will vary directly with the modal time required to obtain definitive feedback from their relevant environment (+, 32).

An example may clarify the essential meaning of the term "time orientation." A productive subsystem that receives feedback about its efforts on a daily basis can be expected to include members with a short time orientation. Conversely, personnel of departments doing basic research or long-range planning will have a long time orientation.

Lawrence and Lorsch (32) measured time orientation with a question that asked for an estimate of the percentage of total time used on activities affecting the organization's profits within a specific time period: less than one month, one month to a year, or one to five years. The findings indicate that the time orientations of members of each subsystem are related to the time span of definitive feedback in market and technical-economic subenvironments.

Action Guidelines: This issue may have special significance in human-service organizations. A worker's time orientation pertains to his sensitivity to and awareness of "events" occurring in his environment, that is, alertness to relevant feedback. This sensitivity and awareness are particularly important in human-service organizations. Feedback may be heightened by activating elements of the environment to send immediate responses on operations to relevant staff members, administrators, or citizen officers. Of course, in certain organizational functions with a longer time perspective (perhaps planning or basic research), personnel occupying such positions might purposely be shielded from ongoing feedback or operational problems.

The subject of interorganizational relationships has received mounting attention in the literature and at sociology conferences. However, most of the writings are still theoretical rather than empirical; they are designed more to develop conceptual frameworks than to test them. The few empirical studies available provide instructive findings that point to potential contributions of further work.

Diverse Exchange Relationships and
Organizational Autonomy

GENERALIZATION 4.4: Organizations may reduce possible environmental controls and maximize their autonomy by forming exchange relationships with many and diverse units of their task environment that can provide needed resources (+ + +, 2, 33, 35, 54).

Exchange refers to flow of diverse resources (money, clients, manpower, etc.) between two organizations. *Task environment* refers to those parts of the environment with which the organization has contact in the process of pursuing its objectives.

Organizations may reduce the possibility of focused control over them by scattering their resource dependencies among several units in their environment. For example, Aiken and Hage (2) suggest that organizations can gain additional resources without loss of agency autonomy (i.e., without greatly increasing the environmental control over them) by participating in joint programs. In such programs, a number of agencies share funds, staff, or physical resources while engaging in defined service areas such as special projects for given target populations. The authors point out that joint programs are one means of reducing the costs of programs without reducing their quality. In terms of this orientation, joint programs may be seen as a form of exchange designed to increase organizational potential by securing additional resources.

In an analogous study, Litwak and Hylton (35) found that social-welfare organizations that diffuse their funding arrangements are better able to control their dependency relations with external organizations, and to resist attempts to lessen their autonomy. Similarly, Tropman's study of social-welfare councils (54) illustrates that broadening council financial inputs (from reliance predominantly on community chests to relations with private foundations and governmental bodies) enabled the agencies to widen the scope of their program activity. Tropman notes that where the councils were heavily dependent on the community chest, severe constraints were placed on their capacity to innovate.

Action Guidelines: Organizations that wish to emphasize their independence might attempt to develop a diversified resource base. The degree to which resource units are not in touch with one another and can be manipulated separately will probably serve to maximize autonomy. The difficulty in this conception is that the agency must expend a relatively high percentage of its energy in cultivating, administering, and maintaining multiple-resource inputs. Also, a shrewd and energetic adversary that wishes to weaken such an organization could probably easily eliminate one source at a time, since the commitment of any single source might not be high.

Joint Programs and Internal Structure

GENERALIZATION 4.5: Organizations having many joint programs with other organizations tend to be more complex, more innovative, have more internal communication channels, and have slightly more decentralized decision-making structures (+, 2).

Organizational complexity refers to the degree of professionalization and diversity of an organization's occupational structure. "Innovativeness" means the number of new programs that are introduced into the organization. "Internal communication" in the cited study pertains to the number of committees in the organization and the number of committee meetings per month. Aiken and Hage (2), in their study of sixteen human-service organizations, examine the issues involved in this proposition. Their implicit assumption is that complexity (namely, higher degree of professionalization and diversity of occupations) leads to intensified communication between different occupational and professional groups, which consequently enriches the organizational package of ideas, programs, etc. Organizations that lack adequate resources may view joint programs with other organizations as a means of establishing new services.

Although a high positive correlation was found between the existence of joint programs and the other organizational variables (complexity, innovativeness, and communication), several qualifying comments are merited. Organizational complexity, as measured by the degree of professionalization and diversity of occupations, may indeed intensify the flow of ideas and the emergence of new programs within the organization. It may, at the same time, lead to increased tension between different professional disciplines and to the weakening of the organization's ability to attain new programs initiated by one of the professional groups. The subject of competitive relationships between different professional groups in organizations has not received much empirical attention in the literature. Some studies (10), however, do raise the issue. Aiken and Hage do not explain the factors that encourage organizations with resources to cooperate with those lacking resources, although they offer hunches along these lines. Also, it is not sufficiently clear why organizations prefer to cooperate with other organizations instead of attempting to mobilize independent resources.

Action Guidelines: Organizations that wish to develop or expand joint programs to increase resources, diversify programs, or foster cooperative relationships should consider incorporating the stated structural elements (professional diversification, decentralization, and intense internal communication) into their organizational framework. A practitioner or administrator wishing to intensify these organizational characteristics, might develop a facilitating environment by arranging joint programs with selected other organizations.

Community Prestige and Organizational Resources

GENERALIZATION 4.6: Organizations may increase their resource support by developing a high prestige image in the community (+, 33, 43).

In his study of the voluntary general hospital, Perrow (43) indicates that the organization created a "favorable image to its salient public" as one means of controlling dependency. The author suggests that if an organization and its ouputs are well regarded, it can more easily attract personnel, influence legislation, and attract clients and donors. In business organizations, prestige is an important quality (as the concept of "good will" implies); "good will," or prestige, has concrete monetary value, which is attached to the sale price of a firm.

Levine and White (33) classified health agencies according to their relative prestige as rated by influential leaders in the community. They found that organizations high in prestige had the highest number of exchanges and received the largest number of communications from other organizations.

Prestige building is not without potential hazards. Perrow (43) suggests that the search for prestige can result in displacement of goals. He states that when organizational resources are overemployed for prestige-furthering activities, efforts not directly related to prestige receive minimal resources even though they are central to the mission of the organization. In human-service agencies similar outcomes may occur. For example, agencies seeking to further the development of their image may restrict services to the poor and seek to service middle- and upper-class clients.[5] The goal of serving high-risk populations may be dislocated by serving instead a segment of the population capable of improving the agency's image among important publics. In addition, prestige-seeking may turn a community-organization agency from controversial goals to conventional ones. When gaining prestige is not detrimental to an agency's core goals, it may be a useful means of winning external support.

Action Guidelines: Organizations having difficulties in mobilizing resources needed for their activities may sometimes improve their situation by developing a high prestige image, particularly among groups which are potential suppliers of resources. However, especially in the case of human services, attempts to build a positive public image in order to

[5] Richard A. Cloward and Irwin Epstein, "Private Social Welfare's Disengagement from the Poor: The Case of Family Adjustment Agencies," Mayer N. Zald, ed., *Social Welfare Institutions: A Sociological Reader* (New York: John Wiley and Sons, Inc., 1965) pp. 623–43.

mobilize funds may detract from the pursuit of the organization's basic goals. Practitioners must be alert to such goal displacement. This underlines the utility of a stable and adequate resources base that makes dependence on "patrons" unnecessary.

Organizations are not only recipients of resources; at the same time they deliver resources to a variety of recipients. This aspect of the organizational behavior was explored by Friedlander and Pickle (17) in their study of small-business organizations.

Multiple External Constituencies

GENERALIZATION 4.7: Organizations differentially satisfy the needs of their environmental constituencies. There is no necessary connection between the meeting of one constituency's needs and the meeting of needs of others (+, 17).

4.7A. Organizations generally are guided by a policy of satisfying only a limited number of constituencies (+, 17).

Constituencies are different for different types of organizations. In the case of business organizations, there are owners, employees, suppliers, creditors, and clients. In the case of human-service organizations, they may include administrators, employees, clients, contributors, board members, primary groups in the community, or political leaders. The study on which this proposition is based points out that small business organizations often have to meet needs of multiple and diverse constituencies. However, the inability to satisfy simultaneously all constituency needs compels organizations to deliver benefits only to certain ones and to neglect others (at least temporarily).

Action Guidelines: Practitioners need to acquire information about the composition of organizational constituencies and the priority order underlying delivery of resources. A community practitioner must generally convince organizations to give the satisfaction of community or client needs a higher priority than those of other competing constituencies.

One of the ways to attain this is to assist these significant constituencies to articulate and communicate wishes and needs.

In considering the contextual framework within which organizations operate, goals loom at least as large as environment. We turn our attention next to goal correlates of organizational behavior.

ORGANIZATIONAL GOALS

In his conceptualization of organizations, Parsons writes:

> As a formal analytical point of reference, primary orientation to the attainment of a specific goal is used as the defining characteristic of an organization which distinguishes it from other types of social systems. This criterion has implications for both the external relations and the internal structure of the system referred to here as an organization.[6]

At least four main assumptions are inherent in this definition. First, organizations have a limited, specified goal; second, the existence of definite goals is the distinguishing characteristic differentiating organizations from other social groups; third, organizations devote considerable energy to the attainment of these goals; fourth, the goal may be viewed as a key independent variable, which affects internal structure as well as external relationships. According to Parsons, in general, an organization's goal component may be viewed as the cornerstone upon which other organizational components are built.

Parsons' approach has been criticized from different points of view. His assumptions about the dominance of a single limited goal in the organizational arena have been rejected on several accounts. Organizations (it is claimed) often have multiple goals rather than a unitary one. Organizational goals are not static. They undergo frequent change, because of the necessary interaction between an organization

---

[6] Talcott Parsons, "Suggestions for a Sociological Approach to a Theory of Organizations, *Administrative Science Quarterly*, 10, no. 1 (1965): 64. For other general discussions, see Charles Perrow, "Hospital Technology Structure and Goals," in *Handbook of Organizations*, James March, ed. (Chicago: Rand McNally and Co., 1965); Charles Perrow, "Organizational Goals," *International Encyclopedia of the Social Sciences* (New York: Macmillan, 1968) 2:305–310.

and its environment. Change of goal is not only an independent variable that affects other organizational features, but is also a dependent variable that is shaped by other factors. In emphasizing the importance of the goal in organization contexts, Parsons discards other equally relevant phenomena for understanding the organization's structure and pattern of interaction. One of those mentioned in the literature is the effort of an organization to survive, even after manifest goals are attained. These counterassumptions lead to the identification of four sets of questions about goals that are important for the practitioner:

1. *The conception of organizational goals.* What are organizational goals; their nature, number, and scale of priority? While there is agreement in the literature on the definition of goal—an end state of the organization as a whole toward which it is moving—there are various conceptualizations of goal. These range from Parsons' view of a limited, specific goal to Gross's (18) global, variegated approach, in which he identifies over 60 different goals in one organizational setting.

2. *The significance of goals in the organizational context.* As mentioned above, Parsons gives goals a dominant position in analyzing an organization. The question, then, becomes what is *its* (according to Parsons) or *their* (according to Gross) effect on the organization? In what phase of organizational development is goal impact particularly felt? Furthermore, what is the significance of the number of goals for the organization's structure and performance pattern?

3. *The creation of organizational goals.* How are organizational goals created? What are the conditions that may generate the kinds and numbers of goals adopted by the organization? What constituencies and forces are important in selecting goals?

4. *Changes in organizational goals.* What are the factors that explain the phenomenon of change in organizational goals, or situations where organizations emphasize their latent maintenance functions rather than their manifest output functions? This question is particularly important in the human-services field, where it has been argued that agencies often do not systematically pursue their manifest goals of providing services to sectors of the population most in need.

Several empirical studies that we have retrieved suggest limited and tentative answers to theoretical-pragmatic questions such as these.

Multiple Goals

GENERALIZATION 4.8: Organizations typically pursue a set of multiple goals when examined behaviorally (+ +, 18, 44).

Most of the empirical studies on the subject of organizational goals reject Parsons' assumption about the dominance of a single goal. While there is general agreement among scholars about the existence of multiple goals, they differ in the way goals should be classified. In an article in the Encyclopedia of the Social Sciences, Perrow distinguishes between six types of goals:

1. SOCIETAL GOALS: those which relate to organizational efforts to mobilize legitimation for its existence from the larger society. (Example: a clinic for drug-addicted youth that wishes to obtain legitimation from the larger society—a legitimation that may insure financial support by emphasizing its possible contribution to the solution of the general drug problem.)

2. OUTPUT GOALS: those which relate to the public constituency or clientele of the organization, that is, to the groups that directly receive organizational outputs. (Example: help provided by the aforementioned clinic to drug-addicted youth.)

3. INVESTOR GOALS: those which relate to the returns received for investing in the organization. These contributions need not necessarily be financial. (Example: the investors may receive favorable newspaper mention for assisting the clinic in its work.)

4. SYSTEM GOALS: those which relate to the organization's efforts to maintain its own equilibrium and stability. (Example: in the case of the clinic, activities designed to insure a solid source base for the organization—money, professional personnel, etc.)

5. PRODUCT GOALS: those which relate to the specific product of the organization. (Example: in the case of a welfare department, the checks that are to be paid to the clients. In human-service organizations, output goals and product goals may not be readily distinguishable.)

6. DERIVED GOALS: those which relate to different functions performed by the organization, which have no direct relation to the organization's main goals. (Example: in the case of the clinic, its in-

volvement in radical political activities, which many of the clients support.)

In another context, Perrow offers a distinction between: a) "official goals," which refer to the general purpose of the organization as put forth in its charter, for example, and b) "operative goals," which refer to the ends sought through the actual operating policies of the organization regardless of what official policies state. This distinction is reminiscent of Merton's earlier discussion of manifest and latent functions.

Gross (18), in his comprehensive study of the goals of universities, offers a somewhat similar typology based on Parsons' scheme. He distinguishes among four types of goals: 1) *goal attainment goals,* which relate to the output of the organization; 2) *adoption goals,* which relate to the organization's relationship with its environment; 3) *integration goals,* which relate to the intraorganizational pattern of relationships; 4) *pattern maintenance goals,* which relate to goals that serve the survival needs of the organization. Pugh et al. (44) approach the question of goals by relating to the degree of operating diversity exhibited by the organization and distinguish between those having narrow and those having broad ranges of activities.

Action Guidelines: In attempting to affect formal organizations (from the inside or from outside), the practitioner should not operate as though organizations have a single, limited goal that guides all their activities. The practitioner should attempt to identify the various goals and goal configurations of the organization, the manifest as well as latent ones. The organization may be differentially vulnerable to attack or influence, or open to coalitions, based on subgoals.

Goal Priority

GENERALIZATION 4.9: Organizations differ from one another in priority given to different kinds of goals. Some organizations emphasize maintenance goals while others emphasize output goals (+ +, 18, 43).

4.9A. The priority order of goals in the same organization is not static, but rather may be subject to considerable flux (+ +, 18, 43). 4.9B. The goal order of priority is determined by the organizations's needs at a given point. Maintenance and adoption goals will be emphasized when the resource base of the organization becomes threatened. "Goal attainment goals" will be emphasized when the organization is under pressure to demonstrate its capacity to explicate its "products" (+ +, 18, 43).

A useful illustration of a shift in an organization's goal emphasis is provided by Perrow (43) in a study of voluntary general hospitals. He shows how changes in organizational needs modify the composition of internal goals. When the hospitals needed financial resources, the trustees constituted the dominant group, shaping major goals. The situation shifted, however, after the organization's financial situation was secured and the need for professional prestige emerged. Domination in the organization was then transferred to the medical staff. With the development and expansion of hospitals, however, the need for coordinating complex functions, including interdependent and specialized health services, paved the way for domination by the administrative staff. Focal organizational goals may be viewed, accordingly, as phases that dominate or fade according to organizational needs.

Goals were described above mainly as dependent variables, shaped by such factors as the organization's interaction with its environment and its needs for resources. In several studies, however, attention is focused on the effects of goals on other organizational variables.

4.9C. The organization's dominant goals generally are those which serve its needs for resources from the environment (+ +, 18, 39, 43, 57).

Several scholars view the need for resources from the environment as crucial for understanding an organization's priority emphasis. Yuchtman and Seashore (57) claim that the fundamental factor guiding organizations is the need to insure survival by acquiring a continuous supply of resources.

Gross (18) does not accept the separation between the organization's goals and its survival efforts. Further, he views the latter as an organizational goal and offers the distinction between output goals and support goals. While output goals relate to the organization's production, support goals are those which guide organizational activities designed to safeguard organizational survival. In this respect, the Messinger study of the Townsend organization (39), Seashore and Yuchtman's study of insurance companies (57), Gross's study of universities (18), and Perrow's study of hospitals (43) have at least one common thread. The weight of "survival needs" of organizations is one of the most important variables that explain their behavior. Gross hypothesizes that the attainment of an organization's support goals is a necessary precondition for the attainment of its output goals.

Action Guidelines: As organizational goals are often in flux, the practitioner should continually evaluate the dominant goals in the organization. A practitioner who wishes to change an organization's goals may move in several ways. First, he might create pressures in the environment that compel the organization to add new goals or to discard existing ones. A client "revolt," for example, may prod organizations to emphasize the goal of serving clients rather than other goals pertaining to maintenance. Second, the practitioner might attempt to challenge the organization and convince it to change its goals by manipulating its resource supply. For example, human-service organizations that need legitimation from the public may be obliged to shift their goal emphasis if this resource is imperiled.

Goals and Agency Constituencies

GENERALIZATION 4.10: The organization's dominant goals reflect the influences of the most powerful individuals or groups in the organization and their vested interests (+ +, 18, 21, 22, 38).

Several studies support this generalization. In a university setting described by Gross, goals such as academic freedom, developing student intellect and creativity, preserving the cultural heritage, and pure research are emphasized in organizations where the faculty has more power than other groups. However, in state-government-controlled universities, more emphasis is placed on such goals as service to the community and vocational training. An interesting point in Gross's study is that despite increased involvement of faculty members in political acitvities, most of them still identify with the more conventional functions of the university.

An illustration of transformation of goals following a change in the social composition of an organization's leadership may be found in Gusfield's study of the Women's Christian Temperance Union (21, 22). In this case, a change in the leadership of the movement led to a shift from an emphasis on humanitarian reform of the underprivileged to a stance of "moral indignation" regarding the middle-class drinker.

Another phase of internal interest-group impact on an organization's goals is revealed by Meniha and Perrow (38) in their case study of a youth commission in a Midwestern city. The commission was established in order to evaluate and recommend programs concerning city youth problems but functioned in practice as a clearinghouse, devoid of substance. The study indicated that the commission's lack of activity stemmed from overlapping membership, that is, the majority of its members belonged to youth organizations that were not interested in the development of a new competitive organization in the youth field. Only after the composition of the commission was changed did it begin to initiate concrete programs according to its original mandate.

Action Guidelines: Practitioners who wish to change organizational goals may approach this task by shifting the division of power in the organization, either by increasing the power of those groups which hold goals compatible with theirs, or introducing into the organization new groups, which have goals compatible with theirs. One of the purposes underlying the introduction of indigenous paraprofessionals into human-service organizations is that of changing goals through the infiltration of new social groups having different

goals. The practitioner may be aided in identifying the dominant goals at a given time by assessing the interests of the
powerful groups dominating an organization at that particular time.

Goal Succession

GENERALIZATION 4.11: When organizations are unable to
achieve their goals, or when the original cause for their existence disappears, they will tend to continue to survive by either adopting new goals and missions, or shifting to maintenance goals (+ +, 21, 39, 58).

Messinger's study of the Townsend Organization (39) and the Zald
and Denton examination of the YMCA (58) illustrate how organizations shift goals in order to adjust to a new social environment, thereby
safeguarding their survival.

The main objective of the Townsend Organization, founded in
1933, was to end the Depression and insure the well-being of the elderly, primarily by retiring all citizens at age sixty on a monthly pension of two hundred dollars. By 1936 the organization had attracted a
membership of over two million and was an important political force.
In 1936 the Social Security Act was adopted, signaling public retire-
ment procedures and encouraging pension plans by private employers. The significance of the Townsend Organization had passed,
with membership declining to just over 50,000 in the early 1950s.

The YMCA case, as described by Zald and Denton, reflects a more
successful episode of goal transformation. The original goals of the Y
included the improvement of the lower classes' social conditions by
means of religious indoctrination and educational activities. Over
time, these goals broadened to more general all-purpose service activities aimed at a middle-class as well as a lower-class clientele. The authors claim that the Y has adapted in a successful way because of its
flexibility in adjusting goals to changing requirements.

Action Guidelines: Organizations are reluctant to disappear.
When their original goals have been attained or lose their

significance, they look for other goals and missions. This is particularly typical of voluntary organizations. Voluntary organizations that have achieved their goals but are not predisposed to disband may possibly be used as a framework for different ideas and programs that are seeking organizational auspices. Those organizations offer manpower facilities and sometimes funds that may be utilized by social planners with sound ideas and programs.

Goals and Structure

GENERALIZATION 4.12: The nature of an organization's goals may have a direct impact on its structure and leadership patterns (+ + +, 23, 43, 49, 58, 59).

Zald (59), in his study of correctional institutions, used the goal concept as the main independent variable. He distinguished among different correctional institutions according to their goal emphasis and showed how goal variations were reflected in a wide range of organizational attributes: structural characteristics, relationships between staff and clients, organization of clients, etc.

4.12A. Multiple leadership is most likely to appear in organizations having a wide range of goals (+ + , 43).

Concentration of organizational authority in the hands of a single leadership unit may be dysfunctional in a situation where the organization has multiple goals and operates in multiple areas. In the case of the general hospital illustrated by Perrow (43), the organization's need for financial aid could be met best by trustees who had access to economic resources. At the same time, the goal of enhancing the reputation of the hospital as a medical institution could be attained best by the medical staff. Multiplicity of goals and activities seem to require leadership inputs from different groups in the organization.

4.12B. A wide range of goals facilitates adaptation and change in organizations (+ + , 23, 49, 58).

4.12C. An organization that has a wide range of goals and must satisfy an external constituency will tend to decentralize, exhibit a strong concern for membership involvement, and emphasize internal communication (+ , 49).

The impact of the number of goals on the organization's ability to adapt to its environment is well illustrated in Zald and Denton's (58) YMCA study.

While the causal order between the existence of several goals and a decentralized hierarchical structure is not clear, the association between these two characteristics is well founded. The organization's decentralization permitted it to keep viable contact with the clientele and to maintain permanent flow of information about client needs. The diversity of goals facilitated making goal transformations, eliminating some activities or adding new ones, based on this information.

Hage and Aiken (23) also lend support to this proposition. In their study of welfare service organizations, they show that agencies having multiple goals were able to exhibit more innovativeness as reflected in their adoption of new technologies. Another dimension is added by Simpson and Gully (49) in their study of voluntary organizations. The authors measured the combined effect of the number of goals and the kind of constituency served by the organization. They found that in voluntary associations with multiple goals and external constituencies, the degree of decentralization, membership involvement, and internal communication was higher than in organizations having delimited goals and internal constituency. They attribute the differences particularly to the pressures imposed on the organization by its external constituencies. These pressures induce the organization to broaden its goals, to decentralize its authority structure, and to make efforts to involve the members in organizational activities. Organizations lacking these external pressures are shielded from this stimulus for change.

Action Guidelines: If a practitioner wishes to decrease the degree of centralization in an organization or develop new or wider leadership, he should work toward broadening the range of goals (and vice versa). If the practitioner wishes to strengthen the innovative tendencies of an organization or encourage greater flexibility, he might attempt to widen its range of goals.

Legitimation Goals

GENERALIZATION 4.13: Organizations that expend much effort on legitimation goals per se (gaining public approval for organizational existence) exhibit a lack of concrete planning or action output (+ +, 54).

Gross (18) sees support goals as a precondition for the attainment of output goals. However, Tropman's study (54) of 154 community welfare councils shows that too much concern for legitimation—a basic support goal—may result in lack of attainment of output goals. These two different emphases probably signal the need for some kind of balance between an emphasis on the organization's survival and on the achievement of its programmatic goals.

Action Guidelines: Too much concern with the survival of the organization may damage its ability to act; therefore, an organization should maintain a proper balance between support and output goals. There is a need for organizations to define their output objectives clearly. Without this, organizations may become dominated by their maintenance needs.

Lawrence and Lorsch's emphasis on the need for a certain degree of differentiation among different units in an organization, rather than on total integration, implies that internal conflicts among units regarding goals or procedures is normal and predictable. This issue of intraorganizational conflict was examined in Smith's study (50) of 250 separate units in six businesses and voluntary organizations.

The difference between voluntary and business organizations suggests a characteristic of voluntary organizations and trade unions. In this latter kind of organization, there is room for a wider range of goal orientations and philosophies among members. An attempt to impose uniformity may crystallize conflicts. In business organizations, the picture is different. Tolerance toward diversity of different units may induce conflicts. Conflicts are not necessarily dysfunctional, as was illustrated in both Smith's (50) and Lawrence and Lorsch's (32) studies. However, they require countervailence through various integrative devices such as staff meetings, mediators, and written communication.

Goals and Intraorganizational Conflict

GENERALIZATION 4.14: Internal goal conflicts may have different consequences in different types of organizations. In voluntary associations, such as unions, member goal consensus may serve in the long run to increase conflict. In business organizations and similar rationalistic structures, goal consensus is a continuing need to preserve organizational cohesion (+ , 50).

The point here is that the potential for conflict tends to be greater and possibly more destructive in centralized bureaucratic organizations. Intraorganizational conflict can be tolerated to a greater degree and may have more positive functions in voluntary organizations. By conflict, the author of the study under consideration means differences in interests or different perceptions or attitudes among members of various echelons of an organization. Smith (50) conducted a study of approximately 250 separate subunits in six different organizational types: an international trade union, the League of Women Voters, a delivery company, an automotive sales company, an insurance company, and a brokerage firm. While there were some variations among the business firms, major distinctions were found between business organizations and voluntary associations. Factors creating interlevel conflict in the business organizations (especially the delivery and insurance companies) did not induce similar results in the voluntary associations. Particularly in the trade union, a high level of consensus created a tendency toward conflict. Consensus, on the other hand, was a precondition for preventing conflict in the rationalistic business organizations.

Action Guidelines: Voluntary associations that wish to prevent sharp and destructive conflicts among their members should not demand from them total agreement or identification. A certain degree of structural flexibility and diversity may be desirable. The practitioner might stimulate conflict in such organizations by assessing that latent tensions should be released or that goals require redefinition or clarification. Conflicts among units in rationalistic business or service organizations often arise by encouraging autonomous tendencies among these units, while conflict in voluntary organizations is often stimulated by attempting to impose uniformity. Sharp conflicts in business or routine organizations may be "cooled off" by using integrative devices such as coordinators who provide linkage between different units.

The third contextual variable we shall consider is that of organizational size. Size is in part an index of structure, in part a reflection of resources, in part a boundary-defining characteristic. As we shall see, the variable of size has important implications for intervention.

ORGANIZATIONAL SIZE

Introduction

Organizational size has been investigated by a number of researchers in terms of its impact on the structure and function of organizations. Theoretical writings on the subject suggest that the following features of organizations may be influenced by size: [7]

1. Organizational efficiency may be contingent on size. The assumption is that certain types of performances (particularly those which demand more resources and staff) are impossible to implement below a basic organizational mass. Obviously, a small organization will be unable to perform tasks that require diverse categories of workers.

2. Larger size permits a range of structural possibilities. Assembly-line operation, for example, is improbable in small organizations.

[7] For general discussion on the impact of size on other organizational aspects, see William H. Starbuck, "Organizational Growth and Development," in *Handbook of Organizations,* James March, ed. (Chicago: Rand McNally and Co., 1965), pp. 451–539; T. Caplow, "Organizational Size," *Administrative Science Quarterly* 4 (1959): 484–505.

3. The size of the organization may influence its stability and its survival over time. The larger the organization, it is argued by some, the greater its potential for longevity.

4. The size of the organization relates to its ability to manage its environment. A larger organization, more widely dispersed or diversified in activities, is less at the mercy of particular events or "accidents" occurring in its environment. Furthermore, the larger the organization, the greater its ability to mobilize needed resources.

5. The size of the organization influences the pattern of distribution of resources. For example, total size may be related to the proportion of resources allocated to program operations.

6. Size is an important factor in shaping internal climate and structure. The trend in the literature is to view larger organizations as more bureaucratic than smaller ones. Smaller bodies, it is argued, tend to be characterized by a "human relations" climate and mode of behavior.

Hypothetically, three main areas may be affected by organizational size: 1) the organization's performance or output; 2) the organization's internal structure; 3) the organization's relationship with its environment. Most of the empirical studies we have retrieved on this subject focus on the second area; only limited data were available on the other two. This again reflects a tendency by researchers to concentrate more on internal characteristics of organizations than on external ones.

Size and General Aspects of Internal Structure

Past studies have generally shown that the larger the size of the organization the greater its bureaucratic tendencies. A range of such studies was reviewed by Hall, Haas, and Johnson (26), who criticized the findings as inconclusive for three main reasons: studies included one or only a few organizations; the organizations that were researched were of limited types; the operational definitions of the major variables—such as size, complexity, and formalization—were poor and inconsistent. In order to overcome those deficiencies the three researchers conducted a highly comprehensive study, which included a sample of 75 organizations ranging in membership from six to 9,000 and representing a wide range of types. They examined the relationship between the size of the organization and the degrees of complexity and formalization. In our pool of literature from the 1964–70 period we found only four studies that dealt specifically with size and general aspects of organizational structure. Another series of studies, which we shall discuss next, dealt with the relationship of size and attributes of the administrative component. Of the former studies, the Hall, Haas, and Johnson investigation is the most comprehensive and substantial. We shall rely heavily upon it in this discussion.

Size as Related to Dispersion, Hierarchy, and Division of Labor

GENERALIZATION 4.15: The greater the organization's size, the greater the degree of a) spatial dispersion, b) hierarchical differentiation, and c) intradepartmental division of labor (+ + +, 26).

Organizational size is measured by the total number of paid employees in the organization. Spatial dispersion refers to the differential geographical location of the organization's departments. Hierarchical differentiation is the number of hierarchical levels in the organization. Intradepartmental division of labor is the division of labor within the departments.

Action Guidelines: To achieve decentralized services (spatial dispersion) it may be necessary to increase general organizational size. Put another way, as an organization moves to decentralize its services, staff should be prepared to eventually deal with problems of increased size. In order to increase the number of hierarchical levels in the organization (to provide for a career ladder, for example), it may be necessary to increase general organizational size. Conversely, when an organization grows in size, it may be necessary to anticipate or plan for additional administrative levels.

Size and Formalization

GENERALIZATION 4.16: With an increase in organizational size, formal surveillance and formal rules will increase relative to informal, personal surveillance (+ +, 44, 46).

This generalization is based in part on Rushing's discussion (46) of aspects of rules and surveillance in organizational settings. In his exploration of the interconnections between structural-contextual features and the mechanisms of control utilized by organizations, Rushing arrives at a set of propositions, some of which are based essentially on previous experimental studies. The generalization offered here is derived from a historical survey of the growth of hospitals. It was found that when hospitals were small, direct, and personal, informal supervision was typically employed; with growth in size, formalization of supervision evolved, with a shift to the mechanisms of rules and regulations. The association between size and organizational formalization is also supported in the Pugh et al (44) study of more than fifty organizations.

Action Guidelines: With increased organizational size, administrators and practitioners should generally plan for or anticipate more use of rules, penalties, and training procedures. This implies increased use of written communication and more strict role definitions. Increased use of rules can be anticipated to a greater degree than increased use of surveillance as an organization grows. A practitioner might plan for and anticipate these changing structural characteristics, attempt to minimize deleterious effects of intensified formalization (by, for example, attempting to maximize informal social relations, and acquire staff with additional and diversified bureaucratic skills).

Organizational Size and Bureaucratic Features

GENERALIZATION 4.17: Increased organizational size is not correlated with an intensification of all bureaucratic features (+ + +, 26, 44, 50).

4.17A. There is no consistent or necessary association between increased size and centralization of authority (+ +, 26, 44).

4.17B. There is no association between increased size and the number of departments in an organization (+ +, 26).

4.17C. There is no association between increased size and lack of communication or coordination among different levels in an organization (+ +, 50).

Hall et al. (26), in their study of relationships between organizational size and other structural characteristics, depart from the usual tendency of organizational researchers to offer general statements based on an examination of one or only a limited number of organizations. They selected a sample representing a wide range of organization types (educational, military, industrial, etc.). Furthermore, they made an effort to provide precise definitions of the variables and to use carefully developed instruments for measurement.

Their most general finding is that relationships between size and other structural components are inconclusive or variable. Although there is a slight tendency for larger organizations to be more complex and more highly differentiated, this relationship is strong for only a few variables (mentioned in the generalization above). Thus, a certain amount of caution is called for in viewing the potency of size in predicting various organizational characteristics. On the other hand, with regard to the variables indicated above, there appears to be a clear relationship.

Pugh et al. (44) also cast doubt on some notions commonly held by students of organizations. The investigators found that increased size was related to structuring of activities (a formalization dimension), but was not related to concentration of authority (a centralization-of-hierarchy dimension). It is necessary to note that Montagna (41) found contradictory results in a study of twelve accounting firms in New York City. The larger firms were more centralized than the smaller ones. Assuming the methodology in both studies is valid, we are left with the conclusion that centralization may or may not be associated with increased size—that is to say, it is variably related to size.

Hall et al. (26) indicate that size does not necessarily influence the number of departments or divisions in an organization, although it is related to division of work within such units. Smith (50) shows that increased complexity in organizations is not correlated with communication and coordination problems in organizations. He points out that complexity may increase potential conflict in organizations when it is associated with centralized authority. Greater size, however, does not by itself generate interlevel conflict.

Contrary to popular belief, then, increased size does not necessarily lead to intensification of all bureaucratic attributes. Or, expressed another way, it does not lead to the acquisition of all the worst features of organizations. Large organizations can be run either democratically or undemocratically, humanely or inhumanely, depending on the style and values of the administrator(s). The uniformity or nonuniformity of task environment and technology seems to be a more critical consideration in influencing these structural features. A large organization has the potential for establishing a highly complicated, variegated division of labor. However, its operations and products may be highly uniform, negating the need for this approach. On the other hand, a small organization may be involved in highly complex but differentiated tasks requiring an intricate division of labor.

Action Guidelines: The practitioner should refrain from drawing the conclusion that larger organizations are necessarily more bureaucratic and therefore may not be flexible and democratic. Size does not lead to the presence of all bureaucratic features in organizations. Large organizations may be run as democratically as small ones and indeed are. Role definitions may be quite loose and broad in large organizations, depending on tasks and functions. Division of labor is likewise more dependent on the nature of the task and the product than on the size of the organization. It is advisable that an administrator or planner build such structural features on the basis of a task analysis concerning the uniformity-nonuniformity dimension, and not allow assessment of these key organizational requirements to be unnecessarily clouded by the sometimes extraneous factor of organizational size.

Size and the Administrative Component

The Terrien and Mills study (52) has prompted researchers to focus considerable attention on the relationship between the total size of an organization and the size of its administrative component. There has been more discussion recently of this particularized question than of the general area of size and structure.

Organizational Structure and Size of the
Administrative Component

GENERALIZATION 4.18: The larger the size of the organization, the greater will be the proportional size of the administrative component (+ +, 52).

Terrien and Mills studied a sample of school districts in California. "Size" related to the number of students attending schools in each district, and they distinguished between small, medium, and large districts. The size of the administrative component was measured by the number of administrative personnel in each district. Anderson and Workow (3) were among the first researchers to be stimulated by the Terrien and Mills findings that the administrative component varies directly with organizational growth. In their study of 49 Veteran's Administration hospitals, they introduced additional variables, "organizational complexity" and "organizational dispersion," and arrived at an interesting qualification of the general proposition.

4.18A. The relative size of the administrative component decreases as the number of persons performing identical tasks increases (+ +, 3, 45).

The administrative component included all employees classified under hospital administration. The proposition is also supported by Montagna's (41) study of accounting firms in New York. The finding was refined by Raphael's study (45) of the size of the administrative cadre in unions.

4.18B. The relative size of the administrative component increases as the number of different tasks performed at the same place increases (+ +, 3).

It is possible to reformulate these statements as follows: the relative size of the administrative component increases as the diversity or complexity of organizational tasks increases. The number of workers in the organization has an effect on the size of the administrative component; however, its effect is mediated by the degree of differentiation and complexity. In organizations where the workers perform a limited number of tasks, the size of the administrative component will be smaller than in organizations where similar numbers of workers perform a larger number of tasks.

Action Guidelines: Practitioners and administrators should expect and plan for proportionally expanded administrative staff components when the organization increases in size, diversifies its tasks (programs and services), or diversifies its staff composition (occupational groupings). The proportion of administrative staff may be safely reduced by reversing these tendencies.

Size of Administrative Component and Spatial Context

GENERALIZATION 4.19: Spatial concentration of the organization may have differential effects on the size of the administrative component, depending on whether the organization is a voluntary membership association or a formal service organization (+ +, 3, 45).

This proposition is derived from the contrasting findings of the Workow and Anderson study (3) of Veteran's Administration hospitals and Raphael's study (45) of trade unions. The latter concluded that spatial concentration of members increases the administrative component; the former found the opposite. The differences between the two studies may be attributed to the different kinds of organizations examined in the studies.

4.19A. In voluntary organizations, spatial concentration of members increases the administrative component (+ +, 45).

In using the term "voluntary organization," Raphael relies on Blau and Scott's typology of organizations, which distinguishes between organizations according to the criterion of *cui bono* (who benefits); voluntary organizations belong to the member-oriented category.

4.19B. In formal service organizations, spatial concentration of members decreases the administrative component. That is to say, the relative size of the administrative component decreases as the number of places at which work is performed decreases (+, 3).

Raphael hypothesizes that in voluntary organizations, the flow of control is from the bottom up—namely, from the members themselves—while in business or service organizations the power is vested in the hands of the higher officials and the control flows down from the top. Thus, in voluntary organizations a larger concentration of members in the same place imposes increased pressures on the administration. Decision making shifts from concentration at the top, in the hands of a limited oligarchy, to a larger number of subadministrators. In a sense, a larger administrative component is associated with democracy in unions.

Action Guidelines: In voluntary membership associations proportionally greater administrative staff components should be planned for when the membership grows in numbers or becomes more concentrated. This spatial concentration (hence *interpersonal* interaction *of members*) has the effect of increasing participation in the organization and the demand for its services, thus placing a strain on the administrative component. Such concentration may also be a strategy for affecting the level of participation and services. The converse should be planned for in formal service organizations. The administrative staff may be reduced when personnel become more concentrated.

Size and Role Conception

GENERALIZATION 4.20: The size of an organizational setting has an impact on the workers' conceptions of their role. In smaller units there may be greater role consensus, greater breadth of role conception, and higher ethical commitment than in medium or large organizations (+ +, 53).

In Thomas's study (53) of public welfare departments the following operational criteria were used: *small size:* two to five workers, no more than two-level hierarchy; *medium size:* five or more workers, no more than three-level hierarchy; *large size:* organizations with a hierarchy of five or more levels; *role consensus:* the degree of agreement between the public-assistance worker and his supervisor about the importance of functions performed by workers; *breadth of role conception:* the number of activities or functions conceived as part of the worker's role; *ethical commitment:* commitment to the ethics of professional social work.

In attempting to explain the findings, Thomas asserts that the size of the organization is often interrelated with community setting of the organizational unit. He indicates that the influence of small community size may account for the service orientations of workers toward clients in small state welfare offices. That is, the role conceptions of the workers in small organizations reflect an interaction of organization and community size.

4.20A. Smaller-sized settings are associated with indicators of quality of job performance in rendering individualized professional services (+ +, 51).

This is derived from the same Thomas study. Job performance was measured by ability of workers to identify family problems and solutions.

Action Guidelines: Small organizations that operate in smaller communities may be more oriented toward the needs of the clientele than those in larger communities located at a considerable distance from their clientele. It may be that planners and administrators who wish to increase the service orientation and job performance of workers should encourage the creation of smaller agencies located close to the clientele, over larger ones, located at a distance. Workers performing individualized or intensified professional service functions (nonuniform events) may gain greater role consensus, scope, and service commitments when placed in smaller operating units. Their quality of job performance may accordingly be enhanced. Role consensus may be an intervening variable in terms of optimizing delivery of professional services. (See Generalization 3.3A.)

This concludes the first part of the review of organizational research. We shall now turn our attention inward and examine additional areas of critical importance to the practitioner—organizational technology, professionalization, and the use of paraprofessionals in human-service organizations.

Chapter Five

Organizational Behavior: Technology and Personnel

TECHNOLOGY IN ORGANIZATIONS

ONLY RECENTLY has the issue of technology employed by organizations received serious coverage in the sociological literature. Although most of this attention is focused on industrial organizations, several works in our data pool relate to technologies in the human-service field, namely technologies that are used in order to change or "process" human beings. Most of the writings in this area are theoretical and aim toward building a conceptual framework that may be used as a basis for empirical studies.[1] The newness of the theoretical initiative in this area may possibly explain the current situation, characterized by a scarcity of relevant empirical studies. The following discussion is therefore based on a restricted number of studies, a limitation the reader should take note of.

The increasing interest in technology as an independent variable stems from the recognition that the "work process" or "techniques" of an organization may profoundly affect other aspects of structure. Perrow, one of the first sociologists to direct his attention toward technologies in human-service organizations, defined technology (and this definition was adopted in several recent empirical studies on this subject) as a series of complex sets of techniques used to alter objects in an appropriate manner. Five basic criteria are emphasized in this definition of technology:

[1] Some of the significant works on technology in organizations are T. Burns, and G. M. Stalker, *The Management of Innovation* (London: Tavistick, 1961); Joan Woodward, *Industrial Organization Theory and Practice* (London: Oxford University Press, 1965); and Charles Perrow, "A Framework for the Comparative Analysis of Organizations," *Administrative Science Quarterly* 32, no. 2:194–208.

1. knowledge of random cause-effect relationship
2. feedback such that the consequences of acts can be assessed objectively
3. possibility of repeated demonstrations of efficacy
4. proportion of successes that can be estimated
5. techniques communicated easily and performed under acceptable limits of tolerance

Perrow makes a distinction between routine and nonroutine technology, a distinction that was adopted by Hage and Aiken (23). This classification of technologies is based on two main dimensions: first, the relative stability vs. variability of the objects upon which the technology is applied; second, the extent to which there is knowledge about the raw materials (or objects) among those who apply the technology. A *routine* technology is one used on stable and known raw materials. A *nonroutine* technology is one used on unpredictable or unknown raw materials, namely, objects that cannot be analyzed in a prescribed way or which pose nonpredictable problems for the technologist. Perrow's definitions and distinctions (especially his category of nonroutine technology) seem to be appropriate for human-service organizations where the "raw material" consists of human beings.

Another conceptual distinction was offered by Harvey (29) for treating technologies used in industrial organizations. Following the pioneering work of Joan Woodward in this area, Harvey differentiated between *technical diffuseness,* which characterizes firms having a high rate of product variation and change, and *technical specificity,* which characterizes firms having lower rates of innovation and technical change.

Despite differences in context, Harvey's conceptual distinction is quite similar to Perrow's definition. Technical diffuseness is parallel to nonroutine technology, while technical specificity is parallel to routine technology.

A third attempt to devise a conceptual framework in this area was made by Pugh and his colleagues (44). While Perrow relates particularly to human-service organizations, and Harvey to industrial ones, Pugh et al. study the entire spectrum of organizational behavior, from hospitals and universities to industrial and commercial organizations.

They propose a scale of *workflow integration* based upon five components that describe different phases of organizational technology:

1. WORKFLOW RIGIDITY: adaptability in the patterns of operations; for example, whether rerouting of work was possible.
2. AUTOMATICITY MODE: the level of automation of the equipment.
3. AUTOMATICITY RANGE: the highest-scoring piece of automated equipment an organization uses.
4. INTERDEPENDENCE OF WORKFLOW SEGMENTS: the degree of linkage between the segments of an organizational process.
5. SPECIFICITY OF CRITERIA OF QUALITY EVALUATION: the precision with which the output measured up to an acceptable standard.

An organization with a higher workflow integration is the one high on workflow rigidity, automaticity range and mode, interdependence of segments, and specificity of evaluation criteria.

Despite the semantic differences, the various conceptual frameworks presented above are similar in many respects. A nonroutine technology has much in common with both technical diffuseness and low workflow integration. It is clear, however, that the concept of "workflow integration" offered by Pugh, et al. encompasses some dimensions not included in Perrow and Harvey. This discussion indicates that it is possible to deal with these studies in comparative perspective.

The reader will have already discerned a striking similarity between routine and nonroutine technology and the earlier discussion of certainty-uncertainty, with its distinction between uniform and nonuniform events. Indeed, the two discussions may simply represent an examination of the identical phenomenon from different vantage points. In the previous analysis, it was pointed out that there is a strong correlation between uniform events and routine, standardized, formalized procedures. Nonuniform events involving a high degree of uncertainty were seen as associated with nonroutine, more open, less formalized organizational procedures. Hence, because the dimensions used in either case possess so much commonality, in a certain sense it is a matter of choice as to whether an organizational analyst wishes to discuss bureaucratic behavior in terms of the character of environmental events or the nature of technological processes.

Nevertheless, within the literature are found research studies and theoretical discussions emanating from one or other of these positions. We shall report to the reader on the current state of the literature. Similarities as well as nuances of difference will appear through pursuing this course.

Technology and Centralization

GENERALIZATION 5.1: Organizations with "routine technology" are more likely to be characterized by centralization of power, with decision making concentrated at the organization's top level (+, 23, 29, 44).

> 5.1A. In organizations with routine work, concrete operational decisions based on the rules determined at the organization's top level tend to be decentralized in the hands of the lower level supervisors and workers (+, 44).
>
> 5.1B. As routine technology increases, the number of levels of authority in the organization increases (+, 29).

Hage and Aiken's study (23) of 16 welfare organizations demonstrates that when an organization faces unanalyzable and unexpected tasks, the authority to deal with them is transferred to those people who have more information on the subject. The authors argue that in organizations with a heterogeneous clientele, authority will be delegated to the workers in lower levels who have direct contact with the clients rather than to people in the higher levels of the organizational hierarchy. Nonroutine technology, therefore, is associated with decentralized authority.

A somewhat different finding is offered by Pugh et al. (44). They indicate the existence of negative correlations between workflow integration and concentration of authority. That is, the higher the integration (parallel to routineness and rigidity), the lower the concentration of authority. The researchers' explanation for this finding is as follows: "because of the increasing control resulting directly from the workflow itself in an integrated technology, decisions tend to become more routine and can be decentralized." It seems that centralization has different meanings in the two studies. While Hage and Aiken place heavy emphasis on the policy-making dimension and character- ize a decentralized organization as the one in which workers in the lower levels of the echelon take an active part in the process of deci- sion making, Pugh, et al. consider decentralized organizations as the ones in which the existence of an integrated body of rules and work ar- rangements (initiated by organization policy makers) permit the work- ers in the lower levels to operate automatically and within set limits of discretion.

It may be argued that the two studies complement rather than con- tradict each other. Both agree that in organizations with routine tasks, the rules are initiated by the organizational hierarchy. Pugh et al. add, however, that in these settings, operational decisions based upon the rules are made by lower level workers on the line or in the field.

Another dimension is added by Harvey (29) in a study of 14 indus- trial organizations. He shows that routine technology brings about a greater number of authority levels in the organization. This finding can be seen to support the argument of Pugh and his associates on the im- pact of technology on organizational concentration of authority. A larger number of authority levels may mean a greater separation be- tween the area of planning and policy making and the area of imple- mentation.

Action Guidelines: In planning for centralized or decentral- ized structures, practitioners should take into account diag- nostically the degree of routine or nonroutine technology required for organizational tasks. A change in the "technol- ogy" and the kind of tasks handled by the organization may lead to a change in the organizational authority structure. Nonroutine tasks and a less rigid technology suggest decen- tralization in decision making. A practitioner who wishes to reduce the centralization of the decision-making process in organizations might attempt to confront the organization with nonroutine tasks and to introduce new and diversified technologies. Organizations requiring routine technologies should plan for a more centralized structure with a greater number of hierarchical levels.

Technology and Formalization

GENERALIZATION 5.2: Organizations with routine technologies are more likely to have greater numbers of rules and structures defining organizational activities and roles: formalization, standardization, and specialization (+ + +, 23, 29, 44).

Definitional clarification may be in order:

FORMALIZATION: rules concerning activities, which indicate what should be done in each instance.

STANDARDIZATION: rules that are fixed rather than flexible and that constrict standards of behavior.

SPECIALIZATION: rules that limit an individual to the confines of his own highly delimited job, such as on an assembly line.

The relationship between technology and formalization was investigated by both Hage and Aiken (23) and Pugh, et al. (44). The former found a greater degree of formalization in organizations that use more routine technologies; the explanation is that organizations dealing with unanalyzable and unpredictable tasks are not able to program for these events through set rules. A tendency to provide established answers for each problematic situation will handicap an organization operating under conditions of such uncertainty.

The Pugh investigation, unlike that of Hage and Aiken, used its own criteria to assess mode of technology rather than relying on the workers' definition. Pugh, et al. preferred the term "workflow integration" to describe rigid, routine, automated work processes. They found a definite correlation between this type of technology and the dimensions of formalization, standardization, and specialization.

Harvey (29) discerned a relationship between routines of technology and both program specification (a formalization-standardization factor) and the number of specialized subunits in the organization (a specialization factor).

Action Guidelines: Reliance on formalized rules in agency settings should be related diagnostically to the routine-nonroutine dimension of tasks and technology. A practitioner who wishes to decrease the degree of formalization might attempt to decrease the level of work routine by introducing more complex technologies.

If the analysis holds up to now, two additional conclusions may follow. When the emphasis is on numbers of clients processed rather than on intensity of service, routine technology would likely be more suitable. Conversely, when clients need highly individualized services, then nonroutine technologies would more likely be the preferred mode. Studies that were reviewed confirm these assumptions and lead to the following generalizations.

Technology and Clients

GENERALIZATION 5.3: Form of technology in human-service organizations is associated with degree of client diversity and production orientation of the agency (+, 23).

> 5.3A. Routine technology is positively related to an emphasis on efficiency (number of clients processed) as a system goal (+ , 23).
>
> 5.3B. Routine technology is negatively but weakly related to the quality of client service, particularly in cases where clients are heterogeneous or need diversified services (+ , 23).

This proposition relies on the Hage and Aiken study (23) of welfare organizations. Those agencies with more routine technologies were found to place emphasis on efficiency (measured quantitatively by the number of clients processed in a given period of time rather than on the quality of services provided). Several explanations may be offered. In the first place, routine technologies permit mass processing of clients, hence it is likely that such criteria of effectiveness will emerge. The criteria play up the unique attributes or potentialities of the technology. Secondly, the emphasis on quantity may comprise a component of the value orientation that leads initially to this technological preference. In addition, quantitative outputs, if available and demonstrable, may insure more public support for the agency's program.

Action Guidelines: These two findings are related to each other: the greater the organization's emphasis on efficiency as a primary goal, the lower its capacity to provide the wide range of services needed by a heterogeneous clientele. The fact that routine technology is correlated negatively with the quality of services in human-service organizations implies that delivery of appropriate professional social services to clients usually requires flexibility, secured only in organizations that apply nonroutine technology, namely a technology that takes into consideration the diversity of the task situation. Thus, effectiveness in delivering individualized or treatment services is correlated with nonroutine technology. Conversely, effectiveness in delivering standardized services such as social security, negative income tax, and prescribed referrals is correlated with routine technology.

A practitioner who wishes to shift the priority of human-service organizations toward quality of individualized services delivered to clients and away from number of clients treated might attempt to change organization technologies by introducing more or varied technologies. In human-service organizations this goal may be attained by demonstrating to the organization that its tasks are diversified rather than uniform. The organization may become aware of the diversity of its tasks if its clients can be mobilized to show in numerous ways that their problems are not uniform.

The relationship between technology and structure is complex and reciprocal. However the fact that there is a correlation between the kind of technology (routine-nonroutine, standardized-nonstandardized) and the structure of the organization does not specify a causal direction. An organization is capable of selecting those technologies which fit its structure or predelictions. In any case, it is obvious that technologies are mediated through human beings—staff, personnel, professionals—who compose the human-service organizations. We shall examine these human-service workers and the literature on professionalization in the next session.

PROFESSIONALS IN ORGANIZATIONS

The cadre of professional workers comprising the manpower of human-service and community-organization agencies is the key to effective task implementation and service delivery. The professionals help shape and execute technology.

The matter of relationships between professionals and organizations has for many years received considerable coverage in the sociological literature. Empirical studies over the period 1964–70 deal with only discrete aspects of the relationship. It may be useful, therefore, for us to summarize succinctly some of the main theoretical trends reflected in the basic literature. This brief overview will be a useful framework for analyzing the empirical studies that we shall discuss later. We shall draw on several key sociological writings for this purpose.[2]

Generally speaking, professionals and bureaucratic settings have been perceived as two "conflicting cultures." Bureaucratic settings place emphasis on structured activities, formal rules, definite job descriptions, and hierarchical control. On the other hand, the professional "culture" values the autonomy of professionals in bureaucratic settings because of their expertise and mastery over a body of knowledge. This autonomy flourishes in more flexible or "human relations" types of organizational settings. These organizations permit the profes-

---

[2] T. Parsons, "The Professional and the Social Structure," in *Essays in Sociological Theory* (New York: The Free Press, 1964), pp. 34–50; William J. Goode, "Community Within a Community: The Professions," *American Sociological Review* 22 (April 1957): 194–200; R. Bucher and S. Strauss, "Professions in Process," *American Journal of Sociology* 66 (January 1961): 325–34. For pertinent literature regarding the social work profession, see, R. Vinter, "The Social Structure of Service," *Issues in American Social Work* Alfred J. Kahn, ed. (New York: Columbia Univ. Press, 1959), pp. 242–69; H. J. Meyer, "Social Work," *The International Encyclopedia of the Social Sciences* (New York: Macmillan, 1968) 14: 415–504.

sional to take part not only in defining his own role in the organization, but also in shaping the overall organizational character (goals, policy, structure, etc.). While the bureaucratic organization demands loyalty to internal goals and processes, professionals strive to maintain contact with and loyalty to their external professional community.

This approach views bureaucratic organizations and professionals as two discrete entities more or less in conflict because their basic premises and interests differ. However, social-work professional literature, for example, traditionally made no such assumption of conflict. It conceived of the practitioner as the servant of the agency, who carried out a consensual "policy" at the bequest of the community for the good of the client.

Another implicit assumption in the literature is that conflict between the bureaucracy and professionals is, in effect, a conflict between progress and stagnation, innovativeness and conservatism, change and status quo. This contrast is evident in the area of relationships between organizations and their clientele. While professionals equipped with "service orientations" wish to provide meaningful assistance to clients, they are constrained (it is argued) by restrictions imposed by administrative managers and boards.

While traces of these "unitary" perceptions still remain in the literature, new trends, which cast serious doubt on the generality of those approaches, have begun to appear. The "unitary bureaucracy"—the classic Weberian approach—is challenged by a new concept, which views the organization from a multidimensional perspective, including alternative models of organization. A more recent theory that professionalization is a "process" involving professional segmentation, rivalry, and evolution questions the "professional community" approach (which emphasizes the coherence of the professional culture).[3]

The multidimensional theories also offer the possibility that organizations may contain not only an element of stagnation, but also the seeds of innovation; professions are not only a source of flexibility, but they may also promote rigidity in organizational settings.

The "inevitability of conflict" position (organization vs. profession)

---

[3] Bucher and Strauss, "Professions in Process," pp. 325–34.

is losing its hold. Although strains toward conflict seem built in, there are also tendencies toward "peaceful coexistence" and cooperation between these two social entities. A more refined, variegated analysis is called for, one that studies the interaction between professionals and organizations in specific organizational settings. (See chapter 3 for further elaboration.)

Recently, empirical studies which we shall review shortly, have departed from the view that professions and organizations are monolithic entities living in separate spheres, and suggest approaches by which interrelationships between them may be analyzed.

Several studies shed light on conditions that permit professionals to mold the organizations in which they are employed. Assuming that under certain conditions professional goals may be more valid in terms of services to clients or to society than organizational goals, it is important to determine the impact of professionals upon organizations.

GENERALIZATION 5.4: Professional impact on organizations is stronger in settings where professional norms are well crystallized and the professional group in the organization is more cohesive (+, 24, 25).

Crystallization of professional norms occurs when the occupation demands a full-time effort, when the profession's knowledge is acquired in an institute attached to a university, and when the occupation is the basis for a professional association. Hall (24, 25) explored the relationships between the degree of professionalization of the occupations and the level of bureaucratization of the work setting. He found that the impact of professionals on an organization is much stronger when their norms are more coherent and crystallized. Such professionals are much more autonomous, and their participation in organizational decision making is more pronounced.

This finding leads to the following assumption: Given that the norms of "established professions" are more coherent and crystallized than those of the "semiprofessions," their impact on organizations will be much stronger. That is, physicians and lawyers have a greater chance of affecting their employing organizations than do social workers and nurses.

Action Guidelines: Practitioners may increase the impact of an occupational group on the organization by intensifying its normative base (a professional ethic linked with a strong professional association and crystallized body of knowledge) or including members of established professions in the staff complement.

GENERALIZATION 5.5: Increased professionalization within organizations is associated with tendencies toward specific structural forms (+ + + +, 2, 5, 6, 10, 23, 24, 25).

5.5A. Increased professionalization is associated with a decentralized authority structure, which means more authority is vested in workers at lower echelons (+ + +, 5, 6, 10, 24, 25).

5.5B. Increased professionalization is associated with less formalization, fewer rules, less standardization, and less job codification; the professionals themselves define their roles (+ + +, 5, 6, 10, 24, 15).

5.5C. Increased professionalization is associated with the use of diverse and less routine technologies (+ +, 10, 23).

5.5D. Increased professionalization is associated with increased organizational complexity in terms of a greater degree of departmentalization and a greater range of occupational diversity within the organization (+ +, 2, 10).

5.5E. Increased professionalization is associated with a broader range of linkages with external organizations (+ , 2).

5.5F. Increased professionalization is associated with adoption of new programs and novel solutions to organizational problems (+ +, 2, 10).

5.5G. Increased professionalization, which includes diversified professionals, will lead to interprofessional conflict over resources and the institution within the organization of bargaining mechanisms for conflict resolution (+ , 23).

Hall (24, 25) examined a range of professional groups, including accountants, engineers, advertising agents, lawyers, librarians, nurses, personnel managers, physicians, social workers, teachers, and stockbrokers. He found that autonomous professional organizations (those dominated by professionals) were generally less bureaucratic in nature than heterogeneous organizations (professionals not dominant).

The association between increased professionalization and decreased bureaucratization is explained in terms of characteristics of professionals: they desire autonomy; they value expertise, which is generally acquired outside of the employing organization; they often identify strongly with an external professional association which is a source of norms. Aiken and Hage (2) found that autonomous professional organizations had a larger network of external relationships with other organizations, as well as a greater tendency to adopt new programs and novel solutions to organizational problems. The study revealed that social-welfare agencies, which employed a larger number of professionals, were more complex (more departments, competition between departments, more contact with the environment). Bucher and Stelling (10), who examined mental-health as well as other health institutes, indicated that multiprofessional organizations are characterized by intense struggles for dominance over resources, which lead to departmentalization and bargaining mechanisms in such organizations.

It should be noted that organizational features described above may result from intervening variables other than direct involvement of professionals. For example, the nature of environmental certainty-uncertainty may have a greater effect on structure. A clear indication of the net effect of the professional factor independent of others requires more elaborate study.

Action Guidelines: A practitioner or agency administrator desiring to create an organization whose characteristics are a decentralized structure, less formalization (fewer rules, less standardization, less job codification), greater departmentalization and occupational diversity, more links with external organizations, new programs, novel organizational solutions, and less routinized technologies may be assisted in moving in such directions by the increased participation of the organization's professionals. This assumes such qualifications as "all things being equal" or "in general." Some professionals and professional groups are not innovative or open to the environment. For some nonuniform or nonroutine events laymen or paraprofessionals may be as good as professionals or better.

Agencies that wish to recruit more professionals or retrain those currently employed should consider optimizing the extent of such structural features into their organizational framework. The character of the optimizing notion will be explored in the next generalization.

Professionals and Moderate Bureaucracy

GENERALIZATION 5.6: Members of established professions, employed in organizational settings, favor moderately bureaucratic features more than highly nonbureaucratic or highly bureaucratic features. They perceive of these organizations as providing necessary resources and autonomy (+, 16).

"Established professions" implies professions that possess a crystallized body of knowledge and technology and that have achieved a stable, high-status position in the public image. Physicians and lawyers are prototypical. By *moderately bureaucratic features* we mean an organization characterized by bureaucratic properties that are not highly emphasized (centralization of authority, formalization of rules, role definition, etc.). These characteristics are existent in the organization, but their intensity is mild in character.

Engle's study (16) of the effects of bureaucracy on professional autonomy of physicians in hospitals underlines mutual interdependence between the two. She compared three hospital settings according to their degree of bureaucracy and found that physicians associated with a moderately bureaucratic setting were most likely to perceive themselves as autonomous. Moderately bureaucratic hospitals apparently contribute to the physician's sense of autonomy to a greater degree than do nonbureaucratic ones. The possible anarchy and inefficiency (with loss or unavailability of resources) of such settings apparently do not facilitate professional task achievement. She further contends that a reasonable amount of bureaucracy is optimal for the realization of the professional's aspirations for autonomy.

Action Guidelines: Professionals usually need resources such as equipment and facilities for practice and research, clerical help, technical support, administrative assistance, etc. These resources may be provided by an organization that possesses bureaucratic features. At the same time, the presence of professionals, and the organization's dependence on them, perhaps serves to neutralize bureaucratic tendencies and to help keep such features at a moderate level. To maximize satisfaction of professionals and, perhaps, to provide them with conditions of optimal effectiveness, organizations should structure themselves at a moderate level of bureaucracy, sufficient to obtain and distribute resources while permitting reasonably autonomous functioning of workers.

Semiprofessionals and Organizational Norms

GENERALIZATION 5.7: "Semiprofessionals" are more predisposed to accept organizational norms and constraints than are "established" professionals (+ + +, 1, 4, 28, 47).

In contrast to the "established" professions, the "semiprofessions" do not enjoy stable support from the public and lack a crystallized, integrated knowledge base. This category of personnel often includes social workers, nurses, and teachers.

A review of the literature indicates that human-service organizations which employ semiprofessionals are typically more bureaucratic than organizations employing established professionals. Aiken and Hage's study (1) of welfare organizations shows that those organizations are characterized by a considerable amount of bureaucracy, including centralized decision making. This point is further reinforced by Scott's study (47) of social welfare agencies, which showed that social workers are predisposed to readily accept supervision from superordinates because of their training.

Action Guidelines: Organizations wishing to employ professionals but desiring to place organizational constraints on their functions might consider employing semiprofessionals.

Semiprofessionals seeking autonomy in their practice should reduce their acceptance of agency norms.

Organizational Impact on Professionals

GENERALIZATION 5.8: Bureaucratic norms will predominate when professionals are vulnerable (small number, weak norms, etc.) and when agency norms are strong (+, 11, 12. [This generalization is the converse of 5.4]).

Daniels's study (12) of the psychiatrist in the military setting lends support to this statement. She shows that the military psychiatrist often violates the ethics of his profession and serves the needs of the organization rather than those of his clients. Among the means the organization may use to accomplish this are isolating the professionals from their "professional community" and attempting to modify some of the basic premises of the profession by emphasizing that there is not necessarily a contradiction between being a professional and serving the organization rather than its clients.

Action Guidelines: To maintain or increase their impact on organizations, professionals should retain strong links (intensive contact) with their professional association and colleagues. Links with professional schools may also serve this purpose. Building a critical mass in terms of numbers in agencies is another source of professional influence.

Supervision and Modes of Power-Influence
Within Organizations

An important aspect of operating human-service organizations concerns the appropriate forms of control and supervision applied to agency personnel. This is often approached ideologically; i.e., democratic supervision is "better" than autocratic supervision. In the discussion that follows, we shall explore this question from an empirical-analytical standpoint and in a way that treats the matter differentially rather than on a unitary basis.

Power, Objectives, and Visibility

GENERALIZATION 5.9: The effectiveness of forms of social power-influence utilized within organizations is dependent on the type of objective sought (attitudinal conformity or behavioral conformity) and the social context of the objective (low or high visibility) (+ +, 55).

The group of subgeneralizations to be discussed is derived from Warren's study (55) of organizational characteristics, administrative style, and staff activities of a sample of 18 schools in the Detroit area. Warren used Etzioni's typology of organizations as a theoretical point of departure. However, he expanded the theory by borrowing the typology of power forms that was developed earlier by French and Raven.

Warren distinguishes among three factors: 1) the particular base of power; 2) the structural conditions under which the power is exercised; 3) the kind of organizational social control that is generated.

Under the category of power base, he includes *coercive power* (the use of physical force), *reward power* (providing rewards), *expert power* (power based on knowledge), *legitimate power* (power based on the utilization of legal or moral norms), and *referent power* (power based on personal identification with the leader, a kind of charismatic legitimation).

Warren further distinguishes between two kinds of conformity created among organization members as a result of the use of power: *behavioral conformity* (compliance in overt behavior but without internalization of norms) and *attitudinal conformity* (conformity accompanied by internalization). Warren stresses that the relationships between these two variables should be viewed through the perspective of structural conditions under which power is exercised. Here he singles out one variable—visibility—and distinguishes between *high visibility* (a situation where the performance of the member is physically observed and supervised) and *low visibility* (where surveillance is absent or impossible).

The predictions from Warren's analysis are presented in the following table:

TABLE 5.1: PREDICTED RELATIONSHIPS AMONG
SOCIAL POWER BASES, TYPES OF CONFORMITY
AND EXTENT OF VISIBILITY

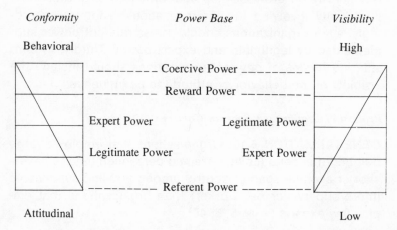

Conformity	*Power Base*	*Visibility*
Behavioral		High
	————— Coercive Power —————	
	————— Reward Power —————	
	Expert Power Legitimate Power	
	Legitimate Power Expert Power	
	————— Referent Power —————	
Attitudinal		Low

This general conceptualization leads to several more refined assertions.

5.9A. Referent power is especially effective in attaining *attitudinal
conformity* (internalization) under conditions of *low visibility* (+ +,
55).

5.9B. Coercive power is especially effective in attaining *behavioral
conformity* under conditions of *high visibility* (+ +, 55).

5.9C. Reward power is effective in attaining *behavioral conformity*
under conditions of *high visibility* (+ +, 55).

5.9D. Legitimate power is effective in attaining *attitudinal conformity* under conditions of either *high or low visibility* (+ +, 55).

5.9E. Expert power is effective in attaining *attitudinal conformity*
(when used with the expert's knowledge field) both under conditions
of *high and low visibility* (+ +, 55).

Action Guidelines: A variety of action guidelines flow from
these propositions. First of all, it is obvious that organizations and change agents should use differential and combined modes of influence, depending on circumstances and

objectives. A single approach will likely lead to limited, ineffective results. Secondly, human-service organizations that rely heavily on professionals deal ordinarily with attitudinal conformity involving the internalization of norms. Accordingly, such organizations should stress referent power supplemented by legitimate and expert power. Thirdly, in considering modes of power, organizations should include the visibility of the behavior or attitude to be influenced.

Professionalization and Span of Control

GENERALIZATION 5.10: Organizations that employ a large number of experts (college-trained personnel) tend to have a shorter average span of control among first-line supervisors (more supervisior per worker) than organizations that employ few experts (+ +, 5, 6, 40).

This proposition is derived primarily from the Blau et al. (6, 40) study of a civil service agency and a finance department. Findings ran contrary to the assumption (based on conventional belief concerning professionals and bureaucracy) that experts tend to maintain considerable distance from their supervisors and to work highly independently. Blau found that as expertise increases, supervision is closer and communication between expert and supervisor is more intense.

The explanation is that in these settings the relationships between the supervisor and the expert are more mutual or collegial in nature. Indeed, Blau indicates that the close relationships established between the two provide the expert with a channel for communication of views and ideas to the higher levels of the organization, and gives the expert a sense of participation in decision making. Thus, immediate supervisors serve as channels of upward communication, not solely as monitoring control instruments or downward communicators. In this sense, "span of control" is a misnomer. "Span of communication" might be a more aptly descriptive concept. Using Warren's terms, the form of power used in the context is "expert power," which may be the most appropriate for these particular settings where the professionals operate under conditions of medium visibility.

Action Guidelines: One of the ways to provide professionals with a sense of involvement in organizations is to reduce the span of supervisory coverage and intensify interaction and communication between professionals and management through supervisory personnel who serve as linking agents. In human-service settings, increasing the worker's sense of participation and involvement may be attained by basing relationships between supervisors and workers on greater mutuality with two-way communication.

Close Supervision and Alienation among Social Workers

GENERALIZATION 5.11: Social workers typically are willing to accept close supervision. At the same time, they experience work alienation (+, 47).

This finding, based on Scott's study (47) of social workers in welfare agencies, is at least partially consistent with the conclusions of Warren and Blau, which stress that professionals are not free of supervision and at the same time favor certain types of supervision. The schoolteachers in Warren's investigation responded in particular to referent influence; the social workers studied by Scott and the financial specialists studied by Blau responded to professional supervision, which may be viewed as parallel with expert influence as reflected in Warren's scheme.

It is interesting to note that, according to Warren, expert power may be the most effective means for attaining attitudinal conformity under conditions of medium visibility, a circumstance under which many social workers and other human-service professionals typically operate.

Scott finds that while social workers tend to accept close supervision, they also express a sense of alienation articulated as a lack of voice in formulating agency policies. Aiken and Hage (1) uncovered a pattern of low staff participation in social-work agencies. While close supervision may achieve sufficient control over performance, it apparently does not create a feeling of satisfaction. To achieve this among professionals, a combination of the three modes of influence—

referent, legitimate and expert—is needed. Referent power may have the potential to instill in members of organizations a sense of personal identification and involvement that may compensate for lack of actual participation in agency decision making.

Action Guidelines: While social workers do accept close supervision, they also experience alienation and a sense of lack of participation. It would be well to augment "expert" supervision with referent and legitimate supervision, as well as to seek opportunities to increase actual participation in agency decision making. Since social-work and other human-service professions appear to be moving in the direction of more established professional status, it would seem appropriate to emphasize autonomy to a greater extent by reducing extensive supervision and employing consultative and supportive relationships or supervisors who perform upward linkage roles.

Supportive Supervision and Job Satisfaction

GENERALIZATION 5.12: Supervisors who use a "supportive" style of leadership (caring about problems of subordinates, refraining from criticizing in the presence of fellow employees, etc.) foster job satisfaction and identification with the organization (+ +, 7, 56).

These findings are based on Wager's study (56) of more than a thousand white-collar workers in industry, as well as the Bowers and Seashore study (7) of insurance company workers. According to Wager, supervisors exhibiting supportive leadership tend to be those with upward influence in the organization. Whether influential supervisors are more secure or whether personal attributes associated with upward influence are also associated with a supportive style is an open question. In terms of our previous discussion, supportive leadership perhaps employs to a considerable degree referent and reward forms of influence.

Action Guidelines: Organizations that wish to encourage the development of job satisfaction and organizational identification by the staff should encourage the use of supportive supervision. Supervisors can perhaps be encouraged to use such supervision by providing them with opportunities for upward influence (as well as through training and socialization experience).

While supervision is found to affect the psychological state or outlook of staff workers, aspects of structure also play a part in this connection.

Hierarchy and Alienation

GENERALIZATION 5.13: Increased hierarchy of authority (centralization and lower degree of worker participation in decision making) is correlated with greater job dissatisfaction and work alienation. Hierarchy of authority is also correlated with expressive alienation (+ + +, 1, 30, 37).

Alienation from work involves a feeling of powerlessness and detachment from the arenas of decision making. *Expressive alienation* implies dissatisfaction with social relations with supervisors as well as with fellow workers.

5.13A. Workers' participation in the organization (as measured by their control over the method and order of performance and their ability to try their own ideas and to utilize their skills independently) tends to increase satisfaction and identification with the organization (+ + +, 1, 37).
5.13 B. Workers participate only slightly in the decision-making process in welfare organizations. Social work agencies tend to have a flat hierarchical structure, but, again, with only low levels of worker participation (+ +, 1).
5.13C. There is generally a low degree of job satisfaction among social-welfare administrators (+, 30).

There is an apparent contradiction within the findings: semiprofessionals accept work in more bureaucratic settings, while on the other hand, these settings create in them a sense of alienation. This probably stems from the fact that for most semiprofessionals the only context in which they can utilize their knowledge (or obtain jobs) is bureaucratic. This is accepted as a given, but personal stresses and dissatisfactions result.

Action Guidelines: An organization that wishes to prevent alienation from work and from expressive relations should decrease the level of hierarchy of authority in the organization by permitting decisions to be made at lower levels, or increase participation of workers by consulting them on decisions made by top administrators and by giving them a certain degree of independence in work. This should help increase job satisfaction and hypothetically aid in retention of workers.

Concluding Note on Professionals

Our discussion would be incomplete if we did not look back to the initial analysis of organizational environments. Although professionals certainly may be considered a basic internal ingredient of an organization, their uniqueness stems from the fact that they represent a limited subculture within the organization, which often differs in some respects from the dominant culture. Furthermore, professionals introduce into the organization knowledge and skills that are ordinarily obtained outside its boundaries. The possibility of viewing the interaction between the organization and the professionals as one aspect of the organization's relationship with the environment is underlined by the fact that the professional is expected to be loyal to his professional association and to identify with its ethical code, which may not necessarily be congruent with organizational norms. The set of generalizations regarding professionals and the organizations in this light signifies conditions under which an occupational group that represents external values and interests is able to affect organizational behavior. Professionals may be viewed as a link between organized professional interests in society on one hand, and formal organizations on the other. In the discussion in chapter 9 on innovations in organizations, the programmatic importance of the linkage of organizational professionals to external environmental associations will become critical.

INDIGENOUS PARAPROFESSIONALS AND
ORGANIZATIONAL SETTINGS

In recent years the use of paraprofessionals as staff members in human-service agencies has increased. An exposition on professionals would be incomplete without a discussion of indigenous paraprofessionals. To clarify our definitions, we should indicate that the term "indigenous" means personnel with socioeconomic or cultural *similarity* with the client population. The term paraprofessional indicates a person with a level of education less than that typically required by fully trained or certified professionals. This new professional role has had an impact not only on agency structures and services, but also on professionals themselves.

Reissman and Pearl have developed a persuasive rationale for the employment of paraprofessionals.[4] We shall review some of their main arguments. First, paraprofessionals can potentially change the image of the poor, because they are both providers of a service and its recipients. This arrangement may lead to a decreased sense of psychological distance and dependence often present in those receiving services. Also, this situation is a therapeutic experience for the helper. Because many indigenous workers were deviant from a social point of view (e.g., unemployed, school dropout, delinquent) their new helping role may promote increased self-confidence and renewal as they grapple with similar problems of their peers.

In addition, from an organizational standpoint, use of paraprofessionals can potentially make services more meaningful and powerful for clients. Using indigenous persons in organizations is a valuable tool for closing the gap between human-service agencies and their clients. This gap includes the cultural distance between middle-class professionals and lower-class clients, as well as the distance between bureaucratic features of many agencies and the poor (as formal organization is alien to the life-style of the poor). Indigenous workers, familiar with lower-class community values and needs, can, by serving as brokers, help bridge this gap by interpreting clients to the organization and vice versa.

[4] Arthur, Pearl and Frank Reissman, *New Careers for the Poor: The Non-Professional in Human Service* New York: The Free Press, 1965.

In addition, employing indigenous paraprofessionals may be a means of dealing with poverty directly by providing jobs and a new career opportunity for a segment of the poor population. It can also be an impetus for increased citizen participation by the poor, by giving them significant roles in community institutions that affect their lives.

There has been a dearth of hard empirical research on the actual tasks and experiences of paraprofessionals in human-service organizations. Many of the writings are case studies. We have retrieved only a smattering of these and will extrapolate from this limited data pool. Our coverage of this topic is narrow, even within the confines of our retrieval frame. Katan, one of our project staff members, has been engaged in a much broader review on the subject, which is reported elsewhere.[5]

Our examination of relevant studies indicates variation among human-service organizations in terms of their conception of the paraprofessional's role and function. The nature of this aspect of experience with paraprofessionals is summarized below.

Differential Use of Paraprofessionals

GENERALIZATION 5.14: Human-service organizations have varying motives for employing indigenous workers, and utilize them in different ways (+ + +, 19, 20, 27, 34, 36, 48).

> 5.14A. In some agencies, indigenous workers operate as linking agents between the service center and its clients (case finders, recruiters, referral agents, etc.) (+, 8, 19, 20).
> 5.14B. Paraprofessionals are sometimes used to deliver services to special client groups because of their presumed similarity to or rapport with such groups (+, 27).
> 5.14C. Some indigenous nonprofessionals direct and operate agency activities. (+, 36).
> 5.14D. Some paraprofessionals are utilized mostly to reduce the clerical burden on the professional staff, and to help overcome manpower shortages (+, 34).

[5] Joseph Katan, "The Interrelationship Between Indigenous Non-Professionals, Professionals and Organizations in Human Service Organizations (Doctoral dissertation, School of Social Work, University of Michigan, 1973).

5.14E. An unintended consequence (from the agency's standpoint) is the acquisition of political and activist skills by paraprofessionals (+, 48).

Although these findings are derived from a limited number of studies (all of them describing specific cases), they point to some interesting trends in the field.

In the Mobilization for Youth case described by Grosser (19, 20) and Brager (8), the main reason for employing indigenous workers was to link the organization and its clientele. Indeed, they were used mostly in the field as representatives of MFY. In this capacity they served as community workers, always under supervision of professional staff.

In the community mental health centers described by Hallowitz (27), the function of the nonprofessionals was similar to that in MFY, although it seems that they had somewhat more autonomy in their work and a greater impact on the operations of the centers. In both cases, however, the main motive underlying their employment was the desire by innovative professionals to reach out to the community and provide new, unconventional services.

In the OEO center described by Lowenberg (36), indigenous workers served in almost all capacities and dominated the scene. This was a social-welfare organization without professionals (except one with limited influence), where paraprofessionals, given resources and authority, were able if so inclined to bring about new programs. The possibility of innovation existed; its realization was unclear.

Leo Levy (34), in an examination of paramedical staff found that employment of paraprofessionals was designed to reduce the work load of the professionals. Seidler's observations of the Detroit Community Action Program (48) highlight socialization into community political roles on the part of paraprofessionals.

These cases suggest that organizations are using paraprofessionals to a large extent for purposes of bridging the gap between services and clientele, and for reallocating work within organizations.

Innovative professionals, who developed this concept of service, recognized the disability of many professionals in communicating with and relating to the poor. While seeking to remedy this deficiency by using the indigenous workers, professionals still maintained their dominance by supervision and by holding the planning and policy-making functions closely under their control. (Interestingly enough, indigenous workers were not involved in the original planning of the series of innovative programs initiated by MFY.)

In both MFY and OEO the "new" careers notion was promulgated by professionals and intellectuals with a sense of social mission. While in MFY the professionals took an active part in the program (this was a local project initiated by people from the School of Social Work at Columbia University and other local institutions), indigenous person-nel in OEO increasingly came to direct and operate services at the local level without the involvement of conventional professionals.

Action Guidelines: Implications regarding these findings are diffuse. It is suggested that a practitioner should probe for further information on roles and functions upon learning that an agency employs paraprofessionals. Further, in planning for the introduction of paraprofessionals into an agency, a range of possible roles should be considered. The linking role appears to be quite important, suggesting that paraprofessionals may be useful linking agents between human-service organizations and culturally distant client populations; they may also relieve professionals of routine components of their jobs. Paraprofessional activity may also serve as a training ground for developing political capability in organizational and community contexts.

Several studies have attempted to provide answers to the question of how firm is the assumption that indigenous workers can create better links between service organizations and their clientele.

Perceptions of Community by Paraprofessionals

GENERALIZATION 5.15: Indigenous paraprofessionals are more knowledgeable concerning attitudes of community residents than are professionals (+, 19, 20).

Grosser (19, 20), in his MFY study, administered similar question-naires to lower-class minority residents of the local community, professional staff members, and indigenous workers. Professionals and indigenous workers were also asked to indicate how they thought local residents would answer. An examination of the responses showed that attitudes and aspects of community awareness on the part of indigenous staff members more closely approximated those of community residents. Furthermore, indigenous workers more accurately predicted the perceptions of community residents on these subjects.

Action Guidelines: Organizations may use indigenous nonprofessionals as a source of information about perceptions of community residents. Professionals should be cautious in acting on their own perception of residents' attitudes and should seek outside validating sources.

Work-Styles of Paraprofessionals

GENERALIZATION 5.16: Paraprofessionals have a different work-style than do professionals (+, 8).

> 5.16A. Paraprofessionals deemphasize bureaucratic features. They tend to be more informal, impervious to bureaucratic authority, and unencumbered by formal role prescriptions (+, 8).
>
> 5.16B. Paraprofessionals tend to relate to clients in a distinct fashion. In assessing social problems they emphasize external life circumstances rather than internalized conditions of the individual, and they accept at face value and act upon information provided by clients (+, 8).

These characteristics of indigenous workers are based on descriptions of three programs conducted within the framework of MFY: a visiting homemaker service, a parent education unit, and a community-development program. In these programs, approximately 40 low-income inner-city residents served as paraprofessional staff.

While the author describes the unique characteristics that appeared, he does not examine the question of whether these were "natural" attributes brought into the organization, characteristics engendered by the organization, or some dual interaction. In other words, we are left with uncertainty about finding similar characteristics in indigenous workers in every setting where they are employed, or only in an innovative setting like MFY, where such nonbureaucratic characteristics may have been accepted or encouraged.

Action Guidelines: The informal characteristics of indigenous nonprofessionals may contribute more in a "human relations" type of organization, where there is more emphasis on openness and collegial relationships, than in more bureaucratic agencies. At the same time, a practitioner seeking to "loosen up" a bureaucratic organization may be able to obtain leverage by introducing paraprofessionals. Indigenous workers may be particularly successful in situations where personal, supportive relationships with clients are important. They may also be effective in nonroutine crisis situations, where quick action on the basis of the available information is needed.

The above proposition hints at possible problems in the web of relationships between paraprofessionals and professionals. We shall attempt to explore this problem and its origins. Studies dealing with the issue identify the following problems:

1. Tension between professionals and indigenous workers when both are present in the organization.
2. Contamination of the indigenous workers' contribution by professionals.
3. Absence of paraprofessional impact on organizations.

Strain in Professional-Paraprofessional Relations

GENERALIZATION 5.17: The potential exists for the development of strained relationships between human-service professionals and indigenous nonprofessionals (+ , 36, 48).

A case in point is illustrated by Lowenberg (36) in a neighborhood center operated with OEO funds in a large Midwestern metropolis. The neighborhood center, in a low-income sector of the city, employed 14 full-time and 30 part-time workers, only two of whom (one a social worker) completed college. Lowenberg graphically describes the discouragement of the professionals working in this paraprofessional atmosphere and indicates four causes:

1. The paraprofessionals are unaware of and unconcerned about bureaucratic rules.
2. Nonprofessionals dislike professionals.
3. The social worker was isolated not only within the organization, but also from colleagues outside its boundaries.
4. The social worker was under nonprofessional control.

Action Guidelines: A balance between the number of professionals and paraprofessionals in an organization may insure professional impact on an organization and keep the morale of the professional at an adequate level. Professionals wishing to work with nonprofessionals should become familiar with the unique characteristics of indigenous workers and construct appropriate modes of interaction through a division of labor between the two parties.

Why should professionals and nonprofessionals function together at all? The ideal solution in the case illustrated by Lowenberg might be for the social worker to depart the agency (it is surprising that Lowenberg found one there at all), and for indigenous workers to operate in that situation without a professional presence or intervention.

Seidler, analyzing the community-action program in Detroit (also an OEO-funded organization), reaches a different conclusion, however.

Professional-Paraprofessional Support

GENERALIZATION 5.18: Rejection of paraprofessionals by trained professional workers creates a situation whereby paraprofessionals receive inadequate supervision and are expected to undertake work demanding expertise they do not possess. The consequence is strain and frustration for them and the organization (+, 48).

According to Seidler (48) the absence of professional workers restricts the range of activities that may successfully be undertaken by paraprofessionals. Indigenous workers often reject professionals and may wish to remove them from the scene. This tendency reflects low-income people's resentments of middle-class professionals, based in part on unhappy previous experiences as clients or employees. However, this may create an unproductive work situation for paraprofessionals. It may be that only through the collaboration of professionals can paraprofessionals actualize their full capabilities.

It should be noted that the point of view expressed in this generalization is based on an analysis by a professional. Nonprofessionals examining the same situation critically might argue that professionals, threatened by the potentialities of nonprofessionals, will always point out the limitations of indigenous workers and the necessity of a "professional presence." Nonprofessionals themselves prefer (as expressed in several studies) to be free of this type of professional presence.

Action Guidelines: On the basis of one study, it is difficult to offer definitive guidance. One may argue that in the case illustrated by Seidler the absence of professionals seemed to limit the capacities of paraprofessionals and of the agency itself. The full utilization of indigenous paraprofessionals may require the collaboration of professionals. Any supervision and guidance offered should fit the characteristics of indigenous workers. Professionals may have to be able to accommodate considerable tension and antagonism in working with paraprofessionals and should be prepared to cope with this in the interest of service to clients. Paraprofessionals need to find suitable ways of working collaboratively with professionals toward attainment of common goals.

When paraprofessionals are working jointly with professionals, another problem emerges—the contamination of the paraprofessionals' contribution. Low-income people interacting intensively with professionals may shed their intrinsic characteristics and through identification adopt the style and mode of behavior of middle-class professionals. This may be welcomed by those who view the employment of indigenous workers as a tool for fostering mobility and entering the mainstream of American life. Those wishing to "cool off" risky situations through co-optation will view the contamination process as useful. Those believing in the uniqueness of the indigenous paraprofessionals will decry the process. For them, contamination signals a loss for the basic merits inherent in the employment of indigenous workers.

Contamination of Paraprofessionals

GENERALIZATION 5.19: Paraprofessionals tend to shift their identification in the direction of middle-class and professional values. This contamination is reflected in mode of dress, language, and aspirations to upward mobility (+, 36, 42).

Morril (42) describes a situation in which considerable contamination occurred and indicates its chief origin, namely, the pressures imposed on paraprofessional workers by the agency. Paraprofessionals were not allowed to play the role of community member and were explicitly instructed to avoid "overidentification" with clients.

5.19A. The probability of contamination is stronger in organizations with a larger proportion of professionals than in organizations where their representation is limited (+, 36).

5.19B. The probability of contamination is stronger in organizations in which paraprofessionals interact intensively with professionals than in organizations in which they work more autonomously (+, 42).

It should be noted that, even if there are conspicuous signs of contamination among paraprofessionals, this development is not necessarily a by-product of "professional impact." Indigenous workers may be middle-class in orientation from the beginning, and their interaction with the professionals may simply be a reinforcement. Grosser (19, 20) found that residents in the community as well as indigenous workers were more moderate in their views than professionals, who tended to express fairly radical opinions. The residents, unlike the staff, believed that local people ought to have an equal chance to get ahead and that any young person ought to earn $10,000 a year. They expressed the opinion that slum children are treated equally in school, that schools are doing an adequate job, and that teachers understand slum children. Staff respondents did not hold such favorable views. The indigenous staff members' views were closer to those of the residents than to those of the professional staff members. In this case, the influence of professionals may have been in the direction of radicalizing indigenous workers. This discussion suggests the addition of a variable: the attitudes of the professionals with whom nonprofessionals work. In MFY, an unusual group of committed, more progressive professionals had been recruited.

Action Guidelines: If the objective is to maintain indigenous values and norms among paraprofessionals, it may be furthered by hiring a relatively high proportion of paraprofessionals and arranging low-intensity relationships with professionals.

The way is now open to synthesize what was offered above.

Variables Affecting Contamination

GENERALIZATION 5.20:
   A. The following factors encourage a process of contamination:
      1. A bureaucratic organizational framework that demands from workers strict loyalty to the organization (42).
      2. Indigenous workers having a middle-class orientation prior to their entry into the organization (8).
      3. An absence of community pressures on indigenous workers (42).
      4. Work arrangements which demand intensive interaction between paraprofessionals and professionals in a moderate, conventional or paternalistic atmosphere.[6]
   B. The following factors discourage a process of contamination:
      1. A flexible human relations organizational structure which does not demand bureaucratic loyalty (8, 19, 20).

[6] This generalization taken by Katan, "Indigenous Non-Professionals."

2. Work arrangements which permit much interaction among indigenous workers themselves, and autonomy in job performance (36).
3. Indigenous workers with strong community identification (19, 20).
4. Exposure to community interaction and pressures (19, 20).

Action Guidelines: Organizations wishing to prevent a contamination process should recruit indigenous workers who identify with the community, deploy indigenous workers in a way that will promote interaction among them and maintain their autonomy (assigning indigenous workers to a specific department would be preferable to dispersing them throughout different departments), placing indigenous workers in teams with professionals committed to the necessity of maintaining the indigenous worker's identity with the community, and expose paraprofessionals to many community interactions.

Studies about the actual performance of indigenous workers, which discuss whether their unique characteristics are actualized in their performance, tend to be cautious in providing information. A longer perspective is needed to assess the effectiveness of this new breed. However, limited findings and descriptive studies permit tentative conclusions.

Community Identification and Paraprofessional
Job Performance

GENERALIZATION 5.21: There is a negative association between accurate prediction of resident views and highly rated performance on the part of paraprofessionals (+, 19, 20).

This finding is derived from the Grosser studies (19, 20), which revealed that the performances of indigenous workers who were successful in identifying with community residents' views were not highly rated by professional supervisors. This finding will confound those believing that knowledge of the community should contribute to better performance.

The negative association is attributed by Grosser to the paraprofessionals' dual status as community residents and staff members. The indigenous workers' accurate knowledge of the community cannot be used as an effective tool at work, because of the workers' simultaneous membership in an organization, where they are controlled by "objective" professionals, and in the community, where they are perceived as representatives of the organization. Grosser assumes that effective performance results from an accurate knowledge of the community, an objective assessment of this knowledge, and an identification with the community.

The knowledgeable worker has the first input, but membership in the community weakens his objectivity in assessing the knowledge, while membership in the organization weakens his identification with the community.

Action Guidelines: An effort should be made to maintain the workers' identification with the community and to ease the tensions stemming from his relationships with two different frameworks—the community and organizations.

Reaching Unserved Populations

GENERALIZATION 5.22: Organizations employing indigenous workers are successful in reaching clients who were not previously receiving services (+, 8, 19, 20).

The ability of indigenous workers to reach out to unserved clients is illustrated in several studies. In the MFY experience described by Grosser (19, 20) and Brager (8), the indigenous workers in part "created" the clientele of the programs and involved clients who were not formerly associated with any agency. The same situation characterized the neighborhood mental-health center described by Hallowitz (27).

Action Guidelines: Organizations may successfully use indigenous workers to attempt to recruit and serve clients who were not previously served.

Making and Keeping Contact

GENERALIZATION 5.23: While indigenous workers may be successful in reaching out to clients, they have difficulty in maintaining relationships between these clients and bureaucratic agencies. This is caused particularly by unfavorable attitudes of personnel in these organizations (+, 8).

Action Guidelines: Limiting the operations of the indigenous workers to the field and to reaching-out functions only may reduce the value of any success they achieve in recruiting new clients. Indigenous workers should also be placed inside agencies in key service and administrative positions. Another possibility is to permit the same indigenous workers who link with clients to take an active part in providing services to them.

Paraprofessional Impact on Organizations

Besides organizational and professional impact on indigenous workers, the latter may have an impact on the organization.

GENERALIZATION 5.24: Indigenous workers are found to be more differential toward the organization after being associated with it one year or more. At the same time, the organization integrates certain of the values of the local culture within its operations (+, 14).

This point is raised in Denhardt's study (14) of the interaction between indigenous workers and bureaucratic human-service agencies in Appalachia. The study shows that through the process of interaction between the two parties (organizational representatives and indigenous workers), two parallel processes occurred: first, the indigenous workers absorbed certain organizational norms; and second, the organization adjusted itself to some of the requisites imposed by the indigenous workers. This study adds an interesting dimension to the findings concerning indigenous paraprofessionals in the Mobilization for Youth described above.

Grosser focused attention on the impact of professionals on paraprofessionals, while he overlooked the possibility that a countervailing force might operate simultaneously; Denhardt identified this phenomenon.

Action Guidelines: Organizations wishing to incorporate elements of the culture of client groups into their organizational norms and operations may accomplish this in part by intensive use of indigenous paraprofessionals. The reverse is also true. Organizations wishing to avoid client "contagion" should refrain from use of paraprofessionals. It may be assumed that an interaction between an organization and an occupational group having a different culture will lead to mutual adjustments. Whether this adjustment will be made for the most part on the organizational or the occupational side depends on such variables as the type of organization, degree of bureaucracy, and the cohesiveness and crystallization of occupational groups.

With this disscussion we conclude the review of organizational literature. While the treatment of the subject is presented in two separate chapters, it is all part of a single whole. The separation was made primarily as an aid in permitting the reader to encompass a preponderance of data, and not because the subject matter itself called for such segmentation. The style and orientation of much of the research lends itself to broader use by planners and administrators than by social actionists and community workers. Perhaps the latter group will be able to construct a greater number of applications from generalizations than I have provided in the action guidelines. For a rounding out of this subject matter, the reader is referred to chapter 9, in which innovations in organizations are discussed, and to chapter 3, in which bureaucratic versus other orientations by practitioners are considered.

BIBLIOGRAPHY FOR PART THREE

1. Aiken, Michael, and Jerald Hage. "Organizational Alienation: A Comparative Analysis." *American Sociological Review* 31, no. 4 (August 1966): 497–507.

2. Aiken, Michael, and Jerald Hage. "Organizational Interdependence and Interorganizational Structure." *American Sociological Review* 33, no. 6 (1968): 912–30.

3. Anderson, Theodore R., and Seymour Workow. "Organization Size and Functional Complexity: A Study of Administration in Hospitals." *American Sociological Review* 26, no. 1 (1961): 23–28.

4. Bar-Yosef, Rivkan, and Erling O. Schild. "Pressures and Defenses in Bureaucratic Rules." *American Journal of Sociology* 71, no. 6 (1966): 665–73.

5. Blau, Peter. "The Hierarchy of Authority in Organizations." *American Journal of Sociology* 73, no. 4 (1968): 453–67.

6. Blau, Peter Wolf V. Heydebrad, and Robert E. Stauffer. "The Structure of Small Bureaucracies." *American Sociological Review* 31, no. 2 (1966): 179–91.

7. Bowers, Daniel J., and Stanley E. Seashore. "Predicting Organizational Effectiveness with a Four-Factor Theory of Leadership." *Administrative Science Quarterly* 11, no. 11 (1966): 238–63.

8. Brager, George. "The Indigenous Worker: A New Approach to the Social Work Technician." *Social Work* 10, no. 2 (1965): 33–40.

9. Brown, E. Michael. "Identification and Some Conditions of Organizational Involvement." *Administrative Science Quarterly* 14, no. 3 (1969): 346–55.

10. Bucher, Rue, and Joan Stelling. "Characteristics of Professional Organizations." *Journal of Health and Social Behavior* 10, no. 1 (1969).

11. Burchard, Waldow. "Role Conflict of the Military Chaplain." *American Sociological Review* 19, no. 4 (1954): 528–35.

12. Daniels, K. Arlene. "The Captive Professional: Bureaucratic Limitations in the Practice of Military Psychiatry." *Journal of Health and Social Behavior* 10, no. 4 (1969): 225–64.

13. Day, Robert C., and R. L. Hamilton. "Some Effects of Close and Punitive Styles of Supervision." *American Journal of Sociology* 69, no. 5 (1964): 499–510.

14. Denhardt, Robert B. "Bureaucratic Socialization and Organizational Accommodation." *Administrative Science Quarterly* 13, no. 3 (1968): 441–50.

15. Eisenstadt, S. N., and Elihu Katz. "Some Sociological Observations in the Response of Israeli Organizations to New Immigrants." *Administrative Science Quarterly* 5, no. 1 (1960): 113–33.

16. Engel, Gloria. "The Effects of Bureaucracy on the Professional Autonomy of Physicians." *Journal of Health and Social Behavior* 10, no. 1: 30–41.

17. Friedlander, Frank, and Hal Pickle. "Components of Effectiveness in Small Organizations." *Administrative Science Quarterly* 13, no. 2 (1968): 289–306.

190 *Organizational Framework*

18. Gross, Edward. "Universities as Organizations: A Research Approach." *American Sociology Review* 33, no. 4 (1968): 518–44.

19. Grosser, Charles. "Local Residents as Mediators between Middle Class Professional Workers and Lower Class Clients." *Social Service Review* 40, no. 1 (1966): 56–63.

20. Grosser, Charles. "Perception of Professional Indigenous Workers and Lower Class Clients." Doctoral dissertation, Columbia University, 1965.

21. Gusfield, Joseph. "Social Structure and Moral Reform: A Study of the Women's Christian Temperance Union." *American Journal of Sociology* 61, no. 3 (1955): 221–39.

22. Gusfield, Joseph. "The Problem of Generations in Organizational Structure." *Social Forces* 35, no. 4 (1947): 323–30.

23. Hage, Jerald, and Michael Aiken. "Routine Technology, Social Structure and Organizational Goals." *Administrative Science Quarterly* 14, no. 3 (1969): 366–75.

24. Hall, Richard. "Some Organizational Considerations in the Professional Organizational Relationships." *Administrative Science Quarterly* 12, no. 3 (1967): 461–78.

25. Hall, Richard. "Professionalization and Bureaucratization." *American Sociological Review* 33, no. 1 (1968): 92–104.

26. Hall, Richard, J. Eugene Haas and Norman J. Johnson, "Organizational Size, Complexity, and Formalization." *American Sociological Review* 32, no. 6 (1967): 901–12.

27. Hallowitz, Emanuel. "The Role of a Neighborhood Service Center in Community Mental Health." *American Journal of Orthopsychiatry* 38, no. 4 (1968): 705–14.

28. Hanlan, Archie. "Organizational Influence on Public Assistance Staff: A Comparative Analysis of Staff Orientations in Three County Welfare Departments." Doctoral dissertation, University of California, Berkeley, 1967.

29. Harvey, Edward. "Technology and the Structure of Organizations." *American Sociological Review* 23, no. 2 (1968): 247–59.

30. Kaloch, Shirley. "A Study of Status Inconsistency Among Social Work Professions." *Social Problems* 15, no. 3 (1965): 365–76.

31. Kaufman, Herbert. *The Forest Ranger*. Baltimore: Johns Hopkins University Press, 1960.

32. Lawrence, Paul, and Jay W. Lorsch. "Differentiation and Integration in Complex Organizations." *Administrative Science Quarterly* 12, no. 1 (1967): 1–47.

33. Levine, Sol, and Paul E. White. "Exchange as a Conceptual Framework for the Study of Interorganizational Relationships." *Administrative Science Quarterly* 5, no. 4 (1961): 583–601.

34. Levy, Leo. "Factors Which Facilitate or Impede Transfer of Medical Functions From Physicians to Paramedical Personnel." *Journal of Health and Social Behavior* 7, no. 1 (1966): 50–54.

35. Litwak, Eugene, and Lydia F. Hylton. "Interorganizational Analysis: A Hypothesis on Coordinating Agencies." *Administrative Science Quarterly* 6, no. 4: 395–420.

36. Lowenberg, Frank M. "Social Workers and Indigenous Paraprofessionals: Some Structural Dilemmas." *Social Work* 13, no. 3 (1968): 65–71.

37. Markus, Nathan. "Staff Participation in Organizational Change, A Study of the Participation of Staff Members of Social Service Organizations in Activities Aimed at Influencing Changes in the Services and Functions of the Employing Agencies." Doctoral dissertation, University of Toronto, 1969.

38. Meniha, John, and Charles Perrow. "The Reluctant Organizations and the Aggressive Environment." *Administrative Science Quarterly* 10, no. 2 (1965): 229–57.

39. Messinger, Sheldon L. "Organizational Transformation: A Case Study of a Declining Social Movement." *American Sociological Review* 21, no. 1 (1955): 3–10.

40. Meyer, Marshall. "Expertness and Span of Control." *American Sociological Review* 33, no. 6 (1968): 744–49.

41. Montagna, Paul D. "Professionalization and Bureaucratization in Large Professional Organizations." *American Journal of Sociology* 74, no. 2 (1968): 138–45.

42. Morrill, Richard G. "Group Identity, Marginality and the Non-Professional." *Archives of General Psychiatry* 19, no. 4 (1968): 404–12.

43. Perrow, Charles. "Organizational Prestige, Some Functions and Dysfunctions." *American Journal of Sociology* 66, no. 4 (1961): 335–41.

44. Pugh, D. C., D. S. Hickson, C. R. Hinings, and C. Turner, "The Context of Organizational Structure." *Administrative Science Quarterly* 14, no. 1 (1969): 91–113.

45. Raphael, Edna. "The Anderson-Workow Hypothesis in Local Unions: A Comparative Analysis." *American Sociological Review* 32, no. 5 (1967): 768–76.

46. Rushing, William A. "Organizational Rules and Surveillance: A Proposition in Comparative Organizational Analysis." *Administrative Science Quarterly* 10, no. 4 (1966): 423–43.

47. Scott, W. Richard. "Reactions to Supervision in a Heteronomous Professional Organization." *Administrative Science Quarterly* 10 (1965): 65–81.

48. Seidler, Murray. "Some Participant Observation Reflections on Detroit's Community Action Program." *Urban Affairs Quarterly* 5, no. 2 (1969): 182–305.

49. Simpson, Richard L., and William H. Gulley. "Goals, Environmental Pressures and Organizational Characteristics." *American Sociological Review* 27, no. 3 (1962): 344–51.

50. Smith, Clagett. "A Comparative Analysis of Some Conditions and Consequences of Intra-Organizational Conflict." *Administrative Science Quarterly* 10, no. 4 (1968): 504–29.

51. Specht, Harry. "Community Development in Low Income Negro Areas." *Social Work* 11, no. 4 (1966): 78–89.

52. Terrien, Frederic C., and Donald C. Mills. "The Effect of Changing Size on the Internal Structure of an Organization." *American Sociological Review* 20, no. 1 (1955): 11–13.

53. Thomas, Edwin J. "Role Conceptions and Organizational Size." *American Sociological Review* 20, no. 1 (1959): 30–37.

54. Tropman, John E. "A Comparative Analysis of Complex Organizations." Doctoral dissertation, University of Michigan, 1967.

55. Warren, Donald I. "Power, Visibility and Conformity in Formal Organizations." *American Sociological Review* 33, no. 6 (1968): 951–70.

56. Weinberger, Paul E. "The Job Satisfaction of Social Welfare Administrators." Doctoral dissertation, University of Southern California, 1966.

57. Yuchtman, Ephraum, and Stanley Seashore, "A System Resource Approach to Organizational Effectiveness," *American Sociological Review* 32 (1967): 891–903.

58. Zald, Mayer, and P. Denton. "From Evangelism to General Service: The Transformation of the YMCA." *Administrative Science Quarterly* 8, no. 2 (1963): 216–34.

59. Zald, Mayer. "Organizational Central Structures in Five Correctional Institutions." *American Journal of Sociology* 68 (1962): 335–54.

Part Four

The Community Setting of Social Change

Chapter Six
Political and Legislative Behavior

INTRODUCTION

WE EXPAND outward now from the organizational context of practice to its community or environmental setting; here we shall be concerned with the broader systemic environment in which action takes place. The concept of community is highly complex, multifaceted, and indeterminate. Even those authors who concentrate on the definitional problem leave their readers with considerable uncertainty and vagueness, and hold varying opinions.[1]

To achieve greater manageability, we have chosen to single out one aspect or subsystem of community: the political subsystem. There are two primary reasons for this choice. In the first place, the political realm is one in which decisions are made concerning communal policies and services that bear importantly on the clientele and constituencies of human-service organizations. Knowledge that may help shape such decisions would likely be of high significance for the audience to whom this book is addressed. Secondly, human-service workers have tended to eschew politically tinged activity, preferring instead to deal with safer matters, to work through professional organs and processes, and to put forth the face of the expert rather than the advocate. There has been a tendency in the past to view politics as sordid—below the level to which an honorable professional will stoop in the conduct of his affairs. When the occasional more heady practi-

[1] Some examples: Conrad M. Arensberg, "The Community as Object and as Sample," *American Anthropologist* 62, no. 2, pt. 1 (April 1961):246–64; Albert J. Reiss, Jr., "The Sociological Study of Communities," *Rural Sociology* 24, no. 2 (June 1959): 118–30; Amos Hawley, *Human Ecology: A Theory of Community Structure* (New York: Ronald Press, 1950); Edward O. Moe, "The Nature of a Community," in *The Planning of Change* by Warren G. Bennis et al. (New York: Holt, Rinehart and Winston, 1961), p. 400.

tioner ventured into this arena, because of lack of knowledge or sophistication concerning the workings of the political system he was
often unsuccessful or suffered damage. Thus, by default or by defeat,
vital decisions pertaining to client well-being were left to others, who
were often less informed and less sympathetic regarding the clients'
plight. The material in this chapter is meant to encourage participation
in the political sphere and to provide a number of strategic options,
which hopefully may contribute to favorable results.

One additional factor gave impetus to the inclusion of a chapter on
political behavior. In surveying political science journals, our staff discovered in the literature a very high percentage of research-based articles dealing with subjects related to community intervention and
social change. Because of the nature of the phenomenon the discipline
treats, political science studies were a "natural" with respect to the
purposes of this work. The subject matter of investigation is inherently
active in nature; thus conversion into applied formulations was effected with considerable ease, requiring fewer inferential extensions
than was true for any of the other practice issue areas.

Another preliminary comment is necessary. While political behavior
has a community referent, it is difficult to confine this discussion to a
locality dimension. Local, state, and national levels of political functioning are highly reactive and intertwined. Roland L. Warren, in *The
Community in America,*[2] has articulately sketched the dissolution of
the concept of local autonomy in understanding the community. The
"Great Change" in community behavior, he maintains, was the development of strong two-way vertical linkages between the locality, and
extracommunity aggregates at the state and federal levels. Through
regulations, availability of program packages, grants-in-aid, and other
resources and mechanisms, larger political units drastically mold the
pattern of local political operations, even in historically local matters
such as education and welfare.

Grodzins gives a kaleidoscopic glimpse of federal penetration into
the local scene in the following passage:

> The federal government has built city halls for many cities and has paid
> for tearing down slums in others. It pays insurance directly to the aged
> and indirectly provides for the health of new mothers. It draws plans for

[2] 2d ed. (Chicago: Rand McNally and Company, 1972).

the best land use for a poor farmer and supplies funds for the construction of a vast manufacturing plant to a multi-million-dollar corporation. It constructs schools here and libraries there. It aids one community in drawing up a city plan, supplies a second community with funds to build a sewer, gives a park to a third, and provides expert advice to the police chief of a fourth when the hardware store is robbed. . . . The typical situation is one in which all governments participate in given activities. To deny the local character of federal activities one would be forced to deny the local character of local governments.[3]

And the importance of this development for human-services planning is expressed by Schottland in this way:

> The health and welfare programs of our federal government do not stand alone. State governments, local governments, and the huge network of voluntary agencies—all are partners and must have a role in social planning and in adding their resources to Federal programs and leadership. The Federal government is the center for planning and leadership in many vital aspects of our life . . . one of the [major] challenges of the second half of the twentieth century might well be the development of a meaningful relationship between Federal government leadership and state and local social planning organizations.[4]

Because of these considerations, the discussion in this chapter will not be confined to locality-based aspects of political and legislative behavior. While the community level will receive some degree of special attention because it is the outer environment which impinges most intimately on most practice situations, wider aspects of the political environment will not be neglected.

We turn now to an examination of the functions of the political subsystem, because such an examination will provide the most useful avenue for discerning ways in which knowledge of political behavior has relevance for community practice.

Most students of politics are in agreement that a key function of government is *provision of services to constituents*. Sanders [5] refers to

[3] Morton Grodzins, *The American System: A New View of Government in the United States* (Chicago: Rand McNally and Co., 1966).

[4] Charles I. Schottland, "Federal Planning for Health and Welfare," in *The Social Welfare Forum, 1963*, National Conference on Social Welfare (New York: Columbia University Press, 1963), pp. 119–20.

[5] Irwin T. Sanders, *The Community: An Introduction to a Social System*, 2d ed. (New York: The Ronald Press, 1966).

this as the "allocation of goods and services" and points out that these are offerings that cannot, or by traditional norms are not expected to be, supplied through private enterprise. He also affirms the truism that in socialist states the scope of such public services is considerably larger than in our own system. Williams [6] alludes to commonly held popular expectations regarding the governmental role in this area. In his survey of citizens and officials of middle-sized cities, respondents perceived of local government in large measure as "the provider of life's amenities." Such amenities and services comprise a formidable laundry list, including police protection, garbage removal, water supply, traffic control and road maintenance, recreational activities and facilities, education, public health, financial assistance, and low-cost housing.

A second function of the political system may be designated *communal decision making*. Here reference is made to the selection of policies and programs to be established and maintained in the community. In part, what is involved is the determination of the number of services to be provided, their character, to whom they should be directed and by what mechanisms and means of service delivery. Also implicated is the question of how services should be funded, land use zoning, the budget process, what sources should be taxed, and in what proportion. Communal decision making extends beyond services per se, and may affect, for example, certain aspects of the institutional character of the community, its moral or value posture, land-use arrangements, growth, patterns of economic development.

As a concomitant of decision making, the political system is the *vehicle through which authority or power in the decision-making process is fixed*. Sanders indicates that "allocation of power" is one of the major operations of a community system. Further, "the governmental institution . . . describes how and to whom power is distributed and the manner in which the power is exercised, particularly with reference to deviant behavior and the introduction of new enterprises or divergent points of view into the community." [7] Thus, government

[6] Oliver Williams, "A Typology for Local Government," *Midwest Journal of Political Science,* May 1961, pp. 150–64.

[7] Sanders, *The Community,* p. 43.

not only makes decisions regarding substantive matters of various kinds, it also decides who shall be responsible for making these decisions. Ward boundary disputes, at-large vs. area-voting schemes, gerrymandering maneuvers, and the like are manifestations of this function in operation.

Social control is still another significant function of the political system, particularly of the governmental apparatus. In its broadest sense social control pertains to the maintenance of conformity in a system, and so understood it may be seen that a great number of groups and institutions play a part in this function—churches, schools, informal friendship cliques, the mass media, etc. A baseline of shared norms and behavioral regularity is necessary for any group or larger system to adhere as a social entity. Hence many parts of the system join in supporting conservative standards. The political system, however, contains within it unusual features of social control, because it has been granted the authority to utilize massive force.

> Such coercive power, or ultimate control, is the special characteristic of the state as opposed to other auspices which may perform parallel or identical functions. Thus, government, to use the more commonly employed term, possesses a control characteristic which differentiates it from other community-based units performing a control function: the power of ultimate coercion. The exercise of this power through the police and court systems is an important and exclusive control prerogative.[8]

A final function of the political system we shall enumerate here has to do with *conflict management.* Banfield and Wilson conceive of this as perhaps the major political function, deriving this view from their thesis that conflict is endemic in social life.

> Politics arises out of conflicts, and it consists of the activities—for example, reasonable discussion, impassioned oratory, balloting, and street fighting—by which conflict is carried on. In the foreground of a study of city politics, then, belong the issues in dispute, the cleavages which give rise to them and nourish them, the forces tending toward consensus, and the laws, institutions, habits and traditions which regulate conflict.[9]

[8] Warren, *Community in America,* p. 180.

[9] Edward C. Banfield and James Q. Wilson, *City Politics* (Cambridge, Massachusetts: Harvard University Press, 1965), p. 7.

Political behavior in this view consists of the means by which social disparities and conflicts are resolved. The outcome of this interaction eventuates in the policies and services referred to in the earlier listing of functions. The character and tone of such conflict resolution inheres in the political process.

The aforementioned display of functions should make plain the stake that community practice has in political affairs. This stake includes defining the types and quality of public services to be provided to citizens, including clients; how these should be delivered; who should pay. Broader policy issues may also be influenced, including structural aspects of the institutional character of the community and the trend of its general social and economic development. There are an opportunity and a challenge to affect the choice of people who will be represented in decision making, the criteria that will be used for the definition and exercise of power, the ways in which shifts of power will be effected. The practitioner should likewise be concerned about personnel and procedures governing coercive social-control mechanisms such as the police and the courts. Left unattended, such institutions are used, sometimes bluntly, sometimes surreptitiously, against the poor, the minorities, the disenfranchised, deviants, and even professionals. A final possibility for the practitioner is to improve the climate of conflict resolution in terms of such attributes as fairness, tone, and breadth of participation.

Many of these areas are terribly difficult and risky to enter into. But the benefits for human-service purposes may be proportionately large. Further, others with more limited, more personalistic perspectives do indeed find it possible to engage themselves in this area and to mold its products. A contemporary practitioner who fails to understand the implications for community practice of the political realm, and neglects to prepare himself with the requisite skills to make an impact there, is tying his own hands and may be shortchanging his clients or constituents.

There remains the task of outlining the components of the political system in order to lay the groundwork for the specific analysis that follows. We will explicate the structural framework of the political system in a way that allows us most expeditiously to organize the data we have gathered, and that is meaningful for the purposes of this book—i.e., highlighting the practice and policy implications of political-science knowledge. The following schematic representation of the political subsystem, then, parallels the structure of the chapter presentation.

One may conceive of the political system in terms of three main components: the body politic, key political actors who guide the process, and policy outputs and impacts.[10] The body politic comprising the basic constituency of politics is the human organism in which the system is embedded. The citizenry, particularly the voting public, may be seen as providing the input that energizes the political system. Next we postulate a series of key political actors, or elites, whose behavior is central in shaping political outputs—political party leaders, legislators, interest groups, and executive officers of political units. In systems terms these functionaries represent throughput; they manipulate the political process. Finally, we focus on the policy outputs and impacts, particularly policy decisions affecting areas of concern to human-service objectives (welfare, education, jobs, housing, mental health, etc.).[11] Three main contextual variables bearing on policy are considered: historical influences, socioeconomic influences and social-structural influences.

The rationale for the selection of these particular components and further elaboration of their content will be provided in the body of the text.

This overview has set the stage for the review of research on political behavior. The reader is advised to consult other portions of this book, which supplement this discussion: voting behavior is treated under Participation (chapter 8); political attitudes and behavior of professional practitioners is considered under Professional Roles (chapter

[10] For a significant discussion of political behavior in social-system terms see David Easton, "An Approach to the Analysis of Political Systems," *World Politics* 9 (April 1957): 383–400.

[11] The concept of policy outputs in political science can be found in Lewis A. Froman, Jr., "An Analysis of Public Policies in Cities," *Journal of Politics* 29 (February 1967): 94–108; Thomas R. Dye, "City-Suburban Social Distance and Public Policy," *Social Froces* 4 (1965): 100–106.

3); and social movement activity as well as client involvements of a political nature are also covered under Participation (chapter 8).

THE BODY POLITIC

The body politic is congruent with what is often referred to as the citizenry or the electorate. Here resides the repository of attitudes, values, interests, that become mobilized in specific political behavior patterns. Banfield and Wilson, taking note of the often dormant, intangible quality of the generalized political constituency, tag it with the label "Unseen Presence."

> Over almost every scene of political activity . . . there hovers an Unseen Presence. At intervals of two or four years it materializes for long enough to mark a ballot or pull the lever of a voting machine, thus deciding who is to be mayor, councilman, judge, and all the rest, and, often, whether a new school is to be built, the water supply fluoridated, or the fireman given a pay raise. At other times the Presence, although out of sight, is seldom out of mind. To the professional politicians who run the . . . government, the voter is the ultimate reality. To please him, or at least to avoid displeasing him, is the goal of much of their endeavors.[12]

The body politic, then, decides who should decide—through its selection of representatives who constitute the lawmaking instrumentality. It also makes direct decisions on taxation matters in some instances, and through referenda and special election procedures, on a variety of other selected issues that are publically acknowledged as significant for community life.[13]

The Body Politic is the first component of the political subsystem to

---

[12] Banfield and Wilson, *City Politics,* p. 224.

[13] While one of the most important functions of the body politic takes place at the ballot box, we will not deal in those specific terms in this discussion. A section of chapter 8 gives considerable attention to voting behavior. In addition, several excellent studies conducted by the Survey Research Center of the University of Michigan have explored voting patterns in considerable depth. See for example: A. Campbell, P. E. Converse, W. E. Miller, and D. E. Stokes, *The American Voter* (New York: Wiley, 1960); A. Campbell, G. Gurin, and W. E. Miller, *The Voter Decides* (Evanston, Ill.: Row, Peterson, 1954); A. Campbell, P. E. Converse, W. E. Miller and D. E. Stokes, *Elections and the Political Order* (New York: Wiley, 1966).

be examined. As the reader can see it is the most general area and will provide the broadest perspectives on political behavior.

Amorphous, Inchoate Nature of Public Attitudes

GENERALIZATION 6.1: Much of the American public's political thinking is ambivalent, cloudy, and inconsistent. Few citizens arrange their opinions in a coherent ideological framework; there is acceptance of much ideological inconsistency (+ + +, 16, 25, 33, 58, 60, 99).

6.1A. In the United States there is a decided absence of ideological cleavage along class lines (+ +, 33, 58).

Glenn and Alston (33) in a 1968 study compared responses to 113 selected questions from a total of twenty Gallup Polls, in an attempt to determine if there were "cultural differences" or "cleavage points" between classes. They found a pronounced lack of "cultural solidarity" within various occupational groups. For example, the average score of the "working class" was around 50 (scale = 100) reflecting the fact that about one-half of the respondents gave the "high status" response and about one-half gave the "low status" response. They conclude that there is no indication of "class crystallization" along ideological lines, and note that there is a definite lack of political consensus within single class groups. These findings are generally supportive of an earlier study by McClosky (58), who observed that "consensus is far from perfect, even among the articulate classes, and will be evidenced on political questions more than on economic ones, on procedural rights more than on public policy, and on freedom more than on equality" (p. 362). Both studies support the conclusion that there is lack of ideological consensus within individual social classes. Those ideological positions which do receive a significant endorsement by members of individual social classes are often inconsistent or mutually incompatible.

6.1B. The proportion of the electorate perceiving politics in ideological terms is to some extent a function of the prevailing political environment (+, 25).

Field and Anderson (25), in a study of voter perceptions in each of three consecutive Presidential elections (1956, 1960, 1964), observed that people's perceptions of political parties and of the candidates in ideological terms differed in each of the three samples. They hypothesized that the differences were due, at least in part, to changes in the external political environment rather than to changes in individual propensity to identify issues in ideological terms. Their study, based on Survey Research Center data, found that voters in general tend to be moderately conservative rather than liberal or radical. Voter choices tended to be more rationally based when the political environment could be characterized as moderately conservative, and more ideologically based when it could not.

6.1C. Americans appear to prefer consensus politics to conflict politics. They look with disfavor upon proposals for sharpening the ideological cleavage between the political parties (+ +, 16, 50, 86, 105).

Dennis (16), in a study assessing the degree of support of Wisconsin citizens for the political party system, found that only 31 percent of his sample population favored increased policy conflicts between parties, while 53 percent believed that governmental efficiency would be increased by *decreasing* interparty conflict. He concludes that the general public does not tend to approve of party competition and controversy. A majority of the public would oppose a shift to a system of ideologically oriented parties (like that of Great Britain). The portrait of American politics that emerges from the Dennis study depicts a tendency to rescue the underdog and a view of politics as an adult game, not a form of group warfare.

6.1D. Ideological conceptualizations of politics are more prevalent among the well-educated and among the politically active (+, 16, 86).

This represents a refinement of the conclusions advanced in several studies already cited. Dennis (16), however, injects an interesting qualification to be considered. If the results of his study are taken at face value, one is faced with a paradox. While all the studies cited demonstrate the well-educated to be more inclined toward ideological conceptualization than other social groups, Dennis has compiled study results that indicate they are *less* favorable than other groups toward the creation of politically responsible parties. The answer to this apparent discrepancy may lie in the strong correlation between higher educational attainment and upper-class socio-economic status. As they are in the minority, it can be seen to the advantage of upper-class groups to keep class-interest matters politically fuzzy.

Action Guidelines: In his dealings with the body politic, the practitioner should learn to expect inconsistency. He will be most successful if he himself can develop a tolerance for ambiguity. When dealing with those who are well educated and politically active he may seek to focus on specific issues, since such individuals are more apt to engage in analytic consideration of issues in terms of ideology. As regards the general public, the practitioner should be careful not to present issues in terms of political conflict and ideological cleavage, as the public by and large does not prefer ideological differentiations along class lines.

A general consideration pertaining to the immediately following series of generalizations will be entered here. Given the existing incoherent, inconsistent, political mentality of the body politic, a practitioner might view one of his important long-run goals to be that of political education. This would particularly involve raising the consciousness of lower-class populations with regard to their objective political and economic situation. Class-based analysis and action for such interest groups stem from this approach. The option for such intervention cuts across all the guidelines that follow.

Additionally, however, there are more short-run, pragmatic political objectives that rely on working within and capitalizing on the existing political environment. These human-service programmatic aims may occasionally be pursued in conjunction with the broader goals of political education; in other instances it would be counterproductive to promote both sets of ends overtly because of inherent strategic or ideological clashes that might be involved in such a posture.

In the following discussion we shall treat action guidelines in terms of pragmatic short-run implications that can be specifically derived from given propositions. This is based on the assumption that it will not be helpful to the reader to reiterate the overarching concept of long-term political education in each instance.

Subgroup Attitudes toward the Political System

GENERALIZATION 6.2: Faith in the American political system, characterized ideologically as "pluralism," varies substantially among different population subgroups (+ + +, 16, 28, 29, 58, 79, 80).

6.2A. Generally speaking, belief in a pluralist model of the political system is greater among politically active persons with high socioeconomic status or high levels of education (+ + +, 16, 28, 29, 58, 79, 80).

6.2B. Such persons are unlikely to support efforts directed at a more equitable distribution of power among the component groups of the society (+ +, 16, 29, 58, 79).

6.2C. Persons who are not politically active, with low socioeconomic status or low levels of education are more likely to invoke elitist or economic models as explanations for the political system (+ + +, 16, 28, 29, 58, 79, 80).

6.2D. Such persons are most likely to desire the attainment of pluralistic ideals (+ +, 16, 29, 58, 79).

6.2E. Ironically, it is not poor blacks but rather *middle-income* blacks in high proportion who are most likely to doubt the existence of equal opportunity (+ +, 28, 29, 79, 80).

Form, Rytina, and Peace (28, 29, 79, 80), investigating the relationship between ideology and a variety of independent variables among different subgroups of the population, have conducted a number of studies in a middle-sized Midwestern community. The Generalizations above represent a summary statement of their main conclusions, some of which are supported by additional studies. Form, et al. (28) observe that, by a variety of indicators, the rich show consistently higher levels of political participation and poor whites consistently lower levels than any other social strata. "The distribution of respondents re: how many elections they had voted followed the income-race hierarchy exactly" (p. 10). The authors also found (80) that lower-income people are more likely (despite lower levels of formal education) to perceive and attempt to deal with structural limitations to social mobility, while upper-income people are more likely to attribute differential social mobility to personal attributes than are the poor of both races or middle-income blacks. Dennis (16) in a study tracing the degree of support of Wisconsin citizens for the political party system, obtained corroborating data regarding the impact of differential education levels of diffuse support for the existing political system as contrasted with specific support for a more representative party structure. Dennis concluded that "this type of reform . . . is not very attractive to general opinion."

Action Guidelines: In interpreting present problems and defining program proposals to social groups, the practitioner should be alert to differential perceptions of the social system held by different social strata. Explanations of programmatic efforts that place strong reliance upon the assumption of a pluralistic political system are likely to be well received by persons of high socioeconomic status, but have less appeal to the middle or lower social strata. This latter audience is more responsive to explanations and arguments within the frame of reference of an elitist or economic model of the political system. However, since lower and middle socioeconomic groups both aspire to attain a system wherein the pluralistic model is the dominant mode, appeals to these groups might be most effective if one can point to ways the program will use the "present situation" to help attain this pluralistic ideal. Arguments aimed at high socioeconomic status groups will probably be better received if they do not attempt to "change" the system, but merely seek to "improve" the quality of services provided by a system that is already "ideal."

Fragmentation of Public Attitudes

GENERALIZATION 6.3: There is considerable division of opinion among the American public concerning fundamental democratic values. A uniform consensus in support of democracy cannot be said to exist (+ +, 58, 70, 86).

6.3A. The public exhibits much greater support for broad abstract statements of democratic beliefs than for specific applications of these very same beliefs (+ +, 58, 70, 86).

According to McClosky (58) 89 percent of those interviewed believe in "free speech for all no matter what their views might be," yet at the same time 50 percent favor censorship of books containing "wrong political views." Prothro and Grigg (70) reported over 95 percent of those polled agreed that "Democracy is the best form of government," "Public officials should be chosen by majority vote," "The minority should be free to criticize majority decisions," but also found that 79 percent would restrict voting to taxpayers, 51 percent would restrict voting to the well informed.

6.3B. Consensus is greater on the principle of freedom than on the principle of equality (+, 58).

Action Guidelines: As in the preceding instance, the primary significance of this proposition is its utility as a guide for the preparation of a policy position in defense of a proposed program or in opposition to an existing program. The subgeneralizations identify the specifics: a general appeal for public support which is presented as an appeal for support of widely held public norms evokes a strong positive response if presented in the abstract, however this response is eroded when the matter is considered in the light of specific issues. As an interesting refinement, it might be noted that public support for "democratic" programs seems most likely if they are both presented in abstract and couched in terms of freedom rather than equality. Individuals more central to the political subsystem appear to offer a more reliable source of support for "democratic" programs than does the public at large, and might serve as the best starting point for the promotion of such programs.

Support for Civil Liberties—Subgroup Variations

GENERALIZATION 6.4: Support for civil liberties varies substantially among different population subgroups (+ + + +, 2, 27, 33, 58, 62, 63, 83, 86, 104).

6.4A. Support for civil liberties is greater among the well-educated than among the poorly educated (+ + +, 2, 27, 58, 62, 86, 105).

In a 1965 study of the "Perceived Legitimacy of Social Protest Actions" Olsen (62) concluded that education, occupation, and income were directly correlated to tolerance for social protest. He viewed age and alienation as inversely correlated to this index of civil libertarianism. The alienation measures utilized in his study are attitudes of political incompatibility (the system is no good; this leads to powerlessness and meaninglessness) and political disenchantment (the system is not worth participating in; one could if he wanted, but to no avail). Under controlled multivariant analysis, the variable of education remained the strongest predictor of protest-action scores, but in a curvilinear fashion. The two political alienation scores were next strongest, followed by age.

6.4B. Support for civil liberties is greater among people with high-status occupations than among people with low-status occupations (+ +, 33, 58).

6.4C. Support for civil liberties is greater among people with high incomes than among people with low incomes (+ +, 27, 62).

A, B and C add up to: *support for civil liberties varies directly with socioeconomic status.*

6.4D. In general, young people exhibit greater support for civil liberties than older people (+ +, 27, 86).

6.4E. Support for civil liberties varies directly with political activity. Political influentials are considerably more libertarian than the general public (+ +, 58, 86, 104).

6.4F. People who are alienated tend to be extremely antilibertarian
(+ +, 62, 65).

Civil liberties are an independent dimension that cuts across the
left-right political spectrum. There is no direct connection between
general political conservatism and anti–civil libertarianism, nor can
attitudes toward civil liberties be predicted from attitudes regarding the
proper level of governmental activity in economic affairs. A prime
example of this is Senator Sam Ervin, who although generally conservative in his political outlook has been an outstanding spokesman for
and defender of civil liberties.

Action Guidelines: In building a "movement," the practitioner should be aware that allies and supporters for civil
liberties can be found in greater proportion among the
young, the well educated, and the politically active. These
variables are more important than position on the left-right
spectrum. People who are politically alienated do not, as a
general rule, support civil libertarian protests. However the
practitioner might be able to intervene to gain the support of
such persons and perhaps even their participation by increasing their sense of political involvement.

Partisan Identification and Social Class—Lack of Correlation

GENERALIZATION 6.5: Partisan division in the United States
is based on a variety of social characteristics. In general, social
class is not the only, or even the overriding, factor in the
determination of party affiliation and partisan attitudes (+ + +,
11, 36, 43, 60, 87, 102).

6.5A. Party affiliation is less strongly associated with social class in
this country than in Britain and West Germany (+, 43).
6.5B. The most powerful variables for explaining party preference
among Americans are region of upbringing, religion, and race.
Southerners, Catholics and Jews, and blacks tend to be Democratic;
northerners, Protestants, and whites tend to be Republican (+, 43,
87).
6.5C. Among workers, there is no apparent causal relationship be-

tween objective economic position and party choice. Workers who are affluent exhibit no greater tendency to vote Republican than their economically deprived colleagues. On the other hand, objective position does not appear to play a significant role in shaping workers' attitudes on domestic and economic issues (+, 36).

6.5D. Among physicians, political ideology is totally uncorrelated with socioeconomic background (parents' socioeconomic status), but is rather highly correlated with religious background. Jewish doctors are substantially more "liberal" than Protestant doctors, and Catholic doctors fall somewhere between (+, 11).

(The term "liberal" in this proposition connotates the identification made by Colombotos (11). It is based on a measurement system utilizing a Guttman scale of four items adopted from *The Authoritarian Personality* [Adorno], measuring levels of general acceptance of social change and of governmental responsibility for the solution of social and economic problems.)

6.5E. In certain sociopolitical contexts, ethnicity can be more important than social class as a determinant of voting behavior (+ +, 101,102).

Wolfinger (102) concluded, on the basis of a study of Italian bloc voting patterns in New Haven, that ethnic voting patterns can best be explained by his "mobilization theory." According to this theory "The strength of ethnic voting (either in support of a party or of a specific ethnic candidate) depends both on the *intensity of ethnic identification* and the *level of ethnic relevance* in the election . . ." (p. 905). He notes that the most powerful and visible ethnic identification is the presence of a fellow-ethnic's name on the ballot. He further notes that attainment of at least middle-class status is a general prerequisite for attaining a nomination in most localities, while a base of support among other middle-class ethnics is necessary for campaign funding purposes. Wolfinger concludes that such ethnic mobilization cannot take place until at least the second or third generations reach maturity, and may be delayed longer. However, shifts in party identification will result from a major ethnic candidacy when it does take place, and study findings indicate such shifts persist beyond the election in which they occur. The author speculates that the tendency toward abandonment of ethnic communities in favor of suburbia, which frequently accompanies attainment of middle-class status, probably reduces the salience of ethnic voting.

6.5F. Among both workers and businessmen, residence in a small town is associated with greater political conservatism (+, 36, 66).

Action Guidelines: The practitioner should avoid overreliance on social class or self-interest as predictors of political outcomes. The body politic is not generally likely to vote along lines of economic interest or social class nor can levels of political participation in specific issues be readily anticipated from such factors. Efforts to achieve mobilization of a favorable constituency, which are based on such predictors, are likely to prove disappointing. Rather one might base his mobilization efforts on such factors as region, religion, race, and ethnicity, as these appear to offer more reliable indicators of who will support or oppose a particular program. As previously stated, long-range efforts, especially by dissident parties, might at the same time emphasize programs that promote consciousness of class-related self interest.

Public Attitudes—Government vs. Politics

GENERALIZATION 6.6: In the mind of the public in the recent past there is apparently a separation between the concepts of "government" and "politics." The public generally has looked approvingly upon that which it perceives as "government" and suspiciously upon that which it perceives as "politics" (+ +, 16, 44, 47, 58, 76, 98).

Illustrative of the conceptualization process suggested by the generalization is Jennings, Cummings, and Kilpatrick's study (44) of the public's perception of appointed officials. The study, part of an extensive investigation of the public perception of the federal service, focuses on the attitudes of four sample groups toward federal appointees. The samples were drawn from four major national populations: general federal employees, the general employed public, high school juniors and seniors, and college seniors. The study found that federal employees are generally held in high regard. In all four sample groups there was little evidence of the ambivalence that frequently comes into play with regard to "politicians." The authors conclude that this is at least partially because appointees are not perceived as politicians.

While the data supporting this generalization have been impressive, it is also evident historically that these attitudes are subject to fluctuations depending on the prevailing political climate. It seems that the given attitudinal configuration held in the period of the early and middle 1960s, but that it was changing in the period that followed—in wake of the Vietnam controversy (including the Pentagon Papers revelations), the Watergate scandals, and the general credibility gap surrounding the Johnson and Nixon presidencies.

Warren Miller, in a study conducted by the Survey Research Center of The University of Michigan, found that "there has been a massive erosion in the trust the American people have in their government." [14] The Center has monitored public attitudes relative to "political cynicism" and "trust in government" on a regular basis since 1958. Their work reveals that these two indicators were relatively stable until 1966, after which they shifted toward the negative direction. In the 1964 national survey 62 percent of the public expressed a "high" level of trust in government; by 1970 that proportion had declined steadily to 35 percent. A study by the American Institute for Political Communication similarly concluded that many Americans "have come to distrust governmental words and actions as well as the media which convey information concerning such words and actions." [15]

Whether the attitudes indicated by the data from the original survey represent a normative base that will be reestablished when an immediate crisis in credibility has passed or whether the trend is toward the stabilization of a new, more cynical norm is impossible to determine. In view of these qualifications, the reader is advised to view this discussion in light of attitudes commonly shared by the body

[14] Reported in *Institute for Social Research Newsletter*, University of Michigan, Winter 1972, p. 5.

[15] *New York Times*, March 7, 1972, p. 38.

politic during the period prior to the mid-sixties but which appear to be less broadly shared at the present time.

6.6A. Generally speaking, the American public has had favorable attitudes toward government and government officials (+ + +, 44, 47, 58, 76, 98).

The strongest support for this proposition comes from a nationwide mail-return survey conducted by McClosky (58) in the late 1950s. A whopping 90 percent of the 1,484 respondents returned questionnaires that expressed agreement with the statement, "I usually have confidence that the government will do what is right" (p. 371). This is indicative of a broad reservoir of popular support for government policy and activity. Widespread and persistent agitation around a single issue or governmental abuse can apparently (at least temporarily) cut into this reservoir of good will.

6.6B. Appointed federal officials, especially cabinet officers, have enjoyed an especially high degree of public trust (+, 44).

6.6C. The public in the past has rarely been critical of government foreign policy (+ +, 47, 76, 98).

A study by Rogers, Stuhler, and Koenig (76) compared the foreign-policy attitudes of a sample of the general public with those of a panel of experts (chosen for their interest in and knowledge of world affairs). The data indicated a wide divergence of opinion between the two groups. By comparison with the experts, the public tended to be uninformed and was more likely to react in an emotion-laden, nonrational manner to foreign-policy issues. This was particularly true if the issues were perceived to involve "national honor," or "patriotism." In addition, members of the public were much less inclined to criticize American actions or to question the validity of official government policies. As an example of a specific disagreement, 73 percent of the panel of experts disapproved of "the way the United States has dealt with Fidel Castro and his government in Cuba," while only 28 percent of the public sample did so. An important subsidiary finding of the study was the absence of any significant difference in foreign-policy attitudes between the college-educated public and the non-college-educated public. The overall remoteness of the general public from information and experience in the foreign-affairs sphere may account for its generally uniform response.

6.6D. In contrast to a generally favorable attitude toward government, the public has had a rather cynical outlook regarding politics (+ +, 16, 44, 58).

A study by Dennis (16) of the public support (in Wisconsin) for the party system found predominantly favorable perceptions mixed with unfavorable ones. The bulk of the public favored retaining at least partial party organization of elections, and approved of citizen participation in campaign-related party activity. However, the general public did not greatly approve of party competition and controversy, and it did not regard party leaders as particularly reliable keepers of campaign promises.

These findings are supported by McClosky's (58) study of consensus among "political actives" vs. the general public regarding democratic values. McClosky compared data taken from a national study of political actives based on a sample group (3,000) of delegates and alternates to the 1956 Presidential conventions with data compiled by the Gallup Poll on a sample of 1,500 members of the general public. The questionnaires used consider personal background, values, attitudes, opinions, political and economic orientations, party outlooks, and personality characteristics. Single answers were analyzed and "scales" formed and validated. The study revealed that about one-half of the sample of the general public felt that *politics* is full of deception, expediency, and self-aggrandizement, but at the same time fully 89 percent of the sample group believed that the *government* will "do what is right."

Action Guidelines: These applications should be evaluated in relation to a shifting attitudinal climate. The studies indicate that the public may be amenable to being mobilized around particular issues perceived as "governmental," but highly volatile around issues perceived as "political." Generally, the body politic has appeared to accept the fact that governance is a specialized skill, to be exercised by technically competent administrators, and that public interference in this process should be limited to instances when "good government" has been disrupted by "politics." In recent years the public seems to have perceived an increase in such contamination.

Advocates of public-policy innovations may avoid some of the stigma attached to "political" issues by presenting their programs in a nonpartisan format. One alternative for achieving this image may be to enlist the high-level (nonelective) and prestigious bureaucrats as primary spokesmen for the proposal. General appeals to widely held norms of "good government" (e.g., freedom, democratic practices, legality) are probably the most effective means for mobilization of broad-based citizen response. The "legitimacy" of the appeal, and therefore the extent of public response, will probably be enhanced if the effort has the endorsement of key governmental, "nonpolitical," figures. Such persons will probably contribute most heavily to gaining public support if they can avoid the aura of "compromise," since this is viewed negatively as "political" by the public. It may be helpful to have appointed government officials show how desired actions may be viewed as "patriotic" or beneficial to our "national prestige," especially if foreign-policy matters are involved.

Parties as Reference Groups

GENERALIZATION 6.7: The American political parties exercise substantial reference group influence over those who vote or are active politically (+ +, 35, 74).

6.7A. Party identification is the major determinant of an individual's evaluation of a political figure. All Democratic aspirants to a particular political office are rated more favorably by Democratic voters than by Republican voters and vice versa. (Or, perhaps, to be more specific: before the national nominating conventions all Democratic aspirants to the Presidency are rated more favorably by Democrats than by Republicans, and vice versa [+, 74].)

6.7B. When a candidate receives the nomination of a particular political party, his rating among the followers of that party immediately improves, while his rating among the followers of the other party immediately worsens (+, 74).

Action Guidelines: One way of building partisan support among political actives for an individual or his programs might be to have him strongly (and publicly) identified with a particular political party. Party members will then tend to perceive both the individual and his programs more favorably.

Other Politically Relevant Reference Groups

GENERALIZATION 6.8: In addition to the political parties, a variety of other reference groups, both formal and informal, are instrumental in molding the political opinions held by the electorate (+ + + +, 24, 27, 36, 72, 74, 86, 93, 98). (See also chapter 7.)

6.8A. Friendship groups and voluntary associations play a key role in transmitting dominant community political attitudes to individual community residents (+ +, 36, 72).

Putnam (72) in a study investigating the transmission of political attitudes at the community (county) level found that "community influence is mediated primarily through numerous personal contacts among members of a community" (p. 641). In general, he found sensitivity to the community environment (dominant voting patterns) to be related to involvement in community associations. In addition Putnam found that active members of community associations were more likely to be sensitive to the dominant political values of the community (as evidenced by voting preferences) than inactive members. Also, respondents who claimed two or more memberships in associations were more likely to be sensitive than those who claimed membership in only one association. The study is based on an analysis of data obtained from the non-Southern respondents to the 1952 Survey Research Center national poll.

6.8B. Among workers, contact with labor unions results in increased political liberalism (+, 36).

6.8C. Segregationist attitudes gradually give way under the impact of strong social pressure in behalf of integration (+, 24).

6.8D. For many voters the "electorate as a whole" represents an important political reference group. Such voters readily alter their opinions to bring them into closer conformity with the expressed will of the majority (+ +, 74, 86).

Partisan polarization diminishes after an election; many voters claim falsely that they have voted for winners.

6.8E. In a highly controversial, emotional issue, such as the war in Vietnam, usual reference group processes may not be pertinent (+, 98).

Action Guidelines: Primary groups and labor unions may be two reference groups that can be employed to influence political opinions. Also, projecting one's view as that of the "electorate as a whole" (a bandwagon effect) can be a useful approach.

Where Partisanship and Social Class are Correlated

GENERALIZATION 6.9: Although social class may be of only limited value in explaining overall patterns of partisanship (see generalization 5), its effects in certain specific issues are present (+ + + +, 2, 27, 28, 29, 30, 33, 37, 58, 62, 79, 80, 86, 104).

6.9A. There is a strong relationship between socioeconomic status and support for civil liberties (+ + +, 2, 27, 33, 58, 62, 83, 104).

6.9B. There is a strong inverse relationship between socioeconomic status and support for government welfare activity. People of high status generally oppose government programs designed to improve the position of the poor (+ + +, 28, 29, 30, 79, 80).

6.9C. On matters of foreign policy, people of high status tend to be interventionist, while people of low status tend to be isolationist (+ +, 33, 35, 86).

Action Guidelines: The practitioner will probably meet with greater success if he seeks support for civil liberties and internationalist policies from high-income groups. Conversely, he will probably do best if he seeks support for welfare policies from low-income groups.

Psychological and Social Psychological Effects
on Political Attitudes

GENERALIZATION 6.10: Psychological and social psychological variables such as alienation, status inconsistency and upward mobility, can have important effects upon political attitudes (+ + + +, 32, 49, 51, 53, 55, 62, 63, 86, 94, 100; see chapter 8 for further discussion of these variables).

6.10A. People who score high on measures of alienation are characterized in aggregate by the following attitude set: support for certain domestic welfare programs such as social security, opposition to foreign aid, suspicion of international organizations (such as the UN), support for restrictions upon civil liberties, hostility toward representatives of the "establishment" (government agencies, big business, the media, etc.) (+ +, 49, 53, 62, 63, 67, 94).

High alienation in these studies embraced the following disparate groups: blacks, unskilled workers, poorly educated persons, persons with low incomes, males. Alienation was found to be more prevalent among persons who express no party preference; with those who do identify with a Party, alienation is more common among Democrats than among Republicans.

Certain aspects of alienation seem to be related to what may be termed populism. That is to say, a number of the characteristics of the alienated cited above are similar to those who supported the Wallace candidacy.

6.10B. Status inconsistency is associated with support for extremist political movements (+ +, 5, 78, 100).

Left- and right-wing extremism seems to be more prevalent among individuals characterized by status inconsistency than among those characterized by consistency. The assumption is that status inconsistency produces psychological stress, which in turn leads to support for political parties advocating *change,* but the change may be of either reactionary or progressive type. There is some indication that the combination of high income plus low education tends to produce right-wing extremism, while that of low income plus high education usually results in left-wing extremism. However, the effects of status inconsistency are in some dispute. Sears (86), for example, believes status inconsistency is largely irrelevant.

Westby and Braungart (100) suggest alternative variables, which are also demonstrated to be associated with political extremism. The authors studied political extremism among each of three sample populations: members of SENSE, a student peace group; members of the Young Americans for Freedom, a rightist student group; and students in an introductory sociology class. The authors found the class and party of the students' families to be significant factors in the prediction of political extremism, and they noted that political extremists of the right share a common bond: they are generally members of groups whose status is threatened by the upward thrust of new minorities. The tendency toward rightist extremism is therefore more typical of lower-middle and working class members. Leftist extremists in the student population tended to be of high status and to have liberal-leaning family political orientations. Thus, Westby and Braungart view student extremists as simply expressing ideological positions which are, in the main, consistent with those of their families.

6.10C. Upward mobility frequently leads either to ultraconservatism or to left-wing radicalism. The former outcome is likely when little or no discrimination is experienced during the upward transition; the latter is likely when substantial discrimination is encountered (+, 55, 80, 86, 93).

6.10D. Relative deprivation creates support for radical political views (+ +, 32, 34).

6.10E. People with "undercontrolled" personality types are higher in political efficacy than people with "overcontrolled" personality types. Moreover, among whites, undercontrol is positively correlated with both general political liberalism and support for civil rights legislation. Among blacks, on the other hand, control type has essentially no impact on ideological orientation: virtually all blacks, the overcontrolled as well as the undercontrolled, are politically liberal and in favor of civil rights legislation (+, 81).

6.10F. People who participate in extremist political movements (partisans of the radical right) do not necessarily demonstrate a tendency to be psychologically disturbed or frustrated in their personal relationships (+, 82, 83).

Action Guidelines: Support for change-oriented political movements can be found among the alienated, the status inconsistent, the status threatened, the upwardly mobile, and those with a greater sense of relative deprivation. Organizers should be alert to the differential expectations of each of these groups; thus the basis for involvement will vary.

GENERALIZATION 6.11: Voters may be more attracted by the "image" they associate with a party than by the party label (+, 26, 57).

In a comprehensive attitude survey Mathews and Prothro (57) interviewed a sample population of 618 black and 694 white southerners. One of the study's findings was that "party image appears to have an effect on voting over and above that of party identification." General propensities to vote for or against candidates of a particular party were largely dependent on the images the voters had attached to the party label. Among the more important components of the party imagery then prevalent were the views that Democrats were better for workers and were liberals (especially regarding race, foreign policy, and social welfare) and that Republicans favored big business, were conservative, and had "objectionable" leadership.

6.11A. Voter support for national political parties is, in part, a function of the degree to which the local party reflects, in personal characteristics of leaders, the national party composition (+, 26).

Flinn (26), in a study of party loyalty in Ohio, looked at voting records of the Ohio House for the 1959 and 1963 sessions. He compared the legislative record of individual representatives to "official" party positions, and attempted to identify significant variables influencing voter reactions to the legislative records so compiled. He determined that support for political parties among local party members is directly related to the amount of similarity between local and national party members, in terms of personal characteristics. Additionally, he found that party members from districts differing in socioeconomic characteristics from the "typical" party district are less likely to support the party position on issues.

Action Guidelines: Since voting behavior frequently appears to result from a contrast by voters of the candidates against the background of their party's image, it may be possible for a particular candidate to win the support of opposition-party voters by stressing the ways he conforms to the image and characteristics popularized by the opposition party. This tactic might be most effective if it can be shown that the opposition candidate exhibits deviations from this popular image. In supporting a particular nominee in primaries, it could be useful to stress the candidate's similarity to national party images and personal characteristics.

BEHAVIOR OF KEY POLITICAL ACTORS

As we move from the body politic seen as a conglomerate whence general political legitimation emanates, we may single out four key types of specialized political actors as central to specific political processes, decisions, and actions. The importance of the key actors that we shall describe emerges from both our understanding of what makes the political system tick and the data that became available to us in our pool of research studies.

PARTY LEADERS: These are officials and functionaries, particularly of the two major parties. They fire the political machinery and are the managers and manipulators of its everyday, routine operations; they keep grass-roots structures intact between major electoral events. These party functionaries, within the limitations of a rather inchoate political culture, sharpen issues and promote particular interests, paving the way for further refinement and formal enactment at the legislative level.

LEGISLATORS: These are the official decision makers. In the American system, many of their prerogatives are shared in a fluid way with the executive branch and may be overruled by the judiciary. As stated above, the party machinery also affects legislative decisions.

INTEREST GROUPS of a great variety of types (ranging from the League of Women Voters to the Chamber of Commerce to the Council of Churches) influence legislative behavior. As noted by Tocqueville and other observers, in the pluralistic American political system there is much viability for activity by interest groups. Lobbying, buttonholing, letter writing, demonstration, are all techniques typically employed by such pressure groups. These groups aim their efforts also at the executive officer, as well as the various departments of government.

EXECUTIVE OFFICERS—mayors (or city managers) governors, the President—share political functions with legislators. Hypothetically the executive officer has the delimited responsibility of carrying out policies that are promulgated by the legislators. In practice the interaction is more complex and subtle. Much potential power lies in the hands of the executive in terms of motivating or prodding legislators to bring into being given policies, and he retains a reservoir of discretion through which he may create policies by interpretation of legislative bills, the use of executive orders and special powers, and the development and control of the departmental machinery of government—all of which may be interlarded with patronage considerations.

The listing does not pretend to cover all actors or even all among these of major importance. Business interests and economic institutions have been excluded, as have labor unions—although these may at times act as interest groups.

Likewise the press is not treated separately, although it may be viewed as embedded in the body politic, playing a singular role in promoting politically relevant attitudes and values, as well as generating specific voting responses. Courts are also not included.

The political actors described above will be discussed in the order in which they have been presented. A short final section will deal with structural factors that more generally affect behavior of political actors, without reference to the specific subcategories.

Party Leaders

Characteristics of Party Leaders and of Their Constituencies

GENERALIZATION 6.12: In terms of ethnic, religious, and socioeconomic background, party leaders generally mirror the communities from which they come (+ +, 3, 12, 17, 92).

Althop and Patterson (3) studied political activism in a rural county in downstate Illinois and found a very strong likelihood that precinct committeemen will be recruited from the locally predominant ethnoreligious group. Conway and Feigert (12) compared party leaders in a rural county with those in an affluent suburban county and discovered that the latter were much more likely to be businessmen, professionals, or housewives.

6.12A. Party leaders tend to have above-average socioeconomic status (+, 5).

Although, on the one hand, the socioeconomic status of party leaders varies directly with the socioeconomic status of their constituencies, it is also true that party leaders taken as a whole are from a higher socioeconomic status than the general population. Apparently, in each particular community the party leaders are recruited from among the upper strata *of that particular community*. As a result, party leaders, while typical in most ways, are above average in socioeconomic status.

6.12B. Within a given community there is little difference in socioeconomic status between the Republican and Democratic party leadership; it is accordingly inappropriate to attribute interparty differences to this factor (+, 3, 27).

6.12C. Within a given community, the leaders of the minority party tend to be younger than the leaders of the majority party (+, 12, 92).

Action Guidelines: The practitioner might choose to intervene in party politics by supporting an alternative party leader. The prospects for success in the effort will be greatly enhanced if the prospective new leader is a person who, although possessing above-average socioeconomic status, is in other respects very similar to the populace. Younger (or atypical) candidates can be more successfully promoted in minority parties.

Background Attributes of Party Leaders

GENERALIZATION 6.13: Party officials tend to possess certain background characteristics and certain attitudes that are conducive to the assumption of leadership roles (+, 5, 58).

6.13A. Involvement in party politics is associated with a high degree of political activity in the childhood home (+, 5).

Bowman and Boynton (5) found that local party officials tended to grow up in families where at least one member was politically active.

6.13B. A large percentage of local party officials have primary occupations that provide politically relevant experiences, involving broker and legal skills (+, 5).

Bowman and Boynton (5) report that 11 percent of their sample of local party officials were lawyers while another 44 percent were "brokers" of some sort. "Brokerage occupations," as described by the authors, are those which tend to develop political skills as a latent function (e.g., insurance salesman, union official). Similarly, the authors hypothesize that some occupations yield legal skills as a side benefit. For example some types of clerical and accounting positions impart specialized legal knowledge and expertise. The authors suggest that three factors critical to success as a candidate are sense of political efficacy, partisan commitment, and the belief that one has a duty to participate in politics. They conclude that occupations which inculcate these attitudes, and which develop needed skills, are logical sources for political candidates.

6.13C. Party actives exhibit a stronger sense of political efficacy, of partisan commitment, and of citizen duty than do members of the general public (+ +, 5, 58).

Action Guidelines: In seeking particular new political leaders, the practitioner might do well to look in the broker and legal professions. Alternatively, he might seek to inculcate broker and legal skills in potential new candidates, especially from minority or poor communities. Good recruits might also be found among people who have had a politically active family or who exhibit traits of political efficacy, partisan commitment, or civic duty.

Motivations of Party Leaders

GENERALIZATION 6.14: Local political leaders are sustained in their political activity by pragmatic motivations of self-interest, although they may be initially motivated by altruism and ideology (+ + +, 3, 6, 12, 92).

> 6.14A. The desire to achieve personally beneficial material and social rewards is the most common motivation for continued involvement in local party politics (+ +, 3, 12, 92).
>
> Conway and Fiegert (12) compared the motivations of local political leaders in two contrasting political units: rural Knox County, Illinois, and suburban Montgomery County, Maryland. They found that the local party leaders they surveyed achieved their greatest rewards in terms of social and business contacts, incidental to the performance of their role. Snowniss (92) in an exploratory study of political recruitment in urban Chicago produced similar results, and also noted a difference in party stability between districts where the party had firm control of the patronage "pork barrel" and districts exhibiting uncertain control over patronage resources. Snowniss found that high patronage districts were characterized by strong party organizations with low worker turnover and strongly materialistic incentives for the maintenance of party loyalty. In low patronage districts there were less stable party organizations, higher worker turnover, and greater emphasis on nonmaterial benefits as rewards for party loyalty. The author suggests that lack of control over a district's patronage and the correlative condition—high worker turnover in the local party structure—are jointly associated with a greater concern for ideology and issues. This appears to support Subgeneralization 6.14D, below.

6.14B. Local leaders often seek political party leadership in hope of later parlaying the position into a public (appointive or elective) office (+, 3, 12).

Althop and Patterson (3) in a study of precinct committeemen in a downstate Illinois County found more than one-half of their respondents claiming to have sought precinct office primarily in hope of using the position as a stepping-stone to public office. It is interesting to note that most of those who sought to parlay their party position in this manner were successful. (This suggests that a good strategy for attaining public office—appointive or elective—is to be a party official first.)

6.14C. Programmatic and ideological concerns are generally insufficient to sustain long-term political-party activity (+, 6, 12).

Conway and Fiegert (12) conclude from their study that programmatic, ideological appeals are a major basis for inducing initial entry into political activity, but that these impersonal appeals do not sustain activists in their performance of party precinct roles. Bowman and Boynton (6) illustrate this observation with their finding that less than 10 percent of the party officials they interviewed were concerned with ideology or policy formation.

6.14D. Programmatic and ideological appeals often provide a motivation for initial entry into local party politics, particularly in high SES communities (+, 12).

Conway and Fiegert (12) in a study comparing rural to suburban political activists found that in low-SES communities party recruits are likely to be paid professionals, oriented toward material rewards or a career in politics, while in high-SES communities party recruits tend toward an amateur model. "Amateur" workers are frequently volunteers and are generally motivated by nonmaterial, issue- or ideology-based concerns.

6.14E. The generalized desire to help one's party may be a factor motivating individuals to seek initial entry into local politics (+, 3).

Althop and Patterson (3) found about one-third of their sample of precinct delegates gave partisan reasons for seeking party office.

The discussion embodied in this proposition is consistent with and to some extent explanatory of Generalization 6.1, which indicates a general state of ideological amorphousness in the body politic. The structure of the party system apparently encourages such ideological vagueness, or at least does not counteract it.

Action Guidelines: Newcomers or "amateurs" involved in local party politics will likely be more responsive than party regulars to ideology- or issue-based appeals. Local party leaders will generally be most responsive to more pragmatic appeals. They may, however, be responsive to endeavors that promise to enhance their public image, since many hold personal political ambitions. For the same reason it may be possible to cultivate key local leaders by generating favorable publicity on their behalf every time they become marginally involved with an activity you sponsor. If the individual politico perceives a particular interest group to be a source of favorable publicity he will be more likely to support it; if the general public identifies him as a part of that group he may be obliged to support it. One way the practitioner might move people with a particular value or program orientation toward elective office would be to secure a local party position for them as an initial step.

Recruitment to Party Leadership

GENERALIZATION 6.15: Local party officials perceive recruitment to be a rather closed process in which the parties themselves function as the primary recruiting agents (+, 3, 27).

Bowman and Boynton (5) asked a sample of local party officials how they first decided to run for party office and found that 60 percent had been urged to do so by the party, 11 percent had been urged by other groups (e.g., labor unions), and 29 percent were "self-recruited." Althop and Patterson (3) report very similar results.

A word of caution: This generalization is valid only to the extent that party officials can be expected to give reasonably accurate and unbiased accounts of their own entry into party politics. Officials may view self-entry as self-seeking or aggressive and therefore deemphasize it, while they may view being sought after as more commendable and thus overemphasize it.

6.15A. Self-recruitment is more common among officials of the minority party than among officials of the majority party (+, 5).

Action Guidelines: To increase recruitment of minorities or other desired individuals into local political parties, one would do well to concentrate one's efforts on finding sympathetic party members to sponsor this endeavor from within the party organization. The chances of success in such efforts would appear to be slightly higher for the minority party than for the majority party, since recruitment into the minority party seems to be less rigidly controlled.

Role Conception of Party Officials

GENERALIZATION 6.16: Local party officials conceive of their jobs primarily in terms of campaign-related activities, particularly those tasks involving building and maintaining an organization base for campaigns (+ +, 3, 6).

In Bowman and Boynton's study (6) of grass-roots party officials in Massachusetts and North Carolina, fully 60 percent of the 138 party leaders interviewed described their jobs in terms of voter mobilization, while nearly 70 percent named a campaign-related task as their single most important responsibility. By contrast, only 1.1 percent described their jobs as having to do with policy formation and only 3.4 percent with recruiting candidates for local office.

6.16A. Local party officials consider ideology and party nominations to be relatively unimportant details (+ +, 3, 6).
6.16B. Minority parties stress building an organization while, appropriately, the majority party is more concerned with maintenance of an existing organization (+, 3).

Althop and Patterson (3), in a study of a downstate Illinois county, conclude: "Organization-oriented activities are more emphasized by majority party leaders, while minority party leaders tended to stress campaign-oriented activities and high involvement in candidate recruitment'' (p. 50).

Action Guidelines: It is generally unproductive to work through local party leaders for help in effecting policy changes or for endorsement of ideological positions. They are only marginally concerned with such matters. Perhaps the best strategy is to make use of them and their organizational bases to promote desirable candidates with appropriate ideological views. If one wishes to penetrate the organization it would be most useful to develop some expertise or expend energy in the areas of campaign management or organizational maintenance, since these are highly valued activities within both the majority and the minority parties.

Ideological Orientation of Party Leaders

GENERALIZATION 6.17: Despite their relative lack of concern for ideological tasks, party leaders are not "issue neutrals." On the contrary, they are highly partisan *organizationally,* that is, loyal to the stands on the issues of their party (+, 27).

Flinn (27) in a study of party leadership in Ohio counties interviewed chairmen and secretaries of the county central and executive committees of the Ohio Democratic and Republican parties, who were elected in 1958 or 1960. The study found that, ''In general, there is a consistent point of view *on national and state issues* within each party which is shared by most of their members and which contrasts with that of the opposing party. . . . In other words, *party leaders are not 'issue neutrals'* '' (p. 95). Evidently party leaders are ideological in an organizational rather than in a personalistic sense.

Action Guidelines: In attempting to influence party officials about given programs or legislative actions, it would be well to emphasize the ideological positions of the party organization. This is made feasible by the often broad platforms or position statements fashioned by the two major parties in their effort to "be all things to all people" within a rather ideologically amorphous American political environment. When organizational ideology coincides with personal ideology, it would seem appropriate to capitalize on this convergence.

Legislators

Legislative Behavior and Party Affiliation

GENERALIZATION 6.18: Party affiliation is associated with particular types of legislative voting behavior—relative to issue categories, responsiveness to interest groups, and attitude toward governmental intervention (+ +, 9, 27, 95).

6.18A. Overall, legislators are more likely to vote along party lines in matters of economic policy than in matters of social welfare. In the latter case, the legislators' constituencies are the key (+ +, 9, 27).

Clausen (9) reviewed the roll call votes of the U.S. House of Representatives for the four Congresses of the Eisenhower Administration, and found party affiliation to be the strongest variable affecting voting behavior relative to economic policy decisions. By contrast, in decisions he defined as welfare policy the most significant variable was the composition of the constituency of the individual legislator. In Clausen's study the distinctions between the two policies related to their impact. If the immediate and direct impact of a proposed policy accrued to the general public it was termed welfare policy, if it accrued to the business community it was defined as economic policy. (The author does not account for the treatment of ambiguities inherent in these definitions.)

An additional finding of interest in this study was the fact that legislative support for "social welfare policy" is strongly correlated with an urbanized and industrialized constituency base. This finding, however, could ultimately point back to party affiliation as a

critical variable, since this type of community is frequently associated with the Democratic party.

6.18B. Democratic legislators are more likely than Republican
legislators to favor government intervention as a problem-solving
option (+ +, 9 27).

Flinn and Wirt (27), in a 1965 survey, described the attitudes of
Ohio county party leaders on issues of public policy. Among their
findings was a rather sharp division along party lines as to the desirability of increased governmental action. Democrats were found to
favor relatively more governmental intervention than Republicans.
The difference was found to be slightly greater with regard to national government than to state government (with the greatest difference coming in the areas of slum clearance and public housing,
federal aid to education, and Social Security benefits).

6.18C. There is a definite tendency for Democratic legislators to be
more favorable in their attitudes toward union-related interest
groups and for Republican legislators to be more favorable in their
attitudes toward business-related interest groups (+, 95).

Teune (95) interviewed all the legislative candidates for and hold-
over senators of the 1961 Indiana General Assembly. This study, in
keeping with generally accepted impressions, found that Democrats
were more favorable toward labor unions and Republicans more favorable toward business organizations. As a sidelight, legislators of
both major parties rated about equal in terms of their predispositions
toward lobbying in general.

Action Guidelines: In gaining support for economic policies
it is advisable to stress modes of influence that involve the
party structure. On broader "welfare" policies, their constituencies would appear to be the vehicle of choice for reaching
legislators. In keeping with popular views on the subject,
Democrats are natural allies for programs necessitating government intervention and tend to be favorable to labor unions. Working through Democratic legislators, or assisting in
their election, would appear to be a useful strategy for furthering many human-service objectives.

Constituents' Opinion and Voting Behavior

GENERALIZATION 6.19: The perceived opinion of constituents appears to be one of the most significant factors affecting the voting behavior of legislators (+ + +, 4, 10, 26, 68).

6.19A. Legislators are more likely to vote in agreement with what they perceive as their constituents' attitudes than on the basis of personal preference (+, 10).

Cnudde and McCrone (10) in a 1966 study confirm the findings of an earlier study by Miller and Stokes,[16] that congressional voting behavior is strongly determined by what are perceived as constituents' attitudes. From their statistical analaysis of the data collected earlier by Miller and Stokes, Cnudde and McCrone conclude that nearly 60 percent of the relationship between constituency and roll call voting behavior is correlated with perceptions of constituency attitude, while less than 13 percent is attributable to the individual legislators' strongly held personal attitudes. The authors suggest that the overwhelming weight given to the constituents' opinion may reflect a general concern for job security among legislators.

6.19B. Legislators whose home districts exhibit weak support for the party are less subject to party discipline, and more sensitive to the constituents' sentiments (+, 26).

Flinn (26) examined 113 roll call votes in the 1959 Ohio House of Representatives that displayed clear evidence of party cleavage, and 50 roll call votes from the 1963 Ohio House exhibiting this same characteristic. He notes that "electoral margin seems to have little to do with loyalty to the party, except that the least secure members of the legislature, i.e., the members of the winning party with the lowest pluralities are less loyal to the party than are other members" (pp. 70–71).

This, too, may be attributable to job-security concerns. The legislator who wins a decisive victory has every reason to believe that his party is in firm control of his voting district and that his future is secure. Partisanship is a form of "career insurance" in this situa-

[16] W. E. Miller and D. E. Stokes, "Constituency Influence in Congress," in *Elections and the Political Order* by A. Campbell et al. (New York, Wiley: 1966), pp. 351–72.

tion. The legislator who wins his seat in a close race, however, may easily perceive his constituency in more bipartisan terms, as a small shift in the constituency in one direction or another might spell his electoral defeat. Or he may feel that his reelection prospects will be enhanced if he can fashion a broader constituency before the next election. In either event the legislator will probably be less likely to support partisan positions.

6.19C. The greater the intensity of division of constituency opinion surrounding an issue, the greater the tendency for legislators to adhere to "official" party positions (+ +, 4, 10).

Anderson (4) studied the relationship between the intensity of controversy surrounding an issue and the dimensional consistency (party loyalty) evidenced in legislative voting. His findings were consistent with the hypothesis that unidimensional consistency is affected by the intensity of controversy surrounding an issue. Scalarity increased as the intensity of controversy increased. This finding is generally compatible with the notion of legislative sensitivity to constituency pressures, and would appear to explain what happens when a legislator confronts a sharply divided constituency. If the constituents' opinions are unclear, he is likely to turn to the next most important reference group and vote his party.

6.19D. Bureaucratic features of legislative structures may preempt or distort legislators' perceptions of their constituents' interests (+, 68).

Polsby (68) reports, in a largely historical study, that government generally is becoming more institutionalized. According to Polsby, the U.S. House of Representatives is a highly complex organization with internal functional specializations (division of labor) on a regular and explicit basis. That is to say, the functions generally serve internal (organizational) as opposed to external (voter-oriented) needs. Polsby suggests that this focus on internal operations (institutionalization) tends to preempt or distort legislators' perceptions of external demands (goal displacement).

There is an indication of task-oriented logic in such legislative behavior. It appears likely that a task-conscious legislator would be sensitive to his immediate working environment. Some writers suggest that bureaucracies breed their own special realities in response to functional needs.[17] In any case, the Polsby article documents a historical trend toward less sensitivity to externally generated issues. Whether or not they are perceived to be issues is not considered as an empirical question. Polsby's observations are particularly relevant to those discussed in Subgeneralization 6.19 A, which indicate that a legislator will readjust his perceptions to those of his constituency if he senses a difference. Polsby has attempted to isolate a key factor which is operative in shaping such perceptions.

6.19E. On some issues a legislator sometimes disregards his constituents and votes independently (+, 10).

In the Cnudde and McCrone (10) study the authors document the view that a legislator's perception of the attitudes held by his constituency tends to shape his own attitudes. The authors specifically note that this situation violates psychological theories which predict that attitudes will shape perceptions. The authors suggest this anomaly might be accounted for by the critical importance of accurate perceptions of constituents' attitudes in the electoral process. They theorize that legislators are, of necessity, ultrasensitive to such attitudes.

As stated earlier, the authors found that in more than 60 percent of the cases studied legislators' votes were in agreement with their perception of constituents' attitudes, while in only 13 percent of these cases was the vote also reflective of personal attitudes. Of particular significance is the remaining 27 percent of the votes studied. In these cases the vote is not explained by a response to perceived attitudes, and must be attributable to other factors.

A number of explanations are possible. Perhaps this 27 percent concerns issues about which the legislator has unshakable convictions and he defies his constituency to vote his own preference on such matters. Alternatively (and more likely), these issues concern matters of relatively minor interest to his constituency and he feels free to support special interest groups or his personal beliefs on such issues. Again, these may be party-relevant issues which require that he prove his loyalty to the party by disregarding constituent pres-

[17] See, for example, John K. Galbraith, *How to Control the Military* (Garden City, N.Y.: Doubleday, 1969).

sures. In the absence of additional data we can but note the fact that in one-fourth of the votes studied, for whatever the reason, legislators (who according to Cnudde and McCrone do not generally alter their perceptions of constituent attitudes to fit personal belief patterns) proved capable of ignoring constituency attitudes and voting on some other basis.

6.19F. Legislators verbalize personal judgment and adherence to personal values as the most appropriate basis for communal decision making (+, 105).

Zisk, Eulaw, and Prewitt (105) observed that about three-fourths of the councilmen in their sample group state they are either indifferent to or antagonistic toward the efforts of organized interest groups to influence their voting behavior. Neither the "tolerants" nor the "antagonists" (who differed little in terms of their objective behavior) considered group claims as essential, or even desirable to the political process. It would appear that fully 75 percent of the councilmen surveyed claim to ignore the potential role (as advisors and allies) which groups might play, and state that instead they determine policy in the "privacy" of their own consciences.

The survey data reported here entail the verbal (as opposed to behavioral) expression of legislator response. The frequency with which such verbal attitudes are translated into actual behavior is not revealed by the study. However, inasmuch as the direction of the study runs counter to the general trend of other studies when behavior itself is the subject of examination, one might assume that the two are different.

Why this discrepancy? It may be that legislators think of it as more honorable to vote independently, and therefore wish to convey such a more lofty view to outside interviewers. Perhaps they wish to shield the "dirty" aspects of politics from public view, conveying instead a junior-high-school-civics ethos. Again, they themselves may not be fully conscious of the degree to which their behavior is dictated by practical political exigencies.

Action Guidelines: A key factor in successful lobbying is to convince the legislator that your opinion is widely held by his constituents. In cases where this is not true an alternative strategy might include organizing to create a broad-based constituency movement. But if the issue generates controversy, and the legislator perceives a split among his constituents, he is likely to retreat to the safety of an "official" party position on the issue. In cases where his adherence to the official party line would serve your ends, you may find it useful to induce controversy, develop competing views, and promote them among conflicting factions. In cases where you seek a departure from the party line, however, consensus policies are generally more productive. If possible, when using public pressure tactics, focus your efforts on "insecure" politicians (i.e., politicians who were elected by narrow margins) since they are both more sensitive to constituency pressures and less bound by party loyalty. Attempt to identify ways your "message" may be distorted as it is perceived by the legislator (such as by bureaucratic processes within legislative bodies), and correct for this. This means you should develop some feedback mechanism to assess the response of the legislator to your efforts. Alternatively, if access or potential is greater there it is possible to work through the bureaucratic machinery of committee structure.

In terms of a personal approach to legislators, one should keep in mind that lawmakers like to think of themselves as voting independently and on the basis of principle. When you yourself have no viable political leverage or when there do not exist strong constituency counterpressures, an approach using persuasion may be effective. This may be based on the principles involved in your policy position, and on an appeal to the legislator to "come to his own conclusions," taking into account the principles and facts you have laid before him.

Interest-Group–Legislator Interaction

Predisposition toward Interest Groups

GENERALIZATION 6.20: Legislators have varying attitudes and responses to interest groups. One can infer the predisposition of a legislator toward interest groups based on attributes of the legislator or characteristics of the interest group (+ + + +, 48, 65, 95, 105).

6.20A. The more a legislator experiences interaction with interest groups the more likely he is to respond positively to interest-group situations (+, 95).

Teune (95) provides the basis for this somewhat circular assertion in his 1967 study of attitudes toward interest groups among Indiana legislators. Among his findings is the observation that "the legislative candidate who is favorably disposed toward interest groups and their functions has most probably had substantial contact with a variety of groups in his constituency" (p. 503). In terms of action implications this statement is handicapped by the tautology it implies (i.e., positive attitudes yield more interactions yield more positive attitudes, and so on). However, it does suggest a possible index for identification of which legislators are more likely to be favorable toward interest groups at a given time. In more general terms, Teune indicates that the legislators' receptiveness to interest groups is associated with a heterogeneous constituency, where there is a higher rate of ongoing interest-group activity.

6.20B. Legislators who are more secure in their personal and political lives tend to be more responsive to interest groups (+, 95).

Teune (95) initially set out to test a hypothesis which suggested a positive relationship between insecurity in office and receptivity to interest-group concerns. He found, instead, evidence to support a counterhypothesis: security is positively correlated with favorable attitudes toward interest groups. A large percentage of his sample not only failed to exhibit the predicted correlation, but in fact demonstrated a reverse relationship. Comparing these results with those of Flinn (26) summarized in Generalization 6.19B one gains some insight into the predispositional attitudes of the two extremes of the legislative security continuum (but little as to the nature of the middle range). It appears that legislators who are least secure operate largely on a minimization-of-risk philosophy. They are more sensitive to their constituency, more willing than others to sacrifice party discipline for the interests of their constituents, but less open to direct interaction with special-interest groups. It would appear they fear unknown repercussions among their constituents more than they desire alliances with available interest groups. In contrast, the most secure legislators are both more loyal to the party and more open to interest-group lobbying. It appears these legislators are less concerned with risk taking, provided the risk offers a reasonable potential benefit. These are tentative assumptions based on some small measure of evidence. Both political parties and interest groups offer significant long-term rewards to their legislative supporters, but a critical factor in reaping such rewards is the ability to get reelected: it is not unreasonable to suppose then that insecure legislators are more likely to minimize these career risks.

6.20C. A legislator's predisposition toward an interest group is strongly influenced by his perception of the individual interest group in terms of its numerical size, geographic distribution, and organization—particularly within his immediate constituencies (+ +, 23, 84, 95, 105).

Studies by Fenno and by Scott and Hunt agree that the geographic distribution, size, and intensity of interest are factors in the success of interest groups in achieving legislative goals. Teune (95) observes that "interest group activity in the constituency stands out as the most important set of variables for explaining attitudes toward interest groups" and concludes that legislators are considerably more sensitive to interest-group activities that take place among their constituencies than they are to lobbying that takes place "in the legislative halls, hotel rooms, and in committee hearings" (p. 504).

6.20D. A legislator is more likely to be receptive to an interest group if the issue involved is of specialized rather than general interest to him (+, 84).

Scott and Hunt report greater involvement by congressmen with interest groups on specialized issues than on peripheral issues. In the Scott and Hunt study an issue was "specialized" if it fell within the jurisdiction of one of the committees of which the congressman was a member. Of the total sample of 34 congressmen, only 22 reported any contact with groups on peripheral issues; 30 did so with regard to their special interests.

6.20E. In their dealings with interest groups, some legislators (at the federal level) are generally more concerned with the "interest" being promoted than with the specific organized groups doing the promoting (+ +, 23, 65, 84).

The studies listed find that for congressmen the "interest" is of much more concern than is the specific organized group. One of these studies states that "congressmen could remember relatively few specific interest groups, but thought in terms of broader interests" (65, p. 783). The implications of these findings for other than federal level legislators, however, are not clear. Since both studies were concerned exclusively with U.S. congressmen, it is not clear that the same relationships would obtain at the state or local levels, where the social distance of constituencies is closer to the legislator.

6.20F. "Respectability" was indicated by local representatives as an important variable influencing their receptivity to interest-group efforts (+, 105).

Zisk, Eulaw, and Prewitt (105) surveyed the perceptions, attitudes, and behaviors of a sample group of 122 councilmen from San Francisco Bay Area cities. Some 84 percent of their sample group listed "respectability" as a basis for group influence, by far the most cited source of influence. The authors indicated that respectability in this context was associated with such factors as honesty, intelligence, and common sense. It should be noted that here again this verbal indication of responsiveness may not coincide with actual behavior. That is to say, councilmen may respond to highly powerful groups regardless of respectability, which may be only one of several bases of potency.

This study also found that *city councilmen overwhelmingly use the city manager as their prime source of information,* followed closely by other councilmen.

Action Guidelines: One who promotes a special interest should seek to establish in the mind of the legislator a firm perception of the group he represents. When possible, one should focus on legislators who are more "secure" and who are members of committees directly concerned with the issue in question, since these are most likely to respond favorably.

If there is a choice, one should select legislators who have a greater degree of contact with interest groups. Present a favorable image in terms of size, geographic scope, and level of organization.

In the case of municipal lobbying chances of success in gaining access (and perhaps exerting influence) are greatly enhanced if the group is presented as "respectable" (honest, factual, practical). When one attempts to get through to local lawmakers with "legitimate" information, the best avenue may be through the city manager; the next best is through other councilmen.

Predisposition toward Interest Groups and Level of Government

GENERALIZATION 6.21: Verbalized predispositions of elected representatives toward interest-group activities are to some extent a function of the level of government served (+, 48, 59, 105).

6.21A. Local councilmen verbalize a less responsive attitude toward interest groups than do national-level legislators (+, 59, 105).

Zisk, Eulaw, and Prewitt (105) reported on the attitudes, perceptions, and behavior of 122 local councilmen from cities in the San Francisco Bay Area toward interest group activity. Among their findings was the fact that only one-fourth of their sample indicated favorable predispositions toward interest groups (although most acknowledged that interest groups did affect their behavior). This appears to be in direct contrast to the popular image of the role of interest groups in government, and to the reported attitudes of legislators operating at higher levels of government. The Kingdon (48) study makes note of the contrast, and refers the reader to Milbraith, *The Washington Lobbyist* (59), for specifics. A review of that source revealed the following: "Most congressional respondents also believe that lobbying is healthy: 50 percent give unqualified approval, 44 percent give qualified approval, and (only) 6 percent think it is more bad than good" (p. 301).

This would appear to document a sizable difference in proportionate support for interest groups between city councilmen and congressmen, with the congressmen indicating more favorable attitudes.

6.21B. Generally speaking, state legislators seem to be more responsive to interest groups than national legislators. National legislators attribute more wisdom to the generalized electorate, and therefore place less reliance on special-interest initiatives (+, 48, 59).

Kingdon (48) states that "other researchers," such as Lester W. Milbraith, have demonstrated state legislators to be more susceptible to interest groups than national legislators. Kingdon's study attempts to establish why this is so. He set out to examine the beliefs of legislative candidates about voter reasoning. The author sought to determine how the legislators' behavior was affected by their personal assumptions of the voters' behavior, implicit or explicit. Kingdon found among winning candidates what he defined as a "congratulation-rationalization effect." This effect, he theorized, leads legislators to conclude that since the voters selected the "best" candidate they must therefore be interested and well informed. Kingdon believes that this effect, particularly at the federal level (where his data indicate it is much stronger than at the state level), leads legislators to assume the voters, viewed in general terms, are much more interested and much better informed than they really are. He suggests that this misperception of the voter, more common at the higher levels of government, helps explain why national legislators may be relatively more responsive to broad-based voter appeals and less responsive to party or special interests than are state legislators.

Kingdon goes on to suggest that the legislators' tendency to overly credit the voter with political awareness may be modified by the distance between a legislator and his constituency. This hypothesis, too, would explain why national legislators (further removed from contact with their constituents) might be more likely to favor broad voter-based appeals than state legislators ("closer" to the voter—more aware of voter apathy). Unfortunately if one extends this line of reasoning to include local councilmen, it would suggest that this group of legislators is the most responsive of all to special interests, being closest of all to the voters and knowing better than anyone how uninformed and apathetic they really are. Perhaps voters are least informed on state matters; more informed on local and national ones.

Without attempting to resolve these explanatory considerations, the limited data do seem to suggest that state legislators indicate the greatest responsiveness to interest-group activities, followed by national lawmakers and next by local councilmen. Because of the small number of studies reported at each level and the explanatory uncertainties, these findings should be viewed as highly tentative.

Action Guidelines: Interest-group members will most likely find easiest access (getting a "foot in the door") to governmental levels as follows: state, federal, local. Since verbal expression of legislators and actual behavior may not coincide, the practitioner will do well to use interest-group "potency" as a conjoint tactic.

Interest Group Potency

GENERALIZATION 6.22: An interest group's success is associated with its "potency" (+ + +, 23, 54, 65, 84, 95, 105).

This statement tends to synthesize some of the preceding data on legislative attitudes toward interest groups and more behavioral findings relative to interest-group success. We have labeled the sum total of the varied characteristics that contribute to an interest group's success as its "potency." The potency of an interest group, then, is defined by its numerical *size,* its *concentration* in a constituency area, its *intensity* of focus on a given issue, its *"respectability,"* and its *alliances* with other interest groups or key political figures. Olson (65) reports that "the geographic distribution, size and intensity of the 'interest' are factors in the success of interest groups in achieving legislative goals" (p. 283). Also, a study by Longley (54) concludes that a significant factor in the legislative success of an interest group is its ability to form alliances with other interest groups or with key political figures (particularly the governor in the case of state-level lobbying).

Action Guidelines: For the practitioner who is seeking to enhance the political efficacy of an interest group, the most important considerations are the ability to recruit large numbers of supporters, the ability to concentrate efforts in key legislative districts, the ability to focus on single issues, the ability to maintain respectability (public-relations image), and the capacity to form alliances with other interest groups and constituencies.

Legislator–Interest-Group–Government Agency

GENERALIZATION 6.23: The interest-group–legislator relationship is frequently a three-way interaction, involving a governmental agency as well (+ +, 23, 54, 65).

Olson (65), drawing on Fenno's data, states that "interest groups cooperate extensively with agencies. Their support of (and their origination from) agency programs is their motive to approach congressmen. The interest group-congress interaction is more of a three-way interaction including agencies" (p. 283).

Longley (54) in assessing success factors in state-level lobbying found that the most significant alliance a state-level interest group could foster was one involving the governor (see Generalization 6.24). Moreover, he found that the type of access associated with maximum success was to be found in "consultation with the governor's experts."

Agency appointments are often based on the perceived "expertise" of the appointee, and it follows that executives or legislators are likely to populate their agencies with "experts" on whom they feel they can rely for advice. Of course such factors as the routinized mechanisms of civil service and the workings of the spoils system muddy the waters and obscure the selection or identification of viable "experts" within many agencies. But such ambiguities notwithstanding, it seems likely that effective lobbyists have discovered ways of filtering out the "real" or influential "experts," and that such individuals probably serve as focal points in these interest-group–agency–legislator success triangles.

Action Guidelines: The practitioner is probably best advised to seek the involvement of relevant governmental agencies in his lobbying efforts. Also, he should attempt to identify and win over "experts" within governmental agencies who serve as consultants to the executive or legislature. If possible, he should form his coalitions so that they involve such individuals, officially or unofficially.

The Executive Officer

Executive Officer Support

GENERALIZATION 6.24: Support by the chief executive is a critical factor in obtaining legislative approval of desired programs (+ + +, 54, 56, 64, 77, 90).

6.24A. Gubernatorial support is a critical factor for the state agency's success in budgetary acquisitons (+ +, 54, 56, 64, 90).

Sharkansky (90) collected data on the budget requests of 592 agencies in 19 states for his study of the relationship between agency success and a number of other variables including gubernatorial support. He measured "success" according to two criteria: 1) short-term attainment in obtaining the requested budget, 2) long-term attainment as indicated by consistent budget expansion. Analysis of the data suggested that the governor's support was crucial for the agency's success. "In 16 states there is a significant positive correlation between the governor's support and short-term success, and in 14 of the states there is a similar relationship between the governor's support and success in budget expansion" (p. 1224). Longley (54) found that the governor's influence on those bills upon which he takes a stand is almost complete.

6.24B. The positions of strong municipal executives, at least on certain issues, are highly correlated with the decisions made by their relevant legislative bodies (+, 77).

Rosenthal and Crain (77) studied the relationship between mayoral or manager positions and issue outcomes with respect to a specific issue: fluoridation. They sought measures of three dimensions in their survey of 1,186 cities: the type of local political organization involved, the level of controversy together with issue positions of key participants, and the outcome. Their data indicated that the position taken by the mayor or city manager virtually determines the decisions made in the locality. This was true when decisions were made by city councils, and also when decisions were submitted to a local referendum. In a supplemental observation the authors note that only *strong* executives appear willing to oppose popular opinion on an issue, and that in such cases their support is virtually indispensable for a favorable outcome.

It might be noted that this study pertains to an issue which is to a certain degree technical-medical in nature, and where factual information and professional expertise may be seen as playing a part in the decision.

Action Guidelines: At the local level, as well as at the state level, for some types of issues (i.e., fluoridation) the most valuable support one can obtain is that of the chief executive. At the state level there is little question that the governor's support is a critical factor in respect to a range of issues. The practitioner should therefore be particularly alert for opportunities to obtain access to the chief executive. Particularly with regard to less popular issues (such as prison reform, welfare benefits, and abortion legislation) the support of the chief executive can spell the difference between success and failure.

Executive-Officer vs. State-Agency Responsiveness to Citizens

GENERALIZATION 6.25: Governors and their executive-office staff appear to be more disposed toward resolution of citizen grievances than are state agencies. State agencies generally appear more oriented toward a defense of the status-quo (+, 64).

Olson (64) analyzed letters written by citizens to the office of the Governor of Wisconsin over a six-month period and the responses these letters evoked. The Olson data reveal that 83 percent of the responses emanating from the governor's office were favorable to the citizen requests. By contrast, most of the responses emanating from state agencies were letters explaining why no favorable action would be taken.

Action Guidelines: Citizen and citizen association grievances concerning state agencies should ordinarily be directed to the governor's office (not the agencies) for maximum effect. (Except perhaps in the case of state agencies whose boards are elected or that are by experience found to be responsive.) Extensive letter-writing campaigns to the governor strengthen his hand in dealing with unresponsive agencies, especially those agencies over which he enjoys limited formal control.

Planning-Agency–Executive-Officer Linkage

GENERALIZATION 6.26: Linkage of city planning agencies with the executive office is associated with better implementation of planning decisions (+ +, 73, 75, 77).

6.26A. A major problem of directors of independent agencies is the lack of a political obligation on the part of the executive to whom they must "sell" their programs (+, 73).

Rabinovitz and Pattinger (73) surveyed 309 directors of local planning agencies in an attempt to determine what form of local planning organization is most effective. They divided their respondents into three categories: agencies (*N*-77) responsible to the chief executive, independent agencies (*N*-76), and agencies that combine aspects of both (*N*-48). The findings show that the major problem for directors of independent planning agencies is that the agency has no person committed to promoting its plans with the general public, and that the agency is isolated from the executive. There is no one with a *political obligation* to forward the agency plans, which impedes the implementation of programs.

Reynolds (75) examined the extent of effective planning and coordinated implementation achieved in the relocation of families from areas designated as urban renewal sites in a sample group of 26 cities. He found the efficacy of the planning process was associated with the type of local government organization, particularly at the executive level. This study is somewhat hampered by its use of value-laden labels for plans and implementation methods which are described in terms of "good" cities and "bad" cities. It was found that of the 15 "good" cities, 10 had strong executives, while the remaining 5 were subject to control by some other strong leadership source. Conversely in the 26 "bad" cities only 7 displayed a formal structure having a strong executive, and in only 4 of the 7 did the executive enjoy the power of appointment over the planning commission.

Rabinovitz and Pattinger (73) observe that planning directors of agencies directly responsible to a strong executive appear to enjoy an advantage over their counterparts who operate under more autonomous arrangements. This may be seen in light of the frequent comment that cities are not "governable" or that veto blocs prohibit needed actions. In such a context coherent planning is in jeopardy, and a strong executive who can coerce or cajole a degree of concerted action is an asset to planning.

Action Guidelines: In seeking to promote planning activities it is particularly helpful to secure the aid of a strong local executive. In some cases it may prove worthwhile to seek ways of increasing executive control over or linkage to the planning agency in order to enhance the effectiveness of the planning process. However, this raises a question of how much direct community control one should willingly surrender in the pursuit of efficiency. The gain in planning purposefulness and capacity may be offset by exposure of planning to some of the more unwholesome concomitants of "politics."

If one is associated with an "independent" agency he would probably do well to develop informal personal ties with the executive if no formal ties are provided. The practitioner might increase the commitment of a reluctant executive to his particular program by a sustained public relations campaign identifying the agency or program with the political administration, and particularly with the chief executive.

An arrangement that combines aspects of agency au-

tonomy on the one hand and constructive working relationships with the executive officer on the other should hypothetically offer an optimal structure.

Influence of Private Consulting Firms

GENERALIZATION 6.27: Governmental officials display a
partial dependency on private consulting firms for "expert"
advice (+, 46).

Kagi (46) in a study of governmental relationships with private
consulting firms, utilized questionnaires and in-depth interviews with
members of some 400 governmental units. He also interviewed a wide
variety of consulting firms. He found that the government officials included in his sample generally displayed a "partial dependency" on
private consulting firms. The author suggests a variety of data-based
reasons for this situation, among them: difficulties in retaining "high-
powered" experts within government, historical ties to such consultants as law firms and financial advisors, accelerating need for more
immediate decisions, and utility of consultants for "blame shifting" if
something goes wrong.

Action Guidelines: Consultants are a newer repository of
power and influence in modern politics. Dictum: Learn who
serve as consultants to the individuals and agencies you
want to influence and work through them. Also, practitioners
can influence local officials directly by instituting consulting
firms or establishing themselves as recognized experts in
given subject areas.

County Officials

GENERALIZATION 6.28: County government officials are
highly oriented toward specialized tasks. They are only
marginally concerned with "general government" issues
(+, 38).

Hanson (38) in a descriptive report on Oklahoma County boards observed major concerns of commissioners as follows: 67 percent roads;

11.8 percent finances; 8.1 percent welfare; 6.8 percent "general government." The study indicated a strong preoccupation by individuals with specialized tasks involved in county government, and only a marginal concern with government in general.

Action Guidelines: In dealing with county officials seek out the person who is clearly responsible for the issue area you are concerned with. Define your problems in specific terms and state the relationship between the problem and the specialized concerns of the official you wish to influence.

Structural Factors and Political Behavior

In concluding this section we shall deal with several structural factors that affect patterns of political performance rather than the behavior of specific political actors. These patterns include such matters as the degree of factionalism involved and the form of governmental functioning (reformed vs. unreformed patterns).

Population Growth

GENERALIZATION 6.29: Municipal governments in communities undergoing rapid population growth have more factionalism and issue conflicts than communities with more stable populations (+, 18).

Downes (18) surveyed population growth patterns for the decade 1950–1960, interviewed 210 councilmen and mayors in 37 suburban cities, and observed a number of council meetings. He categorized his data according to population-growth rate during the decade surveyed: very high (> 500 percent); high (> 100 percent); medium (16–100 percent); low (< 15 percent). From the results Downes concluded that high-growth communities exhibit:

A. Higher degree of issue "visibility" at council level
B. Stronger coalitions among councilmen
C. More public awareness of issues
D. More reliance on "democratic process" to resolve conflicts
E. Less thorough and efficient search for solutions to community problems

Action Guidelines: In communities undergoing rapid growth, practitioners may anticipate involving themselves in situations that include a greater degree of conflict. One must form strong coalitions and sharpen issues when one deals with politicians and political processes. When such a community is undergoing excessive conflict the curtailment of population growth might be sought as a means of enhancing consensus-stability.

Local Governmental Structure and Geographic Region

GENERALIZATION 6.30: Municipal government structure ("reformed" vs. "nonreformed") is associated with geographical region (+ + +, 31, 45, 52, 85, 88, 103).

In the studies cited, "reformed" basically means having a city manager, although it also refers to such features as the nonpartisan ballot and at-large rather than ward representation. These features have implications for the roles of key political actors and the processes by which they pursue their policies.

A number of studies cite correlations between the type of municipal government and the region. Wolfinger and Field (103) found a strong correlation between the mayoral form and region. The incidence of mayor-type governments is reported as: Northeast (65 percent), Midwest (55 percent), South (22 percent), West (15 percent). Froman (31) reports essentially the same conclusion in noting a correlation between manager-council form and region. He found the strongest correlation for this type of local government organization to be "west of the Mississippi." Pursuing a slightly different approach, Sharkansky (88) notes that the correlation also holds true at the level of local congressional districts. He documents a relationship between the type of district organization (or lack thereof—the study looks at apportionment) and region. Region was found to be one of the more salient variables associated with legislative apportionment, outranking even economics as a correlate.

6.30A. There is a recognizable reformist structural configuration: cities with managers tend also to have nonpartisan ballots and at-large elections (+ +, 31, 103).

6.30B. The manager-council form of government is much more prevalent west of the Mississippi than it is east of the Mississippi.
6.30C. Reformed structures are more common in small- and medium-sized cities than in large cities (+ +, 31, 52, 103).
6.30D. In the recent past reformed cities have exhibited more rapid population growth than unreformed cities (+ +, 31, 52).

Scott (84) in a study of council-manager cities in three states (California, Illinois, and Ohio) found that cities adopting the reformed pattern had generally experienced *low* population growth in the decade preceding the change. However, Froman (31) and Lineberry and Fowler (52) both report more rapid population growth in such cities than in their unreformed counterparts following change.
6.30E. Reformed cities tend to have homogeneous, "nonethnic" populations (+ +, 31, 52, 103).

As Wolfinger and Field (103) point out, correlation between reformed-unreformed may be merely a reflection of regional variations. Eastern cities are highly ethnic and have mayors. Western cities are often less ethnic, and have city managers.
6.30F. "Reformed" cities tend to have relatively homogeneous populations in terms of socioeconomic status (+ +, 31, 52, 85).

Froman (31) and Lineberry and Fowler (52) agree that "reformed" cities have relatively homogeneous socioeconomic populations. Froman bases his conclusion on a review of data from the *City and County Data Book,* while Lineberry and Fowler have completed data from a random sample of 200 of the total population of 300 American cities with populations over 50,000 (1960 census).
6.30H. "Reformed" cities tend to display an "urbanization lifestyle" which is moderate rather than either extremely high or extremely low (+, 85).

Scott (85) makes use of a Shevky-Bell index to interpret much of the census data included in his study. One of the dimensions of the index is the urbanization life-style measurement (0–100), which is a combination of "average" measures of fertility, percent of women in the labor force, and percent of single-family dwelling units in the area. The scale is based on the assumption that working women with few children who live in multifamily dwellings are urban. Only one of the "reformed" communities in his sample had a ULS value falling outside the range of 25–50. It is not certain how much weight can be attributed to this finding, however, since the overall sample included only suburbs.

Action Guidelines: The organizer who wishes to have his community change to a council-manager reform type of government will be more likely to succeed if the community in question has some of the following characteristics: is west of the Mississippi, is middle size, is homogeneous white (nonethnic), contains a generally high socioeconomic status population, and has a rapid growth rate. The more of these conditions met the greater the likelihood of success of "reform" efforts. Since such factors appear to exercise a strong influence on the form of government instituted in a given community, the practitioner is probably best advised to direct his energy toward other objectives in communities where many of these prerequisite conditions are not met.

POLICY OUTPUTS AND IMPACTS

We shall next treat factors associated with policy outcomes having a human-service character—i.e., affecting welfare, jobs, mental health. At any earlier time political scientists focused on policy outputs— decisions concerning services and programs of various kinds. Of late there has been an expansion of attention to include the matter of policy impacts—the concrete effects of policies and programs on specific groups and individuals such as the school dropouts, the poor, the physically handicapped. Three particular forces impinging on policies will undergo examination: historical influences, socioeconomic influences, and social-structural influences.

We shall be less concerned here with political actors *per se,* but shall instead attend to the collective products and consequences of their acts—in the form of political policy factors. We shall particularly look to outputs favorable to human values as defined in the framework of this study.

Among those studies which concern themselves with the historical dimension there appears to be agreement that the past experience of a polity is a highly significant factor associated with contemporary policy outcomes. Unfortunately very few studies attempt to focus on an evaluation of this variable.

Where studies considered both the political history of a governmental unit and its socioeconomic environment it was generally suggested that history was a stronger correlate of policy outcome than were SES factors (see, for example, Sharkansky's study [89]). Nevertheless, studies documenting a correlation between socioeconomic environment and policy outcomes were numerous and diverse.

In a sense we might think of propositions concerned with the environment as extensions or refinements of those concerned with political history. Environment can itself be viewed as the cumulative consequences of political history, frozen at a given moment of time. To the extent that social actors perceive their environmental circumstances as a culmination of historical trends and processes, they may base their political behavior on these alone, or on the thrust of accumulated antecedents plus the impact of present circumstances.

It is sometimes difficult to separate social-structural factors from socioeconomic ones. Nevertheless certain structural elements, such as population movements and specific political forms, are in some ways separate variables and will be treated in their own right.

Political History and Policy Outcomes

GENERALIZATION 6.31: The past political experience of a government is strongly associated with its policy outcomes (+ + +, 7, 13, 20, 89).

6.31A. The level of expenditure in various policy categories is strongly associated with previously established levels of expenditure in these categories (+ +, 7, 89).

Sharkansky (89) analyzed data from *Census of Government* for all the state governments for the years 1957–1962. His results show that the level of previous expenditure is "far and away" the most powerful independent variable related to current expenditures. Cepuran (7) compared CAP expenditures per poor person in each of the states with previous levels of state expenditure for welfare-related programs. The results were very similar. He found a strong correlation between higher levels of CAP expenditures and prior support of traditional welfare programs.

6.31B. General response (positive-negative) to antipoverty efforts was strongly related to previous levels of involvement in welfare-related activities (+ +, 7, 13).

Cowart (13), examing similar variables to those described above, considered the extent of support generated for OEO programs at local and state governmental levels and compared the outcomes with previous levels of support for welfare-type programs. He found that, in general, the participation of state and local governments in newly formulated federal programs is a function of their level of previous participation in similar kinds of programs. His investigation of low-policy-level cases indicated that negative experiences with similar past programs was associated with low levels of OEO support.

6.31C. Patterns of policy support fluctuate over time (+, 41, 96).

Hofferbert (41) studied 21 socioeconomic variables over the period 1890–1960. He determined that only two (urbanization and cultural enrichment) remained stable in composition. Further he found that patterns of interrelationship between *all* variables (including these two) and such political factors as voter turnout and partisan preferences, are highly fluid over time. On the basis of these findings the author questions the validity of causal theories based on assumptions of stable social-political correlations. Thomas (96), in a more limited study, found that the impact of socioeconomic factors on the outcomes of four successive constitutional revision referenda (Michigan 1958–1963) varied greatly with the political circumstances surrounding each particular election.

Thus the previous Generalizations are variable over time.

Action Guidelines: Practitioners should be aware of the possibility of causal links between historical factors and policy outcomes, and should also be aware of the possible transitory nature of such correlations. Generally, practitioners are not likely to find significant local or state support for costly new programs, unless these can be viewed as logical outgrowths of established program efforts. When there is a choice, the practitioner should look to states and situations that have committed high levels of expenditure to human-service programs in the past to be most receptive to "innovative" approaches. But even these should be viewed as strongly attached to the goals, if not the methodologies, of established programs. Since periods of high expenditure move in cycles the practitioner might attempt to identify a governmental unit experiencing such a "spurt" and ride the crest. Since funding for programs that have no clear precedent will be extremely difficult to obtain from state or local government sources, he should devote some of his energies to locating alternative funding sources (private, philanthropic, user fees, etc.) for this type of program. If there is any precedent for funding from any source, that is probably the best place to begin looking. The practitioner should avoid structuring proposals in ways reminiscent of other programs that have met with failure, and when possible emphasize aspects of proposals that are consistent with traditionally endorsed goals and methodologies.

Economic Development and Policy Outcome

GENERALIZATION 6.32: Policy outcomes are frequently associated with the level of economic development of the environmental system (+ + + +, 7, 8, 13, 39, 40, 52, 69, 97, 99).

6.32A. Wealthier, more industrialized, more urbanized states exhibit more responsiveness to human-service needs (+ + +, 7, 13, 21, 39, 40).

Numerous studies cited offer examples of this association. Studies 21, 39, and 40 all cite relations between such indicators and the level of social services provided. Hofferbert (39) notes a strong correlation between industrialization and the degree of "welfare orientation" exhibited by a state. In a separate study (40) he notes that urbanization, percent of nonagricultural employment, and per capita income all exhibit strong positive correlations with the level of (mostly human-service type) services provided. In this study per capita income is identified as the strongest and most consistent correlate. This correlation is also supported by Dye (21), who sees "wealth" as closely related to levels of welfare benefits provided.

Studies by Cowart (13) and Cepuran (7) cite specific instances of this correlation. Cowart notes that wealthier states were more likely to support antipoverty programs; Cepuran points out that measures of personal income were strongly correlated with levels of expenditure in support of the Community Action Program. Finally, Dye (21) notes that, in the case of states, income is the strongest factor associated with support for civil rights legislation.

6.32B. Larger, wealthier, more industrialized states adopt new programs more rapidly (i.e., are more innovative) (+ +, 7, 13, 99).

This finding appears as a corollary to that cited above and is supported by several of the same studies. The most specific treatment of the Generalization occurs in a national study by Walker (99) who concludes that wealth, industrialization, large size, turnover in office, and full representation of urban areas (apportionment) are those characteristics of states which are positively correlated with the adoption of new programs.

Among cities, per-pupil expenditure for public education is directly correlated with measures of median family income and property value per pupil (+, 20).

6.32C. In relatively underdeveloped countries, policies consistent with democratic political values are related to the level of social and economic development. Diffusion and adaptation of democratic values and practices appear to increase in an underdeveloped country as socioeconomic conditions improve (+, 97).

Neubauer (61), using data from 23 nations, found that a positive correlation between his index of democratic political development (combining equality and competition in elections) and four measures of socioeconomic development (education, communication, urbanization, and employment in agriculture) did not exist among relatively developed, complex countries. Since other authors have posited a positive correlation between similar measures among underdeveloped countries, Neubauer concludes that the relationship only obtains below a certain "threshold point" of socioeconomic development.

Socioeconomic factors may also be related to policy outcomes involving specific issue categories at the national level. Polumbo and Williams (69), for example, in a study of 133 countries with public health departments conclude that 92 percent of the variance in public-health policy is accounted for by urbanization.

6.32D. Poor states often devote more per capita resources to human services than wealthier, more "urbanized" communities but still provide lower levels of client service (+ +, 22, 52, 89).

Sharkansky (89) used *Census of Government* data for the years 1957–1962 to determine that on a per capita basis poor states generally devote more of their resources to the support of state government (i.e., services) than do wealthier states. This finding appears to run counter to nearly all the Generalizations listed in this section. Careful examination of the study reveals, however, that Sharkansky's measurements are of total per capita population expenditure—not per eligible recipient expenditures. Thus the level of expenditure cited does not necessarily reflect the level of service provided.

Dye (22) obtained comparable results at the level of local government in 67 large cities. In the case of local areas he found poorer communities put forth more effort to provide a less adequate education than did wealthier cities.

One might explain these findings through a hypothesis that the number of potential recipients (per capita) in need of public services decreases as per capita income increases. Thus the proportionate expenditure per recipient (level of service provided) will increase as per capita income increases. Assuming these dynamics, a large, wealthy community with a relatively low proportion of its population classified as potential clients can provide for more adequate services at a lower per capita cost than can a smaller, poorer community where a high proportion of the population uses public services. This interpretation is underscored by another important Sharkansky study (91) revealing absence of a close relationship between current measures of government expenditures and quality of public services.

Action Guidelines: Areas most able to support human-service programs financially are large, wealthy, urban, industrial. Efforts to acquire or expand services in such areas are likely to have a quick and substantive payoff. Support for innovative new programs is also more likely in such areas. Concomitantly, the level of absolute need for such services is probably lower. Thus, practitioners should look to such communities to be the proving grounds for new ideas, rather than as a focus for their major efforts. In particular the practitioner might communicate the comparative inability of poorer communities to cope with their problems by utilization of internal resources as a line of argumentation to encourage channeling of more "outside" resources into such communities.

For the practitioner who is concerned with community growth in developing nations (and perhaps also of poorer political subdivisions of more developed nations) more democratic values and practices might be more readily obtained indirectly, by concentrating efforts on economic development, than directly. In more complex political environments, however, economic advances cannot be assumed to contribute to the democratic policies and procedures.

Policy and Social Class Rank

GENERALIZATION 6.33: Policy outcomes are influenced differentially by social class rank (+ +, 8, 97).

Uyeki (97) surveyed 22 cities of population in excess of 5,000 within the boundaries of Cuyaloga County, Ohio. He ranged the cities on a scale according to social rank, urbanization, and segregation, and compared the results of this ranking to the political outcomes of a number of countywide electoral events. The results of the study reveal that social rank was related to 90 percent of the outcomes of all electoral events considered. (Urbanization was related to 42 percent and segregation to 20 percent.) Social rank was most strongly related to bonds for physical improvement (95.5 percent) and "good government" issues (94.1 percent), while urbanization was most strongly associated with tax levies for public welfare (66.7 percent).

6.33A. Social stratification is associated with decentralized decision making (+, 8).

Using 51 American cities as his sample, Clark (8) compiled data to test his hypothesis that horizontal and vertical differentiation in the social system (stratification) is associated with more decentralized forms of decision-making organizations, and that this in turn is associated with a lower quantity of policy outputs. The results confirmed the correlation between stratification and centralization of decision making but, interestingly, failed to support the hypothesized impact on policy decisions. In fact, positive correlations were found to exist between decentralized decision-making structures and policy outputs in the case of total budget expenditures and also of urban renewal.

One might explain this situation by hypothesizing that, in the case of "fragile" decisions (Clark's term—connotes controversy), the existence of conflicting social strata leads to a crystallization of issues and thus ultimately contributes to the formation of coalitions and the resolution of issues. This process could also apply to the less "fragile" issues, since social groups might conceivably have already crystallized their opinions about such issues. Of course the consensus that characterized less stratified communities with more centralized control also permits the resolution of "fragile" issues. In this case the process could be interpreted as the avoidance of conflict, which is facilitated by the ability of such bodies to make rapid decisions in the quiet, orderly atmosphere of consensus politics. The study suggests that the two modes of decision making are both effective means of producing policy outcomes, but perhaps differentially so in relation to specific patterns of social stratification.

Action Guidelines: If one is concerned with influencing the outcome of a particular electoral event, he may do well to make separate appeals to various levels of the social strata. Arguments stressing the "good" of the community will probably be most effective with the upper social strata. The existence of conflicting social strata, particularly in the presence of decentralized governmental structure, may provide more favorable conditions for the resolution of "fragile" (controversial) issues than does the existence of social homogeneity and its corollary: strong, centrally controlled government. However, if community decision-making authority is centralized, one's policy might achieve greater impact if one maintained low levels of direct participation and sought direct access to the decision makers. In such a situation, broad participation, which greatly increases the level of controversy surrounding an issue, might spell defeat. Therefore, if administrative support seems likely the best tactic might be to keep public awareness at a low level and work for a central decision. (See also Action Guidelines for Generalization 6.19.)

Party Competition and Policy Output

GENERALIZATION 6.34: Party competition is associated with increased policy output (+ + + +, 7, 13, 15, 39, 71, 88, 99).

One can find a sizable number of studies documenting the correlation between high degrees of party competitiveness and increases in some types of policy output. Cowart (13), for example, suggests a causal sequence of: high party competitiveness → high political participation → positive response to antipoverty programs. Hofferbert (39) observes the same basic relationship, noting that when party competitiveness decreases there is also a decrease in the passage of welfare-oriented policies. (However, he held the correlation to be uncertain because competitiveness in his sample was found to correlate strongly with industrialization.) Pulsipher and Weatherby (71) also document the correlation, finding an association between the degree of party competition and the level of governmental (per capita) expenditure in the following categories: total education, higher education, categorical public welfare, total public welfare, and total expenditures. Walker (99) found the correlation to be inconsistent with regard to the innovativeness of policy outputs, but also indicates some support for the idea that "turnover" fosters change.

There is a major problem in the evaluation of this association in view of probable intercorrelations between the independent variable (party competitiveness) and broader "environmental" variables (such as "urbanization"). An additional study concerning the relationship by Crittendon (15) is illustrative. Crittendon found high party competition to be associated with "development" (modernization). "Development," like "urbanization" is a gross environmental variable and both may harken back to socioeconomic factors.

Several other variables are identified in the studies as associated with increased party competitiveness. Among these are per capita income level (88), Community Action Program expenditures (7), and public political participation (13, 15).

In summary, then, the most that can be said with respect to the relationship between party competition and policy outputs is that generally when party-competitiveness increases policy outputs also increase, although the relationship may not be direct. There is reason to suspect that increases in both party competitiveness and policy outputs are rooted in some third causal factor. In studies that controlled for intercorrelations between party competition and other (generally environmental variables) party competitiveness was found to have little independent effect on policy outcomes (see, for example, Dye [21] on the impact of competitiveness on civil rights policy outcomes).

Action Guidelines: Efforts to increase party competitiveness may effect the "amount" of outputs, particularly in terms of quantitative dimensions. However, several environmental factors also appear to be strong determinants of policy. Given the opportunity, it is probably best to manipulate both variables (environmental and structural). "Spontaneous" party competition might be seen as a somewhat reliable predictor of the likelihood of increased policy outputs.

Decentralization-Centralization and Policy Output

GENERALIZATION 6.35: The effects of centralized-decentralized decision-making structures on policy outputs vary with the issue (+, 8, 14).

Crain and Rosenthal (14) found that certain issue outcomes could be associated with the degree of centralization of decision-making control in determination of policy. In this example the issue was fluoridation of water. The authors found that a critical factor in obtaining a positive community policy response on fluoridation was the presence of a strong centralized decision-making authority (i.e. city manager, partisan mayor, etc.). They attribute this observation to the fact that the centralized structure in this instance tended to "insulate" the decision makers from the "irregular" pressures of an "organized minority."

In his more general study, Clark (8) found decentralization to be positively associated with levels of budget expenditures of local communities and with support for urban renewal.

We conclude that centrality may have varying effects based on the nature of the issue or other sociological variables in the community. Further research is necessary to clarify and elaborate the relationship.

Action Guidelines: Direction here is rather general and obvious. Depending on the issue, the practitioner would work through or attempt to establish centralized or decentralized decisional structures. Further research may specify which structure is facilitative for which type of policy issue. A further source of guidance may be found in Generalization 4.1.

Reform vs. Nonreform Governmental Structures

GENERALIZATION 6.36: Policy outputs of city governments vary systematically with reform vs. nonreform governmental structure (+ +, 20, 22, 52).

6.36A. "Reformed" governments are less responsive to minority and dissident policy aims than are "unreformed" governments (+, 52).

6.36B. Manager cities spend a larger proportion of their income for education than do nonmanager cities (+, 22).

6.36C. Manager cities are significantly more successful in annexing suburbs than are nonmanager cities (+, 20).

Each of the above illustrates the fact that a particular governmental structural form can have an impact on policy outcomes. Lineberry and Fowler (52) found that cities with higher proportions of ethnic and religious minorities tend to have higher taxes and expenditures (per unit of income), but that the correlation is considerably stronger for unreformed cities than for reformed cities. In this case, and perhaps in the other subgeneralizations as well, it appears that social cleavage (mirrored by degree of ethnicity) produces pressures to increase taxation and expenditure levels, and that reformed governments are more successful than unreformed ones in resisting these pressures. Further it appears that reformed governments, by remaining "above politics," effectively prevent low-status populations who do not possess bureaucratic skills or informal status resources from exerting meaningful influence on professional public administrators.

Generally it can be stated that correlations of the type noted here (governmental structure → policy outcome) are weak in comparison to correlations that obtain between policy outcomes and system environmental factors (size, wealth, SES, enthnicity, etc.). This is the case, for example, in data offered by Dye (22). While reporting the (weak) correlation noted here, Dye also observes that, in most cases, urban environmental forces appear to directly influence educational outcomes without being mediated by structural variables.

However, in another study Dye (20) finds that manager-type governments are significantly correlated with success in annexation efforts. Of interest in this study was that, with regard to this issue, type of government structure was significant while some of the major environmental variables (e.g., size of population) were not. Dye concluded that the most important factor appeared to be the social class distance between the central city and the surrounding suburbs, with age of settlement also a strong correlate. He suggests that for younger cities annexations can serve an integrative function, and will be the likely choice of tactics of manager-administrators who generally seek to discount conflict and work for consensus and the general good of the entire community. He notes, however, that in older urban areas, where suburbs have become socially differentiated from the central city, conflicts have already crystallized and cannot be discounted. For such communities, he suggests that efforts at annexation as an integrative tactic are much less likely to succeed.

Action Guidelines: For the practitioner seeking to increase or coordinate municipal services in a metropolitan area, a major tactical consideration may be the type of city government structure (reformed-nonreformed). Other important factors he should evaluate are homogeneity of the population (ethnicity), age of settlement, and "social distance" between component metropolitan units. Then, depending upon his objectives, he may wish to employ the following strategies: if the city is young and has a reform-type government he may wish to seek integration of services through annexation. In this event he should seek to avoid crystallization of conflicts and work directly with professional city administrators. If he is concerned that such efforts are ignoring the interests of low-status minorities, he should attempt to develop ways for spokesmen of these groups to penetrate the administrative buffers that surround the professional city manager and make their demands felt. In such instances threats of "politization" and "mobilization" are probably good strategies (if the threat is credible).

If the focus of one's efforts is an older, highly differentiated urban area, the need for coordination and integration of services will have to be met through devices other than annexation. Possibilities for practitioner goals include the formation of any of a wide range of cooperative boards or agencies (e.g., specialized service agencies, interjurisdictional agreements and contracts, joint programs or boards of directors). In such situations constituency interests are generally protected by political participation and are best served by the involvement of minority representatives in such activities. Thus, in this circumstance, political mobilization is probably the most effective tactic.

Policy Innovation

GENERALIZATION 6.37: Some types of policy innovation are associated with community population characteristics (+, 1, 31).

6.37A. Homogeneous communities favor population-wide policies; heterogeneous communities favor population-segmented policies (+, 31).

Froman (31) in a national sample found evidence that homogeneous communities tend to adopt policies that affect the total population simultaneously, whereas heterogeneous communities tend to adopt policies that affect different subpopulations at different times. Communities that are homogeneous with regard to social and economic diversity (in many areas one might well read "suburbs") generally promulgated "area" policies, such as nonpartisan elections, annexations, intermunicipal cooperation, fluoridation, and educational services. Heterogeneous communities (here one might read "central city areas") were associated with segmental policies, such as urban renewal for specific neighborhoods and per capita expenditures for welfare programs aimed at particular population groups.

6.37B. City participation in urban renewal is associated with outward population migration (+, 58).

Aiken and Alford (1) studied data on 582 American cities, concluding that the degree of participation (presence or absence; speed and level of participation—in dollars per capita committed) in urban renewal efforts was most directly related to the community level of outward population migration. Also directly (but less so) related with participation were such factors as percentage of Democratic voters, age of city, size of city, and level of voter turnouts.

Action Guidelines: Practitioners who become involved in community planning activities are well advised to design their program proposals to "fit" community population characteristics. That is to say, proposals will be more likely to elicit favorable responses if the client population is universalistically defined (general public) in homogeneous communities, or conversely if it is particularistically defined (specific subpopulations) in heterogeneous communities. Cities with high outward migration might be seen as good potential for certain types of programs, such as urban renewal.

Apportionment and Policy Output

GENERALIZATION 6.38: Malapportionment has little, if any, effect on policy outcomes (+ + +, 19, 39, 42, 71, 88).

The consensus of a number of studies on malapportionment is summarized by Dye (19) in his report comparing all 50 states with regard to three indicators of policy output—education, welfare, and taxation, compared with an "index of representativeness" (1 man = 1 vote→ 100 points). Dye concludes that "On the whole, the policy choices of malapportioned legislatures are not noticeably different from the policy choices of well apportioned legislatures" (p. 599).

For the most part studies on malapportionment discover no significant relationship between this variable and policy decisions. Jacob (42) finds malapportionment uncorrelated with "ills" of state government. Sharkansky (88) reports correlations with economic development to be weak and inconsistent. Hofferbert, in another study (39), indicates examples of noncorrelation with industrialization, party composition, welfare orientation, aid to cities, and division of control between executives and legislatures. And Pulsipher and Weatherby (71) report an even longer list of noncorrelates including elementary education, secondary education, public-welfare cash assistance, police, fire, highways, sanitation, and recreation. In short, nearly every measurable category of output shows no association with malapportionment. There is, however, an exception to this trend. This is reported, with explanation, below.

6.38A. Well-apportioned legislative systems tend to adopt new ideas more quickly—but this advantage may "wash out" over a longer period of time (+, 99).

Walker (99) discovered one of the correlates of innovation among American states to be full representation of urban areas in state legislative bodies. As this correlation runs counter to much of the preceding, it warrants an explanation. The writer tends to attribute the significance of this result to a probable intercorrelation between malapportionment and region (region was determined by Walker to be significantly correlated with innovativeness). Malapportionment appears to be an essentially historical phenomenon (i.e., determined by the accidents of history) for it does not correlate with any of the other structural or environmental variables except slightly with region (see Sharkansky, 88).

Action Guidelines: On the whole, apportionment appears to have little effect on the legislative product of state governments. Efforts previously invested in general reform activities would probably be better spent in focusing on program objectives. A program of economic improvement will probably be much more effective at inducing desired policy outcomes, and may yield desirable side benefits of more equitable apportionment as well.

It is of interest to note that Dye's (22) examination of school boards in 67 American cities revealed that the form of selection to the board (election vs. appointment) had no relationship to the quality of education provided. The implications of his study similarly suggest that practitioners devote efforts to increased funds for educational services rather than to elective procedures (assuming that the goal of increased services is seen as salient).

CONCLUSION

This chapter has tread through a wide expanse of the terrain of political science. While it would not be profitable to attempt a detailed summary, highlighting several important themes may be useful.

We started by describing the amorphous, fluid character of the body politic, a constituency that avoids ideological precision and eschews value cleavage. There is variation among social classes on such values as civil liberties or the interpretation of pluralism. Ideological unevenness exists across the left-right spectrum—with many conservatives, for example, standing in firm support of civil libertarian principles. Social class identity and class-based self-interest are by and large not influential with respect to partisan behaviors.

Four types of political actors came under scrutiny: party leaders, legislators, interest groups, and executive officers. Party leaders generally define their tasks around organization building and maintenance, not in ideological terms (although concern for maintenance produces a status quo mentality). At the same time they are not ideologically neutral, but rather espouse the particular principles advanced by their party at a given time. They are motivated largely by self-interest and they tend to be recruited by the existing party machinery.

Legislators have different attitudes toward attempts at influence by interest groups. They tend to be more favorable if they have had a greater amount of interaction with such groups, are more secure in their political office, and if the interest being represented is of particularized relevance to them (with regard to committee appointments and the like). Some evidence points to differential predisposition according to level of government (local, state, federal), with distance from accurate feedback regarding constituents' knowledge and effectiveness as a factor that affects predisposition. Interest-group effectiveness is bound up with its "potency," namely its size, concentration in a constituency, intensity of focus on a given issue, its respectability, and the viability of its alliances. Success is also enhanced by linking up with a relevant government department or with appropriate experts in government who can legitimate or buttress the position being advocated.

Support of the executive officer is critical in achieving some legislative aims. In addition, the executive office, being more politically sensitive and vulnerable, responds more favorably to citizens' appeals and grievances than do the operating departmental bureaucracies of government. Governmental planning agencies increase the possibility of having plan designs implemented if they can form structural relationships with the executive branch.

Historical influences appear to be a significant factor in predicting policy outcomes; past experience is a vital precursor of current policy formulations. Degree of economic development is an important indicator of policy level, with wealthier, more urbanized, more industrialized communities ranking higher on policy development. An evident connection exists between availability of resources and the capacity to employ these resources to optimize policy outputs. Several social structural factors appear to affect policy, such as the extent of party competition, the existence of reform vs. nonreform governmental composition, and certain population characteristics. Reapportionment, on the other hand, does not bear a strong relationship to human-service oriented policy enactments.

More abstractly, political science literature is rich in research data highly germane to community intervention aims. Much of the research has an applied caste in its original form and often touches on vital human-service related decisional areas. Using the customary categories and theoretical perspectives already prevalent in the discipline, one can easily make translations geared to community practice concerns. Further, manipulating the variables considered can have a powerful impact on social change. Community organizers and planners have leaned heavily toward sociology for their knowledge base; they would stand to gain a great deal by availing themselves of this additional social science resource more fully than has been common up until now.

BIBLIOGRAPHY FOR PART FOUR

1. Aiken, Michael, and Robert R. Alford. "Community Structure and The Case of Urban Renewal." Paper presented to American Sociological Association Annual Meeting, June 1969.

2. Alford, Robert R., and Harry M. Stable. "Community Leadership, Education, and Political Behavior." *American Sociological Review* 3, no. 2 (1968): 259–72.

3. Althop, Phillip, and Samuel Patterson. "Political Activism in a Rural Country." *Midwest Journal of Political Science* 10, no. 1 (1966): 39–51.

4. Anderson, Lee F. "Variability in the Unidimensionality of Legislative Voting." *Journal of Politics* 26, no. 3 (1964): 568–85.

5. Bowman, Lewis, and George R. Boynton. "Recruitment Patterns among Local Party Officials: A Model and Some Preliminary Findings in Selected Locales." *Journal of American Political Science Review* 60, no. 3 (1966): 667–76.

6. Bowman, Lewis, and George R. Boynton. "Activities and Role Definitions of Grassroots Party Officials." *Journal of Politics* 26, no. 1 (1966): 121–40.

7. Cepuran, Joseph. "CAP Expenditures in the Fifty States: A Comparison." *Journal of Urban Affairs Quarterly* 4, no. 3 (1969): 325–41.

8. Clark, Terry N. "Community Structure, Decision Making, Budget Expenditures and Urban Renewal in 51 American Communities." *Journal of American Sociological Review* 33, no. 4 (1968): 576–93.

9. Clausen, Aage R. "Measurement Identity in the Longitudinal Analysis of Legislative Voting." *American Political Science Review* 61, no. 4 (1967): 1020–35.

10. Cnudde, Charles F., and Donald J. McCrone. "The Linkage between Constituency Attitudes and Congressional Voting Behavior: A Causal Model." *American Political Science Review* 60, no. 1 (1966): 66–72.

11. Colomibotos, John. "Social Origins and Ideology of Physicians. A Study of the Effects of Early Socialization." *Journal of Health and Social Behavior* 10, no. 1 (1969): 16–29.

12. Conway, Margaret M., and Frank B. Feigert. "Motivation, Incentive Systems, and the Political Party Organizations." *Journal of American Science Review* 62, no. 4 (1968): 1159–73.

13. Cowart, Andrew T. "Anti-Poverty Expenditures in the American States: A Comparative Analysis." *Midwest Journal of Political Science* 13, no. 2 (1969): 219–36.

14. Crain, Robert L., and Donald B. Rosenthal. "Structure and Value in Local Political Systems: The Case of Fluoridation Decisions." *Journal of Politics* 28, no. 1 (1966): 169–95.

15. Crittendon, John. "Dimensions of Modernization in the American States." *American Political Science Review* 64, no. 4 (1967): 989–1001.

16. Dennis, Jack. "Support for the Party System by the Mass Public." *American Political Science Review* 60, no. 3 (1966): 600–15.

17. Downes, Bryan T. "Municipal Social Rank and the Characteristics of Local Political Leaders." *Midwest Journal of Political Science* 12, no. 4 (1968): 514–37.

18. Downes, Bryan T. "Issue Conflict, Factionalism, and Consensus in Suburban City Councils." *Urban Affairs Quarterly* 4, no. 4 (1969): 477–97.

19. Dye, Thomas R. "Malapportionment and Public Policy in the States." *Journal of Politics* 27, no. 3 (1965): 586–601.

20. Dye, Thomas R. "Urban Political Integration: Conditions Associated with Annexation in American Cities." *Midwest Journal of Political Science* 8, no. 4 (1964): 430–66.

21. Dye, Thomas R. "Inequality and Civil Rights Policy in the States." *The Journal of Politics* 31, no. 4 (1969): 1080–97.

22. Dye, Thomas R. "Governmental Structure, Urban Environment and Educational Policy." *Midwest Journal of Political Science* 11, no. 3 (1967): 353–80.

23. Fenno, Richard F. *The Power of the Purse: Appropriation Politics in Congress* (Boston: Little, Brown and Co., 1966).

24. Fergin, Joe R. "Prejudice, Orthodoxy and the Social Situation." *Journal of Social Forces* 44, no. 1 (1965): 46–57.

25. Field, John O., and Ronald E. Anderson. "Ideology in the Public's Conceptualization of the 1964 Election." *Public Opinion Quarterly* 33, no. 3 (1969): 380–98.

26. Flinn, Thomas A. "Party Responsibility in the States: Some Causal Factors." *American Political Science Review* 68, no. 1 (1964): 60–71.

27. Flinn, Thomas A., and Frederick M. Wirt. "Party Leaders in Ohio." *Midwest Journal of Political Science* 9, no. 1 (1965): 77–98.

28. Form, William H., and Joan Rytina. "The Rich and the Blacks: Two Views of Politics and Government." Paper presented at a meeting of the American Sociological Association. San Francisco, September 1969.

29. Form, William H., and Joan Rytina. "Ideological Beliefs on the Distribution of Power in the U.S." *American Sociological Review* 34, no. 1 (1969): 19–31.

30. Frederickson, H. George. "Exploring Urban Priorities—The Case of Syracuse." *Urban Affairs Quarterly* 5, no. 1 (1969): 31–43.

31. Froman, Lewis A., Jr. "An Analysis of Public Policies in Cities." *Journal of Politics* 29, no. 1 (1967): 94–108.

32. Geschwender, James A. "Social Structure and the Negro Revolt: An Examination of Some Hypotheses." *Journal of Social Forces* 43, no. 2 (1964): 248–56.

33. Glenn, Norval D., and John P. Alston. "Cultural Distances among Occupational Categories." *American Sociological Review* 33, no. 3 (1968): 365–82.

34. Gurr, Ted. "A Causal Model of Civil Strife: A Comparative Analysis Using New Indices." *American Political Science Review* 62, no. 4 (1968): 1104–24.

35. Hacker, Andrew. "Does a 'Divisive' Primary Harm a Candidate's Election Chances?" *American Political Science Review* 59, no. 1 (1965): 105–10.

36. Hamilton, Richard F. "Skill Level and Politics." *Public Opinion Quarterly* 29, no. 3 (1965): 390–99.

37. Hamilton, Richard F. "A Research Note on the Mass Support for 'Tough' Military Initiative." *American Sociological Review* 33, no. 3 (1968): 439–45.

38. Hanson, Bertil. "County Commissioners of Oklahoma." *Midwest Journal of Political Science* 9, no. 4 (1965): 388–400.

39. Hofferbert, Richard. "The Relation Between Public Policy and Some Structural and Environmental Variables in the American States." *American Political Science Review* 60, no. 1 (1966): 73–82.

40. Hofferbert, Richard. "Ecological Development and Policy Change in the American States." *Midwest Journal of Political Science* 10, no. 4 (1966): 464–85.

41. Hofferbert, Richard. "Socioeconomic Dimensions of the American States, 1890–1960." *Midwest Journal of Political Science* 12, no. 3 (1968): 401–18.

42. Jacob, Herbert. "The Consequences of Malapportionment: A Note of Caution." *Journal of Social Forces* 43, no. 2 (1964): 256–61.

43. Janowitz, Morris, and David R. Segal. "Social Cleavage and Party Affiliation: Germany, Great Britain, and the United States." *American Journal of Sociology* 72, no. 6 (1967): 601–18.

44. Jennings, M. Kent, Milton C. Cummings, Jr., and Franklin P. Kilpatrick. "Trusted Leaders: Perceptions of Appointed Federal Officials." *Public Opinion Quarterly* 30, no. 3 (1966): 368–84.

45. Jones, Garth N. "Integration of Political Ethos and Local Government Systems: The Utah Experience with Council-Manager Government." *Human Organization* 23, no. 3 (1964): 210–23.

46. Kagi, Herbert M. "The Roles of Private Consultants in Urban Governing." *Urban Affairs Quarterly* 5, no. 1 (1969): 45–58.

47. Katz, Fred, and Fern Piret. "Circuitous Participation in Politics." *American Journal of Sociology* 69, no. 4 (1964): 367–73.

48. Kingdon, John W. "Politicians' Beliefs about Voters." *American Political Science Review* 61, no. 1 (1967): 137–46.

49. Kosa, John, and Clyde Z. Nunn. "Race Deprivation and Attitude toward Communism." *Phylon* 25, no. 4 (1964): 337–46.

50. Laponce, J. A. "An Experimental Method to Measure the Tendency to Equibalance in a Political System." *American Political Science* 60, no. 4 (1966): 982–93.

51. Lenski, Gerhard E. "Status Inconsistency and the Vote: A Four Nation Test." *American Sociological Review* 32, no. 2 (1967): 298–301.

52. Lineberry, Robert, and Edmund Fowler. "Reformism and Public Policies in American Cities." *American Political Science Review* 61, no. 3 (1967): 701–16.

53. Lipsitz, Lewis. "Work Life and Political Attitudes: A Study of Manual Workers." *American Political Science Review* 58, no. 4 (1964): 951–62.

54. Longley, Lawrence. "Interest Group Interaction in a Legislative System." *Journal of Politics* 29, no. 3 (1967): 637–58.

55. Lopreato, Joseph. "Upward Social Mobility and Political Orientation." *American Sociological Review* 32, no. 4 (1967): 586–92.

56. Mars, David. "Localism and Regionalism in Southern California." *Urban Affairs Quarterly* 2, no. 4 (1967): 47–74.

57. Mathews, Daniel R., and James W. Prothro. "Southern Image of Political Parties: An Analysis of White and Negro Attitudes." *Journal of Politics* 26, no. 1 (1964): 88–111.

58. McCloskey, Herbert. "Consensus and Ideology in American Politics." *American Political Science Review* 58, no. 2 (1964): 361–82.

59. Milbraith, Lester W. *The Washington Lobbyist*. Chicago: Rand McNally and Co., 1963.

60. Mitchell, Robert E. "Class-Linked Conflict between Two Dimensions of Liberalism-Conservatism." *Journal of Social Problems* 13, no. 4 (1966): 418–27.

61. Neubauer, Deane E. "Some Conditions of Democracy." *American Political Science Review* 61, no. 4 (1967): 1002–10.

62. Olsen, Marvin E. "Perceived Legitimacy of Social Protest Actions." *Social Problems* 15, no. 3 (1963): 297–310.

63. Olsen, Marvin E. "Alienation and Political Opinions." *Public Opinion Quarterly* 29, no. 2 (1965): 200–212.

64. Olson, David M. "Citizen Grievance Letters as a Gubernatorial Control Device in Wisconsin." *Journal of Politics* 31, no. 3 (1969): 741–55.

65. Olson, David M. "Studies in American Legislative Process." *Public Administration Review* 23, no. 3 (1968): 280–86.

66. Photiadis, John D. "Community Size and Aspects of the Authoritarian Personality among Businessmen." *Rural Sociology* 32, no. 1 (1967): 70–77.

67. Polansky, Norman A. "Powerlessness among Rural Appalachian Youth." *Rural Sociology* 34, no. 2 (1969): 219–22.

68. Polsby, Nelson W. "The Institutionalization of the U.S. House of Representatives." *American Political Science Review* 62, no. 1 (1968): 144–68.

69. Palumbo, Dennis J., and Oliver P. Williams. "Predictors of Public Policy: The Case of Local Public Health." *Urban Affairs Quarterly* 2, no. 4 (1967): 75–92.

70. Prothro, James W., and Charles M. Grigg. "Fundamental Principles of Democracy: Bases of Agreement and Disagreement." *Journal of Politics* 22, no. 2 (1960): 276–94.

71. Pulsipher, Allan G., and James L. Weatherby, Jr. "Malapportionment, Party Competition, and the Functional Distribution of Governmental Expenditures." *American Political Science Review* 62, no. 4 (1968): 1207–19.

72. Putnam, Robert D. "Political Attitudes and the Local Community." *American Political Science Review* 60, no. 3 (1966): 640–54.

73. Rabinovitz, Francine F., and Stanley S. Pattinger. "Organization for Local Planning: The Attitudes of Directors." *Journal of AIP* 33, no. 1 (1967): 27–32.

74. Raven, Bertram H., and Phillip S. Gallo. "The Effects of Nominating Conventions, Elections and Reference Group Identification upon the Perception of Political Figures." *Human Relations* 19, no. 3 (1968): 217–31.

75. Reynolds, Harry W., Jr. "Local Government Structure in Urban Planning, Renewal, and Relocation." *Public Administration Review* 24, no. 1 (1964): 14–20.

76. Rogers, William C., Barbara Stuhler, and Donald Koenig. "A Comparison of Informed and General Public Opinion on U.S. Foreign Policy." *Public Opinion Quarterly* 31, no. 2 (1967): 242–52.

77. Rosenthal, Donald B., and Robert L. Crain. "Executive Leadership and Community Innovation: Fluoridation." *Urban Affairs Quarterly* 1, no. 3 (1966): 39–57.

78. Rush, Gary R. "Status Consistency and Right-Wing Extremism." *American Sociological Review* 32, no. 1 (1967): 86–92.

79. Rytina, Joan, William H. Form, and John Pease. "Income and Ideological Beliefs about the Distribution of Power in the United States." Convention paper, ASA, 1969.

80. Rytina, Joan, William H. Form, and John Pease. "Income and Ideology: General and Situated Beliefs about the American Opportunity System." Convention paper, ASA, 1969.

81. St. Angelo, Douglas, and James Dyson. "Personality vs. Political Orientation." *Midwest Journal of Political Science* 12, no. 2 (1968): 202–23.

82. Schmuck, Richard, and Mark Chesler. "Superpatriot Opposition to Community Mental Health Programs." *Community Mental Health Journal* 3, no. 4 (1967): 382–88.

83. Schoenberger, Robert A. "Conservatism, Personality, and Political Extremism." *American Political Science Review* 62, no. 3 (1968): 868–79.

84. Scott, Andrew M., and Margaret A. Hunt. *Congress and Lobbies: Image and Reality.* Chapel Hill: The University of North Carolina Press, 1964.

85. Scott, Thomas M. "The Diffusion of Urban Governmental Forms as a Case of Social Learning." *Journal of Politics* 30, no. 4 (1968): 1091–1108.

86. Sears, David O. "Political Behavior." In *The Handbook of Social Psychology.* Gardner Lindsay and Elliot Aronson, eds. 2d ed. Reading, Mass.: Addison-Wesley, 1969. 5: 315–48.

87. Segal, David R., and David Knoke. "Social and Economic Bases of Political Partisanship in the United States." Paper for American Sociological Association, 1969.

88. Sharkansky, Ira. "Economic Development, Regionalism and State Political Systems." *Midwest Journal of Political Science* 12, no. 1 (1968): 41–61.

89. Sharkansky, Ira. "Economic and Political Correlations of State Government Expenditures: General Tendencies and Deviant Cases." *Midwest Journal of Political Science* 11, no. 2 (1967): 173–92.

90. Sharkansky, Ira. "Agency Requests, Gubernatorial Support and Budget Success in State Legislatures." *American Political Science Review* 62, no. 4 (1968): 1220–31.

91. Sharkansky, Ira. "Government Expenditures and Public Services in the American States." *American Political Science Review* 61, no. 4 (1967): 1066–77.

92. Snowniss, Leo M. "Congressional Recruitment and Representation." *American Political Science Review* 60, no. 3 (1966): 627–39.

93. Stacey, Barrie. "Intergeneration Mobility and Voting." *Public Opinion Quarterly* 30, no. 1 (1966): 133–39.

94. Templeton, Fredric. "Alienation and Political Participation: Some Research Findings." *Public Opinion Quarterly* 30, no. 2 (1966): 249–61.

95. Teune, Henry. "Legislative Attitudes toward Interest Groups." *Midwest Journal of Political Science* 11, no. 4 (1967): 489–504.

96. Thomas, Norman C. "The Electorate and State Constitutional Revision: An Analysis of Four Michigan Referenda." *Midwest Journal of Science* 12, no. 1 (1968): 115–29.

97. Uyeki, Eugene S. "Patterns of Voting in a Metropolitan Area: 1938–1962." *Urban Affairs Quarterly* 1, no. 4 (1966): 65–77.

98. Verba, Sidney, et al. "Public Opinion and the War in Vietnam." *American Political Science Review* 61, no. 2 (1967): 317–34.

99. Walker, Jack L. "The Diffusion of Innovations among the American States." *American Political Science Review* 63, no. 3 (1969): 880–99.

100. Westby, David L., and Richard G. Braungart. "Class and Politics in the Family Backgrounds of Student Political Activists." *American Sociological Review* 31, no. 5 (1966): 690–92.

101. Wilson, James Q., and Edward C. Banfield. "Public Regardingness as a Value Premise in Voting Behavior." *The American Political Science Review* 58, no. 4 (1964): 876–87.

102. Wolfinger, Raymond E. "The Development and Persistence of Ethnic Voting." *American Political Science Review* 59, no. 4 (1965): 896–908.

103. Wolfinger, Raymond E., and J. O. Field. "Political Ethos and the Structure of City Government." *American Political Science Review* 60, no. 2 (1966): 306–26.

104. Zeitlin, Maurice. "Revolutionary Workers and Individual Liberties." *American Journal of Sociology* 72, no. 6 (1967): 601–18.

105. Zisk, Betty, Heinz Eulaw, and Kenneth Prewitt. "City Councilmen and the Group Struggle: A Typology of Role Orientation." *Journal of Politics* 27, no. 3 (1965): 618–46.

Part Five

Citizen Participation in Social Change

Chapter Seven

Participation: Voluntary Associations and Primary Groups

INTRODUCTION AND OVERVIEW
ON PARTICIPATION

THE MATTER of citizen participation has been a continuing major concern for community organization practitioners and theorists, predating by some time the Office of Economic Opportunity's popularization of the concept in its slogan "maximum feasible participation." Neighborhood and community development workers, including those in the early settlement-house movement, viewed grass-roots participation as a cardinal requisite of their efforts, and planners in such institutions as Community Welfare Councils and United Funds have long embraced "voluntarism," by which operationally they meant the involvement of a cross section of community elites in policy formulation and program implementation.[1] Unfortunately, participation has been inadequately developed as a specific conceptual area of social science, although, since de Tocqueville's [2] early insightful writings, American social scientists have included the question of collective voluntary action as an item on their intellectual agenda. In more recent years, under the impact of such social developments as OEO, the Civil Rights and Black Power movements, student activism, and women's liberation sociologists and political scientists have raised the saliency of this subject in their research and writings.

[1] For a historical overview on the subject see Sidney Dillick, *Community Organization for Neighborhood Development—Past and Present* (New York: Women's Press and Morrow, 1953).

[2] Alexis De Tocqueville, *Democracy in America* (New York: Oxford University Press, 1947).

A multitude of forms of participation exist and new forms appear to be emerging. Individuals have had primary-group, kinship, and friendship associations over the centuries. With the advent of industrialization and its concomitant increased societal complexity, voluntary associations and formal organizations have come into being, proliferating the number and diversity of associational structures. As societies have increased in scope and expectations of oppressed people have risen, the potential and need has developed for individuals to organize themselves on a large-scale basis through social movements.

Voluntary associations are often viewed as mechanisms for mediating between the individual, made small by the growing size and complexity of society, and larger community and bureaucratic structures that affect one's life. In this sense, voluntary associations represent collective instrumentalities through which individuals in concert, especially those with little power or resources, may make a greater impact on their social environment than if they acted independently.[3] Citizen education, creative expression, and societal change are also seen as functions of associations. Since citizen participation in these associations is critical to their performance, the manipulation of types and rates of participation is of considerable importance to change agents and community operatives of various kinds. Ironically—as Kornhauser, Hausknecht, Foskett, and other sociologists who have studied voluntary associations have suggested—participation is unevenly distributed in the community, and those who have most to gain from such involvement, the poor, show the lowest rates of membership.

In the area of community organization, participation has been viewed in various and not always compatible ways. Sometimes participation is spoken of as a goal in its own right. That is to say, in an impersonal urban environment, where associational ties have supposedly been weakened, the core objective of practice has been viewed by some to be the restoration of potential ties for meaningful human interaction through participation.[4] Substantive results, such as specific

---

[3] Arnold Rose, "A Theory of the Function of Voluntary Associations in Contemporary Social Structure." "Some Functions of Voluntary Association" from his book, *Theory and Method in the Social Sciences* (Minneapolis: The University of Minnesota Press, 1954), ch. 3.

[4] For a prototypical representation of this position see William W. and Loureide J.

health and welfare programs, are not so important in this formulation as is the more fundamental objective of providing channels for meaningful interaction.

Sometimes participation is viewed as a means for achieving more concrete programmatic ends—but as a constant, unvarying means.[5] There are two main suppositions here. On the one hand, it is argued that democratic values require the broadest possible involvement of affected community actors in the development and enactment of policies and programs. Hence, maximum participation represents a fundamental philosophical creed of practice. On the other hand, it is held that only those programs which are determined by citizens will be vigorously carried out; that is to say, when people take part in determining policies, they will lend themselves to and support these policies over the long run. Lewin's classic studies on the effects of group participation on carrying out personal decisions buttress this position. Thus, participation is correlated on a more practical basis with effectiveness of program implementation.

A third view of participation is more relativistic, and, one might say, analytical. It looks at participation also as a means, but as a conditional means to be employed selectively for certain goals and under given circumstances.[6] Not all valued social objectives, in this conception, will be achieved or maximized through broad participation. Some research studies, for example, suggest that raising the level of community involvement has had a negative impact on the institution of pro-

---

Biddle, *The Community Development Process: The Rediscovery of Local Initiative* (New York: Holt, Rinehart and Winston, 1965).

[5] Murray G. Ross in his widely read book on community organization advocates this view. He states: "Community organization as it has been described here requires the participation of the people of a community. For what is to be united in common action is people. And what is to be changed is to be changed by people." Murray G. Ross, *Community Organization: Theory, Principles and Practice* (New York: Harper and Row, 1967), pp. 168–69. This view may also be inferred from John M. Foskett, "The Influence of Social Participation on Community Programs and Activities," *Community Structure and Analysis,* Marvin B. Sussman ed. (New York: Thomas Y. Crowell, 1959), pp. 311–30.

[6] This more analytical orientation is suggested in William Gamson, "Community Issues and Their Outcome: How to Lose a Fluoridation Referendum," in *Applied Sociology: Principles and Problems,* eds. A. Gouldner and S. M. Miller (Glencoe, Illinois: The Free Press, 1965).

gressive programs such as school desegregation and fluoridation. With this third orientation the practitioner should weigh the costs and benefits of participation in terms of specific social-welfare outputs.

As an aid to presenting findings, we have considered the matter of typologies of participation. In our review of efforts by researchers to categorize forms of participation, we found a multiplicity of approaches that attempt to achieve theoretical and empirical utility. Typologies have been constructed utilizing such concepts as expressive and instrumental behavior, temporary and permanent structures, public and private auspices, remunerative and nonremunerative motives.[7] These typologies have not been related to a general theory of participation; no such theory or conventional typology has emerged which enjoys widespread consensus among researchers or practitioners in the field.

For purposes of presentation we have found it convenient to classify types of participation in a pragmatic fashion on the basis of the major kinds of social groupings with which community practitioners ordinarily engage in conducting their work. These include the following:

1. Voluntary associations made up of citizen actors, usually at the grass-roots level. We define voluntary associations in terms of expressive as well as instrumental activities, and we *exclude* for purposes of this discussion those organizations specifically engaged in militant social action or political work. Voluntary associations in this sense deal with middle-range social change when they are task-oriented rather than expressive in character.

2. Primary group units including friendship, kinship, and local neighborhood groups, which have informal interpersonal ties that often cut across interest-group associations.

3. Social movements aimed at inducing radical social change at the community or societal level and often made up of disaffiliated, deviant, or socially oppressed populations. Often such groups in their proximate goals seek to change policies and programs of bureaucratic organizations such as welfare departments and boards of education. Broadening the decision-making structure in such organizations is also a common goal.

---

[7] See for example, C. Wayne Gordon and Nicholas Babchuk, "A Typology of Voluntary Associations," *American Sociological Review* 24, no. 2 (February 1959): 22–29.

4. Politically oriented groups, which gear their activities largely toward modifications of the existing political system and which operate through established political structures and instrumentalities.

5. Client organizations composed of individuals who receive services from a variety of formal organizations related to the human-services-agency network and those activities are focused on affecting service delivery patterns and modifying decision-making structures in the welfare field.

These five types of participation, hence, will comprise the basic analytical categories and topical rubrics we shall use in presenting the pertinent research we have reviewed. In the following sections these types of participation will be treated separately and sequentially. While we have differentiated them for analytical purposes, the categories are not considered mutually exclusive in an absolute sense. Nevertheless this scheme appears to be useful. In a two-part presentation on participation we shall use this initial chapter to treat participation in voluntary associations and primary groups, and a second one to deal with more specifically action-oriented participation in mass movements, political affairs, and client-based organizations.

We found a considerable volume of research studies on participation in the journals we reviewed. We have therefore summarized and synthesized a formidable body of writings in a small amount of space, as we found it impossible to engage in elaborate discussion of generalizations or to provide much descriptive content from studies. Occasionally, when a specific study seemed of particular interest or lent special clarification, we have selectively summarized its salient points. At the conclusion of this part we have provided a brief recapitulation of major generalizations on participation as well as the bibliography of research studies on this subject.

PARTICIPATION IN VOLUNTARY ASSOCIATIONS

Since the voluntary association is probably the most common type of organization with which community practitioners work, research findings concerning participation in them are of considerable interest for our purposes. Voluntary associations are usually defined by social-science researchers as organized groups of people having the following characteristics:

1. CONTINUITY: the association persists over some discernible period of time.

2. GOALS: the association is formed for specific, shared purposes.

3. MOTIVATION: membership in the association is voluntary, the result of individual choice rather than compulsion.

4. STRUCTURE: the association has developed some definition of member obligations and rights, some hierarchical configuration, and some patterns of organizational activity.

Social-science research on voluntary associations has been largely directed to answering such questions as Why do persons join voluntary associations? or What are the characteristics of individual participants? There has been less research concerned with the characteristics (structure and atmosphere) of the voluntary associations themselves, the different types of existing voluntary associations, and the influence of associational structure on individual participation patterns.

The reader should be aware of the context of research studies that were reviewed in this chapter. The studies cover a wide range of types of voluntary associations, such as those related to occupations, professional associations, unions, church-related associations, neighborhood self-help groups, or associations organized under the influence of a sponsoring agency. At the same time, the highly informal, flat organizational types, of which there are many in ghettos and poor neighborhoods,[8] are generally excluded. Few studies compare participation in these different types of associations, so that one is limited in making applications of the findings. In addition, participation is generally defined as "membership in voluntary associations." Few studies attempt to distinguish between different degrees of intensity of association participation.[9] These limitations notwithstanding, a number of generalizations of interest to practitioners may be formulated.

[8] See Nicholas Von Hoffman, "Re-Organization in the Casbah," *Social Progress* 52, no. 6 (April 1962): 33–44

[9] Chapin, in his participation scale, suggests five levels of intensity of participation: official membership, meeting attendance, financial contributions, committee participation, holding an office. F. Stuart Chapin, *Experimental Designs in Sociological Research* (New York: Harper Bros., 1955).

The Demography of Involvement in Voluntary Associations: Who Participates

Scope of Adult Participation

GENERALIZATION 7.1: Most adults are members of voluntary associations (+ +, 12, 141).

An example of research supporting this proposition is the study by Babchuck and Booth (12) who interviewed a representative cross section of persons age 21 to 63 in a Midwestern state. Babchuck and Booth found that 84 percent of their respondents belonged to at least one voluntary association. However, it should be noted that the authors use "voluntary association" to refer to a broad range of groups (such as church- and job-related associations, recreational groups, and fraternal and service clubs) in addition to the task-oriented planning and action groups with whom the community practitioner usually works.

Action Guidelines: Since most adults in this country have been members of voluntary associations, the practitioner may rely on this form of participation as an initial organizing device rather than using other forms (such as social or political action) with which persons may not be so familiar or may not accept as legitimate. Second, the practitioner may use the many existing voluntary associations in any community to recruit members to spread information, and to diffuse innovations and programs. In addition, programs or activities promoted in the context of or as an expression of voluntary association behavior may gain legitimation or support in the community.

Social Class

GENERALIZATION 7.2: Participation in voluntary associations varies with an individual's social class (+ + + +, 12, 46, 82, 90, 141, 203, 235).

7.2A. Participation in voluntary associations varies directly with level of education. As an individual's level of education increases, so does participation in volunatry associations (+ + +, 46, 82, 90, 203).

7.2B. Participation in voluntary associations varies directly with an individual's family income (+ +, 90).

7.2C. Participation in voluntary associations varies directly with an individual's perceived social status (reputational prestige) in the community (+, 234).

7.2D. One's social class not only influences his rates of participation but also his type of association. Lower-class persons have higher rates of participation in expressive than in instrumental organizations (see Generalization 7.10). Middle- and upper-class persons appear to have high participation in both types of organizations (+ +, 141).

Action Guidelines: Persons with high social class—as measured by the dimensions of level of education, social prestige, and income—appear to be the easiest persons to recruit for membership in voluntary associations. To the degree that voluntary associations are influential in the community, interests of such persons may be disproportionately favored. The findings also suggest that a low level of education is associated with lower participation; thus community-sponsored adult-education programs might potentially result in an increase in associational participation in lower-class communities.

Occupation

GENERALIZATION 7.3: Participation in voluntary associations varies with certain characteristics of an individual's occupation. One's amount of participation and the type of association one joins are influenced by one's occupation. (+ + +, 52, 82, 83).

7.3A. Participation in voluntary associations appears to be highest among members of "professional" occupations (+ +, 52, 83).

The relationship between occupational professionalization and patterns of community participation was studied by Faunce and

McClelland (52). They examined an industrial community whose proportion of professionals in the labor force was increasing because of automation. The researchers found that professionals have a high rate of participation in community activities and were becoming the most influential group in the community.

7.3B. Participation in voluntary associations is associated with occupations that provide the individual with a leadership role (+, 82).

7.3C. Occupation influences the type of association in which persons participate. Persons tend to participate in organizations whose prestige ranking corresponds to their occupational prestige ranking (+, 82).

This proposition was explicitly tested by Hagedorn and Labowitz (82) who studied the participation patterns of persons in eight occupational categories—managers, engineers, scientists, skilled and semiskilled workers, technicians, technologists, clerical workers, servicemen, and janitors. They found that occupational status was related both to rate of participation (persons in high-status occupations had higher rates of participation in community and professional associations) and to type of participation. (The higher a person's occupational prestige, the higher the prestige of the organizations of which he was a member.)

7.3D. Participation in "bureaucratized" occupations is associated with high rates of voluntary association membership (+ +, 21, 82).

This finding contradicts the theory that bureaucratization leads to the development of a highly alienated "middle mass." Instead the experience of participating in bureaucratic organizations appears to increase association membership. Skills and attitudes fostered by one context may perhaps be easily transferred to the other context.

7.3E. Small businessmen have the lowest level of participation in voluntary associations, particularly in small communities undergoing industrialization and in larger cities. This group also shows a high degree of alienation and the highest resistance to change-orientated, government-sponsored programs (+ +, 21, 166, 167).

(*Occupation and Race*)

7.3F. For whites, participation varies directly with the status of an individual's occupation (+ +, 21, 82).

7.3G. For blacks, low-status occupational groups may have higher

288 Citizen Participation

rates of membership in voluntary associations than do the higher status occupational groups (+, 195).

This apparent racial difference in participation may be explained by the high participation of blacks with low occupational status in expressive organizations such as churches, and recreational and fraternal organizations. However, none of the empirical articles covered in this project specifically investigated the relationship between race, occupational status, and type of association membership.

Action Guidelines: These propositions relating participation to occupational characteristics are helpful in predicting persons who would be likely to join a voluntary association, suggesting that it is easier to recruit members of higher status occupations, except in the black community, where the converse may hold. The practitioner in a community undergoing a change in its occupational structure can anticipate changes in voluntary association membership. The practitioner will probably be more successful in recruiting new members who have occupational status similar to that of existing members: if the practitioner is able to recruit high- or low-status members whose status differs from that of the existing membership, the prestige of the association will raise or lower accordingly. Attempts to open opportunities for low-income people—particularly by employing them in responsible positions in large, bureaucratic organizations—may also increase their rates of participation in voluntary associations.

Sex

GENERALIZATION 7.4: Men and women have different rates of participation in voluntary associations (+ + +, 12, 160, 195).

7.4A. White men have higher rates of participation in voluntary associations than white women (+ +, 12, 160).

7.4B. Black women have higher rates of participation in voluntary associations than black men (+, 195).

7.4C. Women on the whole appear to have more stable patterns of participation in voluntary associations than do men. They tend to retain their membership in the same organization for longer periods of time (+, 12).

Action Guidelines: White men have more experience in voluntary associations and would probably be easier to recruit for a wide range of organizations. Black women appear to be the better recruitment source. For ease in recruitment, the practitioner might lean toward attracting black women. However, an important practice objective might be to increase the rate of participation of black males. The practitioner might consider recruiting women for participation in long-range programs and recruit men for shorter-run change efforts.

Life Cycle

GENERALIZATION 7.5: Rates of participation in voluntary associations differ at different stages in an individual's life cycle (+ + +, 12, 114, 160).

7.5A. Participation is greatest among persons of middle age (+ +, 12, 160).

This finding may not necessarily reveal a lack of interest in participation among older and younger persons, but rather a lack of opportunity for participation and barriers to participation—for example, lack of transportation. A study by Lambert, Guberman, and Morris (114), for instance, showed that one-third of a sample of 297 elderly persons were willing to donate their services to agencies, but administrators were unwilling to use them. As has been suggested elsewhere (209), participation rates are associated with opportunity, motivation, capacity.

7.5B. Participation is greater for married than for single persons. Married people with school-age children have higher participation rates than those with very young children (+, 12, 160).

Middle age correlates with marriage. Persons in their middle years have firm roots in the community, children in school, business inter-

290 Citizen Participation

ests to promote—all of which serve to act as a stimulus for participation.

Action Guidelines: Persons in their middle years, especially those who are married, should be the easiest group to recruit. The practitioner attempting to increase participation of other age groups will have to deal with the factors that limit the participation of these groups, such as lack of transportation and attitudes of citizens and professionals regarding older persons.

Multiplier Effect

GENERALIZATION 7.6: Persons who are already members of voluntary associations are most likely to join other organizations. Persons who have never been members are least likely to join a new organization (+ +, 76, 82).

Action Guidelines: A primary pool of recruits for association membership is composed of persons who already belong to voluntary associations. A practitioner seeking active participants in new projects should consider approaching people with a strong record of activity. Also, one of the benefits of participation is that it may stimulate people to expand their organizational memberships.

Lower-Class Participation—Participation of the Poor

The preceding propositions have illustrated some general attributes of individuals, which influence their participation in voluntary associations. The practitioner may take into account and use these characteristics in recruiting various groups into membership in voluntary associations or determining where greater effort is required to increase participation. Clearly, the practitioner cannot change individual characteristics, such as age, sex, and social class, which are associated with participation, but he may be able to manipulate directly such other variables as attitudes and values, which in turn influence the participation patterns of different groups. We shall be dealing with these types of variables to a greater degree in the sections that follow. We shall also add specificity to the discussion by focusing on participation among different class levels.

Attitudes and Motives of the Poor

GENERALIZATION 7.7: Many of the attitudes and values associated with low-income life-style seem to limit participation in voluntary associations (+ + +, 176, 188, 235).

7.7A. Low-income persons have a low sense of efficacy and an attitude of powerlessness. They tend to see their low status as the result of strong external forces over which they have no control (+ + +, 176, 188, 235).

Efficacy here refers to an individual's belief that through his own actions he is able to exert some influence over his own life and external environment.

Of course, not all lower-income persons share these feelings equally; but it does appear that in aggregate these attitudes are more common among the poor than among higher-status groups, and that, among the poor, the persons who have the most feelings of powerlessness are least likely to participate in voluntary associations. For example, Chemmie (30) studied AFDC mothers in terms of their participation in a welfare rights organization. He found that, in comparison with low-level participants or nonparticipants, mothers with high participation in the organization were less likely to subscribe to a belief in fate, higher in optimism, and held significantly lower feelings of powerlessness, social isolation, and alienation. The three groups had similar feelings of normlessness and manifest anxiety.

Action Guidelines: Practitioners need to provide low-income persons with opportunities to increase their sense of efficacy. For example, if the practitioner can select immediate activities and goals that are delimited and more readily achievable, he can increase the probability that the community organization he is staffing will successfully accomplish its initial goals. Such short-range goal attainment may increase morale and provide an impetus for working on long-range goals.

Experience of the Poor

GENERALIZATION 7.8: Low-income persons may lack the experience of participation in specific social roles that facilitate membership in voluntary associations. They frequently acquire social role behaviors that inhibit membership (+ + +, 14, 112, 235) (See Subgeneralization 7.3B).

7.8A. Low-income persons generally have high experience with dependency roles and little experience with leadership roles (+, 235).

7.8B. Because of these dependency roles, lower-class persons may be extremely reluctant to take action and express their grievances against persons whom they perceive as powerful oppressors (+, 112).

7.8C. Low-income persons may develop tendencies to displace their frustration by in-group aggression, dependency attitudes, or regression rather than taking direct action toward the source of their frustration (+, 14).

Action Guidelines: Practitioners may help low-income persons overcome feelings of dependency by placing them in positions of leadership within voluntary associations and by maximizing their responsibility for participation in group decision making. The practitioner can encourage low-income persons to express their frustrations and attempt to define the external sources of these frustrations. The practitioners may have to rely initially on strategies that do not invoke high fear of reprisal from powerful oppressive forces. Alternatively, through humiliating or disarming such forces or by building protective group solidarity, the poor may take courage to oppose oppressive forces.

Resources of the Poor

GENERALIZATION 7.9: Low-income persons have few of the objective resources necessary for participation in voluntary associations. Lack of these resources can be a barrier to association membership and to the association's ability to function (+ + +, 20, 40, 146).

> 7.9A. Low-income persons contribute less money to voluntary associations (and are less able to contribute) than higher income persons (+ +, 20, 146).
>
> 7.9B. Low-income persons may not have funds to spend on transportation, child care, and other kinds of domestic help that may be necessary in order for them to participate in voluntary associations (+, 40).

Practice Guidelines: The practitioner may have to seek funding for a voluntary association outside its low-income membership (such as foundations, government grants, etc.). This can have the effect of limiting autonomy or making budgets unstable. Many low-income members may have to be provided with aids such as transportation and child-care services in order to facilitate their participation in associations.

Time Perspective on Gratification

GENERALIZATION 7.10: Low-income persons have unique attitudes and interests, which potentially may motivate them to participate in certain kinds of voluntary associations. The practitioner may rely on or act to enhance these motivations in attempting to increase the participation of low-income persons in voluntary associations (+ + +, 154, 187, 188, 195).

> 7.10A. Low-income persons show more interest in participating in activities that have direct, immediate benefits than in long-term activities with long-range payoffs (+ +, 187, 188).
>
> This generalization has been tested in several studies of time ori-

entation of lower- and middle-class persons. In comparison with their middle-class counterparts, lower-class individuals have a greater present-time orientation as compared to a future-time orientation. Some researchers have hypothesized that this difference in time orientation is due to pressure on the low-income person to be preoccupied with immediate, recurrent daily problems of survival. An example of class differences in time orientation was found in a study by Schneiderman (187), who compared a sample of welfare recipients with a sample of middle-class school teachers and social workers. Welfare recipients were significantly more likely to emphasize "present time" over "future time" on a value orientation scale based on an instrument developed by Kluckhohn and Strodtbeck.

7.10B. Low-income persons seem to prefer participation in activities that provide opportunities for spontaneous, expressive behavior (+ + +, 154, 187, 188, 195).

Action Guidelines: Lower-class persons seem to require a high amount of immediate benefit or payoff in order to sustain their participation in voluntary associations. Low-income persons seem to prefer voluntary associations that provide high levels of two kinds of participation benefits: instrumental resolution of immediate problems and expressive performance, with immediate social gratification. Rather than initially attempting to induce the poor to participate in long-range planning organizations, it would seem advisable to encourage formation of community organizations that can assist in the solving of daily problems, such as getting the landlord to repair substandard housing, and that can provide members with strong social satisfactions. At least some short-range projects with quick payoffs should be built into organizational programs for the poor.

Immediate Economic Gains vs. Changes
in Life-Style

GENERALIZATION 7.11: Low-income populations are more likely to participate in programs that aim at improving eco-

nomic and social conditions obviously affecting them ad-
versely than in programs aimed at changing their life-styles,
attitudes, and behaviors (+ + + +, 20, 46, 76, 129, 183, 210).

7.11A. Low-income persons show interest in participating in activities that have direct, specific economic benefits: activities specifically aimed at reducing their poverty (+ +, 20, 46).

7.11B. Low-income persons are on the whole more likely than other
groups to perceive social-system barriers that limit upward mobility.
Higher-income groups are more likely to perceive barriers to mobility in terms of individual differences in ability and achievement
(+ +, 183).

7.11C. Voluntary associations that stress "self-help" as the major
strategy for dealing with the problem of poverty seem to have little
general participation by low-income persons (+ +, 76, 210).

Although social-welfare projects that fail are not usually the subject of empirical research reports, some studies that support the
above proposition are available. Spitze (210), for example, reported
the failure of a self-improvement housekeeping program for welfare
recipients. She compared a group of mothers who were enrolled in
the program with a control group of mothers who did not participate. The groups were studied after the housekeeping program was
completed, and no differences in behavior were found. In addition,
attendance at the program meetings was very low.

7.11D. Low-income persons with low levels of participation are not
entirely isolated from organizations, even if their participation is at
a low level. Many low-income persons have contact with economically oriented welfare institutions such as employment agencies or
welfare departments (+, 129).

7.11E. Self-help groups that attempt to change values and behaviors
of lower-class persons without changing their poverty may be ineffective, since many of the behaviors of lower-class persons are
adaptive and functional for a low-income life-style. The adaptive
practices appear to be held *in addition to* (a "value stretch") rather
than *instead of,* a general set of middle-class values and aspirations
that the poor hold in common with the rest of society (+, 178).

7.11F. "Problematic" behaviors exhibited by many low-income

persons cannot be seen as the consequence of a particular lower-class family structure (+ +, 224).

The effect of family structure on behavior of lower-class persons was studied by Wasserman (224), who compared 55 intact families to 62 father-absent families in a public housing project. The presence or absence of a father failed to differentiate families in terms of dependency attitudes, scholastic achievement of children, and juvenile delinquency. The data were obtained by interviewing mothers, inspecting school records, and reviewing housing authority records.

Action Guidelines: Practitioners attempting to build participation of the poor should concentrate on forming organizations that can deal effectively with problems of poverty. Low-income persons will participate in programs they perceive as directly beneficial (i.e., realistic job training, employment as paraprofessionals by human-service agencies, attempts to increase welfare budgets). The practitioner can anticipate less sustained lower-class participation in self-help civic programs that do not attempt to deal with their economic problems. Since the poor have high contact with organizations that influence their economic status (such as employment and welfare agencies), organizing the poor on the basis of their client status as welfare recipients or as clients of employment agencies may be a useful strategy. Also welfare agencies and employment agencies might be used by practitioners as resources for contacting and recruiting low-income persons. (These agencies may also serve as useful referral centers.) Practitioners should develop improved services or oganize low-income clients in an attempt to improve services rather than sponsor programs directed toward changing ("improving") the poor themselves.

The practitioner should not assume that the poor have totally different values; they also appear to share many of the aspirations of middle-class persons. The practitioner should be aware that self-help programs which seek to modify adaptive behaviors may make it more difficult for low-income persons to function in their social situation. In addition, attempts to change lower-class family structure may be ineffective for reducing certain "problematic" behaviors of low-income persons which agencies are trying to reduce. In summary, self-help programs (such as neighborhood improvement associations) should be evaluated to make sure that the behaviors one is attempting to change are actually dysfunctional, and self-help programs should be undertaken along with, rather than in place of, attempts to reduce poverty.

Class Identity and the Poor

GENERALIZATION 7.12: Lower-class persons have little tendency to participate in voluntary associations organized explicitly and publicly for the purpose of improving "working-class interests" (+ + +, 21, 22, 52, 73).

7.12A. Lower-class persons show relatively high levels of informal participation in religious, neighborhood, and friendship groups but have low membership in voluntary associations and low levels of political participation (+ , 21).

7.12B. Lower-class persons have low class consciousness (+ +, 21, 22, 52, 73; for an expanded discussion see chapter 5).

7.12C. Working-class persons by and large do not experience a sense of relative deprivation because they are likely to perceive that they have a high degree of potential job mobility (+, 22).

This proposition was supported in a study of the job mobility perceptions of a sample of 162 manual workers and 63 salaried managers (22). It was found that as high as 57 percent of the working-class sample perceived opportunities for advancement in their job situation, although managers did have even higher levels of perception of advancement.

Action Guidelines: These generalizations suggest that the practitioner will have little success in gaining participation of workers solely on the basis of their class position or class interests. Other bases for organizing need to be employed.

Middle-Class Participation

Resources of Middle- and Upper-Class Participants

GENERALIZATION 7.13: Persons with high socioeconomic status have specific resources for participation, which the practitioner can utilize (+ + + +, 132, 146, 179, 187, 212).

> 7.13A. Persons with high socioeconomic status have more economic resources for participation than low-income persons and are thus able to have higher commitment to community involvement in terms of willingness to give time and money than are persons of lower socioeconomic status (+, 146).
>
> 7.13B. Highly educated persons have greater future orientation, greater interest in long-range planning activities than persons with less education (+, 187).
>
> 7.13C. Persons with high educational and occupational status are more aware and have more information about general community problems (such as public health and environmental pollution) than lower-class persons (+ +, 132, 179, 212).
>
> An example of research supporting this proposition is a study conducted by Rosenstock, Haefner, Kegelis, and Kerscht (179). They interviewed a sample of 1,493 adults about their knowledge of three public health problems: fallout, pesticides, and fatty foods. Better educated groups and persons with higher incomes were significantly more likely to be well informed about all three issues.

Action Guidelines: Stimulating participation of high-socioeconomic-status persons in a voluntary association is most useful if the association needs money, needs members who can give a large amount of time to association activities, or needs members who have the interest and skills necessary to engage in long-range planning. Also, highly educated persons are well informed about public-health issues and can be used to spread information about those issues both inside and outside the voluntary association. For example, they might be useful in speaking to other community groups about these issues.

Motives and Values of High-Income People

GENERALIZATION 7.14: Highly educated, high-status persons have particular attitudes and values which influence them to participate in specific kinds of organizations (+ + +, 28, 46, 131).

> 7.14A. Self-actualization and self-fulfillment are important factors motivating highly educated persons to participate in community voluntary associations. Economic benefits are less important (+, 46).
>
> Higher-status persons have other means available to them to promote their economic interests. Their own business organizations or professional associations may serve these purposes. Participation in community organizations may thus supplement these other organizational affiliations.
>
> 7.14B. Highly educated persons prefer discussion to lectures (+, 28).
>
> 7.14C. Middle- and upper-class persons appear to prefer use of cooperative group strategies to the use of intergroup conflict (+, 131).

Action Guidelines: To recruit middle- and upper-class persons the practitioner should stress the opportunities for personal growth and development participation offers, provide opportunities for self-evaluation within the organization (for example, group discussions about what the members have learned from a particular participation experience, about the contributions participation has made to their own lives), use discussion rather than or in addition to lecture methods in educating highly educated persons about a particular issue, and try to stress common goals and group values (public-regarding orientation) rather than focusing on divisive issues.

Occupational Rank Among High-Income People

GENERALIZATION 7.15: Persons of high socioeconomic status are likely to be professionals and to have relatively high levels of participation in professional associations.

Their involvement in such associations may reduce the support for innovation in relevant occupations fields (+ +, 13, 51, 53, 221).

7.15A. Professionals may not support innovations in their field,[10] even though such innovations may have considerable support among the general public (+ +, 13, 53).

A comparison of the attitudes of citizens and professionals toward a particular human-services innovation was studied by Baker and Schulberg (13). They compared the degree of support for the idea of community mental health among a sample of nonprofessional citizens and a group of psychologists and psychiatrists. The citizens all served on state mental health area boards. The citizens had higher support for community mental health ideology and were less dogmatic and less conservative in their attitudes concerning mental health services than were the professional psychiatrists and psychologists.

7.15B. Persons who have been members of a profession for a length of time may have a more conservative, less change-oriented approach to innovations in occupational roles (+, 219).

7.15C. The greater the involvement of a profession within a specific occupational area, the less likely the members are to support occupational innovations within that area (+, 51).

Action Guidelines: The practitioner can expect that the increasing "professionalization" of occupations will result in an increase in the formation of professional interest groups, whose members will probably be middle- and upper-class persons. Professional interest groups can constitute a powerful potential source of opposition to radical occupational innovations that a practitioner or citizen groups may wish to see instituted. Rather than trying to modify attitudes and interests within the profession, the practitioner might seek organized support for such occupational innovations among citizen groups, nonprofessional agency board members, or persons who have been in the profession for only a short

[10] One assumes in this discussion occupational innovations that fall outside established norms, values or technical processes within the profession. Fuller discussion of professionals and innovation will be found in chapters 3, 5, 9.

period of time. Practitioners could also attempt to make professionals aware of the degree of community support for occupational innovations.

Benefits and Participation

Benefits of Participation

GENERALIZATION 7.16: The amount of participation in voluntary associations varies directly with both the number of benefits (rewards, satisfactions) offered by an organization, and the degree to which the benefits are contingent upon participation (+ + +, 141, 222, 225).

7.16A. "Lower-class and especially minority members [of voluntary associations] may be likely to find a participation-contributions equation relevant because they have fewer opportunities than middle-class whites to participate" (+ +, 141).

7.16B. There appear to be four important kinds of benefits that community-oriented voluntary associations can offer to the members in exchange for their contributions: achievement of specific goals, personally rewarding goal-achievement procedures, structural devices (such as formal offices), and informal friendships (+ +, 225).

The concept of a benefit-participation contingency that influences participation was utilized by Warner and Hefferman (222) in a study of farmers' organizations. They based the study on a sample of 238 persons, using attendance at meetings as the measure of participation, and measuring the benefits by responses to interviews. They found that the greater the number of benefits contingent upon participation, the higher the attendance at association meetings.

Action Guidelines: Practitioners may raise the amounts of organizational participation by increasing the benefits of participation, especially if members cannot receive these benefits in other ways. Raising benefits is particularly important to sustaining the participation of lower-class persons who have greater limitations on their participation in voluntary associations. Participation benefits the practitioner might manipulate include achieving more goals, using strategies members find personally rewarding, letting persons who enjoy talking speak to community groups, allowing artists to draw posters, increasing the number of association offices and committees, and encouraging the formation of friendships among members.

Benefits to Participants

GENERALIZATION 7.17: Participation in voluntary associations yields a number of personal internal benefits for individuals who participate (+ + +, 30, 102, 145, 165, 237).

> 7.17A. Participation in voluntary associations may lead to increased tolerance of divergent attitudes (+, 237).
> 7.17B. Participation in voluntary associations is associated with the development of a more positive self-image (+ +, 102, 145, 165).
> 7.17C. Participation in voluntary associations is associated with a decrease in feelings of powerlessness (+, 30).

Action Guidelines: Practitioners may increase individuals' desires to participate in voluntary associations by demonstrating the benefits of such participation. The practitioner may also deliberately use participation to promote greater tolerance of divergent viewpoints, enhanced self-image, and an increased sense of mastery.

Some Dynamics of Participation

Intensity of Participation and Group Consensus

GENERALIZATION 7.18: An intensely high level of active participation is not necessary in order to achieve consensus about actions in a voluntary association. In a large organization, active participation may serve to increase the level of conflict within the association (+ +, 141, 202).

Etzioni has suggested that the degree of participation for effective organizational operation varies. He indicates a rising level of participation by members in the following organizational contexts: prison, the peacetime army, industrial plants, trade unions, schools, mental hospitals, religious organizations. The degree to which member commitment is vital for achieving organizational goals is a factor to be weighed in viewing modes of participation.[11]

Action Guidelines: If participation is sufficient to sustain motivation and attain goals in a task-oriented organization, the practitioner would be advised not to be overly concerned about raising the level of participation. In conflict situations, the practitioner may actually want to decrease the level of participation, at least temporarily.

Minority Domination

GENERALIZATION 7.19: Voluntary associations may become co-opted by a small group of members so that they no longer represent the interests of all members of the association (+, 53).

Action Guidelines: To maintain democratic control of a voluntary association, the practitioner can foster utilization of group decision-making processes; for example, he may require that issues be voted upon by group members rather than being decided in small executive committees. This generalization and its implications can be seen as a contradiction—or better still a limitation—on the previous generalization. The practical reality, however, is that practitioners have to balance strategies that may limit the level of participation with strategies that stress democratic control of the association, depending on circumstances and goals.

Physical Location and Participation

GENERALIZATION 7.20: Physical features such as seating arrangements may affect differential participation at a meeting. Persons who sit in the front of the room or directly facing the chairman usually make the largest number of comments (+, 207).

[11] Amitai Etzioni, *Complex Organizations: A Sociological Reader* (New York: Holt, Rinehart and Winston, Inc., 1962).

Action Guidelines: The practitioner may possibly affect to some degree the amount of participation by individuals in a meeting by the way he arranges the seating. To increase participation of individuals, he should locate them in the front of a room or facing the chairman. To decrease participation of individuals, he should locate them in the back of the room, or not facing the chairman. To equalize participation he should attempt a fluid physical arrangement.

Effects of Irregular Events–Community Disasters

GENERALIZATION 7.21: During times of disaster, traditional interest barriers to participation often break down. At these times the community is most willing to develop multiclass voluntary associations, and to extend the opportunity for participation to low-income groups and other groups whose participation in the community is traditionally marginal (+ +, 49, 174).

Studies of participation patterns that emerge during periods of natural disaster have been studied by Dynes (49). Drawing on a series of case studies of natural disasters made by the Disaster Research Center at Ohio State University, Dynes found that in disasters feelings of community solidarity emerged and that persons placed a higher priority on community interests than on self interests. Community identification increased, and personal and intergroup conflicts decreased.

Action Guidelines: Stress situations such as disasters may provide opportunities to incorporate unrepresented groups and interests in the community participatory structure. A practitioner seeking to promote such participation should reenforce these changes to give them continuity.

Scope of Participation and Unintended Consequences

GENERALIZATION 7.22: Failure to utilize existing patterns of "horizontal integration" of community associations results in a higher proportion of unfavorable consequences in "consensual" or "rational" planning efforts. Higher community participation in planning may lead to fewer unintended negative effects (+, 29, 158).

7.22A. Voluntary associations are important components of the community's horizontal integration pattern, necessary in planning. They are usually not part of the community vertical integration pattern utilized in some types of community planning (+, 29).

Horizontal integration refers to the pattern of linkages among organizations within the community. *Vertical integration* refers to the linkages of local organizations with larger "parent" organizations at the regional, state, or national level.

Callahan's (29) study of 116 planners in nine cities showed that they utilized two different networks of organizations in planning. Planners who were affiliated with voluntary associations utilized horizontally integrated organizations in planning. Planners in public agencies involved vertically linked networks in planning.

Action Guidelines: Voluntary planning processes often involve use of the network of horizontally linked local organizations. Practitioners should be alert to the necessity of such interorganizational linkages. Planners in public agencies are least likely to utilize such horizontal networks, thus practitioners should make them aware of this deficiency when additional horizontal linkages are necessary. Also, planners in private agencies may need to make greater use of vertically linked organizations for some types of planning activities—for example, community economic development.

PRIMARY GROUP MEMBERSHIP

The activity of "participation" is not, of course, limited to formally organized voluntary associations and other task-oriented collectivities. Individuals are also "natural" members of informal "primary groups," which are characterized by diffuse and intense relationships between members. Examples of primary groups include friendship groups, kinship groups, neighborhood social networks, and racial, ethnic, or religious informal groupings. Often the practitioner who is attempting to influence patterns of participation in voluntary associations may be unaware of the types of primary group participation that exist in a particular community, and of the effect of this, actual or potential, on his own work.

Awareness and utilization of existing group ties may be an important strategy for increasing the effectiveness of voluntary associations, committees, and other task groups with which the practitioner typically works. Primary groups can provide support for organization activities and may be used to induce individuals to participate in voluntary associations. Primary groups also provide a variety of functions outside the scope of the traditional "community organization." The adequate functioning of primary groups is sometimes necessary for the evolution of communities that can mobilize to solve their own problems through development of "community competence." [12] Thus the practitioner may find it necessary or useful to assess and improve the functioning of these groups and to provide individuals with a greater opportunity to participate in them.

Patterns of group participation may also exist as barriers to changes the community practitioner is attempting to implement. One example is the opposition by some white ethnic groups to certain minority-group advancement programs. Group participation may reinforce attitudes the practitioner is attempting to change or it may serve as a barrier to membership in voluntary associations. Neighborhood primary group distrust may be a deterrent to the practitioner's very ability to establish himself in the community in a legitimate role. Often the practitioner must modify a program in the face of primary group opposition, or bargain for and attempt to promote primary group support. It is safe to assume that failure to recognize basic grass-roots primary group participation patterns has often reduced the effectiveness of community organization intervention efforts. The relative importance of these forms of participation in low-income areas together with the practitioner's unawareness of their existence and impact can be especially handicapping.

Studies of primary group participation and its relationship to com-

[12] Roger M. Lind and John E. Tropman, *Delinquency Planning and Community Competence: A Preliminary Assessment* (Ann Arbor, Michigan: Community Systems Foundation, 1969).

munity organization have usually utilized two main types of research methodology. Most common is survey research, in which a sample of persons from a given community are interviewed about their activities. Another frequent technique is participant observation, whereby the researcher enters into the life of a given community by examining at first hand group participation over a period of time. The following discussion draws on both types of studies.

The Context of Primary Group Participation: Demography, Mobility, Community Structure

Extent of Primary Group Participation

GENERALIZATION 7.23: Almost all persons have at least a moderate level of primary group participation. Groups and categories of persons usually described as "anomic," or lacking ties to communities and organizations and having low rates of political and associational participation, do nevertheless usually maintain informal social group relationships (+ + + +, 1, 6, 21, 26, 101, 113, 117, 159, 192, 214).

7.23A. Urban residents cannot generally be characterized as isolated individuals. Residents of inner-city areas generally maintain kinship ties and develop friendships (+ + +, 1, 117, 214).
7.23B. Urban residents may identify themselves with their neighborhoods. This tendency is associated with consensus about the physical area comprising the neighborhood (what blocks are included), social ties that exist among local residents, and use of local institutions such as stores, churches, theaters and clubs (+, 117).
7.23C. Migrants to urban areas retain kinship ties, and frequently settle near relatives or move into an ethnic community with which they identify (+ +, 6, 26, 192).
7.23D. Low-income ethnic immigrants, in particular, develop strong locality friendship ties (+, 159).
7.23E. Low-income persons may have strong kinship and friendship ties, and geographical stability, although they may possess few organizational memberships (+, 113).

These findings were reported by LaBarre in her study of 32 self-supporting poor families in Durham, North Carolina (113). The families were interviewed as part of a child health care project. Although the families had few contacts with social groups and organizations outside their locality and kin groups, they had close ties to a large, extended kinship group.

7.23F. Religious organizations are substantially comprised of individuals who have few other organizational ties (+ , 101).

More abstractly, one may theorize that primary-group membership has not diminished as a consequence of industrialization. The hypothesis that industrial society is becoming a "mass society" of isolated individuals with few ties to other persons and groups was tested explicitly by Bonjean (21) in a study of participation patterns of persons in a town undergoing industrialization. Interviewed were 104 businessmen, 108 managers, and 120 workers. Managers had high social and neighborhood participation, although they had few contacts with relatives. Workers had high kin and religious participation. Small businessmen displayed the lowest degree of social participation but were not isolated.

Action Guidelines: The practitioner should be aware of the friendship, kinship, and neighborhood participation patterns of groups popularly characterized as "anomic" or isolated. These patterns do not appear to be disrupted by urbanization and industrialization to the extent predicted by some theorists.

Since many groups with low formal organizational participation, such as low-income persons, ethnic immigrants, and migrants from rural areas, have these primary group ties, the practitioner can utilize these primary group ties for "organizing the unaffiliated." For example, the practitioner involved in a community health care project might contact potential participants through relatives of a core group or through the local church.

One important primary group unit still retained (to a greater or lesser extent) in urban areas is the neighborhood. The neighborhood can be utilized by the practitioner as the basis of organizing or as a unit for planning. People's perceptions of neighborhood (geography and social composition) can also be helpful in defining the parameters of neighborhood community organization. The practitioner can use local institutions as a means of contacting and recruiting neighborhood residents. For example, a local store-owner might be used to spread information about a program. Low-income neighborhoods also seem to contain a group of persons who are geographically stable and have worked in the area for several years. These persons might become members or be used as indigenous workers to recruit voluntary association members.

Finally, the studies suggest that practitioners need not be overly pessimistic about industrial development in terms of its alleged consequences for primary group relationships. Industrialization does not seem automatically to produce socially isolated, fragmented individuals. Community organization practitioners might attempt to strengthen existing primary group association patterns as a way of balancing some of the negative social consequences of industrialization.

Geographic Mobility and Participation

GENERALIZATION 7.24: Migrants to urban areas often seem to rapidly develop primary group participation patterns that assimilate them into the community. Geographic mobility does not necessarily result in increased isolation (+ + +, 1, 101, 117, 192; see also chapter 10).

7.24A. Migrants to urban areas frequently settle near people whom they know, close to relatives, or in a relevant ethnic community +, 117, 192).

7.24B. The church is used as an important integrating mechanism by migrants to urban areas. Migrants have higher church attendance than natives of similar socioeconomic status (+, 101).

Migrant status and church attendance was studied by Jitodai (101) in a sample of 3,083 residents of a large metropolis. Migrants from both rural and urban areas had higher rates of church attendance than did natives of similar age, sex, religion, and socioeconomic status. The highest rate of church attendance was among white-collar migrants.

7.24C. Native American Indian migrants have high initial participation in community organizations, which they use to establish friendship and work ties (+ , 1).

7.24D. Migration patterns change during the course of industrialization. Originally, most migrants to urban areas came from rural regions but over time the composition of migration groups changed to persons who were young, well-educated, and residents of other urban areas (+ , 215).

The changing characteristics of urban migrants were studied by Taeuber and Taeuber (215) for the period 1955–1960 using data from the 1960 Census. They found that, contrary to the popular stereotype, black urban immigrants were of higher socioeconomic status than the resident black population and equal to or higher than the resident white population. Black migration patterns are thus coming increasingly to resemble those of whites. For whites, and increasingly for blacks, migration is becoming intermetropolitan rather than rural to urban. Most recent black migrants to northern metropolitan areas have had previous experience in urban living. Older descriptions of black migration patterns appear to be no longer applicable.

Action Guidelines: The practitioner can encourage urban migrants to utilize resources that will aid in assimilating them into new urban areas of settlement. Churches and local voluntary associations are often used by migrants to establish work and friendship ties, and the practitioner might influence such organizations to maximize these functions. Practitioners can assist in assimilation by helping migrants locate members of their ethnic and kinship groups, or by establishing within ethnic communities information centers that new migrants can utilize.

In addition, the practitioner should be aware that the char-

acteristics of migrants change during the course of industrialization. Services in developing countries need to be
geared to the requirements of rural-to-urban migrants—
acquiring job skills, obtaining information about jobs, utilizing social welfare agencies in urban areas. Services to migrants in industrialized countries need to be geared to a
younger, better-educated, already urbanized population.

Social Mobility and Ethnic Identity

GENERALIZATION 7.25: Social mobility does not necessarily
lead to the displacement of kinship, ethnic, racial, or religious groups and the substitution of group ties based on
social class. Instead, social differentiation is often imposed
on the preexisting group ties (+ + + +, 7, 8, 41, 162, 177,
192, 229).

Social mobility refers to the individual's movement from one social
class to another, usually as the result of changes in level of education, occupation, or income.

7.25A. Migrant residence patterns are a function both of social class
and kinship ties. Upwardly mobile ethnic groups acquire a middle-
class life-style, but they also retain their participation in ethnic and
religious groups (+ +, 7, 8, 162, 192).

An example of research supporting this proposition is a study by
Penalosa and McDonagh (162) of social mobility among Chicanos
in California. Upward mobility was measured in terms of socioeconomic status; degree of acculturation was also measured, through
indicators such as use of English. It was found that upwardly mobile
Chicanos do not shed their ethnic identification significantly and that
Catholicism rather than Protestantism was most associated with upward mobility. The authors concluded that it is the shedding of
lower-class culture rather than ethnicity which is most related to
upward mobility.

If an ethnic group's status is highly disparaged in the larger society and operates as a significant barrier to mobility, group members
may reject their ethnic identification (148).

7.25B. Health practices reflect both racial and class differences between groups. In order to predict health practices, a community practitioner must know both a person's race and social class (+ , 177).

7.25C. Patterns of ethnic voting increase rather than diminish with an ethnic group's attainment of middle-class status (+ , 229).

The relationship between ethnic voting and social class was studied by Wolfinger (229) through an analysis of voting patterns of Italians in New Haven. Ethnic-group voting patterns have traditionally been explained by the "assimilation theory," which hypothesizes that ethnic voting is strongest during the earliest period of residence of the group and declines as the group members leave the working class. However, Wolfinger found that his data contradicted this theory; ethnic voting *increased* as Catholics acquired middle-class status. Alternatively, Wolfinger formulated a "mobilization theory" of ethnic voting, hypothesizing that "Middle-class status is a virtual prerequisite for candidacy for major office; an ethnic group's development of sufficient political skill and influence to secure such a nomination also requires the development of a middle class, and of leaders with middle-class attributes such as education and political sophistication. Therefore, ethnic voting will increase when the ethnic group has produced a middle class" (p. 905).

NOTE: This finding applies here to a city with a homogeneous urban ethnic community. Ethnic voting could decrease if suburbanization occurs.

7.25D. A tendency to choose friends within one's own social stratum (differential association) is greatest among persons who are nonmobile, status consistent, and whose perceived and objective perceptions of their status coincide (+ , 41).

This finding is interesting because it contradicts the idea that mobility is associated with an increase in exclusive identification with the higher social class. From the finding, it appears that the opposite is true, that nonmobile persons derive most of their friendships from persons of their own social class.

Although upwardly mobile groups may retain their ethnic and kinship identifications, once persons have solidified new class-based association patterns, it may be difficult to get them to replace these ties with neighborhood and friendship ties to persons of different social classes. A study that supports this qualification analyzed persons who returned or moved to the downtown Detroit area to live in a high-income apartment complex (227). They showed little association with the low-income residents of the surrounding community. For example, the residents were not willing to send their children to neighborhood schools, and they had little social contact with neighbors outside the complex.

Action Guidelines: Social class does not appear to be replacing traditional bases of primary group association such as kinship and ethnicity. Instead, upwardly mobile persons seem to form primary group ties with persons of the same "ethclass"—persons who have similar social status and who also have a similar "traditional" group membership, such as ethnicity or religion. Thus, for example, middle-class Catholics are likely to form friendships with other middle-class Catholics. This suggests to the practitioner that ethclass and more traditional primary group ties are useful bases for organizing persons.

Traditional ethnic and religious ties do not appear to be barriers to upward mobility. The practitioner who is working in a setting of community development, helping groups to become upwardly mobile, should not consider attempting to weaken traditional primary group associations to promote upward mobility.

The practitioner can anticipate the emergence of ethnic groups as political interest groups, as mobility provides them with sophisticated in-group leadership and the resources necessary for political organization. The practitioner can look to ethnic group members who have achieved some upward mobility as potential political candidates.

The group for whom social class appears to be a relevant basis for participation are persons who are nonmobile and status consistent. Highly mobile persons might be good sources of recruitment to multiclass associations.

Community Structure Variables

GENERALIZATION 7.26: Community structural variables affect patterns of informal group participation (+ + +, 26, 88, 116, 117, 189).

7.26A. The higher an ethnic community's institutional completeness, the higher its ability to attract as residents ethnic immigrants who have high identification with the community (+ +, 26, 117).

Institutional completeness as used here refers to the number of social institutions located within a given community rather than outside it.

The relationship of community institutions to ethnic immigrant residence was investigated by Breton (26). Interviews were obtained with 230 male immigrants to Montreal. The measurement of "institutional completeness" was based on a rating of churches, welfare organizations, newspapers, and periodicals within each ethnic community. Breton found that although ties with the native community showed a substantial increase after the immigrants had lived in the country for six years, there were important differences among communities. Some 89 percent of members of institutionally complete communities had most of their relations with that ethnic community, as compared with 21 percent of those from communities with low institutional completeness. Of the types of institutions, churches had the greatest effect in maintaining the immigrant's associations with the ethnic community.

7.26B. The higher the ethnic homogeneity of a community, the higher the participation in ethnic organizations (+, 88).

The effect of population composition on differences in ghetto organization was studied by Hill and Larson (88). They compared the participation patterns of members of three communities—one with 100 percent black population, one with 89 percent, and one with 27 percent. The community with the highest proportion of blacks had the highest participation in local organizations, sensitivity to local problems, and the most geographically stable residents.

In this connection, it is worth noting that Southern cities have a residential distribution of blacks which may be an impediment to neighborhood organizing. Although Southern cities are becoming increasingly segregated, the original residential pattern was to disperse blacks throughout the city in the "backyard" residence pattern developed during slavery (189).

Action Guidelines: Using the above characteristics, the practitioner can predict in which communities participation may be promoted on an ethnic basis—those with a high number of local institutions, and those with high ethnic homogeneity. By working to strengthen local institutions, the practitioner may also increase the community's potential for local community organizing.

When a practitioner is attempting to mobilize ethnic groups in heterogeneous areas, he probably should not try to develop residentially based organizations. Instead, he would be well advised to use the ethnic group's occupational and organizational ties to recruit members; for example, a confederation of black churches working to end discrimination in employment might be developed.

Primary Group Participation and Other
Forms of Participation

Primary Groups and Voluntary Associations

GENERALIZATION 7.27: Informal patterns of primary group participation may affect and enhance modes of participation in voluntary associations with which the practitioner works (+ + + +, 41, 79, 82, 83, 93, 100, 109, 164, 167, 185, 186, 206, 211).

7.27A. Persons are often recruited for membership in voluntary associations by their friends (+, 186).
7.27B. Primary groups are sources of information about the activities of voluntary associations and are utilized by individuals in making decisions about whether or not to join such associations (+, 93).

Support for this proposition was obtained from a study of decisions by young adults to participate in higher education programs. Persons who enrolled were interviewed and it was learned that *all* of them had discussed enrolling with their parents and most had consulted with friends and former students.

7.27C. Friendships that develop within voluntary associations are an important source of satisfaction, which sustains participation (+, 164).

7.27D. Primary group ties are important for the development of trust within a larger association and for reducing communication barriers that arise when members are ignorant of one another's true feelings about a situation requiring such shared awareness (+, 109).

7.27E. Primary groups are sometimes a source of motivation to participate in voluntary associations because such participation may raise an individual's prestige within the primary group (+ +, 79, 82, 167).

7.27F. Individuals may join voluntary associations because they provide a means to make needed contacts with primary groups such as occupational associates and friendship groups (+ +, 79, 83).

It is important to note that if this is the only reason for joining and maintaining participation, individuals will probably soon leave the organization and maintain their friendships outside the organization. Such a finding was reported by Ablon (1) in a study of participation patterns among Indian migrants to the San Francisco area. She found that initially they had high participation in community organizations such as clubs and churches, but as they developed friendships and work and neighborhood ties, their participation in these associations declined.

7.27G. Primary group support reinforces *commitment* to participate in voluntary association programs and activities (+, 206).

7.27H. Primary group influences may provide both positive and negative sanctions to control behavior (+ +, 185, 211).

7.27I. Primary groups within voluntary associations are more effective in changing individual attitudes than are voluntary associations alone. They have a reinforcing or multiplier effect (+, 41).

This proposition was tested by Curtis, Timbers, and Jackson (41) in a study of the effects of types of social participation upon prejudice. The relationships were investigated using a white male sample which was controlled in terms of status, age, religion, and ethnicity. It was found that participation in primary group structures had no effect upon prejudice or even increased it. Participation in secondary associations was associated with a slight decrease in prejudice, but the decrease in prejudice was greatest where primary relationships developed within a voluntary association.

7.27J. Amount of interaction with kin has no effect—positive or negative—on participation in voluntary associations (+, 77).

This finding, reported by Greer et al., seems to indicate that quantitative differences in amount of kinship participation do not raise participation in secondary associations. However, it should be noted that kinship participation does not *decrease* participation in voluntary associations, as has been sometimes assumed.

Action Guidelines: By utilizing existing primary group memberships and by developing primary groups within an organization, the practitioner can contribute to the effectiveness of voluntary associations. The practitioner can encourage persons to recruit potential voluntary association members through their friendship networks, as well as to spread information to friends and relations in order to encourage individuals to support voluntary associations. Also, as a recruitment strategy, the practitioner can stress the primary group advantages of joining a voluntary association: increased friendships, how association membership increases prestige within existing primary groups such as one's work associates, and more contacts with other groups. However, the practitioner should stress these as secondary benefits; they should not be the individual's sole reason for joining the organization.

By developing close personal relations within the voluntary association, the practitioner can build the trust necessary for communication, develop commitment to participate in various programs, influence behavior, and change individual attitudes. Finally, primary groups within the voluntary association might be used by the practitioner as a substitute social referent for moving individuals out of participation in deviant or "undesirable" primary groups.

Primary Group Correlates of General Social Participation

GENERALIZATION 7.28: One of the most important functions performed by primary groups is the inculcation of attitudes that motivate and sustain an individual's pattern of participation (+ + + +, 24, 50, 56, 61, 90, 104, 105, 108, 144, 154, 163, 173, 206, 207, 217).

7.28A. Patterns of participation in secondary associations are transmitted intergenerationally. Children have patterns of participation in organizations similar to those of their parents (+ + + , 24, 90).

7.28B. Parents actively transmit values that influence their children to participate in specific kinds of secondary associations. For example, Kenniston found that student participants in social-action organizations had parents who transmitted a philosophy of "political liberalism" (+ + +, 56, 61, 108, 144, 206).

7.28C. Peer groups transmit values that influence their members to participate in specific kinds of secondary associations (+ + + +, 61, 105, 108, 154, 163, 207, 217).

7.28D. The transmission of parental values about participation is affected by family structure. There is less transmission of participation-related attitudes in one-parent families (+, 104).

7.28E. Socialization of attitudes affecting participation can be acquired early in life. Children of eight have developed differences in sense of political efficacy (+ , 50).

7.28F. Attitudes acquired through primary group socialization are not necessarily fixed, but can vary as a person and his environment change over the course of one's life (+ +, 34, 172).

As an example of this fluidity, in a study of the consequences of the effects of early socialization on physicians' ideology, Colombotos (34) found that early socialization experiences had a greater effect on general and diffuse attitudes such as mobility aspirations and political ideology than on restricted work-specific attitudes toward the formal organization of medical practices and colleague controls. Another study, by Prewitt, Eulau, and Zisk (172), found that political experiences in childhood were less important than immediate situational demands in orienting politicians to their jobs.

7.28G. Political attitudes of residents in a particular community are acquired through social participation to a greater extent than through the amount of their exposure to political party propaganda (+, 173).

This proposition was tested by Putnam (173) using data obtained in a national survey. Political attitudes were found to be less related to the level of party activity in a community than to identity with the community and articulation of clear community political standards, and informal social relationships.

7.28H. Lack of strong community ties may produce individuals who are less committed to community norms and therefore more willing to engage in militant demands for radical social change (+ +, 67, 126, 157).

Action Guidelines: The practitioner can predict the predisposition of individuals to participate in secondary associations by knowing the attitudes of their primary group memberships. If a practitioner is trying to modify attitudes that influence participation he may work through parents to reach children or young people. To influence political attitudes of adults he should engage informal friendship networks. Alternatively, he could encourage individuals to develop new primary group memberships. Militant organizations may find success in recruiting by approaching individuals without strong associational ties.

Local Community Identification and Linkage

Linkage-Identification-Participation

GENERALIZATION 7.29: An individual's pattern of linkage in a neighborhood affects his identification with the neighborhood as well as his rate of participation (+ + +, 7, 15, 26, 117, 180).

7.29A. The greater the length of residence, the greater the individual's involvement in his neighborhood (+ +, 26, 117).

7.29B. Employment in the local area increases the individual's involvement in and identification with the neighborhood (+ + +, 122, 180).

7.29C. Association with neighbors leads to increased information about local issues (+, 77). Limitation: While this was found true of suburban residents, social participation of urban residents did not similarly, in this study, affect information about local issues.

The reader should recognize that developing neighborhood identification is not always desirable from the standpoint of community organization (9, 180). This is brought out clearly by Roth and Boynton (180) in a study of attitudes toward metropolitan government. Antimerger attitudes were held by persons who had a strong local community ideology, as measured by their liking for the community and their feeling that the community had distinctive characteristics that should be preserved. Persons with the highest communal ideology worked in the area, were less educated, and did not hold professional occupations. Accordingly, localism may operate as a counterforce with respect to larger issues and developments.

7.29D. Individuals who have high social participation within the neighborhood are more likely to be aware of the neighborhood's inadequacies (+, 15).

Action Guidelines: Individuals who have strong occupational and friendship ties to a community are good sources for recruitment to neighborhood voluntary associations. They tend to have high awareness of and much information about local problems and hence possess potentialities for effective membership. By encouraging social participation and involvement in local institutions, the practitioner may eventually affect the development of neighborhood voluntary associations.

The practitioner attempting to consolidate local units in the interests of a plan to coordinate and solve large-scale social problems may, under some conditions, want to decrease neighborhood identification or seek out individuals whose neighborhood ties are weak.

Primary Group Structure and Group Identification

GENERALIZATION 7.30: Characteristics of primary group structure affect the degree of identification with the group (++, 2, 4).

7.30A. Group identification increases with high opportunity for participation, with high opportunity for upward mobility within the group, and with increased clarity of group structures and norms (+ , 2).

7.30B. Group identification increases as the members' awareness of their common interests increases (+, 4).

Action Guidelines: If the practitioner wishes to increase identification with primary groups, he should work to provide all members with maximum opportunity for participation, keep channels open for access to diverse positions of leadership, and explicate group norms and structures. He should also stress the common interests of the members. If the practitioner wants to discourage an individual's participation in a particular group, such as a delinquent gang, he would operate in a converse fashion.

Primary Group Opinion Leaders as Linking Agents

GENERALIZATION 7.31: Individuals with critical locations in primary group networks may be utilized by the practitioner to link primary group members to voluntary associations (+ +, 19, 38, 85, 208).

7.31A. Persons with high social participation can be utilized as indigenous workers to recruit members for community organizations (+, 208).

7.31B. Certain individuals are utilized by other community members as sources of information when making decisions about whether to adopt innovations (+, 38).

7.31C. Factory foremen can be successfully utilized to encourage groups to adopt participation in a health service program (+, 19).

7.31D. Use of primary group contacts with a change agent plus participation in a voluntary association was more effective in changing attitudes than voluntary association membership alone (+, 85).

Action Guidelines: Opinion leaders and others with common membership may be used to good advantage when a practitioner wishes to link primary groups with voluntary associations, or to recruit or gain support for an association's program among community primary groups.

Negative Features of Primary Group Membership

Primary Groups Sustaining Prejudice and Extremism

GENERALIZATION 7.32: Primary groups can socialize individuals to develop attitudes and values that oppose specific changes or forms of participation (+ + + +, 55, 81, 95, 103, 130, 161, 186).

> 7.32A. Primary groups may encourage individual members to develop attitudes of prejudice (+ + +, 55, 95, 161).
>
> 7.32B. Primary groups may socialize persons so that they develop extremist political attitudes, which lead them to oppose various social-welfare innovations (+, 186).
>
> In the Schmuck and Chesler (186) study of superpatriots who opposed the introduction of community mental health programs, it was found that, contrary to popular belief, superpatriots were not disturbed, alienated individuals. Instead, they were dogmatic persons who had become highly involved in a tight network of local primary group and secondary associations—such as church, neighborhood, and voluntary associations—which sustained those beliefs. Further, they derived a great deal of satisfaction from this participation.

Action Guidelines: Practitioners will have great difficulty changing negative attitudes of persons with a high amount of social participation and reinforcement which supports these beliefs. One might instead attempt structural or legal strategies or select some other group or problem for attention.

Primary Groups as Forces of Fragmentation

GENERALIZATION 7.33: Formation of community organizations based only on primary-group ties may be too narrow a base of participation, and may impede the ability to form coalitions and develop a broad base of support (+, 232).

The practitioner should regard this proposition as a limitation on utilizing primary-group memberships as a basis for stimulating other kinds of participation. Often the practitioner must unite a range of groups in support of a given goal, and this requires playing down the primary-group differences that might otherwise be sources of cleavage, and prevent groups from forming coalitions.

Primary Groups as Forces Sustaining Traditionalism

GENERALIZATION 7.34: Emergence of new attitudes in modernizing communities is associated with a shift from informal primary group associations to experiences in formal structures (+ +, 63, 97, 194).

> 7.34A. Development of "modern" attitudes, especially values favorable to social change, is related to increased participation in rationalistic organizations (+ +, 97, 194).
>
> 7.34B. Development of "modern" attitudes is associated with increasing experience in formal education (+, 194).
>
> 7.34C. Development of nationalistic identification is associated with increased participation in formal education (+, 63).
>
> 7.34D. Increased participation in rational and formal organizations may have feedback effects, leading to changes in primary-group relationships (+, 194).
>
> In a study of the effect of industrialization on family size and organization, Scott (194) interviewed 107 employed and 99 unemployed women in a small Puerto Rican town. Employed and higher-educated women had a self rather than a family orientation, higher communication with their husbands concerning family issues, sharing of family decision making, a greater number of organizational memberships, and higher social participation in general.

Action Guidelines: Community development practitioners need to structure and facilitate participation of individuals in new forms of secondary association, rather than relying heavily on traditional primary groups as resocializing agents to promote modern attitudes. These new secondary associations may have disturbing consequences for established primary-group patterns. The practitioner can perhaps be ready to help the community anticipate and adjust to these consequences.

Parenthetically, the existence of formal organizations and voluntary associations can serve to strengthen primary-group participation within the community rather than to detract from it. Breton's study (26) of ethnic communities in Montreal indicated that the presence of community institutuons such as churches, newspapers, and clubs increased informal social ties to the community—even among immigrants who do not participate directly in these institutions.

Practitioners' Awareness of Primary-Group Influences

GENERALIZATION 7.35: Community practitioners and human-service professionals in general are sometimes unfamiliar with patterns of informal group participation. Lack of knowledge of these patterns can hamper the development of effective services for these groups (+ + +, 15, 30, 54, 116, 155, 171, 233).

7.35A. Failure to utilize local organizations in planning sometimes results in a higher number of unplanned, unfavorable consequences (+, 30).

7.35B. Planners and residents may diverge in their concept of what constitutes a desirable neighborhood. The lower an individual's social class, the greater the divergence between him and the planner in conceptions. (+, 116).

7.35C. Professionals may have little information about the social behavior of their low-income clients (+, 171).

7.35D. Individuals may hold certain attitudes toward their community which lead to their opposition to social plans such as urban renewal (+ +, 15, 54).

A study of communities that opposed urban renewal was conducted by Fellman (54) in Boston and Cambridge, Massachusetts. A low-income community, the proposed location for a freeway, was studied by interviewing, historical research, and field observation. The majority of the residents appeared to experience their neigh-

borhoods as self-contained social units where they could visit with friends and relatives, attend churches and schools, shop, and visit doctors and dentists. Relocation of such people meant disruption of entire ways of life, not just the inconvenience of moving. The residents had no part in the planning of the urban-renewal project.
7.35E. Institutionalization of new programs may require the support of existing social networks within a community. Bypassing existing social networks often leads to opposition to a new program (+, 155, 223).

Action Guidelines: Practitioners can become aware of primary group norms and participation patterns by involving local groups in the planning process. Without such participatory inputs, planning has sometimes disrupted traditional patterns of primary-group participation, and it is difficult for individuals to find replacements for the functions these patterns perform. Individuals and groups will attempt to maintain primary-group relationships, and this attempt may lead to their opposition to planning activities. When the local group is of a different social class than the planner, it is especially likely to have divergent concepts of what constitutes a desirable neighborhood. Individuals with high primary-group participation (such as people with strong ethnic ties) are particularly likely to resist planning efforts that threaten to disrupt such relationships. If the practitioner is trying to arrest a particular planning effort, which is viewed as undesirable, he might deliberately recruit such individuals. Also, the practitioner might stress the disruption of primary-group relationships as a recruiting and organizing issue.

In this chapter we have discussed the broadest and most common forms of participation—primary groups and voluntary associations. These participation modes include some activities that are largely expressive, creative, and social in character. In the next chapter we shall describe participation that is explicitly and specifically social-change oriented: social movements, political activity, and client organization.

Chapter Eight

Participation: Social Movements, Political Action, Client Organization

PARTICIPATION IN SOCIAL-ACTION MOVEMENTS

SOCIAL MOVEMENTS have gained increasing prominence in recent years as low-power groups—blacks, students, women—have organized to press demands. "Up against the wall" and "Black Power" in the late 60's became part of the everyday vocabulary of Americans.

A social movement can generally be differentiated from other types of voluntary associations in terms of its larger size, its strain toward major structural changes in the social order or in designated social institutions, and reliance on mass action and often militant tactics as an important medium for achieving its goals. Examples of this form of organization include the Civil Rights–Black Power Movement, Chicano and Native American developments, the Peace Movement, Women's Liberation, and Student Activism. We shall use the terms *social movements* and *social-action movements* interchangeably, although the latter suggests radical organizations and tactics.

Social movements have been the object of recent empirical investigation to an increased degree. Most of this work has been directed toward the study of contemporary phenomena, presenting several problems for the practitioner who is attempting to develop practice guidelines from these findings. The overall limitation is that study of phenomena taken at a fixed point in time makes it difficult to develop hypotheses or make predictive statements about the "life history" of fast-changing social movements—the ways in which they evolve historically. For example, it is questionable whether studies of the earliest joiners of the civil rights and peace movements (the subject of many of the available findings) are useful for making statements about recruitment strategies later, when these movements were more established and had more widespread support. This problem may be dealt with in part by indicating the dates when studies were conducted and noting these as constraints in the formulation of practice derivations.

Illustratively, a "big question" in the study of social-action movements has been whether there is a relationship between mass protest, which includes militant tactics or attitudes, and collective violence. Some theoretical and practical issues that have been considered are whether there are certain conditions under which violence emerges as a consequence of protest and if participants in collective violence and militant social action have similar characteristics. For example, does potential for collective violence increase or decrease as the size of a social action movement is magnified? Lack of good longitudinal studies of social movements prevents definitive answers to such questions, a limitation the reader of this section should keep in mind when evaluating a set of generalizations based on the study of "emerging phenomena."

The Demography of Social Action—Who Participates

Age

GENERALIZATION 8.1: The highest rate of participation (and potential for participation) in social action movements is found among young persons—between 15 and 25 years (+ + +, 33, 35, 126, 151, 196, 233).

8.1A. Support for militant protest as a legitimate action is greatest among young persons (+, 151).

8.1B. Willingness to use violence and militant action to reduce social injustices is greatest among young persons (+ +, 33, 126, 196).

8.1C. Young persons are more willing than their elders to engage in actions that violate traditional norms regarding racial discrimination (+, 42).

8.1D. Young blacks show a greater potential for generational change in the direction of militant social action than do young whites. Young blacks are more likely to reject the American work ethic than are whites, and young blacks score lower in anomie than do their elders. Youth of both races show a decline in family identification (+ , 233).

8.1E. Older persons, because they have a longer history of participation in traditional political parties, are more likely to continue their support of those parties than are young persons, who have little or no experience of traditional political participation. Conversely, young persons are more likely than older persons to support nontraditional political movements (+ , 35).

This last Subgeneralization helps explain why young people have a high degree of participation in social movements. Our hypothesis is that the tendency of the young to support new movements is caused not only by their youth (rashness, inexperience, rebelliousness) but also by their lack of strong ties to more traditional forms of participation. This hypothesis was tested by Converse, Miller, Rush, and Wolfe (35), who studied support for George Wallace in the 1968 presidential election. They found a negative correlation between age and support for Wallace, especially outside the South. Older people had much stronger ties to established political parties than did youth, and the correlation between age and Wallace support was greatly reduced when strength of partisan identification was controlled. Thus commitment to traditional political organizations may be viewed as acting as a counterpressure that prevented older people from supporting the conservative Wallace campaign, while younger persons who lacked traditional ties were more likely to lend themselves to the new "radical right" political movement.

Action Guidelines: The practitioner may view younger persons—especially blacks—as potential participants in social-action movements. Movements that emphasize nontraditional ways of thinking and acting are especially likely to attract young persons. Young people are likely sources of support for the protest actions of other groups even though they may not be actual participants in the movement.

Since young people participate in social movements outside of traditional participation channels, the practitioner who is trying to build a movement should increase opportunities for participation within new organizational arrangements. Alternatively, the practitioner who is trying to defuse a movement (such as support for Wallace) should attempt to increase opportunities for participation acceptable to youth in traditional political organizations. Alternatively the practitioner might build nontraditional outlets more favorable to the ideological position he favors.

Education

GENERALIZATION 8.2: Participation in social-action movements is associated with persons who have a higher level of education (+ + + +, 65, 69, 105, 108, 151, 153, 154, 157, 168, 193, 217).

Limitation: This generalization is especially true for the earliest joiners of social movements (+, 193). (There were no longitudinal studies in our research pool of how the composition of a social movement varies over time.)

8.2A. Students who participate in protest activities have higher academic achievement and intellectual interest than nonprotesting students (+ + +, 105, 108, 217).

Most studies have found the early student protestors to be a highly select group of students. For example, Trent and Craise (217) studied attitudes of three groups—a national sample of college students, a sample of Berkeley seniors, and a sample of students arrested in the Free Speech Movement. In comparison with the national sample and the Berkeley seniors, the arrestees scored higher on measures of complexity, autonomy, intellectual interest, tolerance of ambiguity, objectivity and independence of thought, freedom, and imaginativeness of thinking.

8.2B. Protesting students are more frequently found at colleges and universities of high academic quality (+ + +, 105, 108, 153, 154, 193).

8.2C. Persons who participate in social-action movements have a high awareness of the issues and a great amount of political information (+ +, 65, 157).

8.2D. Lack of political information is an important factor in reducing participation of the poor in social-action movements (+, 168).

8.2E. Acceptance of protest as legitimate is directly correlated with level of education (+, 151). (However, when alienation is controlled, persons with a low amount of education are more willing to accept protest activities than are those with a moderate amount. Highly educated persons have the highest acceptance of protest activities.) [1]

8.2F. For participation in urban disturbances, education is curvilinearly related to participation, with most rioters having medium levels of education (high-school graduates). According to the Kerner Commission, rioters appear to be better educated than nonrioters but less well educated than counterrioters (+ + +, 69, 157).

Action Guidelines: In looking for early joiners of social movements, practitioners should seek to recruit highly educated persons. High-quality educational institutions are a good source of social-movement recruits. Providing people with educational experiences that stimulate intellectual in-

---

[1] There are seemingly discrepant tendencies in this type of data in the generalizations in this chapter. It may be useful to provide the reader with a frame of reference for interpreting the material. The upper and middle classes, which contain a disproportionate percentage of the more educated, in general view the workings of the society favorably and "support the system." However, from this strata—in particular from the highly educated segment—come a group of politically sophisticated dissidents who are sensitive to social injustices and who are sympathetic to protest and related civil libertarian activities. While comprising only a small percentage of the middle and upper classes, they makeup a large and influential percentage of that population universe which approves of or is invloved in more militant approaches to social and political issues.

The poor are aware of some of the reality factors that block and limit them in specific ways. However, they do not in general have a systematic analysis of society. This makes for ambivalence within the group. Ideologically the large majority tend to accept elements of the "American Dream" with its supposition of potential upward mobility for everybody. And they avoid a crystallized identity as working or lower class. Consequently they do not in large proportion vote or move politically on a bloc basis across issues in terms of working-class interests or a radical perspective.

terest and free and creative thinking may increase the propensity to participate in social-action movements.

Intensive discussion of issues, and spreading of information about issues—especially among the less educated—is an important potential device for stimulating participation in social movements. The practitioner should expect that less educated persons with high alienation and moderately educated persons will have little support for protest, with the exception of young, moderately educated blacks, who have high support for militant protest.

Some Psychological Correlates of
Social-Action Participation

Relative Deprivation

GENERALIZATION 8.3: Participation in social-action movements is associated with an individual's sense of relative deprivation (+ + + +, 78, 108, 138, 139, 142, 150, 168, 169, 182, 193).

Relative deprivation refers to the perceived gap between one's aspirations, and one's expectation of achieving them. Relative deprivation is that which an individual perceives in terms of a psychological standard. It is not an absolute, objective measure of deprivation (such as level of income). A central hypothesis of the relative deprivation theory is that persons who are high in terms of absolute deprivation may not be very high in feelings of relative deprivation, because their aspirations are low. While an improvement in their objective conditions may reduce absolute level of deprivation, it may also raise aspirations. If aspirations rise faster than expectations, a person's relative deprivation may increase while his absolute deprivation decreases.

The relationship of relative deprivation to participation in social movements was investigated by Morrison and Steeves (138) in a study of the National Farmers Organization. Compared with other farmers, NFO members were generally in economically advantaged farm situations, but they expressed higher dissatisfaction and were employing somewhat drastic means to change the economic institutions affecting farm marketing. Before their participation NFO members had had higher income aspirations than nonmembers, but they also exhibited a greater belief in the structural sources of obstacles to their reaching these aspirations.

8.3A. Relative deprivation among blacks is increasing, partly as a consequence of urbanization. Rural to urban migration within the South leads for blacks to a decrease in absolute deprivation but to an increase in relative deprivation. Although they improve their circumstances materially, they become less equal to the white population around them in terms of education, occupation, and income (+ , 78).

8.3B. Relative deprivation may increase as a consequence of modernization in developing countries, by bringing traditional peasant groups into contact with upper- and middle-income life-styles and values (+ , 139).

8.3C. A high degree of participation in social-action movements, at least at the very beginning, does not come from the very poor but from persons who have experienced some limited amount of upward mobility (+ + + , 138, 168, 169, 193).

8.3D. The very poor will participate in social-action movements if there is a severe absolute worsening of their economic conditions (+ , 168).

This finding may appear to be incompatible with the relative deprivation hypothesis. One explanation may be that economic crises shatter the expectations of the poor, thus increasing their relative deprivation. This variant of the relative deprivation hypothesis remains to be examined. Nevertheless, at present we can say with some degree of confidence that a modest improvement in economic status will increase the participation in social movements of the very poor, and that a *drastic* worsening in economic conditions will also increase their participation.

8.3E. Level of aspiration is an important factor in predicting support for violence among blacks at both low and high occupational levels. The highest support for violence is found among persons with both higher occupational status and higher levels of aspiration (+ , 142).

A word of qualification is necessary here. This latter proposition was tested by Murphy and Watson (142) in a study of black participation in urban disturbances. The study showed that while relative deprivation was useful in predicting support for violence, it was *not* related to *actual* participation among blacks in high-status occupations, although there was a slight relationship between aspiration level and urban-disturbance participation among blacks in low-status occupations. In terms of support for violence, blacks in both occupational categories had high support when they had high levels of aspiration *combined* with high levels of discontent. This finding accents the idea that "relative deprivation" is measured not only by level of aspiration, but also by the *gap* between aspirations and expectations. Low- and high-income blacks with high relative deprivation appeared equally likely to support violence.

8.3F. Potential for participation in social-action movements involves observable and perceived deprivation by members of a social group (+, 150).

Because of their relatively high social isolation, certain groups of poor persons—such as rural farmers, migrants, or persons in isolated areas such as Appalachia—may have low feelings of relative deprivation (182). High isolation means little opportunity for groups to compare their chances in life with those of other groups; they have few standards for measuring how "bad off" they really are and are thus less likely to develop feelings of relative deprivation.

For example, a representative study by Rushing (182) consisted of interviews with 1,029 farm workers, who were defined as living in poverty, and a comparison group of middle- and upper-class farm owners. All subjects were from the state of Washington, in wheat-, fruit-, and vegetable-growing areas. It was found that the farm workers, many of whom were migrants, were limited in upward mobility as a class because of lack of education, job skills, and income levels. Farm workers perceived that they were experiencing deprivation to a greater extent than growers (22 percent of the workers agreed that life was "unhappy and would not get better" as compared to only 6 percent of the growers). But while the workers felt deprived, the small degree of deprivation they sensed as compared to their objective state was associated with the geographic isolation and the low social visibility that was found to be true of the group. Little contact was found with middle- and upper-class persons. The analysis of perceived deprivation revealed a false consciousness of their objective position.

Action Guidelines: The practitioner might determine which persons in a community are likely to be high in relative deprivation and recruit actively from among this population, if he is interested in building membership for a social-action movement. The very poor are unlikely to be the first joiners of social movements, because of their low aspirations, except perhaps when they experience a severe worsening of economic conditions. Similarly, groups which are physically and socially isolated from the rest of the population are not likely to be joiners. However, these groups might join at a later time after a movement has experienced some success. Early joiners of a social movement include persons who are slightly better off than their neighbors in a low-income community, groups which have recently migrated to cities from rural areas, and groups which are experiencing a slight improvement in their economic conditions.

The practitioner may be able to influence a person or group's sense of relative deprivation in several ways. First, persons can be encouraged to participate in such activities as adult education, which may raise levels of aspiration and thus increase relative deprivation. Second, by emphasizing unequal life chances and experiences of discrimination as an organizing issue, the practitioner can make groups aware of the gap between their aspirations and the likelihood of their achieving them. Third, practitioners might dramatize deprivation by bringing socially isolated oppressed or deprived individuals into contact with more privileged individuals or communities. School busing may have this effect, for example.

In addition, the concept of relative deprivation has implications for the life history of social movements. The consequence of limited success in achieving goals for a movement may be increased militancy on the part of the members as long as aspirations continue to rise as a result of that success.

Status Inconsistency

GENERALIZATION 8.4: Participation in social-action movements is associated with a high level of status inconsistency (+ + + +, 66, 67, 69, 126, 169, 181).

Status inconsistency refers to the degree to which rankings in terms of the various dimensions of socioeconomic status fail to coincide for a particular individual. Socioeconomic status is usually measured on several dimensions: level of education, occupation, income, and social status or prestige. Thus examples of persons who have high status inconsistency would be persons who have high education and low income (college students), high education and low-status occupations (blacks with professional training who suffer from discrimination in employment), high education or income and low social status (minority groups who are labelled as "socially inferior" because of their ethnic status).

8.4A. Different types of status inconsistency may result in different types of participation in social movements. High income–low education status inconsistency is associated with right-wing political extremism. Low income–high education inconsistency is associated with left-wing political extremism (+, 181).

8.4B. Actual amount of status inconsistency is increasing among blacks (+ +, 66).

A comparative study of black and white status dimensions was conducted by Geschwender (66), who compared changes among blacks and whites in levels of education, occupation, and income over time. He found that blacks were improving their level of education relative to whites, moving into middle-status but not upper-status occupations, and were falling farther behind whites in terms of income. Thus, the researcher concluded, the proportion of status inconsistents (high education–low income) among blacks is increasing.

8.4C. Participation in civil disorders is associated with high status inconsistency (+ + +, 67, 69, 126).

Rioters are found to have education-occupation status inconsistency. They are better educated than nonrioters, but are more likely to be employed in low-status occupations or to be underemployed.

Action Guidelines: Status inconsistency is an important source of personal tension and sense of grievance, which the practitioner can capitalize on to increase participation in social movements. The practitioner might explicitly increase awareness of status inconsistency through communication or educational programs. Certain kinds of social welfare programs may also increase status inconsistency. For example, participation in adult education activities that elevate a lower-class person's educational level but not his income may raise his status inconsistency. Conversely, adult education may reduce the status inconsistency of high-income–low-education persons and thus reduce their tendency to participate in right-wing extremist movements. Another source of status inconsistency may be civil rights legislation or black studies programs, which raise a group's ethnic status but not its income. Thus the practitioner can anticipate increased or decreased militancy in community-action programs as the consequence of participation in some human-service and education programs.

Alienation

GENERALIZATION 8.5: Alienated individuals who participate in social movements are likely to have both a high sense of personal mastery or control and a high sense of "system blame" (awareness of structural obstacles) (+, 80).

Findings concerning the relationship between powerlessness-alienation attitudes and participation in social-action movements have been unclear and contradictory. Several empirical studies report that participants in social action have high feelings of alienation (175, 205); other studies report that alienation and powerlessness are inversely related to participation in social-action movements (151, 168); finally, participation in social movements has been found to be unrelated to feelings of alienation (213). Two recent studies, however, suggest more refined hypotheses, which may prove to be helpful in resolving this ambiguity in findings concerning powerlessness-alienation attitudes and participation in social movements.

Gurin, Gurin, Rosina, and Beattie (80) suggest that the concept of "alienation" can be broken down into two components: an individual sense of personal control and a sense of "system blame" (high awareness of the impact of the system on social problems). They conclude that various combinations of these two dimensions of alienation can result in different types of participation:

SENSE OF SYSTEM BLAME

Sense of Personal Control	*High*	*Low*
High	Participation in collective protest, social action	Individual attempt to achieve, individual status striving
Low	Extreme militancy, violence	The authors do not discuss this cell; probably apathy and withdrawal

From this analysis we derived the above generalization.

8.5A. Social-action participation may reduce feelings of powerlessness (+, 119).

Levens (119) found that participation in social movements was inversely related to powerlessness; participation appeared to reduce powerlessness. Moreover, she hypothesizes that this relationship may be due to the consequences of participation in social action—that is, such participation reduces feelings of powerlessness. Thus, attitudes of participants in social movements may change over time. While assumptions underlying this proposition are incorporated in writings by Haggstrom and others,[2] the study by Levens is one of the few empirical tests of the assertion.

[2] Warren C. Haggstrom, "The Power of the Poor," in *Poverty in America,* Louis A. Ferman et al., eds. (Ann Arbor: University of Michigan Press, 1965), pp. 315-34.

Action Guidelines: Although powerlessness is inversely related to participation in other kinds of activity, such as membership in voluntary associations, it has an ambiguous relationship to participation in social movements. Joining social
movements seems to require awareness of the need for collective action to change structural arrangements, not belief
in the efficacy of individual action. Thus in organizing persons (either with a high or low sense of powerlessness), the
practitioner should stress the efficacy of collective action as
opposed to individual action and convey a sense of system
blame. Participation in a successful social-action movement
may increase sense of personal mastery, which would reinforce propensities toward participation in social action.

Awareness of Structural Effects

GENERALIZATION 8.6: Participation in social-action movements increases as awareness of social system or structural
causes of social problems increases (+ + + +, 33, 59, 60,
65, 80, 108, 138, 142, 157, 183, 184).

This is a broader and more highly supported form of the previous
generalization.

8.6A. Attributing poverty to social-system causes varies inversely
with income. The poor are the most likely to be aware of the structural blockages to upward mobility, while the rich are most likely to
perceive poverty as the consequence of individual differences in
ability and motivation (+ +, 60, 183).

8.6B. An improvement in economic conditions accompanied by
high aspirations (relative deprivation hypothesis) is associated with
high awareness of structural blockages to mobility (+ +, 138, 142).

8.6C. Student participants in social-action movements have an acute
sense that the system is violating their rights (+, 108).

8.6D. Participation of blacks in militant protest and collective violence is associated with a high awareness of discrimination
(+, 142).

Awareness of discrimination was found by Murphy and Watson

(142) to be an important variable in explaining black support for violence. They interviewed a sample of residents of south central Los Angeles, an area that had been under a curfew during the 1965 civil disorder. Support for violence was associated with the *combination* of high aspirations and high awareness of discrimination. For persons in high-status occupations, the greatest source of discontent was awareness of police malpractice. Persons in low-status occupations showed the highest discontent with consumer discrimination, including the practices of ghetto merchants.

8.6E. Neighborhoods with high participation in civil disorders also have high proportions of residents who report experiencing actual economic discrimination and police brutality (+, 33).

8.6F. Participation in social-action movements is associated with a low degree of trust in the political system (+ +, 33, 65, 157).

8.6G. Low-income persons support the concept of a pluralistic power structure as an ideal; however, more than any other group, they are likely to perceive that the power structure actually works in elitist terms (+ +, 59, 184).

Action Guidelines: To encourage social-action participation, the practitioner might emphasize group experiences of injustice as an organizing issue. The practitioner should reinforce and document the belief, already held by many of the poor, that their poor life chances are the result of structural blockages to mobility, not lack of individual effort. Persons who have striven and even taken steps upward but have failed to "really make it" are likely to have high awareness of structural blockages; they can potentially be utilized to educate others concerning the need for collective action.

Particular issues seem likely to increase awareness of structural barriers to mobility. These include organizational practices that individuals perceive as violating their rights (an issue effective in organizing students), consumer discrimination (an important source of dissatisfaction among low-income blacks), and police brutality (important grievance for high-income as well as low-income blacks). Individuals who have had recent experiences of discrimination are thus probably good sources for participation in social movements. Two other sources of dissatisfaction among the poor are the ineffectiveness of the political system in handling their grievances, and the inadequacy of opportunities for general economic mobility.

*Some External Social Correlates of
Social-Action Participation*

Effects of Membership Groups and Reference Groups

GENERALIZATION 8.7: Participation in social-action movements is influenced by the attitudes and values of an individual's membership groups and reference groups (+ + + +, 56, 61, 75, 108, 153, 163, 205, 206).

Membership groups are those groups of which an individual is currently a member. *Reference groups* are those groups which an individual uses as a source of norms and values, whether or not he is currently a group member.

8.7A. Participation in social-action movements is associated with parental support for such action (+ + +, 61, 205, 206).

8.7B. Participation in social-action movements is associated with parental support of the goals and values of the movement. Parents of participants often share the values advocated by the movement (+ + +, 56, 75, 108).

The influence of parental values on student participation in social action has been reported by Kenniston (108). Student protesters often come from liberal political families; a majority report that their parents hold views essentially similar to their own and accept or support their activities. Parents of protesters are usually liberal Democrats and a large number are pacifists and socialists. Propensities for militant social action may be viewed as an extension of rather than rebellion against parental values.

8.7C. Student participation in social movements is associated with faculty support at an institution for the goals of the movement (+ +, 108, 153).

8.7D. Continuing participation in social movements is associated with a *change* in membership groups. Persons who change their membership groups to include more friends who support a movement or actually participate in it are more likely to continue their participation than are persons who do not change their friendship groups (+, 61).

8.7E. Development of a radical social action organization requires a high level of interaction between members in many areas of life, not just in movement activities. Ability to spread the movement and to attract new supporters requires ability to be in close and permanent contact with other groups who can be influenced to join (+, 163).

8.7F. Detachment in the community may reduce an individual's acceptance of established norms and foster a predisposition toward deviant or militant movements (+ +, 67, 126, 157).

Action Guidelines: Membership groups and reference groups are important sources of attitudes and values motivating and sustaining an individual's social-action participation. Individuals with supportive families and friends are good sources of recruitment to social-action movements. The practitioner might want to stimulate participation by trying to develop support of important reference groups such as members' parents, or faculty on college campuses, or members' friends. Encouraging the development of friendships within the movement assists in the creation of new reference groups, which help to sustain member participation. When these reference groups are intense and cover many areas of an individual's life, reinforcement of social-action participation is magnified.

One might also utilize members' existing ties to recruit new members to the social-action movement. For example, members would be likely to recruit their friends, neighbors, and work associates into a social movement. Developing new ties and increasing interaction with other groups increases the ability to spread movement membership to other groups. Recruiting new members seems to be easier if the movement can develop close personal ties with potential recruits. The tendency of movements to antagonize and alienate those not fully in sympathy works in opposition to these possibilities.

Previous Participation in Voluntary Associations

GENERALIZATION 8.8: Persons with a history of successful experience of participation in traditional voluntary associations are not good recruits for social movements (+ +, 65, 68, 126, 157).

Findings concerning the previous participatory experiences of social-movement members appear to be somewhat inconsistent. For example, one set of findings shows that participants in civil disorders have very low levels of "normal" organizational participation (68, 126). A second group of findings shows that such participants have only moderate levels of organizational participation and define these participation experiences as unsuccessful and unsatisfying (65, 157).

Action Guidelines: Practitioners should not expend efforts to recruit persons with a history of participation in more traditional forms of participation for social-movement membership, especially if their participation has been satisfying.

*Effects of Social-Movement Participation
on Other Participation*

GENERALIZATION 8.9: Participation in social-action movements may increase some other forms of participation (+ +, 119, 205).

> 8.9A. Persons who participate in one social-action movement often have high participation in other social movements (+, 205).
> 8.9B. Persons who participate in a social-action movement may increase their political participation (+, 119).

Action Guidelines: A practitioner promoting social action should look to other social-action movements for support and recruits. Multiple memberships, which may develop as a consequence of social-movement participation, are a potential source of linkages to other groups that can be utilized for purposes of coalition-formation. When considered effective, social-movement participants can be mobilized to engage in more traditional political action. (This may be especially true for short-term campaigns and actions.)

*Sources of Support for Social Action
and Violent Protest*

Popular Support of Protest Actions

GENERALIZATION 8.10: Acceptance of nonviolent protest as legitimate is associated with highly educated persons and low-educated persons who are also low in political alienation. Rejection of protest is associated with persons who are low in education and high in political alienation, and is greatest among moderately educated persons (+, 151).

Action Guidelines: Groups most likely to reject the legitimacy of protest are the alienated with low education, and persons with moderate education levels. Since these groups comprise the majority of the population, social movements can anticipate that much of their activity will be regarded as illegitimate by the majority. They will probably have to rely on some highly educated community members as sources of legitimation for protest actions, or shun legitimation as a tactical variable.

GENERALIZATION 8.11: Professionalization is associated with a decrease in support for social-action movements (+ + +, 51, 197, 219).[3]

8.11A. Support for social action decreases as the length of employment in a professional occupation increases (+, 219).

8.11B. The greater the institutional involvement of social workers in

[3] See also Generalizations 3.9–16.

a problem area, the more conservative their perceptions of effective social-action strategies and the greater their differentiation of social-action roles for professional and lay groups (+ +, 51).

A survey of 1,020 members of the New York chapter of the National Association of Social Workers revealed a general disapproval of protest as a strategy of social action among groups representing the profession (51). Social workers were more likely to approve of protest in the housing field and less likely to endorse protest and more likely to monopolize leadership roles in issue areas, such as public welfare, where they have greater institutional involvement.

Action Guidelines: The practitioner should not look to professional social workers (and other professionals) for support as members of social-action movements. Since this professional tendency exists, the practitioner should be aware of it and make sure that he himself is not attempting to assume nonmilitant roles and steer social movements into adopting less militant strategies.

Some Dynamics of the Social-Action Process

Leadership Factors and Militancy

GENERALIZATION 8.12: An increase in competition for leadership leads to increased activity within a social movement (+ +, 98, 127).

8.12A. Organized competition for leadership occurs when leaders are able to develop several independent bases of support. Independent competition occurs where there is a weak community prestige structure (+, 127).

Development of competition among civil rights leaders was studied by MacWorter and Crain (127) in 14 cities. Two forms of competition were found: between organizations and between individuals. Interviews with community decision-makers and analyses of documentary materials were used to test the above subgeneralization. Both forms of competition were associated with increased militancy. It is important to note, however, that while competition for leadership increased militancy, it did not necessarily increase effectiveness in achieving goals. Organized competition led to intensive activity but inadequate outcomes, individual competition to more sustained outcomes, and no competition to disciplined drives for specific goals.

Action Guidelines: In competitive leadership situations, the practitioner can anticipate an increase in militancy and activity within the social movement. The practitioner can work to stimulate competition in order to raise the level of participation in a social movement. However, this may result in a decrease in the movement's ability to achieve specific goals. The practitioner will have to weigh the relative advantages of increased participation against the attainment of delimited short-range goals.

Leadership in Different Phases of Social Movement

GENERALIZATION 8.13: Over time, social movements may experience a change in the composition of the leadership. Two basic leadership types emerge and compete with each other during the course of a social movement: accommodative leadership and militant leadership styles (+ +, 89, 98).

8.13A. A period of protest and crisis may be followed by a period of negotiation in which protest leaders replace and are in turn replaced by accommodative leaders. This is particularly likely in communities where accommodative leaders are local residents and protest leaders are outsiders (+, 89).

This emergence and alternation of two different leadership structures is described by Hines and Pierce (89) in a case study of civil rights leadership in Montgomery, Alabama, at the time of the bus boycott. The local accommodative leadership structure, which was based on (self) interest-group rather than community goals and had very little community power, was replaced during the boycott by a militant leadership of independent, nonsalaried persons. After the protest, when Dr. King left the city, there was a quick return to the accommodative leadership structure.

8.13B. Militancy may be opposed by existing accomodative leaders who perceive the new protest leadership as a threat (+, 89, 98).

Action Guidelines: Black and other minority social-action movements may require the emergence of a new power structure relatively independent of the white community. Some black community leaders may oppose the new leadership. Some of this competition might be handled by encouraging accommodating leaders to continue to play negotiating roles, to serve as communication links with the white community. However, militant leaders face the problem of how to avoid being displaced by accommodative leaders during periods of low protest activity.

Types of Action Goals

GENERALIZATION 8.14: Militancy may be opposed by members within a particular social movement because social-action conflicts with other task goals of the movement. Militancy may be supported by members of an organization because of its effect in achieving the process goals of providing symbolic satisfactions and increasing commitment to the organization (+, 44).

Action Guidelines: Practitioners should be aware of the problem of the displacement of task goals by process goals with socioemotional benefits for movement members. Decisions to utilize protest in preference to other strategies should be based on careful evaluation of the functions and dysfunctions of protest strategies for both task accomplishment and group process.

Needed Resources and Strategies

GENERALIZATION 8.15: Successful social-action movements must appeal to four different constituencies to survive and to achieve immediate goals: *members, mass media, third parties,* and *target organizations capable of granting* *goals.* Success in the long run requires building a powerful, independent resource base (+ +, 124).

The dilemmas of social action are highlighted by a study (124) of a rent strike headed by Jesse Gray in New York City. Gray spent a good deal of time organizing groups and speaking throughout the city, thus neglecting administrative detail, failing to collect dues systematically, and alienating lawyers, who were often not paid. College students who staffed the rent strike offices helped this situation, but this sort of help was transient and often not applicable in the emphasis on Black Power. A further difficulty in satisfying the conflicting demands of constituent groups arose with regard to the mass media. To satisfy the media's demands for "news," Gray often exaggerated the size and success of the protest to the mass media, which printed his claims. However the media later demanded documentation of his claims, which he could not supply. In the short run, by meeting the demands of his organizational members, he had satisfied them; but, in doing so, he was labeled irresponsible by more established groups.

The target agency (in this case the New York City government) responded with symbolic rewards rather than significant change in the protester's situation. In a crisis, Mayor Lindsay took a "walking tour" of the ghetto. The programs adopted for responding to the crisis gave the impression they met the protestors' demands, but they were without substance.

Action Guidelines: Social-action movements require a minimum amount of resources in order to survive and achieve goals. In the short run this requires that coalitions be formed with other groups that have these resources and are willing to give some support to the movement's goals. In the long run movements must build their own independent resource base to achieve their long-term, wider-ranging demands. The need to develop short-term coalitions may place some constraints on the strategies the movement can utilize. The dilemma for the practitioner is to be able to devise strategies for forming coalitions while avoiding the problems of co-optation.

To illustrate, following are leadership modes and tactics

that may be employed with regard to each constituent group social activists must address:

1. *Organizational members:* If these are from low-income groups, the leader may have to adopt a militant style, promising rewards that will satisfy the members' needs for, e.g., immediate economic gains or emotional expressive release.

2. *Mass media:* The practitioner should plan some organizational events and public tactics with an eye to what is "news" to the mass media; therefore, some of the tactics should be dramatic with perhaps the hint of conflict—e.g., demonstrations, sit-downs, sensational statements. In addition, the worker must cultivate relationships with reporters assigned to his organization or to the area of civic rights or social problems and attempt to meet the reporters' special needs for "news." The practitioner may try such tactics as letting the reporters know of events ahead of time (e.g., giving them a "scoop") or deliberately distorting or enlarging the scope of the organization's activity to attract the media's interest.

3. *Third parties:* Appeals should be made to third parties, which are likely to be established human-service organizations or the more conservative civil rights organizations. The practitioner must consider the long-term relationships and interdependencies these organizations are likely to have with target agencies, their modes of operating (which are likely to be less sensational than those of the protest agency), and their penchant for careful organization and administrative detail. Appeals to these groups, then, may require that the protest organization adopt a more moderate leadership style (perhaps a different leader can be trained for these skills), and the presentation of less dramatic appeals to these groups.

4. *Target agency:* A combination of the above strategies and leadership styles is likely to be necessary in moving the target agency—e.g., dramatic protests, involving the use of the mass media—in order to embarrass the target agency and provide negative publicity to which the agency is sensi-

tive, combined with a less militant, organizationally conscious style in order to gain long-term rewards of actual admission to decision-making bodies, and in order to gain the added support of third parties.

The above approaches, according to the study, should be considered short-term, since protest as a tactic is a limited strategy because of its inherent difficulties in organizational maintenance and in meeting the conflicting needs of constituent groups while sustaining the participation of members.

Still another case study of rent strikes produces a related type of observation (143). The author points out that the rent strike failed because toward the end the social action organization became heavily involved in a complicated technicallegal process. Most of its energies became enmeshed in court procedures, burning out its resources and dampening the spirits of members who were not given a continuing channel for active participation. The implication here is that grass-roots activist groups should not engage with bureaucracies on their own terms, in their own area of competence. It is not possible for the grass-roots organization to bring to bear the organizational sophistication and technical resources involved in what has been termed "going the bureaucratic route." At the same time such an approach has a detrimental effect on participatory tendencies, which are vital to a social-action strategy.

Elite Responses and Violence

GENERALIZATION 8.16: The response of other groups, especially elites and gatekeepers, to social-movement initiatives is an important factor influencing the likelihood that a particular social-action protest will result in collective violence (+ + +, 16, 91, 122, 134, 137, 149, 221).

8.16A. The greater the amount of unsuccessful communication between the complaining group and the political or administrative system before a social-action protest, the greater the likelihood that the protest will become violent (+, 137).

The conditions under which collective protest results in violence were studied by Morgan (137) in a questionnaire survey of students, faculty, and administrators at 106 colleges that experienced protests against armed-forces recruiting in the fall of 1967. Morgan found that the demonstrations were usually preceded by student attempts to communicate their grievances to the school administration through a variety of channels: newspapers, student-government resolutions, petitions, leaflets, conversations with administrators or faculty. There was a positive correlation between protests that resulted in civil disobedience and the amount of efforts the students made at communication before the demonstration. Thus, the greater the number of unsuccessful attempts student groups experienced in trying to implement their change goals peacefully through negotiation and communication, the more likely the groups were to engage in civil-disobedience rather than orderly protests.

8.16B. Protestors often use violent means only after they have attempted other nonviolent means of seeking redress for their grievances (+ + +, 137, 149).

8.16C. Oppressive actions by officials are a prime course of violence (+ +, 149).

Obershall points out that violence is more often initiated by the authorities and their agents than by protestors, as when peaceful assemblies, etc., are broken up and fired upon. The magnitude of casualties will be even greater if the agents of social control know that the public will not hold them accountable for the casualties they produce during repression (149).

8.16D. Third parties may serve to reduce the possibilities of violence (+ +, 149).

According to Obershall, the probability of violence decreases when there is an impartial third party available to serve as a buffer or mediator in the conflict.

8.16E. Higher likelihood of collective violence (civil disorders) is associated with cities with a low number of minority group members on the police force and lack of direct contact between minority group members and local government (+, 122).

8.16F. Severity of collective violence has been associated with the presence of a special police riot plan (+, 221).

8.16G. Movements that rely on civil-disobedience protests are more effective than orderly protests in achieving immediate objectives but are also more likely to produce repression, and regulations sanctioning future activity (+ +, 137).

8.16H. Repressive violence on the part of social-control forces leads to increased acceptance of militant protest actions and increased support of the movement's goals among persons who have some initial sympathy with the movement (+, 16, 137).

8.16I. Repressive violence initiated by social-control forces is associated with expansion of protest activities by movement members (+, 137).

8.16J. The attempt to crush a social movement through the elimination (assassination) of its leaders leads to an increase in militancy among the movement's members and to increased distrust of the political system (+ +, 91, 134).

Action Guidelines: The practitioner can influence the likelihood that a particular social protest will result in violence. First, the practitioner must try to assess the response "authorities" will make to that protest. If a protest has been preceded by an unsuccessful period of intergroup communication, there is a greater likelihood that the protest will become violent. One strategy for avoiding violence in such a situation is to persuade a third party to intervene and act as a mediator in the conflict. By making administrative and political authorities aware of the high possibility for violence, the practitioner may increase the possibility for peaceful resolution of grievances.

Violence is also more likely to occur in situations where there is a lack of opportunities for expression and resolution of grievances between social movements and the political system. Nonreform governments in cities with small election districts seem to provide the most opportunities for direct contact with political officials.

The practitioner should carefully weigh the costs and gains of using civil-disobedience strategies. They may be more effective than orderly protests, in achieving short-run objectives, but they may hamper the long-range effectiveness of a social movement by stimulating repressive sanctions against future activity. The practitioner should attempt to make the movement aware of these costs and gains.

Finally, violence may have some positive consequences for a social movement. A practitioner can utilize it. By viewing the action guidelines in a converse fashion, they can be used to escalate the level of conflict. For example, by publicizing repressive action initiated by the authorities, greater support for the movement can be developed among initial sympathizers. In this context, the practitioner can gain a psychological advantage by pointing to the movement's attempt to communicate, in order to peacefully resolve grievances without a protest. Violence may also result in movement members having a greater commitment to the movement and possibly increased willingness to support militant action.

While we are terminating the discussion of social action at this point, the reader is advised that additional treatment of participation in social action will be found in the section on client participation later in this chapter. Those studies of social action which had a client referent were placed in the client section for convenience of discourse. The reader with a special interest in social action might go immediately to that section for purposes of continuity. (See especially Generalizations 8.34, 8.35, 8.36, 8.38, 8.39, 8.40.) Meanwhile, we shall proceed with the subject of political participation, which embodies social action also, but in a more particularized sense.

POLITICAL PARTICIPATION

Many social-welfare objectives, whether involving new programs, fiscal rearrangements in the community, or modified social practices or structures, require manipulation of the community political process. The institutionalization of health, education, and welfare reforms often takes place by transformation of social problems into public issues, proposal of solutions to these issues, and a transformation of these "solutions" into laws by placing them on an election ballot to be approved or rejected by the voting public. Or a community group may wish to elect legislators who are generally sympathetic to a given progressive policy line. Hence, we shall attempt to formulate practice guidelines derived from current research which enable practitioners to predict and influence broad community participation in electoral politics. Aspects of political participation not confined to the area of voting are found in chapter 6.

Most of the studies from which the action guidelines in this section are derived concern two interrelated aspects of voting—level of voting participation, and specific issue content. There are few studies that combine simultaneous analysis of both aspects of the voting process; for example, charting voting patterns of given groups over time to determine how voter turnout varied on different issues. This has imposed limitations on the specificity with which action guidelines can be drawn.

It would be of use to the reader to supplement this review by examining the series of reports on voting patterns issued by the Survey Research Center of the University of Michigan. Some of these books and monographs, written by such researchers as Campbell, Converse, Stokes, and Miller, are cited in chapter 6.

The studies we shall report on relate voter participation to three main categories of variables: attributes of the individual voter, community characteristics, and the structure of the election process itself. The most widely investigated variable is social class, or an aspect of class such as education, occupation, or income. The methodological quality of the studies appears generally to be good; most researchers rely on systematic demographic data to measure concepts.

The Demography of Political Voting Behavior—Who Votes?

Voting and Socioeconomic Status

GENERALIZATION 8.17: For individuals within a given community, there is a direct relationship between a variety of dimensions of social class and voting participation. The higher the social class level of a population group, the higher its rate of voting (+ + + +, 60, 73, 107, 200, 216, 238).

8.17A. Voter participation varies directly with an individual's level of education (+ + +, 107, 216, 238).

8.17B. Voter participation varies directly with an individual's level of income (+ + +, 60, 200, 238).

8.17C. Voter participation varies directly with an individual's occupational status (+ +, 73, 238).

The political interest and activity of different occupational groups was investigated by Glenn and Alston (73) in their analysis of studies conducted by the National Opinion Research Center from 1953 to 1965. Persons in different occupational groups were ranked in terms of their political activity and information about issues. In terms of political activity, the occupational groups ranked, in the order from highest to lowest activity rates, as follows: professionals, business and executives, clerical and sales workers, skilled workers, service workers, farmers, and nonfarm laborers.

It is of interest to note a limitation on the above. Zikmuod and Smith (238) found that the proposition was generally supported with the exception that persons with jobs requiring high scientific or technical training had a rate of voter participation lower than one might predict from their high occupational status. This may reflect the scientist's reputed detachment and aloofness from public affairs.

Action Guidelines: The practitioner can use the above generalizations to predict the relative degrees of voter turnout on the basis of social class variables. If the practitioner has a reliable guide for determining whether persons of a particular social class or race are likely to support or oppose a given issue, he can begin to assess the numbers of persons who will likely be voting for or against that issue. The generalizations also suggest to the practitioner which groups are easiest to mobilize politically for voting participation. For example, few resources may be needed to ensure high voter turnout among the highly educated, but mobilizing low-income persons might require extensive resources to overcome their typically low rate of participation. The findings hint that community adult education programs might have the consequence of raising the political participation of low-socioeconomic-status groups and hence could be a mobilizing tool. Community organizations, such as the League of

Women Voters, whose goals include increased voter participation, can use these generalizations to identify target populations with the lowest levels of voter participation and the greatest need for education and support.

Racial Variables

GENERALIZATION 8.18: Blacks generally have lower rates of voter participation than whites (+ + +, 60, 92, 216).

8.18A. The very lowest level of voter participation is found among lower-class whites (+, 60).

When voter participation among racial groups of the same social class is compared, these groups have voter turnout, ranked from highest to lowest, as follows: upper-class whites, middle-class whites, middle-class blacks, lower-class blacks, lower-class white (+, 60).

Action Guidelines: Traditionally, blacks have had lower political participation than whites. However, these studies have not usually evaluated the differential consequences of voter registration drives, civil rights laws, or the recent emergence of blacks as candidates for major political offices on black voter participation. The generalizations here suggest that as blacks and other minorities achieve middle-class economic status, their voter participation increases. The practitioner might mobilize the middle-class group and employ them organizationally as a means of achieving still broader minority participation. The most difficult group of all to involve in voter participation, and thus the one requiring the greatest effort to activate, appears to be low-income whites.

Age

GENERALIZATION 8.19: Age is related to voter participation in a curvilinear fashion. Highest voter turnout is found among middle-aged persons (30 to 60 years). Lowest voter turnout is found in the under-30 age group. It is assumed that voting declines after age 60, but findings are somewhat unclear (+ +, 18, 74, 238).

Zikmuod and Smith (238) found that voter participation declined after age 60. Glenn and Grimes (74), however, discovered in a cohort analysis of Gallup Poll interviews concerning voting in *presidential* elections, that political activity actually *increased* with age. Glenn and Grimes found that interest in political issues remained high as age increased. Lack of voter participation in *behavioral terms* among the elderly was not related to a decline *attitudinally* of interest in political issues, but instead to the fact that physical disability and transportation problems made it difficult for many of the aging to vote in elections.

Action Guidelines: It appears that mobilizing younger persons to vote is a serious problem.[4] The practitioner would have to work hardest at raising the political interest of this group. Middle-aged persons should be the easiest to mobilize. The practitioner may not need to work to increase the interest of elderly people in political activity, but rather should attempt to remove barriers to their participation, such as lack of transportation. For example, local political parties or civic organizations could be encouraged to make transportation and escort services available to elderly persons on election day.

Personal Variables—Alienation, Information

Alienation

GENERALIZATION 8.20: Participation in voting generally is associated with low feelings of alienation and with high feelings of political efficacy (+ + + +, 27, 36, 60, 152, 170, 204, 216, 228).

Political efficacy is defined as the belief that one's actions can influence the political system. Alienation is defined as a sense of power-

---

[4] The studies in our data pool preceded the 1972 McGovern campaign, in which there was considerable youth participation. Whether that campaign represents a basic change in youth voting patterns or whether it was an isolated phenomenon remains to be seen.

lessness: the feeling that one's actions make no difference to the operation of the political system.

8.20A. High alienation is found among the following groups of potential voters: low-educated, low-income blacks and whites, low-income rural whites, and low-income white migrants from rural areas. These groups are also low in political efficacy (+ + +, 60, 170, 216).

8.20B. Persons who have high feelings of alienation display more withdrawal from political participation in *national* elections than in *local* elections (+, 216).

8.20C. Participation by alienated groups at the local level is often "negative" in character; persons high in alienation oppose or veto issues supported by the local community power structure (+, 216).

8.20D. Political alienation is positively associated with voting against traditional political parties by joining nontraditional political movements when they arise (+ + +, 36, 204, 228).

This generalization was supported by a study of the bases of support for Governor George Wallace in the 1968 election. Findings, reported by Wolfe (228), are based on interviews, held before and after the election, of 1,394 citizens in 48 states. The typical Wallace voter was found to be negative about the Johnson administration, cynical about the federal government, and doubtful about his own ability to influence government policy.

Hence we see that alienation is related in various ways to whether a citizen will vote or not, the context of the vote (local or national election), and the direction of the vote as well. The question is obviously complex and has a number of dimensions requiring clarification. A more thorough review of several studies may facilitate such clarification.

One general assumption that runs throughout various studies is that national elections provide voters with only a very limited chance to express their views or influence policy on specific issues. Thus, on the national level, the politically alienated are typically the nonvoters. On the local level, however, it is easier for the voter to perceive his vote as being directed at specific targets and actually influencing decision making. For this reason, feelings of alienation are likely to be expressed through a negative vote rather than no vote at all. Some researchers hypothesize that this opposing vote is not issue-specific, but rather a demonstration of the desire not to let a given "them" put something over on an alienated "us."

Dwight G. Dean (43) attempts to correlate alienation with political apathy. Dean defines alienation in terms of powerlessness, normlessness, and social isolation. He relates it to *political apathy,* which he also breaks down into *interest apathy, influence apathy, behavior apathy,* and *voting apathy.* Scales developed to measure alienation were extracted from the literature and applied to a sample drawn from four of the 19 wards in Columbus, Ohio. Dean hypothesized a positive correlation between alienation and political apathy. In fact, the correlation was not statistically significant. In explaining this, Dean suggests that normlessness need not be related to political apathy, since individuals often engage in politics for such reasons as conformity or the meeting of psychopathological needs.

Horton and Thompson (94) explore the issue of powerlessness and the translation of negative attitudes into action through the referendum. Alienation, according to these researchers, involves popular discontent: commitment to existing norms but frustration of efforts to be politically effective within the framework of these norms. The authors contend that the referendum is an area of community politics that provides a ready-made institutional channel for the expression of protest. They note that voter turnout is generally higher for defeated than for passed referendums and that this defeat follows a consistent pattern of negative voting among the socially and economically deprived segments of the population, the same segments that usually contribute a disproportionate number of nonvoters.

Interviews with nearly 400 voters in two upstate New York communities shortly after these communities voted on and defeated school-bond proposals form the basis for this study. In both towns, defeat of the school-bond proposal was accompanied by an increased turnout among persons of low income and education. According to the researchers, an atmosphere of controversy generalized beyond the specific issues and directed against the experts and local leaders pervaded each campaign and was provoked and perpetuated through attacks by self-appointed leaders of the opposition.

8.20E. Persons who are high in political alienation and participate in extremist political movements are not necessarily psychologically maladjusted or frustrated in their interpersonal relationships (+, 186, 190, 228).

For example, organized opponents of mental health programs were not found to be "crackpots" but rather had stable psychological and social characteristics. While the above was confirmed in several careful studies, it was not supported by Marcus (128), who found that psychopathology was associated with participation in nontraditional political activity. Hence it should be viewed as tentative.

Action Guidelines: Practitioners should be aware of the psychological attitudes of alienation that reinforce the low level of voter participation among particular groups, especially low-income, low-educated persons, blacks, whites in rural areas, and recent white migrants to cities from rural areas. The practitioner who wants to increase electoral participation in the conventional political system among these groups will have to work to reduce these feelings. For example, achieving some measure of success on issues through a local community organization might increase individual feelings of efficacy. Likewise, providing information on issues might dispel some negativism. On the other hand, if the practitioner is attempting to defeat traditional political candidates and policies, he might look to highly alienated groups for support. Groups high in political alienation may be more easily mobilized to vote in local than national elections (such as school-bond issues), and to vote against issues supported by local political elites rather than for them. Being able to defeat an issue may itself lead to an increase in group feelings of efficacy. Thus the practitioner might want to begin working with a highly alienated group by encouraging its members to vote against a particular issue or through nontraditional channels. The practitioner should not assume that persons who have nontraditional forms of political participation on the right are necessarily psychologically maladjusted and hence to be written off.

They share many of the individualistic concerns of the left and may possibly be open to persuasion regarding voting or coalition action on an issue basis.

Political Information

GENERALIZATION 8.21: Voter participation is associated with an individual's level of political information (+ + +, 25, 73, 133).

8.21A. Political information is directly related to social class (+ +, 25, 73).

8.21B. Educational programs that provide new information about how the political system works can be effective in raising the level of political information (+ +, 115, 133).

In a study of the effects of high school civics curricula conducted by Langton and Jennings (115), the authors found that educational programs were effective in raising political information and efficacy among black adolescents. However, these programs had no effect on white adolescents, who already seemed familiar with the information being taught in the program.

Action Guidelines: Better informed people may be more easily mobilized to vote. Educational programs that increase political information may have some effect in changing attitudes that affect the level of political participation. However, the practitioner must evaluate educational programs to make sure that they are in fact imparting new political information to target groups. In the recent past, blacks seemed to be better able to use and to be in greater need of such educational programs than whites.

Perception of Legitimacy

GENERALIZATION 8.22: Support for the political system's legitimacy varies with socioeconomic status, especially with level of education (+ +, 25, 45).

This generalization was tested by Boynton, Patterson, and Hedlund (25) in a survey of a sample of Iowa residents in November 1966.

Support for the political system was measured in terms of two dimensions: *compliance factor,* willingness to comply with decisions reached in the legislative system, and *institutional commitment factor,* willingness to maintain the legislative system in the face of generally unsatisfactory performance. The researchers found that the greatest overall support for the legislative system in terms of both compliance and commitment came in aggregate form from college-educated groups, high-income groups, and professional and managerial occupational groups. Those with high school educations were higher on compliance than commitment; those with grade school educations were low on both dimensions. As indicated earlier, relatively high levels of support for protest against the system also comes from the highly educated group.

Action Guidelines: Educational development programs that increase political information may increase commitment to the legitimacy of the political system, and hence by inference to electoral participation—providing, one assumes, that system is operating to allocate resources in a reasonably just manner. It may be important to convey this equitable principle in an educational program. However, if the political system is operating unjustly, giving people accurate information about how it works will probably not increase their commitment to it, but could rather stimulate nonconventional political behavior.

Structural Variables—The Electoral Situation and the Community Context

Structure of the Electoral Situation

GENERALIZATION 8.23: The amount of voter participation varies with the structure or characteristics of the election process itself (+ + +, 107, 220).

8.23A. Voter turnout is associated with the type of election. Popular elections, for example, have higher rates of voter turnout than bond issues. National elections in the United States have higher turnout rates than local elections (+, 220).

Action Guidelines: One can anticipate different propensities for voting depending on the electoral situation. The practitioner in general will have to work harder to foster participation in local elections and in specialized elections focusing on such matters as school-bond issues. One needs to assess the desirability of promoting greater turnouts. For example, if the practitioner has assurances that the majority of a small group expected to vote on school bonding matters will go in his direction, he might want to keep the issue contained and at a low level of political awareness so as not to stir up the opposition (see Generalization 8.26).

Registration and Voting

GENERALIZATION 8.24: Differences in voting rates can be accounted for in part by differences in registration procedures and rates (+, 107).

8.24A. Registration rates increase as election competitiveness increases (+, 107).
8.24B. Permanent registration systems are associated with higher rates of registration than are periodic registration systems (+, 107).
8.24C. Changing the election process by simply removing legal barriers to registration and voting (especially for minorities) has not automatically resulted in large changes in rates of voting participation (+ + +, 18, 32, 38, 92, 147).

Most of the support for this proposition comes from studies of attempts to register black voters in the South. For example, Holloway and Olson (92) found that from 1954 to 1963 black voter registration remained fairly stable at about 30–35 percent and in 1964 increased to only 43.8 percent. Thus while the Voting Rights Act resulted in some gains in participation, the majority of blacks still remained unregistered. Furthermore, the increase in black registration was offset by a corresponding increase in white registration. Clubek, DeGrove, and Farris (32) found that an increase in black registration in Florida towns, even when they involved increased voting because of manipulative political practices by the power structure, did not have any effect on local policies of segregated facilities and did not result in improved municipal services. Nimms and McClesky (147) found that abolition of the poll tax resulted in no gains for black voters, some gains among Chicanos, and the highest gains among young voters. However, the *majority* of previously unregistered voters remained unregistered. Beck and Jennings (18) found that voting had low salience for high school seniors and that lowering the voting age to 18 could not be expected to produce high voter participation in the 18 to 21 age group.

Action Guidelines: Changing the structure of the election process appears to be a potential but certainly not sufficient means for raising voting participation of disenfranchised groups. A high rate of voter participation appears to require maximum opportunity for participation (which can be achieved through legal changes such as abolishing the poll tax, lowering the voting age, and establishing permanent registration) as well as motivation and opportunity to participate. Thus practitioners must be alert to follow up structural changes that involve manipulation of political instrumentalities with motivational changes requiring attitudinal shifts and the provision of opportunities through services such as transportation or baby-sitters.

Community Structural Factors

GENERALIZATION 8.25: Characteristics of community structure are related to voter support of various human welfare issues (+ +, 3, 123, 218).

8.25A. Degree of urbanization is positively related to voter support for tax levies for welfare and bonds for physical improvement (+, 218).

8.25B. Cities with a reform type of government, as opposed to mayor-council, partisan government, are less responsive to the social welfare needs of community minority groups (+, 3, 123).

Governmental structure appears to depend more on geographical than sociological variables. In a study of the governmental structures of 309 cities, Wolfinger and Field (230) reported that city governmental structure (reform versus partisan) was not related to a city's population composition or to its public-regarding or private-regarding ethos, but rather to the region of the country in which it was located. Reform governments are more often found in the South and West, partisan governments in the Northeast.

Action Guidelines: The community planner who is interested in supporting long-range, community-wide planning activities such as metropolitan government or planning for regional urban transportation systems will find the greatest support for these activities among high-educated, high-income suburban residents, and in communities that have high urbanization and are high in proportions of these residents. Persons who are engaged in community action efforts to improve human-service programs for the poor may recruit the greatest voter support for those programs in cities with a partisan type of government.

Although communities with a high proportion of low-income persons may have higher taxes and expenditures, the poor do not appear to be receiving their proportionate share of the benefits. Practitioners need to communicate to low-income and ethnic minority groups the amount of direct benefits they receive in proportion to the taxes they pay as well as to mobilize their effective use of the polls.

In regions where the city government structure and population composition are unfavorable to the interests of the poor, a useful strategy for the practitioner would be to combine various voter proposals so that they might receive a broader base of community support. For example, job training programs could be incorporated into school tax levies, since education is a high-priority issue for all voter groups. Finally, more middle- and upper-class whites may be willing to support human-welfare issues if the more general community-wide benefits of these issues are anticipated.

Issue Variables—Conflict and Class Correlates

Issue Conflict and Voting Rate

GENERALIZATION 8.26: Elections with a high amount of competition and conflict are associated with higher rates of voter turnout (+ + +, 5, 39, 48, 135, 140).

8.26A. Elections with a high amount of competition are more characteristic of communities with a high degree of socioeconomic cleavage—that is, heterogeneous communities with a large number of low-income residents (+ , 5).

Dimensions of community structure that affect voter turnout were studied by Alford and Lee (5), who analyzed data on 1961 and 1962 local elections held in 676 cities with a population of over 25,000. Their measure of voter turnout was the proportion of registrants who voted. They found that cities with more highly ethnic or less-educated populations had higher levels of voter turnout. The authors note that this finding is somewhat surprising because highly educated individuals are more likely to vote than low-educated individuals. However, at the community level, the existence of a high proportion of lower-class persons increases the visibility of socioeconomic cleavages, which seems to result in highly competitive elections that increase the voter turnout among all social classes.

8.26B. Higher conflict over political issues is associated with cities with a high population growth rate. Low political conflict is associated with cities with a stable growth rate (+, 47).

8.26C. Higher issue conflict is associated with the degree of cleavage between opponents on a particular issue as well as with leadership turnover in the community (+ , 64).

All of the above subpropositions support the general position that community heterogeneity is associated with socioeconomic cleavage and conflict, which in turn increases voter turnout. However, it should be kept in mind that this proposition seems to be true only in situations where low-income groups have some opportunity to organize and participate in the political process. For example, the proposition would not apply to certain areas of the South where political participation of blacks has been restricted. In a study of the consequences of income inequality, Dye (48) found that states with greater income inequality between blacks and whites had low party competition and low voter turnout.

8.26D. A high degree of competition and voter turnout are associated with partisan elections and a mayor-council form of government, rather than with nonpartisan elections and a reform city manager type of government (+, 5).

8.26E. While conflict serves to elevate voter turnout, it may bring about some disadvantages the practitioner should anticipate. For example, raising the level of community conflict seems to increase voter opposition on some issues, such as fluoridation (+ +, 39, 140).

Action Guidelines: The generalizations indicate that motivation to participate in electoral politics may be increased by elevating the emotional level of an election campaign. The practitioner may attempt to raise voter turnout by encouraging the development of competition or conflict during an election. A strategy for raising the level of conflict might involve stressing the socioeconomic and other cleavages that exist in the community, and the cleavages between the groups supporting and opposing an issue. Other, more long-range strategies involve development of partisan elections, nonreform governmental structures, and support of a high rate of community growth.

Under certain circumstances, the practitioner may wish to discourage community conflict, for example, if one is a planner trying to fluoridate the water supply in a rapidly growing town or to promote desegregation in a split community with strong oppositional forces. In this case, the practitioner might want to play down the cleavages dividing the issue's supporters and opponents and work quietly from inside bureaucratic structures. Raising community conflict seems especially useful when the practitioner is trying to mobilize community groups to oppose a particular issue, and when he has no access to or faces stiff opposition from "gatekeepers" and power elites.

Social Issues and Social Class in Voting

GENERALIZATION 8.27: There are significant differences in the types of issues supported by persons of different social classes (+ + + +, 60, 84, 118, 125, 152, 168, 180, 183, 218, 231).

8.27A. Voters of low socioeconomic status support issues that provide them with direct economic and social benefits: "bread and butter" issues that favor their specific group interests. Persons of high socioeconomic status support issues that are formulated in terms of more general, diffuse benefits for the entire community (+ +, 180, 218).

The lowest socioeconomic status groups show the highest support for "social welfare" issues, such as improved low-income housing, which are important to their own specific needs and interests. High-status groups are most likely to support issues involving metropolitan government and such physical community improvements as highway construction and control of water pollution.

Banfield and Wilson's study (226) of "public interest" or "self interest" as the dominant motivation in voting behavior indicated that other variables also cut across the relationship between interest motivation and social class. They found that blacks in *both* low- and middle-income classes were more supportive of public expenditures than were white ethnic groups. Low-income renters were more favorable to public expenditures than were middle-income homeowners. Anglo-Saxon and Jewish upper-income homeowners were also more likely to support public expenditures, even when these operated outside of class interests.

8.27B. Support for social welfare issues that directly benefit the poor varies inversely with social class. Greatest opposition to welfare, job training programs, and open housing comes from whites in aggregate at the highest income level. Highest support for these programs comes from poor blacks, although poor whites and middle-income whites also show some support for these programs (+, 60).

8.27C. Persons with high alienation (which correlates in these studies with low education and income) lean toward supporting government involvement in domestic affairs, while persons with low alienation give less support to government involvement in domestic affairs and more support to involvement in foreign affairs (+, 152).

8.27D. All groups rank education as the highest-priority government issue (+, 62).

8.27E. Support for social change regarding the economic system is not associated with the most impoverished classes, but with individuals who have experienced some degree of economic progress (+ +, 168, 231). (See Relative Deprivation generalizations.)

8.27F. Support for major changes in the political system is associated with persons who have high status inconsistency (+ +, 118). (See Status Inconsistency generalizations.)

8.27G. Lack of support for social-welfare issues is associated with a belief in individual ability and motivation as the source of social mobility (+ +, 60, 183).

Upwardly mobile persons who have experienced discrimination as a block to advancement are less likely to adopt this ideology and are more likely to adopt "radical" political attitudes (125).

8.27H. Attitudes by social class are not consistent from the standpoint of a liberal-conservative ideological framework, but rather vary from issue to issue (+, 136).

Mitchell (136), for example, compared voting patterns in the 1960 school tax proposal in Berkeley, California, with those of the 1956 presidential election. He found that electoral support for the liberal school tax proposal was greatest among upper-class persons, but that they did not support Stevenson, the liberal presidential candidate in the 1956 election. The reverse was true for lower-class persons. Glenn and Alston (73) also found that persons in various social classes had attitudes that varied from issue to issue. For instance, persons in professional occupations were tolerant of minorities, conservative in general attitudes, supportive of civil rights, negative toward labor unions, and favorable to the policy of United States intervention in foreign affairs.

The reader is cautioned not to overemphasize the issue of social class. A number of studies suggest that social class is not the major cleavage influencing attitudes on major political issues in the United States. Janowitz and Segal's (99) study of the bases of political cleavage in the United States, Great Britain, and West Germany showed that the United States had the lowest association between social class and party affiliation, social class as a basis of political cleavage was declining, and new bases of political cleavage, based on race and religion, were emerging. Segal and Knoke (198) found that race and region were important variables in explaining political party preferences. They concluded that these variables were more important then economic (or occupational) variables as bases of political cleavage.

Action Guidelines: Despite the specified qualifications, social class is a variable the practitioner should consider as an aid in predicting whether persons will support or oppose particular issues. The poor will have the highest support for a number of social-welfare issues that benefit them directly, while high-income groups will show little support for these issues. One source of hostility on the part of the latter to social-welfare programs for the poor is their belief in the American work ethic. The paractitioner should attempt to educate upper-income groups concerning the barriers to mobility that exist in this country, while at the same time he should enhance the political power of the lower class. Rationality and persuasion alone are not to be considered a sufficient force for shifting economic resources.

If a practitioner is a planner interested in gaining support for social-welfare activities with community-wide, "public regarding" benefits, such as pollution control, he should try to involve upper-class groups. Support of lower-income groups on such issues will be obtained only if they can see direct benefits, such as the relationship between pollution and their own health problems. The practitioner should at the same time be aware that "public regarding" issues may in fact be differentially beneficial to different subgroups within the community and should therefore not be misled by interest-group claims that a particular proposal is "for the good of all."

Since the data indicate that different social classes have different priorities, it might be a reasonable strategy for the practitioner to encourage low-income groups to form coalitions with other social classes, instead of competing with them in setting priorities. Thus ghetto organizations could perhaps agree to support road construction in exchange for the business community's support of more low-cost housing.

It is advisable to utilize variables other than social class for predicting whether or not a particular issue will be supported. Race, religion, region, and property ownership also influence issue attitudes. Finally, the practitioner should be aware that an individual's or a group's attitude toward a specific issue will not be consistent in terms of a general ideological stance. Support must be appraised on an issue-by-issue basis.

Some Dynamics of the Voting Process

Ethnic Voting Participation and Middle-Class Status

GENERALIZATION 8.28: Increases in ethnic bloc voting are associated with the development of middle-class status among ethnic groups, primarily because middle-class status seems to be necessary if a person of ethnic background is to run for public office (+, 229).

Action Guidelines: Practitioners can anticipate and work to organize the development of ethnic voting patterns as blacks, Chicanos, Native Americans, and Puerto Ricans attain middle-class status. Recruiting ethnic candidates to run in local elections may increase the voter participation of these groups.

Primary Group Affects on Voting Behavior

GENERALIZATION 8.29: Community attitudes, as reflected in voting patterns, appear to a greater degree to be formed through a process of social participation than directly through the activity of political parties (+ +, 173; see chapter 7).

Action Guidelines: The practitioner who is attempting to change voter attitudes may work through existing patterns of participation in primary groups and voluntary associations, rather than relying only on political party activity. Such a strategy could include the recruiting of persons with a wide range of organizational memberships and friendship ties to act as "socializers" who would attempt to change their friends' and fellow members' attitudes. Also, the practitioner could encourage existing groups who support an issue to influence their membership politically.

Letter Writing as an Index of Voting Propensity

GENERALIZATION 8.30: Using the opinions of letter-writers is a less realistic guide to voting behavior than are opinion polls (+, 35).

The majority of letters to public officials and to newspapers and magazines come from a small number of people, about one to three percent of the electorate, who tend to write very frequently. This small group accounts for over two-thirds of all mail received by officials.

Action Guidelines: The practitioner who is attempting to assess voter opinion on a particular issue should disregard the amount of support or opposition by letters written to officials or to the mass media. Practitioners may indicate to public officials whom they support that letter writers are not accurate guides to voter opinion. Alternatively, it is possible through a well-organized mail campaign to convey a sense of generalized public opinion.

As a concluding comment, we advise the reader to keep firmly in mind that these studies on voting behavior cannot readily be applied cross-culturally. In one sense the culture-bound quality of the findings can be viewed as a limitation or negative feature of the studies. On the other hand, one might state this point affirmatively with a generalization to the effect that political processes are found to vary across national systems and cultures. For example, Kesselman (110) found that in France, competition was not related positively to increased voter turnout and that further, unlike in the United States, voter turnout was higher in local than in national elections. Kuroda (111) found some similarities and some differences between Japanese and American voter participation. In both countries, voter participation was related to socioeconomic status, but Japanese women were much less politically active than women in the United States, and newspapers played a less significant part in Japanese than in American elections. We shall not treat cross-national political factors in this book, but only call the readers' attention to them. From here we shall proceed with a consideration of participation by client populations.

CLIENT PARTICIPATION

The term "client participation" will refer to the involvement of clientele of human-service agencies in the decision-making processes of those agencies which have been created to provide services to them. Traditionally, social agencies have utilized two major forms of community involvement in decision making. The first of these is characterized by the appointment of community persons, usually well-known community elites—"leaders"—to agency boards, primarily through appointive action by the board itself. The second employs the public election or official political appointment of board members according to the requirements of law, as for example in the case of local school boards. The latter election procedure has not been common for private human-service agencies.

As a result of the customary mode of selection, most boards have been composed of a disproportionate number of individuals from the middle and upper classes. In reviewing the empirical literature on this subject, Morris reports that agency governance has been dominated by employers, professional men and women, managers, and housewives whose husbands are in one of the listed categories.[5] In his study of the

---

[5] Robert Morris, "Social Planning" in *Five Fields of Social Service: Reviews of Research*, Henry S. Maas, ed. (New York: National Association of Social Workers, 1966), pp. 185–208.

Indianapolis Community Chest, Seeley [6] found that campaign leaders were mostly drawn from a thin stratification layer in the middle class. And in examining participation in community-welfare decision making in Syracuse, Willie's data [7] indicated that about one percent of the population of that city played a key role in major decisions.

As is typical, these participation procedures did not provide for input of clients in agency policy matters. In recent years, however, some new forms of client participation have been implemented under the impact of the OEO Community Action Programs, the local community control ideology, and as a consequence of demands by client groups (predominantly those of low income and of racial and ethnic minority backgrounds) who receive the bulk of services to have a role in agency policy making. In these developments, "client participation" has sometimes been conceived of broadly in terms of participation of ethnic, racial, or neighborhood populations from which most clients come. The collectivity was officially referred to as "Target Area Residents." Thus, styles of participation are reflected variously by the involvement of clients themselves, people who have high potential for becoming clients or acquiring some of the problems of clients, or people with similar social-class, geographic, or ethnic characteristics of clients. Because this latter group resembles clients in important ways, it can presumedly authoritatively articulate their needs and desires. In this sense one may use the term "client system" as developed by Lippitt and associates to describe aptly generalized client entities in the community, such as "the poor," "blacks," "youth." [8]

Most of the empirical work on client participation has utilized case-study methodology, investigating specific attempts to develop client participation, and has relied heavily on participant observation. Since reasonably extensive client participation is a fairly recent phenomenon, few empirical studies have appeared in the journals in the past, although the number has been increasing. In addition, the entire matter

---

[6] John R. Seeley, et al., *The Community Chest* (Toronto: The University of Toronto Press, 1957).

[7] Charles Willie, "Trends in Participation of Businessmen in Local Voluntary Affairs," *Sociology and Social Research* 48, no. 3 (April 1964): 289–300.

[8] Ronald Lippitt, et al., *The Dynamics of Planned Change* (New York: Harcourt, Brace and Company, 1958).

of client "presence" within organizations has come in for more serious sociological analysis.[9] A sizable proportion of the available empirical studies deal with programs of client participation set up under the Community Action Programs of OEO. These programs have been distinct in three ways. First, participation was developed in the context of a set of explicit federal guidelines and requirements. Second, organizational resources for establishing client participation were available; that is to say, an agency was created with funds ostensbily for organizing and involving low-income client population groups in agency policy making. Thirdly, the client population is conceived of as including potential clients as well as the broader client-system notion. Hence, the reader is cautioned that the findings of these particular case studies are somewhat distinctive and may not be highly generalizable to other models of client participation, especially when one also considers the limited number of studies. By and large, literature support ratings of generalizations in this section are low.

Demography of Client Participation

Participant Characteristics

GENERALIZATION 8.31: Target-area representatives in community-action programs were found to have distinct characteristics as compared to the rest of the low-income population (+, 23, 201).

8.31A. Most poverty board candidates who participated in the election of representatives were women (+, +, 23, 201).

8.31B. Representatives have a high degree of contact with community residents and participation in community activities (+, 23, 201).

Bowen and Masotti (23) studied 43 of the 48 candidates for election to Cleveland's Council for Economic Opportunity. They found that the candidates had a history of membership in voluntary associ-

[9] See for example, William R. Rosengren and Mark Lefton, *Organizations and Clients: Essays in the Sociology of Service* (Columbus, Ohio: Charles E. Merrill Publishing Company, 1970).

ations, had held offices and leadership positions in those groups, and had active political participation. The candidates also had a high amount of primary-group community ties. They were long-time area residents, had high social participation with persons in the community, and had many friends.

A listing of traits possessed by and lacking in candidates as determined by this study may be summarized as follows:

Traits possessed:
Belong to voluntary associations and exhibit leadership
Have many friends
Vote regularly
Are enthusiastic about the Poverty Program
Want to help others
See themselves as equal

Traits not possessed:
Family stability
Group consciousness as poor
Strong feelings for the poor as oppressed
Feelings of the middle class as oppressors
Understanding of liberal politics and service programs

The characteristic of *voting regularly seemed especially important in predicting candidacy.*

8.31C. Representatives had a high sense of efficacy and a strong belief in the possibility of nonviolent change (+, 23).

8.31D. Candidates who received organizational support (i.e., NAACP, settlement house, local clubs) had a better chance of being elected than candidates who did not receive it (+, 201).

One of the first studies of local client participation focused on Philadelphia, a city where in February 1965 the Mayor established a command group for the War on Poverty. The Mayor, in a sharp break with the past, instructed the eighteen-member committee to expand to include a dozen direct representatives of the poor. Shostak (201) in an intimate descriptive study reviews the background of the Philadelphia Antipoverty Action Committee and discusses such matters as the problems of including direct representatives of the poor, the character of the town meetings held to rally public support, the significance of the election returns, and performance of the new representatives. Attention is also given to four central race-related controversies that were manifested: the debate over the alleged homogeneity of the poor black population, the rift between the poor blacks and social workers, the rivalry among factions in slum neighborhoods, and the uncertainty of the preference of the poor blacks for racial self-advancement and separatism on the one hand or for interracial advancement and integration on the other.

The findings suggest that the town meetings, held throughout the city, brought irregular representation of the significant categories of the poor. Poor whites did not attend in proportion to their representation (30 percent rather than 55 percent); the same was true of the city's Puerto Rican population. The vast majority of the audiences were women, especially black women. A large number of candidates contested the 144 open seats, and as predicted the organized slates backed by settlement houses, the NAACP, and local civic and political clubs appeared, and succeeded in electing a majority of the 12 council members. This early experiment with at-large, town-meeting type of elections was successful in bringing in representation of some of the poor. The experience led to a discounting of certain preconceived notions of the poor blacks being a disorganized, homogeneous mass, dependent on social agencies, and with leadership by one or two established spokesmen taken for granted.

Action Guidelines: In seeking for persons to serve as client representatives, one may anticipate response more readily from women and persons who have social participation, voluntary association membership, and are long-time area residents. In other words, good candidates are persons with many contacts, who are known throughout the community. Consistent past voting behavior is a particularly good predictor. The practitioner can encourage potential candidates to serve as client representatives by stressing the theme that client participation offers candidates an opportunity to use their personal resources and abilities to get things done, that their participation can make a difference, and that client participation offers opportunities for nonviolent change. The typical candidate does not appear likely to support radical social change strategies, preferring instead to work "within the system." Spokesmen of the poor may be expected to need political education to increase their sophistication and social consciousness. In addition, the social action practi-tioner wishing to gain representation will need to aggres-sively promote participation of individuals who have a more "radical" orientation, who would not ordinarily or naturally desire to participate in Establishment politics.

Client Participants and Broader Community Participants

GENERALIZATION 8.32: Client representatives have a dif-ferent type of board participation than do agency-selected representatives from the larger community (+ +, 57, 236).

8.32A. Target-area representatives had much less board experience than do board members from the private sector of the larger commu-nity (+, 57).

8.32B. Target-area representatives were underrepresented in the number of positions they held on the most powerful administrative and executive committees (+, 57).

8.32C. Target-area representatives were more likely to see them-selves as accountable to a constituency than were private board members (+, 57).

8.32D. Target-area representatives were more willing to delegate participation in decision making to neighborhood councils (+, 57).

Interviews with 387 Community Action Agency board members were conducted by the Florence Heller School for Advanced Studies in Social Welfare (57) to compare members from the private sector of the larger community and members who were selected from the poverty target area (we shall describe this study in greater detail later). The two groups differed in their attitudes about the participa-tion of local target-area groups in the community action agency. Target-area members were more likely than private members to approve strongly of the CAA's developing neighborhood councils, and to believe that the neighborhood councils should make final decisions on target-area programs.

8.32E. Typical contributions of target-area representatives have been anecdotal histories, insistence on paraprofessional opportunities, a sense of constituency, a reform orientation, and antipathy toward bureaucratic red tape (+, 201).

8.32F. Private agencies with high-status board members are associated with higher financial contributions. Low-status boards have higher attendance at meetings and higher board program leadership (+, 236).

8.32G. Private agencies (YMCA) serving areas of high average income are much more likely to recruit board members residing in the area than are agencies in low-income areas (+, 236).

Zald (236) studied 37 branches of the Chicago YMCA located in the inner city, outer city, and suburbs. The major variables used were demographic characteristics, socioeconomic status, and effectiveness of the board as measured by financial contributions, program leadership, meeting attendance, and a reputational measure of effectiveness.

The results were that there are marked differences in types of effectiveness of YMCA boards, with the crucial variable being where the board members are recruited. Zald concludes that for this type of private board, median income of the population is the best predictor of board membership.

Action Guidelines: Since target area representatives had less participation experience as board members than persons from the larger community, the practitioner may have to work with these members to help them acquire such board-member skills as preparing agendas. The practitioner should be concerned that target-area members are adequately represented in administrative positions and on powerful executive committees so that they have access to decision-making positions.

Target-area members are the best sources of support for increased neighborhood involvement in policy making. Representatives from the larger community are less likely to see themselves as accountable to area residents. The practitioner should try to increase the sense of accountability of this group, possibly by helping neighborhood groups to gain access to them.

Finally, local and nonlocal residents seem to perform different functions on the boards of private agencies like the YMCA. Nonlocal, higher status board members are useful for increasing agency funds. If the practitioner wants to decrease the use of this group as agency board members, he will have to seek alternative sources of agency funding. When trying to persuade agencies to recruit more local residents as board members, the practitioner should stress the willingness of this group to participate in terms of meeting attendance. Recruiting local residents as agency board members is particularly important in low-income communities, since these areas seem to have the lowest local representation on agency boards.

Another way of stating this is as follows: If it is thought that high financial contributions and higher levels of programming are desirable, then board members should be recruited from the higher income levels. However, if the board is to be a training ground in political effectiveness, and if local interests are considered more important than programming per se, then an effort should be made to recruit residents on to boards, even when the area is of low-income status. This pattern is likely to be associated with higher board attendance and local leadership in programming.

Types of Client Participation

Advisory and Adversary Models

GENERALIZATION 8.33: Client participation in recent agency policy-making has tended to assume one of two major organized forms: advisory and adversary (+ +, 10, 58, 70).

Advisory participation is characterized by client groups that communicate information to the agency and advise it in policy making without authority or power to enforce decisions. The process usually involves a low level of agency-community conflict and the advisory group members are often agency-selected and limited in number.

Adversary participation refers to the development of organized client groups that either operate outside the agency (external adversary participation) or are represented by clients on committees within the agency (internal adversary participation). Client groups here are more likely to have widespread community membership and to act as pressure groups utilizing conflict strategies to influence agency policy making. (The reader will note the absence on agency policy boards of nonadversary, nonadvisory direct client participation as decision makers.)

8.33A. Degree of adversary participation was directly associated with the proportion of blacks and Chicanos in a city population (+, 10).

8.33B. Adversary participation usually took the form of a federated structure composed of coalitions of neighborhood groups (+, 11).

This finding is based on a study (11) of 52 black neighborhood-associations sponsored by community action agencies in urban areas. It was found that an agency-wide focus on neighborhood organizing tends to foster militant social action by associations to a greater extent than when such activities are decentralized to individual neighborhood service centers.

8.33C. Use of adversary or militant participation was associated with the development of a citywide interassociation council created by the associations themselves and not a part of the community action agency structure (+, 11).

8.33D. There was no direct relationship between federal directives for community participation and what occurred at a local level: a diversity of patterns of participation (+, 10).

Action Guidelines: Client participation in agency decision making tends to assume one of three forms: advisory, internal adversary, or external adversary. The practitioner can anticipate adversary participation in cities with a high proportion of blacks or Chicanos. To encourage militant adversary participation, client participation should be supported by a

citywide federation of neighborhood associations independent of the official agency structure. Finally, federal guidelines for client participation programs should be flexible;
they should allow cities to develop their own patterns of
client participation. For example, advisory participation
might develop in a smaller, ethnically homogeneous community, while a large, heterogeneous city would develop external adversary participation.

Type of Participation and Outcome

GENERALIZATION 8.34: Types of client participation vary in
terms of outcome and community response. The way in
which a particular type of participation is structured can produce varying degrees of effectiveness in attaining goals
(+ + +, 10, 54, 58, 70, 87, 156).

8.34A. Adversary participation is associated with the achievement
of specific, short-run objectives, but internal adversary participation
may produce a great deal of intraagency conflict, and external adversary participation may produce much public criticism of the
agency (+, 10).

8.34B. External adversary participation may be effective in halting
programs, but adversary groups typically are limited in developing
plans for alternative programs and having their plans adopted
(+ +, 54, 70).

8.34C. Effective adversary client participation in decision making in
controversial issues requires that the community practitioner play
the role of advocate rather than mediator (+, 70).

Action Guidelines: Adversary participation appears to be
most useful in attaining short-run, specific goals and in
stopping particular programs the client group opposes. If
the practitioner is trying to work with a client group to formulate and gain agency acceptance of long-range plans, he
should develop another type of client participation, or at
least not rely solely on external adversary participation. Effectiveness of adversary participation requires that the prac-

titioner utilize an advocate role rather than attempt to mediate between the client and the agency.

Changes in Type of Participation Over Time

GENERALIZATION 8.35: Different client populations prefer different styles of participation. These preferences may change over time (+ , 106).

Motivating client groups to join organizations acting in their behalf is of vital importance in making such organizations viable. A study conducted in Israel looked at communication patterns employed by different client groups in dealing with welfare officials (106). Typically clients from traditional (rural, less modern) ethnic backgrounds preferred altruistic appeals that were more passive, covered a narrower range of reasons, and were nonnormative, while those from more modern backgrounds tended to employ normative appeals based on the target organization's goals and ideology. With the passage of time and the gaining of experience, traditional clients shifted to increased use of normative appeals.

Action Guidelines: In working with client groups, the practitioner should take into account their personal predilections. One might induce people into participation initially through activities most compatible with their outlook (starting where people are) and shift to more functional or aggressive strategies as people become "ready" for these. The suggestion made in the study report is that in some cases when clients gain more experience with agencies, they tend to move toward more assertive styles of action, perhaps from advisory to adversary modes of participation.

Structural Variables and Client Participation

Community Structure and Extent of Participation

GENERALIZATION 8.36: Communities vary in their degree of client participation (+ +, 10, 58, 201).

Limited participation in CAP programs was characteristic of cities with a low proportion of minority groups and a small population (+ +, 10, 58, 201).

This finding was reported by Austin (10) in a study of community agencies in 20 cities with a population of 50,000 to 500,000. Cities with a population of less than 150,000 had little participation by community residents. Involvement in all types of participation was low. There was little conflict in any of the programs. Limited participation in the program was also characteristic of cities with a low proportion of minority group residents.

> 8.36A. Poor white communities showed the lowest participation in community-action programs (+, 10, 201).
>
> 8.36B. A limited amount of client participation is associated with less impact on agency decision making (+, 10).

Action Guidelines: In cities with a small population or a small proportion of minority group members, the practitioner can anticipate that it will be difficult to organize client participation. These cities might require more funds for organizing and allow a longer time to develop client participation. Poor whites will also be a difficult group to organize; the practitioner may have to devote more resources to organizing this group and try to make sure that its interests are represented in client participation, for example, by allowing poor whites a certain amount of proportional representation. Since generally a high level of client participation appears to be necessary if they are to influence agency decision making, the practitioner will have to devote much attention and energy to maximizing client participation. This may apply to a lesser degree for adversary participation (see Generalization 8.37).

Community Structure Correlates of
Advocacy Participation

GENERALIZATION 8.37: Emphasis on advocacy (or militant) client action styles is associated with cities characterized by the following:

Large cities with a large black population and a pattern of
black mobilization
Cities with a council-manager type of government
Cities where the target area participation is moderate
Cities where a citywide, adversary coalition or support
group is operating outside the arena of the CAA community itself (+ +, 10, 11, 58).

The Florence Heller research study (58), referred to earlier, was a
major effort to evaluate the types of participation patterns of local
CAA groups. The study was conducted as a descriptive field investigation, which examined a range of variables in Community Action
Agencies: the participants in the original CAA organization, the Board
of Directors, operational experiences from 1967–68 of the CAA
boards, neighborhood associations that were formed, and interassociation councils that developed, as well as numerous attitudes and judgments of individuals in the CAA network. The study examined similarities and differences among the group of twenty CAA's located in
urban areas (centers from 50,000 to 1,000,000 population) including
cities such as Hartford, Cleveland, Charlotte, and Laredo.

Among the general findings of the study was that opportunities for
citizens of low-income neighborhoods to participate in decision making had to some degree been realized. Local conditions and local
forces—such as governmental type, city size, ethnic population—were
intervening factors in determining the characteristics of participation of
the local CAA board. In particular, the cities that emphasized the militant or political model of participation rather than a service delivery
organizational model were those cities where a council of associations
had been formed, with the council functioning as an action coalition
among target-area associations.

Among the systematic relationships found was that large cities with
large black populations and council-manager governments tended to
have external adversary participation, with the arena of adversary action being the community itself. In similar cities with mayor-council
governments the arena may be the CAA.

Where there was adversary CAA participation, there was also support for such tactics as mass protest and political action by neighborhood associations.

Practice Guidelines: This generalization suggests the types of cities in which militant client participation is likely to develop. Furthermore, it suggests some ways to politicize a community if it is not yet militant. The practitioner should help the group to use as its arena of involvement the community at large, and not focus on the CAA itself. Adversary participation is likely to appear in large cities with large black populations, and when the representatives are almost entirely minority group members. In any case, it is important to form an external citywide supportive council of associations, including representatives of the CAA neighborhoods, if militant strategies are being pursued.

Cities with a council-manager type of government are more likely than cities with a mayor-council government to be involved in militant political action—i.e., using mass-protest techniques. Such cities might be selected out, in conjunction with other variables, as offering potential for militant action. Attaining a moderate level of communitywide participation is sufficient to sustain adversary or social-action forms of client participation.

Organizing Clients for Advocacy Participation

Group Cohesion and Explicit Issue Conflict

GENERALIZATION 8.38: Adversary client participation is effective only under given conditions. Among them are a highly unified client constituency group, operating under circumstances of explicit issue conflict, and the presence in a key administrative position of a staff person with a commitment to social change (+ +, 58, 70, 87, 156, 199).

8.38A. The advisory form of client participation is ineffective in situations where there are conflicts of interest between groups. Advisory participation in such situations may be associated with client influence only in noncontroversial issues, in ambiguously resolved issues, in discussion of issues rather than negotiation, and in the "ratification of decisions rather than in the actual decision-making process itself " (+, 70).

8.38B. Effective adversary participation (as well as internal advisory participation) in decision making requires that the client group be a coordinated body that has developed unity concerning major controversial issues (+ +, 70, 87).

8.38C. The degree of internal disunity will decrease if the client group that advises or negotiates with the agency is preceived by the community as representative of neighborhood interests. Procedures for selection of client representatives must insure that all neighborhood interests either be directly represented or have high access to client representatives (+ +, 58, 87, 156).

8.38D. Representatives who see themselves as responsible to their constituents take a more active role in influencing agency decision making (+, 70).

8.38E. Participation in community action programs has served to train the poor for involvement in political action (+, 199).

8.38F. Adversary client participation is enhanced when minority-group community leadership was involved in the original formation of a community action agency and represented in sufficient strength on the policy board (+, 58, 156).

Action Guidelines: The practitioner should attempt to determine whether there are differing interests between clients and agencies, which need to be resolved by conflict through the use of an adversary model of participation. The advisory model of participation often does not permit full expression of these conflicts and does not provide opportunities for their resolution; instead, it attempts to minimize the possibility of conflict. Use of clients in making controversial decisions within the agency (internal adversary model of participation) requires that they be involved in the broad decision-making process, in making a range of decisions, and that they be involved in both the discussion and the negotiation aspects of decision making. If internal participation is not structured in this way, the agency will attempt to avoid conflicts with clients by deemphasizing their opportunities for participation. Using the client group to make decisions within the agency will probably require use of both internal advisory and internal adversary models of participation, depending on the issue.

Client representatives should be supported by neighborhood groups that have achieved some consensus on major issues. If neighborhood groups are divided on many issues, their client representatives will increase internal agency conflict and the clients may be excluded from decision making. Client representatives will not be supported by the community if they are not perceived as representative of community interests. The practitioner can increase community support of client representatives by setting up democratic election procedures and by providing community groups with easy access to client representatives. Clients elected in this way and who maintain contacts with their constituents take a more active role in agency decision making. Clients who have been active in agency participation may be encouraged to participate in more political forms of social action.

Decentralized Line Personnel—A Target Group

GENERALIZATION 8.39: Welfare workers use different styles of "defense" reaction when confronted by client groups. Grass-roots adversary participation by clients directed at line or decentralized personnel can modify staff behavior and service delivery patterns (+ , 17).

In a suggestive study (17), 67 officials of six social-service organizations in Israel were interviewed regarding their customary responses to client pressures. It was found that practitioners respond to clients with individual forms of defense, which are related to societal norms, or with structural defenses, which include "joint defense" (group consolidation) among professionals, or the use of a "pressure specialist," that is, a practitioner who acts as a buffer between the clients and the other workers. Use of structural defenses was found to be associated with the degree of professionalization of the organization (proportion of professionals employed). Line personnel were found to be responsive to local grass-roots client pressures.

Action Guidelines: This study indicates that organizational changes can come about as a result of participation by clients at the service unit level. As a consequence of multiple stresses, local line officials are vulnerable as well as in a position to bring about changes in organizational operations, despite constraining regulations of central headquarters. Accordingly, it is not necessary for client groups always to exert political or legal pressure at the top in order to effect changes in human-service organizations. Intervention through grass-roots participation aimed at more available direct-service personnel may also be effective. Vulnerability to client pressure is enhanced if professionals can be prevented from forming a joint defense group or if the client group refuses to deal with a singled-out pressure specialist.

Factors Facilitating Client Participation

Support by Central Staff and Neighborhood Groups

GENERALIZATION 8.40: High participation rates of the poor in decentralized or neighborhood community action agencies is associated with support for participation by the central staff and board and support for participation by significant neighborhood organizations (+ + +, 11, 58, 70, 71, 120, 156, 199, 204).

8.40A. Greater support for decentralized or neighborhood participation came from target-area representatives than from private city-wide board members (+ , 11, 58).

8.40B. More successful neighborhood participation requires from the very beginning the involvement of low-income citizens and neighborhood groups (+, 156).

8.40C. Staff roles in technical-assistance capacities rather than as program directors were associated with higher rates of neighborhood participation (+, 156).

An illustrative study (156) of CAP programs was conducted through conversations, observations, and written field reports. The findings of the report suggest that CAA decentralization was accomplished through an initial central or downtown agency, rather than by local areas. The CAA role in decentralization became that of supervising neighborhood corporations, channeling funds, and providing technical assistance. Successful decentralization involved central Community Action Agency support, local support, and early involvement by the local representative in the decentralization process. Neighborhood boards needed training and technical assistance. The report finds that the central CAA must have a staff that is willing to provide technical assistance rather than to perform the role of program director.

Included in this report are case studies of Neighborhood Service Programs in seven cities. A major problem was that with funds coming from downtown, there was a feeling that most decisions were continuing to be made there as well. Other problems were present in the decision-making and participation area, which caused serious questions to be raised concerning the power of the neighborhood CAA to effect desired change.

Action Guidelines: To achieve greater participation of the poor, decentralization of neighborhood organizations is necessary. The community practitioner should work to secure the support of the board and staff towards this structure. One can help the staff members to agree to the change by emphasizing their new role—i.e., expertise and technical assistance—and play down their loss of power. The practitioner may find support for decentralization from local representatives, and may develop this support into a conscious voting coalition on the central board, at the same time as he tries to secure support from some of the private members.

The practitioner may function initially as an advocate, because the involvement of the target-area representatives and neighborhood groups is needed in the early, planning stages, of decentralization. Acknowledging the limited expertise of the TAR's in administrative functions, the community practitioner may try to prevent hostility to the decentralization program by designing training experiences prior to the actual decentralization experience. The same can be done for the neighborhood representatives who are on interim boards.

It is crucial that the practitioner assist the neighborhood groups to maximize their participation. To do so, he must help to involve significant neighborhood organizations (for which he must have knowledge and contacts). Also, one must attempt to have the local CAA boards be representative, which may mean stepping on some local political toes. Involving and representing new groups is crucial, but painful, and the practitioner must anticipate and help the constituents be prepared for an active attack by the groups already in power.

Technical Skills

GENERALIZATION 8.41: A strong barrier to increased legitimation of client participation in agency decision making is the client's lack of technical skills and professional expertise (+ + +, 31, 54, 72, 96, 121, 156).

8.41A. Professionals have increased their participation in decision making over time by defining decisions as requiring professional judgment, phrasing issues in technical, expert terms (+, 72).

A study of participants in educational decision making in New York City was conducted by Gittell (72) over a 25-year period. She found that, over time, the city political system became decreasingly involved in educational decision making and technical expertise came to be accepted as the basis for policy making. Involvement of public-interest groups in educational issues has also decreased over time, while the decision-making power of the professional staff of the central school bureaucracy has increased. Definition of issues as requiring expertise has decreased the public's resources for participation in educational decision making.

8.41B. When conflict increases so that issues can no longer be so defined only in technical terms, the involvement of public groups in the decision-making process also increases (+, 72).

8.41C. Client participation increases when clients are given training and technical assistance in decision making (+, 156).

8.41D. Training and expertise is an important consideration if groups wish to obtain acceptance of their new programs by agencies (+, 54, 121).

8.41E. The major conflict between experts and local board members occurs over technically difficult issues (+, 31).

Action Guidelines: Giving clients some level of technical training or enabling them to hire experts as consultants will increase their status as legitimate decision makers within the agency. If clients are not given technical assistance, the practitioner can anticipate planner-client conflict in making decisions about issues which require expertise. This conflict can be minimized if planners formulate their plans in terms of community norms and values rather than presenting them to clients in terms of technically difficult concepts.

If the practitioner wishes to broaden client participation in decision making, he should attempt to stress the nontechnical elements of a decision, and to increase the amount of conflict between various agency groups so that the decision cannot be resolved professionally within the agency and will come to be defined in less technical terms.

Time Dimension and Program Scheduling

GENERALIZATION 8.42: Client participation in decision making must involve a time period adequate for gaining information and achieving consensus. Program timetables may conflict with development of such a community decision-making process (+, 156, 199).

The importance of adequate time for client participation in decision making was reported in a case study of Neighborhood Service Programs in seven cities. (156) The structure of decision-making timetables left local residents with the sense that they were not being delegated adequate powers and resources. Pressure to produce quickly alternated with extended deadlines, made community people feel that they were being rushed to produce programs which were "acceptable" and could be funded according to the timetable but which were not necessarily in the interest of the local area.

Action Guidelines: The practitioner should attempt to design ample, flexible timetables which give clients sufficient time to inform themselves about issues and plans and to make decisions about implementing those which they feel are adequate. Client participation programs should have funds for an initial long-term planning phase, rather than requiring clients to quickly adopt service delivery programs.

Social Agency Executives and Client Participation

Attitudes of Agency Executives Toward Client Participation

GENERALIZATION 8.43: Most agency administrators support only limited client participation in decision making (+ +, 86, 120, 191).

8.43A. Agency administrators are more opposed to adversary then to advisory participation in decision making (+, 86, 191).
8.43B. The majority of agency administrators oppose the appointment of clients to administrative and policy-making positions (particularly at the state level) (+, 86, 191).
8.43C. Administrators have the greatest amount of opposition to "socially stigmatized" clients functioning in agency decision-making roles (+ , 120, 191).

Schwartz and Chernin (191) studied attitudes toward client participation in public-welfare agencies in a survey of 35 agency administrators and 25 employees of a university. Participation favored by the majority of both groups was in local advisory committees made up of recipients, agency director, staff members, and board members. There were more favorable attitudes toward participation of the blind and disabled than toward participation of AFDC welfare recipients, although private agency administrators were less likely

than public agency administrators or university personnel to differentiate between participation of the two groups.

Action Guidelines: The practitioner trying to initiate client
participation can expect agency opposition to such activity.
Administrators are most likely to support client advisory participation at the local level in an organization which also
includes staff and other board members. However, this type
of participation probably minimizes client influence in
agency decision making and thus is useful primarily in the
initiating stage of a program. Also, in trying to bring about
greater client participation, the practitioner might as a matter of strategy try at first to include less-stigmatized clients,
such as the blind and disabled, on advisory committees. The
practitioner might start out using this type of participation
and then move into such other forms as adversary participation or client involvement on policy-making committees at
the state level.

By-Product of Client Participation

Development of Political Skills

GENERALIZATION 8.44: Participation as an agency board
member provides the client with an opportunity to learn the
necessary skills for political participation (+, 199).

Practice Implications: The practitioner can expect a payoff
from client participation in terms of increased political skills
of client board members. These persons can be useful in
terms of facilitating the political organization of the local
community.

OVERVIEW SUMMARY OF
PARTICIPATION GENERALIZATIONS

This chapter has dealt with three distinct aspects of political and activist participation. A general summary of such disparate subject mat-

ter is difficult, and perhaps would not be very useful taken alone. Instead, on the following pages will be presented an overall summary of generalizations covered in chapters 7 and 8.

Scope of Participation

VOLUNTARY ASSOCIATIONS: Most adults are members of voluntary associations.

SOCIAL MOVEMENTS: Only a minority of the population becomes involved in social-movement participation.

POLITICAL PARTICIPATION: Most adults participate politically at least through voting; less engage in collective interest-group participation.

CLIENT PARTICIPATION: Organized client activity is a newly developing type of participation, which has as yet involved few persons. Traditionally, agencies have had little client participation in decision making.

PRIMARY GROUP MEMBERSHIP: This is the most widespread form of participation. Almost every person has primary group ties of one sort or another.

Age

VOLUNTARY ASSOCIATIONS: Highest participation for persons of middle age.

SOCIAL MOVEMENTS: Highest participation among youth.

POLITICAL PARTICIPATION: Lowest participation among youth. High participation among persons of middle age. Participation will remain high among older persons if physical impediments can be overcome. Youth participation is proportionately high in deviant political movements.

CLIENT PARTICIPATION: Highest participation among middle-aged persons.

PRIMARY GROUP MEMBERSHIP: High participation for all age groups.

Socio-Economic Status

VOLUNTARY ASSOCIATIONS: Participation varies directly with socio-economic status; those of higher status have higher rates of participation.

SOCIAL MOVEMENTS: Participation varies with status inconsistency; those with great status inconsistency participate more. Participation varies with amount of relative deprivation, so that participants are likely to be persons who have experienced a limited amount of upward mobility.

POLITICAL PARTICIPATION: Participation varies directly with socio-economic status. Those of higher status have the highest rates of participation.

CLIENT PARTICIPATION: This has traditionally been highest for persons of high socioeconomic status who customarily served as agency board members. New public programs requiring client participation are increasing the involvement of persons of low socioeconomic status.

PRIMARY GROUP MEMBERSHIP: High for all socioeconomic status groups.

Education

VOLUNTARY ASSOCIATIONS: Participation varies directly with education; those of higher education have higher rates of participation.

SOCIAL MOVEMENTS: Earliest joiners are likely to be persons with high education. Level of education varies directly with rate of participation in the student civil rights movements. Persons with moderate levels of education are most likely to participate in very militant forms of social action.

POLITICAL PARTICIPATION: Participation varies directly with education; those with higher education have higher rates of participation.

CLIENT PARTICIPATION: Low-income client participants are slightly better educated than the rest of their community. Traditional agency-selected board members have high education.

PRIMARY GROUP MEMBERSHIP: High for all levels of education.

Information and Awareness of Issues

These vary directly with participation in all five types of structures. The higher the individual's participation in any one structure, the higher his information about and awareness of issues. Alternatively, one may state the proposition that the higher an individual's information and awareness of issues, the higher his level of participation.

Feelings of Powerlessness and Alienation

VOLUNTARY ASSOCIATIONS: Inversely related to this type of participation; high feelings of powerlessness are associated with low levels of participation.

SOCIAL MOVEMENTS: Participation may be related to powerlessness plus some combination of other factors, such as awareness of structural blockages to mobility. Findings are contradictory.

POLITICAL PARTICIPATION: Inverse relationship.

CLIENT PARTICIPATION: Inverse relationship.

PRIMARY GROUP MEMBERSHIP: No relationship. Persons with high or low degree of powerlessness can both have strong primary-group relationships. However, primary groups can socialize these kinds of attitudes.

Attitudes toward "System"

VOLUNTARY ASSOCIATIONS: Participation is associated with awareness of problems, but the belief exists that concerns are shared by many and that cooperative action is possible. There is a belief that disagreements can be worked out.

SOCIAL MOVEMENTS: Participation is associated with high system blame, high system distrust.

POLITICAL PARTICIPATION: Same as for voluntary associations.

CLIENT PARTICIPATION: Same as for voluntary associations.

PRIMARY GROUP MEMBERSHIP: No relationship to level of participation. However, primary groups serve as socialization mechanisms so that persons develop attitudes toward the system which are similar to those of other group members.

Attitude Change

All types of participation appear to have the capacity to change their members' attitudes. Through participation, persons can develop an increased sense of power, a more positive self-image, and more tolerance of divergent attitudes. However, if participatory experiences are dissatisfying, participation may lead to higher system distrust.

Conflict

VOLUNTARY ASSOCIATIONS: No relationship between level of conflict and level of participation is discussed in research findings.

SOCIAL MOVEMENTS: Conflict raises intensity of participation.

POLITICAL PARTICIPATION: Conflict raises intensity of participation.

CLIENT PARTICIPATION: Conflict raises intensity of participation.

PRIMARY GROUP MEMBERSHIP: No consistent relationships.

Interrelationships among Different Types
of Participation

VOLUNTARY ASSOCIATIONS: Membership in voluntary associations is associated with high social participation and participation in other organizations.

SOCIAL MOVEMENTS: Membership in social movements is associated with low participation in other categories or with a moderate level of participation, which an individual defines as dissatisfying.

POLITICAL PARTICIPATION: Political participation is positively related to other types of participation, except social movements.

CLIENT PARTICIPATION: Client participation is related to high involvement in political, associational, and social participation.

PRIMARY GROUP MEMBERSHIP: High for all persons, whether or not they have other types of participation.

Group Support

All types of participation are influenced by the attitudes and participation models, which the individual acquires through previous participation in other groups, associations, or organizations. The support of other reference and membership groups is necessary for an individual to engage in a particular form of participation. Previous participatory experiences affect future patterns of participation.

BIBLIOGRAPHY FOR PART FIVE

1. Ablon, Joan. "Relocated Indians in the San Francisco Bay Area: Social Interaction and Indian Identity." *Human Organization* 23, no. 4 (Winter 1964): 296–304.

2. Adomek, Raymond, and Edward Doger. "Social Structure Identification and Change in a Treatment-Oriented Institution." *American Sociological Review* 33, no. 6 (December 1968): 934–44.

3. Aiken, Michael, and Robert R. Alford. "Community Structure and Innovation: The Case of Urban Renewal." Paper presented at a meeting of the American Sociological Association, San Francisco, September 1969.

4. Alexander, C. Norman, and Ernest Q. Campbell. "Balance Forces and Delinquent Drinking." *Social Forces* 46, no. 3 (March 1968): 367–75.

5. Alford, Robert R., and Eugene C. Lee. "Voting Turnout in American Cities." *American Political Science Review* 42, no. 3 (September 1948): 796–813.

6. Amanullah, Mohammod. "The Lumbee Indians and Their Adjustment Patterns in Urban Society." *Digest of Urban and Regional Research* 16, no. 1 (Spring 1969): 26–27.

7. Anderson, Charles H. "Religious Communality among White Protestants, Catholics, and Mormons." *Social Forces* 46, no. 4 (June 1968): 501–8.

8. Antonovsky, Aaron. "A Study of Some Moderately Successful Negroes in New York City." *Phylon* 28, no. 3 (Fall 1967): 246–60.

9. Archer, Morton, Seymour Rinzler, and George Christakis. "Social Factors Affecting Participation in a Study of Diet and Coronary Heart Disease." *Journal of Health and Social Behavior* 8, no. 1 (March 1967): 22–31.

10. Austin, David M. "Dilemmas of Participation." Paper presented at a meeting of the National Conference on Social Welfare, May 1969.

11. Austin, David M. "Organizing for Neighborhood Improvement or Social Change?" Dissertation, Brandeis University, Florence Heller School, 1969.

12. Babchuck, Nicholas, and Alan Booth. "Voluntary Association Membership: A Longitudinal Analysis." *American Sociological Review* 34, no. 1 (February 1969): 31–45.

13. Baker, Frank, and Herbert C. Schulberg. "Community Mental Health Ideology, Dogmatism, and Political-Economic Conservatism." *Community Mental Health Journal* 5, no. 6 (December 1969): 433–36.

14. Ball, Richard A. "A Poverty Case: The Analgesic Subculture of the Southern Applachians." *American Sociological Review* 33, no. 6 (December 1968): 885–95.

15. Barresi, Charles M. and John H. Lindquist. "The Urban Community: Attitudes toward Neighborhood and Urban Renewal." Paper presented at a meeting of the American Sociological Association. San Francisco, September 1969.

16. Barton, Allen H. "The Columbia Crisis: Campus, Vietnam, and the Ghetto." *Public Opinion Quarterly* 32, no. 3 (Fall 1968): 333–51.

17. Bar-Yosef, R. and E. O. Schild. "Pressures and Defenses in Bureaucratic Roles." *The American Journal of Sociology* 71, no. 6 (May 1966): 5–14.

18. Beck, Paul Allen, and M. Kent Jennings. "Lowering the Voting Age: The Case of the Reluctant Electorate." *Public Opinion Quarterly* 33, no. 3 (Fall 1969): 370–79.

19. Blanco, Antonia, and Sheila Akabas. "The Factory: Site for Community Mental Health Practice." *American Journal of Orthopsychiatry* 38, no. 3 (April 1968): 543–52.

20. Bonem, Gil and Philip Reno. "By Bread Alone, and Little Bread: Life on AFDC." *Social Work* 13, no. 4 (October 1968): 5–11.

21. Bonjean, Charles M. "Mass, Class, and the Industrial Community: A Comparative Analysis of Managers, Businessmen, and Workers." *American Journal of Sociology* 72, no. 2 (September 1966): 149–62.

22. Bonjean, Charles M., Grady D. Bruce, and J. Allen Williams Jr. "Social Mobility and Job Satisfaction: A Replication and Extension." *Social Forces* 45, no. 4 (1966): 492–501.

23. Bowen, Don R. and Louis Masotti. "Spokesman for the Poor: An Analysis of Cleveland's Poverty Board Candidates." *Urban Affairs Quarterly* 4, no. 1 (September 1968): 84–110.

24. Bowman, Lewis, and G. R. Boynton. "Recruitment Patterns among Local Party Officials: A Model and Some Preliminary Findings in Selected Locales." *American Political Science Review* 40, no. 3 (September 1966): 667–76.

25. Boynton, G. R., Samuel Patterson, and Ronald Hedlund. "The Structure of Public Support for Legislative Institutions." *Midwest Journal of Political Science* 12, no. 2 (May 1968): 163–80.

26. Breton, Raymond. "Institutional Completeness of Ethnic Communities and the Personal Relations of Immigrants." *American Journal of Sociology* 70, no. 2 (September 1964): 193–205.

27. Burnham, Walter Dean. "The Changing Scope of the American Political Universe." *American Political Science Review* 59, no. 1 (March 1965): 7–23.

28. Buttedahl, Knute, and Coolie Verner. "Characteristics of Participants in Two Methods of Adult Education." *Adult Education* 15, no. 2 (Winter 1965): 61–73.

29. Callahan, James J., Jr. "Obstacles to Community Planning for the Elderly." Dissertation, Brandeis University, 1968.

30. Chemmie, Peter. "A Study of Differential Participation in an Indigenous Welfare Rights Organization as Related to Value Orientations and Patterns of Alienation." Dissertation, University of Minnesota, 1969.

31. Clavel, Pierre. "Planners and Citizen Boards: Some Applications of Social Theory to the Problem of Plan Implementation." *Journal of the American Institute of Planners* 34, no. 3 (May 1960): 130–39.

32. Clubek, Alfred, John DeGrove, and Charles Farris. "The Manipulated Negro Vote: Pre-Conditions and Consequences." *Journal of Politics* 26, no. 1 (February 1964): 112–29.

33. Cohen, Nathan. "The Los Angeles Riot Study." *Social Work* 12, no. 4 (October 1967): 14–21.

34. Colomibotos, John. "Social Origins and Ideology of Physicians: A Study of the Effects of Early Socialization." *Journal of Health and Social Behavior* 10, no. 1 (March 1969): 16–29.

35. Converse, Phillip E., Aage R. Clausen, and Warren E. Miller. "Electoral Myth and Reality: The 1964 Election." *American Political Science Review* 59 (June 1968): 21–36.

36. Converse, Phillip E., Warren E. Miller, Gerold G. Rusk and Arthur Wolfe. "Continuity in Change in American Politics: Parties and Issues in the 1868 Election." Paper presented at the American Political Science Association, New York, 1969, 1–30.

37. Cook, Samuel Dubois. "Political Movements and Organizations." *Journal of Politics* 26, no. 1 (February 1964): 130–53.

38. Coughenow, C. Milton. "The Rate of Technological Diffusion among Locality Groups." *American Journal of Sociology* 69, no. 4 (1964): 325–39.

39. Crain, Robert L. and Donald B. Rosenthal. "Structure and Value in Local Political Systems: The Case of Fluoridation." *Journal of Politics* 28, no. 1 (February 1966): 169–95.

40. Cullen, James S. "Determinates of Participation in Parents Education Courses." *Journal of Health and Social Behavior* 7, no. 4 (Winter 1966): 302–8.

41. Curtis, Richard F., Dianne M. Timbers, and Elton F. Jackson. "Prejudice and Urban Social Participation." *American Journal of Sociology* 73, no. 2 (September 1967): 235–46.

42. Davis, Morris, Robert Seibert, and Warren Breed. "Interracial Seating Patterns on New Orleans Public Transit." *Social Problems* 13, no. 3 (Winter 1966): 298–306.

43. Dean, Dwight G. "Alienation and Political Apathy." *Social Forces* 38 (March 1960): 185–90.

44. Demerath, N. J. III, Gerald Marwell, and Michael T. Aiken. "Tactics and Tensions in a Summer of Yesteryear: Results of a Panel Analysis of 1965 Southern Civil Rights Workers." American Sociological Association Convention, San Francisco, 1969.

45. Dennis, Jack. "Support for the Party System by the Mass Public." *American Political Science Review* 60, no. 3 (September 1966): 600–15.

46. Douglah, Mohammad, and Gwenna Moss. "Differential Participation Patterns of Adults of Low and High Educational Attainment." *Adult Education* 18, no. 4 (Summer 1968): 247–59.

47. Downes, Bryan. "Issue Conflict, Factionalism, and Consensus in Suburban City Councils," *Urban Affairs Quarterly* 4, no. 4 (June 1969): 477–597.

48. Dye, Thomas R. "Inequality and Civil Rights Policy in the States." *The Journal of Politics* 31, no. 4 (November 1969): 1030–97.

49. Dynes, Russell R. "Community Conflict: An Explanation of its Absence in Natural Disasters." Paper presented at a meeting of the American Sociological Association, San Francisco, California, September, 1969.

50. Easton, David, and Jack Dennis. "The Child's Acquisition of Regime Norms: Political Efficacy." *American Political Science Review* 61, no. 1 (March 1967): 25–39.

51. Epstein, Irwin. "Social Workers and Social Action: Attitudes toward Social Action Strategies." *Social Work* 13, no. 2 (April 1968): 101–8.

52. Faunce, William, and Donald McClelland. "Professionalization and Stratification Patterns in an Industrial Community." *American Journal of Sociology* 72, no. 4 (January 1967): 341–50.

53. Feinbaum, Robert. "The American Medical Association: A Case Study of Professional Practices." Paper presented at a meeting of the American Sociological Association. San Francisco, 1969.

54. Fellman, Gordon. "Planning Implications of Neighborhoods' Resistance to Proposed Housing and Highways." *Digest of Urban and Regional Research* 15, no. 2 (Winter 1968): 61.

55. Fendrich, James M. "Perceived Reference Group Support: Racial Attitudes and Overt Behavior." *American Sociological Review* 32, no. 6 (December 1967): 960–90.

56. Flacks, Richard. "The Liberated Generation: An Exploration of the Roots of Student Protest." *Journal of Social Issues* 23, no. 3 (July 1967): 52–75.

57. Florence Heller School for Advanced Studies in Social Welfare. "Community Representation in Community Action Programs." August 1968.

58. Florence Heller School for Advanced Studies in Social Welfare. "Community Representation in Community Action Programs." March 1969.

59. Form, William, and Joan Rytina. "Ideological Beliefs on the Distribution of Power in the United States." *American Sociological Review* 34, no. 1 (February 1969): 19–31.

60. Form, William H., and Joan Rytina. "The Rich and the Blacks: Two Views of Politics and Government." Paper presented at a meeting of the American Sociological Association. San Francisco, September 1969.

61. Frank, Jerome, and Jacob Schonfield. "Commitment to Peace Work: A Closer Look at Determinants." *American Journal of Orthopsychiatry* 37, no. 1 (January 1967): 112–19.

62. Fredrickson, H. George. "Exploring Urban Priorities—The Case of Syracuse." *Urban Affairs Quarterly* 5, no. 1 (September 1969): 31–43.

63. Frey, Frederick. "Socialization to National Identification among Turkish Peasants." *Journal of Politics* 30, no. 4 (November 1968): 934–45.

64. Gamson, William A. "Rancorous Conflict in Community Politics." *American Sociological Review* 39, no. 1 (February 1966): 71–81.

65. Geschwender, James A. "Civil Rights Protest and Riots: A Disappearing Distinction." *Social Science Quarterly* 49, no. 3 (December 1968): 474–84.

66. Geschwender, James A. "Social Structure and the Negro Revolt: An Examination of Some Hypotheses," *Social Forces* 43, no. 2 (December 1969): 248–316.

67. Geschwender, James A. "Status Inconsistency, Social Isolation, and Individual Unrest." *Social Forces* 46, no. 4 (June 1968): 477–84.

68. Geschwender, James A., Benjamin D. Singer, and Richard Osborn. "Social Isolation and Riot Participation." Paper presented at a meeting of the American Sociological Association, San Francisco, September 1969.

69. Geschwender, James A., Benjamin D. Singer, and Judith Harrington. "Status Inconsistency, Relative Deprivation, and the Detroit Riot." Paper presented at a meeting of the American Sociological Association, San Francisco, September 1969.

70. Gilbert, Neil. "Clients or Constituents: A Case Study of Pittsburgh's War on Poverty." Dissertation, University of Pittsburgh, 1968.

71. Gilbert, Neil. "Maximum Feasible Participation? A Pittsburgh Encounter." *Social Work* 14, no. 3 (November 1969): 84–92.

72. Gittell, Marilyn. "Professionalism and Public Participation: New York City, A Case Study." *Public Administration Review* 27, no. 3 (September 1967): 237–51.

73. Glenn, Norval, and John Alston. "Cultural Distances among Occupational Categories." *American Sociological Review* 33, no. 3 (June 1968): 365–82.

74. Glenn, Norval D., and Michael Grimes. "Aging, Voting, and Political Interest." *American Sociological Review,* 33, no. 4 (August 1968): 563–76.

75. Goldrich, Daniel. "Peasant's Sons in City Settings: An Inquiry into the Politics of Urbanization in Panama and Costa Rica." *Human Organization* 23, no. 4 (Winter 1964): 328–33.

76. Gove, Walter, and Herbert Costner. "Organizing the Poor: An Evaluation of a Strategy." Research report to the Office of Economic Opportunity, 1969.

77. Greer, Scott A., Donald E. Carns, and Robert F. Winch. "Social Participation and Formal Voluntary Organizations." Paper presented at a meeting of the American Sociological Association, Washington, D.C., September 1970.

78. Grindstaff, Carl F. "The Negro, Urbanization, and Relative Deprivation in the Deep South." *Social Problems* 15, no. 3 (Winter 1968): 342–52.

79. Gurin, Arnold. "The Functions of a Sectarian Welfare Program in a Multi-Group Society: A Case Study of the Jewish Welfare Federation of Detroit." Dissertation, University of Michigan, 1965.

80. Gurin, Patricia and Gerald, C. Rosina, and Muriel Beattie. "Internal-External Control in the Motivational Dynamics of Negro Youth." *Journal of Social Issues* 25, no. 3 (Summer 1969): 29–53.

81. Hadden, Jeffrey K., and Raymond Rymph. "Social Structure and Civil Rights Involvement: A Case Study of Protestant Ministers." *Social Forces* 45, no. 1 (September 1966): 51–61.

82. Hagedorn, Robert, and Sanford Labovitz. "An Analysis of Community and Professional Participation among Occupations." *Social Forces* 45, no. 4 (June 1967): 483–91.

83. Hagedorn, Robert, and Sanford Labovitz: "Participation in Community Associations by Occupation—A Test of Three Theories." *American Sociological Review* 33, no. 2 (April 1968): 272–83.

84. Hamilton, Richard F. "Skill Level and Politics." *Public Opinion Quarterly* 29, no. 3 (Fall 1965): 390–99.

85. Hardee, Gilbert J. "Planned Change and Systematic Linkage in a Five-Year Extension Program with Part-Time Farm Families." *Rural Sociology* 30, no. 1 (March 1968): 23–32.

86. Hartman, Chester W., and Gregg Carr. "Housing Authorities Reconsidered." *Journal of the American Institute of Planners* 35, no. 1 (January 1969): 10–21.

87. Hasenfled, Yeheskel. "The Character of the Community Action Center." Paper presented at a meeting of the National Conference on Social Welfare, May 1969.

88. Hill, Richard, and Calvin J. Larson. "Differential Ghetto Organization." Paper presented at a meeting of the American Sociological Association. San Francisco, September 1969.

89. Hines, Ralph H., and James E. Pierce. "Negro Leadership After the Social Crisis: An Analysis of Leadership in Montgomery, Alabama," *Phylon* 26, no. 2 (Summer 1965): 162–71.

90. Hodge, Robert W., and Donald Treiman. "Social Participation and Social Status." *American Journal of Sociology* 33, no. 5 (October 1968): 722–40.

91. Hofstetter, C. Richard. "Political Disengagement and the Death of Martin Luther King." *Public Opinion Quarterly* 33, no. 2 (Summer 1969): 174–79.

92. Holloway, Harry, and David Olson. "Electoral Participation by White and Negro in a Southern City." *Midwest Journal of Political Science* 10, no. 1 (February 1966): 99–122.

93. Horner, James T., and Alan B. Knox. "Encouraging Non-College-Bound Rural Young Adults to Participate in Continuing Education." *Adult Leadership* 14, no. 6 (December 1965): 186–88.

94. Horton, John E., and Wayne E. Thompson, "Political Alienation as a Force in Political Action." *Social Forces* 38 (March 1960): 190–95.

95. Hough, Richard L., Gene F. Simmers, and James O'Meara. "Parental Influence, Youth Contraculture, and Rural Adolescent Attitudes toward Minority Groups." *Rural Sociology* 34, no. 3 (September 1969): 383–86.

96. Hyman, Herbert Harvey. "Organizational Response to Urban Renewal." Dissertation, Brandeis University, 1967.

97. Inkeles, Alex. "Making Men Modern: On the Causes and Consequences of Individual Change in Six Developing Countries." *American Journal of Sociology* 75, no. 2 (September 1969): 208–225.

98. Jackman, Norman, and Jack Dodson. "Negro Youth and Direct Action." *Phylon,* 28, no. 1 (Winter 1967): 5–15.

99. Janowitz, Morris, and David Segal. "Social Cleavage and Party Affiliation: Germany, Great Britain, and the United States." *American Journal of Sociology* 72, no. 6 (May 1967): 601–18.

100. Jansyn, Leon R. "Solidarity and Delinquency in a Street Corner Group." *American Sociological Review* 31, no. 5 (October 1966): 600–614.

101. Jitodai, Ted T. "Migrant Status and Church Attendance." *Social Forces* 43, no. 2 (December 1964): 241–48.

102. Johnson, David. "Racial Attitudes, Negro Freedom Schools Participants and Negro and White Civil Rights Participants." *Social Forces* 45, no. 2 (December 1966): 266–73.

103. Jones, Garth N. "Integration of Political Ethos and Local Government Systems: The Utah Experience with Council-Manager Government." *Human Organization* 23, no. 3 (Fall 1964): 210–23.

104. Juras, Dean, Herbert Hirsch, and Frederic J. Fleron, Jr. "The Malevolent Leader; Political Socialization in an American Subculture." *American Political Science Review* 62, no. 4 (January 1966): 184–97.

105. Kahn, Roger. "Rank and File Student Activism: A Contextual Test of Three Hypotheses." Paper presented at a meeting of the American Sociological Association. San Francisco, September 1969.

106. Katz, Elihu, and Brenda Danet. "Petition and Persuasive Appeals: A Study of Offical-Client Relationships." *American Sociological Review* 37, no. 6 (December 1966): 811–21.

107. Kelley, Stanley, Jr., Richard E. Ayres, and William G. Bowen, "Registration and Voting: Putting First Things First." *American Political Science Review* 61, no. 2 (June 1967): 359–77.

108. Kenniston, Kenneth. "The Sources of Student Dissent." *Journal of Social Issues* 23, no. 3 (July 1967): 108–38.

109. Keruloff, Arthur H., and Stuart Atkins. "T-Group for a Work Team." *Applied Behavioral Science* 2, no. 1 (January–March 1966): 63–93.

110. Kesselman, Mark. "French Local Politics: A Statistical Examination of Grass Roots Consensus." *American Political Science Review* 60, no. 4 (December 1966): 963–73.

111. Kurdao, Yasumasa. "Political Attitudes in a Japanese Community." *Public Opinion Quarterly* 29, no. 4 (Winter 1965–66): 602–13.

112. Kurzman, Paul A. "The Native-Settler Concept: Implications for Community Organization." *Social Work* 14, no. 3 (November 1969): 58–64.

113. LaBarre, Maurine. "The Strengths of the Self-Supporting Poor." Paper presented at a meeting of the National Conference on Social Welfare, May 1968.

114. Lambert, Canille, Jr., Mildred Guberman, and Robert Morris. "Reopening Doors for Older People: How Realistic." *Social Service Review* 38, no. 1 (March 1964): 42–50.

115. Langton, Kenneth P., and M. Kent Jennings. "Political Socialization and the High School Civics Curriculum in the United States." *American Political Science Review* 62, no. 3 (September 1968): 852–67.

116. Lansing, John B., and Robert W. Murans. "Evaluation of Neighborhood Quality." *Journal of the American Institute of Planners* 35, no. 3 (May 1969): 195–99.

117. Lee, Terence. "Urban Neighborhood as a Socio-Spatial Scheme." *Human Relations,* 21, no. 3 (August 1968): 241–69.

118. Lenski, Gerhard E. "Status Inconsistency and the Vote: A Four-Nation Test." *American Sociological Review* 32, no. 2 (April 1967): 298–301.

119. Levens, Helene. "Organizational Affiliation and Powerlessness: A Case Study of the Welfare Poor." *Social Problems* 16, no. 1 (Summer 1968): 18–32.

120. Levin, Jack, and Gerald Taube. "Bureaucracy and the Socially Handicapped: A Study of Lower Status Tenants in Public Housing." Paper presented at a meeting of the American Sociological Association, San Francisco, September 1969.

121. Edward Levine. "A Political Perspective of Environmental Planning." Paper presented at a meeting of the American Sociological Association, San Francisco, September 1969.

122. Lieberson, Stanley, and Arnold R. Silverman. "The Precipitants and Underlying Conditions of Race Riots." *American Sociological Review* 30, no. 6 (December 1965): 887–98.

123. Lineberry, Robert, and Edmund Fowler. "Reformism and Public Policies in American Cities." *American Political Science Review* 61, no. 3 (September 1967): 701–16.

124. Lipsky, Michael. "Protest as a Political Resource." *American Political Science Review* 62, no. 4 (December 1968): 1144–58.

125. Lopreato, Joseph. "Upward Social Mobility and Political Orientation." *American Sociological Review* 32, no. 4 (August 1967): 506–22.

126. Luby, Elliot, et al. "The Detroit Riot: Some Characteristics of Those on the Street." *Psychiatric Opinion* 5, no. 3 (June 1968): 29–35.

127. MacWorter, Gerald A., and Robert L. Crain. "Subcommunity Gladitorial Competition: Civil Rights Leadership as a Competitive Process." *Social Forces* 46, no. 1 (September 1967): 8–21.

128. Marcus, George E. "Psychopathology and Political Recruitment." *The Journal of Politics* 31, no. 4 (November 1969): 913–31.

129. Marsh, C. Paul, Robert J. Dolan, and William L. Riddich. "Anomia and Communication Behavior: The Relationship Between Anomia and the Utilization of Three Public Bureaucracies." *Rural Sociology* 32, no. 4 (December 1967): 435–45.

130. Marx, Gary T. "Religion: Opiate or Inspiration of Civil Rights Militancy." *American Sociological Review* 32, no. 1 (February 1967): 64–72.

131. McGinn, N. F., E. Hartburg, and G. P. Gisburg. "Responses to Interpersonal Conflict by Middle-Class Males in Gaudalajara and Michigan." *American Anthropologist* 67, no. 6 (December 1965): 1483–95.

132. Medalia, Nahurn Z. "Air Pollution as a Socio-Environmental Health Problem, A Survey Report." *Health and Social Behavior* 5, no. 4 (Winter 1964): 154–65.

133. Metz, A. Stafford. "The Relationship of Dental Care Practices to Attitudes toward Fluoridation." *Health and Social Behavior* 8, no. 1 (March 1967): 55–59.

134. Meyer, Philip. "Aftermath of Martyrdom: Negro Militancy and Martin Luther King." *Public Opinion Quarterly* 33, no. 2 (Summer 1969): 160–73.

135. Minar, David W. "The Community Basis of Conflict in School System Politics." *American Sociological Review* 31, no. 6 (December 1966): 822–34.

136. Mitchell, Robert Edward. "Class-Linked Conflict between Two Dimensions of Liberalism-Conservatism." *Social Problems* 13, no. 4 (Spring 1966): 418–27.

137. Morgan, William R. "Faculty Mediation of Student War Protests." Paper presented at a meeting of the American Sociological Association, San Francisco, September 1969.

138. Morrison, Denton E., and Allan D. Steeves. "Deprivation, Discontent, and Social Movement Participation: Evidence on a Contemporary Farmers' Movement, the NFO." *Rural Sociology* 32, no. 4 (December 1967): 414–34.

139. Mubeccel, Kiray. "Values, Social Stratification, and Development." *Journal of Social Issues* 24, no. 2 (April 1968): 87–100.

140. Mueller, John E. "Fluoridation and Attitude Change." *American Journal of Public Health* 58, no. 10 (November 1968): 1876–80.

141. Mulford, Charles Lee, and Gerald E. Klonglan. "The Significance of Attitudes for Formal Voluntary Organizations: A Synthesis of Existing Research and Theory." Paper presented at a meeting of the American Sociological Association, Washington, D.C., September 1970.

142. Murphy, Raymond J., and James M. Watson. "Level of Aspiration, Discontent, and Support for Violence: A Test of Three Hypotheses." Paper presented at a meeting of the American Sociological Association, San Francisco, September 1969.

143. Naison, Mark. "The Rent Strike in New York." *Radical America* (November–December 1967): 7–49.

144. Nasitir, David. "A Note on Contextual Effects and the Political Orientation of University Students." *American Sociological Review* 33, no. 2 (April 1968): 210–13.

145. Nash, A. "The Impact of Adult Education on Taxi Drivers During an Organizing Drive." *Adult Education* 16, no. 5 (November 1967): 183–85.

146. Nelson, Merwyn, Verl R. W. Franz, and D. G. Marshall. "The Franz-Marshall Scale of Commitment for Community Action." *Rural Sociology* 34, no. 3 (September 1969): 396–401.

147. Nimms, Dan, and Clifton McCleskey. "Impact of the Poll Tax on Voter Participation: The Houston Metropolitan Area in 1966." *Journal of Politics* 31, no. 3 (August 1969): 682–99.

148. Noel, Donald. "Group Identification among Negroes: An Empirical Analysis." *Journal of Social Issues* 20, no. 2 (April 1964): 71–84.

149. Oberschall, Anthony. "Group Violence: Some Hypotheses and Empirical Uniformities." Paper presented at a meeting of the American Sociological Association. San Francisco, September 1969.

150. Oberschall, Anthony. "The Los Angeles Riot of August 1965." *Social Problems* 14, no. 3 (Winter 1968): 322–41.

151. Olsen, Marvin E. "Perceived Legitimacy of Social Protest Action." *Social Problems* 15, no. 3 (Winter 1968): 297–310.

152. Olsen, Marvin E. "Alienation and Political Opinions." *Public Opinion Quarterly* 29, no. 2 (Summer 1965): 200–212.

153. Orbell, John M. "Protest Participation among Southern Negro College Students." *American Political Science Review* 61, no. 2 (June 1967): 446–56.

154. Orum, Anthony M. "Structural Sources of Negro Student Protest: Campus and Community." Paper presented at a meeting of the American Sociological Association. San Francisco, September 1969.

155. Osborne, Oliver H. "The Yoruba Village as a Therapeutic Community." *Journal of Health and Social Behavior* 10, no. 3 (September 1969): 187–200.

156. "OSTI Revised Decentralization Training Program." *Protest and Prejudice* (Cambridge, Massachusetts, April 1969).

157. Paije, Jeffrey M. "Political Orientation and Riot Participation." Paper presented at a meeting of the American Sociological Association. San Francisco, September 1969.

158. Paiva, J. F. "A Study of Unplanned Effects of Planned Change in Community Development." Dissertation, Brandeis University, 1968.

159. Palisi, Bartholomew J. "Ethnic Patterns of Friendship." *Phylon* 26, no. 3 (Fall 1965): 217–25.

160. Payne, Raymond and Barbara, and Donald Shoemaker. "Social Background Factors and Participation in Voluntary Associations." Paper presented at a meeting of the American Sociological Association, Washington, D.C., September 1970.

161. Peck, Sidney, and Sidney Rosen. "Influence of the Peer Group on the Attitudes of Girls toward Color Differences." *Phylon* 26, no. 1 (September 1965): 50–63.

162. Penalosa, Fernando, and Edward C. McDonaugh. "Social Mobility in a Mexican-American Community." *Social Forces* 44, no. 4 (June 1966): 498–505.

163. Petras, James, and Maurice Zeitlin. "Miners and Agrarian Radicialism." *American Sociological Review* 32, no. 4 (August 1967): 578–86.

164. Phelps, David W. "Parent Perceptions of Cooperative Nursery School Evening Meetings: Implications for Professional Education." *Adult Education* 14, no. 3 (September 1965): 87–88.

165. Phillips, Derek L. "Mental Health Status, Social Participation, and Happiness." *Journal of Health and Social Behavior* 8, no. 4 (December 1967): 285–91.

166. Photiadis, John D. "Community Size and Aspects of the Authoritative Personality among Businessmen." *Rural Sociology* 32, no. 1 (March 1967): 70–77.

167. Photiadis, John D. "Social Integration of Businessmen in Varied Size Communities." *Social Forces* 46, no. 2 (December 1967): 229–36.

168. Pinard, Maurice. "Poverty and Political Movements." *Social Problems* 15, no. 2 (Fall 1967): 250–63.

169. Pinard, Maurice, Jerome Kirk, and Donald von Eschen. "Processes of Recruitment in the Sit-In Movement." *Public Opinion Quarterly* 33, no. 3 (Fall 1969): 355–69.

170. Polansky, Norman A. "Powerlessness among Rural Appalachian Youth." *Rural Sociology* 34, no. 2 (May 1969): 219–22.

171. Pratt, Lois. "Level of Sociological Knowledge among Health and Social Workers." *Journal of Health and Social Behavior* 10, no. 1 (March 1969): 59–65.

172. Prewitt, Kenneth, Heinz Eulau, and Betty H. Zisk. "Political Socialization and Political Roles." *Public Opinion Quarterly* 30, no. 4 (Winter 1966–67): 569–582.

173. Putnam, Robert D. "Political Attitudes and the Local Community." *American Political Science Review* 60, no. 3 (September 1966): 640–54.

174. Quarantelli, E. L., and Russell R. Dynes. "Interorganizational Relationships and Stress Situations." Paper presented at a meeting of the American Sociological Association. Boston, 1968.

175. Ransford, H. Edward. "Isolation, Powerlessness, and Violence: A Study of Attitudes and Participation in the Watts Riot." *American Journal of Sociology*, 73, no. 5 (March 1968): 581–91.

176. Rhodes, Lewis. "Anomia, Aspiration, and Status." *Social Forces* 42, no. 4 (May 1964): 434–40.

177. Roach, Jack, and Lionel Lewis. "The Effects of Race and Socio-Economic Status on Family Planning." *Journal of Health and Social Behavior* 8, no. 1 (March 1967): 40–45.

178. Rodman, Hyman. "The Lower-Class Value Stretch." *Social Forces* 42, no. 2 (December 1963): 205–15.

179. Rosenstock, I., D. Haefner, S. Kegeles, and J. Kerscht. "Public Knowledge, Opinion, and Action Concerning Three Public Health Issues, Radioactive Fallout, Insect and Plant Sprays and Fatty Foods." *Journal of Health and Social Behavior* 7, no. 2 (Summer 1966): 91–98.

180. Roth, Marian, and G. R. Boynton. "Communal Ideology and Political Support." *The Journal of Politics* 31, no. 1 (February 1969): 167–85.

181. Rush, Gary. "Status Inconsistency and Right-Wing Extremism." *American Sociological Review* 32, no. 1 (February 1967): 86–92.

182. Rushing, William. "Aspects of Deprivation in a Rural Poverty Class." *Rural Sociology* 33, no. 3 (September 1968): 269–87.

183. Rytina, Joan, William Form, and John Pease. "Income and Ideology: General and Situated Beliefs about the American Opportunity System." Paper presented at a meeting of the American Sociological Association. San Francisco, September 1969.

184. Rytina, Joan, William Form, and John Pease. "Income and Ideological Beliefs about the Distribution of Power in the United States." Paper presented at a meeting of the American Sociological Association, San Francisco, September 1970.

185. Salem, Richard G., and William J. Bowers. "The Deterrent Effects of Formal Sanctions." Paper presented for a meeting of the American Sociological Association. San Francisco, September 1970.

186. Schmuck, Richard, and Mark Chesler, "Superpatriot Opposition to Community Mental Health Programs." *Community Mental Health Journal* 3, no. 4 (1967): 382–88.

187. Schneiderman, Leonard. "The Culture of Poverty: A Study of the Value Orientation Preferences of the Chronically Impoverished." Dissertation, University of Minnesota, 1963.

188. Schneiderman, Leonard. "Value Orientation Preferences of Chronic Relief Recipients." *Social Work* 9, no. 3 (July 1964): 13–18.

189. Schnore, Leo F., and Philip C. Evenson. "Segregation in Southern Cities." *American Journal of Sociology* 72, no. 1 (July 1966): 58–67.

190. Schoenberger, Robert A. "Conservatism, Personality, and Political Extremism." *American Political Science Review* 62, no. 3 (September 1968): 868–73.

191. Schwartz, Jerome, and Milton Chernin. "Participation of Recipients in Public Welfare Planning and Administration." *Social Service Review* 41, no. 1 (March 1967): 10–22.

192. Schwarzweller, Harry, and James Brown. "Social Class Origins and Rural-Urban Migration and Economic Life Chances: A Case Study." *Rural Sociology* 32, no. 1 (March 1967): 6–19.

193. Scott, Joseph. "Social Class Factors Underlying the Civil Rights Movement." *Phylon* 27, no. 2 (Summer 1965): 132–44.

194. Scott, Joseph. "Sources of Social Change in Community, Family, and Fertility in a Puerto Rican Town." *American Journal of Sociology* 72, no. 5 (March 1967): 520–30.

195. Seals, Alvin, and Jiri Kolaja. "A Study of Negro Voluntary Organizations in Lexington, Kentucky." *Phylon* 25, no. 1 (Spring 1964): 27–31.

196. Sears, David, and John McConahay. "Participation in the Los Angeles Riot." *Social Problems* 17, no. 1 (Summer 1969): 3–20.

197. Segal, Bernard E. "Dissatisfaction and Desire for Change among Chilean Hospital Workers." *American Journal of Sociology* 75, no. 3 (November 1969): 375–88.

198. Segal, David, and David Knoke. "Social and Economic Bases of Political Partisanship in the United States." Paper presented at a meeting of the American Sociological Association. San Francisco, September 1969.

199. Seidler, Murray. "Some Participant Observer Reflections on Detroit's Community Action Program." *Urban Affairs Quarterly* 5, no. 2 (December 1969): 183–205.

200. Sharkansky, Ira. "Economic Development, Regionalism, and State Political Systems." *Midwest Journal of Political Science* 12, no. 1 (February 1968): 41–61.

201. Shostak, Arthur B. "Promoting Participation of the Poor: Philadelphia's Antipoverty Program." *Social Work* 11, no. 1 (January 1966): 64–72.

202. Smith, Clagett. "A Comparative Analysis of Some Conditions and Consequences of Intra-Organizational Conflict." *Administrative Science Quarterly* 10, No. 4 (March 1966): 504–29.

203. Smith, Joel, and Horace Rawls. "Standardization of an Educational Variable: The Need and its Consequences." *Social Forces* 44, no. 1 (September 1965): 57–66.

204. Soares, Glaucio, and Robert Hamblin. "Socio-Economic Variables and Voting for the Radical Left: Chile, 1952." *American Political Science Review* 61, no. 4 (December 1967): 1053–66.

205. Solomon, Frederic, and Jacob Fishman. "Youth and Peace: A Psycho-Social Study of Student Peace Demonstrators." *Journal of Social Issues* 20, no. 4 (October 1964): 54–73.

206. Solomon, Frederic, and Jacob Fishman. "Youth and Social Action: Action and Identity Formation in the First Student Sit-In Demonstration." *Journal of Social Issues* 20, no. 2 (April 1964): 36–46.

207. Sommer, Robert. "Classroom Ecology." *Applied Behavioral Science* 3, no. 4 (October–December 1964): 487–503.

208. Specht, Harry. "Community Development in Low-Income Negro Areas." *Social Work* 11, no. 4 (October 1966): 78–89.

209. Spiro, Shimon E. "Effects of Neighborhood Characteristics on Participation in Voluntary Associations." Ph.D. Dissertation, University of Michigan, 1967.

210. Spitze, Helen Taylor. "Project HEVE." *Adult Education* 15, no. 9 (March 1967): 311–12.

211. Stephenson, Richard, and Frank Scarpitti. "Argot in a Therapeutic Correctional Milieu." *Social Problems* 15, no. 3 (Winter 1968): 384–95.

212. Suchman, Edward A. "Preventative Health Behavior: A Model for Research on Community Health Campaigns." *Journal of Health and Social Behavior* 8, no. 3 (September 1967): 197–209.

213. Surace, Samuel, and Melvin Seeman. "Some Correlates of Civil Rights Activism." *Social Forces* 46, no. 2 (December 1967): 197–207.

214. Sutcliffe, J. P., and B. D. Crabbe. "Incidence of Degrees of Friendship in Urban and Rural Areas." *Social Forces* 42, no. 1 (October 1963): 60–64.

215. Taeuber, Karl, and Alma. "The Changing Character of Negro Migration." *American Journal of Sociology* 70, no. 4 (January 1965): 429–41.

216. Templeton, Fredric. "Alienation and Political Participation: Some Research Findings." *Public Opinion Quarterly* 30, no. 2 (Summer 1966): 249–61.

217. Trent, James, and Judith Craise. "Commitment and Conformity in the American College." *Journal of Social Issues* 23, no. 3 (July 1967): 34–52.

218. Uyeki, Eugene. "Patterns of Voting in a Metropolitan Area," *Urban Affairs Quarterly* 1, no. 4 (June 1966): 65–77.

219. Varley, Barbara. "Are Social Workers Dedicated to Service?" *Social Work* 11, no. 2 (April 1966): 84–91.

220. Vines, Kenneth, and Henry Glick. "The Impact of Universal Suffrage: A Comparison of Popular and Property Voting." *American Political Science Review* 61, no. 4 (December 1967): 1073–87.

221. Wanderer, Jules. "An Index of Riot Severity and Some Correlates." *American Journal of Sociology* 74, no. 5 (December 1969): 500–505.

222. Warner, W. Keith, and William Hefferman. "The Benefit-Participation Contingency in Voluntary Farm Organizations." *Rural Sociology* 32, no. 2 (June 1967): 133–53.

223. Warriner, Charles. "Traditional Authority and the Modern State: The Case of the Maranao of the Philippines." *Social Problems* 12, no. 1 (Summer 1964): 51–56.

224. Wasserman, Herbert. "Father-Absent and Father-Present Lower-Class Negro Families: A Comparative Study of Family Functioning." Dissertation, Brandeis University, 1968.

225. Weissman, Harold. "An Exploratory Study of a Neighborhood Council." Dissertation, Columbia University, 1966.

226. Wilson, James Q., and Edward C. Banfield. "Public Regardingness as a Value Premise in Voting Behavior." *American Political Science Review* 63, no. 4 (December 1964): 876–84.

227. Wolf, Eleanor, and Mel Ravitz. "Lafayette Park: New Residents in the Core City." *Journal of the American Institute of Planners* 30, no. 3 (August 1964): 234–39.

228. Wolfe, Arthur. "Challenge from the Right: The Bases of Voter Support for Wallace in 1968." Paper presented at a meeting of the American Sociological Association. San Francisco, September 1969.

229. Wolfinger, Raymond. "The Development and Persistence of Ethnic Voting." *American Political Science Review* 59, no. 4 (December 1965): 896–903.

230. Wolfinger, Raymond, and John Osgood Field. "Political Ethos and the Structure of City Government." *American Political Science Review* 60, no. 2 (June 1966): 306–26.

231. Wood, Arthur. "Political Radicalism in Changing Sinhalese Villages." *Human Organization* 23, no. 2 (Summer 1964): 99–107.

232. Wright, Theodore. "The Muslim League in South India Since Independence: A Study in Minority Group Political Strategies." *American Political Science Review* 60, no. 3 (September 1966): 579–600.

233. Youmans, E. Grant, S. E. Grigsby, and H. King. "Social Change, Generation and Race." *Rural Sociology* 34, no. 3 (September 1969): 305–12.

234. Younis, El-Farouk. "Differential Citizen Participation in Rural Community Development: A Comparative Study." Dissertation, University of Pittsburgh, 1964.

235. Zahn, Jane. "Some Adult Attitudes Affecting Learning: Powerlessness, Conflicting Needs, and Role Transition." *Adult Education* 19, no. 2 (December 1969): 91–97.

236. Zald, Mayer N. "Urban Differentiation, Characteristics of Boards of Directors, and Organizational Effectiveness." *American Journal of Sociology* 73, no. 3 (November 1967): 261–72.

237. Zeitlin, Maurice. "Revolutionary Workers and Individual Liberties." *American Journal of Sociology* 72, no. 6 (May 1967): 601–18.

238. Zikmuod, Joseph, and Robert Smith. "Political Participation in an Upper-Middle Class Suburb." *Urban Affairs Quarterly* 4, no. 4 (June 1969): 443–58.

Part Six

Two Social Change Processes

Chapter Nine
The Diffusion and Adoption of Innovations

INTRODUCTION

THE HUMAN-SERVICE professions in general and the area of community organization in particular are frequently characterized as change-oriented fields. For this reason, scholarly endeavor referred to as the diffusion and adoption of innovations seems of special interest to these areas. While the subject of diffusion and adoption was not one of the original "practice issue areas" designated for literature retrieval by this project, the existence of this school of research within the journals in our sampling frame quickly became apparent, as did the relevance for our purposes of the general subject matter covered: i.e., the process by which new ideas or practices are propagated and gain acceptance by groups of people.

Our treatment of diffusion will have two foci, which will be presented sequentially: diffusion of innovations among community population groups, and diffusion of innovations in organizations. The first is more centrally located within the traditions of diffusion studies: how new agricultural practices are learned by farmers; how new medicines come to be prescribed by physicians; how new public-health techniques are introduced by community-development workers to villagers in underdeveloped nations. The second focus, innovation in organizations, is newer as a discrete area of concern, and does not have so firm a theoretical and research base as does the former area. However, in some ways it more fundamentally touches the typical problems and issues faced by community-organization practitioners, most of whom are inextricably enmeshed in organizational entanglements. While this material may in some respects be seen as more primary or important for community planning and organizing, we shall hold it for later presentation in the interests of a more orderly, holistic development of ideas on the general subject. In actuality, the organizational discussion may be seen as a special case of the diffusion principles covered in the earlier analysis.

For the treatment of diffusion, we wish to acknowledge our special debt to Everett Rogers for his singular scholarly contribution (116). His conceptual constructs served as the basis for the theoretical formulations underlying our discussion. Throughout the chapter, the reader will encounter much of Rogers's terminology, as well as generalizations adopted or transposed from his book. Although Rogers's work is not directly or self-consciously aimed at community planning and action as a field, his framework of analysis is compatible with and indispensable to this presentation. Rogers's more immediate consultation with the project about the methodology of retrieval is also gratefully acknowledged.

The section on diffusion among population groups, below, is a direct outgrowth of Rogers's groundbreaking formulations. This initial presentation may be viewed as:

1. The collecting and synthesizing of diffusion research literature and the application of it to community-organization practice issues and to the problems of the human-service fields. The attempt here is to package succinctly a wide range of research endeavor so as to make it easily understandable and available to practitioners and activists in these fields. The mainstreams of research dealing with diffusion studies include anthropology, rural sociology, medical sociology, education, industry, and agricultural extension. Some human-service fields, such as agricultural extension and adult education, are familiar with and have actively incorporated elements of the diffusion tradition. Other areas, such as social work and city planning, have virtually ignored this tradition, remaining uninformed and uninfluenced by its potentialities for practices and programs. It is to the latter groups in particular that the contents of this chapter are addressed.

2. A replication of Rogers's work, bringing in more recent studies

and studies from supplementary streams of literature which are more directly concerned with community organization and human services. This replication, essentially confirms the validity and the utility of Rogers's original formulations.

3. The addition of pertinent studies and contexts and the casting of materials in a specialized light, which makes the study of diffusion comprehensible and usable by those concerned with community intervention: social planners, neighborhood workers, and social activists. In this sense, we shall attempt a reinterpretation and a unique coloration of Rogers's work with explicit action guidelines specified. This involves not only the collection and systematizing of diffusion research but also going beyond to treat it in a specialized fashion.

Because of the substantial formative role that Rogers's work played in diffusion research theory, additional comments seem in order. Rogers's *Diffusion of Innovations* is generally considered a classic in its field. In this book, the author reviewed over 500 publications on the diffusion and adoption of innovations and collated their findings into a consistent theoretical framework. Many research investigations reviewed were specifically related to Rogers's work and often elucidated issues Rogers felt needed further investigation. For this reason, many of the generalizations cited here are similar, sometimes identical, to the generalizations that appear in Rogers's work. His theory and discussion seems to have become virtual gospel for the diffusion and adoption researcher and thus most studies use "Rogerian" concepts, theoretical orientation, and terminology, thereby making similarity to his work unavoidable.

The studies to follow involve a wide range of contexts, materials, and processes. New technical products, services, and practices, new political policies and structures, are but a very few examples of the range of innovations covered. In discussing the question of innovation, we have generally accepted the self-definition of researchers. Products and services described by authors as innovations have been assumed to be so. While this method of coding undoubtedly has defects, we felt that any personal decisions as to the innovativeness of a product or service might unnecessarily restrict certain relevant information. The reader should therefore take into account that our treatment of innovation involves diverse definitions employed by different researchers. We did not attempt to screen out studies which did not meet a preestablished and consistent conception of innovation. Our approach has the virtue of inclusiveness involving a multifaceted perspective. It possesses the resulting deficit of definitional looseness and possible inconsistency. The discussion should be appraised in that light.

The following brief glossary will introduce the reader to the technical language and major concepts of diffusion. It will be followed by a conceptual chart, which illustrates the terms in such a way as to convey the dynamic flow of diffusion as a social process.

Some Key Definitions (listed in order of logical development of ideas)

1. INNOVATION: Generally speaking, an innovation may be viewed as any idea perceived as new by a population group or organization, in our terms, a target system. An innovation, as most often operationalized in the research literature, refers to technical-professional-commercial novel ideas and practices such as population planning devices, mechanical improvements, and farming techniques. These are generally legitimate, conventional, and within the normative consensus of a community and its elites. In the few instances when a more radical type of innovation is being considered, this departure from the general conceptualization of an innovation will be indicated.

2. TARGET SYSTEM: A group, organization, community or society toward which an innovation is directed.

3. INNOVATIVE, INNOVATIVENESS: These two general terms are used to indicate the tendency of a target system to adopt innovations. A target system is innovative or has innovativeness if it adopts many innovations and adopts them at a rapid rate. When possible, distinctions will be made. In either case, *innovative* and *innovativeness* are general descriptive characteristics of one target system relative to others and not absolute measures of adoptive behavior.

4. MASS MEDIA, COMMUNICATIONS: A general term which signifies

a communication source that is cosmopolite, impersonal, institutional, and formal. Although some researchers have made distinctions among these above four characteristics, the relationships between them and the diffusion and adoption of innovations are consistent enough to group them under one classification.

5. FACE-TO-FACE COMMUNICATIONS: The opposite of mass media. A general term which signifies a communications source that is localite, personal, noninstitutional, and informal. The discussion of mass media with respect to these four characteristics and their similarities and differences also applies here.

6. INNOVATION ACTORS (innovotors, early adopters, early majority, late majority, laggards): Rogers's five adopter categorizations based on a relative time of adoption of innovations. The five categories are listed in terms of their innovativeness. Innovators are the first to adopt innovations and laggards the last.

7. OPINION LEADERS: Individuals who are influential in approving or disapproving new ideas, and from whom others seek advice and information regarding innovations.

8. ADOPTION RATE: The relative speed with which an innovation is adopted by the members of a target system, usually measured by the length of time required for a certain percentage of the members to adopt an innovation.

9. STAGES IN THE ADOPTION PROCESS (*awareness, interest, evaluation, trial, adoption*): These are Rogers's five stages in the adoption process. Behaviors associated with each of these stages are *exposure to innovation, increased interest and information gathering, decision whether or not to try innovation, trial of the innovation,* and *decision as to further continuation.*

10. ADOPTION PERIOD: The length of time required for a target system to pass through the adoption process from awareness to adoption.

11. COSMOPOLITE: A term which signifies an orientation external to a target system's particular social system, interest in, association with, and openness to external system information and influences.

12. LOCALITE: The opposite of cosmopolite. It signifies an orienta-

tion limited to the target system's own social system and lack of openness to external system inputs and influences.

A general scheme embracing and illustrating this set of terms, borrowed from Rogers, will be found below.

DIFFUSION OF INNOVATIONS AMONG POPULATION GROUPS

Target System Variables Associated with Receptivity to Innovation

Probably the most basic finding of diffusion and adoption literature is that all target systems do not adopt innovations at the same rate. Numerous researchers (probably a majority of those included in our research pool) have been concerned with identifying those variables which distinguish between target systems that are receptive to innovation and those that are not. Their studies reveal clearly demonstrated relationships of variables such as traditionalism, socioeconomic status, and value orientation, which affect the innovativeness of a target system. This section will present 17 main generalizations and a number of subgeneralizations regarding the propensity of system innovation.

Our main purpose in this treatment is to alert the practitioner to indicators that enable one to gauge the probable rate of adoption of an innovation brought into a given target system. We shall sugget various target systems on which the practitioner may focus, in order to maximize potentialities for the adoption of innovations. We shall not assume, however, that it will always be most advantageous to choose target systems likely to be receptive to innovation, since other considerations besides a propensity for adoption are often salient.

Cultural Values

GENERALIZATION 9.1: The innovativeness of a target system is inversely related to the extent to which that target system adheres to traditional norms. Target systems with a

FIGURE 9.1 PARADIGM OF THE ADOPTION OF AN INNOVATION BY AN INDIVIDUAL WITHIN A SOCIAL SYSTEM

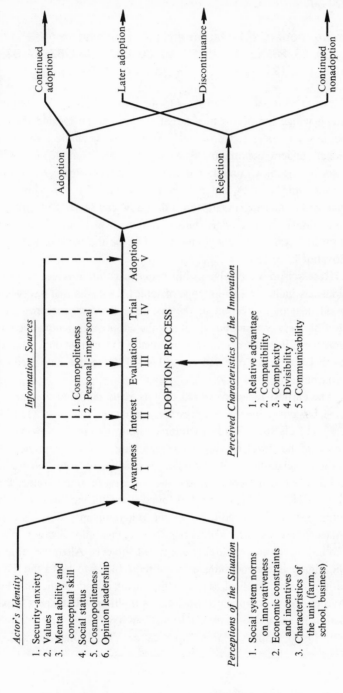

more modern orientation are more innovative (+ + + +, 1, 6, 20, 23, 28, 42, 44, 45, 57, 59, 66, 68, 76, 80, 83, 87, 92, 105, 107, 110, 124, 128, 132, 133, 134, 141, 145).

Traditional and *modern* refer to the two end points of a continuum along which the norms of a target system can be located. Numerous authors have stressed different variables as the indices of the traditional–modern continuum. Rogers (116), for example, states that a "social system with modern norms is more technologically developed, cosmopolite, literate, rational and empathetic" (p. 61). This generalization and the subgeneralizations to follow can serve to identify for the practitioner those modern target systems which are likely to place a positive value on change and therefore be the most receptive to innovations.

Research into the relationship between cultural values and innovations has included a wide range of topics. One area that has received a good deal of discussion in the last several years concerns the relationship between traditionalism and the adoption of innovative medical practices. Researchers have consistently found that individuals who have a traditional orientation are less likely to use new medical approaches.

The earliest report reviewed on this issue involved attitudes rather than behavior, but its findings are consistent. Suchman (133) found that subjects from highly traditional ethnic groups in New York City had a higher level of skepticism regarding medical care and a lower level of scientific health attitudes than subjects from less traditional ethnic groups. In another study, dealing with behaviors rather than attitudes, Nall and Speilberg (92) found that Chicanos who were highly integrated into the traditional ethnic subcommunity were less willing to accept the standard TB treatment (e.g., institutionalization in a sanitarium) than were less highly integrated subjects. Also, they found that the highly integrated subjects were most likely to leave the TB sanitarium against medical advice. Other investigators in the area include Archer (6), who replicated Suchman's findings with respect to participation in an anticoronary clinic in New York City, and Press (107), who found a direct relationship between a traditional orientation and use of a "curer" rather than a physician among a sample of Bogota residents.

9.1A. The innovativeness of a target system is inversely related to the extent of ruralism found in that target system. Target systems in an urban setting or with an urban orientation are more innovative (+ + + +, 44, 57, 59, 66, 68, 87, 124, 132, 141).

Research investigation of the relationship between the rural-urban continuum and innovativeness has involved target systems ranging from the level of the individual to that of cities and townships. One example is a study by Harp and Gagan (59) which indicated that participation by rural New York State townships in a federal government renewal plan (adoption of renewal program) was directly related to the amount of accessible information and the presence of an urban setting in the township. In the absence of an urban setting within the township itself, proximity to an external urban setting was also related to participation in renewal.

9.1B. The innovativeness of a target system is inversely related to the degree to which that target system emphasizes extended family norms. Target systems stressing nuclear family norms are more innovative (+ +, 44, 68).

In a study related to human services, Freedman, et al. (44) found that efforts at planned limitation of family size in Taiwan was most likely among nuclear families.

9.1C. The innovativeness of a target system is directly related to the extent to which that target system utilizes the mass media. Target systems that utilize the mass media at the expense of face-to-face communication are generally more innovative (+ + +, 23, 28, 44, 45, 83, 105, 134).

Daxjupta's illustrative study (28) of the use of farm products among Indian farmers revealed that proven innovators (i.e., those who had previously adopted the most improved farm practices) used cosmopolite sources of information whereas late adopters used localite sources. Early adopters were found to use both types.

Another study more closely related to the field of human service was conducted by Freedman, et al. (44). The study demonstrated that married couples in Taiwan who were readers of newspapers were more likely to use birth control than were married couples who did not read papers. The variables related to a modern orientation, such as urban background and high education, were also directly related to the use of population control techniques.

9.1D. When the mass media are conservative (i.e., opposed to certain innovations) contact with the mass media is inversely related to innovativeness (+, 76).

In most of the studies on mass media, researchers have shown that the information obtained from such sources has a liberalizing effect on a target population. These works implicitly assume that mass media sources present a viewpoint favorable to change. One study by Lane (76) demonstrated that the media may have a conservative bias and therefore act as a check on innovation. In this study conducted in Brazil, the conservative national communications media were found to be opposed to certain radical leaders and ideas. Rural Brazilians, who were isolated from this conservatizing influence, were found to be more favorable toward these activist leaders than were urban Brazilians.

9.1E. The innovativeness of a target system is inversely related to the degree of residential stability within that target system. Target systems with higher levels of geographic mobility are more innovative (+ +, 1, 50, 63, 110).

Sociologists have recurrently demonstrated that more modern urban systems (cities are the usual focus of investigation) are characterized by highly mobile populations and that rural areas are more traditional. Raphael (110) found that the strongest predictor of rates of usage of a Chicago children's psychiatric clinic was a high level of population migration within a community. She noted, however, that severity of illness among clinic cases was not related to the level of population migration.

9.1F. The innovativeness of a target system is inversely related to the degree to which its population is homogeneous. Heterogeneous (with respect to political affiliation, income, race and ethnicity, etc.) target populations are more innovative than homogeneous ones (+ + +, 6, 80, 92, 109, 133).

Quite clearly, the heterogeneity of a target population is closely related to population migration, as well as to general factors related to urbanization. As individuals move from one area to another (especially rural to urban), the mixing of demographic characteristics takes place. Homogeneous target systems are generally less innovative because of a consensus as to fixed attitudes and behaviors. Linsky (80) found that the propensity to institutionalize the mentally ill is higher in culturally homogeneous communities, presumably because of a greater consensus as to what constitutes unacceptable or dangerous deviant behavior. It should be noted, however, that once accepted by the elite of a homogeneous target population, an innovation can have rapid diffusion and adoption throughout the general population.

9.1G. The innovativeness of a target system is inversely related to the degree to which that target system relies on folk concepts. Target systems with a high level of scientific knowledge are more innovative (+ + +, 23, 42, 128, 131, 133, 145).

In a study applicable to community development, Foster (42) studied a number of peasant societies in Latin America and Africa, and found that the folk concept of "limited goods" was a significant barrier to the peasants' readiness to take part in individual efforts to improve their own situation. "Limited goods" implied, in the peasant world view, that there were only a limited amount of resources available to any one community.

Other studies, such as Coughenow's (23), have demonstrated the converse idea that target systems with a scientific attitude are more innovative. Coughenow sampled Kentucky farming communities in order to compare their rates of adoption fo five innovative farm practices. The median score on scientific attitude held by the community was found to have a correlation with the rate of adoption.

Action Guidelines: The practitioner desiring rapid or extensive adoption of an innovation should concentrate his efforts on target systems in a modern setting and with more modern orientation. Such a target system will generally possess the following tendencies:

1. an urban character or orientation
2. a nuclear family structure
3. a high level of utilization of mass media (when they are not conservative)
4. a high level of residential mobility
5. a more heterogeneous population
6. a high level of scientific knowledge

In certain situations, these variables may be employed as indices of receptivity to innovation.

In order to increase the innovativeness of a traditional target system, the practitioner could attempt to introduce one or more of the above modern characteristics into it. By and large, the latter must be viewed as a long-term strategy and probably necessitates a societal effort, as exemplified in certain nationally sponsored community-development programs.

Socioeconomic Status

GENERALIZATION 9.2: The innovativeness of a target system is directly related to its socioeconomic status. High-SES target systems are more innovative (+ + + +, 3, 8, 13, 17, 23, 24, 28, 30, 43, 44, 45, 47, 51, 58, 61, 62, 66, 68, 69, 70, 73, 83, 102, 107, 110, 111, 123, 124, 130, 131, 137, 141, 146).

Because socioeconomic statistical indicators are easily obtainable, a large number of researchers have studied the relationship between such indicators and diffusion and adoption behavior. With the exception of the issue of participation in social-movement organizations, the results have been highly consistent: high-SES target systems adopt more innovations than low-SES target systems.

It should be noted that a substantial number of the studies in this research pool dealt with such issues as use of technical novelties and improved farm equipment; and because of the cost of the innovations considered, it is obvious that only high-SES target systems would have resources available to adopt the innovations. Other studies, however, were concerned with innovations that had no or relatively low costs.

Since these studies also confirmed the general proposition, the cost factor bias is not seen as the sole source for the direct relationship between SES and innovativeness. At this junction, it should be noted that the relationship between SES and innovativeness has been well established, so that researchers need not burden themselves further in reiterating this association; if anything, only refinement and exception need be stated. Moreover, practitioners should make more conscious use of this established fact in their intervention plans.

One study in this area was conducted by Dohrenwend and Chin-Song (30). This study revealed a direct relationship between SES and recommendation for outpatient care versus hospitalization for individuals with mental disorders among a sample of New York City residents. Low-SES individuals were less tolerant of deviance. Similarly, Press (107) found that high-SES subjects in Bogota were more likely to use a modern physician than a traditional curer, whereas low-SES subjects showed the opposite tendency.

9.2A. The innovativeness of a target system is directly related to its level of educational attainment. Target systems with high educational attainment are more innovative than those with low educational attainment ($+ + + +$, 3, 8, 23, 24, 30, 44, 45, 62, 83, 102, 110, 111, 123, 124, 130, 137).

Bennett (8) found that earlier (with respect to age) use of birth-control techniques was associated with high educational attainment among a sample of patients at a Tuscon Planned Parenthood Center.

In a study of sample Michigan precincts, Thomas (137) attempted to identify the demographic variables of individuals who were the first to support constitutional revision. Both high education per se and high SES in general were found to be strong predictors of initial support for constitutional revision.

9.2B. The innovativeness of a target system is directly related to its income level. Target systems with a high income level are more innovative than those with a low income level ($+ + + +$, 13, 23, 24, 58, 61, 68, 73, 130, 131, 141, 146).

In a representative study, Kivlin and Fliegel (73), using a sample of Pennsylvania farmers, found that small-scale operators were slower to adopt new farm practices than were medium-size farmers.

9.2C. The direct relationship between wealth and innovativeness is not linear, but curvilinear. Wealthy target systems innovate more than poor target systems, but middle-rank target systems innovate less than would be expected if the relationship were linear (+, 17).

Cancian's (17) graphic presentation of data from seven previous studies concerning the adoption of improved farm practices in developing rural areas, found results corresponding to both of the following graphs:

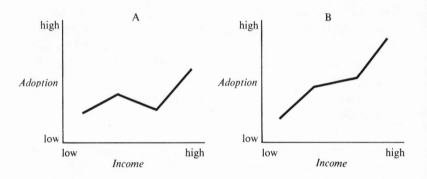

Graph *A* depicts the results found in three studies; Graph *B* represents those from the other four studies. In both cases, the innovativeness of middle-rank target systems was found to be less than would be expected from the assumption of a direct linear relationship between wealth and innovativeness.

9.2D. The innovativeness of a target system is directly related to its levels of occupational status. Target systems with members from high occupational status groups are more innovative than those with members from low occupational status groups (+ + +, 3, 69, 86, 124).

In one study (86) a relationship was found between teenagers' stated use of marijuana and the occupational status of their parents. In another (69), Canadians of higher occupational status were more willing to accept newcomers to the country.

9.2E. The innovativeness of a target system is directly related to majority-group status. Target systems composed of minority-group members are less innovative than are those composed of members of the majority group (+ +, 8, 13, 45, 51, 110).

Goldschneider and Uhlenberg (51) indicate that minority-group status has a separate effect, independent of status, with respect to use of family-planning procedures. Here again, it is important to indicate that the innovations examined in most of these studies dealt with technical equipment and processes, not innovation related to changes in social statuses and definitions.

9.2F. The innovativeness of a high-SES individual may be influenced by the social context in which that individual is functioning. Certain environments may be more conducive to innovation (+, 33, 70).

Kahn (70), in a national sample of college students, found that the direct relationship between SES and student activism was operative only at highly selective (but not necessarily top ranking) institutions. High SES and participation as rank-and-file members of a social-action movement were not compared at less selective institutions. Thus the quality and character of the educational institution itself was strongly associated with student activism.

9.2G. Unrewarded, status-inconsistent target systems (low income, high status) are the most likely participants in radical innovative action (+, 47).

Geschwender (47), through an examination of collective behavior studies, suggests that persons high in ethnicity or education but low in income or occupation evidence the most discontent and are most prone to be receptive to participants in social movements. (See chapter 8 for a more complete treatment of status inconsistency.)

Action Guidelines: The practitioner desiring rapid or extensive adoption of an innovation should concentrate efforts on target systems with high socioeconomic status. The major indices of socio-economic status are: income, education, occupation, majority group membership.

The reader is again reminded, however, that the innovations considered here are by and large of the legitimate, technical, and nonradical type. There is considerable evidence that adoption of radical innovations is not solely related to socioeconomic status but is influenced by such factors as feelings of relative deprivation and status inconsistency.

Past Experience

GENERALIZATION 9.3: The innovativeness of a target system is directly related to previous experience with innovations and inversely related to previous negative experience. Target systems that have previously experienced successful innovations are more innovative than those which have not; target systems that have previously experienced unsuccessful innovations become even less innovative (+ + +, 24, 32, 100, 126, 129).

The basic elements of the generalization can be viewed in terms of learning theory. In simplistic terms, behaviors that are rewarded are learned and repeated again; behaviors that are not rewarded are not so likely to be repeated. The matter of transfer of learning also enters; presumably, innovativeness will be greatest with respect to innovations that are similar to those successfully experienced in the past.

In a study of community development, Sibley (126) compared two rural communities in the Philippines and found that a more modern community was less open to change than a traditional one, because of the former's previous detrimental experience with change and change agents.

In another study concerning more modern target systems, Cowart (24), using a national sample, found that a state's financial participation in the Economic Opportunity Act (EOA) could best be predicted by its previous expenditures for social-welfare programs. States that previously had the highest expenditures for such programs expended the most financial resources in the implementation of the EOA.

Action Guidelines: The practitioner wishing to maximize the adoption of an innovation should approach target systems that have had previous positive experiences with innovations, particularly if these past innovations were similar to the present one. In order to facilitate the eventual adoption of a particular innovation, the practitioner may want to have secondary innovations adopted first in order to make the primary innovation more likely to be adopted. This incremental strategy may be particularly useful in cases where the primary innovation would seem too risky or radical if it were introduced without prior experience. Finally, the practitioner should be cautiously analytical when introducing innovations, in that it may be better to wait for more favorable circumstances than to develop a negative set toward innovation in general as the result of one or more failures in a target system.

Felt Need for Change

GENERALIZATION 9.4: The innovativeness of a target system is directly related to the extent to which it feels a need for change. Discontented target systems generally are more innovative than contented ones (+ + + +, 3, 19, 22, 35, 53, 61, 65, 72, 74, 85, 135, 139).

An innovation involves a change in the status quo. Thus it naturally follows that to adopt an innovation a target system ordinarily would want to change. Oftentimes, a key task of a practitioner is to convince the target system of the need for change. Target systems that are already discontented will be likely to adopt innovations sooner than will target systems that accept the current situation with satisfaction and are not motivated to change. This concept of "felt need" has become institutionalized in the community-development literature. The social-work precept "start where the client is" has a similar connotation.

In a study of agricultural practices, Tulley et al. (139) found that among Australian farmers recognition of a problem and an understanding of its nature and consequences were important in the adoption of effective remedial agricultural measures.

In another study, which is more applicable to human-service organizations, Horner and Knox (61) found that participants in a continuing

education program were significantly more likely to be dissatisfied
with their jobs than were nonparticipants.

9.4A. The use of moderate appeals to fear may increase the innovativeness of a target population (+, 72, 135).

Swinehart (135) found tentative evidence that the use of appeals
to fear may increase rather than decrease an elderly (over 65) person's willingness to receive health messages. Presenting moderate
appeals to fear (in a reassuring context) can enhance learning of
their content.

9.4B. The adoption of innovative actions in social movements is
related to the extent to which the target system casts its discontent in
societal terms—i.e., views its problems as caused by social rather
than personal inadequacy (+, 65, 72).

Jhirad-Reid (65), in a small sample of black Americans, found
that users of conventional social agencies tended to see their problems as being caused by personal inadequacies whereas nonusers
were more likely to see structural and environmental causes. She
found that expressed solutions for the first group were internalized
whereas those of the second group were structure-directed.

Action Guidelines: The practitioner desiring to maximize the
rate of adoption of an innovation should concentrate on
those target systems which are discontented and therefore
more predisposed in favor of change. According to Murray
Ross, discontent should systematically be "focused, chan-
neled, and widely shared in the community." [1] (It may also
be heightened through the use of moderate appeals to fear.)
In order to promote community organization approaches,
the practitioner must understand the social etiology of discontent.

Value Orientation

GENERALIZATION 9.5: The innovativeness of a target system is directly related to its acceptance of supportive value

[1] Murray Ross, *Community Organization: Theory Principles and Practice* (New York:
Harper and Row, 1967).

orientations. These include liberalism, scientism, and non-authoritarianism. Conservative, fatalistic, and authoritarian target systems are less innovative (+ +, 7, 20, 83, 147).

In this context, *liberal* refers to a favorable attitude toward progress or reform and open inquiry; *scientific* refers to a systematic knowledge of the physical world, and having technical skill and proficiency; and *authoritarian* implies favoring the principle of subjection to authority as opposed to that of individual freedom.

Chattopadkyay and Pareek (20), in a sample of Indian farmers, found that the three positive value-orientation dimensions accounted for over half of the variance in the adoption of five improved farm practices.

Action Guidelines: If possible, the practitioner would find it of benefit to measure certain value orientations—such as liberalism, scientism, and nonauthoritarianism of the members of a target system—in order to determine which members will be most innovative, or whether or not the system as a whole will be receptive to innovation. Through adult education or mass media approaches these values might be inculcated in order to prepare a system to be more receptive to innovation.

Social Participation

GENERALIZATION 9.6: The innovativeness of an individual is directly related to his level of social participation. Persons who are active in formal organizations or voluntary associations are more innovative than persons who are not (+ +, 23, 26, 58, 83, 134).

While it may be true that social participation in itself makes an individual more innovative, the practitioner can expect individuals with a high level of social participation to be more innovative. The extent to which a person is socially active may serve as an indicator of potential innovativeness.

In one of the comparatively few studies concerned with the relationship between social participation and innovativeness, Hardee (58) found that linkage of part-time North Carolina farm families with County Extension Education Program agents was associated with higher levels of general social participation and higher economic status. Families who became highly linked with the Extension Agent were characterized both by an initially higher level of SES and social participation and by greater gains on these two variables after a certain point of linkage activity.

Action Guidelines: The practitioner should contact individuals who are active in formal organizations or voluntary associations in order to maximize the rate of adoption of an innovation. In order to make individuals more innovative, the practitioner might encourage and facilitate such mechanisms of social participation. Increased social participation may connect a person with other variables (social skills that can be used to increase business contacts) that may more directly affect innovativeness.

Attributes of the Innovation Proper That Affect the Diffusion and Adoption Process

A target system's receptivity to innovation is not the only factor that determines whether or not an innovation will be adopted. Just as different target systems have characteristics that indicate varying levels of receptivity to innovation, the innovations themselves have characteristics that indicate how well they will be diffused and adopted. In this section, we shall discuss six variables: relative advantage, value compatibility, divisibility, communicability, complexity, and geographical accessibility.

Certain variables among these (i.e., divisibility, complexity, communicability, and geographical accessibility) lean toward being intrinsic variables in that they are to some degree inherent in innovations, and can be analyzed independently from the diffusion process. On the other hand, relative advantage and value compatability are more extrinsic variables, which are generally the result of an interaction between intrinsic innovation characteristics and the characteristics of target populations, and of the diffusion and adoption process. For this reason, the specific actions of the diffusion agent are more immediately salient with regard to these factors. Although this distinction may not always be so clear-cut as is suggested, the main function of this section is to alert the practitioner to variables embedded in the innovation itself that can affect its adoption rate.

Relative Advantage

GENERALIZATION 9.7: The rate of adoption of an innovation is related to people's perception of its advantages relative to other innovations or the status-quo. More advantageous innovations will have a higher adoption rate than less advantageous ones (+ + +, 22, 73, 74, 93, 105, 139, 140).

Relative advantage implies a cognitive-evaluative decision-making process. Thus, what is involved here are advantages as perceived in personal or psychological terms rather than in some absolute material sense. They are usually calculated according to economic profit, but may have other referents, depending on the target system's goals or values.

Coe and Barnhill (22) found that one of the major reasons why an innovative program designed to improve the method of distributing medications in a large urban hospital failed was that the physicians and nursing staff did not feel that the improvements in technical efficiency were sufficient to overcome the disadvantages associated with a loss of familiarity with the previous procedures.

In another study, Polgar et al. (105) found that the high cost and low visibility of a mosquito abatement program were sufficient to thwart efforts aimed at initiating such a program in California.

9.7A. A crisis situation may emphasize the relative advantage of an innovation. The adoption rate of such innovations will be higher during or shortly after a crisis period (+, 93, 140).

During a crisis, the relative advantage of an innovation may be increased primarily because the liabilities of a continuation of the status quo become dramatically apparent.

Whether or not the crisis will result in a higher rate of adoption of an innovation depends on whether or not the crisis diminishes the amount of resources the target system has at its disposal. If resources are diminished, innovations will not be adopted immediately, but rather soon after the crisis subsides. Empirical support derives primarily from a study by Varon (140), which found that there was greater working-class acceptance of intervention by a children's protective agency when the situation was drastic; for example, when children are abandoned in their homes.

Action Guidelines: The practitioner wishing to maximize the adoption rate of an innovation should either behaviorally or psychologically underline the advantage of the particular innovation relative to the status quo or other possible innovations. If a crisis situation occurs, one may use it as leverage for introducing an innovation. If such a situation does not exist, the practitioner may want to create one, if not in reality, at least in the minds of the potential adoptees.

Value Compatibility

GENERALIZATION 9.8: The rate of adoption of an innovation is related to the degree to which it is perceived to be compatible with the existing values of the target system. More compatible innovations will have a higher adoption rate than less compatible innovations (+ + + +, 7, 10, 35, 36, 40, 53, 73, 77, 88, 95, 96, 118, 140).

Compatibility refers to a judgment by the target system and may or may not have any objective reality. Standards by which compatibility is measured include, for example, cultural values, previously accepted practices, and professional standards of conduct.

Emerson, et al. (35) reported a large increase in the use of birth control methods following the birth of a second child, and the attainment of the desired family size.

Another example of this concerns problems often faced by community developers, as reflected in a case study by Fathi (36). This study describes an attempt to introduce movies about innovative public health programs to a particular community—an attempt that met with severe resistance (stoning). A "detached worker" was able to gain acceptance into the community and to receive the approval of the local religious leaders to first show films of a more compatible nature (religious films), and was then later permitted to show the intended films.

9.8A. Professionals are more innovative (than nonprofessionals) with respect to innovations compatible with their professional self-image and values. They are less innovative with respect to incompatible innovations (+ +, 7, 77, 118, 125).

In a national sample of medium-sized cities, Rosenthal and Crain (118) found that when the fluoridation issue (a technical professional matter) was controversial, professional city managers were more likely to support it openly than were nonprofessional city managers.

Baker and Schulberg (7) found that a sample of eastern Massachusetts nonprofessional citizens groups were more accepting of community-mental-health ideology than were professional psychologists and psychiatrists. It would seem that the professionals were hesitant to lend approval because certain ramifications of the adoption of community-mental-health ideology were not consistent with the professionals' norms and their self-interest.

Action Guidelines: With respect to compatibility, the practitioner has three alternatives. First, he can obtain maximum adoption of innovations by introducing only those innovations which are compatible with the existing values of the target system. If the situation is obscure, opinion leaders or elites might be prevailed upon to endorse an innovation, thus legitimating its compatibility with community values. Second, he may work toward the emergence of values within the target system which are compatible with the innovation to be introduced. The third alternative consists of a middle ground between these two. Since the issue of compatibility refers to the target system's perception, the practitioner may be able to interpret an innovation to the target system in a manner consistent with its existing values (sometimes this compatibility may be cloudy or tenuous). A variation here is to introduce that aspect or phase of a divisible innovation most compatible with a given population, leaving less compatible aspects for later introduction if feasible.

Partialization

GENERALIZATION 9.9: The rate of adoption of an innovation may be related to its partialization. Innovations amenable to trial on a partial basis (part of the innovation or part of the target population) will have a higher adoption rate than innovations necessitating total adoption without an anticipatory trial (+ +, 105).

There are at least two factors concerning the partialization of an innovation: the nature of the innovation itself and the proportion of individuals in a target system who are initially involved in adoption. Innovations that can be tried on a partial basis or by a partial segment of a more general target system will be adopted at a higher rate.

Polgar, et al. (105) sampled California farmers and found that mosquito eradication procedures were not adopted because they could not be implemented gradually.

Although only one of the empirical research reports included in our research pool was directly concerned with the issue of the partialization of an innovation, Rogers (116) gives it strong support and offers two related generalizations, which have important implications for the practitioner.

1. The divisibility of an innovation is more important for earlier adopters than it is for later adopters.
2. Early adopters try innovations on a smaller scale than late adopters.

The rationale behind both of these generalizations is that early adopters face a larger risk when adopting an innovation in that they do not have benefit of information concerning suitability or effectiveness of the innovations from previous adopters. Thus they wish to "try out" the innovation with as minimal a risk as possible. Late adopters, on the other hand, have the benefit of the experience of the early adopters and therefore know what to expect.

Action Guidelines: In order to maximize the adoption rate of an innovation, the practitioner should attempt to formulate it in such a way that it can be experienced initially in part or by a limited portion of a target system. The utilization of demonstration projects in communitywide innovations is a frequently used method employing this principle.

Communicability

GENERALIZATION 9.10: The rate of adoption of an innovation is related to its perceived communicability. Innovations which can be explained or demonstrated with ease will have a higher adoption rate than those which are difficult to explain or demonstrate (+ + + +, 11, 29, 38, 41, 62, 67, 74, 95, 104, 105, 106, 122, 144).

Rogers defines communicability as the degree to which aspects of an innovation may be conveyed to others. Communicability is closely related to partialization and complexity.

9.10A. The rate of adoption of an innovation is related to the amount of positive direct contact the target system has with the innovation. Innovations that are successfully experienced by target systems will have a higher adoption rate than innovations that are interpreted to the target system (+ + + +, 16, 29, 38, 62, 67, 104, 106, 112, 122, 144).

Johnson et al. (67) found that positive trial experience teaching illiterates had more favorable impact on future teachers' attitudes concerning the illiterates than did a short-term training program.

Festinger's cognitive dissonance theory seems to be relevant since direct contact is related to behavioral change. According to the theory, a target system's attitudes can be changed by first changing its behavior. Attitude-discrepant behavior results in cognitive dissonance which is then reduced by attitude reorganization. In an empir-

ical study by Feagin (38), the author found support for the dissonance theory with respect to race relations in Dallas. Attitude
change with respect to integration resulted from the gradual desegregation of businesses and schools.

9.10B. The oral transmission of technical information about innovations may result in distortion (+ , 41).

Fliegel and Sekhow (41), in a study of oral transmission of agricultural innovations in India, found that a good deal of distortion
takes place, particularly during early communications between professional change agents and farmers.

9.10C. Innovations communicated to a target system in its native
language will have a higher adoption rate than innovations communicated in a foreign tongue because of the higher communicability of the former diffusion (+, 11).

In a relevant study, Blanco and Akabas (11) investigated the
health and emotional problems of a sample of factory workers. Although no control group was used, the authors state that offers of
services in response to an original information-gathering questionnaire had a high rate of acceptance because these offers were written
in the language in which the subjects completed the original questionnaire.

9.10D. Innovations may be effectively diffused through subcultural
communication networks (+, 95).

O'Donnell and Jones (95) found that involvement in a drug subculture facilitated the spread of intravenous administration of heroin
by providing the specific channels of communication, the social
structure, and the system of values supportive of the I.V. technique.

Action Guidelines: In order to maximize the adoption rate of
an innovation, the practitioner should try to make it as easy
as possible to explain or demonstrate. This can be facilitated
by enabling the target system to have direct contact with the
innovation, since the oral transmission of knowledge is often
subject to much distortion. Oral communication should be
supplemented by visual aids or experiential exposure if
possible, or with feedback interactions to check grasp and
interpretation of information inputs.

In addition, if the practitioner can induce the target system toward innovative behavior, attitudinal changes in the direction of the behavioral change may result. The language of the communication message is also quite obviously related to its communicability. Generally, the closer the communication to the target's language or vernacular, the better. Similarly, a subculture may facilitate the communication of information about an innovation when the innovation and communication are compatible with the values of that subculture. Thus, the practitioner should attempt to reach a subculture, through its own communication channels (i.e., former addicts or indigenous structures such as Synanon).

Geographical Accessibility

GENERALIZATION 9.11: The rate of adoption of an innovation is related to the geographical accessibility of the innovation to the target system. Innovations that are highly accessible to the target system will have a higher adoption rate than innovations that are not (+ +, 35, 64, 96).

Two of the studies related to this proposition deal with birth control. In the first, Jaffe (64) based his findings on a national sample of family-planning services. He concluded that the single most important factor facilitating acceptance of family planning is the establishment of free subsidized services, which are geographically accessible to the population in need. In the second study, Emerson et al. (35), discuss one example of the way in which geographical accessibility can be achieved. In this case, the integration of birth-control methods with maternity care was successful. A high percentage of women were induced to use birth-control techniques when services were offered in a hospital where they were already receiving maternal care.

9.11A. Geographical accessibility of the target system to an innovation can be increased by diffusing information about the innovation in social environments in which the target system functions (+, 11, 89).

This points to the advantages "outreach" programs can have on the adoption rate of innovations. Surprisingly, only one study in the research pool was concerned with this approach. In it, Blanco and Akabas (11) stress the importance of conducting surveys and distributing to workers within a factory letters offering services to them. We can make no comparisons with the effectiveness of other approaches, however, because of the lack of any control groups in this study.

Another study, by Monk et al. (89), demonstrates that when an innovation is not diffused in a social environment in which the related behavior takes place, adoption will be low. The authors analyzed the ineffectiveness of an antismoking campaign conducted in a high school. One factor contributing to this failure was that students who smoked the most were also the most difficult to reach through normal school activities. Heavy smokers were generally the least involved in normal school activities.

Action Guidelines: The practitioner should be aware that innovations must be made accessible to the target systems for which they are designed, or they will not be used. One method of at least communicating the existence of an innovative service is to approach the target system in the social environment (work, religion, voluntary association) in which it functions. Thus, the information can be brought to the target system rather than waiting for the system to discover the innovation on its own before it initiates contact with the diffusion agency. When the innovation is related to a particular behavior, it should be diffused in the social setting in which that behavior most frequently takes place.

Complexity

GENERALIZATION 9.12: The rate of adoption of an innovation is inversely related to its degree of perceived complexity. Less complex innovations will have a higher adoption rate than highly complex ones [2] (+ + +, 116).

[2] This proposition was taken directly from Rogers's work and although it was not verified by any empirical research reviewed by the project, it is offered here because of its importance and applicability to the current discussion.

Complexity is defined by Rogers (116) as "the degree to which an innovation is relatively difficult to understand and use." Once again it is not the objective complexity of an innovation alone that determines its diffusibility but rather the amount of complexity as perceived by the target system.

Action Guidelines: In order to maximize the adoption rate of an innovation, the practitioner should formulate the innovation at a level of complexity which can be accommodated by a target system. Since the issue of complexity must be viewed in the framework of the system's perception, complexity is closely related to communicability. As much as possible, the practitioner should explain the innovation in simple or familiar terms. A less than complete explanation of the nature of an innovation but conveying its essential character may enhance its adoption rate more than a complete description, particularly when the complete description is highly complex.

Attributes of the Diffusion and Adoption Process

Having scrutinized variables related to both target system and innovation, we shall now turn our attention to the even more complex process by which innovations are diffused and adopted. Diffusion occurs among population groups or systems while adoption is often an individual action of persons or social units. Although it is conceptually useful to make a distinction between these two concepts, this section will deal with both elements of the process in a unitary way.

In this discussion a wide rage of variables will be considered. The fact that there are fewer studies per proposition in this section than the first two reflects a bias toward obtaining demographic variables (SES, age, sex) as contrasted with less tangible variables such as opinion leadership and peer support. Finally, we should indicate that the variables of traditionalism and compatibility appear again in the upcoming set of generalizations. Such a recurrence seems to reflect mutual interrelationships between target systems norms, innovation characteristics, and the diffusion and adoption process.

Compatibility of the Diffusion Process

GENERALIZATION 9.13: The rate of adoption of an innovation is directly related to the extent to which it is diffused in a manner compatible with the target system's norms, values, and customs. Innovations with a compatible diffusion process will have a higher adoption rate than innovations with an incompatible diffusion process (+ + + +, 18, 36, 37, 49, 75, 89, 110, 117, 120, 126, 127, 128, 131, 144, 148, 149).

Although this is similar to Generalization 9.8, which relates the perceived value compatibility of an innovation to its adoption rate, the reader's attention is directed to the difference between the compatibility of the innovation per se and the compatibility of the process by which it is diffused, vis-à-vis a target population.

Evidence in support of the importance of a compatible diffusion process is aptly demonstrated in a research investigation concerning community development (143). The author discusses the failure of a community development program in the Philippines with respect to the structure and operations of the local Maranao community or *agana*. According to the analysis, the government would have been more effective in its community development program if, instead of working through the municipality and the barrio, it had used traditional authority systems and social control mechanisms of the *agana* level of organization.

9.13A. The rate of adoption of an innovation is related to the extent to which it is diffused in a manner compatible with the target system's power structure. Innovations that are diffused with the cooperation of the target system's power structure generally have a higher adoption rate than innovations that are not (+ + +, 36, 48, 49, 117, 126, 127, 143).

In the previously discussed study of efforts to introduce public-health movies in a rural Mideastern community by Fathi (36), the cooperation of the local religious leaders was found to be critical.

In another study, Goldberg (48) identifies two types of power structures (open and closed) in developing countries and discusses the implications of both types for gaining legitimacy.

9.13B. Target systems with a traditional orientation are more likely to use informal, personal sources of information. The rate of adoption of an innovation in such a setting is directly related to the extent to which the innovation is diffused through those channels (+, 75, 110).

A study by Kurtz (75) focuses on channels of information used in problem solving by persons with Spanish surnames in Denver. Kurtz studied the way in which information circulated among this traditional urban-dwelling minority group. Using the criteria of reputation, nomination techniques, and interviews, Kurtz identified a number of "gate-keepers." The study showed that these individuals used informal channels to link individuals who had problems to the urban resources available to meet those problems.

9.13C. In traditional lower-class target systems, cultural norms may inhibit communication between relevant members of a target system and thereby inhibit the rate of adoption of certain innovations (+ +, 98, 131, 149).

Empirical evidence in support of this proposition comes directly from a study by Yaukey, et al. (149) concerning attitudes toward birth control in East Pakistan (Bangladesh). Their thesis was that in the traditional context of East Pakistan, the family structure is highly segregated, and the communication between husband and wife is therefore very limited. The authors found that a significant portion of the high degree of concurrence between the spouses concerning the desired family size could be attributed to similar life conditions rather than as a result of explicit discussion. Only about one-fourth of the husbands and wives indicated that they based their estimates on communication with their spouses.

Action Guidelines: Guidelines concerning the value compatibility of the diffusion process are similar to the earlier set dealing with the value compatibility of the innovation itself. The practitioner can either diffuse innovations in a manner compatible with existing norms, values, and customs, or attempt to change these values. The latter constitutes a formidable undertaking.

Communication Media Used by Different Categories of Adopters

GENERALIZATION 9.14: Different modes of communication are used by different adopters. Relatively early adopters of innovations tend to use mass media information sources whereas later adopters tend to use face-to-face information sources. The rate of adoption of an innovation is related to the degree to which information is passed through the appropriate communication mode (+ + +, 3, 28, 64, 75, 89, 113, 121).

In a sample of farmers in India, Daxjupta (28) found that those who were innovators (on the basis of previous adoptions of improved farm practices), used institutionalized sources of information whereas late adopters relied more on noninstitutionalized sources.

Another study by Aldrich (3) examined participation in a petition drive on the issue of daylight saving time. He found that mass media communications were sufficient to secure participation in the drive by many individuals. Later supporters of this action, however, were best reached through personal contacts with the early adopters.

9.14A. Utilization of communication modes is related to the target system's SES. High-SES populations use mass-media information sources whereas low-SES target systems use face-to-face sources (+ +, 75, 113, 121).

This proposition also suggests a correlation between early adoption and higher SES. Sawhney (121) sampled farming families in India, and found that users of cosmopolite information sources tended to be younger, more highly educated, owners of larger farms with more income, and more active in formal organizations than were users of localite information sources.

Kurtz's study (75) of Spanish-surnamed individuals in Denver lends indirect evidence to this subproposition. This traditional minority group used face-to-face communication to obtain information regarding urban problems.

9.14B. Socioeconomic status is related to the number of communication modes used as information sources. High-SES populations use more sources of information than low-SES populations (+, 113).

Rieger and Anderson (113), in a sample of Michigan residents, found a direct relationship between education and 1) the number of information sources used, and 2) the use of educational facilities as an information source. Age was inversely correlated with the two dependent variables.

In addition, there are four generalizations from Rogers that are related to the issue of communication modes:

1. Impersonal (mass) information sources are most important at the awareness stage, and personal sources are most important at the evaluation stage in the adoption process.
2. Cosmopolite information sources are most important at the awareness stage, and localite information sources are most important at the evaluation stage.
3. Earlier adopters utilize information sources that are in closer contact with the origin of ideas than later adopters.
4. Earlier adopters utilize a greater number of different information sources than later adopters.

Action Guidelines: The practitioner should gauge the type of information source he wishes to employ to the type of target system he wishes to contact and to the purposes for which the diffusion of information is intended. Utilization of a mass-media information source can be expected to result in a limited general awareness of the innovation by the target system as a whole and in some trial of the innovation by innovators and other early adopters. Face-to-face communications are more important for later adopters, particularly at the evaluation stage. Upper-class populations can be readily reached through mass media as well as through multiple communications. In order to reach lower-class populations, the practitioner should use more limited, intense, focalized communications, which have a face-to-face character.

Peer Support

GENERALIZATION 9.15: The rate of adoption of an innovation is related to the extent to which the target system receives peer support in favor of adoption. Innovations that are supported by the peers of a target system will have a higher adoption rate (+ + + +, 1, 16, 23, 25, 34, 39, 43, 61, 74, 78, 79, 86, 94, 103, 134, 146).

Social psychologists have long known that an individual changes his attitudes or resists change not only on the basis of his own psychological characteristics, but also because of the social influence of his peers. Similar effects can also be shown for target systems of more complex social organization.

Frank and Schonfield (43), in a sample of individuals active in peace work, found that persons who received support for their activities from family and friends were more likely to continue or increase their efforts. Shifts in friendship patterns occurred for persons who continued but did not receive support from their original friends.

9.15A. The rate of adoption of an innovation is directly related to the extent to which members of the target system discuss the innovation with other members. Target systems that discuss an innovation will have a higher rate of adoption (+, 23, 79, 134).

Individuals who are more open to new information are more likely to be willing to change. In addition, mutual exchange of information is likely to result in a clearer understanding or appreciation of the innovation by target-system members. It should be noted, however, that discussion per se is not enough; informed discussion prompts a higher innovation-adoption rate.

Evidence in support of this position comes from research by Suchman (134), who found that the frequency of use of an accident-preventing glove among Puerto Rican sugar-cane workers was directly related to discussion with other workers about the glove.

9.15B. The rate of adoption of an innovation is facilitated by a consensus of goals among peers within the target system (when the innovation is compatible with these goals) (+, 146).

Wilkening and Guerrero (146) found that in Wisconsin farm families, consensus between a husband and wife on high aspirations for the farm was associated with a higher adoption rate of improved farm practices than when only one spouse had high aspirations for farm improvement.

9.15C. People with certain characteristics tend to seek personal advice from persons with similar characteristics (+, 78).

Liberman (78) studied the influences bringing about a decision to enter a state mental hospital in Baltimore. He found significant in-group flow of influence with respect to sex, religion, and socioeconomic status (males influenced males, females, females; Catholics, Catholics; Jews, Jews; upper-SES, upper and lower-, lower). A high degree of consensus between those influenced and those influencing them was also noted with respect to their attitudes regarding community mental health facilities. Out-group influence patterns were older to younger and upper-SES to lower (when influences crossed SES boundaries).

Rogers proposed a number of generalizations relevant to the issue of peer influence and not covered by our pool of studies:

1. Personal influence from peers is most important at the evaluation stage in the adoption process and less important at other stages.
2. Personal influence from peers is more important for relatively late adopters than for earlier adopters.
3. Personal influence from peers is more important in uncertain situations than in clear-cut situations.
4. Each adopter category is mainly influenced by individuals of the same or a (slightly) more innovative adopter category.

Action Guidelines: The practitioner should attempt to gain peer support around a target individual or group he wishes to influence toward adoption of an innovation. When such a peer group appears favorable or when the innovation is clearly advantageous, the practitioner should encourage peer discussion. Arriving at a peer consensus regarding the innovation and making it publicly explicit will speed adoption. Persons should be encouraged to seek advice from others with similar characteristics, when those others are likely to be supportive. Alternatively, the practitioner might seek out a segment of such influential peers and urge them to advocate the innovation with the target population. The practitioner should especially emphasize personal peer influence at the evaluation stage of adoption with relatively late adopters or when the situation is unclear with early adopters.

Opinion Leaders

GENERALIZATION 9.16: Certain individuals of a target system are more influential in expediting the diffusion and adoption process. The rate of adoption of an innovation is directly related to the extent to which these "opinion leaders" promote it (+ + + +, 4, 36, 63, 75, 81, 105, 110, 118, 127, 132).

As defined at the beginning of this chapter, opinion leaders are those individuals who are influential in the approving or disapproving of new ideas; in that, they are those persons from whom others seek advice. Opinion leaders are not necessarily innovators, although with respect to their followers they generally tend to be more innovative. Rather than comprising a single adoption category, opinion leaders are usually present in every adopter category, and persons from a particular adoption category usually choose opinion leaders from a similar adoption category or one slightly higher. Individuals in an adopter category far removed from a particular individual are often considered too deviant or distant from the individual's own norms to be considered a valid source of knowledge and influence. Opinion leaders *within* a given adopter category may be early adopters within that category. (Additional discussion of opinion leaders is found in chapter 3 under Linking Roles.)

9.16A. Opinion leaders and innovators are usually different individuals. Although opinion leaders are more innovative than their followers, they are not necessarily innovators (+, 81).

Rogers (116) indicates that each adopter category is influenced mainly by individuals of the same or slightly more innovative adopter categories. "Innovators" are among the most radical adopter category, and thus, their influence is relatively limited. Late adopters and laggards, for example, might consider innovators to be deviants, and would not consider them to be opinion leaders.

Lionberger and De Francis (81) studied a southern Missouri community, and found that farmers almost always considered opinion leaders and innovators to be discrete sets of individuals. When seeking advice, farmers did not usually approach those who had first adopted a particular innovation but instead others whose advice they respected.

9.16B. Opinion leaders have more education than their followers. They tend to use sources of information that are more impersonal, cosmopolite, and technical than their followers (+ +, 4, 63, 105, 132).

Jacobs (63) found that key communicators (opinion leaders) in urban Thailand were more educated and exposed to more mass society (cosmopolite) than were their followers.

In the Polgar, et al. study (105), farmers in California were asked whom they consulted concerning improved farm practices. The persons named by farmers as advisors had, in aggregate, a significantly higher level of education, formal participation, and cooperation with government agencies than did the total group of families.

Although the concept of opinion leadership has been the subject of considerable empirical investigation, few of the innovation studies reviewed in this project focused on this topic. In order to supplement these, we present the following series of generalizations about opinion leadership taken from Rogers (116). We shall also summarize at this time Rogers's generalizations concerning early adopters.

Opinion Leaders:
1. Opinion leaders conform more to social-system norms than do the average members of a community.
2. There is little overlapping among the different types of opinion leaders. (The area of expertise of an opinion leader is usually limited to a small number of issues.)
3. Opinion leaders are slightly higher in social status and social

position, and more cosmopolite and innovative than their followers.

Early Adopters:

1. Earlier adopters have more specialized operations (i.e., concentration on fewer different enterprises) than later adopters.
   Adoption agencies (as compared to public welfare agencies,
   for example) would have more specialized operations.
2. Earlier adopters have a type of mental ability different from
   that of late adopters. (Rogers does not define the concept of
   "mental ability," but indicates that because early adopters
   must be able to adopt or synthesize a new idea largely from
   mass-media sources of information and not from the example
   of others, there is an implicit difference.)
3. Earlier adopters are more cosmopolite than later adopters.
4. Earlier adopters have more opinion leadership than later adopters.
5. Relatively late adopters are more likely to discontinue innovations than are earlier adopters.
6. Other members of the social system often perceive innovators
   as deviants. (On the other hand, opinion leaders, by definition
   are almost never considered deviants.)

Action Guidelines: In order to maximize personal influence
in favor of an innovation, the practitioner should identify the
target system's opinion leaders with respect to the *relevant
issue area* and enlist their support in favor of adoption. One
can usually best identify opinion leaders by asking people to
whom they go for advice and information about an idea.
Since opinion leaders use more mass-media sources of information than do their followers, opinion leaders can
usually be reached through this type of communication.
Opinion leaders are not necessarily individuals with a history
of being innovative. If, however, for a given issue or program
they can be motivated either to innovate or encourage
others to innovate, their influence on the adoption process
can be significant. Opinion leaders can be reached somewhat more readily through mass media and technical modes
of communication. They can be located among the some-

what better-educated, more cosmopolitan, higher-social-status segments of a larger population. They will likely have higher rates of social participation.

The practitioner can expect target systems that deal in specialized (nonroutine) products and services to be more innovative. For maximum efficiency, he should introduce innovation among these target systems.

The practitioner can also expect later adopters to discontinue innovations at a higher rate and so may want to work closely with such persons in order to minimize this problem.

Innovators may not be effective sources of influence on other members of a target system; they may be considered deviants by the community. Opinion leaders should be utilized, especially if they are also early adopters.

The Innovation Message

GENERALIZATION 9.17: Generally, innovations communicated with a clear and unambiguous message are more likely to be adopted than those subject to unclear and confusing interpretations (+ +, 18, 21, 91, 97).

Mueller (91), in a sample of Los Angeles County residents, found that subjects given a partially positive professional argument in favor of fluoridation were less favorable toward the innovation than a control group receiving no arguments.

Carmack (18), in a case study of a citizens' committee in Dallas, found that the committee was able to facilitate desegregation by presenting the general community with a "united front" of favorable opinion held by influential individuals.

Chetkow (21) found that members of a Community Services Council in Indianapolis were more apt to use a novel priority plan when it contained minimal vagueness and imprecision.

Action Guidelines: Whenever possible, the practitioner should endeavor to present a clear, unified, and unambiguous communication in favor of an innovation.

The Process of Diffusion and Adoption

Once again there are a number of issues concerning the diffusion process that were not touched upon by our pool of studies, but which are of importance to the community-organization practitioner. Therefore, the following observations are stated as they appear in Rogers's work:

1. Awareness occurs at a more rapid rate than does adoption.
2. The first individuals to adopt innovations require a shorter adoption period than do later adopters.
3. The awareness-to-trial period is longer than the trial-to-adoption period.
4. The awareness-to-trial period is shorter for relatively earlier adopters than for later adopters.
5. The trial-to-adoption period is longer for relatively earlier adopters than for later adopters.
6. Commercial change agents are more important at the trial stage than at any other stage in the adoption process.
7. Change agents have more communication with higher-status than with lower-status members of a social system.

Action Guidelines: The practitioners should be aware of time differences between adoption stages, and particularly that existing between adopter categories, so that results can be maximized. Specifically, one can expect early adopters to try out a new innovation soon after they become aware of it, but to take longer after trial to adopt it. With such target systems, the practitioner should concentrate on the trial-to-adoption stage in order to maximize the adoption rate. With later adopters, the practitioners should exert more effort during the awareness-to-trial stage, since a trial is more difficult to implement with such target systems.

In the next section, we shall concentrate on a particular target system, the organization. We shall present generalizations that emphasize the relationship between various structural and functional variables, and the innovativeness of an organization. The reader should remember that the generalizations presented in this first section may be applicable to all types of target systems. Thus, what follows may be considered as a supplement to or special case of the above material.

INNOVATION IN ORGANIZATIONS

General Introduction and Overview

We shall emphasize the organization here because community practice is intrinsically organizational in nature. It is difficult, if not impossible to conceive of a community organizer who is not intimately involved with organizations in the course of his work. Given this fact and the change orientation of community practice mentioned earlier, the importance to the practitioner of principles relating to organizational innovation becomes obvious.

The following section includes generalizations that relate a number of structural and functional variables to organizational innovativeness. Although a wide range of research has been utilized to formulate these propositions, the work of Hage and Aiken is of particular importance. In addition to the research articles developed from their data on sixteen social welfare and health agencies (2, 55, 54), their book (56), which includes research data in addition to their own, was of great assistance in the development of the section that follows.

See chapters 4 and 5 for further discussion.

Professional Factors

Professional Staff Structure

GENERALIZATION 9.18: The adoption rate of innovations in organizations is directly related to various structural aspects of the organization's professional staff complement. Organizations with professional staff structures are more innovative than organizations without these structures (+ + +, 2, 9, 15, 27, 46, 54, 55, 56, 90, 99, 100).

In this context, *innovation* refers to programmatic and technical changes compatible with professional norms. Earlier in this chapter, we briefly discussed the high degree of innovativeness of professionals toward innovations compatible with their professional norms (see Subgeneralization 9.8B), but the concept deserves further elaboration at this point. A number of authors, including Mohr (87), have pointed out that by being innovative professionals accomplish one of the basic missions of their role: they further their knowledge by learning from new experiences through participation in innnovative activities.

Innovativeness may be viewed as a tool designed to enhance the professional's status, self-image, and prestige. However, in order to enhance the professional's status, an innovation must be consistent with his professional norms. Characteristically, professionals are not innovative with respect to the radical change inherent in social-action strategies in the field of community organization. This tendency is extenuated as the professional in an organizational setting moves up the organizational hierarchy and thereby becomes more closely identified with the goals and controlling elites of that organization (see chapter 3).

It is also possible that innovations motivated by concern for professional status rather than client service may be neutral or detrimental relative to the needs of clients. Although one should not conclude that such innovations are necessarily frivolous, it remains uncertain whether value choices that advance a professional group also advance the interests of clients. Professionally tinged innovation is sometimes at the root of profound progress while at other times it squanders resources. This is not to say that all innovations are adopted to further professional status interests. Undoubtedly, many professionals place the needs of their clients first and strain to create new approaches in the clients' best interests.

Diversity of Professional Staff

9.18A. The adoption of innovations by organizations is directly related to the degree of diversity of its professional staff specialities (+ +, 2, 9, 54, 55, 56).

Hage and Aiken (56) hypothesize that a greater range of different professions results in more diverse employee perspectives and values. Innovation is fostered by multiple inputs from varied sources. By attempting to demonstrate the need for its own programs, each profession will produce interactive tension encouraging the process of seeking new ways to improve organizational performance.

In an empirical test (2, 54, 55) of this hypothesis, the authors found a positive correlation between the number of occupational specialities and program change during a five-year history of sixteen social welfare and health agencies within a large Midwestern metropolitan community. Program change was operationalized simply by the number of new programs added to the organization. No differentiation between the traditionalism or nontraditionalism of these new programs was made. Any new program was considered an innovation. This approach to the adoption of innovation may account for at least some of the differences between the results found by Hage and Aiken and those of other researchers such as Mohr (87), who defined innovation in terms of new nontraditional programs.

Friedson and Rhea (46) suggest some qualifications to this subgeneralization with their finding that very little communication flows between parallel specialities in a hospital setting. This suggests the need for internal communication networks between the different specialities in order to promote an exchange of ideas.

9.18B. The adoption rate of innovations in an organization is directly related to the number of extraorganizational professional linkage interactions engaged in by its employees (+ +, 54, 55, 56, 90).

Hage and Aiken (56) theorize that extraorganizational professional linkages provide a means for employees to learn of new developments in their respective fields. Organizational innovation will result as these developments are made known to and adopted by the decision-making hierarchy. The authors' study of social-welfare and health agencies (54, 55) revealed a positive correlation between three measures of the amount of extraorganizational professional activity of employees and the rate of program change.

A study of the results of consciously planned attempts in seven American communities to develop services for the elderly, conducted by Morris and Randall (90), supplies additional support for this subproposition from a somewhat different point of view. This study demonstrated that the professional community organizer who worked from an external position and linked up with a number of social-welfare agencies in a community was the most effective in stimulating new programs for the elderly. Although this study involves an outside professional practitioner linking up with organizations, instead of the converse, the same general implications can be drawn.

9.18C. The adoption rate of innovations in organizations is related to the length of professional training required of the organization's employees (+, 54, 55, 56).

Hage and Aiken (56) believe that an emphasis on professional training is roughly equal to an emphasis on the acquisition of knowledge: an employee's concern with keeping abreast of developments in his field. Thus, the adoption of professionally compatible innovations is facilitated through the mechanisms described earlier in subgeneralization 18A. However, since the amount of professional training here refers to job requirements and not continued intellectual activity, it is not surprising that the authors (54, 55) found only a slightly positive correlation between length of professional training and rate of program change.

9.18D. The adoption rate of innovations in organizations is directly related to the number of professionals employed by the organization (+, 27, 100).

The number of professionals is a crude indicator of the presence of the professional staff structure mentioned earlier. Pappenfort and Kilpatrick (100) offer support in their study of private agencies in Chicago that provide group work services to children and youth. They found that agencies with a high number of professional employees were more likely to have special programs for handicapped children than were similar agencies with fewer professionals.

A study by Daniels (27) of psychiatrists in the military also lends support here. She demonstrates how organizational norms will predominate when there is limited professional presence, leading to isolation and constraint by the organization. In her study, Daniels indicates how the military psychiatrist remains primarily an evaluator and referral agent rather than a therapist, because the position separates him from other professionals and imposes strict organizational norms.

9.18E. Certain professionals function as opinion leaders for other employees within an organization. Innovation may hypothetically be facilitated by gaining the support of these opinion leaders (+, 4, 125).

Scott (125), in an analysis of a public-welfare agency located in an urban setting, found that agency workers preferred professional qualities in supervisors to bureaucratic ones. This attitude was manifested particularly among professionally trained agency workers. A large majority of workers under professionally oriented supervisors selected supervisors as their primary source of professional stimulation.

9.18F. Paraprofessionals represent a potentially important source of organizational innovation, particularly with respect to making organizations more responsive to the needs of lower-income populations (+ , 15). (This area is discussed more fully in chapter 5.)

In a detailed exploration of three New York City Mobilization for Youth Programs, Brager (15) indicates that this concept holds despite the fact that the use of indigenous persons in program roles tends to be challenged by existing institutions. The author indicates that nonprofessionals function best when given a considerable measure of autonomy, responsibility, and freedom to sustain their own identity. Brager found that their effectiveness in activizing the MYF program and in recruiting large numbers of previously unreached low-income persons resulted from a lack of felt social distance between the nonprofessionals and clients. Offsetting this effectiveness, however, was their relative inability to pressure the conventional social agencies to move in a more responsive and activist direction, because of the low legitimacy such organizations accorded them.

Action Guidelines: In order to increase the potential innovativeness of an organization (innovations compatible with professional norms), the pracitioner should do one or more of the following:

1. Increase the number of occupational specialities within the organization.
2. Encourage and facilitate staff participation in extraorganizational professional activities.
3. Increase the amount of formal and informal training required of employees.
4. Hire more professionals.
5. Encourage external professional inputs.

6. Employ supervisors who are professionally stimulating.

The practitioner who is external to an organizational setting, and who wishes to introduce professionally compatible innovation in as little time as possible, should seek out those organizations which display the above characteristics. One might also inject more external professional influences, thereby "opening up" the agency from the outside.

In order to increase the accountability of an organization to its client population (a possible source of innovation), the practitioner should urge the employment of indigenous paraprofessionals. These people should not be highly "professionalized," but should be accorded role legitimacy within the employing organization and other organizations as well.

Structural Factors

Formalization

GENERALIZATION 9.19: The innovativeness of an organization is inversely related to the organization's degree of formalization. Organizations with many specific, strictly enforced rules are less innovative than organizations which have few rules and allow discretion in employee functioning (+ + +, 15, 54, 55, 56, 90, 99).

Hage and Aiken (56) indicate that *formalization* refers to the degree of codification of jobs in an organization. It is best measured by the number of written rules specifying what is to be done, although informal rules or customs may also be important. Also to be considered is the degree to which the rules are enforced, either by formal or informal sanctions.

The authors theorize that high formalization is detrimental to innovativeness for a number of reasons. First, a highly formalized job provides the worker little latitude for considering alternative procedures or practices. Second, the existence of rules is based on the assumption that the rule represents the best way to handle a particular situation; there is little incentive to search for new methods. Finally, the existence of rules is a significant obstacle to the implementation of new programs in that new programs will necessitate changes in rules, thus disturbing the existing network of procedural operations in the organization.

In other studies (54, 55) it was found that a measure of the sheer number of regulations was significantly and negatively correlated with program change.

Palumbo (99), in a study of fourteen large public-health departments, revealed that departments high in role specification tended to be more formalized and have less innovation. Factors directly connected with role specification were centralization, specialization, and costs. Morale, professionalism, productivity, and participatory management were inversely correlated with role specification.

Action Guidelines: To increase the innovativeness of an organization, the practitioner should decrease the number of written regulations that must be followed or the sanctions that are to be applied if the rules are not followed. The practitioner desiring organizational adoption of innovations should seek out those organizations which are low in formalization.

Centralization

GENERALIZATION 9.20: Usually, the innovativeness of an organization is inversely related to its degree of centralization. Highly centralized organizations are usually less innovative than decentralized organizations, provided that the chief executives of the organization are not initially predisposed in favor of innovation (+ + +, 2, 9, 54, 55, 56, 90, 99, 114, 136).

Centralization refers to the proportion of organizational positions and occupations whose occupants participate in the decision-making process, as well as the proportion of decision-making areas in which they are involved. *High centralization* means that only a few positions located at the top participate in the decision-making process.

Hage and Aiken (56) theorize that high centralization is detrimental to innovation in several ways. First, it has been widely observed that individuals in power often act to maintain or enhance that power. Thus, innovativeness may represent a threat to the existing power definitions and for that reason may be vetoed. A related point here is that a centralized decision maker may have a psychological stake in the policies and practices he has formulated and may therefore be personally resistant to modifications. Second, a centralized decision-making structure presupposes that only a few individuals will consider innovations, and thus fewer different perspectives will be involved. Third, high centralization usually leaves open only a few channels of communication for members on the lower levels to reach the elites at the top. Uusally, these lines of communication are through established channels and over various echelons, which means that there are a number of opportunities for the ideas to be vetoed or to be set aside as they rise through the administrative hierarchy.

In a test of their hypotheses, Hage and Aiken (2, 54, 55) found that decentralization, as measured by the degree of employee participation in four areas of decision making, was significantly and positively correlated with the rate of program change.

In another study, Bernard et al. (9) provide evidence regarding the relationship between decentralization and organizational innovativeness in a case study of the Neighborhood Service Organization in Detroit. In this particular agency, a decentralized administration (together with other factors) was seen as conducive to innovation.

Finally, in another more empirical investigation, Palumbo (104) surveyed fourteen large public health departments, and found centralized organizations to be less innovative.

In order to understand the effects of centralization on the innovativeness of an organization, the reader should consider the effect of the attitudes of a chief executive on the innovativeness of an organization. Research evidence indicates support of the following propositions:

9.20A. The innovativeness of an organization may be facilitated by the presence of a chief executive who is in favor of innovation. Organizations that have an innovative chief executive are likely to adopt more innovations than are organizations that do not (+, 31, 82, 87, 118).

The attitudes of the chief executive have both a direct and an indirect facilitating effect on organizational innovation. A chief executive, particularly in a highly centralized organization, may expedite innovation simply by edict or fiat. For example, one study reports success in introducing new police practices by working down through the chain of command (3). Indirectly, a chief executive can facilitate innovations by creating an organizational climate receptive to innovation. A middle level of facilitation by a chief executive is also possible; e.g., by establishing research subunits within an organization.

Mohr (87) has conducted a thoroughly documented investigation of the importance of attitudes of a chief executive on the innovativeness of an organization, through interviews with local health officers (chief executives) from 93 health departments in the United States and Canada. Mohr analyzed their public-health ideology and inclination toward activism with respect to 26 kinds of medical and health-care programs.

A simple variable combining these two attitudinal measures—the total number of personnel added in all nontraditional program areas during a specific five-year period—was found to be moderately connected with "progressive programming." A smaller subsample of the local health offices revealed that activist ideology was moderately correlated with the total number of nontraditional programs adopted within the same five-year period. Thus, the executives' attitude toward change was important in the actual implementation of change. There is also some indication that a chief executive sometimes may be more willing to innovate than are subordinates.

9.20B. A person of higher social position in an organization loses less esteem than a subordinate if he successfully deviates from organizational norms, but he loses more esteem if the deviation has an unsuccessful outcome (+, 5, 136).

The chief executive has prestige, power, and a position that conveys dedication to the goals and well-being of the organization. He is able to deviate from established norms and definitions without subjecting his loyalty to question.

This conclusion is based primarily on Alvarez's (5) study of informal reactions to deviance in simulated work organizations. This laboratory experiment involved sixteen work groups (organizations), each of which included a research confederate and nine subjects. Each group was assigned the task of generating creative ideas for the manufacture of greeting cards. The hierarchical status of the deviating confederate and a feedback communication indicating each group's success or failure were experimentally controlled. The results of the experiment were consistent with the above generalization, with esteem measured from the evaluations by the subjects of the confederate. Various studies in small-group research are consistent with this discussion.

9.20C. The attitudes of the staff concerning innovation are not necessarily associated with the innovativeness of an organization (+ +, 54, 55, 56).

The investigation of sixteen human-services organizations conducted by Hage and Aiken (54, 55, 56) is the source of this somewhat surprising supposition. The authors found that neither pro nor antichange orientations on the part of agency staff members were related to program change. Other structural factors were more important.

This series of generalizations suggests that the attitudes of the chief executive of an organization are critical to the innovativeness of an organization, whereas the attitudes of the staff may not be. Executives are much less likely to be regarded as deviants when they violate organizational norms. In addition, chief executives are more likely to innovate if there is a likelihood of success.

Now that we have clarified several of the assumptions made in the overarching generalization on executive input, we are able to look at two additional subgeneralizations more related to the issue of centralization.

9.20D. Lower-level workers have greater capacity than their supervisors to formulate novel decisions (+, 142).

This statement (on the surface a contradiction of the previous one) is based on Walter's (142) study of three neighboring cities with city managers and nonpartisan boards of aldermen. He conceptualized novel decisions as those which refer to situations that are new to an organization and are therefore not covered by existing rules and procedures. Since lower-level workers are often closer to the boundaries of the organization, they are in touch with and influenced more directly by changes in the environment. Their situation enables them to become better informed about these new developments, and this knowledge is the basis of their expertise. Hence, they are better equipped to introduce novel ideas. Using observations and interviews, Walter was able to empirically substantiate this relationship. Unlike the previous subgeneralization, this one deals with *capacity for* or *capability of* introducing innovations, not with *attitudes*.

9.20E. Innovation is not facilitated when employee participation does not result in a decentralized decision-making structure, but instead increases employee identification with management (+, 101).

In a great many organizations, periodic meetings between employees and the administration are touted as indicators of a decentralized organizational structure or participatory democracy. In many of these organizations, however, although opinions are shared, decisions are not made. Patchen (101) studied the TVA's "cooperative program," a series of conferences and committee meetings between representatives of management and of the unions that represent TVA employees. The author found that identification with the TVA did result, but that general interest in innovation (i.e., change in policy and procedures) did not. Interest in innovation was negatively correlated with interest in the program. Co-optation rather than a sharing of decision-making power had occurred.

Action Guidelines: The guidelines from the preceding set of generalizations follow a developmental sequence. First, generally speaking, the practitioner should assume that centralized organizations will be less innovative than decentralized organizations, and therefore, if the practitioner wants to maximize the adoption rate of an innovation, he should ordinarily approach or develop the latter type.

Also, the practitioner can increase the innovativeness of an organization by increasing the participation of its employees in decision making. Such participation must, however, be a genuine sharing of influence, not merely periodic discussions between employees and management in set status roles.

When the chief executive of a centralized organization is innovative and the practitioner has access to him, it may be effective to penetrate such organizations through the chief executive. Once the latter has adopted the innovation in principle it can be rapidly implemented, since high centralization facilitates the downward transmission of information and policy. The practitioner should realize that the quality of implementation may be low in such situations, however, since adoption directed by others may be superficial and unstable. Some innovations may require significant participation by employees, particularly if they are nonroutine or cannot be monitored.

Under more typical conditions (i.e., a chief executive who is not innovative), the practitioner can perhaps affect innovation by working through the lower-level workers, especially in a human-relations structure.

Size

GENERALIZATION 9.21: The size of an organization does not appear to have a consistent relationship with its innovativeness. Instead, size is important either for or against innovation depending on other variables that interact with it (+ + +, 1, 53, 54, 55, 87, 90, 100, 119, 141).

At first glance, the variable of organizational size appears to be either inconsistently or not at all related to innovativeness. Researchers such as Mohr (87), and Pappenfort and Kilpatrick (100) found size to be directly related to innovativeness whereas Hage and Aiken (54, 55) found it to be inversely related. Upon further scrutiny, it seems likely that size itself is not critical to innovativeness, and that it becomes significant only when it is linked with other variables, which are critical. The following series of subgeneralizations should serve to underline this relationship. The potential range of important variables should not be considered limited to those discussed here. Rather, the variables introduced are restricted to those which received empirical support from the research found in our data pool. Others that come immediately to mind, but that are not mentioned, include formalization, job satisfaction, and division of labor.

The following three subgeneralizations concern organizational slack, numbers of professionals, and centralization. While the last two of these variables are considered elsewhere, their inclusion here in addition will help clarify the relationship between organizational size and innovativeness. We trust that such clarification will offset the obvious redundancy.

9.21A. Large organizations tend to have more organizational slack (uncommitted resources), which can be applied to innovative programs. When organizational size is associated with organizational slack, large organizations will be more innovative than smaller ones (+, 53, 87, 119).

Organizational slack as discussed by Mohr (87) is the difference between those resources obtained or obtainable from the environment and those required to maintain the organization. In his analysis of public-health departments, Mohr identified important specific slack resources held by larger organizations but not by smaller ones. These resources enabled large public-health departments to adopt many more nontraditional programs than smaller ones. Thus, large size makes available greater resources, which then facilitate innovativeness, rather than size per se. In other words, large organizations may have available uncommitted resources, which can be applied to innovation; smaller organizations may have to apply all their resources to existing commitments and the overriding imperative of organizational survival.

9.21B. Large organizations can afford to employ more and higher-level professionals, who may serve as an innovative force. When organizational size is directly related to the number of professionals employed, an organization will be innovative (+, 100).

As previously noted, the Pappenfort and Kilpatrick (100) study found that the larger group work organizations in Chicago offering services to youth and children had more professionals than did smaller organizations. This was presumably because the larger organizations had more resources that could be used to employ professionals. Also, top professionals are attracted to agencies with resources and "high standards." The relationship between professionals and the innovativeness of an organization has already been discussed at length and need not be repeated here.

9.21C. Larger organizations tend to be more centralized. Hence, larger organizational size may be negatively associated with innovativeness (+, 12).

Although Blankenship and Miles (12) did not consider innovation, the results of their work are sufficient to suggest this subgeneralization, because centralization has already been shown to be inversely related to innovativeness. In their study of eight light-manufacturing organizations, the authors concluded that in large organizations, the locus of the decision making is at the top level of the administrative hierarchy. In small organization, however, lower-level managers also take part in decision making.

9.21D. Smaller organizations devote their resources to fewer and smaller nontraditional programs, but implement them more intensively and comprehensively than do larger organizations (+, 87).

This subgeneralization is also based on Mohr's (87) study, which showed that smaller agencies devoted their increased resources to relatively fewer nontraditional programs but to a more intensive degree.

Action Guidelines: The practitioner desiring to assess the potential innovativeness of an organization should not be concerned with the size of the organization per se. Instead, one must attempt to gauge the balance among various size-related factors, some of which are conducive to innovation and some of which are detrimental. Perhaps the most important facilitating variable is the availability of slack resources that might be used for innovation, coupled with a higher level of professionalization in some agencies. Centralization also may be related to size and is often detrimental to innovativeness. Furthermore, since there seems to be a tendency for larger organizations (when they are able) to adopt a larger number of innovations and for smaller organizations to adopt innovations more comprehensively, the practitioner might wish to approach either type, depending on specific goals.

Production Emphasis

GENERALIZATION 9.22: The innovativeness of an organization is inversely related to the degree to which the organization places an emphasis on production. Organizations which emphasize low costs and the quantity of products and services are less innovative then those which emphasize quality (+, 2, 119).

Innovation, being a change in established patterns of an organization's operations, sometimes necessitates a period of disruption during which production is decreased or profits are reduced. In addition, the results of an innovation are often not known beforehand, and innovation therefore presents a risk. Consequently, organizations concerned with maximizing production are more likely to favor continuation of the status quo. While innovations directly related to efficiency of output would be adopted at a relatively higher rate by organizations concerned with production, they would nevertheless be subject to the same considerations.

A clear example of this relationship is found in a study of 24 Chicago area hospitals by Rosner (119). In the study, many hospitals showed an emphasis on quantity through their high economic orientation—i.e., a concern with costs of new services as opposed to the benefits to patients. Rosner found that a high economic orientation had a significant negative correlation with the frequency of trial of new drugs among the hospitals. Those hospitals highly concerned with keeping costs at a minimum were less likely to try new drugs as frequently. High economic orientation also was weakly and negatively correlated with the promptness of trial of the new drugs.

Action Guidelines: In order to increase the innovativeness of an organization, the practitioner should attempt to move the organization from an emphasis on low costs and the quantity of products and services to an emphasis on the quality of products and services. A practitioner wishing to maximize the adoption rate of an innovation should approach organizations that emphasize quality of services.

Job Satisfaction

GENERALIZATION 9.23: Job satisfaction is not independently related to organizational innovativeness. Both high and low morale may motivate attempts toward organizational change or be sources of resistance to change. Similarly, innovation in an organization may result in either high or low job satisfaction. (+ +, 54, 55, 85, 99).

From the research reviewed for this text, it was impossible to discern a consistent relationship between job satisfaction and innovativeness, either independently or in conjunction with other variables. After reviewing the relevant findings, we shall present a discussion of other possible relationships between job satisfaction and organizational innovativeness. Although that discussion will not be based on empirical evidence, it does appear to be logically consistent with available research.

Evidence in support of a direct relationship between job satisfaction and innovativeness comes from Hage and Aiken's studies (54, 55). The authors found a significant and positive correlation between the level of job satisfaction and program change. Partially offsetting this finding is Markus's study (85) of five large social-welfare organizations. Although he did not measure the extent of organizational innovativeness, Markus found that employees who were more discontented with their work and were bothered by incongruities and inconsistencies in organizational operations were more likely to be participants in organizational change. What this implies is that the innovativeness of certain agencies studied by Hage and Aiken may have resulted in higher job satisfaction, not vice-versa. This suggests two possible subgeneralizations:

9.23A. Organizations which are innovative have higher job satisfaction (+, 54, 55).
9.23B. Job dissatisfaction is likely to be a motivating force for organizational innovation (+, 85).

Intuitively, these two subgeneralizations do not appear to cover all of the possibilities and dimensions of the generalization. For example, in some instances, innovation may be so disruptive that job satisfaction is lowered. Also, high job satisfaction may result in complacency and protectiveness of the status quo. Finally, high job satisfaction may be a motivating force for organizational innovation when an organization's norms favor change.

In summary, then, it appears that job satisfaction cannot be consistently related to organizational innovativeness. Clearly needed is more empirical research, which can refine this issue by isolating the key variables and clarifying their relationships.

Action Guidelines: The practitioner should not assume that high job satisfaction will make an organization more innovative. Rather, it seems that when an organization has innovative goals and norms, high job satisfaction may facilitate that effect. In situations in which the organization is characterized by inertia and low innovativeness, the practitioner may find that low job satisfaction will motivate innovation, if this low morale can be attributed to the inertia of the agency. The practitioner should also not assume that the adoption of innovations will increase job satisfaction. It is important to consider the balance between a number of variables, such as social relationships and job responsibilities, both before and after the innovation.

Joint Programs

GENERALIZATION 9.24: The innovativeness of an organization is associated with the openness of its boundaries. Organizations with many linkages to external influences (as demonstrated by the number of joint programs with other organizations) are more innovative than organizations with few linkages (+, 2).

Aiken and Hage (2) found that interdependence between organizations, as operationalized in the form of joint programs, is not a casual factor of innovativeness but rather a result of other organizational factors conducive to innovativeness. Internal organizational diversity (with respect to occupations and philosophies) stimulates organizational innovativeness. The resulting innovations necessitate additional resources, and one method of gaining these needed resources is to establish joint programs. Thus, the significance of this generalization is that it helps the practitioner identify innovative organizations by observing the extent of their involvement in joint programs. Aiken and Hage do not deal directly with another possibility, however. It seems reasonable to assume that the establishment and operation of a joint program also introduces some innovations. Thus, while our primary hypothesis is that innovations lead to joint programs, there is a strong possibility that joint programs may also lead to more innovations.

In an empirical test of their hypothesis, Aiken and Hage (2) found that organizations with many joint programs were more occupationally diversified, innovative, decentralized, and had more active internal communications. One might say that organizational openness can be facilitated both by external professional linkages and linkages to external organizations through joint programs.

Action Guidelines: The practitioner wishing to maximize the adoption rate of an innovation should concentrate on organizations that are participating in joint programs, as they will tend to have open boundaries. The practitioner should be able to increase the innovativeness of an organization by establishing joint programs with other agencies. Such a strategy would appear particularly beneficial when the target agency alone does not have the resources to adopt the innovation or it does not want to adopt the proposed innovation without some prior experience with it.

Innovation in and Applications of Research

GENERALIZATION 9.25: Research conducted in mixed or applied settings is more likely to be both innovative and implemented than research conducted in a purely academic setting (+, 52, 105).

Characteristically, research performed in universities is subject to pressure to pursue the classical problems of science (basic research) rather than to attempt to solve immediate problems (applied research). Investigation has been directed toward the question of which type of research is more innovative. Although the research pool for this paper contained only two such investigations, the above generalization is offered as a tentative conclusion.

A study by Gordon and Marquis (52) provides evidence in support of the first portion of this proposition: that "marginal" or applied settings are more conducive to innovation. In this study, the authors had a panel of well-known medical sociologists rate the innovativeness of project proposals submitted by the directors of 245 projects being conducted in universities, health agencies, medical schools, hospitals, and clinics. In general, the data showed that research conducted in "marginal" institutions tended to be more innovative than research in the purely academic settings. Innovation in this study was implicitly defined, individually, by the panel of qualified researchers. Additional evidence suggested that the ease with which the consequences of research could be assessed in applied institutions accounted for the greater innovation found there. Another way of viewing this is to conceptualize the mixed situation as one involving more diverse professional inputs, and hence with more conduciveness to innovation (Generalization 18A).

With respect to the second half of this generalization—that innovations developed through collaboration between pure and applied research are more likely to be adopted than those developed through pure research—evidence is found in a study by Price (103). The study compared the Fish Commisssion and the Game Commission in Oregon. After Price verified that the Game Commission had been significantly more successful in introducing new wildlife-management knowledge, he attempted to discover the reason why. Price found that the Fish Commission had a high percentage of biologists with graduate degrees. This was taken as a rough measure of the "pure research" versus the "applied" orientation of the Fish Commission researchers. Because of this considerable difference in type of knowledge between the researchers and the appliers, or practitioners (the hatchery men), the practitioners felt social distance from and lowered respect for the researchers. This discrepancy led the hatchery men to resist accepting and using the findings of the research biologists. The Game Commission, having more applied as distinct from pure researchers, with knowledge closer to that of practitioners (gamekeepers), was able to have more of its innovations adopted, because the gamekeepers had a higher level of respect for (felt less social distance from) the researchers.

Action Guidelines: In order to increase the innovativeness of research, the practitioner might locate pure researchers in such applied settings as agencies rather than in universities. In such settings, the relationship of the research to the organization's goals should be emphasized and the researchers should be given a moderate amount of freedom. Alternatively, pure research projects, located in universities and dealing with human-service problems and issues, should attempt to include applied researchers or researchers with experience in applying research. In general, it is useful to have research conducted by mixed or applied personnel if innovation is an objective. Applied researchers—i.e., those with educations, attitudes, etc., similar to practitioners—should be used to convey research to the practitioners. This role differentiation tends to reduce social distance as well as resistance by practitioners to the research findings.

VARIABLES AFFECTING THE SUCCESS
OF IMPLEMENTATION OF INNOVATIONS

Introduction

In this final section we shall focus on the implementation of innovations. Two main areas of interest will be covered. First, we shall discuss the characteristics of a relatively new breed of organization—the agency whose primary purpose is creating, testing, and demonstrating the practice of intra- or extraorganizational innovation. We shall review three case studies of such ''organizations for innovation'' and shall make comparisons and generalizations where applicable.

The second major area of interest concerns the barriers to successful implementation of an innovation by an organization. Up to this point, the primary emphasis has been on the adoption of innovations and, because not all innovations adopted by an organization are successfully implemented, some consideration of the sources of resistance to organizational implementation of innovations is therefore necessary. On the basis of the research studies drawn from our pool, some subgeneralizations will be developed and their implications discussed.

"Organizations for Innovation"

GENERALIZATION 9.26: Certain characteristics are associated with the effectiveness of an organization that introduces innovation into other organizations. "Organizations for innovation" with these characteristics will be more successful in introducing innovation into other organizations (+ +, 9, 31, 90).

The three studies on which this proposition is based focus on "organizations for innovation" which represent a range of organizational structures and goals. Before discussing the characteristics of these organizations, it is necessary to briefly describe each case study.

Doig (31) presents a case study of the Vera Institute of Justice, an organization that attempts to change the policies and procedures of the New York City Police Department. This particular study deals with attempts to effect bail reform, but also discusses the structure and functioning of the Vera Institute in general. A number of particular characteristics of the relationship between the Vera Institute and the Police Department are noteworthy. The relationship between the two organizations is a relatively stable and enduring one, involving joint planning, shared personnel, and considerable participation by the police hierarchy. Also important is the fact that the institute has chosen important projects, but ones presenting little threat to the target organization (which undoubtedly helps to account for the continuing relationship).

The Neighborhood Service Organization (NSO) is the subject of a case study by Bernard, et al. (9). The NSO is primarily concerned with service innovations in the area of social welfare. It differs from the Vera Institute in that it has a larger range of projects and a higher level of direct participation in them. NSO tends to conduct its own demonstration projects, whereas the Vera Institute usually limits itself to mutual planning efforts. In addition, the NSO's relationships with target organizations are generally much closer than the relationship between the Institute and the New York Police.

The third case study is by Morris and Randall (90). It is a cross-community, cross-organizational investigation of planning organizations that attempt to develop new services for the elderly.

We have offered as subgeneralizations only characteristics of an "organization for innovation" that were reflected in at least two out of the three studies.

9.26A. The effectiveness of an "organization for innovation" is associated with organizing innovations into demonstration projects (+, 9, 31).

A demonstration project approach, as indicated by Doig (31), puts little pressure on an organization to commit itself to new practices on a system-wide basis until they have been validated adequately on a small scale. This clearly is beneficial to an agency because it minimizes potential risk. Note the parallel to partialization, identified earlier as an attribute facilitating innovation.

9.26B. The effectiveness of an "organization for innovation" is associated with a decentralized administration that allows the staff to influence and stimulate others with a minimum of organizational constraints on role performance (+, 9, 90).

This subgeneralization is a reformulation of Generalization 9.20, which related the centralization of an organization inversely to its innovativeness.

9.26C. The effectiveness of an "organization for innovation" is associated with having a staff particularly able to deal with the target organizations or clients for whom the innovations are intended (+, 9, 31, 90).

At first glance, there seem to be contradictory findings in these studies. Both Doig (31) and Morris and Randall (90) stress the importance of technical knowledge, whereas Bernard, et al. (9) indicate that heavy use of social work students and paraprofessionals is conducive to innovation. This apparent contradiction is resolved, however, when one considers the differing orientations of the organizations studied. The agency studied by Bernard, et al. works largely with the poor, whereas the New York Police Department and a group of social-welfare agencies, both highly technical organizations, were the targets of the organizations studied by Doig, and Morris and Randall. Thus these studies indicate that organizations whose staffs are close to the target systems for which the innovations are intended are likely to be effective.

It should also be noted that Doig (31) stresses the importance of technical knowledge as a source of power behind innovative suggestions. Thus, it seems that technical knowledge is a valuable weapon for an organization attempting to introduce low threat innovations while maintaining a long-term continuing relationship. For other situations (e.g., high threat innovations or short-term crisis intervention) other sources of power would be more effective.

Action Guidelines: The practitioner attempting to establish an organization that will act as a source of innovation in other organizations should make sure that the "organization for innovation" has the following characteristics:
1. Functioning through demonstration projects.
2. Low centralization.
3. A staff able to relate well to the target system.
    a. Highly technical staff members to deal with technical organizations.
    b. Paraprofessionals to deal with low-income clients.

Barriers to Innovation Implementation

GENERALIZATION 9.27: Mere formal adoption of an innovation does not assure its implementation. Both intra- and extraorganizational actors may offer resistance to the implementation of the innovation (+ +, 14, 22, 60, 115, 147).

It is indeed a rare innovation that everyone, even within the comparatively small-scale confines of an organization, favors. Resistance to an innovation is normal. However, we are here concerned with resistance strong enough to block the implementation of an innovation. From several investigations in our research pool, we can identify a number of actors who are sources of resistance. (There is no claim that this list exhausts all possibilities.)

9.27A. Resistance to the implementation of an innovation may come from lower level workers in an agency or individual members of a voluntary association (+ +, 14, 22, 60, 147).

A study by Wood and Zald (147) concerning the Methodist Church and racial integration is a graphic example of an instance where lower-level members of an organization resisted the implementation of an innovation. The study indicated that many Southern churches resisted integration, contrary to the adopted national church policy of integration on the local level. These churches acted by reducing financial contributions at the local level on "Race Relations Sunday," decreasing their use of strictly Methodist literature, and using various pressures against liberal ministers.

9.27B. Resistance to the implementation of an innovation may come from other organizations intimately involved with the innovation (+, 115).

This factor is particularly salient when an innovation involves referrals to other organizations. Robinson (115) analyzed the relative failure of a well-baby clinic offering referral services. The study found that the failure was partially caused by the poor response of other social-welfare and health agencies to the clinic's referrals.

9.27C. Resistance to the implementation of an innovation may come from the clients of a target system that the innovation is intended to serve (+, 115).

In the previous study of a well-baby clinic located in a public housing project, Robinson (115) also found that almost one-half of the clients referred to other agencies failed to follow through on those referrals. The well-baby clinic itself was also found to have a relatively low percentage of attendance.

Action Guidelines: We have identified three major possible sources of resistance to an innovation. Hypothetically, resistance might be reduced by directly involving the relevant actors in the development of the innovation, giving them sufficient knowledge or attitudinal influence about the innovation prior to its implementation, or through structural means programming compliance with the innovation.

While the previous section has synthesized the available research findings from our data pool, it has not exhausted the extent of the writings concerning innovation in organizations. Just as we expanded the parameters of our retrieved data in the first section of this chapter by drawing on the writings of Rogers, we shall again expand our data here by utilizing an article by Thompson (138), which summarizes studies dealing with innovations in organizations.

Below we shall present some of the main conclusions drawn by Thompson. They suggest ideas that can readily be presented in the form of generalizations, because confirming data are related to them. According to Thompson, innovative organizations can be characterized as follows:

1. *An absence of production ideology.* One that emphasizes detailed, assembly-line tasks for employees. This results in jobs that draw on only a small portion of a worker's store of knowledge or training, thus restricting his potential creative inputs and contributions to the organization.
2. *Encouragement of conflict and uncertainty.* Organizations that permit and stimulate a reasonable level of conflict and ambiguity allow the introduction of multiple perspectives on any given issue.
3. *The use of intrinsic rewards.* Organizations that use an extrinsic reward system, administered by the hierarchy of authority, foster conformity rather than innovation. More conducive to change are reward systems that involve internal commitment, esteem by colleagues, and benevolent competition.
4. *Elimination of hierarchy through which an innovation must pass to win acceptance.* Those organizations which require approval of new ideas up through a long chain of command place restraints on innovation, because any new idea can be vetoed by multiple sources.
5. *Placing a high value on goal attainment rather than internal distribution of power and status.* Organizations focused on internal power relations tend to be conservative and to support the

status quo. New ideas are likely to be scrutinized primarily in terms of maintenance issues.

6. *Nonsegregation of innovation units.* When such specialized innovation units and mechanisms as research and development departments are highly segregated, their influence becomes blocked.

7. *Uncommitted money, time, skills, and good will.* In this statement Thompson is in another way dealing with the matter of organizational slack, which was discussed earlier in the chapter.

8. *Ease of communication.* Unless new ideas are circulated they cannot be learned and used. Thus, ease of communication is seen as important, together with its converse: a low level of parochialism or departmentalization.

9. *A middle range of member identity, between total commitment and complete alienation from the organization.* The point here is that neither total commitment nor total alienation provides the combination of openness and motivation to innovate. Perception of the organization as an avenue of professional growth fosters motivation.

10. *A psychological sense of personal security and autonomy, coupled with a moderate level of problem challenge and uncertainty.* The challenge provides motivation to change existing procedures; security and autonomy give the confidence to strike out in new directions.

11. *The general characteristic of "structural looseness."* This includes broader participation in decision making, less stratification, overlapping and vague jurisdiction and role definitions, use of group processes, overlapping and multiple group membership, temporary and rotating assignments, and ongoing organizational and subunit restructuring. Thompson sees all these attributes operating to prevent rigid, standardized, recurrent, or narrow patterns. By employing such arrangements, an organization would constantly be in a fluid state, never permitting any given procedure to become set or ritualized.

12. *More diffused evaluation procedures.* This includes a multiple ranking system with multiple salary scales, peer evaluations, and elimination of procedures relating to secrecy and loyalty.

This removes a unitary hierarchy from allocating rewards so rigidly that conformity results. Multiple sources of evaluation and reward are viewed as more conducive to innovation.

Thompson equates the innovative organization with a professional one. He places high value on internalized norms, autonomy, collegial relationships, organizational openness and looseness, and receptivity to multiple inputs. Whether or not this characterizes all or most professions is open to question.

Leaving this matter aside for the time being, the attributes themselves, whether supported by most professions or not, appear on the surface to be those which are consistent with innovation, or, as stated previously, with the capacity to deal with nonuniform events. Thompson's conclusions in general supplement the propositions introduced earlier in the chapter.

CONCLUSION

Innovations are by nature creative, idiosyncratic, artistic actions of individuals and groups of individuals. Here we have attempted to codify or "routinize" innovativeness by specifying regularities in the making and sharing of innovations. Let there be no misunderstanding: a practitioner cannot use the foregoing in cookbook fashion, employing recipe A to produce innovation B. We have attempted to indicate certain conditions that can facilitate or remove blocks to innovation. Just as with all the other generalizations and guidelines, these need to be carried to fruition by a knowledgeable, dedicated, imaginative individual: a practitioner or change agent who is able to delicately fuse science and art in the interests of creating a social order more conducive to humanistic values.

Chapter Ten

Movement and Assimilation of Populations

INTRODUCTION

"MOVEMENT OF POPULATIONS" is a term that refers to the transmigration of individuals or groups from one area of residence or settlement to another, whether by choice or on a nonvoluntary basis (as a consequence of, e.g., urban renewal programs, economic dislocations). Population movement has been neither a distinctive nor a systematic area of study in the professional schools or in the practice literature, although it has been an important functional problem for community practitioners.

Many social planners and welfare workers are deeply involved in urban-renewal and development projects and have first-hand experience through relocation services in coping with the hardships of forced population movement that often accompany such programs. Travelers' Aid has long been a basic service for persons in transit, as have been the Red Cross and Salvation Army under emergency conditions. The neighborhood settlement house historically played a role in helping to assimilate overseas immigrants and rural migrants into new urban settings, while often attempting to preserve the unique features of divergent cultural backgrounds. Other activities of practitioners in working with communities on problems of neighborhood racial integration, city planning, and economic redevelopment suggest the usefulness of raising the subject of population movement to the level of explicit study and analysis.

It may be of interest to the reader that this subject was not included on our original list of practice issue areas. However, during our initial examination of research writings it became obvious that this was an area of concern to social scientists from a variety of disciplines, who often had little interconnection with or even awareness of researchers in other disciplines. At the same time the connection between the subject matter and problems of community-organization practice was apparent.

In an earlier time the topic of cross-cultural movement, acculturation, and assimilation engaged the minds of the major figures in sociology. Individuals such as Robert Park, Louis Wirth, W. I. Thomas, and Florian Znaniecki placed this subject in a central position in their work. Numerous anthropologists and ethnologists likewise gave it sustained theoretical attention. Trends and fashions change; the great waves of immigration to this country stopped, and other areas such as organizational theory increased in saliency, with a resulting decline in interest in population movements and assimilation as a predominant theme in the social sciences. In recent years there has been evidence of a revival of consideration of population movements as an area of study by social scientists and practitioners, as evidenced by the founding of such journals as the *International Migration Review,* published by the Center for Migration Studies.[1]

In our review of research we have found many studies that pertain to the United States and a smaller number that deal with foreign countries. Both types have been included in our analysis. We shall view population movements in terms of the shift in residence of population groups from one location (the area of origin) to another location (the area of settlement, or the host community). We discovered a number of differences in the character of movements when they involve relocation within a given metropolitan area (intraurban migration) as contrasted with movements to an urban center from a rural community or from a different urban area (interarea migration). Intraurban migrations constitute shorter distances, are often compulsory in character as a result of formally organized urban redevelopment programs, and frequently are correlated with neighborhood racial change patterns. Interarea movement generally involves immediate economic considerations to a greater degree—migration to seek work or to obtain a better job.

[1] Joseph E. Eaton, ed., *Migration and Social Welfare* (New York: National Association of Social Workers, 1971); Norman W. Lowrie, "The Migration Mess," *Social Work* 17, no. 1 (January 1972): 77–86.

We shall discuss intraurban and interarea movements separately in the following sections. Subsequently we shall consider in a more general way the process of assimilation of populations into new cultural environments. We shall consider rates of assimilation for different population groups, the temporal dimension in assimilation, and variables associated with the character of both the migrant population and the host community as they impinge on the dynamics of assimilation.

In this instance, it seems advisable to make use of the initial introductory remarks to deal with an important general assumption that is held by many practitioners concerning attributes of people who move frequently, and which may unfavorably color the issue. Implicit in much professional opinion is the view that high mobility rates are correlated with mental instability, social pathology, deviancy, and other negative or problematic conditions. However, scrutiny of the literature leads the reviewer to mark this belief a professional myth and to frame a counterproposition along the following lines:

GENERALIZATION 10.1: There is no general correlation between degree of residential mobility and social-psychological pathology or deviancy (+ + +, 4, 7, 44, 54, 57).

Studies concerning drug addiction, educational underachievement, juvenile delinquency, the occurrence of mental illness, and participation in urban disorders revealed no difference in the manifestation of these behaviors between persons high and low in residential mobility. The assumption that persons with histories of residential mobility tend to be more likely candidates for expression of social and psychological problems is not supported by the research findings reviewed. For example, Simpson and Van Arsdal (57) in a carefully designed study found that youths defined by the courts as delinquent did not systematically differ from nondelinquent youths in geographic migration patterns. Both groups had similar profiles concerning moves from city to city and moves from residence to residence in the same city. According to these investigators, migration was ruled out as a factor associated with delinquency. Similarly, Ball and Bates (7) found that the residential mobility history of narcotic addicts treated at Lexington was no different from that of a sample of the general population. Drug users and persons in the general population showed little difference in residential mobility from birth to the onset of addiction. One explanation of this phenomenon may be that frequent change of residence has become so common in the population that it is not now a correlate of psychological stress, as it once might have been.

Some degree of caution should be exercised in drawing inferences from this data. A study by Levine (31) runs counter to this trend. According to Levine's data, frequency of movement on an intraurban basis for *low income populations* may be associated with mental-health problems of school-aged children; the result would be poor scholastic achievement. Family tension was found to be a correlate of frequent residential changeover in the sample.

Action Guidelines: In selecting clients for services, agencies dealing with the prevention and treatment of social problems should not generally use residential mobility as a prime criterion. Residentially mobile persons may perhaps best be served by providing environmental support services related to migration needs such as employment aid, financial assistance and programs designed to foster rapid assimilation. Some delimited subpopulation groups, however, may need treatment services in connection with residential mobility.

INTRAURBAN MIGRATION

This section will focus on movements within the same geographic region, usually within a given city or urban area. We shall pay special attention to the effects of urban renewal and other public projects that result in forced residential shifts of large numbers of people, and shall attempt to describe the attributes of persons who tend to be frequent intraurban movers and the character of neighborhoods as they affect migration patterns. We shall also examine aspects of neighborhood racial change, placing particular emphasis upon who suffers from urban renewal and other forced migratory processes, and how damaging effects on people and neighborhoods may be minimized.

Forced Migration and Social Class

GENERALIZATION 10.2: Persons differ in the ease with which they are able to manage forced relocation. This difference is related largely to social class and degree of locality identification (+ + +, 8, 18 59).

> 10.2A. Relocation is relatively difficult for persons who have less than a high school education, are employed in unskilled occupations, or are foreign born. They tend to be lower class (+ + +, 8, 18, 59).
>
> 10.2B. Relocation is relatively easy for persons who have a high school education or more, are employed in highly skilled occupations, and are native born. They tend to be middle class (+ + +, 8, 18, 59).
>
> 10.2C. Relocation is difficult for persons who have high neighborhood identification, have friends located in the neighborhood, and plan to resettle in the same neighborhood (+ + +, 8, 18, 59).
>
> 10.2D. Relocation is less difficult when persons do not identify with their neighborhood, have friends outside the neighborhood, and plan to resettle in areas outside it (+ + +, 8, 18, 59).

Action Guidelines: This proposition spotlights categories of persons who can be predicted to be in greatest need for relocation services. Practitioners should concentrate their efforts on those persons who need intensified services when forced to move; i.e., lower-class residents, those with low skills and education, those with strong neighborhood identification, those who plan to relocate within the neighborhood, or those having no friends or kin outside the neighborhood.

Forced Migration and Lower Class Status

GENERALIZATION 10.3: Forced movement because of urban renewal or other government programs tends to disrupt low-income and ethnic minority group neighborhoods, and to increase the economic and social instability of persons already in marginal positions (+ + +, 13, 21, 33, 58).

10.3A. Forced movement tends to increase overcrowding and occupancy of substandard housing in adjacent areas, which necessitates future moves (+ + +, 13, 21, 33, 58).

A number of independent studies of families replaced by urban renewal uniformly found that, for a sizable group of families, displacement led to overcrowding and new residence in substandard dwellings. Logan, et al. (33) reports that 40 percent of the families displaced in Springfield, Massachusetts, found it necessary to move within four years of displacement because of these factors.

10.3B. For blacks, forced movement tends to increase population density, partly because of racial discrimination (+ + +, 13, 21, 33).

Hartman (21) and Logan et al. (33), in separate studies, report that displacement increased population density for blacks; racial discrimination was given as a factor accounting for this outcome.

10.3C. For whites, forced movement need not increase population density or clustering in one area (+ + +, 13, 21, 33).

The findings of Logan et al. (33) suggest that displaced white families, have a wider range of possible locations for housing than blacks, which decreases white people's relocation problems.

10.3D. Forced movement tends to increase housing costs for those displaced (+ + +, 13, 21, 33).

Three studies on this subject uniformly found that, compared with housing costs prior to displacement, new housing increased monthly expenditures for a majority of families.

10.3E. Persons forced to move may receive little aid from existing relocation programs (+, 21).

Hartman (21), studying displaced families from Boston's East End, found that only 15 percent of the families received assistance from the Renewal Agency.

Action Guidelines: The findings in this area raise serious questions concerning the basic premises of urban renewal, in that forced movement without also making available adequate alternative housing only increases the social and economic hardships of lower-class residents. For blacks, the vicious combination of forced movement and racial discrimination in housing tends to intensify ghettoization in other areas of the city—"slum shifting" as characterized by Jane Jacobs.

Practitioners should make it a very strong precondition that adequate housing be made available for residents before urban-renewal projects are begun. Whether they hold planning positions or whether they are engaged in organizing neighborhood residents, practitioners need to address this issue vigorously. Also, money for moving expenses and other relocation costs should be made available so that the financial burden does not fall upon residents who can least afford it. Rent subsidies may be one way of compensating for increased rents for persons who are victimized by forced public migration. Even within existing parameters of renewal, better implementation of services appears to be necessary.

To punctuate the issue we shall close with an excerpt from testimony by Dr. Hartman before a Federal Civil Rights Commission Hearing (in January 1970 in St. Louis).[2] Hartman characterized the matter as follows:

> The urban renewal program is clearly being used as a means of redistributing the black population. This is beyond doubt a violation of the law and public policy. Although the program was introduced as part of the Housing Act of 1949, which stated in its preamble the national housing goal of "a decent home and suitable living environment for every American family," as far as many black families have been concerned, urban renewal has meant not only worse housing conditions but an involuntary reshuffling from one city to another or from one part of the city to another. This is done as local renewal officials decide how they want land used on which black families reside and where they want black families to live.
>
> There is nothing to be said about this pattern other than it must be ended at once. Local renewal authorities may propose programs of this sort but it is up to the U.S. Department of Housing and Urban Develop-

[2] Reported in *Civil Rights Digest*, 3, no. 2 (Spring 1970): 36.

ment (HUD)—and there is no question but that it has the power—to en-
join localities from blatantly pursuing such racist urban renewal projects.
This is something that must be demanded of the U.S. Department of
Housing and Urban Development.

Lower Class-Status and Frequency of Movement

GENERALIZATION 10.4: Low-income groups tend to make
more intraurban moves than other income groups (+, 31).

10.4A. Intraurban moves for lower income groups are associated
with economic instability and family strains (+, 31).

As suggested earlier, one study on the subject indicated that low
income groups tend to move within cities because of a variety of
economic and family problems. Levine (31) indicates that children
of low income people with high intraurban movement rates are often
unable to succeed in school because of strains within the family and
the tension that results from frequent changing of schools. Thus,
poor school achievement is correlated with the interacting variables
of family tension, economic instability, and frequent moving. These
data should be viewed in juxtaposition with Generalization 10.1,
which discounts a relationship between mobility and pathology.

Action Guidelines: High levels of intracity movement may
for some groups be correlated with family and economic
problems. High movers within the low-income population
may particularly benefit from family-centered problem services and economic assistance. Schools may need to develop more services for rapid integration of students from
families that move often. Treatment and support services in
some instances ought to involve consideration of the movement factor in the design of a service strategy.

Working-Class Neighborhood Cohesion and Urban Renewal

GENERALIZATION 10.5: Working-class neighborhoods differ in the extent to which residents identify positively with
their locality and support local subcultural institutions

within it. This has consequences for the planning of urban renewal projects (+ + +, 8, 10, 18, 44, 59).

10.5A. High concentrations of subcultural institutions in working-class neighborhoods are associated with

1. Identification with and commitment to the neighborhood (+ +, 8, 10, 18).
2. Identification with a minority-group subculture (+ +, 8, 10, 18).
3. Concentration of friends, neighbors, and kin within the neighborhood and high degrees of interaction with these groups (+ +, 8, 18, 59).
4. Residence in the neighborhood by choice (+ +, 10, 18, 59).

10.5B. Low concentrations of subcultural institutions in working-class neighborhoods are associated with

1. Low identification with and commitment to the area (+ +, 6, 59).
2. Choice of residence based more on economic necessity than social ties to the area (+, 59).
3. Restricted social ties on the block of residence (+, 59).

In studies of working-class Italian (10, 18, 20) and Puerto Rican (12) ethnic neighborhoods, investigators found that subcultural institutions (ethnic churches, clubs, food stores, bars) supported an active neighborhood-centered social life, where friendships and neighborliness were intertwined with organization membership and leisure-time activities. Most of these were case studies of one community or neighborhood. Briton (10) and Wolf and Lebeaux (59) took a comparative approach and found that working-class neighborhoods differ in their capacity to support subcultural institutions. Wolf and Lebeaux (59) compared data from a working-class Italian neighborhood in Boston with data from a working-class black neighborhood in Detroit. The Boston neighborhood supported an active subcultural life while the Detroit neighborhood did not. The investigators suggested a variable that differentiated the two neighborhoods: Residents in Detroit did not live in the neighborhood by choice, but because of economic restrictions and the force of racial discrimination. The Boston area was one preferred by its residents even when moving was economically feasible.

Action Guidelines: Forced migration because of government redevelopment programs may disrupt vigorous neighborhoods supporting a viable social life. Under these circumstances, such programs should be discouraged in favor of rehabilitation approaches that do not result in movement from the neighborhood. Local support of an active social life based upon long-term interpersonal ties and area identification suggests the existence of social benefits that should not be discarded in deference to physical improvements; whenever possible, physical improvements ought to be made in such a way as to enhance the quality of social life, not to injure it.

Practitioners are well advised to concentrate their efforts on developing neighborhood-level institutions as a means of increasing identification and social interactions in neighborhoods lacking these conditions. The absence of such characteristics should not be used as a justification for area renewal unless adequate housing is available for displaced families. The studies reviewed in this section reveal that areas of residence can be important social units for improving the quality of social life of persons living in them. Residents are capable of developing primary and secondary group memberships in their residence areas, which may contribute to their sense of participation in society. Urban living need not necessarily signify isolation and alienation. (See Generalizations 7.23 and 7.24.) The importance of the preservation and rehabilitation of areas is punctuated by studies (13, 21, 33) indicating that displaced families often tend to locate in dwellings that are inferior physically and cost more to rent or buy. Local institution-building might include developing block organizations and free or low-cost medical and social-service facilities located in the neighborhood.

When social ties and local identification are largely lacking in a local area that is in other ways a slum, an important ethical as well as empirical question arises: is it better to move people quickly to new housing projects or to engage in the slower process of area rehabilitation and institution-building in the original neighborhood? A definitive answer on this issue is lacking.

Neighborhood Organization and Renewal Planning

GENERALIZATION 10.6: Neighborhood residents can influence renewal plans in their areas (+ +, 12, 44).

> 10.6A. Neighborhood residents can exercise veto power on renewal plans by utilizing existing neighborhood organizations, developing new neighborhood organizations, and linking with communitywide organizations (+ +, 12, 44).
>
> 10.6B. Neighborhood residents without linkages to communitywide organizations but having neighborhood organizations are less able to influence renewal programs in their areas (+ + , 12, 44).
>
> 10.6C. Neighborhood residents having neighborhood organizations and technical assistance can develop independent planning for their localities (+ + , 12, 44).
>
> In a case study by Davies (12), neighborhood groups were, with assistance from agencies, able to formulate a redevelopment plan that was later adopted with minor changes by the City Planning Department.

Action Guidelines: It seems evident that neighborhood residents, through local organizations and linkages with communitywide organizations and influentials can develop veto power over renewal plans. To move beyond the veto function to neighborhood-initiated planning, neighborhood groups require technical assistance (i.e., from planners or lawyers). Neighborhood workers should concentrate on developing both neighborhood-based organizations and communitywide contacts in order to block renewal programs. For neighborhood-level planning, neighborhood organization, extraneighborhood ties, and technical assistance by expert individuals or agencies is needed.

Racially Changing Neighborhoods
and Property Values

GENERALIZATION 10.7: The movement of minority populations to formerly white residential areas does not generally lead to declining property values. In some cases, black immigration is associated with an increase in property values (+ + +, 35, 36, 37, 38, 40).

Studies in the East and Midwest have revealed little relationship between property values and the movement of blacks into white residential areas. Investigators have used a variety of source information and statistical procedures, and have concentrated for the most part on census data covering a number of years.

To illustrate, Palmore (40) examined the relationship of property value fluctuations and racial integration in Washington, D.C., and found that areas where integration took place did not generally experience a decline in housing values. In some cases, property values increased. The investigator used housing data for a period of years before integration and the same type of data after integration.

One is struck by the consistency with which findings by a variety of investigators working with different regional and geographic units strongly support the proposition. The findings are also congruent with the earlier *Residence and Race: Report for the Commission on Race and Housing.*This Report was prepared under the sponsorship of the Fund for the Republic (University of California Press, 1960).

Action Guidelines: To increase the stability of racially changing residential areas—i.e., to help check flight of white residents when blacks move into new areas—practitioners might
1. Inform residents of the facts concerning the relationship between residential integration and property values in order to dispel myths on the subject.
2. Work to curtail blockbusting, panic selling, and distorted

lending practices, which are the more fundamental causes of instability.

This author has elsewhere pinpointed institutional forces that operate in racially changing neighborhoods to manipulate the process artificially, especially real-estate agents and financial institutions.[3] A practitioner with responsibility for area planning or community development can feel comfortable in planning integrated patterns without concern about deleterious economic consequences for already-residing populations.

In the next section we shall enlarge our scale and deal with longer interarea movements—those involving shifts from one urban area to another or from rural areas to urban areas.

INTERAREA MIGRATION

We can now take a more macroscopic view and examine the characteristics of populations involved in movements between geographical regions as distinguished from those who move within the same urban locale. We shall be concerned primarily with immigration to urban centers, either from areas of origin in rural locations or from other cities. Employment factors, occupational status, and support patterns of different population groups will play an important part in the analysis.

The majority of research studies reviewed here were based on national samples using United States census statistics or other nationwide data. Some studies were confined to only white or black populations. Studies that in a more limited way focused on migration of groups into a particular city resulted in findings consistent with studies utilizing national samples. The data incorporate different time periods which extend over a three-decade period from the 1930s through the 1960s. A small number of studies pertaining to Latin American and European countries are also included.

---

[3] See Jack Rothman, "The Ghetto Makers," *The Nation* 193 (October 7, 1961): 222–24. Reprinted in *Race and Poverty: The Economics of Discrimination,* John F. Kain, ed. (Englewood Cliffs, N.J.: Prentice-Hall, Inc., 1969), pp. 122–27.

Economic Basis of Movement

GENERALIZATION 10.8: The main factor in voluntary interarea movement is the difference between the opportunity
structure in the area of destination and the area of departure. People (regardless of race or class) tend to move to
new urban centers for the purposes of economic betterment
(+ + + +, 1, 2, 30, 47, 51, 54, 59).

> 10.8A. Interarea movement to fill a previously acquired job tends to
> be associated with white-collar and professional occupational status
> (+ + +, 30, 47, 51, 54), a 21–40 age range (+, 54), and high
> school education or above (+ + +, 30, 47, 51, 54).
> 10.8B. Interarea movement to seek new employment (or without
> having previously acquired a job) is associated with lower status and
> manual occupations (+ + +, 30, 47, 51, 54), persons below age 21
> and above age 40 (+, 54), and less than a high school education
> (+ + +, 30, 47, 51, 54).

Middle-aged, middle-class people go to a new region to fill a
position they have already acquired. Lower-class people, as well as
the very young and the very old, move between regions without
necessarily having acquired a job. Their move is linked with their
hopes of obtaining one.

Persons of higher occupational status and high educational level
have resources and knowledge of employment procedures that enable them to make job transitions smoothly and over larger distances. As cosmopolites, they tend to have both a wider range of contacts and associations as well as a pool of information that aids in
their movement.

By contrast, lower-status occupational groups, low-educated populations, and the young and old are motivated by the same basic
aims (better economic opportunity) but lack resources, knowledge,
and marketable skills. Movement involves more uncertainty, since
these groups depart to new locales for the purpose of seeking work,
which may not be available or which may take time to find.

The Tilly and Brown study (54) of migrants of Wilmington, Delaware, documents these points. Higher-status migrants came to

Wilmington already having a new job. They had the capacity to use professional agencies or had other contacts in the Wilmington area. They moved long distances and tended to use professional movers for resettlement. Lower status groups migrated to seek work. They relied on kinship and family ties for information and support. They did not have personal resources or channels to facilitate job location and resettlement.

Action Guidelines: For persons of low occupational rank, the young and old, and persons of low education, services are needed to support interarea migration, including job counseling, job retraining, relocation aid, and financial support in the area of destination. A national job locating and support service might ease the uncertainty over employment for persons fitting these characteristics. This would require developing a national job information center with subcenters in various areas to facilitate job seeking and area relocation. The Swedish system provides a model that might be adopted.

To encourage greater interarea movement, employment opportunity in the areas of destination might be stressed. To discourage interarea movement, areas of departure should develop greater attractions—such as increased occupational and educational opportunities. This is especially true of rural areas on a world wide basis.

Social Class and Migration Distance

GENERALIZATION 10.9: The geographic distance traversed in interarea movement varies according to social class (+ + +, 30, 47, 54).

10.9A. Middle-class and white-collar groups tend to move over longer geographic distances (+ + +, 30, 47, 54).

10.9B. Lower-class and blue-collar groups tend to move either seldom or to move short distances. Successive moves tend to be over progressively longer geographic distances (+ + +, 30, 47, 54).

As one example, Schwartzweller and Brown (47) found that high-status groups in a rural Kentucky area were both more likely to migrate and migrated further distances than lower-status groups. Lower-status groups tended to be more locally oriented both in terms of having less of a tendency to move out of the area as well as moving to a destination close to the original area of residence when relocating.

That middle- and upper-class groups move over longer distances is owing to various factors: having the security of a job on the other end, having contacts and associates at the new location, having the ability to afford long-distance travel, etc. These reasons seen in converse (often in addition to a locality-orientation) explain why the poor are more likely to move in short hops, perhaps becoming more affluent and less locality-oriented with sequential moves. Assuming that more upwardly mobile people are likely to move in the first place, these shifts can be seen as stepping-stones toward middle-class status, with the distance between stones increasing as one comes closer to the goal.

Action Guidelines: In attempting to encourage or support migration of low-income populations (to foster better educational or economic opportunities, for example), the practitioner might take advantage of their natural tendencies in geographic mobility. Thus, one might reduce proximity to the area of origin and increase the distance of the move incrementally. Supportive services in job seeking, retraining, and relocation are useful to sustain this group in its migration efforts.

Occupation and Migration

GENERALIZATION 10.10: Occupational groups vary in their propensity for interarea movement (+ + +, 3, 30, 47, 50, 54).

10.10A. Professional people are most likely to move and blue-collar workers are least likely to move (+ + +, 3, 30, 47, 50, 54).

10.10B. Frequent movers among the professionals tend to be employed in small organizations, salaried, and members of professional associations (+ +, 3, 30).

10.10C. Infrequent movers among the professionals tend to be self-employed or tied to a local clientele or job market. Among this group may be found medical doctors and lawyers in private practice (+, 30).

10.10D. Better working conditions serve as a strong incentive for professionals to migrate to new urban areas (+ +, 3, 30).

Action Guidelines: To encourage interarea moves among professionals (and to aid recruitment):

1. Use national professional associations as a linkage into the professional job information network.
2. Recruit in small organizations and stress improved working conditions in the new positions.
3. For professionals who tend to become tied to the local job market or local clientele, recruit before they graduate from professional schools.

On the other hand, to discourage or redirect migration of professionals, seek to equalize economic remuneration and working conditions on a national basis. Such an arrangement might contribute to bringing medical services, for example, to locales where they are currently lacking or inadequate.

Use of Urban Institutions According to Class

GENERALIZATION 10.11: Experience with the use of urban institutions and sources of aid in migration differs by social class (+ + +, 25, 26, 47, 54).

10.11A. Middle-class groups tend to be characterized by experience in the use of impersonal urban institutions (+ + +, 25, 26, 54) and use of impersonal sources of aid in migration such as "mobility specialists" (movers). They need not rely solely upon kin and friends during and after migration (+ +, 47, 54).

10.11B. Lower-class groups tend to be characterized by lack of experience with impersonal urban institutions (+ + +, 1, 25, 26) and major reliance upon kin and friends for sources of aid during and after migration. This tends to partially counterbalance the limitations of inexperience with the urban setting (+ + + , 1, 47, 54).

10.11C. Persons under 21 or over 40 tend to depend upon kin and friends for assistance before and after migration (+ , 54).

The young and the old are not so likely to be attached to institutions, particularly economic ones. Thus they are not able to use professional associations, business contacts, etc. as linkage mechanisms.

These propositions are illustrated in various studies. For example, it is shown that middle-class migrants become easily involved in civil, political, and other voluntary associations while lower-class migrants do not become involved so quickly (25, 26). In her study of relocation problems, Ablon (1) describes the difficulty that American Indians experienced when they migrated to an urbanized setting in which such everyday but impersonal institutions as banks, post offices, and welfare organizations were foreign and inaccessible to them.

Action Guidelines: The immediate implication here is that lower-class people and the young and old need special aid in linking with urban institutions that can be of assistance to them. This suggests the need for educational efforts to inform them of the availability of services. In addition, it may be necessary to help socialize people in the use of unfamiliar institutions; mere information about their existence will probably not be enough. One should not be overly pessimistic concerning prospects. In a recent study of usage of a community social-service agency, Raphael (43) found evidence that working-class migrants used agency services to a greater degree than nonmigrants of the same social class. This suggests that migrants needing services can and will use them when they are made available and accessible.

Primary Group Linkages

GENERALIZATION 10.12: Regardless of social class, primary group kinship and friendship ties play an important role as linkage to the new setting and as a source of aid after migration (+ + +, 1, 20, 49, 54).

The importance in migration of relatives and friends is for different social classes a matter of degree. As noted previously, lower-class populations rely chiefly upon these primary groups. Middle- and upper-class populations also use kinship and friendship ties, in addition, to numerous other sources of aid (movers, employment agencies, voluntary associations). This point is significant, since it suggests that the family in an industrial society continues to play a significant role even in middle-class groups, which have been characterized in terms of an isolated nuclear family unit with few extended familial linkages.

Action Guidelines: Middle-class populations with many linkages to a new area require little assistance during and after migration. Middle-class populations that have no linkages to their new locations may benefit from services that help integrate them into a new neighborhood setting. Litwak and Fellin (32) suggest that neighborhoods having a positive orientation to new residents develop neighborhood-based voluntary associations in which both husbands and wives can participate, and through which new arrivals can be quickly integrated at a primary group level.

Lower-class populations lacking kinship ties may need to be aided in settlement through the use of close personal contacts by practitioners in detached-worker and other high-intensity professional roles.

Linkage Constellation and Social Class

GENERALIZATION 10.13: The linkage constellation (number and types) between the migrant and the area of destination differs by social class (+ +, 47, 49, 54).

Linkage implies sources that provide aid, information, or encouragement to the migrant. Linkage may include friends, relations, employers, professional organizations, or work associates. It is also possible that the migrant may move on his own with no preexisting linkage. Persons may move into the new setting with a single type of linkage or a combination of linkages.

10.13A. For middle-class populations there tend to be two major patterns of linkage: multiple linkages (job ties, kinship, friendship, etc.), or movement without prior ties to the area of destination (+ +, 47, 54).

10.13B. For lower-class populations movement generally occurs in one linkage pattern: a limited range of linkages largely comprised of friends or relations (+ +, 47, 54).

Action Guidelines: This proposition again underlines the importance of supplementing primary linkages of low-income migrants with contacts to urban institutions and secondary associations, or, if the migrant comes without primary group ties, attempting to replicate these in the new location.

In this section we have dealt with several variables that touch on the assimilation or absorption of migrant populations. This is a subject that requires more extended treatment, for the crux of concern by human-service agencies with population movement centers on the welfare and adjustment of people who migrate. In the discussion to follow, therefore, we shall deal with variables associated with the assimilation or acculturation of populations in motion.

THE PROCESS OF ASSIMILATION OF MOBILE POPULATIONS

Our focus of inquiry here is the rate and process of assimilation of migrant peoples, mostly into new urban settings. We have touched upon aspects of assimilation in earlier sections; here we shall give it concentrated inspection. We shall attempt to develop generalizations about assimilation, whether intraurban or interarea in character.

Assimilation refers to the process by which migrants become involved with new cultural groups in the community of settlement, and concomitantly develop new customs, skills, and attitudes. At the same time, the host community may also develop new characteristics as a consequence of the presence and impact of new population groups.

Some indicators or measures of assimilation found in the research reviewed include organizational participation (10, 25, 26), primary group relationships (2, 22, 23), and political involvement (6, 34). Assimilation may be said to be affected by the attributes, attitudes, and communal organization of the migrant population; the structure and receptivity of the host community; and situational factors that affect the course of assimilation. As summarized by Berry,[4] assimilation is not inevitable; it proceeds at a slow and uneven pace, and includes objective and subjective, as well as conscious and unconscious components. In addition to variables related to the migrant population and the host community, according to Berry, assimilation is affected by such things as the relative numbers of the groups involved in the contact situation, migratory rates of entry, the manner of settlement, and the influence of significant personalities and institutions in either encouraging or opposing assimilation. Our search of the literature illuminates many but not all of these considerations. The manner of presentation of findings will, however, be within the framework of discourse as developed above.

Assimilation Rates and Social Class

GENERALIZATION 10.14: Rates of assimilation into new locations vary according to social class; higher rates of assimilation are correlated with higher social class (+ + + +, 6, 14, 22, 23, 25, 26, 41, 44, 58).

10.14A. People of higher economic status assimilate into new locations at a relatively more rapid rate (+ + + +, 6, 22, 23, 25, 26, 41, 58).

Native-born American migrants of higher economic standing tend to become quickly involved with such voluntary organizations as civic, political, and church groups and tend also to participate in their new setting by voting (6, 25, 26). Similarly, investigators of immigrants to the United States and Australia found, by using acculturation questionnaire items, that more economically advantaged

---

[4] Brewton Berry, *Race Relations: The Interaction of Ethnic and Racial Groups* (New York: Houghton Mifflin Company, 1951).

groups scored high on acculturation scales in their new settings (22, 23, 41, 58).

10.14B. Assimilation rate varies with occupational status (+ + + +, 1, 2 6, 25, 26, 41).

A variety of studies of mobile populations, including Italian Americans, Hungarian refugees, and American Indians, suggested that individuals in positions of low occupational status (such as manual workers) showed low acculturation to their new environment. Measures of primary-group contacts between these groups and the host community groups showed a pattern of few cross-group contacts.

10.14C. Individuals who have or aspire to occupational mobility assimilate more rapidly (+ + +, 14, 22, 42, 58).

Studies of Cuban and Hungarian immigrants to the United States and Italian immigrants to Australia uniformly found that those immigrants who either desired mobility or were actually experiencing occupational mobility scored high on measures of acculturation.

10.14D. People with higher educational attainment assimilate more rapidly (+ + +, 1, 2, 41, 48).

Studies suggest that having a high school education or more is associated with more rapid assimilation. The implications of these social class indices are that having such resources as money, educational abilities, or occupational skills facilitates assimilation. Education would appear to be a particular factor that permits cross-cultural communication to take place.

One hypothesis for understanding the relationship between assimilation and occupational status or mobility is that high occupational status not only increases the economic resources available to the migrant but also tends to bring him into increased contact with others who are different, opening up possibilities for new kinds of social relationships, new social experiences, and new values that facilitate integration into an urban environment.

Curtis (11) states explicitly that interpersonal skill is gained in part from occupational mobility. Inkels's study (24) of components of modern attitudes in six developing countries also adds evidence to the relationships among assimilation, occupational experience, and education. He defines a modern attitude in terms of openness to new experiences, independence from traditional family ties, and active participation in civil affairs. The experiences that were found to be critical for the development of a modern attitude were education and employment in a modern, rational organization, where persons learned new ways of orienting themselves to others and were socialized within a formal or rationalistic organizational structure. There seems to be a connection between what Inkels has defined as a modern attitude and integration into an urban setting. The driving forces for change toward a modern attitude are education and occupational mobility, which are also related to high levels of assimilation.

Action Guidelines: In selecting or recruiting populations for migration, or in anticipating absorption patterns of mobile populations, the practitioner can predict more rapid assimilation from populations of a higher social class. On the other hand, practitioners can anticipate greater needs for service and support in assimilation from lower-class populations. Some services that might tend to facilitate assimilation include financial support, job training, upgrading and placement, educational programs, and subsidies. Programs designed to increase occupational mobility, such as job training, job retraining, and adult education, are especially important.

Assimilation Rates and Race

GENERALIZATION 10.15: Assimilation rates are associated with race. Blacks have lower rates of assimilation (+ + + +, 9, 15, 16, 21, 29, 46).

10.15A. Probably the major factor inhibiting assimilation of black migrants is hostile attitudes in the host community (+ +, 51).

Studies prove racial-exclusion mechanisms make integration of blacks difficult. For example, Taeuber and Taeuber's study (51) of Metropolitan Chicago blacks showed that even when economically affluent, blacks were unable to find housing in white areas.

Action Guidelines: The lack of connection between occupational status, occupational mobility and assimilation for minorities suggests that racial attitudes and practices of the dominant white population must be as important a focus for change as providing such services as educational and occupational advancement programs, aimed at increasing mobility for blacks and other minorities.

Assimilation Rates and Attitudes

GENERALIZATION 10.16: Such attitudes as level of expectation and level of satisfaction are related to assimilation rates (+, 22, 42).

Two studies of immigrant groups (22, 42) independently reported positive statistical relationships between expressed satisfaction with the host environment and measures of acculturation. Hungarian and Italian immigrants to the United States and Australia respectively scored low on measures of acculturation when unhappy with their host environment. One possible explanation involves the circular reasoning that poor acculturation has hindered these groups from developing the skills of the host culture required to fulfill expectations, thus further inhibiting assimilation. It is suggested in these studies that level of satisfaction is linked to the level of expectation experienced by the individual prior to migration; greater dissatisfaction is expressed when the host-community experience does not match the level of expectation held prior to migration.

Action Guidelines: These studies imply that realistic expectations should be conveyed to migrant populations even prior to their departure. A mental set based on actual mobility possibilities apparently aids assimilation and fosters a more favorable psychological outlook.

Assimilation Rate and Length of Settlement

GENERALIZATION 10.17: Assimilation is associated with lenth of residence in the host community. An initial time period for adjustment appears to be necessary before assimilation is facilitated (+ + +, 10, 25, 26, 32).

The longer persons spend in their new community, the more likely they are to become integrated. New arrivals tend to have an adjustment period before assimilation occurs. For example, in a study of ethnic group communities in Montreal, Briton (10) found that group members tend initially to become involved in primary- and secondary-group associations of their own ethnic background. These contacts provide familiarity, protection, and mutual aid, but then do not preclude simultaneous ties to the native population. However, these latter ties increase after six or more years of residence. Similarly, Litwak and Fellin's study (32) of middle-class residents and Jitodai's studies (25, 26) of a more general population of residents found that there is an initial period after relocation in which involvement in voluntary associations is low; later, involvement may increase to a level equal to that of the host population.

10.17A. First- and second-generation migrants of minority-group origins tend to have more ties than their parents to the host culture (+, 39).

Palisi (39), for example, reported that first-generation Italians, as compared with their foreign-born parents, had a higher diversity of friendships with host population groups, indicating in part that children of immigrants tend to be more integrated than their parents.

Migrants may themselves be deeply involved with their own subculture and still encourage their children to become more integrated into the dominant culture (17). Portes's study (42) of Cuban immigrants showed that, although adults were fairly isolated culturally in their new setting, they nevertheless wanted their children to learn English, become educated, and associate with both Americans and Cubans.

Action Guidelines: It appears that migrant populations should be provided with a period of accommodation and adjustment, possibly in a familiar in-group setting, before active assimilation behavior can be expected or encouraged. "Slow" assimilation should neither be frowned upon, nor should it cause practitioners to feel a sense of discomfort or failure. One might well take a considerably longer range view of assimilation, anticipating gradual acculturation on a cross-generational basis.

Settlement in Highly Concentrated Ethnic Areas

GENERALIZATION 10.18: Mobile ethnic and minority-group populations tend to settle in sections of host communities having high concentrations of persons of similar ethnic or minority-group origin (+ + + +, 1, 22, 28, 29, 54).

10.18A. Lower-class ethnic and minority-group populations especially tend to settle in areas of high concentration of similar ethnic populations (+ + +, 1, 2, 33, 39).

For example, studies of American Indians migrating to a large northern California city report settlement in areas with a high American Indian population (1, 2). This tendency is reported also for blacks, as well as Italian, Hungarian, and Cuban immigrant groups (22, 28, 29, 54).

10.18B. Settlement in areas of high ethnic- and minority-group concentration is associated with linkages to these areas based on friendship and kinship ties (+ + +, 28, 33, 54).

Research suggests that settlement in high-concentration ethnic- and minority-group areas tends to be associated with lower-class status, although middle-class ethnic groups also show this tendency to a lesser degree. For lower-class migrants, settlement in ethnic areas permits assistance and emotional support to be given by friends and relatives to those facing a strange life in a new urban environment.

Tilly and Brown (54) found that lower-status migrants to the city of Wilmington, Delaware, relied heavily before, during, and after migration upon friends and relations for job information, material assistance, and support. Similarly Schwartzweller and Brown (47), studying migration patterns of persons from rural Kentucky, found that migrants used friendship and kinship ties to the city for information and assistance.

Action Guidelines: To encourage or to assist natural movements of minority and ethnic groups, especially those of the lower-class, practitioners should provide opportunities for settlement in areas of high ethnic concentration. This may involve making contacts with associations and organizations of similar minority- and ethnic-group origins in the area of destination to aid these groups during and after migration.

Ethnic Composition of the Host Community

GENERALIZATION 10.19: Assimilation rates of ethnic groups are affected by the ethnic composition of the host community (+ + + +, 6, 7, 22, 28, 42, 56).

> 10.19A. Settlement in areas of high ethnic concentration generally tends to slow down assimilation (+ + +, 1, 2, 6, 22).
>
> Where residence, interactions, and identification with the ethnic subculture intensify minority or ethnic consciousness, integration with the dominant culture may be limited. Studies of minority groups and immigrant groups (Native American, blacks, Hungarian, Cubans, etc.) consistently found that persons living in high-concentration minority- or ethnic-group communities had little contact with host population groups or score low on measures of acculturation.
>
> 10.19B. Ethnic-area subcultural institutions (particularly the church) that view assimilation in a favorable light can facilitate integration into the larger community (+, 25, 42).
>
> Two studies cite involvement in the ethnic church as a mechanism for increasing contact with the larger community. The church can be a context for in-group protection, mutual aid, and subcultural survival, while at the same time serving as a structured linkage channel for integration or contact with the larger community. The significance of this subproposition in juxtaposition to the previous one is the understanding that settlement by migrants in an in-group subcommunity can serve either to foster or restrain assimilation, depending on the posture of subcultural institutions toward the larger community.
>
> 10.19C. Residence by individuals in areas of mixed ethnic-host population or in areas of mostly host population tends to accelerate integration (+ + +, 22, 42, 58).

Studies of three immigrant groups to the United States (Italians, Cubans, and Hungarians) revealed that residence in mixed or predominantly host population areas is associated with high acculturation scores for immigrants located in these types of settings. This short-circuits the initial adjustment period experienced by most immigrants.

Action Guidelines: When seeking to preserve ethnic- or minority-group subcultures, practitioners should encourage movement to areas of high ethnic-group or minority-group concentration and should assist in the preservation of subgroup institutions. When seeking to encourage rapid integration into the host community, practitioners might attempt to settle migrants in mixed areas or areas having a high concentration of the host population. Alternatively, assimilation may be facilitated through a process of initial settlement in an ethnic community, with encouragement by subcultural institutions of broader community involvement as well as the provision by these institutions of channels for wider community contact.

Host-Community Blocks to Assimilation

GENERALIZATION 10.20: Assimilation of minority groups may be hampered by resistances and blocks imposed by the host community (+ + + +, 15, 16, 19, 27, 29, 46, 52, 53).

10.20A. Job discrimination hampers occupational mobility for racial minorities while residential discrimination hampers integration into the larger community (+ + +, 19, 52).

One especially revealing study was conducted by Taeuber and Taeuber (52). Blacks were viewed as an immigrant group and compared with other ethnic migrant groups, including Puerto Ricans and Mexicans, with regard to residential segregation. The investigators found that over the past 30 years, black residential segregation has remained high, but that all other immigrants have experienced decreasing residential segregation. Secondly, there was a positive relationship between income and residential dispersion for all immigrant groups except blacks. For blacks, higher socioeconomic status did not increase residential dispersion.

10.20B. Residential segregation of ethnic and racial groups because of discrimination and racism has remained fairly constant in the past ten years and has even increased in some sections of the country (+ + +, 29, 46, 53).

Action Guidelines: This proposition points out that assimilation, particularly in the form of integration, is a two-way process in which minority-group migrants must often face a hostile host environment. It has a reciprocal character in that migrants go through a process of preparation for assimilation, but the new community must also be ready to accept them into its social life. Discrimination toward newcomers may be one of the strongest barriers to assimilation into a host community. Accordingly, practitioners may help minority groups organize to counteract discrimination, work with groups in the host community to eliminate discriminatory practices, or encourage higher level governmental action against discriminatory practices.

Host Community Preferences

GENERALIZATION 10.21: Host communities and their subgroups vary in terms of preferences for different migrant populations (+, 27).

The study on which this generalization is based explored the attitudes of Canadians at different occupational levels toward immigrants of varying occupations. It was conducted in a central Canadian town of 12,000, which had experienced an influx of immigrants after the war. Two samples were taken, totaling 155 subjects in all. This research report was based on two questions included in the survey:

1. "If you were in a position to suggest what types of immigrant workers can enter Canada, how would you decide?" (Followed by a list of ten occupations to be rated on a five-point acceptability scale.)

2. "How do you feel about . . ." (Followed by a list of ten occupations and the corresponding service they offer the individual
   to be rated on a five-point scale of willingness to use the service
   offered by immigrants.)

The responses confirmed the hypothesis that immigrants are differentially legitimized in terms of their occupations and services. Immigrants in high-status jobs were more acceptable as candidates for
admission to the country. Natives as a whole were less willing to use
services of immigrants in high prestige occupations than those in low.
Further, natives employed in high-prestige occupations were more
willing to admit immigrants and use their services than were those
employed in low-prestige occupations.

This leads to the following set of subgeneralizations:

10.21A. Host population groups, regardless of status, prefer admission of immigrants of high occupational status (+, 27).

10.21B. High-status natives are more willing to use services of immigrant populations (+, 27).

Action Guidelines: Higher status host population groups
may be helpful in breaking down resistances of other groups
toward the services offered by new immigrants. Political mobilization or functional involvement of such groups may be a
useful tactic. On the other hand, educational and "human
relations" programs might be directed at lower-class host
populations to foster acceptance, possibly by using the influence and attitudes of higher-class persons in an instructive
capacity.

Impact of Migrant Populations

GENERALIZATION 10.22: Migrant populations may effect
structural changes in the host community (+ + +, 5, 6, 20,
34, 58).

This statement reiterates that assimilation involves a two-way or reciprocal dynamic: the mobile population is changed or absorbed within
the host community, while at the same time the host community may

be modified through the impact made on it by the incoming population.

10.22A. Population changes may result in modified voting patterns and political alignments in the host community (+ +, 5, 6, 20, 34).

Studies in the United States suggest that the migrants may have a decided impact in changing voting patterns and political alignments. One study (34) reports that the influx of migrants into urban areas of the Southern states has (among other factors) contributed to the change in political alignment of the South from a predominantly Democratic Party structure to a two-party structure with increasing Republican strength.

10.22B. The social status of migrants and the stability of the political system tend to influence the character of political involvement by migrants (+ +, 5, 6, 20, 58).

Two studies (20, 58) of developing countries in Latin America suggest that when the political system is unstable and unable to provide necessary social and economic services for rural migrants to the urban centers, left-wing party voting and political violence may occur. This is more likely to occur among low-status migrants who are unable to find employment and who experience value flux as a result of a change in the authority structure within the urban setting. Higher-status migrants are less likely to engage in political violence or left-wing voting, because their skills allow them to achieve economic integration; but they too may be activated for political change efforts when the political system cannot create economic and social conditions conducive to their assimilation. Studies (5, 6) in the United States indicate that higher status migrants are more likely to involve themselves in voting and other conventional political behavior than are lower class migrants.

Action Guidelines: Migrants may be viewed as a resource for social change. Lower-class migrants show potential for social action, upper-class migrants for conventional political action. In developing countries, progressive governmental policies should stress economic development in rural areas in order to meet needs and discourage excessive urban migration, especially when jobs are unavailable in urban centers. Workers seeking support for radical movements will find recruits among migrants who are new to the city or un-employed.

CONCLUSION

From the foregoing discussion it becomes clear that economic varia-bles—especially social-class and occupational factors—are highly sig-nificant to an understanding of the nature of population movements and the planning of appropriate strategies for intervention. Not only do the human-service needs of different class groups vary, but these groups also require different social and communal environments for easy relocation. Urban renewal tends to have a disrupting and debili-tating influence on families while racism places a uniquely invidious burden on nonwhite populations involved in migration.

BIBLIOGRAPHY FOR PART SIX

A: Chapter Nine

1. Aiken, Michael and Robert R. Alford. "Community Structure and Innovation: The Case of Urban Renewal." Paper presented to American Sociological Association Meeting, June 1969.

2. Aiken, Michael and Jerald Hage. "Organizational Interdependence and Inter-Organizational Structure." *American Sociological Review,* 33, no. 6 (December 1968): 912–30.

3. Aldrich, Howard. "Non-Racial Political Movements: Political Mobilization and the Middle Class." *Working Papers on Center for Research on Social Organization, University of Michigan,* Paper 35 (June 1968), pp. 1–35.

4. Allen, Thomas J. and Stephen J. Cohen. "Information Flow in Research and Development Laboratories." *Administrative Science Quarterly* 14, no.1 (March 1969): 12–19.

5. Alvarez, Rudolfo. "Informal Reaction to Deviance in Simulated Work Organization, A Laboratory Experiment." *American Sociological Review* 33, no. 6 (December 1968).

6. Archer, Morton, Seymour Rinzler, and George Christakis. "Social Factors Affecting Participation in a Study of Diet and Coronary Heart Disease." *Journal of Health and Social Behavior,* 8, no. 1 (March 1967): 22–31.

7. Baker, Frank and Herbert C. Schulberg. "Community Mental Health Ideology, Dogmatism and Political-Economic Conservatism." *Community Mental Health Journal* 5, no. 6 (December 1969): 433–36.

8. Bennett, Claude F. "Diffusion within Dynamic Populations." *Human Organization.* 28, no. 3 (Fall 1969): 243–47.

9. Bernard, Sydney, Emeric Kurtagh, and Harold Johnson. "The Neighborhood Service Organization: Specialist in Social Welfare Innovation," *Social Work* 13, no. 1 (January 1968): 76–84.

10. Birkby, Robert H. "The Supreme Court and the Bible Belt: Tennessee Reaction to the Schempp Decision." *Midwest Journal of Political Science* 10, no. 3 (August 1966): 304–19.

11. Blanco, Antonio and Sheila Akabas. "The Factory Site for Community Mental Health Practice." *American Journal of Orthopsychiatry* 38, no. 3 (April 1968): 543–52.

12. Blankenship, L. Vaughn and Raymond E. Miles. "Organizational Structure and Managerial Behavior." *Administrative Science Quarterly* 13, no 1 (June 1968): 106–20.

13. Blau, Zena Smith. "Exposure to Child-Rearing Experts: A Structural Interpretation of Class-Color Differences." *American Journal of Sociology* 69, no. 6 (May 1964): 596–608.

14. Bok, Marcia. "A Motivation Model of Participation in Activities among Chronic Geriatric Mental Patients." Doctoral dissertation, University of Michigan, 1968.

15. Brager, George. "The Indigenous Worker: A New Approach to the Social Work Technician." *Social Work* 10, no. 2 (April 1965): 33–40.

16. Bucher, Rue. "The Psychiatric Residency and Professional Socialization." *Health and Social Behavior* 6, no. 4 (Winter 1965): 197–206.

17. Cancian, Frank. "Stratification and Risk-Taking: A Theory Tested on Agricultural Innovation." *American Sociological Review* 32, no. 6 (December 1967): 912–26.

18. Carmack, William R. "Communication and Community Readiness for Social Change." *American Journal of Orthopsychiatry*. 35, no. 3 (April 1965): 539–543.

19. Cauffman, Jay. "Motivating University Women to Positive Health Behavior." *Journal of Health and Social Behavior* 7, no. 4 (Winter 1966): 295–302.

20. Chattopadkyay, L. N. and Udai Pareek. "Prediction of Multi-Practice Adoption Behavior from Some Psychosocial Variables." *Rural Sociology* 32, no. 3 (September 1967): 324–33.

21. Chetkow, B. Harold. "Some Factors Influencing the Utilization and Impact of Priority Recommendations in Community Planning." *Social Service Review* 41, no. 3 (September 1967): 271–82.

22. Coe, Rodney M. and Elizabeth A. Barnhill. "Social Dimensions of Failure in Innovation." *Human Organization* 26, no. 3 (Fall 1967): 149–56.

23. Coughenow, C. Milton. "The Rate of Technological Diffusion among Locality Groups." *American Journal of Sociology* 69, no. 4 (January 1964): 325–39.

24. Cowart, Andrew T. "Anti-Poverty Expenditures in the American States: A Comparative Analysis." *Midwest Journal of Political Science* 13, no.2 (May 1969): 219–36.

25. Crain, Robert L. "Fluoridation: The Diffusion of an Innovation among Cities." *Social Forces* 44, no. 4 (June 1966): 467–77.

26. Curtis, Richard F., Dianne M. Timbers, and Elton F. Jackson. "Prejudice and Urban Social Participation." *American Journal of Sociology* 73, no. 2 (September 1967): 235–46.

27. Daniels, Arlene K. "The Captive Professional: Bureaucratic Limitations within the Practice of Military Psychiatry." *Journal of Health and Social Behavior* 10, no. 4 (December 1969): 255–65.

28. Daxjupta, Satadal. "Communication and Innovation in Indian Villages." *Social Forces* 43, no. 3 (March 1965): 330–37.

29. deFleur, Melvin and L. B. "The Relative Contribution of Television as a Learning Source for Children's Occupational Knowledge." *American Sociological Review* 32, no. 5 (October 1967): 777–89.

30. Dohrenwend, Bruce P. and Edwin Chin-Song. "Social Status and Attitudes toward Psychological Discord: The Problem of Tolerance of Deviance." *American Sociological Review* 32, no. 3 (June 1967): 417–33.

31. Doig, Jameson W. "Police Problems, Proposals and Strategies for Change." *Public Administration Review* 28, no. 5 (September–October 1968): 393–406.

32. Dunmore, Charlotte J. "School Bureaucracies and Family Acceptance of Educa-

tional Opportunity Programs.'' Paper presented to American Sociological Association Meeting, San Francisco, September 1, 1969.

33. Edinger, Lewis J. and Donald S. Searing. "Social Background in Elite Aanlysis: A Methodological Inquiry." *American Political Science Review* 61, no. 2 (June 1967): 428–46.

34. Edmonds, Vernon H. "Logical Error and Function of Group Consensus: An Experimental Study of the Effect of Erroneous Group Consensus Upon Logical Judgments of Graduate Students." *Social Forces* 43, no. 1 (October 1964): 33–38.

35. Emerson, Luther et al. "Acceptance of Family Planning among a Cohort of Recently Delivered Mothers." *American Journal of Public Health* 58, no. 9 (September 1968): 1738–45.

36. Fathi, Asghar. "Leadership and Resistance to Change: A Case from an Underdeveloped Area." *Rural Sociology* 30, no. 2 (June 1965): 204–12.

37. Faunce, William A. and M. Joseph Smucker. "Industrialization and Community Status Structure." *American Sociological Review* 37, no. 3 (June 1966): 390–99.

38. Feagin, Joe R. "Prejudice, Orthodoxy and the Social Situation." *Social Forces* 44, no. 1 (September 1965): 46–57.

39. Fendrich, James M. "Perceived Reference Group Support: Racial Attitudes and Overt Behavior." *American Sociological Review* 32, no. 6 (December 1967): 960–90.

40. Fliegel, Frederick C. "Differences in Prestige Standards and Orientation to Change in a Traditional Agricultural Setting." *Rural Sociology* 30, no. 3 (September 1965): 279–90.

41. Fliegel, Frederick C. and Gurmeet S. Sekhon. "Balance Theory and the Diffusion of Innovations, an Empirical Test." Paper presented to the American Sociological Association, San Francisco, 1969.

42. Foster, George M. "Present Society and the Image of Limited Good." *American Anthropologist* 67, no. 2 (April 1965): 293–310.

43. Frank, Jerome D. and Jacob Schonfield. "Commitment to Peace Work: A Closer Look at Determinants." *American Journal of Orthopsychiatry* 37, no. 1 (January 1967): 112–19.

44. Freedman, Ronald, John Y. Taklshita, and T. H. Sun. "Fertility and Family Planning in Taiwan: A Case Study of the Demographic Transition." *American Journal of Sociology* 70, no. 1 (July 1964): 16–27.

45. Frey, Frederick. "Socialization to National Identification among Turkish Peasants." *Journal of Politics* 30, no. 4 (November 1968): 934–65.

46. Friedson, Eliot and Buford Rhea. "Knowledge and Judgment in Professional Evaluations." *American Sociological Review* 10, no. 1 (June 1965): 107–24.

47. Geschwender, James A. "Status Inconsistency, Social Isolation, and Individual Unrest." *Social Forces* 46, no. 4 (June 1968): 477–84.

48. Goldberg, Harvey. "Elite Groups in Peasant Communities: A Comparison of Three Eastern Villages." *American Anthropologist* 70, no. 4 (August 1968): 718–32.

49. Goldkind, Victor. "Social Stratification in the Peasant Community." *American Anthropologist* 67, no. 4 (August 1965): 863–83.

50. Goldschmidt, Walter. "Theory and Strategy in the Study of Cultural Adaptability." *American Anthropologist* 67, no. 2 (April 1965): 402–7.

51. Goldschneider, Calvin and Peter R. Uhlenberg. "Minority Group Status and Fertility." *American Journal of Sociology* 74, no. 4 (December 17, 1969): 12.

52. Gordon, Gerald and Sue Marquis. "Freedom, Visibility of Consequences and Scientific Innovation." *American Journal of Sociology* 72, no. 2 (September 1966): 195–202.

53. Gross, Neal, Joseph B. Giacquinta, and Marilyn Bernstein. "Complex Organizations: The Implementation of Major Organization Innovations." Paper presented to American Sociological Association Meeting, Boston, August 1968.

54. Hage, Jerald and Michael Aiken, "Program Change and Organizational Properties." *American Journal of Sociology* 72, no. 5 (March 1967): 503–19.

55. Hage, Jerald and Michael Aiken. "Routine Technology, Social Structure and Organizational Goals." *Administrative Science Quarterly* 14, no. 3 (September 1969): 366–75.

56. Hage, Jerald and Michael Aiken. *Social Change in Complex Organizations*. New York: Random House, 1970.

57. Hall, Julian Craven. "The Conflict between Income Guarantee Proposals and the Value of Work." Doctoral dissertation, Washington University, 1968.

58. Hardee, Gilbert J. "Planned Change and Systemic Linkage in a Five-Year Extension Program with Part Time Farm Families." *Rural Sociology* 30, no. 1 (March 1965): 23–32.

59. Harp, John and Richard J. Gagan. "Renewal Plans: A General Systems Analysis of Rural Townships." *Rural Sociology* 33, no. 4 (December 1968): 460–73.

60. Hemmens, George C. "Planning Agency Experience with Urban Developmental Models and Data Processing." *Journal of the American Institute of Planners* 34, no. 5 (September 1968): 323–27.

61. Horner, James T. and Alan B. Knox. "Encouraging Non-College Bound Rural Young Adults to Participate in Continuing Education." *Adult Leadership* 14, no. 6 (December 1965): 186.

62. Inkeles, Alex. "Making Men Modern: On the Causes and Consequences of Individual Change in Six Developing Countries." *American Journal of Sociology* 75, no. 2 (December 8, 1968): 18.

63. Jacobs, Milton. "A Study of Key Communicators in Urban Thailand." *Social Forces* 45, no. 2 (December 1966): 192–99.

64. Jaffe, Frederick S. "A Strategy for Implementing Family Planning in the United States." *American Journal of Public Health* 58, no. 4 (April 1968): 713–25.

65. Jhirad-Reid, Judith. "Patterns of Problem-Solving Activities of the Users and Non-Users of Social Agencies." Doctoral dissertation, Bryn Mawr College, 1969.

520   Two Social Change Processes

66. Jitodai, Ted T. "Urban-Rural Background and Formal Group Membership." *Rural Sociology* 30, no. 1 (March 1965): 75–82.

67. Johnson, Raymond L., Richard W. Cartwright, and Jessie V. Cooper. "Attitude Changes among Literacy Teachers Coincident with Training and Experiences." *Adult Education* 18, no. 2 (Winter 1968): 71–80.

68. Johnson, Cyrus M. and Alan C. Kerckhoff. "Family Norms, Social Norms, Social Position and the Value of Change." *Social Forces* 43, no. 2 (December 1964): 149–56.

69. Jones, Frank E. and Wallace E. Lambert. "Occupational Rank and Attitudes toward Immigrants." *Public Opinion Quarterly* 29, no. 1 (Spring 1965): 137–44.

70. Kahn, Roger. "Rank and File Student Activism: A Contextual Test of Three Hypotheses." Paper presented to American Sociological Association Meeting, 1969, pp. 1–9.

71. Katz, Elihu and Brenda Danet. "Petition and Persuasive Appeals: A Study of Official Client Relationships." *American Sociological Review* 37, no. 6 (December 1966): 811–21.

72. Kegeles, S. Stephen. "A Field Experimental Attempt to Change Beliefs and Behavior of Women in an Urban Ghetto." *Journal of Health and Social Behavior* 10, no. 2 (June 1969): 115–24.

73. Kivlin, Joseph E. and Frederick Fliegel. "Differential Perceptions of Innovations and Rates of Adoption." *Rural Sociology* 32, no. 1 (March 1967): 78–91.

74. Klein, Julius, and Derek L. Phillips. "From Hard to Soft Drugs: Temporal and Substantive Changes in Drug Usage among Gangs in a Working Class Community." *Journal of Health and Social Behavior* 9, no. 2 (June 1968): 139–45.

75. Kurtz, Norman R. "Gatekeepers: Agents in Acculturation." *Rural Sociology* 33, no. 1 (March 1968): 64–70.

76. Lane, Jonathan P. "Isolation and Public Opinion in Rural Northeast Brazil." *Public Opinion Quarterly* 33, no. 1 (Spring 1969): 55–68.

77. Lay, John W., Jr. "Social Psychological Characteristics of Innovators." *American Sociological Review* 34, no. 1 (February 1969): 73–82.

78. Liberman, Robert. "Personal Influence in the Use of Mental Health Resources." *Human Organization* 24, no. 3 (Fall 1965): 231–35.

79. Linn, Lawrence. "Social Identification and the Seeking of Psychiatric Care." *American Journal of Orthopsychiatry* 38, no. 1 (January 1968): 83–88.

80. Linsky, Arnold. "Community Structure, Mental Hospitalization and Reaction to Deviant Behavior." Paper presented to American Sociological Association Meeting, Boston, 1968, pp. 1–7.

81. Lionberger, Herbert F. and Joe De Francis. "Views Held of Innovator and Influence Referents as Sources of Farm Information in a Missouri Community." *Rural Sociology* 34, no. 2 (June 1969): 197–211.

82. Longley, Lawrence. "Interest Group Interaction in a Legislative System." *Journal of Politics* 29, no. 3 (August 1967): 637–58.

83. Loomis, Charles P. "In Praise of Conflict and Its Resolution." *American Sociological Review* 32, no. 6 (December 1967): 875–91.

84. Maddox, George L. and Joseph H. Fichter. "Religion and Social Change in the South." *Journal of Social Issue* 22, no. 1 (January 1966): 44–59.

85. Markus, Nathan. "Staff Participation in Organizational Change: A Study of the Participation of Staff Members of Social Service Organizations in Activities Aimed at Influencing Changes in the Services and Functions of the Employing Agencies." Doctoral dissertation, University of Toronto, 1969.

86. Mauss, Amand L. "Anticipatory Socialization toward College as a Factor in Marijuana Use." *Social Problems* 16, no. 3 (Winter 1969): 357–64.

87. Mohr, Lawrence B. "Determinants of Innovation in Organizations." *American Political Science Review* 63, no. 1 (March 1969): 111–26.

88. Molotch, Harvey. "Racial Integration in a Transition Community." *American Sociological Review* 34, no. 6 (December 1969): 878–93.

89. Monk, Mary, Matthew Tayback, and Joseph Gordon. "Evaluation of an Anti-Smoking Program among High School Students." *American Journal of Public Health* 55, no. 7 (July 1965): 994–1004.

90. Morris, Robert and Ollie A. Randall. "Planning and Organization of Community Services for the Elderly." *Social Work* 10, no. 1 (January 1965): 96–103.

91. Mueller, John E. "Fluoridation Attitude Change." *American Journal of Public Health* 58, no. 10 (November 1968): 1876–80.

92. Nall, Frank C., II, and Joseph Speilberg. "Social and Cultural Factors in the Responses of Mexican Americans to Medical Treatment." *Journal of Health and Social Behavior* 8, no. 4 (December 1967): 299–308.

93. Nash, A. "The Impact of Adult Education on Taxi Drivers During an Organizing Drive." *Adult Leadership* 16, no. 5 (November 1967): 183–85.

94. Nasitir, David. "A Note on Contextual Effects and the Political Orientation of University Students." *American Sociological Review* 33, no. 2 (April 1968): 210–13.

95. O'Donnell, John A. and Judith P. Jones. "Diffusion of the Intravenous Techniques among Narcotic Addicts in the United States." *Journal of Health and Social Behavior* 9, no. 2 (June 1968): 120–30.

96. Orum, Anthony. "Structural Sources of Negro Student Protest: Campus and Community." Paper presented to American Sociological Association Meeting, August 1969.

97. Paageorgis, Demetrios. "Prevention and Treatment in Mental Health Communications." *Public Opinion Quarterly* 29, no. 1 (Spring 1965): 107–19.

98. Palisi, Bartolomeo J. "Ethnic Patterns of Friendship." *Phylon* 26, no. 3 (Fall 1966): 217–25.

99. Palumbo, Dennis J. "Power and Role Specificity in Organizational Theory." *Public Administration Review* 29, no. 3 (May–June 1969): 237–48.

100. Pappenfort, Donnell M. and Dee Morgan Kilpatrick. "Opportunities for Physi-

cally Handicapped Children: A Study of Attitudes and Practices in Settlements and Community Centers." *Social Service Review* 41, no. 2 (June 1967): 179–88.

101. Patchen, Martin. "Labor-Management Consultation at TVA: Its Impact on Employees." *Administrative Science Quarterly* 10, no. 2 (September 1965): 149–74.

102. Perrucci, Robert and Robert A. Rothman. "Obsolescence of Knowledge and the Professional Career." Working paper # 12, Institute for the Study of Social Change, Purdue University, 1969.

103. Petras, James and Maurice Zeitlin. "Miners and Agrarian Radicalism." *American Sociological Review* 32, no. 4 (August 1967): 578–86.

104. Plotnick, Morton. "Education and Mass Mailing: Its Impact on Volunteers." *Adult Education* 15, no. 2 (Winter 1965): 87–88.

105. Polgar, Steven, Howard Dunphy, and Bruce Cox. "Diffusion and Farming Advice: A Test of Some Current Notions." *Social Forces* 42, no. 1 (October 1963): 104–11.

106. Pratt, Lois. "Level of Sociological Knowledge among Health and Social Workers." *Journal of Health and Social Behavior* 10, no. 1 (March 1969): 59–65.

107. Press, Irwin. "Urban Illness: Physicians, Curers and Dual Use in Bogota." *Journal of Health and Social Behavior* 10, no. 3 (September 1969): 209–18.

108. Price, James L. "Use of New Knowledge in Organizations." *Human Organization* 23, no. 3 (Fall 1964): 224–34.

109. Putnam, Robert D. "Political Attitudes and the Local Community." *American Political Science Review* 60, no. 3 (September 1966): 640–54.

110. Raphael, Edna E. "Community Structure and Acceptance of Psychiatric Aid." *American Journal of Sociology* 69, no. 4 (January 1964): 340–58.

111. Reeder, Leo G. and Goteti B. Krishnamurty. "Family Planning in Rural India: A Problem in Social Change." *Social Problems* 12, no. 2 (Fall 1964): 212–23.

112. Reynolds, Harry W., Jr. "Public Housing and Social Values in an American City." *Social Service Review* 39, no. 2 (June 1965): 157–64.

113. Rieger, Jon H. and Robert C. Anderson. "Information Source and Need Hierarchies of an Adult Population in Five Michigan Counties." *Adult Education* 18, no. 3 (Spring 1968): 155–75.

114. Riley, John M. "A Comparative Study of Social Workers' Role Orientation in the State Mental Hospitals with Differing Organizational Structures." Doctoral dissertation, Brandeis, 1967.

115. Robinson, Derek. "Effectiveness of Medical and Social Supervisors in a Multiproblem Population." *American Journal of Public Health* 58, no. 2 (February 1968): 252–62.

116. Rogers, Everett. *Diffusion of Innovations*. New York: Free Press, 1962.

117. Rosenfeld, Henry. "Changes, Barriers to Change and Contradiction in the Arab Village Family." *American Anthropologist* 70, no. 4 (July 1968): 732–53.

118. Rosenthal, Donald B. and Robert L. Crain. "Executive Leadership and Community Innovation: Fluoridation." *Urban Affairs Quarterly* 1, no. 3 (March 1966): 39–57.

119. Rosner, Martin M. "Economic Determinants of Organizational Innovation." *Administrative Science Quarterly* 12, no. 4 (March 1968): 614–25.

120. Salem, Elie. "Local Elections in Lebanon." *Midwest Journal of Political Science* 9, no. 4 (November 1965): 376–87.

121. Sawhney, M. Mohan. "Farm Practice Adoption and the Uses of Information Sources and Media in A Rural Community in India." *Rural Sociology* 32, no. 3 (September 1967): 310–23.

122. Schmuck, Richard A. "Helping Teachers Improve Classroom Group Processes." *Applied Behavioral Science* 4, no. 4 (October–December 1968): 401–35.

123. Scott, Joseph W. "Sources of Social Change in Community, Family and Fertility in a Puerto Rican Town." *American Journal of Sociology* 72, no. 5 (March 1967): 520–30.

124. Scott, Thomas M. "The Diffusion of Urban Governmental Forms as a Case of Social Learning." *Journal of Politics* 30, no. 4 (November 1968): 1091–1108.

125. Scott, W. Richard. "Reactions to Supervision in a Heteronomous Professional Organization." *Administrative Science Quarterly* 10 (June 1965): 65–81.

126. Sibley, Willis E. "Social Organization, Economy, and Directed Cultural Change in Two Philippine Barrios." *Human Organization* 28, no. 2 (Summer 1969): 148–54.

127. Silverman, Lydel F. "An Ethnographic Approach to Social Stratification: Prestige in an Italian Community." *American Anthropologist* 68, no. 4 (July 1966): 899–919.

128. Spiro, Melford E. "Buddhism and Economic Action in Burma." *American Anthropologist* 68, no. 5 (October 1966): 1163–74.

129. Spitzer, Stephen P. and Norman K. Denzin. "Level of Knowledge in an Emergent Crisis." *Social Forces* 44, no. 2 (December 1965): 234–38.

130. Stycos, J. Mayone. "Haitian Attitudes toward Family Size." *Human Organization* 23, no. 1 (Spring 1964): 42–47.

131. Stycos, J. Mayone. "Social Class and Preferred Family Size in Peru." *American Journal of Sociology* 70, no. 6 (May 1965): 651–58.

132. Stycos, J. Mayone. "The Potential Role of Turkish Village Opinion Leaders in a Program of Family Planning." *Public Opinion Quarterly* 29, no. 1 (Spring 1965): 100–130.

133. Suchman, Edward A. "Sociomedical Variations among Ethnic Groups." *American Journal of Sociology* 3 (November 1964): 319–31.

134. Suchman, Edward A. "Preventive Health Behavior: A Model for Research on Community Health Campaigns." *Journal of Health and Social Behavior* 8, no. 3 (September 1967): 197–209.

135. Swinehart, James W. "Voluntary Exposure to Health Communications." *American Journal of Public Health* 58, no. 7 (July 1968): 1265–75.

136. Tannenbaum, Arnold S. and Jerald G. Bachman, "Attitude Uniformity and Role in a Voluntary Organization." *Human Relations* 19, no. 3 (August 1966): 309–23.

137. Thomas, Norman C. "The Electorate and State Constitutional Revision: An Analysis of Four Michigan Referenda." *Midwest Journal of Political Science* 12, no. 1 (February 1968): 115–29.

138. Thompson, Victor A. "Bureaucracy and Innovation." *Administrative Science Quarterly* 10, no. 1 (June 1965): 1–20.

139. Tulley, Joan, E. A. Wilkening, and H. A. Presser. "Factors in the Decision-Making in Farming Problems." *Human Relations* 17, no. 4 (November 1964): 295–320.

140. Varon, Edith. "Communication: Client, Community and Agency." *Social Work* 9, no. 2 (April 1964): 51–57.

141. Walker, Jack L. "The Diffusion of Innovations among the American States." *American Political Science Review* 63, no. 3 (September 1969): 880–99.

142. Walter, Benjamin. "Internal Control Relations in Administrative Hierarchies." *Administrative Science Quarterly* 11, no. 2 (September 1966): 179–206.

143. Warriner, Charles K. "Traditional Authority and the Modern State: The Case of the Maranao of the Philippines." *Social Problems* 12, no. 1 (June 1964): 51–56.

144. Weeks, Kent M. "Public Servants in the New Zealand Ombudsman System." *Public Administration Review* 29, no. 6 (November–December 1969): 633–38.

145. Whitten, Norman E., Jr. "Power Structure and Sociocultural Change in Latin American Communities." *Social Forces* 43, no. 3 (March 1965): 320–30.

146. Wilkening, E. A. and Sylvia Guerrero. "Consensus in Aspirations for Farm Improvement and Adoption of Farm Practices." *Rural Sociology* 34, no. 2 (June 1969): 182–96.

147. Wood, James R. and Mayer N. Zald. "Aspects of Racial Integration in the Methodist Church: Sources of Resistance to Organizational Policy." *Social Forces* 45, no. 2 (December 1966): 255–65.

148. Wyllie, Robert W. "Ritual and Social Change: A Ghanian Example." *American Anthropologist* 70, no. 1 (February 1968): 21–34.

149. Yaukey, David, William Griffiths, and Beryl J. Roberts. "Couple Concurrence and Empathy on Birth Control Motivation in Dacca, East Pakistan." *American Sociological Review* 32, no. 5 (October 1967): 716–26.

B: Chapter Ten

1. Ablon, Joan. "American Indian Relocation Problems of Dependency and Management in the City." *Phylon* 24, no. 4 (Winter 1965): 362–71.

2. Ablon, Joan. "Relocated American Indians in San Francisco." *Human Organization* 23 (1964): 290–304.

3. Alexhamson, Mark. "Cosmopolitan, Dependency, Identification and Geographic Mobility." *Administrative Science Quarterly* 10 (June 1965): 98–106.

4. Alford, Robert, and Michael Aiken. "Community Structure and Innovation." American Sociological Association Report, 1969.

5. Alford, Robert and Edward Fee. "Voting Turnout in American Cities." *American Political Science Review* 62, no. 2 (September 1968): 798–813.

6. Alford, Robert and Harry Scoble. "Sources of Local Political Involvement." *American Political Science Review* 62, no. 4 (December 1968): 1192–1207.

7. Ball, John C. and William A. Bates. "Migration and Residential Mobility of Narcotic Drug Users." *Social Problems* 14, no. 1 (Summer 1966): 56–69.

8. Barresi, Charles M. and John H. Lindquist. "The Urban Community: Attitudes toward Neighborhood and Urban Renewal." American Sociological Association Report, 1969.

9. Blumberg, Leonard and Michael Folli. "Little Ghettos: A Study of Negroes in the Suburbs." *Phylon* 27, no. 2 (1966): 117–31.

10. Briton, Raymond. "Institutional Completeness of Ethnic Communities and the Personal Relations of Immigrants." *American Journal of Sociology* 70, no. 2 (September 1964): 193–205.

11. Curtis, Richard F. "Differential Association in the Stratification of the Urban Community." *Social Forces* 42, no. 1 (October 1963): 68–76.

12. Davies, J. Clarence. *Neighborhood Groups and Urban Renewal* (New York: Columbia University Press, 1966).

13. Davies, James F. "The Effect of Freeway Displacement on Racial Housing Segregation in a Northern City." *Phylon* 26, no. 3 (Fall 1965): 209–15.

14. Duncan, Beverly and Otis D. "Minorities and the Process of Stratification." *American Sociological Review* 33, no. 3 (June 1968): 356–64.

15. Elshort, Hansjorg. "Two Years After Integration—Race Relations in the Deep South." *Phylon* 38, no. 1 (Spring 1967): 41–51.

16. Fagan, James F. and R. A. Brody. "Cuban In Exile." *Social Problems* 11, no. 4 (Spring 1964): 384–401.

17. Fellman, Gordon. "Planning Implications of Neighborhood Resistance to Proposed Housing and Highway." *Digest of Urban and Regional Research* 15, no. 2 (Winter 1968): 61–66.

18. Freed, Marc. "Functions of the Working Class Community in Modern Urban Society." *Journal of the American Institute of Planners* 33, no. 2 (March 1967): 90–103.

19. Glen, Norvale D. "Relative Size of Negro Population and the Negro Occupational Status." *Social Forces* 43, no. 1 (October 1964): 42–49.

20. Goldrich, Daniel. "Peasants' Sons in City Schools." *Human Organization* 23, no. 4 (Winter 1964): 328–33.

21. Hartman, Chester. "The Housing of Relocated Families." *Journal of the American Institute of Planners* 30, no. 4 (November 1964): 266–86.

22. Heiss, Jerold. "Factors Related to Immigrant Assimilation." *Human Organization* 26, no. 4 (Winter 1967): 265–71.

23. Heiss, Jerold. "Sources of Satisfaction and Assimilation among Italian Immigrants." *Human Relations* 19, no. 2 (May 1966): 165–79.

24. Inkeles, Alex. "Making Man Modern: On the Causes and Consequences of Individual Changes in Six Developing Countries." *American Journal of Sociology* 75, no. 2 (December 1969): 18–30.

25. Jitodai, Ted. T. "Migrant Status and Church Attendance." *Social Forces* 43, no. 2: 241–48.

26. Jitodai, Ted T. "Urban Rural Background and Formal Group Membership." *Rural Sociology* 30, no. 1 (March 1965): 75–82.

27. Jones, Frank E. and Wallace Lambert. "Occupational Rank and Attitudes toward Immigrants." *Public Opinion Quarterly* 29, no. 1 (Spring 1965): 137–44.

28. Jones, Lancaster F. "Ethnic Concentration and Assimilation." *Social Forces* 45, no. 3 (March 1967): 412–23.

29. Kantrowitz, Nathan. "Ethnic and Racial Segregation in the New York Metropolis." *American Journal of Sociology* 74, no. 6 (December 1969): 685–95.

30. Ladinsky, Jack. "Occupational Determinants of Geographic Mobility among Professional Workers." *American Sociological Review* 32, no. 2 (April 1967): 253–64.

31. Levine, Murray. "Residential Change and School Adjustment." *Community Mental Health* 2, no. 1 (1966): 61–69.

32. Litwak, Eugene and Phillip Fellin. "Neighborhood Cohesion under Conditions of Mobility." *American Sociological Review* 28, no. 3 (June 1963): 364–76.

33. Logan, M. et al. "Evaluation of Housing Standards of Families within Four Years of Relocation by Urban Renewal." *American Journal of Public Health* 58, no. 7 (July 1968): 1256–61.

34. Mathews, Daniel and James Prothro. "Southern Images of Political Parties." *Journal of Politics* 26, no. 1 (February 1964): 88–111.

35. Matityahu, Marcus. "Racial Composition and Home Price Changes." *Journal of the American Institute of Planners* 34, no. 5 (September 1968): 334–38.

36. Molotch, Harvey. "Racial Change in a Stable Community." *American Journal of Sociology* 75, no. 2 (December 1969): 12–20.

37. Molotch, Harvey. "Racial Integration in a Transitional Community." *American Sociological Review* 34, no. 6 (December 1969): 878–93.

38. Neer, B. and F. Freeman. "Impact of Negro Neighbors on White Homeowners." *Social Forces* 45, no. 1 (September 1966): 11–18.

39. Palisi, B. J. "Ethnic Patterns of Friendship." *Phylon* 36, no. 3 (Fall 1966): 217–25.

40. Palmore, Erdman. "Integration and Property Values in Washington, D.C." *Phylon* 27, no. 1 (September 1966): 15–19.

41. Penalosa, Fernando, and Edward C. McDonaugh. "Education, Economic Status and Social Class Awareness of Mexican Americans." *Phylon* 29, no. 2 (September 1968): 119–26.

42. Portes, A. "Dilemmas of a Golden Exile." *American Sociological Review* 34, no. 4 (August 1969): 505–18.

43. Raphael, Edna E. "Community Structure and Acceptance of Psychiatric Aid." *American Journal of Sociology* 69, no. 4 (1964): 340–58.

44. Rasmussen, Darrel. "Effects of Regional and Occupational Mobility on Non-White Income Changes." *Digest of Urban and Regional Research* 15, no. 2 (Winter 1966): 19.

45. Robins, Lee N., et al. "School Milieu and School Problems of Negro Boys." *Social Problems* 13, no. 4 (Spring 1966): 408–36.

46. Schnore, Leo F. and Phillip C. Evenson. "Segregation in Southern Cities." *American Journal of Sociology* 72, no. 1 (July 1966): 58–67.

47. Schwarzweller, Harry and J. Brown. "Social Class Origins, Migration and Economic Life Change." *Rural Sociology* 32 (March 1962): 6–19.

48. Shryock, Harry S. and Charles Ham. "Educational Selectivity of Interregional Migration." *Social Forces* 43, no. 3 (March 1965): 299–310.

49. Silverman, Clyde F. "An Ethnographic Approach to Social Stratification: Prestige in an Italian Community." *American Anthropology* 68, no. 4 (July 1966): 899–919.

50. Tarver, D. "Occupational Migration Differentials." *Social Forces* 43, no. 2 (December 1964): 231–41.

51. Taeuber, A. and K. "Changing Character of Negro Migration." *American Journal of Sociology* 70, no. 4 (January 1965): 429–41.

52. Taeuber, A. and K. "Negroes as an Immigrant Group." *American Journal of Sociology* 69, no. 4 (1964): 374–82.

53. Taeuber, Karl. "Negro Residential Segregation." *Social Problems* 12, no. 1 (Summer 1964): 42–49.

54. Tilly, Charles and James Brown. "On Uprooting, Kinship and the Auspices of Migration." *International Journal of Comparative Sociology* 8 (September 1968): 139–64.

55. Turner, R. J. "Social Mobility and Schizophrenia." *Health and Social Behavior* 9, no. 3 (September 1968): 194–203.

56. Useen, John and Ruth. "The Interfaces of a Binational Third Culture." *Journal of Social Issues* 23, no. 1 (June 1967): 130–44.

57. Van Arsdol, Maurice D., Sr., and Jon E. Simpson. "Residential History and Educational Status of Delinquents and Non-Delinquents." *Social Problems* 15, no. 1 (Summer 1967): 25–40.

58. Weinstock, S. D. "Some Factors that Retard or Accelerate the Rate of Acculturation with Hungarian Immigrants." *Human Relations* 14, no. 4 (November 1964): 321–40.

59. Wolf, E. and C. Lebeaux. "On the Destruction of Poor Neighborhoods by Urban Renewal." *Social Problems* 15, no. 1 (Summer 1967): 3–8.

60. Wolf, E. and M. Ravitz. "Lafayette Park." *Journal of the American Institute of Planners* 30, no. 3 (August 1964): 234–39.

Part Seven

From Theory into Practice

Chapter Eleven

Research Utilization
as a Process

I. RESEARCH UTILIZATION METHOD:
A NEGLECTED AREA

THE PREVIOUS CHAPTERS have been concerned with substantive areas of knowledge as derived from social-research findings. Now we shall turn inward, and examine the method and process entailed in carrying out this endeavor. The specifics of our methodology were given in chapter 1, and are elaborated upon in appendix A. Here we shall conceptualize at a higher level the process of transposing knowledge from cognitive to active form. Fundamentally, this will be a discussion of various theoretical and conceptual aspects of the research utilization process.

Research findings represent only one of several areas of social-science knowledge; others include discrete facts, concepts, hypotheses, and information about the methodology of scientific inquiry. The research utilization process may be viewed as an innovative phenomenon. Mohr [1] discusses innovation as distinct from invention: invention implies bringing something new into being; innovation implies bringing something into new use.

Social-science theory and knowledge are rarely produced in a form immediately translatable into action directives or practice principles. There is an "engineering" task [2] or "knowledge linking role" [3] that

---

[1] Lawrence Mohr, "Determinants of Innovation in Organizations," *American Political Science Review* 63, no. 1 (March 1969): 11–126.

[2] Edwin J. Thomas, "Selecting Knowledge from Behavioral Science," in *Behavioral Science for Social Workers,* Thomas, ed. (New York: The Free Press, 1967), 416–24.

[3] Ronald G. Havelock, *Planning for Innovation through Dissemination and Utilization of Knowledge* (Ann Arbor, Mich.: Institute for Social Research, 1969).

needs to be performed if the products of the social sciences are to be employed by the practitioner. Numerous scholars have written about various aspects of the knowledge utilization or application process,[4] yet one senses this is still a largely intuitive, underdeveloped intellectual area.

Neither social scientist nor social practitioner has in the past judged the process of utilization to be a question that warrants serious attention in its own right. Gouldner states:

> Traditionally, sociological theory has ministered to the needs of pure or basic researcher, rather than those of applied research. Indeed, the cas-

[4] Martin Bloom, "The Selection of Knowledge from the Behavioral Sciences and Its Integration into Social Work Curricula," *Journal of Education for Social Work* 5 (Spring 1969): 15–27; Emmett Dedmon, "Barriers to Communication: Another Journalist's View," in *Behavioral Sciences and the Mass Media,* Frederick T. C. Yu, ed. (New York: Russell Sage Foundation, 1966), pp. 184–88; Joseph W. Eaton, "A Scientific Basis for Helping," in *Issues in American Social Work,* Alfred J. Kahn, ed. (New York: Columbia University Press, 1959), pp. 270–92; Joseph W. Eaton, "Science, 'Art,' and Uncertainty in Social Work," *Social Work* 3 (July 1958): 3–10; Mabel A. Elliott, "Social Problems and Social Theories: Dilemmas and Perspectives," in *Applied Sociology,* Alvin W. Gouldner and S. M. Miller, eds. (New York: The Free Press, 1965), pp. 398–411; Tony Tripodi, Phillip Fellin, and Henry J. Meyer, "Utilization of Research: Principles and Guidelines," in *The Assessment of Social Research* (Itasca, Ill.: F. E. Peacock, 1969), pp. 94–130; Charles Frankel, "The Relation of Theory to Practice: Some Standard Views," in *Social Theory and Social Invention,* Herman D. Stein, ed. (Cleveland: Case Western Reserve University Press, 1968), pp. 3–26; Alvin W. Gouldner, "Explorations in Applied Social Science," in *Applied Sociology,* Gouldner and S. M. Miller, eds. (New York: The Free Press, 1965), pp. 5–22; Ernest Greenwood, "The Practice of Science and the Science of Practice," *Brandeis University Papers in Social Welfare* (Waltham, Mass.: Brandeis University, 1959); Ronald G. Havelock, "Ideas for Research on Utilization of Knowledge" (Ann Arbor, Mich.: Center for Research on Utilization of Scientific Knowledge, Institute for Social Research, University of Michigan, July 1966); Alfred Kadushin, "Assembling Social Work Knowledge," in *Building Social Work Knowledge,* Report of a Conference (New York: National Association of Social Workers [NAWS], 1964), pp. 16–37; Ralph L. Kolodny and Hyman Rodman, "Organizational Strains in the Researcher-Practitioner Relationship," in *Applied Sociology,* pp. 93–113; Paul F. Lazersfeld et al., *The Uses of Sociology* (New York: Basic Books, 1967); Eugene Litwak, "Policy Implications in Communications Theory with Emphasis on Group Factors," in *Behavioral Science for Social Workers,* pp. 105–17; Henry S. Maas, "Developing Theories of Social Work Practice," in *Building Social Work Knowledge,* pp. 48–59; Jack Rothman, "Community Organization Practice," in *Research in the Social Services: A Five Year Review,* Henry S. Maas, ed. (New York: National Association of Social Workers, 1971); Edwin J. Thomas, "Types of Contributions Behavioral Science Makes to Social Work," in *Behavioral Science for Social Workers,* pp. 3–13; Harold L. Wilensky and Charles N. Lebeaux, *Industrial Society and Social Welfare* (New York: Russell Sage Foundation, 1968).

ual observer may almost think it a contradiction in terms to speak of a methodology of applied social sciences. Yet the fact is that the applied social sciences are badly in want of such a methodology. For as a result of this deficiency, the very meaning and character of applied social science remain obscure and those concerned with it often reflexibly reiterate received formulae.[5]

The social scientist's general outlook frequently leaves him insensitive to or unconcerned with the social utilization of his efforts and products. The reward system of the disciplines typically offer little in the way of either money or prestige to encourage those with interests in application. In fact, they discourage such efforts.

Thomas presents a cogent analysis of the requisites of systematic research utilization:

> There is another focus of conceptualization that is sufficiently important to merit separate emphasis. I am speaking of the very process of utilizing behavioral science knowledge. Both the increasing knowledge of behavioral science and its selective applicability to [practice] necessarily compel conceptualization of what contributes to [practice] and what does not. Behavioral science knowledge must be selected for use, assimilated by educators and practitioners, amalgamated into the larger fabric of [practice] knowledge, introduced into educational and agency contexts, and subsequently evaluated and tested. This process, which begins with selection from the heartlands of the academic disciplines of behavioral science and terminates in the front lines of practice in the . . . profession, is a complex intellectual, practical, and institutional transition in the engineering of behavioral science knowledge. This "engineering transition" is just beginning to receive the analysis it deserves.[6]

While appreciating the value of the practical applications of social-science research, a precaution is in order; it has to do with the limitations of social science: Few theoretical issues are resolved in a definitive and ultimate way. Social phenomena are of such complexity, and the power and scope of current methodologies are so limited, that much of what goes under the name of social-science knowledge must be considered as tentative. There is the danger of "oversell," particularly for the enthusiastic but naive consumer of social-science wares.

[5] Alvin W. Gouldner, "Explorations in Applied Social Science," in *Applied Sociology*, pp. 5–6.

[6] Edwin J. Thomas, "Selecting Knowledge from Behavioral Science," in *Behavioral Science for Social Workers*, pp. 6–7.

Indeed, unrealistically high expectations or overoptimism may be a grave impediment to utilization of the social sciences. Eaton tells us that "science is neither a faith nor a panacea"; [7] practitioners ought therefore to be skeptical and scientists reserved.

Kadushin alludes to this frailty of social science research, and yet points to the inevitable conclusion that it is the best verified knowledge we have and that it ought to be exploited maximally for what it may offer:

> Given the complexity of the human condition, given the changing nature of the problems we seek to understand even as we are seeking to understand them, given accident and happenstance and individual, group and community uniqueness, it is not likely that even the best research will give us all the answers necessary. . . .
> Research may never be able to give us as much as we want. But research may be able to give us some increasingly modest increment of what we need. [8]

In this spirit we now turn to an examination of processes through which research may be identified and consciously, systematically applied so as to aid in addressing some of the troubling social problems that confront human-service workers.

II. MODELS OF RESEARCH UTILIZATION

A particular model of research utilization shaped the contents of this book. This approach in its overall formulation starts with the body of basic research and moves along a continuum to wide application by practitioners in the field. It would be useful to explicate the components of this model, demonstrating the various phases and tasks involved in carrying it out. This will be followed by a description of some alternative modes of relating research to practice-policy matters.

Let us begin with a schematic representation of the model (Figure 11.1). This can be visualized in terms of several operational steps and material stages. The steps are conceived of as subprocesses or tech-

[7] Joseph W. Eaton, "A Scientific Basis for Helping," in *Issues in American Social Work,* p. 292.

[8] Alfred Kadushin, "Child Welfare," in *Research in the Social Services: A Five-Year Review,* Henry S. Maas, ed. (New York: National Association of Social Workers, 1971), p. 64.

nical operations along the continuum. Each operation results in a stage that is a landmark product (including experience or data) that provides materials for the next operation. The model encompasses six basic stages, interconnected by five operational steps. The steps are located within arrows in the figure below in order to indicate their more active, processual function in the model.[9]

To go on now to describe the various subparts of the scheme:

Material Stage I: Basic Research Pool

Here we are referring to the reservoir of existing research data available in the formal literature of the disciplines and professions, as well as less formal sources, such as agency reports, dissertations, and project memoranda. Some of this material stands independently in raw form; some is referenced in index books or computer banks of various types; other material is both referenced and abstracted in index books or computer banks. While the model begins at this stage, it is obvious that it emerges from prior research efforts in the scientific community.

From Raw Basic Research to
Consensus Generalizations

Operational Step 1: Retrieval,
Codification, Generalization

1. This step requires the location of pertinent research data sources in terms of some practice problem or objective. Both primary and secondary sources are possible, including the use of stored information pools.
2. Selection from the source pool of those studies bearing on the problem or issue at hand. Here one encounters problems of nomenclature, including the appropriate selection of descriptors. Problems of traversing the disparate taxonomies of knowledge in social science and social practice present themselves. Practice perspectives ordinarily need to be translated into typical scientific linguistic analogs in order for scientific sources to be exploited.

[9] This is to acknowledge the contribution to these ideas of my colleague Jesse Gordon, with whom I shared an experimental seminar on The Research Utilization Process.

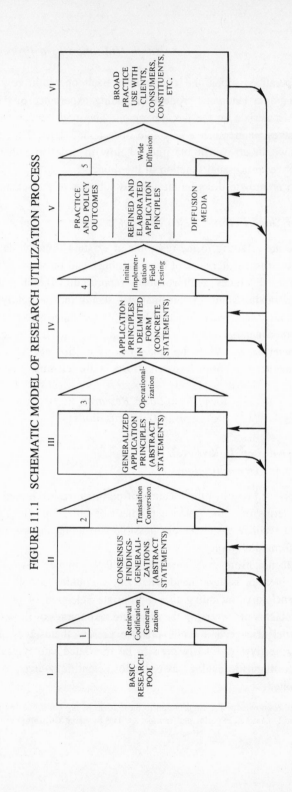

FIGURE 11.1   SCHEMATIC MODEL OF RESEARCH UTILIZATION PROCESS

3. Assessing data for reliability, validity, applicability.
4. Codifying data into suitable categories of knowledge.
5. Constructing consensus findings within the selected data.
6. Drawing appropriate generalizations and propositions from consensus findings.

Material Stage II: Consensus Findings,
Generalizations, Propositions

As implied in the description of operations, the product here is one or more generalizations based on the convergence of a number of findings of research studies. Where numerous studies in varying circumstances, using different subjects and methodologies, are in substantial agreement, one can have a greater degree of confidence in the validity of these generalizations, particularly when there are few if any findings that yield counterconclusions.

The generalizations will be abstract as a result of their tendency to synthesize diverse studies. Likewise they will tend to describe social phenomena rather than provide intervention prescriptions, in that most social-science research deals with understanding the social world rather than changing it.

Consensus findings may be descriptive of a simple empirical regularity or they may be propositional in describing a consistent uniform relationship between two variables.

From Research Generalizations to
Generalized Application Principles

Operational Step 2: Translation
and Conversion

Here the essential task is that of cognitive application.
1. Translations now need to be made from scientific language back to language more suitable to the categories of normative usage in the professions.
2. Conversion from descriptive to prescriptive formulations entails making an "inferential leap" across the gap between generalization and practice principle. The size of this leap and the range

of directions of application need to be considered (toward organizational stability or organizational change, for example).
3. "Reality" dimensions—such as feasibility, or implementability,
   of a given application, limiting conditions and qualifiers that restrict or channel use—must be taken into account.

Stage III: Generalized Application Principles

These are the output of the translation-conversion process. The Action
Guidelines enumerated in this volume are representative of products in
this stage. These prescriptive statements, while now of more immediate relevance to practitioners, are derived from broad consensus generalizations, and tend also to be constituted in rather abstract form. At
this level, the concrete implementation of application principles is left
to the creative efforts of practitioners, unless the utilization process is
carried forward into further stages.

From Generalized Application Principles
to Operationalization

Operational Step 3: Operationalization

Operationalization involves more finite specification of locations, contexts, and behaviors for implementation: two examples are the type of
agency setting and the types of people to whom the intervention pertains.

Operationalization may be a largely cognitive-perceptual task or it
may include actual experimental implementation as a way of developing the specifications. The former procedure may include use of existing theory or of cumulative practice wisdom in relating principles to
operations; the latter procedure may require the conducting of a field
test in the intended implementation setting (in that case stages IV and
V blend).

Material Stage IV: Application Principles
in Delimited Form

Operationalization results in a much more detailed, narrowed practical
exposition of application principles. It may involve the concretization

of each of what have become identified as the key elements contained in the application statement. In this form application may be discussed in mental-health centers as compared to, for example, city-planning agencies; large cities as compared to small cities; agencies with sizable budgets as compared to those with limited budgets, etc. Often the operationalization in its entirety is designed specifically for a given agency setting (public housing) or type of practitioner (school administrators). An operationalized statement of application gives the practitioner a great deal more direction, demanding less of him in terms of cognitive effort or intellectual creativity. At the same time it facilitates his getting on with what he conceives as his main function, taking action in the field.

From Delimited Application to Refined and Tested Application Principles

Operational Step 4: Initial Implementation—
Field Testing

1. This step assumes the availability of working documents, audio-visual materials, manuals, etc., which can be put in the hands of representative practitioners.
2. The purpose of field testing is to determine whether the materials are usable by practitioners in their present form; to modify, expand, and more clearly operationalize the application principles; and to assess the effectiveness of the action principle with respect to its intended outcome with clients. This form of reality testing may yield feedback that modifies the action principle or the basic theory that generated it. This step incorporates elements of dissemination and of evaluative research.
3. Some dissemination tasks include selection of sites or users, recruitment and training incentives for use, entry problems, clarification of role of practitioner, and of relationship to role of disseminator-researcher.
4. Research tasks include development of a suitable methodology for study and of instruments; monitoring; adjustment for special problems such as practitioner resistance or Hawthorne effects; evaluation of effectiveness; and development of criteria for re-

jecting, modifying, or authenticating the application principle.

It should be noted again that when operationalization leading up to Stage IV is developed through limited field implementation, Steps and Stages IV and V can be combined functionally.

Material Stage V: Practice and Policy
Outcomes; Tested, Refined and Elaborated
Application Principles; Diffusion Media

At this stage several useful products should have been brought into being. In the first place, it may be possible to determine whether the application principle holds together in action. While it was derived originally from basic research, this may be the first instance of its being tried out in its prescriptive form. Thus, the "inferential leap" can become subject to at least tentative confirmation or rejection. This type of evaluation may be carried through by means of formal research procedures or less formal observational and assessment approaches. Because of the complexity of most community intervention settings, testing through rigorous experimental designs is precluded. Secondly, the application principle and its elements may be sharpened, qualified, or recast as a result of field experience. This means an elaboration involving such matters as steps and stages in the implementation process, tools and resources required by the practitioner, etc. Finally, based on the field experience, diffusion materials incorporating results of the field work—practitioner manuals and handbooks, audiotapes, videotapes, documents, charts, etc.—may be crystallized.

From Refined Application Principles and Media
to Wide Diffusion

Operational Step 5: Wide Diffusion

This step includes:
1. Isolation of a universe of practitioners or organizations who are potential target users.
2. The determination of their attributes, attitudes, and needs.
3. Selecting appropriate materials and packaging them in an attractive, responsive way.
4. Reaching and motivating potential users.

5. Locating functional gatekeepers, opinion leaders, or informal professional networks as diffusion channels.
6. Providing initial training and continuing support and reinforcement to users.
7. Developing procedures for scanning results of wider application, etc.

Stage VI: Broad Practice Use

The end result of the process should be widespread utilization of the application principle in the field. By this time the principle should have withstood testing, and means of effectively communicating its appropriate implementation to practitioners should have been developed. The eventual beneficiaries are clients, consumers, and constituents in the human-services system. Broader experience with clients, involving both method and outcome, should again hypothetically feed back on the entire process, suggesting modifications and refinements for every stage, right back to the basic research.

Next, we shall compare this model with other formulations of research utilization. Later in the chapter we shall give examples that hopefully will further tie down some of the notions briefly described above.

Havelock, who has conducted one of the most extensive reviews of the utilization of social-science knowledge, describes a process basically similar to the one presented above.[10] He designates it the *research, development and diffusion* perspective. He states that it is characterized as placing a premium on rationality, use of systematic planning, division of labor, and high investment payoff relative to long-term benefit, to capacity to reach a mass audience, and to both quality and quantity of services. Prototypes are the federal Agricultural Research and Extension System and research and development operations in industry. Some typical spokesmen for the approach include David Clark, Egon Guba, and Henry M. Brickell.

Two other common perspectives are brought out by Havelock. The *social interaction* model focuses on the dynamics of diffusion. It concerns itself with the social structure of adoption of innovations: how farmers come to use new agricultural implements or physicians new

[10] Ronald G. Havelock, *Planning for Innovation: Through Dissemination and Utilization of Knowledge* (Ann Arbor, Michigan: Institute for Social Research, 1969).

drugs. The availability of useful knowledge, techniques, or programs is assumed, and the focal issue is their dissemination to potential users who can benefit from them.

This perspective is characterized by attention to such themes as the personal relationships among members of a diffusion system, opinion leaders and informal influence networks, group memberships and identifications, and local-cosmopolitan outlook as a variable in receptivity to new ideas. The basic unit of concern is "individual receivers," especially their perception of and response to knowledge directed to their attention. Much emphasis is placed on the stages through which individuals pass in the process of deciding to utilize a new practice, usually starting at "awareness" and terminating at "adoption": the initiation of the process is in the hands of a "sender"; the "receiver" plays a relatively passive role, although solutions are formulated on the basis of the receiver's perceived needs. Some typical spokesmen for this orientation include Everett Rogers, James Coleman, Elihu Katz, Richard Carlson, and Paul Mort. Havelock's schematic representation of this model is given below.

FIGURE 11.2   THE SOCIAL INTERACTION PERSPECTIVE

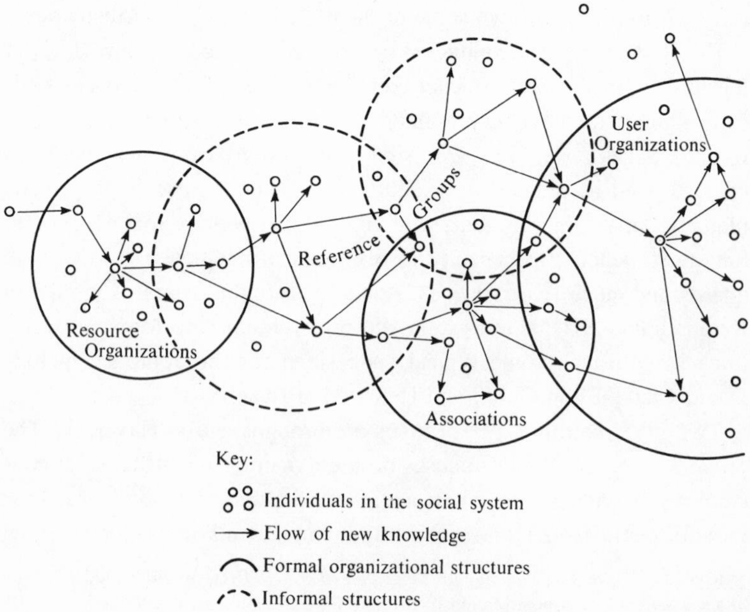

Key:

$\circ\circ\atop\circ\circ$ Individuals in the social system

⟶ Flow of new knowledge

⌒ Formal organizational structures

⌒ Informal structures

The other model delineated by Havelock is labeled the *problem-solver*. This model hypothetically starts with the user (client, consumer, receiver, recipient, etc.); his need is the paramount consideration and he participates with a change agent in diagnosing his own problem. The change agent is an outside catalyst, consultant, or collaborator, guiding the user to find beneficial solutions himself. Thus, the change agent helps the user to link back from his problem situation to sources of knowledge that may provide individually tailored answers. Self-determined change is seen as offering the firmest motivational basis and best prospects for long-term maintenance. While change may be initiated by the change agent, as well as by the client, the latter must desire the change and be prepared to take an active part in bringing it about. Prototypes of this approach include mental-health consultation, organizational self-survey (or self-renewal) projects, and the programs that have been identified with the National Training Laboratories. Among proponants of this model are Ronald Lippitt, Herbert Thelen, Goodwin Watson and Mathew Miles. Havelock's schematic depiction of this model is given below:

FIGURE 11.3   THE PROBLEM—SOLVER PERSPECTIVE

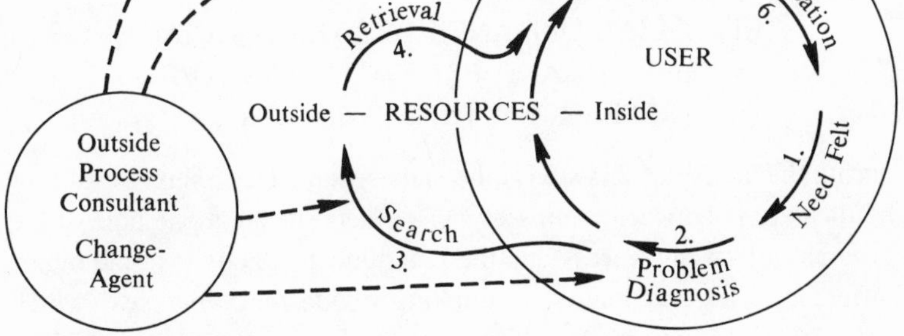

While different proponents advocate different models, and while these can be conceptualized independently, as Havelock indicates, the models are not necessarily antagonistic or mutually exclusive. It is evident, for example, that the *social interaction* model can be located in Stages V and VI of our project model. Social interaction takes as a given that earlier work had occurred and it proceeds from the point at which there is available a tested action principle and diffusion vehicle. The problem solver, when he has clarified with the user what the focal problem is, may then proceed by moving back through Stages I–III of the project model, as he seeks solutions in the research literature. Diffusion is not at issue, because the receiver has already been identified and is motivated to make use of research-based knowledge. The emphasis is on intensive, personalized contact; scope is thus not a consideration with regard to diffusion. This points to the factors of high cost and heavy investment of personnel inherent in the problem solver conception.

Existing research literature and storage banks are a resource that may be harnessed by researcher-developers who are instrumental in the first model, by diffusion specialists of various kinds who animate the second, and by change agents who figure heavily in the third. Clients, or practitioners as clients, hypothetically may themselves tap into these research sources. Our experience indicates that practitioners and clients lack the sophistication required to directly exploit this type of knowledge; this is in part because the knowledge is not developed and contained in such a way as to facilitate their use of it. In the next section we shall analyze this problem; we shall discuss the gap between researchers and users, including barriers to effective communication and collaboration.

III. SOCIAL DISTANCE BETWEEN SOCIAL SCIENTISTS AND PRACTITIONERS: THE RESEARCH UTILIZATION GAP

During the course of this study, the staff became increasingly aware of the dichotomy between the researcher or theoretician at one pole of the research utilization process and the practitioner or activist at the other. Different styles and modes of thinking divide the two types, which makes communication difficult and utilization of each other's contributions and products problematic. There exists formidable social distance—characterized by mistrust, differing outlooks, and ostensibly contrasting goals—which in the past has inhibited fuller articulation between social scientist and social practitioner. A number of the writers previously cited have looked into this subject and have made note of varying dimensions of this social distance. Some of the barriers to collaboration that have been delineated include the following:

Basic Professional Definitions
  Different focal concerns (Kolodny and Rodman)
  Different role perceptions (Kolodny and Rodman)
Value Considerations
  Differing value systems (Havelock, 1969)
  Variations in definition of professional ethics (Gouldner)
Communication Difficulties
  Inadequate communication (Dedmon)
  Lack of two-way direct relationships (Schwartz)
  Information overloads (Havelock, 1969)
  Different languages and jargonistic styles (Angell)
Methodological Assumptions
  Different methodological grounding (Gouldner)
  Conflicting views of the utility of practical experience and
    common sense (Wilensky and Lebeaux)
  Differing standards for measuring achievement (Dedmon)
  Differing views of the utility of negative criticism (Wilensky
    and Lebeaux)
Orientation toward Clients
  Different understandings of client needs (Lazersfeld, et al.)
  Different conceptions of risk to clients (Havelock, 1969)
Interprofessional Conflicts
  Conflicts over recognition (Kolodny and Rodman)
  Perceived conflicts of interest (Gouldner)
  Different loyalties and identities (Angell)
Perceptions and Attitudes
  Prejudicial attitudes toward one another (Dedmon)
  Misunderstandings concerning interests (Gouldner)

Perhaps the fundamental difference is one of function. This then affects training, which in turn colors values, cognition, style, and the rest. The social scientist has the primary function of *comprehending the world:* producing knowledge that permits him and others to understand it better. The practitioner has the key function of *changing the*

world (or more specifically, parts thereof): producing material effects
that permit clients, organizations, or communities to behave more ad-
vantageously in terms of specific desired outcomes.

It is possible to construct a profile depicting the view each of the
two principals in this forced but unstable relationship holds toward the
other.

The Researcher's Perception of the Practitioner

If we start with the critical views (or stereotypes) social scientists have
of practitioners, we may see the latter as placing low value on intellec-
tuality and high value on action or change for its own sake. Practitioners are too uninterested or busy to read, study, or develop in a
truly professional way. Instead of orderly, systematic examination of
issues, which requires time and scholarly objectivity, practitioners
tend to come to hasty conclusions and engage in actions unsubstan-
tiated by adequate data. They are uninterested in self-criticism and of-
fended by outside criticism. They manifest a distrust and fear of research, which unmasks their own limitations and their unwillingness to
grapple with difficult or abstract material, including scientific methodology. This is related also to a narrow professionalism: such intense
engagement in the specifics of a given problem situation that generalizations on a more abstract basis cannot be carried over from one context to another. This kind of raw empiricism generates an indefinite
number of discrete problem situations. As Zetterberg points out,
"where common sense sees different problems, scientific theory sees
the same problem. This is an extremely comforting idea. It implies
that if we can find scientific solutions to a small number of theoretical
problems we really have solutions to a large number of practical issues." [11] Because of his immersion in given agencies or problems, the
practitioner tends to become a captive of a limited perspective, without
theory or comparative exposure to permit a broad, cosmopolitan grasp.
This leads to a conservative posture, made up of loyalty to the organization and defensiveness regarding any perceived threat to its survival.

In addition, practitioners are restricted by their inability to utilize

[11] Hans L. Zetterberg, *Social Theory and Social Practice* (New York: Bedminster Press,
1962), p. 43.

terms from basic scientific technical language for their own purposes. Thomas has illustrated comparable vocabularies by listing a number of substantive areas of sociology ordered by objects of analysis in social work. For example information about "clients," the terminological referent in social work, may be found in sociology under such rubrics as social stratification, race and ethnic relations, personality and social structure, social disorganization and deviant behavior, sociology of mental illness, and criminology. Says Thomas, "It is clear that there are substantive domains of sociology relevant to all of the specific analytic areas of social work, that some substantive domains are either uniquely or most particularly associated with certain social work areas and not others, and that altogether a large portion of the knowledge of sociology bears upon one or another aspect of social work." [12]

Social scientists also resent the smugness of the practitioner who feels that only he understands worldly problems or real people because of his direct, everyday engagement. The social scientist believes that his relative distance from phenomena under study gives him perspective, and that he has developed means (participant observation, pilot studies, etc.) by which he is able to acquire a sufficient degree of familiarity and "feeling" for social phenomena to permit him to understand and master them. In addition, the social scientist maintains it is not his but the practitioner's responsibility to draw implications for policy and action from research. This indeed, according to the social scientist, is the specific obligation of the practitioner; it falls on him to have at least the minimum amount of mental capacity and technical ability to comprehend social-science research and theory and to proceed from the theoretical to the practical, from data to dicta, in areas of professional concern.

The Practitioner's Perception of the Social Scientist

Practitioners see social scientists as engaged in studies of low social relevance. The subject matter areas are largely asocial, trivial or esoteric, abstract, and reflect narrow scientism rather than humanistic

[12] Edwin J. Thomas, "Selecting Knowledge from Behavioral Science," in *Behavioral Science for Social Workers,* p. 11.

concern. Quite often, if there is a social value orientation expressed in their work, it is one of conservatism, supportive of the status quo. The whole systems theory approach, for example, is viewed as indicative of this static orientation. Social scientists avoid the policy implications of their work, and their failure to relate the outcome of the research efforts to important social issues is perceived as stemming either from ignorance or a lack of compassion. There is also a kind of compromised intellectualism involved in the bending of research pursuits to such exigencies of the moment as the availability of federal or foundation grants or to subject areas that will yield the largest payoffs in dollars and professional prestige. Here one detects a form of professional faddism that is unbecoming in an allegedly science-based field of endeavor. As one observer has noted,

> Just as there are styles and changing fashions in community organization practice, there are styles and changing fashions in social research and theory. Two decades ago the great thing was stratification studies. A decade ago the great power structure surge began. And, a few years ago poverty and civil rights began to capture the imagination of many sociologists. Today the big thing is systems analysis. What will it be tomorrow? [13]

The social scientist's preoccupation with methodological "gimmickry" and its attendant overinflated jargon serves only to confuse and to alienate the practitioner who seriously wishes to draw on social-science knowledge. In addition, the faulty level of conceptualization in many social-science writings repels the practitioner. Data are often correlated only peripherally with the concepts and conclusions set forth. There is frequently a "forced" sense to these writings, giving the impression that the social scientist is straining to shape data to fit his hypothesis or to produce a publishable article at any cost.

In addition to their ponderous and pretentious quality, social-science writings exhibit a sponginess about conclusions that can be reached. The practitioner is interested in definite answers to specific questions; instead he finds inconclusive generalities about broad theoretical matters. Researchers often couch those specific critical evaluations of practice they do make in arrogant terms; they strike a pose of detach-

[13] Roland L. Warren, "Applications of Social Science Knowledge to the Community Organization Field," *Journal of Education for Social Work* 3, no. 1 (1967): 70.

ment, but actually show no appreciation of the real problems with which the practitioner is faced and the limited resources and authority he has available to cope with them. In fact, according to practitioners, such criticisms typically constitute hostile, dilettantish attacks rather than constructive, responsible assistance.

The author has had occasion to receive from graduate students training for social work practice comments about their reactions to social-science writings that were assigned for their analysis. These comments, which are reproduced below as direct quotations, convey some of the feeling attached to the stereotypes, problems and hostilities noted above:

> From my standpoint, that of a practitioner, there are several problem areas relating to the utilization of social science knowledge to practice areas. One problem surrounds the area of the validity of the research on which the knowledge is based. Can the material be applied with confidence? Often the knowledge accessible to the practitioner is of questionable value due to the research design. A practitioner is not apt to take a course of action which uses knowledge that has not been proven reliable in a variety of situations, i.e.: research that has not been replicated. As a practitioner I worry about how easily one can translate a piece of knowledge from the place where it is found to the place where it is to be applied.
>
> I have had a very difficult time finding social science articles that were of real relevance to me. Most of the articles contained information which might be necessary background but which was not of immediate applicability. Typical of the articles in this category are "Transactional factors in the determination of delinquent status," and "Factors related to student participation in campus social organizations," from *The Journal of Social Psychology*. Both of these articles contained information that a practitioner, be he a community organizer, case worker, or group worker, would need in order to work with a population consisting in one case of delinquents, or people termed delinquents, and in the other case of people in college who are not participating as much as would be expected.
>
> In neither case does the article discuss any way of putting the knowledge to use, nor does it discuss the relative transferability of the knowledge about this group to slightly different groups. The extent of the knowledge in the first case is simply a discussion of what types of things are likely to be reported when they are discovered by the police or the school janitor. The findings in the second case were made on the basis of 1,200 people in a large, Midwestern university. The results are discussed in terms of women participating more than men, and full-time work cut-

ting down participation. Traveling to campus and the manner of transportation also had an effect. This knowledge would be extremely helpful if one were trying to increase participation at a similar university where one would have reason to believe that participation trends were similar, for one would know which populations to aim the appeal at.

Quite often the research available to the practitioner is too specific to be readily applied to practice situations. What may be valid under one set of variables may not be valid under a different set. Further, much of scientific knowledge in social science is not in a finished state—i.e. it has only partial confirmation or confirmation under certain conditions. Unless the user of knowledge can recognize what research is ready for use and what is only perhaps exploratory with certain implications that may or may not be usable, utilization becomes a faulty process. Findings may be inconsistent, contradictory, and rather confusing to the practitioner. There's a great deal of disagreement on some issues and the practitioner is caught in the middle.

I found a number of articles that gave useful knowledge for the practitioner, but with the press of the practitioner's responsibilities he is unable to systematically review the literature and integrate this information. Also, these articles are not written with practice in mind so that the practitioner has to be able to pick out what is useful to him and what is not. Because of this there seems to be a danger in the practitioner depending upon the findings of only one article even if the research design may not be the best. The conclusions of a given study should be clear enough to allow the practitioner to extract them with a minimum of effort and uncertainty. Often it is time consuming to pull all the necessary relevant material from a research report because it is scattered. Such a lack of organization can seriously inhibit utility.

There is a broad expanse of social science knowledge in a variety of periodicals, reports, and books. To date, little effort has been made to catalog the bulk of this material in a consistent, comprehensive manner. As a result, the first task of the practitioner, should he desire certain knowledge, is to find it. Only then can he judge its quality and consider it for use.

Several students commented on difficulties in understanding statistical and technical language in the social sciences. One student commented on the statistical area as follows:

The journals I read contained a number of articles using various scales and measures, such as "Response sets and the Maudsley Personality Inventory," and "A comparison of the Rosenzweig P-F Study and the Brown Interracial version (Hawaii)." While some of the subjects for these articles are fascinating, and they sound like they might be extremely relevant to something (although to what is not always clear), our training, happily, does not go into these things in much detail. This makes it difficult to understand the articles and leads to a great deal of frustration—so much that I felt that the percentage of such articles in journals was very high.

There were many statistical terms and symbols that I do not know about. For the most part, although this is something that I want to learn, the demands of field instruction and of required classwork, and the many things I want to know about practice, make it difficult to acquire this information. I have the feeling that those of us in social work for the most part are not particularly good at or interested in mathematics and therefore the students do not enjoy learning and the faculty does not enjoy teaching this material, since it is cut-and-dried memorization for the most part. In spite of the lack of popularity of the suggestion, I must suggest that we take more work in statistics.

Another able student listed terms that he did not understand in eight selected journals that he reviewed. Examples from three of the journals are given below:

Journal of Sociology

Arationality, separate multivariate analysis, dissipated adaptive flexibility, urban fertility, totn $+ 1$, 2, 3, . . . , $n =$ relative A.D.R., innovative permeability, spatiotemporal characterizations, probabilistic covariations, the Delta Index.

Journal of Human Relations

Signed digraphs, veridicality, the Mann-Whitney "U," nonscale types, controverted results, P-O-X situations, cognitive deviation, cube root transformation, test vectors.

Journal of Health and Human Behavior

Coefficient of concordance W, unimpaired percentages, screening score, cluster analysis, two-tailed test, crude indexes, EPPS test, the expansion n, Kolomozorov-Smirnov one-tailed test, Yates corrections, normalized scores Fisher's R [7], correlative replication.

The student concludes:

Are we as practitioners failing to insist loudly enough that social science progress be brought about by giving "meaning" to such words as those presented in this paper—or will they continue to be used as mere "shibboleths"? Perhaps there is nothing we practitioners can do but continue to rationalize our way along, pretending we comprehend. As a last resort, we can always reply, "These findings only confirm what we practitioners already know."

Based on reactions such as these, is it any wonder that one study on the subject found that social-work professionals do not value research findings as much as other resources for the improvement of their practice? This research reported that four out of five practitioners approached felt that, "reading research articles is the least useful or second least useful activity in improving their practice." [14] The study found fault in two quarters: the social worker is not sufficiently scientifically oriented and the research that is available to practitioners is not especially valuable; it does not tell the practitioner specifically how to carry through in a practice situation.

IV. FACILITATING COMMUNICATION BETWEEN RESEARCHERS AND PRACTITIONERS

A number of barriers to movement across the continuum from basic research to application in practice should have by this time become explicit and vivid. Now we shall confront the difficult but essential task of suggesting approaches to removing some of the blockages. This will be attacked from two different vantage points, one close to the research-pool end of the continuum and the other at the opposite pole of diffusion to practitioners. These choices for emphasis are based on pragmatic considerations. A few (although not many) useful articles were located, which offer assistance on selecting studies from the research literature. With regard to diffusion, I have been engaged in a study of this matter, and thus am prepared to offer some substantive materials based on that experience. Concerning the research terminus, I shall indicate aids in the form of criteria for selecting and evaluating appropriate knowledge that have been proposed by some of the few

---

[14] Aaron Rosenblatt, "The Practitioner's Use and Evaluation of Research," *Social Work* 13, no. 1 (Jan. 1968): 56.

authors who have studied this problem systematically. I shall treat the diffusion aspect more extensively through a number of principles for communicating with practitioners and illustrative materials that demonstrate the principles.[15]

So far we have been dealing with Stages I, II, and III of the utilization process: the retrieval, codification, and generalized application of research. One begins with some specific environmental concern—a problem or objective in practice. Retrieval studies have taken as their environmental concern such subjects as reducing intergroup tensions, promoting organizational effectiveness, or improving decision making in task-oriented small groups. This then is narrowed down in terms of a particular focus on several subareas of attention. For example, while this study was concerned in general with social planning and community action, it dealt more specifically with such practice-issue areas as participation, political behavior, and diffusion of innovations. In examining small-group decision making, Collins and Guetzkow delineated several subareas; among them were interpersonal relations, power, communication, satisfaction, and leadership. Next, the type of literature to be searched needs to be determined, and then refined further into specific data sources and methods of selection. This procedure is elaborated in the Appendix.

There remains then the need to establish criteria or principles by which to guide the selection and evaluation of specific materials from the research pool. Such criteria are meant to facilitate utilization potentialities. Assistance has become available in this connection through an orienting framework suggested by Thomas.[16]

Thomas suggests research be examined in terms of what he refers to as *knowledge power* (the soundness of the intrinsic content of the social-science knowledge) and *referent features* (the implementability, manipulability, or engineerability of the knowledge). Under knowledge power one is advised to be alert for such factors as:

1. VALIDITY: Is the methodology of the study acceptable? Are there corroborating studies?

---

[15] These were prepared by the staff of this project who have been conducting a follow up action-research study aimed at disseminating action guidelines in the field.

[16] Edwin J. Thomas, "Types of Contributions Behavioral Science Makes to Social Work," in *Behavioral Science for Social Workers*, pp. 3–13.

2. PREDICTIVE POTENCY: Does this particular theory or construct link with more inclusive systems of theory? Is the formal logical structure of the theory soundly continuous with other bodies of theory?

3. VARIABLE POTENCY: Does this variable explain a sizable portion of the variance; this is, does it account for the results of a given study to a greater degree than other variables which also effect the results?

With regard to referent (implementability) features, the following criteria are highlighted:

Variable Availability for Control:

1. REFERENT IDENTIFIABILITY: Is the variable observable and operational in the real world? The "collective unconscious" is not easily identifiable in these terms; a given state legislature is.

2. REFERENT ACCESSIBILITY: Can the variable be approached, touched, addressed? Can the practitioner gain access? The "power structure" may be seen as a mechanism for fostering change, but do channels exist for communicating with the seats of power?

3. REFERENT MANIPULABILITY: If identifiable and accessible, does the practitioner have sufficient resources or leverage to put his variable to work? Many social problems may be resolved if the distribution of resources in the economic system can be reallocated. Control over the economic system, however, is elusive.

Feasibility Factors:

4. MANIPULATION COST: How costly is the strategy or program involved, and are finances available?

5. POTENCY: How much influence or impact will this variable have if injected into a given practical situation?

6. ETHICAL SUITABILITY: Given the value system of the profession or the norms of a particular community or population group, how appropriate is the use of the implied mode of intervention?

To the above consideration, Fellin, Tripodi, and Meyer add the implementability factor of "organizational constraints." [17] The practitioner must weigh factors existing within his agency structure that may place restrictions on his capacity to manipulate the given variable.

[17] Tripodi, et al., *The Assessment of Social Research.*

A more expanded scheme (somewhat overlapping the above) for screening and selecting studies for practice is suggested by Tripodi, Fellin, and Meyer.[18] Their outline, in somewhat modified form, is presented below:

GENERAL AIDS TO UTILIZATION

I. Should the Research Report be read at all?
   A. Does the reader have a particular practice problem?
   B. Is the research likely to bear on the reader's practice area?
   C. Is the research important to practice generally?
II. To what aspect of practice is the research relevant?
   A. What objects of interest and activity are addressed?
      1. Recipients?
      2. Process of service?
      3. Purveyance of service?
   B. Does the research pertain to current or potential objects of practice?
   C. From what value perspective are the objects of the study viewed?
   D. On what levels does the research visualize the objects of interest?
      1. Recipients:
         a. Individual
         b. Group
         c. Organization
         d. Community
         e. Society
      2. Process of serving:
         a. Interpersonal intervention
         b. Manipulation of organizational patterns
         c. Interorganizational and intergroup manipulation
         d. Policy proposals and development
      3. Purveyance of service:
         a. Professional arrangements
         b. Organizational arrangements

[18] *Ibid.*

E. What practice purpose does the research serve?
1. Treatment?
2. Enhancement?
3. Prevention?
III. What knowledge content of the research may be useful?
A. Empirical knowledge?
B. Conceptual knowledge?
C. Methodological knowledge?
IV. How useful can the research be for practice?
A. How sound is the research?
B. How engineerable are the variables?
1. How available are variables for control by the practitioner?
2. How much difference in the practice situation will it make if the variables are manipulated?
3. How feasible is it to manipulate variables of the research in the practice situation?
a. Economic feasibility?
b. Ethical suitability?
c. Organizational constraints?
V. What types of use can be made of the research?
A. Direct application
B. Indirect or complementary application
C. General stimulation

These formulations can be seen as useful in helping practitioners, researchers, and linkers to select and apply research in such a way as to expedite its consumption by practitioners. One senses that the matter of selecting and assessing research for practice is still a largely undeveloped subject from both a conceptual and technical standpoint. At the same time, research retrieval and utilization has been receiving increasing attention in the disciplines and professions, as well as from federal agencies. An expansion of intellectual productivity in the area may probably be anticipated as a result in the period immediately ahead.

The following discussion concerns the dissemination phase of utilization (assuming that appropriate selection of knowledge has been made); it will be based on the experience of our project staff in operationalizing action guidelines and readying them for implementation by practitioners in the field. During this phase of the project a limited number of guidelines were chosen for field testing, using such criteria as their implementability, and their applicability across diverse agency settings. Based on an experimental pilot year, a preliminary practitioner's manual was prepared and is being employed in a full field study.[19] The discussion that follows is drawn from the thinking that went into the construction of the manual, which was aimed at maximizing the potential acceptance and use of given action prescriptions. Here we shall emphasize how the written word was used to encourage utilization.[20] The approach was supplemented by interpersonal contact, training, and structural arrangements.

One of the four guidelines used in the study had to do with the diffusion of innovations. It was based on work done by Everett Rogers and others in the diffusion area, and supported the concept of partialization: innovations are often readily accepted by a population group following their successful usage with a smaller subpart of that population. Sections of the practitioner manual were set up according to communication principles geared to reaching potential practitioner users. In the presentation below we shall state the principle of communication for that section and follow with illustrative text drawn from the same section of the manual. For ease of presentation the manual text has been abbreviated and somewhat modified.

1. Provide the research basis for an action principle.

2. Convert the research generalization into its specific applied form.

Practitioners are concerned with and interested in the basis for a research generalization. They want a reasonable measure of assurance that the generalization has valid scientific support. At the same time they do not wish to be encumbered with a great deal of verbiage concerning the research itself, especially when it is written in highly tech-

---

[19] A description of the study will be found in Jack Rothman, Joseph Teresa, and John Erlich "The Community Intervention Project: Reviving Action Research," (Paper given at American Sociological Association Annual Conference, New York City, August 1973). This full staff group participated in preparation of the manual materials that will be described.

[20] Obviously such media as audiotapes, videotapes, and programmed instructional techniques may also be employed as dissemination tools.

nical language, including numerous statistical terms. If the research review can report studies in the specific circumstances of the practitioners' situation—setting or problem area or clientele—this will be reassuring and will reduce doubts over transferability of findings from one context to another.

The practitioner seeks a clear, direct conversion of a research generalization into its active or applied form. Often practitioners with very limited research backgrounds are left with a vague or confused sense concerning the practice or policy implications of a finding. Those with more sophisticated backgrounds tend to dwell on limitations or qualifications in a finding, and to consider to a greater degree its relevance for future research than for present application. For this reason a straightforward statement concerning practice or policy directions is vital if research products are to stand a chance of being put to work in the real world of community intervention.

These principles were given material form in the manual as follows:

GENERALIZATION: The rate of adoption of an innovation may be related to its divisibility. Innovations amenable to trial by part of a target population will have a higher adoption rate than innovations necessitating total adoption by the population without prior trial.

Steven Polgar, Howard Dunphy, and Bruce Cox, "Diffusion and Farming Advice: A Test of Some Current Notions," *Social Forces,* 42, no.1 (October 1963): 104–11.

Also numerous studies reported in Everett Rogers, *The Diffusion of Innovations* (New York: Free Press, 1962).

Action Guideline: Practitioners wishing to promote acceptance of an innovation, should attempt to formulate it in such a way that the innovation can be experienced initially by a limited portion of the target system.

*3. Provide an example showing the implementation
of the action guidelines with regard to a problem
situation or practice context familiar
to the practitioner.*

*4. The example should be as close as possible
to the practitioner's perspective, using practice
language or the actual words of
similar practitioners.*

Practioners, we have found, tend to think more in terms of problems than of theories, and to have an inductive cognitive style whereby general principles are evolved from specific commonsense reasoning, based on exposure to direct experience. Therefore, in the manual, the narrative episode described below was actually the first textual material presented. The narrative was prepared by a practitioner who had implemented the guideline in the first-year pilot study.

The report below was written by a community practitioner based in a Family Service Agency in a conservative, middle-sized community in Michigan. The practitioner was new to the agency, which had over the years conducted a traditional casework program, geared to serving essentially middle-class clients who went to the agency offices for assistance. This worker, the first staff member with a community orientation to be hired by the organization, viewed the job as an opportunity to introduce innovative programs with a community focus and to service neglected client populations. She employed this Guideline as one way of formulating a strategy geared to promoting an innovative program.

The innovation Guideline works very well! In fact I would recommend it highly to any worker wanting to get a new program or new practice accepted. I tried it with two different kinds of 'innovations' in very different situations and it worked well in both. The first was a program designed for mentally retarded adults to prove that such a program could be done with volunteer help, and that response from volunteers would be forthcoming.

Two small groups of adults were selected initially be using some Department of Social Services community care homes and their residents. Eventually we had other home operators asking that their residents be allowed to participate, and ultimately we used our experiences in this program to write a proposal to the Wilson Public Schools Adult Education Department for a weekly socialization program for 200 mentally retarded adults. All of this took planning in great detail initially because we could not afford for those first few programs to fail.

To promote acceptance I wrote up the project carefully and presented it to the Executive and the Board, the Department of Social Services staff, and the Association for Retarded Children staff. We recruited and trained volunteers; we selected the initial group with some care; and we tried to monitor everything constantly.

Through demonstrating with a small portion of the target population, we could then open up the program to the larger target population—which we did. If we had not limited the group initially we would have had disaster, because we did not have the volunteers, the space, the equipment or the knowhow to handle a large group. In addition we did not have the acceptance of the agency that this was a viable way to proceed in this program. This particular test of the guideline was a rather large scale programmatic effort requiring a considerable amount of time to test it; but it was a basic need in program development for the agency.

----

5. The specific action principle contained
in the narrative example should be
clearly and simply explicated.

The possibilities for ambiguity, uncertainty, and confusion are manifold in relating theory to practice. The action principle should be "pinned down" (linking back into the narrative example of practice if useful). This was done as follows.

The Principle of Partialization

The practice principle demonstrated in the illustration and embodied in the Guideline is that of partialization. That is to say, select a part of a total target system to initially carry out a new technique, and use the delimited demonstration of success as the basis for promoting the idea, or having it spread spontaneously, across a wider target population. There are a considerable number of familiar analogs: the demonstration project, the modeling of roles or behavior, the "free sample."

6. State the relevancy of the action guideline
to the general practice outlook of the practitioner:
his objectives, tasks, problems, needs.

It is important to relate the action guideline to the perspective of the practitioner, demonstrating how it can be of value to him in terms of the kinds of things he is likely to think are important in doing his job. Why is this guideline significant? How does it fit into the spectrum of concerns of the typical practitioner? This consideration took the following form.

Innovation and Community Practice

The human-service professions generally, and the area of community organization in particular, have sometimes been characterized as *change-oriented fields*. For this reason the process of the diffusion and adoption of innovations is of special importance. Practitioners are constantly involved in promoting new programs, new techniques, new tactics, and new ideas, which they wish to propagate in working with target and client systems of various kinds. Sometimes such novel programs are already well-established elsewhere and only "new" in terms of being transposed to a particular situation (as with the outreach notion in the practitioner's narrative). On the other hand the innovation is sometimes unique creation of the practitioner and those he is associated with (as with the teach-in as a tactic or Mobilization for Youth as a program).

> *7. Provide definitions, qualifications and elaborations as appropriate to clarify or amplify use of the action principle.*

Although applied statements should be written in fairly nontechnical language, it nevertheless may be necessary to define terms or clarify concepts. Even before operationalization, obvious limitations and qualifications implicit in the guideline may be indicated. Special theoretical or conceptual notions associated with the guideline may be offered. With the innovation guideline the following elaborations were included.

Some Definitions and Distinctions

A fairly comprehensive and systematic literature has sprung up around the idea of diffusion of innovations. Thus in this area one has available a distinct terminology and set of concepts. (Everett Rogers has codified much of this literature in two important books).[21] It might be useful to draw on the diffusion literature for purposes of clarification, as in the following enumeration.

1. INNOVATION: Generally speaking, an innovation may be viewed as any program, technique, or activity perceived of as new by a population group or organization—in our terms, a target system. An innovation as most often operationalized in the research literature refers to technical-professional and commercial novel ideas and practices such as use of contraceptive devices for population planning, new medical equipment, and farming techniques. These are typically legitimate, conventional, and within the normative consensus of a community and its elites. In general, the promotion of broad and radical political change is not encompassed by the diffusion literature, though it seems likely that some applications can be made in this area.

2. TARGET SYSTEM: An individual, group, organization, community or society toward which an innovation is directed. In the context of our work we shall be dealing largely with the organizational and subcommunity level.

3. STAGES IN THE ADOPTION PROCESS: Rogers in reviewing the agricultural extension literature suggests five typical stages in the Adoption Process: awareness, interest, evaluation, trial, adoption. Behaviors associated with each of these stages are exposure to innovation, increased interest and information gathering, decision to try innovation or not, trial of the innovation, and decision as to further continuation.

4. INNOVATION ACTORS (innovators, early adopters, early majority, late majority, laggards): Rogers's five adopter categorizations based on a relative time of adoption of innovations. The five categories are listed in terms of their innovativeness, with innovators being the first to adopt innovations and laggards being the last.

[21] *The Diffusion of Innovations* (New York: The Free Press, 1962); revised edition, Rogers and F. Floyd Shoemaker, *The Communication of Innovations* (New York: The Free Press, 1971).

*8. Provide concrete practice examples of
all elements of the guideline
that have empirical referrents.*

In our work we found that an action guideline can be divided into a number of analytical elements. It was useful to give concrete examples of how these various elements were concretized in several different practice situations. (The column heads in the following table give the elements of the innovation guideline.) Operationalization illustrations in this instance were as follows:

Operationializing the Concept

In the example given at the outset, a means of operationalizing this guideline was depicted: a program was provided to a small segment of the mental retardate population within a city. It might be noted that this example also involved certain transfer mechanisms for facilitating diffusion from the smaller to the larger population. The board of directors of the Family Service agency, a key decision-making unit with authority to act, voted to extend outreach services to the mentally retarded after having witnessed the smaller demonstration program.

It may be useful to illustrate some other instances of innovation promotion in order both to show a range of types of innovations to which this guideline has been applied by practitioners as well as to demonstrate how other practitioners have concretized the concepts of a general and a partial target system. We shall also indicate mechanisms by which the transfer from the smaller to the larger target system was effected. Perhaps this can most concisely be summarized through the use of the following table.

It is interesting to observe that in all these illustrations a formal decision-making unit was necessary in order to foster or legitimate the transfer and broadening of the innovation. This is of particular concern, because in much of the diffusion literature such mechanisms are infrequently acknowledged. In part this may be so because many diffusion studies deal with agricultural extension and like enterprises, where a single practitioner or change agent is dealing with a geographically limited and homogeneous population of individuals or families.

TABLE 11.1

Setting	Innovation	General Target System	Partial Target System	Transfer Mechanism
Traditional Settlement House Serving a Largely Black Population	Introducing an intensive educational focus into a program that had been largely recreational	Entire school age membership of the settlement house	A group of teen members were involved in two educational counseling sessions	Board of Directors voted an allocation for hiring an educational director to serve the membership
A Regional Planning Council Serving Several Counties	Have the planning council gain responsibility for advising HUD on housing applications from all regional municipalities	All municipalities in the region	With HUD approval, reviewed and assessed trial applications from four municipalities	HUD approved review procedure for all municipality applications
A Community Mental Health Center in a Semi-Rural County	Stimulate local unions to accept the function of community caregivers for their members	All local unions in the county	A limited number of union members and leaders participated in a workshop on community care giving	The county-wide (all inclusive) AFL-CIO Labor Education Committee voted sponsorship of a follow-up workshop to be offered to all county locals
A Social Welfare Employees Union in a Metropolitan Community	Decentralize program implementation through building level unit committees	All building level units in the union (thus, the total membership)	Shop Stewards at a single building location were involved successfully in union program implementation functions	The Union Executive Board instituted a policy of building level program implementation

In such work diffusion may take place more informally, either with a demonstration by the change agent, followed by "spontaneous" social contagion throughout the target population, or by means of opinion leaders who are encouraged to adopt the innovation, and through their example, and based on their prestige and respect in the community, influence others to try some new approach or procedure. Clearly, community practice is largely an organizationally based activity, requiring more formal and structured procedures in order to execute processes similar to those carried out by extension agents.[22]

> *9. Show various possible patterns of implementation*
> *of a given action guideline. These patterns*
> *represent different general modes of action*
> *within a common intervention strategy.*

In attempting to move from a theoretical formulation to a complex practice arena, practitioners may find difficulty in pinning down pertinent points of application. They may discover one possible mode of action and settle on this without considering other alternatives. For this reason it is useful to provide a range of implementation patterns the practitioner may consider for use. Showing such a range may suggest additional possibilities to the practitioner. This was accomplished as follows:

Patterns of Implementation

There are two basic patterns or models of implementation of this Guideline. One proceeds from the practitioner *P* to the partial target system *PTS* to the general target system *GTS*. This is typical of the agricultural extension approach. It may be depicted as follows:

"SPONTANEOUS" CONTAGION MODEL

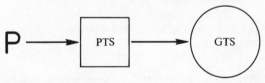

---

[22] In the revised book, *Communication of Innovations,* Rogers and Shoemaker include a section entitled "Authority Innovation Decisions," which considers the effects of decision-making units in organizational settings.

The second model moves from the practitioner, also to a partial target system, now to a relevant decision-making unit *DMU* and thence as above to the general target system. This process typically is involved in organizational contexts. It appears below:

DECISION-MAKING UNIT MODEL

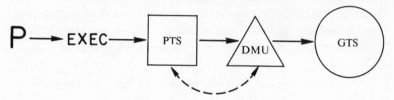

In our preliminary work we discovered that these basic or "pure" forms were rarely utilized. Rather, elaborations and refinements of various kinds became necessary. In the initial example, given at the beginning of this guideline chapter, the worker first sought the approval of the director, then the agency board, to carry out a trial program for the mentally retarded. She then conducted the program with a partial population, reported back to the board, and won approval for the expanded program. This can be visualized as follows:

THE REPEATED DECISION-MAKING UNIT MODEL

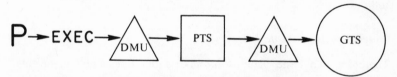

(The welfare workers' union situation noted in Table 11.1 was identical, except that the practitioner, as union president, was serving as the top executive, and could go directly to the executive board. Thus the second step was eliminated.)

DECISION-MAKING UNIT MODEL, WITH PRIOR DIRECT EXPOSURE

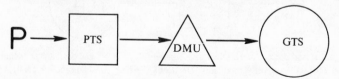

When the practitioner has the sanction of his agency and is carrying out an officially mandated innovation, it may not be necessary to work through intraorganizational structures. The community-mental-health, union-caregiver program is a case in point. Here the worker first spoke with an opinion leader who had associations with a small number of unions. Through this contact an experimental workshop was conducted with a cluster of union groups. The program caught the attention of an outside countywide decision-making unit and was spread through their involvement. The process appears as below:

EXTERNAL DECISION-MAKING UNIT MODEL,
WITH OPINION LEADER

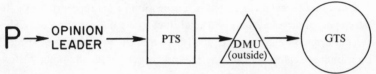

An infinite number of other possibilities can be conceived. The purpose has not been to run through an exhaustive listing, but rather to suggest a fluid range of patterns, based on actual experience. Some of these may fit exactly the reader's situation, but more likely they may help to point up unique features of his own situation, which call for different implementation patterns for this guideline.

10. As an aid to the practitioner, possible problems
("pitfalls") in implementing the guideline
should be presented.

11. Useful avenues of attack
("tips") should be offered.

It is easy to oversell the virtues of a guideline. However, to do so leaves the practitioner unprepared for the difficulties he may face or frustrated when things do not work out as well as he had anticipated. By presenting some of the possible problems that have been encountered by others, the practitioner may be more prepared to cope with them. Also, when successful techniques based on the experiences of others are available, these should be shared to ease the way. Whenever possible we have presented these "nitty-gritty" practice matters in the actual words of practitioners who have had specific prior experience.

Problems and Prospects in Implementation

Pitfalls. Practitioners, although they have had mostly favorable experiences with this guideline, also allude to certain problems in using it. Here are some of their comments:

    a. "Hard to conceptualize what 'promote acceptance of an innovation' actually means: what is acceptance, how is it measured, how many have to accept?"

    b. "Identification of what is meant by a 'partial target.' "

Tips. As has been suggested, the selection of an appropriate, facilitative partial target system is crucial in carrying out the approach. This selection must be done strategically, so that the probability of success on a limited scale is enhanced. The practitioner who attempted to foster a building-level–program-implementation arrangement discusses the factors he took into account in selecting an initial target building as follows:

> The basic consideration for the successful application of this guideline, at least in my case, was the selection of the target subpopulation. I was able to employ the following factors: Geographic location; history of organizational activity leading to cohesiveness (how long had the folks been relating to each other organizationally); leadership (both actual and potential) within the partial target population; level of skill and experience within the target population.

Another practitioner suggests the strategic snowballing effect of the guideline in the following statement:

> I believe that the guideline's use produced a favorable result in that the organizations represented in the target system were not able to block the Planning Council's housing review system. I think that had we confronted all elements of the target system simultaneously—particularly if we had dealt with all the local governments without first gaining agreements with HUD—we would have been defeated before we were even ready to begin.

*12. In order to promote and facilitate use of the
action guideline, and of the manual, it is necessary
to convey a reasonable amount of encouragement,
reinforcement, and optimism in order to give the
practitioner a pushoff toward utilization.
If possible, such encouragement should include
legitimation from colleagues.*

Since it is our observation that practitioners tend to rely heavily on personal experience and the advice of peers, it may be assumed that in order to facilitate use of research-based, fairly abstract written material, it will be necessary to offer special encouragement or impetus to proceed, based on the experience and advice of fellow professionals. Attempts along these lines were incorporated into the manual as follows:

It might be said that among pilot-year practitioners there was a general consensus that this guideline would be useful to others.

Several practitioners felt that it would be useful in terms of long- and medium-range planning to at least point out operational problems on a small scale before the innovation was attempted on a large scale.

Specific comments as to why it might be useful to others include the following:

1. Helpful when a situation is negotiable or when a relationship is being built.
2. Provides a simple and fairly uniform, concrete way of introducing new ideas.
3. Helpful in a number of ways; attempting to change attitudes of the board; clearer identification of needs and methods of meeting client needs.
4. Useful for gaining the acceptance of new ideas that do not have major implications for the existing power relationships.

Perhaps a good way to end this general discussion of the guideline and its use, and to form a bridge with its actual implementation in the field, is to heed the words of one practitioner: "Once one determines how the innovation can be experienced initially by the partial group there is no problem in carrying it out."

*13. Provide guidance on how to take the initial steps
toward active implementation of the guideline
in a practice situation.*

*14. Structure an opportunity to take initial
steps toward implementation.*

Toward this end we have included a section on "getting started,"
which listed some basic steps to consider during planning stages. This
was followed by an "Initial Log Form," in which the practitioner was
asked to set down in writing his preliminary notions concerning operationalizing the elements of the guideline: the main individuals and
groups to contact, and what might be some of the major conditions
that would impinge upon the usage of the guideline. In the design
of the project we were able to provide feedback on the initial log
writeup, which permitted further encouragement for forward movement, and clarified or corrected the practitioner's preliminary imple-
mental thrust. If possible such encouragement and feedback should
be established. Use of peers under agency or professional sponsorship is one possible way of accomplishing this. The Getting Started
section included:

1. Think of some new program, technique, or other activity that
   you have been planning to carry out, or that ties in with general
   tasks and objectives of your current position or assignment.
2. Attempt to set this down as a goal, but of moderate scope and
   time dimension—something that could be completed in a reasonable period of time (two to three months).
3. Conceptualize the general or "total" target system at which this
   innovation is directed: who are the people who would be bene-
   fiting from, utilizing, or participating in this innovation.
4. Think through a smaller segment of that target system, a more
   delimited subgroup who:
   a. might be drawn into a trial or demonstration of the innovation
      with relative ease.
   b. might very likely succeed in an initial trial.
   c. by succeeding would likely have an impact on the larger
      target system, or on a relevant decision-making unit that

could legitimate or authorize transfer of the innovation to the larger target system.

5. Our review of patterns of implementation suggests that early in the game authorization or legitimation is often needed in order to proceed. This may be obtained from a superordinate or from the agency board. Also persons or organizations who can provide resources to carry through the small-scale demonstration, or who can offer access to the smaller target system, may need to be approached at an early stage. Think through those individuals, groups, or organizations whose acceptance needs to be gained.

6. When you have worked the issue through in your mind to this point, begin to fill out the Initial Log. This is meant to assist you to formulate some tentative early steps that you might take in starting to carry out this Guideline.

These principles and concepts are still in a developmental phase and are being given a field trial in our current research effort. The contents of the manual will be revised and expanded as a result of that experience and perhaps the communication of principles will be modified. As stated earlier, we are presenting one discrete mode of diffusion: printed matter.[23]

V. THE LINKING SPECIALIST ROLE

The discussion of solutions to gaps in the research utilization processes has suggested certain specialized linking roles. I once believed that research utilization could be optimally enhanced simply by practitioners becoming more research oriented and researchers more application minded. Upon further reflection and experience this avenue for removing barriers to utilization seems less promising. As stated previously, social scientists and practitioners have essentially different basic functions, and these create distinct mental sets, intellectual skills, attitudinal and value predispositions, and general professional

[23] It is important to take into account other types of communications media, personal contact approaches, and structural effects. The latter may involve working through organizational channels, including invoking the authority structure of the agency, providing monetary or professional rewards, or prevailing upon informal peer influences in the agency or organized professional system.

styles. One might even argue that in order to perform these basic functions to capacity the particular segmented orientations of the two parties are entirely appropriate; indeed a considerable amount of intermingling might have contaminating consequences detrimental to the effectiveness of both. This is not to say that some small percentage of practitioners and social scientists may not take out intellectual "dual citizenships." But from a practical point of view, the number of people who can be relied on to develop such multiple outlooks and capacities can be anticipated to be small (although increasing). The sheer volume of knowledge that must be acquired in order to master the two disciplines is inhibiting to large-scale developments along these lines.

From an examination of Figure 11.1, it becomes obvious that there is an immense distance between the researcher in the academy and the practitioner in the field. The space between them is both extensive and interspersed with various critical transition junctures and roadblocks. As stated earlier, there are a series of engineering tasks that must be performed along the way in order to keep the flow of knowledge and experience in motion along the continuum. This requires the interjection of additional roles, performed by linkage specialists.

These linkage specialists may include individual *linking agents* or formal *linking institutions*. Linking agents are expected to have some intermixture of social-science and practitioner competencies. They should be able to understand the language and professional set of each of the parties and to be conversant with typical problems and concerns of both. The methods of scientific inquiry as well as the methods of practice intervention should be familiar to them. Linking agents may emanate from either the social sciences or from the professions; they may be researchers with applied interests and commitments, or professional practitioners with scientific inclinations and concerns. In some instances they may be individuals with full training in both the professional field and the scientific discipline (such as a masters degree in city planning and a doctorate in political science). Several universities offer joint programs that equip students with such combined capabilities.

Linking institutions are organizations given a full or partial mandate to further research utilization endeavors. They may be composed of hybrid linking agents as described above or they may acquire their dual capability through a careful blending of personnel by recruitment from both practice fields and academic disciplines. Certain types of university units pertain, such as urban studies centers or community development institutes which design or actually conduct community-based programs.[24] Some private foundations are constituted this way, and in some instances such operating agencies as Mobilization for Youth have been so conceived.

Perhaps the chief institutions with linking functions as described are the graduate schools in human-service professions. These schools are composed in large measure of practitioners who teach professional skills in their capacities as faculty members. In addition, many of these schools engage a sizable percentage of faculty members from the academic disciplines, either to teach fundamental social-science courses, or courses in research methodology. (The compositions of the academic departments themselves are rarely so eclectic.) Because of this faculty configuration the professional schools are singularly endowed structurally with the wherewithal to promote research utilization activities. This is not to say that such potential is typically exploited, only to imply that the potential uniquely exists in such institutional settings. In a special report on the use of social-science knowledge, the National Science Foundation lends support to this view of the professional schools. The report states: "The professions—law, medicine, engineering, social work, journalism, mental health work, and education—are among the main social institutions through which social science knowledge can be translated into day-to-day practice. . . . The professions have a distinctive role in the translation of knowledge into action." [25]

The other advantage in the professional setting is that effort can be focused on given reality problems. This provides a useful basis around which to organize contributions of several disciplines. A problem focus can break down the insularity and the departmentalized categories inherent in the disciplines; one is then forced to put theories

---

[24] Only a few fully specialized linking institutions with utilization as a central mission come to mind; among them are the Center for Research on the Utilization of Scientific Knowledge at the University of Michigan.

[25] National Science Foundation, *Knowledge into Action: Improving the Nation's Use of the Social Sciences* (Washington, D.C.: Government Printing Office, 1969), p. 21.

and conceptual distinctions to work on complex, multifaceted phenomena, which defy or cut across these rigorous but static categories. Faculty members teaching practice-method courses often endeavor to formulate curricula in such a way as to interweave intervention and
social-science components. They naturally become knowledgeable in
the two areas. Research centers and institutes located within profession
schools are particularly suited to undertake knowledge-linkage roles.

Are there few or many linkage roles? Both the "Social Interaction"
and the "Problem Solver" models of research utilization posit a limited range of linkage roles. In the one instance roles are confined to
dissemination of previously processed prescriptions and materials; in
the other, the interpersonal helping and motivating of clients and practitioners encompasses a heavy concentration of effort.

Alternatively, in the project model of research-development-dif-
fusion a wide range of roles is possible and necessary. One might, for
example, emphasize data-collection, storage, and codification as in the
case of the ERIC (Educational Research Information Centers) Centers
or the *Poverty and Human Resources Abstracts.* Some individuals
concern themselves primarily with developing generalizations and application principles from existing data. This volume and the books on
retrieval and utilization cited in chapter 1 are of this genre. Sometimes
publishing firms and other individuals give special attention to operationalizing general-action principles in practice terms and preparing
materials for communicating this information. Examples are practitioners' handbooks and manuals, films, and video and audio tapes.
Others attend to the related activity of training—including the scheduling of special conferences, workshops, staff development institutes,
and the like—geared to helping practitioners learn new developments
in the social sciences and relate them to practice problems and tasks.
Continuing education departments of universities and staff development departments in agencies feature such roles. Some linkage agents
deal fundamentally with the diffusion function, going out into the natural setting of the practitioner or client, and promoting new ideas,
techniques, and materials gleaned from the social sciences. Agricultural extension agents are prototypical here, but other functionaries
also come to mind, among them drug company salesmen who in-

troduce new products to physicians and publishing house representatives who promote new publications.

Some linking agents and institutions restrict themselves exclusively to one of these role categories. Others cut across several. In a few instances agents span the length of the continuum. In the light of our current limited knowledge concerning this area, and the obvious need that exists, both role-extensive and role-intensive activities are to be accepted and encouraged.

The linkage notion is a major theme in Havelock's *Planning For Innovation*. Another aspect of linkage that he suggests involves physically bringing together individuals occupying the varying delimited subroles across the continuum from basic researcher through "applied researcher developer" and on to the practitioner. Such interaction and exchange among specialized roles may be accomplished by way of special conferences, symposia, or problem-focused workshops. Havelock also suggests somewhat different ways of viewing some of the subspecialist roles listed above. For example he delineates a role of "conveyer"—one who is aggressively engaged in passing on prepackaged knowledge (such as the extension agent)—or of the "consultant": an agent who makes himself available to disseminate scientific knowledge if called upon (such as certain mental health professionals). Havelock suggests that directors of human-service agencies, because of their authority and an overall perspective on an organization's program, are in a highly advantageous position to play linking roles if so inclined and equipped. Opinion leaders in professional associations and agency settings can also be of critical importance in fostering linkage.

The reader is referred to Havelock for more extensive analytic consideration of linkage factors. Here it will suffice to reiterate the importance of such linking roles. The National Science Foundation, after an extensive study of the subject, concludes that the social sciences "can contribute to solving the nation's problems if full advantage is taken of their strengths." [26] Unfortunately, the study group declares, there are formidable obstacles and gaps to the utilization of the fruits of the

[26] *Ibid.*, p. xii.

social sciences for these purposes. In another publication Ronald Lippitt, a long-time leader in the research utilization movement, stresses the importance of universities and training institutes increasing their efforts to produce specialists equipped to meet this need. As Lippitt notes:

> Our own experience with graduate seminars and practicums has revealed that there are significant numbers of students, both in the behavioral science departments and the professional schools, who are eager to explore these new roles. These students seek new skills quite different from the research production skills typically taught in behavioral science departments and from the skills of operating practice taught in the professional schools. Certainly the training of utilization agents requires grounding *both* in behavioral science discipline and in professional values and technology. This obviously puts a new strain on the fairly segregated curriculum designs and training sequences which still exist in most of our graduate programs. The challenge is great—*and* surmountable.[27]

In this book the author and the staff have assumed a specialized linking role in developing generalizations from research literature and converting them into action principles. Robert Lynd asked the compelling question underlying the entire effort: "Knowledge for What?" One sort of answer has been set down here. Whether this answer has meaning will have to be determined, to a greater degree than is true in publications generally, by the extent to which the words become connected up with specific behavioral iniatives by readers (or by those whom they teach or whom they work with). In other words, there is a special relationship here between author and reader. The author has performed one aspect of linkage. The process can only be carried forward to completion if the reader takes on a complementary linking role, that of putting action guidelines into operation to meet real problems. The ultimate answer to Lynd's question is contingent on what happens eventually out in the community, as a consequence of those roles and those actions undertaken by the community of readers.

[27] Ronald Lippitt, "The Process of Utilization of Social Research to Improve Social Practice," in *Sociology in Action: Case Studies in Social Problems and Directed Social Change,* Arthur B. Shostak, ed. (Homewood, Ill.: The Dorsey Press, 1966), p. 280.

Appendix A
Notes on Methodology

A SUBSTANTIAL EFFORT was devoted to the development of methodological procedures. The general framework of the methodology was outlined in chapter 1. Supplementary information will be provided here.

Initially, I attempted to use an advanced group of graduate students in a research course to do a preliminary survey of journals and report on articles. It was found that this did not produce reliable results: many students did not possess the intellectual capacity to move with facility between social science and social practice; reporting of research findings was inadequate and application was frequently inept. In a second approach, I and one more advanced student assistant undertook to carry out the project. This also was found to be an unsuitable procedure. The process was considerably more time consuming than was originally estimated. Treatment of a substantive research article required a two- to three-hour period in order to digest, select the most significant aspects, abstract, code in terms of the various practice dimensions, and draw implications in terms of these dimensions. Our original estimates on time for this were off by a factor of four or five. Using highly sophisticated staff while insuring reliable reportage is an extremely expensive procedure for obtaining the volume of coverage intended.

A third avenue evolved, which seemed to provide a better balance of technical capability and sheer manpower necessitated by the endeavor. In the first place, coverage of journals was reduced from the originally envisioned ten-year span to one of six years (1964–70). Secondly, employed as reviewers were doctoral and master's students who were screened in terms of appropriate undergraduate and graduate social-science background and familiarity with community planning and organizing processes. Seven research assistants were hired to work twenty hours a week. This was arranged to permit intermittent short work periods, because of the tediousness and concentration required by the task. Experience in the early stage showed that efficiency was markedly reduced after several hours. It was better to stagger one's activities than to engage in this procedure on a sustained basis. Also, it is possible on a university campus to assemble rather easily and quickly a large research staff on a part-time, short-term basis.

Staff Composition and Supervision

I was initially directly responsible for all work. Research assistants were expected to turn in reports to me weekly. These were closely monitored in order to check, for example, comprehension, clarity, and logical interconnections. Each reviewer was given a three- or four-week training period. At the outset the study was defined and explained. The reviewer completed a sample report of an article and this was critiqued. The journal being surveyed was brought into the conference so that the reviewer's approach to selection of articles could be assessed. Review and discussion of the staff member's work was continued on an intensive basis until the staff member and I were agreed that an appropriate level of performance had been reached. I held a regular weekly conference with each staff member for purposes of feedback to him as well as to deal with questions of clarity and the need for further information or development of implications. In addition, I had weekly (later bi-weekly) staff seminar sessions as a way of further orienting the staff, maintaining morale in what is otherwise a lonely undertaking in the library, and improving the effectiveness of staff members through exchange and mutual criticism.

After a year, in the fall of 1969 I was obliged, owing to my regular faculty position, to reduce my work on the project to a one-third time commitment. I therefore evolved still another modification. Three staff units were composed, made up of three or four reviewers, each of whom was directed by a unit supervisor. The staff during this period consisted of between 10 and 12 reviewers and three supervisors. The supervisors were graduate students who had been trained by serving as reviewers the previous year. The procedures outlined above were carried out through these unit heads and unit personnel. I supervised the unit heads on a weekly basis and reviewed all reports submitted by all reviewers. This tended to contribute to consistency in the format and content level of reports. In addition, formal definitional statements explicating the practice issue areas helped achieve uniformity among reviewers.

Conference Papers

In addition to the search of selected journals, several supplementary avenues were investigated. There is a time lapse between the completion of research and its report in professional journals. In light of the already substantial time between the conducting and the completion of research, as well as the fluidity of social situations being investigated, it is important to obtain results early. In addition, much applied research is not accepted in the journals or becomes buried in agency files or libraries.

Conference program announcement bulletins were screened for the 1968 and 1969 annual conventions of the American Sociological Association and the National Conference on Social Welfare, and letters were written to presenters of what appeared to be relevant research papers requesting copies of reports. The purpose of the study was explained and cooperation was invited. Returns from this procedure were approximately 80 percent, higher than had been anticipated from previous experience. The difference may be explained by the nature of the request (part of a research retrieval project) and the fact that we requested only research papers, that is, those for which authors have likely written formal reports rather than informal jottings, because of the concreteness and complexity of the subject matter. Among those papers were many useful studies for the purposes of the project, which might not have formally been in print for perhaps two to five years. These conference papers were reviewed on the same basis journal articles were.

Dissertations

Dissertations are another source of research information that in some instances does not find its way into print or that may be delayed. An attempt was made to investigate dissertation production in the field of social work. Completed dissertations have been reported on a yearly basis in the *Social Service Review*. When these were reviewed over a six-year period for content pertinent to the study, some 100 dissertations were noted as relevant. The process of obtaining and reading each of these would be highly time consuming. The following procedural shortcut was therefore devised: Each dissertation author was written to directly; the purpose of the study was explained and his cooperation was requested in making his investigation available for the project. A short questionnaire was enclosed with the latter, with four categories under which dissertation authors were requested to summarize their study. These categories (and instructions) include the following:

1. Research problem or area of investigation (indicate hypotheses if indicated).
2. Study method and design.
3. Major findings (please be as specific as possible).
4. Specific implications for practice (including qualifications and chief potentialities).

Through this procedure 40 research dissertations were reviewed and added to the data pool of the study. One part-time staff member was assigned to deal exclusively with dissertations; she would occasionally have to check the actual dissertation document when information given on the reporting form was too brief.

Specialized Sources

Sources were also sought out for less readily available research and evaluation reports. An excellent vehicle was found in the *Quarterly Digest of Urban and Regional Research* of the Bureau of Community Planning, University of Illinois. Here were located summaries of research efforts conducted by, for example, universities, governmental bureaus and departments, OEO Community Action Agencies, and private research institutes. Another staff member selected relevant summaries for a five-year period and coded and processed these. It was necessary to discard from this collection such items as announcements of research projects, interim progress reports, and conceptual writings.

Existing Compilations

A variation in the retrieval procedure was considered for a number of subject areas: schools of study or research in which we knew of compilations or inventories of research already completed. These areas included organizational theory, small group theory, diffusion and adoption of innovations, and persuasion-mass communications. We explored the possibility of reviewing these research compendiums, selecting generalizations that seem to have the greatest relevancy for practice, and suggesting the application principles that might readily be derived. After completing this procedure with organizational-theory material, it was decided that this approach did not have so much utility for our purposes as did the more intensive article-by-article (or study-by-study) review, in which we had more control over the data. Problems included variations in variables treated, inconsistency in level of conceptualization, and insufficient data in order to have confidence in assertions made.

Research Data Pools

One additional approach to retrieval was attempted. A staff member was assigned specifically to seek out and use various research data pools, both computerized data banks and software indexes of various kinds. The following systems were investigated:

Educational Research Information Center (ERIC)
U.S. Department of Commerce Clearinghouse for Federal Scientific and Technical Information
Universal Reference System (URS)
National Clearinghouse for Mental Health Information (NIMH)
National Council on Crime and Delinquency Abstracts

The experience in this project with such established systems was essentially negative. Various problems became evident: 1) The system may be too cumbersome, complex, or expensive to use; 2) information is simply in reference form, suggesting which articles to examine on various subjects in another step rather than providing abstracts that can be used directly; 3) if abstracts are provided, sometimes they give so little data about findings or methods that they are virtually unusable except as a reference to the original studies; 4) an important limitation is that the system generally does not yield research data exclusively; one has to plod through an incredibly massive hodgepodge of theoretical, speculative, conceptual, and experiential reports to extract the occasional research-based materials; 5) some of the systems primarily give information on studies or projects in progress rather than the findings of completed studies.

At any rate, this latter avenue was abandoned for purposes of this report and no studies included in the data pool of this report were obtained by this procedure. The project has prepared a full summary of the experience with formal data systems, but space precludes its inclusion here.

Report Form for Abstracting Studies

The main instrument of the investigation was the Study Report Form, on which was recorded information for each study included in the data pool. A preliminary version was developed and given a pretest with students in a graduate research class. The revised form was used by the principal investigator and one sophisticated assistant. Based on this experience the final version was developed. This is reproduced in slightly abbreviated form at the back of this Appendix. The instrument has three main sections:

1. *Background information concerning the study.* This is a kind of "vital statistics" overview: the variables studied or themes covered; the study design and methodology; the national and community context in which the study was conducted. This section also provided a mechanism for screening articles into the data pool (a check for variables related to community organization practice and whether empirical methods were used), or screening them out (eliminating studies that had major methodological defects).

2. *An abstract or summary of the study.* This included: a) elaboration on the theoretical perspective or problem investigated including conceptual framework or hypotheses; b) a reasonably well developed

description of the methodology; c) a statement of the major findings. Reviewers were instructed to "stay close to the data," that is, to report in mainly quantitative form what the outcome of the study was, not to accept as primary data the conclusions, implications, or conjectures of the author, which were elaborations of basic data considerations. The elaborations could be reported also, but not as a substitute for data, and with the explicit clarification that these are the author's extrapolations from the data. Tables, charts, or sections of studies were Xeroxed when appropriate.

3. *Coding of data into practice issue areas (such as participation, organizational behavior, practitioners roles, etc.) and drawing policy or practice implications based on the data.* Here the reviewer coded the study within all categories into which it fell and was urged to consider matters of application and utilization for each of these categories. In making applications the reviewer was urged to hold speculation within reasonable bounds, that is, to make inferential statements that were based solidly in the data and that did not involve extensive leaps from the data. Such applications were not to be so abstract that they failed to offer direct prescriptive behavioral initiatives for intervention. This step in particular necessitated continuing training and mutual exchange between reviewer or supervisors and the principal investigator, and was the place where the principal investigator was required to be most active in revising and expanding on materials produced through the retrieval procedures.

In addition, the reviewers had an open-ended section in which to make general comments and notes: For example, reflections on the importance or quality of the study, relationship to other studies reviewed, limitations of the study.

Processing Report Forms

After reports had been reviewed and were considered accurate and complete they were Xeroxed and filed. The original report was filed by journal in chronological order, and a second copy was filed alphabetically according to the first author of the article. A Xerox copy was made for each Issue Area into which the article was coded. Thus there was a separate file for each Practice Issue Area, which included every study that had been identified with that area. Typically individual studies were coded in anywhere from one to five Issue Areas. For example, an investigation providing data about participation might also contain information about organizational behavior (organizational structure and forms or participation) as well as about diffusion of innovations (use of new techniques to encourage people to participate in service programs). The particular study was seen as providing independent data for each Practice Issue Area to which it was related, whether the author had identified or recognized that relationship or not. No attempt was made to place a study in the Issue Area into which it mainly fit; rather the approach was to code a study into as many areas as it logically fell.

Development of "Issue Area" Summaries

In developing chapters for this report, staff members worked from these Practice Issue Area files. An attempt was made to proceed in two directions. First, we went directly into the data and attempted to discern inductively the kinds of categories into which material naturally fell. Subsequently we surveyed the literature of that area in order to determine the topology of the field as developed theoretically by scholars who had written in the area. We then sought the most useful way to assemble our data into subcategories based on an understanding both of conventional treatments and of our personal assessment of how our particular data tended to group together. In some instances where there was a strong established theoretical school we leaned in that direction in devising subcategories (as with organizational theory and the diffusion of innovations). In other instances, where no commonly accepted overarching framework existed among scholars, we leaned in the direction of composing our own subcategories (as with practitioner roles and participation).

The next stage was on the one hand an extremely tedious one of sifting through sometimes hundreds of studies in order to group similar elements, and on the other a highly imaginative one of visualizing connections among distinct languages, concepts, and findings from diverse disciplines and contexts. Clusters of data comprising consensus findings were constructed and appropriate statements constituting generalizations were composed. Finally Action Guidelines were drawn, based in part on application derivations suggested in the report forms for each of the studies.

Limitations of the Methodology

There are a number of limitations inherent in the methodology. In the first place, some measure of judgment was exercised in the selection of investigations to be included. Some rejected investigations might have been included by some other reviewer. Thus our selection of studies may not have been so broad as was theoretically possible.

In addition, in grouping investigations into Practice Issue Areas and into generalizations and subgeneralizations within these Issue Areas, the coder may not have placed investigations from the data pool into all the categories in which they potentially belonged. Thus, the reader may find that he is aware of an investigation pertaining to a given generalization which is not included there. Given the volume of materials being treated, and the basically "manual" procedures employed, a "satisfying" rather than a totally comprehensive level of coverage may be anticipated. There is no claim of exhaustiveness in relating studies to generalizations, but it is hoped that a useful level of such matching has been achieved.[1]

In compiling consensus findings on given subjects, we brought together data that crossed social aggregate levels (such as small group, organization, and community), or that included interventions carried out by practitioners working with individuals and small groups as well as communities. Some studies on the state and national level were also used. Judgment was employed concerning whether particular studies could be grouped together. It is possible to argue that traversing aggregate levels and contexts in this way may tend to diminish the strength of derived generalizations. We viewed the matter alternatively, to the effect that consensus findings which converge although

---

[1] The procedures that have been developed and the categories arrived at should make possible a computer-assisted processing procedure in an updating of the study five or ten years hence. At that time perhaps greater comprehensiveness of coverage may be attained. Rogers's work has proceeded stepwise in such a manual-to-machine direction as reflected in his two retrieval studies on the subject of innovation.

drawn from a wide range of different contexts lend strength to generalizations.[2] The tendency was to include disparate settings and subjects whenever such a mix seemed reasonable. We were propelled additionally in taking this approach by the assumption that the state of relevant research is such that few problems have been studied systematically or comparatively in several studies, while at the same time the state of practice is such that guidance needs to be drawn from as many available sources as possible. The tentative nature of the generalizations and particularly of the action guidelines should, nevertheless, be recognized. They represent a developmental stage in the scientific process, requiring in any case further refinement and controlled empirical testing.

This leads also to consideration of a general strategy of data seeking. It is our view that few single studies exist with extremely far-reaching, ubiquitous implications—on the one hand because of the complexity and manysidedness of human behavior and on the other because of the inadequacy of existing social-science tools and resources. For this reason we did not attempt to rely on a select number of refined, definitive studies. Rather we aimed for cumulative aggregation of diverse investigatory efforts. Bulk with situational variety rather than methodological elegance was considered the mark of a better generalization.

More generally, the methodology represented an attempt to synthesize and draw policy and practice guidelines from a huge volume of social-science research in a subject area in which this has not occurred before. The project was a learning experience for the staff at every step and the product clearly reflects this encounter with unruly materials and the absence of established methodology. The effort nevertheless has to some degree broken new ground and has hopefully provided a base upon which others, as well as this author, can build in future efforts along these lines.

[2] In this sense our approach is consistent with Collins and Guetzkow in their retrieval study of group decision-making processes. They state: "We were fortunate to be able to support many of our contentions with studies in both field and laboratory settings as well as with data obtained from many different kinds of subjects. These generalizations are greatly strengthened by this breadth." (Barry E. Collins and Harold Guetzkow, *A Social Psychology of Group Process for Decision Making,* New York: John Wiley & Sons, 1964, p. 2.)

Appendix B

Study Report Form (Modified)

Reporter ————————————————

Journal ———————————————— Vol. —— Issue ——

Date ———————— Pages ——————

Author(s) ————————————————————————

Title ————————————————————————

  I. *Basic check list*

      a) Variables related to CO practice   Yes ————————

          Major variables or themes ————————————

      b) Empirical ———— Other ————

      c) Study Design: Exploratory ————

                  Quantitative-Descriptive ————————

                  Experimental —— Other ————

      d) Study Methods Survey — Case study ————————

                  Part. Obser. ————————————

                  Doc. ———— Demograph date ————

                                Other ————

      e) Any major defects (sample size or representativeness, logical inconsistancies, major statistical problems, etc.) ——————————————————————

      f) Context: U.S.: South-Urban ———— Foreign: Developing Urban ————

                        Rural ————   Rural ————

                      Other-Urban ————   Developed Urban ————

                        Rural ————   Rural ————

                      National ————

                      Institutional ————
                        total institutions—
                        mental hospitals, etc.

II. *Abstract:* 1.) *General area of inquiry and conceptual framework* (hypotheses if any) 2.) *Methodology,* 3.) *Findings*—you may copy abstract of article if given.

III. Practice Issue Areas:

1. Communication_____
2. Decision Making_____
3. Diffusion and Adoption____
4. Legislative-Political-Governmental Process_____
5. Movement of Populations___
6. Participation_____
7. Planning Process_____
8. Power_____
9. Practitioner Roles_____

10. Resistance to Change_____
11. Service Structure and Delivery_____
12. Social Influence_____
13. Strategy_____
    a. Conflict_____
    b. Consensus_____
    c. Bargaining_____
    d. Other_____

For each item checked, indicate *major findings* from abstract and *practice implications.* Emphasize and develop implications. *Name below* those *issue areas* relevant to a given set of findings-implications. General guidelines—stay close to the *actual data;* push ahead from findings to practice implications. Be specific about directives suggested to the practitioner. What does this finding tell the C.O. practitioner about what he should *do.*

IV. *Comments* (other findings, significance of study, relationship to other studies, important references and their implications or findings, etc.):

Index of Subjects

Accommodative leaders, 345, 346; *see also* Leaders, Leadership
Accountability (of) community action agencies, 377; organizational, 462
Acculturation, 485, 506–9, 510
Activism: *see* Militancy; Political and legislative behavior; Radicalism; Social participation
Activist, role of, 66
Actor-teacher role, 39
Adaptability: assimilation and, 508–9; (in) Peace Corps volunteers, 40
Adjustment: *see* Adaptability
Administrators: defined, 48; organizational influence on, 144–45, 147–50; outside influences on, 48–49; perception of member liberalism, 73; resistance to client decision-making, 392–93; types, 48–49; use of media, 49–50; *see also* Executives; Government officials; Professionals-Practioners
Adoption goals: defined, 133; emphases, 134; *see also* Organizations, goals
Adoption of innovations: *see* Innovation, diffusion and adoption of
Adoption period, defined, 421
Adoption process, stages, defined, 421
Adoption rate, defined, 421
Adult education: innovation and, 435; job satisfaction and, 433–34; political participation and, 354; status inconsistency and, 336; *see also* Education; Educational Attainment
Adults: social movement participation, 328; voluntary association membership, 285
Adversary participation: (in) community action agencies, 380–82, 384–87; *see also* Militancy; Radicalism; Social participation

Advisory participation: (in) community action agencies, 379, 380–81, 385–87; *see also* Social participation
Advocate: perception of delinquency, 56; roles of, 62, 66, 382, 389–90
Advocate-observer role, 40
Age: employment and, 497; social movement participation by, 327–29, 394; social protest and, 209; use of institutions and, 501; use of media and, 449; voluntary membership by, 289–90; voter participation and, 355–56; *see also* Aged; Youth
Aged: attitude change in, 434; services for, 459–60
Agricultural extension agents: *see* County extension agents
Agricultural innovation: acceptance and adoption of, 72, 427, 429–30, 433, 448, 450–51; *see also* Farmers; Innovation, diffusion and adoption of
AID advisors, effectiveness, 58–59
Alienation: defined, 356–57; organizational innovation and, 482; political behavior and, 209, 210, 219, 356–62, 367–68; social participation-activism and, 336–38, 343, 396; (of) workers in organizations, 171–74; *see also* Frustration
Allocative-fund (layman) value system, 101
Ambiguity, organizational innovation and, 481
American Public Health Association, 17
Annexation of suburbs: municipal government type and, 263; social factors in, 264–65
Antipoverty programs: *see* Community action agencies and programs;

Motivator role, 62

Municipal government, type of: administrative structure and, 263–65; community action agency participation and, 383–84; geographical location and, 251–53; militancy and, 42; population characteristics and, 250–51, 265–66, 383–84; response to social welfare needs and, 363, 439; voter turnout and, 366

Narcotic addiction, residential mobility and, 486–87; subculture of, 442

National Opinion Research Center, political behavior studies, 354

Nationalistic identification, educational attainment and, 323; *see also* Race

Native Americans: migration of, 501, 509; primary group participation, 310; *see also* Blacks; Chicanos; Minorities; Race

Needs: community and client, 129–30; low income groups, 45–46; (as) met by service organizations, 159; (as) met by urban social structure, 76; social change and, 433–34

Neighborhoods: councils, 46–47; institutions, 491–93; integration, 495–96; involvement and identification with, 319–20, 488, 491–93; organization, 494–95; political change in, 514–15; (as) primary group units, 305–7; voluntary associations in, 502; working class, 491–93; *see also* Ethnic neighborhoods; Institutions, subcultural; Neighborhood service organizations and programs

Neighborhood service organizations and programs: decision-making and participation in, 389, 392–93; professional-paraprofessional relationships, 180–81; *see also* Community action agencies and programs; Neighborhoods; Office of Economic Opportunity centers and programs; Social welfare programs

New York City: Mobilization for

Youth Program, 461; police department and innovation, 477–78, 479

Nonprofessionals: *see* Indigenous workers; Paraprofessionals; Semi-professions

Nonroutine technology, 153–55; client needs and, 158–59; (in) decentralized organizations, 155–57; defined, 153; *see also* Organizations, technology; Routine technology

Norms: bureaucratic, 166–67; community influence on, 42–45; diffusion of new, 445–47; executive deviation from, 466; innovation and, 422, 424–28; leader adherence to, 453; (of) linking agents, 77–78; professional, 84–88, 99–102, 162–63, 457–58; *see also* Customs; Values

Nurses: norms and values of, 77–78; role orientations of, 85

Occupations: awareness of community problems among, 298; innovation among, 299–301, 430, 458–59, 461; mobility and assimilation among, 297, 488, 499–500, 505–6, 512–13; social discontent among, 339; voluntary association membership among, 286–88; voting behavior among, 354

Office of Economic Opportunity centers and programs: client characteristics, 374–76; client participation, 373, 374; indigenous workers in, 177, 178; professional-paraprofessional relationships, 180–81; support for, 255; *see also* Community action agencies and programs; Economic Opportunity Act; Neighborhood service organizations and Programs; Social welfare programs

Opinion leaders: characteristics, 454; defined, 421; innovation and, 452–55, 565, 567; (as) linking agents, 77, 79–80, 82; professionals as, 460; *see also* Change agents; Leaders; Leadership

Organizational slack, defined, 469

Personal information sources: *see* Information, sources

Personality, practitioner roles and, 53–54, 58–59

Physicians: bureaucracy and, 165; (as) linking agents, 80, 82; (in) mental health planning, 44; *see also* Psychiatrists; Psychologists

Planning (social), 496; action guidelines, 38–41; executive officer influence, 247–49; professional-resident relationships, 324–25; sources of support for, 304–5; *see also* Change agencies; City planning; Community action agencies and programs; Community organization; Innovation, diffusion and adoption of

Planning (council) orientation value system, 101

Police: brutality, 339; (as) linking agents, 80, 82; outside influences on, 50–51, 477–78, 479; (as) perpetrators of violence, 355

Political efficacy: defined, 356; *see also* Political and legislative behavior; Voting

Political leaders: characteristics and background, 224–26; defined, 222; ideological orientations, 230–31; motivation, 226–28; recruitment, 228–29; role conceptions, 229–30; *see also* Executive officers; Government officials; Governors; Leaders; Legislators; other headings beginning with the term Political

Political and legislative behavior, 195–203, 222–23, 268–70, 394, 395, 396, 397; attitudes toward "politics," 212–16; decision-making in, 262–63; democratic values and, 208–9; development of skill in, 393; educational attainment and, 204–5, 206–7, 360, 429; (of) ethnic groups, 313; external influences on, 217–18; geographical location and, 251–53; local economic levels and, 256–59; past experience and, 254–56, 342–43; population change rate and, 250–51,

514–15; primary group influence on, 318–19, 322; psychological influences, 219–21; roles and variables, 90–105; socioeconomic status and, 203–7, 209, 210–12, 218–19, 220, 259–61; *see also* Community organization; Voting; other headings beginning with the term Political

Political parties: age and, 328; influence on voters, 216–17; legislator loyalty toward, 231–32; recruitment of leaders, 228–29; social class and, 210–12, 368–69; social legislation and, 261; voter images of, 221–22; *see also* Voting; other headings beginning with the term Political

Politico: defined, 48; means of influencing, 49; *see also* Political leaders

Poll tax, 363

Poor: *see* Socioeconomic classes

Population change rate: political aspects, 250–51, 514–15

Population groups: *see* Clients; Hetereogeneous population groups; Homogeneous population groups; Target systems

Population movement, 484–87; assimilation and, 310–11, 503–15; characteristics of participants, 310; primary group participation and, 307, 309–11; social psychology of, 486–87; *see also* Migration, interarea; Migration, intraurban; Relocation services; residential mobility

Power structures: innovation and, 446, 479, 481–82; (in) organizations, 167–70, 464, 479, 481–82; violence and, 349–52

Powerlessness: *see* Alienation

Practitioners: *see* Professionals-Practitioners

Prejudice, 16; primary groups and, 322; social participation and, 316–17; *see also* Discrimination; Segregation

Press, use of by government officials, 49–50

Pressure groups: *see* Interest groups

Prestige (of) organizations in the community, 127–29 (within) primary groups, 316, 317; (of) professions, 458; (of) voluntary associations, 287

Primary groups: *see* Social participation, (in) primary groups

Primary-like groups, formal organizations and, 76

Problem solving: groups and, 54, 74–75; models, 543; *see also* Decision-making

Production ideology: innovation and, 481; *see also* Profit motive

Professionalization: (of) community organization practitioners, 102–3; organizational communications and, 126; organizational structure and, 162–66; social movement support and, 343–44; *see also* Professionals-Practitioners; Professions

Professionals-Practitioners, 160–62, 174

——bureaucracy and, 165–66

——(in) cross-cultural consultation, 58–60

——defense mechanisms, 387–88

——defined, 48

——goals, 4–8

——means of influencing, 49

——meeting community and client needs, 129–30

——organizational relationships, 26, 121, 133, 135, 145, 147, 149, 159, 162–65

——personality attributes, 53–54

——political activity: *see* Political and legislative behavior

——power base, 50

——(as) problem solvers, 54

——relationship of training to norms and performance, 58, 86, 87

——relationships with indigenous workers, 177–78, 180–83

——roles, 35–36, 60, 61, 105–6; adversary, 381–82; advocacy, 389–90; assertiveness of, 72–75; autonomy of, 88–90; community factors in, 42–46; conceptions of, 150–51; conflict and compromise in, 64–71, 92–94; defined, 144–45, 147; diversity of performance in, 37; effectiveness in cross-cultural consultation, 58–60; linking agent, 63, 76–83; major orientations of, 83–88; organizational factors in, 46–53; personal attributes and, 53–58; political and activist, 90–105; scope of, 61–64; social change process and, 38–41; stages of, 89

——social science research and, 1, 13–32, 475–76, 544–76

——supervision and modes of influence, 167–74

——value orientations, 55–56, 99–102

——*see also* Administrators; Change agents; Clients; Community organization; Executives; Paraprofessionals; Professionalization; Semi-professions; Social workers; Supervisors

Professions: defined, 165; innovation and, 299–300, 439, 457–62, 469–70, 482–83; mobility among, 499–500; *see also* Paraprofessionals; Professionals-Practitioners; Professionalization; Semi-professions

Profit motive, innovation and, 471–72

Propaganda, political, 318–19

Property values, integration and, 495–96

Protest: *see* Social action and change; Social participation; Violence

Protest leaders: *see* Leaders

Psychiatrists: bureaucracy and, 167; community mental health attitudes, 300, 439; Mental Health Ideology Scale and, 104; professional norms, 460; values, 55; *see also* Physicians; Psychologists

Psychologists: community mental health attitudes, 300, 439; Mental Health Ideology Scale and, 104; *see also* Physicians; Psychiatrists

Public assistance: *see* Social welfare programs

Public health, attitudes and resistance toward, 80, 439

Public health departments: *see* Health agencies

Public health nurses: *see* Nurses

Index of Names

The Index consists primarily of authors of studies making up the data bank from which generalizations and action guidelines were drawn. A separate bibliography has been composed for each data-based Part. Page numbers are keyed to Parts (designated by roman numerals) and to position in the bibliography (in parentheses) for authors cited within Parts.

The Index includes also in italics a smaller listing of the main authors quoted in the text and footnoted below in the body of the text.

Fahn, Jane C.
II(29): 58
Farris, Charles
V(32): 362
Fathi, Asghar
II(30): 76, 79, 80
VIA(36): 438, 446, 452
Faunce, William
V(52): 286, 287, 297
Feagin, Joe R.
VIA(38): 441, 442
Fee, Edward
VIB(5): 513, 514
Feigert, Frank B.
IV(12): 224, 226, 227
Feinbaum, Robert
V(53): 300, 303
Feldman, Ronald A., 66
Fellin, Phillip
VIB(32): 502, 507, 508
Fellman, Gordon
V(54): 324, 381, 390, 391
VIB(17): 508
Fendrich, James M.
V(55): ' 322
VIA(39): 450
Fenno, Richard F.
IV(23): 239, 240, 243, 244
Fergin, Joe R.
IV(24): 217, 218
Field, John Osgood
IV(25): 203, 204; (103): 251, 252
V(230): 364
Fishman, Jacob
V(205): 336, 340, 342; (206): 315, 316, 318, 340
Flacks, Richard
V(56): 318, 340
Fleron, Frederic J., Jr.
V(104): 318
Fliegel, Frederick C.
VIA(40): 438; (41): 441, 442; (73): 428, 429, 437, 438
Flinn, Thomas A.
IV(26): 221, 233, 238; (27): 209, 217, 218, 224, 228, 230, 231, 232

Florence Heller School for Advanced Studies in Social Welfare
II(50): 37, 42
V(57): 377; (58): 379, 381, 382, 383, 384, 385, 386, 388
Folli, Michael
VIB(9): 506
Form, William H.
IV(28): 206, 218; (29): 206, 218; (79): 206, 218; (80): 206, 207, 218, 220
V(59): 338, 339; (60): 338, 353, 354, 355, 356, 357, 367, 368; (183): 295, 338, 367, 368; (184): 338, 339
Foster, George M.
VIA(42): 424, 427
Fowler, Edmund
IV(52): 251, 252, 256, 258, 263
V(123): 363
France, William A.
VIA(37): 446
Frank, Jerome D.
V(61): 318, 340, 341
VIA(43): 428, 450
Franz, Verl R. W.
V(146): 293, 298
Frederickson, H. George
IV(30): 218
V(62): 368
Freed, Marc
VIB(18): 488, 492
Freedman, Ronald
VIA(44): 424, 425, 428, 429
Freeman, F.
VIB(38): 495
Frey, Frederick
V(63): 323
VIA(45): 424, 425, 428, 429, 431
Friedlander, Frank
III(17): 129
Friedman, John
II(31): 37, 39
Friedman, Robert
II(32): 37, 48
Friedson, Eliot
VIA(46): 457, 459